The Catechism Of The Council Of Trent

Catholic Church

THE

CATECHISM

OF

THE COUNCIL OF TRENT.

PUBLISHED BY COMMAND

OF

POPE PIUS THE FIFTH.

TRANSLATED INTO ENGLISH

BY THE REV. J. DONOVAN,

PROFESSOR, &c., ROYAL COLLEGE, MAYNOOTH.

BALTIMORE:

PUBLISHED BY FIELDING LUCAS, JR.

NO. 138 MARKET STREET.

DECREE

OF THE COUNCIL OF TRENT.

.THAT the faithful may approach the Sacraments with greater reverence and devotion, the Holy Synod commands all Bishops not only to explain, in a manner accommodated to the capacity of the receivers, the nature and use of the Sacraments, when they are to be administered by themselves; but also to see that every Pastor piously and prudently do the same, in the vernacular language, should it be necessary and convenient. This exposition is to accord with a form to be prescribed by the Holy Synod for the administration of all the Sacraments, in a Catechism, WHICH BISHOPS WILL TAKE CARE TO HAVE FAITHFULLY TRANSLATED INTO THE VERNACULAR LANGUAGE, AND EXPOUNDED TO THE PEOPLE BY ALL PASTORS.

Conc. Trid. Sess. 24. de Reform. c. 7

THE

TRANSLATOR'S PREFACE.

THE ROMAN CATECHISM, of which an English translation is now submitted to the public, was composed by decree of the Council of
Trent; and the same venerable authority commands all Bishops " to
take care that it be faithfully translated into the vernacular language, and expounded to the people by all pastors." [1]

The Fathers of the Council had examined with patient industry,
and, in the exercise of their high prerogative, had defined, with unerring accuracy, the dogmas of faith which were then denied or disputed: but the internal economy of the Church, also, solicited and
engaged their attention; and accordingly, we find them employed
in devising measures for the instruction of ignorance, the amelioration of discipline, and the reformation of morals.

Amongst the means suggested to their deliberative wisdom for the
attainment of these important ends, the Roman Catechism has been
deemed not the least judicious or effective. The ardour and industry
of the " Reformers" were actively employed, not only in the publication of voluminous works, " to guard against which required, perhaps, little labour or circumspection;" but, also, in composition · of
" innumerable smaller works, which, veiling their errors under the
semblance of piety, deceived with incredible facility the simple and
the incautious." [2] To meet the mischievous activity of such men,
and to rear the edifice of Christian knowledge on its only secure and
solid basis, the instruction of its authorized teachers; to afford the
faithful a fixed standard of Christian belief, and to the Pastor a prescribed form of religious instruction; to supply a pure and perennial
fountain of living waters to refresh and invigorate at once the Pastor

[1] Conc. Trid. Sess. 24. de Reform. cap. 7.   [2] Pref. page 15

and the flock, were amongst the important objects contemplated by the Fathers of Trent in the publication and translation of the Roman Catechism.[1]

They, too, are amongst the objects, which were contemplated by those, who urged the present undertaking, and which influenced the Translator's acceptance of the task. Coincidence of circumstances naturally suggests a concurrence of measures; and it requires little discernment to discover the coincidence that exists between the present circumstances of this country and those which awakened and alarmed the vigilance of the Fathers of Trent. Ireland, indeed the Empire, has been inundated with pernicious tracts, teeming with vituperative misrepresentations of the dogmas of the Catholic faith, and loaded with unmeasured invective against the principles of Catholic morality. "Innumerable smaller works, veiling their errors under the semblance of piety," have been scattered with unsparing hand " amongst the ignorant and incautious:" efforts are still made (the object is avowed) " to promote the principles of the Reformation," by unsettling the religious convictions of the people; and we are fortified by the example of the Fathers of Trent in the hope, that an antidote eminently calculated to neutralize the poison, which has been so industriously diffused, to abate prejudice, instruct ignorance, promote piety, and confirm belief, will be found in a work containing a comprehensive summary of the dogmas of the Catholic faith, and a no less comprehensive epitome of the principles of Catholic morality

To another, and, happily, an increasing class of the community, the present volume cannot fail to prove a useful acquisition—to those who, anxious only for truth, desire to know the real principles of Catholics, could they arrive at a knowledge of them through the me dium of a compendious and authoritative exposition. Whilst inquiry struggles to burst the bonds in which prejudice and interested mis representation have long bound up its freedom, and would still oppress its energies, it would not become Catholics to look on with in difference. We owe it to truth, to aid these growing efforts of en. .lightened reason : the voice of charity bids us assist the exertions of honest inquiry : we owe it to our ourselves to co-operate in removing the load of obloquy under which we still labour; and, if it were pos sible for us to be insensible to these claims, there is yet an obligation from which nothing can exempt us—it is due to religion to make her known as she really is. To these important ends we cannot, perhaps, contribute more effectually, than by placing within the reach

[1] Pref. pages 13, 14.

of all, a Work explanatory of Catholic doctrine, and universally acknowledged authority in the Catholic Church.[1]

To the Pastor, upon whom devolves the duty of public instruction, the " Catechismus ad Parochos" presents peculiar advantages. In its pages he will discover a rich treasure of theological knowledge, admirably adapted to purposes of practical utility. The entire economy of religion he will there find developed to his view—the majesty of God, the nature of the divine essence—the attributes of the Deity, their transcendent operations—the creation of man, his unhappy fall—the promise of a Redeemer, the mysterious and merciful plan of redemption—the establishment of the Church, the marks by which it is to be known and distinguished—the awful sanction with which the Divine Law is fenced round, the rewards that await and animate the good, the punishments that threaten and awe the wicked—the nature, number and necessity of those supernatural aids instituted by the Divine goodness to support our weakness in the arduous conflict for salvation—the Law delivered in thunder on Sinai, embracing the various duties of man, under all the relations of his being—finally, the nature, necessity and conditions of that heavenly intercourse that should subsist between the soul and its Creator; the exposition of that admirable prayer composed by the Son of God—all this, comprehending as it does, the whole substance of doctrinal and practical religion, and at once instructive to Pastor and people, the reader will find in the " Catechismus ad Parochos," arranged in order, expounded with perspicuity, and sustained by convincing argument.

Besides a general index, one pointing out the adaptation of the several parts of the Catechism to the Gospel of the Sunday will, it is hoped, facilitate the duty of public instruction, and render this Catechism, what it was originally intended to be, the manual of Pastors.

Such are the nature and object of the present work: a brief sketch

---

[1] On this subject the following observations, from the pen of a Protestant Clergyman, are as candid as they are just :—" The religion of the Roman Catholics ought always, in strictness, to be considered apart from its professors, whether kings, popes, or inferior bishops; and its tenets, and its forms, should be treated of separately. To the acknowledged creeds, catechisms, and other formularies of the Catholic Church, we should resort for a faithful description of what Roman Catholics do really hold, as doctrines essential to salvation; and as such held by the faithful in all times, places, and countries. Though the Catholic *forms* in some points may vary in number and splendour, the Catholic *doctrines* cannot ;—though *opinions* may differ, and change with circumstances, *articles of faith* remain the same. Without a due and constant consideration of these facts, no Protestant can come to a right understanding respecting the essential faith and worship of the Roman Catholics. It has been owing to a want of this discrimination, that so many absurd, and even wicked tenets, have been palmed upon our brethren of the Catholic Church: that which they deny, we have insisted they religiously hold; that which the best informed amongst them utterly abhor, we have held up to the detestation of mankind, as the guide of their faith, and the rule of their actions. This is not fair: it is not doing to others as we would have others to do unto us."—*The Religions of all Nations, by the Rev. J. Nightingale, p. 12.*

of its history must enhance its worth, and may, it is hoped, prove ac
ceptable to the learned reader.

It has already been observed, that the Roman Catechism owes its
origin to the zeal and wisdom of the Fathers of Trent: the Decree
of the Council for its commencement was passed in the twenty-fourth
session; and its composition was confided to individuals recommended,
no doubt, by their superior piety, talents and learning. That, during the Council, a Congregation had been appointed for the execution of the work, is matter of historic evidence;[1] but whether, before the close of the Council, the work had actually been commenced,
is a point of interesting, but doubtful inquiry.[2] It is certain, however, that amongst those who, under the superintending care of the
sainted Archbishop of Milan, were most actively employed in its composition, are to be numbered three learned Dominicans, Leonardo
Marini, subsequently raised to the Archiepiscopal throne of Lancia-
no,[3] Francisco Foreiro, the learned translator of Isaias,[4] and Ægi-
dius Foscarrari, Bishop of Modena,[5] names not unknown to history
and to literature.[6] Whether to them exclusively belongs the completion of the Catechism, or whether they share the honour and the
merit with others, is a question which, about the middle of the last
century, enlisted the zeal and industry of contending writers. The
Letters and Orations of Pogianus, published by Lagomarsini, seem
however, to leave the issue of the contest no longer doubtful. Of
these letters one informs us, that three *Bishops* were appointed by
the Sovereign Pontiff to undertake the task:[7] of the three Dominicans
already mentioned, two only had been raised to the episcopal dignity;
and hence a fourth person, at least, must have been associated to
their number and their labours. That four persons had been actually
appointed by the Pontiff appears from the letter of Gratianus to
Cardinal Commendon:[8] and after much research, Lagomarsini has
discovered that this fourth person was Muzio Calini, Archbishop of
Zara.[9] The erudite and accurate Tiraboschi has arrived at the

---

[1] Pogianus, vol. 2. p. xviii. [2] Palavicino, lib. xxiv. c. 13.

[3] Epistolæ et Orationes Julii Pogianni, editæ a Lagomarsini, Romæ, 1756, vol. 2. p. xx.

[4] Oltrochius de vita ac rebus gestis, S. Caroli Borromæi, lib. 1. c. 8. annot. 3. apud Pogianum, vol. 2. p. xx.

[5] Tabularium Ecclesiæ Romanæ. Leipsic, 1743.

[6] Foreiro's translation and commentary on Isaias may be seen in the "Recueil des grands critiques."

[7] "Datum est negotium a Pontifice Maximo tribus *episcopis*," &c. Pog. Ep. et Orat. vol. 3. p. 449.

[8] " . . . . "ad eam rem quatuor viros Pius delegit," &c. Pog. vol. 1. p. xvii.

[9] Calini assisted at the Council, as Archbishop of Zara, and died Bishop of Terni, in 1570. It would appear from Tiraboschi that he belonged to no religious order. He is called " huomo di molte lettere e molta pietà." See MSS. notes found in the library of the Jesuit College in Fermo; also MSS. letters of Calini, apud Pogian. vol. 2. p. xxii. Palavicino Istoria del C. di Trento, l. 15. c. 13.

same conclusion : he expressly numbers Calini amongst the authors of the Roman Catechism.[1] The MSS. notes, to which Largomarsini refers in proof of this opinion, mention, it is true, the names of Galesinus and Pogianus with that of Calini: Pogianus, it is universally acknowledged, had no share in the composition of the work ; and the passage, therefore, must have reference solely to its style. With this interpretation, the mention of Calini does not conflict ; the orations delivered by him in the Council of Trent prove, that in elegance of Latinity he was little inferior to Pogianus himself ; and the style, therefore, might also have employed the labour of his pen.

Other names are mentioned as possessing claims to the honour of having contributed to the composition of the Trent Catechism, amongst which are those of Cardinal Seripandus, Archbishop of Salerno, and legate at the Council to Pius the Fourth, Michael Medina, and Cardinal Antoniano, secretary to Pius the Fifth; but Tiraboschi omits to notice their pretensions; and my inquiries have not been rewarded with a single authority competent to impeach the justness of the omission. Their names, that of Medina excepted, he frequently introduces throughout his history; in no instance, however, does he intimate that they had any share in the composition of the Roman Catechism ; and his silence, therefore, I am disposed to interpret as a denial of their claim.

The work, when completed,[2] was presented to Pius the Fifth, and was handed over by his holiness for revisal to a Congregation, over which presided the profound and judicious Cardinal Sirlet.[3] The style, according to some, was finally retouched by Paulus Manutius;[4] according to others, and the opinion is more probable, it owes this last improvement to the classic pen of Pogianus.[5] Its uniformity, (the observation is Lagomarsini's) and its strong resemblance to that of the other works of Pogianus, depose in favour of the superiority of his claim.[6] The work was put to press under the vigilant eye of the laborious and elegant Manutius,[7] published by authority of Pius the Fifth, and by command of the Pontiff translated into the lan-

---

[1] See Tiraboschi Storia della Letteratura Italiana, T. vii. part 1. p. 304, 308. vid. Script. Ordin Prædic. vol. 228. Romæ, 1784.

[2] It was finished anno 1564. Catechismum habemus jam absolutum, &c. Letter of S. Charles Borromeo to Cardinal Hosius, dated December 27th, 1564, Pog. 2. lvii.

[3] Ibid. To Cardinal Sirlet, Biblical literature owes the variæ lectiones in the Antwerpian Polyglot.

[4] Graveson Hist. Eccl. T. 7. p. 156. Ed. Venet. 1738. Apostolus Zeno. Anotat. in Bibl. Elog. Ital. T. 11. p. 136. Ed. Venet. 1733.

[5] Lagomarsini Not. in Gratian. Epist. ad Card. Commend. Romæ, 1756

Vol. 2. p. xxxiv.   [7] Pog. vol. 2. p. xxxix

guages of Italy, France, Germany, and Poland.[1] To the initiated no
apology is, I trust, necessary for this analysis of a controversy which
the Translator could not, with propriety, pass over in silence, and on
which so much of laborious research has been expended. To
detail, however, the numerous approvals that hailed the publication
of the work, recommended its perusal, and promoted its circulation,
would, perhaps, rather fatigue the patience, than interest the curiosity of the reader.[2] Enough, that its merits were then, as they are
now, recognised by the Universal Church; and the place given
amongst the masters of spiritual life to the devout A'Kempis, "second
only," says Fontenelle, "to the books of the canonical Scripture,"
has been unanimously awarded to the Catechism of the Council of
Trent, as a compendium of Catholic theology.

Thus, undertaken by decree of the Council of Trent, the result of
the aggregate labours of the most distinguished of the Fathers who
composed that august assembly, revised by the severe judgment, and
polished by the classic taste of the first scholars of that classic age,
the Catechism of the Council of Trent is stamped with the impress
of superior worth, and challenges the respect and veneration of
every reader.

In estimating so highly the merits of the original, it has not, however,
escaped the Translator's notice, that a work purely theological and
didactic, treated in a severe, scholastic form, and, therefore, not
recommended by the more ambitious ornaments of style, must prove
uninviting to those who seek to be amused, rather than to be instructed. The judicious reader will not look for such recommendation·
the character of the work precludes the idea: perspicuity, and an
elaborate accuracy, are the leading features of the original; and the
Translator is, at least, entitled to the praise of not having aspired to
higher excellencies. To express the entire meaning of the author,
attending rather to the sense, than to the number of his words, is
the rule by which the Roman Orator was guided in his translation
of the celebrated orations of the two rival orators of Greece.[3] From
this general rule, however just, and favourable to elegance, the Trans-

---

[1] It was printed by Manutius before the end of July, 1566, but not published until the Sep-
tember following, when a folio and quarto edition appeared at the same time, accompanied
with an Italian translation, from the pen of P. Alessio Figgliucci, O. P. Sabutin. in vitâ Pii. V.
Pog. vol. 2. xl.

[2] Amongst these authorities are Bulls 102, 105, of Pius V. in Bullar. p. 306, 307; Brief of
Greg. XIII. 1583; Epist. Card. Borrom; Synods of Milan, 1565; of Beneventum. 1567; of Ra-
venna, 1568; of Meaux, 1569; of Geneva, 1574; of Melun. (national) 1576; of Rouen, 1581; of
Bourdeaux, 1583; of Tours, 1583; of Rheims, 1583; of Tolouse, 1590; of Avignon, 1594; of
Aquileia, 1586, &c. &c.

[3] De opt. gen. orat. n. 14.

lator has felt it a conscientious duty not unfrequently to depart, in the translation of a work, the phraseology of which is in so many instances, consecrated by ecclesiastical usage. Whilst, therefore, he has endeavoured to preserve the spirit, he has been unwilling to lose sight of the letter: studious to avoid a servile exactness, he has not felt himself at liberty to indulge the freedom of paraphrase: anxious to transfuse into the copy the spirit of the original, he has been no less anxious to render it an express image of that original. The reader, perhaps, will blame his severity: his fidelity, he trusts, may defy reproof; and on it he rests his only claim to commendation.

By placing the work, in its present form, before the public, the Translator trusts he shall have rendered some service to the cause of religion: should this pleasing anticipation be realized, he will deem the moments of leisure devoted to it well spent, and the reward more than commensurate to his humble labours.

MAYNOOTH COLLEGE.

June 10th, 1829.

PREFACE

TO THE CATECHISM

OF

THE COUNCIL OF TRENT.

INTENTION OF THE COUNCIL—OBJECT AND AUTHORITY OF THE
WORK—ITS USE AND DIVISION.

SUCH is the nature of the human mind, so limited are its in- *Insufficiency of human reason.* tellectual powers, that, although by means of diligent and laborious inquiry it has been enabled of itself to investigate and discover many divine truths; yet guided solely by its own lights it could never know or comprehend most of those things by which eternal salvation, the principal end of man's creation and formation to the image and likeness of God, is attained. "The invisible things of God, from the creation of the world, are," as the *Necessity of revelation.* Apostle teaches, " clearly seen, being understood by the things that are made: his eternal power also and divinity."[1] But "the mystery which had been hidden from ages and generations" so far transcends the reach of man's understanding, that were it not "manifested to his saints to whom God," by the gift of faith, "would make known the riches of the glory of this mystery, amongst the Gentiles, which is Christ,"[2] it had never been given to human research to aspire to such wisdom.

But, as "faith cometh by hearing,"[3] the necessity of the assi- *And of authorized teachers.* duous labour and faithful ministry of a legitimate teacher, at all times, towards the attainment of eternal salvation is manifest, for it is written, "how shall they hear without a preacher? And how shall they preach unless they be sent?"[4] And, indeed, never, from the very creation of the world, has God most merciful and benignant been wanting to his own; but "at sundry times and in divers manners spoke, in times past, to the Fathers by the

[1] Rom. i. 20.   [2] Coloss. i. 26, 27.   [3] Rom. x. 17.   [4] Rom. x. 14, 15.

2

Prophets;"[1] and pointed out, in a manner suited to the times and circumstances, a sure and direct path to the happiness of heaven. But, as he had foretold that he would give a teacher, "to be the light of the Gentiles and salvation to the ends of the earth;"[2] "in these days he hath spoken to us by his Son,"[3] whom also by a voice from heaven, "from the excellent glory,"[4] he has commanded all to hear and to obey; and the Son "hath given some apostles, and some prophets, and others evangelists, and others pastors and teachers,"[5] to announce the word of life; that we be not carried about like children with every wind of doctrine, but holding fast to the firm foundation of the faith, "may be built together into a habitation of God in the Holy Ghost."[6]

The pastors of the Church to be heard. That none may receive the word of God from the ministers of the Church as the word of man, but as the word of Christ, what it really is; the same Saviour has ordained that their ministry should be invested with such authority that he says to them; "he that hears you, hears me; and he that despises you, despises me;"[7] a declaration which he would not be understood to make to those only to whom his words were addressed, but likewise to all who, by legitimate succession, should discharge the ministry of the word, promising to be with them "all days, even to the consummation of the world."[8]

Peculiar necessity of pastoral instruction in these days. As this preaching of the divine word should never be interrupted in the Church of God, so in these our days it becomes necessary to labour with more than ordinary zeal and piety to nurture and strengthen the faithful with sound and wholesome doctrine, as with the food of life: for "false prophets have gone forth into the world"[9] "with various and strange doctrines"[10] to corrupt the minds of the faithful; of whom the Lord hath said *Activity of the "Reformers."* "I sent them not, and they ran; I spoke not to them, yet they prophesied."[11] In this unholy work, to such extremes has their impiety, practised in all the arts of Satan, been carried, that it would seem almost impossible to confine it within bounds; and did we not rely on the splendid promises of the Saviour, who declared that he had "built his Church on so solid a foundation, that the gates of hell should never prevail against it,"[12] we should be filled with most alarming apprehension lest, beset on every side by such a host of enemies, assailed by so many and such formidable engines, the Church of God should, in these days, fall beneath their combined efforts. To omit those illustrious

---

[1] Heb. i. 1.	[2] Is. xlix. 6.	[3] Heb. i. 2.	[4] 2 Pet. i. 17.
[5] Eph. iv. 11.	[6] Eph. ii. 22.	[7] Luke x. 16.	[8] Matt. xxviii. 20.
[9] 1 John iv. 1.	[10] Heb. xiii. 9.	[11] Jerem. xxiii. 21.	[12] Matt. xvi. 18.

states which heretofore professed, in piety and holiness, the Catholic faith transmitted to them by their ancestors, but are now gone astray, wandering from the paths of truth, and openly declaring that their best claims of piety are founded on a total abandonment of the faith of their fathers : there is no region however remote, no place however securely guarded, no corner of the Christian republic, into which this pestilence has not sought secretly to insinuate itself. Those, who proposed to themselves to corrupt the minds of the faithful, aware that they could not hold immediate personal intercourse with all, and thus pour into their ears their poisoned doctrines, by adopting a different plan, disseminated error and impiety more easily and extensively. Besides those voluminous works, by which they sought the subversion of the Catholic faith; to guard against which, however, containing, as they did, open heresy, required, perhaps, little labour or circumspection; they also composed innumerable smaller books, which, veiling their errors under the semblance of piety, deceived with incredible facility the simple and the incautious.

The Fathers, therefore, of the general Council of Trent, anxious to apply some healing remedy to an evil of such magnitude, were not satisfied with having decided the more important points of Catholic doctrine against the heresies of our times, but deemed it further necessary to deliver some fixed form of instructing the faithful in the truths of religion from the very rudiments of Christian knowledge; a form to be followed by those to whom are lawfully intrusted the duties of pastor and teacher. In works of this sort many, it is true, have already employed their pens, and earned the reputation of great piety and learning. The Fathers, however, deemed it of the first importance that a work should appear, sanctioned by the authority of the Holy Synod, from which pastors and all others on whom the duty of imparting instruction devolves, may draw with security precepts for the edification of the faithful; that as there is "one Lord, one faith," [1] there may also be one standard and prescribed form of propounding the dogmas of faith, and instructing Christians in all the duties of piety. *Object and authority of this work.*

As, therefore, the design of the work embraces a variety of matter, the Holy Synod cannot be supposed to have intended to comprise, in one volume, all the dogmas of Christianity, with that minuteness of detail to be found in the works of those who pro- *Its subject matter.*

[1] Eph. iv. 5.

fess to treat of all the institutions and doctrines of religion. Such a task would be one of almost endless labour, and manifestly ill-suited to attain the proposed end. But, having undertaken to instruct pastors and such as have care of souls in those things that belong peculiarly to the pastoral office and are accommodated to the capacity of the faithful; the Holy Synod intended that such things only should be treated of as might assist the pious zeal of pastors in discharging the duty of instruction, should they not be very familiar with the more abstruse questions of theological disputation.

Principal things to be observed by the Pastor in communicating instruction. Such being the nature and object of the present work, its order requires that, before we proceed to develope those things severally which comprise a summary of this doctrine, we premise a few observations explanatory of the considerations which should form the primary object of the pastor's attention, and which he should keep continually before his eyes, in order to know to what end, as it were, all his views and labours and studies are to be directed, and how this end, which he proposes to himself, may be facilitated and attained.

First. The first is always to recollect that in this consists all Christian knowledge, or rather, to use the words of the Apostle, "this is eternal life, to know thee, the only true God, and Jesus Christ whom thou hast sent."[1] A teacher in the Church will, therefore, use his best endeavours that the faithful desire earnestly "to know Jesus Christ and him crucified,"[2] that they be firmly convinced, and with the most heart-felt piety and devotion believe, that "there is no other name under heaven given to men whereby they can be saved,"[3] for he is the propitiation for our sins."[4]

Second. But as "by this we know that we have known him, if we keep his commandments,"[5] the next consideration, and one intimately connected with the preceding, is—to press also upon their attention that their lives are not to be wasted in ease and indolence, but that "we are to walk even as Christ walked,"[6] "and pursue," with unremitting earnestness, "justice, godliness, faith, charity, patience, mildness;"[7] for, "he gave himself for us, that he might redeem us from all iniquity, and might cleanse to himself a people acceptable, a pursuer of good works."[8] These things the Apostle commands pastors to speak and to exhort.

Third. But as our Lord and Saviour has not only declared, but has also proved by his own example, that "the Law and the Prophets

[1] John xvii. 3.   [2] 1 Cor. ii. 2.   [3] Acts iv. 12.   [4] 1 John ii. 2.
[5] 1 John ii. 3.   [6] 1 John ii. 6.   [7] 1 Tim. vi. 11.   [8] Tit. ii. 14.

depend on love," [1] and as, according to the Apostle, charity is the end of the commandments, and the fulfilment of the law,[2] it is unquestionably a paramount duty of the pastor, to use the utmost assiduity to excite the faithful to a love of the infinite goodness of God towards us ; that burning with a sort of divine ardour, they may be powerfully attracted to the supreme and all perfect good, to adhere to which is true and solid happiness, as is fully experienced by him who can say with the Prophet; " What have I in heaven but thee ? and besides thee what do I desire upon earth ?"[3] This, assuredly, is that more excellent way[4] pointed out by the Apostle, when he refers all his doctrines and instructions to charity which never faileth ;"[5] for whatever is proposed by the pastor, whether it be the exercise of faith, of hope, or of some moral virtue ; the love of God should be so strongly insisted upon by him, as to show clearly that all the works of perfect Christian virtue can have no other origin, no other end than divine love.[6]

But as in imparting instruction of any sort, the manner of communicating it is of considerable importance, so in conveying instruction to the people, it should be deemed of the greatest moment.—Age, capacity, manners and condition demand attention, that he, who instructs, may become all things to all men, and be able to gain all to Christ,[7] and prove himself a faithful minister and steward,[8] and, like a good and faithful servant, be found worthy to be placed by his Lord over many things.[9] Nor let him imagine that those committed to his care are all of equal capacity or like dispositions, so as to enable him to apply the same course of instruction, to lead all to knowledge and piety ; for some are, " as it were new-born infants," others grown up in Christ, and others in some sort, of full maturity. Hence the necessity of considering who they are that have occasion for milk, who for more solid food, [11] and of affording to each such nutriment of doctrine as may give spiritual increase, " until we all meet in the unity of faith, and of the knowledge of the Son of God into a perfect man, into the measure of the age of the fulness of Christ." [12] This the example of the Apostle points out to the observance of all, for, " he is a debtor to the Greek and the Barbarian, to the wise and to the unwise :" [13] thus giving all who are called to this ministry, to understand that in announ-

Fourth.

[1] Matt. xxii. 40. [2] 1 Tim. i. 5. Rom. xiii. 8. [3] Psalm lxxii. 25.
[4] 1 Cor. xii. 31. [5] 1 Cor. xiii. 8. [6] 1 Cor. xvi. 14. [7] 1 Cor. ix. 22.
[8] 1 Cor. iv. 1, 2. [9] Matt. xxv. 23. [10] 1 Pet. ii. 2. [11] 1 Cor. iii. 2. Heb. v. 12.
[12] Eph. iv. 13. [13] Rom. i. 14.

2*   C

cing the mysteries of faith, and inculcating the precepts of morality, the instruction is to be accommodated to the capacity and intelligence of the hearers; that, whilst the minds of the strong are filled with spiritual food, the little ones be not suffered to perish with hunger, "asking for bread, whilst there is none to break it to them." [1]

Fifth. Nor should our zeal in communicating Christian knowledge be relaxed, because it is sometimes to be exercised in expounding matters apparently humble and unimportant, and, therefore, comparatively uninteresting to minds accustomed to repose in the contemplation of the more sublime truths of religion. If the wisdom of the eternal Father descended upon the earth in the meanness of our flesh, to teach us the maxims of a heavenly life, who is there whom the love of Christ does not compel [2] to become little in the midst of his brethren; and, as a nurse fostering her children, so anxiously to wish for the salvation of his neighbour, that as the Apostle testifies of himself, he desires to deliver not only the Gospel of Jesus Christ to them, but even his own life for them. [3]

Where the doctrines of Christianity are contained. But all the doctrines of Christianity, in which the faithful are to be instructed, are derived from the word of God, which includes Scripture and tradition. To the study of these, therefore, the pastor should devote his days and his nights, always keeping in mind the admonition of St. Paul to Timothy, which all who have the care of souls should consider as addressed to themselves; "Attend to reading, to exhortation, and to doctrine, [4] for all Scripture divinely inspired, is profitable to teach, to reprove, to correct, to instruct in justice, that the man of God may be perfect, furnished to every good work." [5]

Division of the work. But as the truths revealed by Almighty God, are so many and so various, as to render it no easy task to comprehend them, or, having comprehended them, to retain so distinct a recollection of them as to be able to explain them with ease and promptitude when occasion may require; our predecessors in the faith have very wisely reduced them to these four heads—The Apostle's Creed—The Sacraments—The ten Commandments—and the **First part.** Lord's Prayer. The Creed contains all that is to be held according to the discipline of the Christian faith, whether it regard the knowledge of God, the creation and government of the world; or the redemption of man, the rewards of the good and the pu-

---

[1] Heb. v. 14. Lamen. iv. 4.   [2] 2 Cor. v. 14.   [3] 1 Thess. ii. 7, 8.
[4] 1 Tim. iv. 13.   [5] 2 Tim. iii. 16, 17

nishments of the wicked. The doctrine of the seven Sacraments comprehends the signs, and, as it were, the instruments of grace. The Decalogue, whatever has reference to the law, "the end whereof is charity." [1] Finally, the Lord's Prayer contains whatever can be the object of the Christian's desires, or hopes, or prayers. The exposition, therefore, of these, as it were, common-places of sacred Scripture, includes almost every thing to be known by a Christian. *Second Part. Third Part. Fourth Part.*

We, therefore, deem it proper to acquaint pastors that, whenever they have occasion, in the ordinary discharge of their duty, to expound any passage of the Gospel, or any other part of Scripture, they will find its substance under some one of the four heads already enumerated, to which they will recur, as the source from which their exposition is to be drawn. Thus, if the Gospel of the first Sunday of Advent is to be explained, "There shall be signs in the sun and in the moon, &c. [2] whatever regards its explanation is contained under the article of the creed, "He shall come to judge the living and the dead," and by imbodying the substance of that article in his exposition, the pastor will at once instruct his people in the creed and in the Gospel. Whenever, therefore, he has to communicate instruction and expound the Scriptures, he will observe the same rule of referring all to these four principal heads, which, as we have already observed, comprise the whole force and doctrine of Holy Scripture. *Application of the Catechism to the Gospel of the Sunday.*

He will, however, observe that order which he deems best suited to persons, times and circumstances. Walking in the footsteps of the Fathers, who to initiate men in Christ the Lord and instruct them in his discipline begin with the doctrine of faith, we have deemed it useful to explain first in order what appertains to faith. *Why it begins with the explanation of the Creed.*

As the word faith has a variety of meanings in the Sacred Scriptures, it may not be unnecessary to observe that here we speak of that faith by which we yield our entire assent to whatever has been revealed by Almighty God. That faith thus understood is necessary to salvation no man can reasonably doubt; particularly as the Sacred Scriptures declare that "Without faith it is impossible to please God." [3] For as the end proposed to man as his ultimate happiness is far above the reach of the human understanding, it was, therefore, necessary that it should be made known to him by Almighty God. This know- *Faith, how understood here.*

---

[1] 1 Tim. i. 5.   [2] 2 Luke xxi. 26.   [3] Heb. xi. 6.

ledge is nothing else than faith, by which we yield our unhesitating assent to whatever the authority of our Holy Mother tho
Church teaches us to have been revealed by Almighty God: for
the faithful cannot doubt those things of which God, who is truth
itself, is the author. Hence we see the great difference that exists
between this faith which we give to God, and the credence which
we yield to profane historians.   But faith, though comprehensive, and differing in degree and dignity, [for we read in Scripture these words, " O thou of little faith, why didst thou doubt"[1]
and " great is thy faith," [2] and " Increase our faith,"[3] also
" Faith without works is dead"[4] and " Faith which worketh by
charity ;[5]"] is yet the same in kind, and the full force of its
definition applies equally to all its degrees.   Its fruit and advantages to us, we shall point out when explaining the articles of
the Creed.   The first, then, and most important points of Christian faith are those which the holy Apostles, the great leaders and
teachers of the faith, men inspired by the Holy Ghost, have divided into the twelve articles of the Creed: for as they had received a command from the Lord to go forth " into the whole
world," " as his ambassadors, and preach the Gospel to every
creature, [6] they thought proper to compose a form of Christian
faith, " that all may speak and think the same thing;" [7] and
that amongst those whom they should have called to the unity
of faith, no schisms should exist; but that they should be perfect in the same mind, and in the same spirit.   This profession
of Christian faith and hope, drawn up by themselves, the Apostles called a " symbol," either because it was an aggregate of the
combined sentiments of all ; or because, by it, as by a common
sign and watch-word, they might easily distinguish false brethren, deserters from the faith, " unawares brought in," [8] " who
adultered the word of God,"[9] from those who had pledged an
oath of fidelity to serve under the banner of Christ.

The Creed why composed by the Apostles.

---

[1] Matt. xiv. 31.	[2] Matt. xv. 28.	[3] Luke xvii. 5.	[4] James ii. 17.
[5] Gal. v. 6	[6] 2 Cor. v. 18, 19, 20.	Mark xvi. 15.	[7] 1 Cor. i. 10.
	[8] Gal. ii. 4.	[9] 2 Cor. ii. 17.	

THE

CATECHISM

OF

THE COUNCIL OF TRENT.

PART I.

ON THE TWELVE ARTICLES OF THE CREED.

ARTICLE I.

"I BELIEVE IN GOD, THE FATHER ALMIGHTY, MAKER OF HEAVEN
AND EARTH."

AMONGST the many truths which Christianity proposes to our Division of
belief, and of which separately, or collectively, an assured and the Creed.
firm faith is necessary, the first and one essential to be believed
by all, is that which God himself has taught us as the foundation
of truth, and which is a summary of the unity of the divine
essence, of the distinction of three persons, and of the actions
which are peculiarly attributed to each. The pastor will inform
the people that the Apostles' Creed briefly comprehends the doctrine of this mystery. For, as has been observed by our predecessors in the faith, who in treating this subject, have given proofs
at once of piety and accuracy, the Creed seems to be divided into
three principal parts, one describing the first Person of the divine nature, and the stupendous work of the creation—another,
the second Person, and the mystery of man's redemption—a
third, comprising in several most appropirate sentences, the doctrine of the third Person, the head and source of our sanctification.
These sentences are called articles, by a sort of comparison frequently used by our forefathers; for as the members of the body
are divided by joints (*articulis*) so in this profession of faith,
whatever is to be believed distinctly and separately from any
thing else, is appositely called an article.

"I BELIEVE IN GOD."] The meaning of these words is this; Import of
I believe with certainty, and without a shadow of doubt profess the words
my belief in God the Father, the first person of the Trinity, who in

21

by his omnipotence created from nothing, preserves and governs the heavens and the earth, and all things which they encompass: and not only do I believe in him from my heart, and profess this belief with my lips, but with the greatest ardour and piety tend towards him, as the supreme and most perfect good.   Let it suffice thus briefly to state the substance of this first article: but as great mysteries lie concealed under almost every word, the pastor must now give them a more minute consideration, in order that, as far as God has permitted, the faithful may approach, with fear and trembling, the contemplation of the glory of the divine Majesty.

· The word "believe," therefore, does not here mean "to think," "to imagine," "to be of opinion," but, as the Sacred Scriptures teach, it expresses the deepest conviction of the mind, by which we give a firm and unhesitating assent to God revealing his mysterious truths.   As far, therefore, as regards the use of the word here; he, who firmly and without hesitation is convinced of any thing, is said "to believe." [1]   Nor is the knowledge derived through faith to be considered less certain, because its objects are not clearly comprehended ; for the divine light in which we see them, although it does not render them evident, yet sheds around them such a lustre as leaves no doubt on the mind regarding them. "For God, who commanded the light to shine out of darkness, hath shone in our hearts,"[2] "that the Gospel be not hidden to us, as to those that perish." [3]

Certainty of Faith.

From what has been said, it follows that he who is gifted with this heavenly knowledge of faith, is free from an inquisitive curiosity ; for when God commands us to believe, he does not propose to us to search into his divine judgments, or inquire into their reasons and their causes, but demands an immutable faith, by the efficacy of which, the mind reposes in the knowledge of eternal truth.   And indeed, if, whilst we have the testimony of the Apostle, that "God is true and every man a liar;"[4] it would argue arrogance and presumption to disbelieve the asseveration of a grave and sensible man affirming any thing as true, and urge him to support his asseveration by reasons and authorities ; what temerity and folly does it not argue in those, who hear the words of God himself, to demand reasons for the heavenly and saving doctrines which he reveals ?   Faith, therefore, excludes not only all doubt, but even the desire of subjecting its truths to demonstration.

Excludes curiosity.

But the pastor should also teach, that he who says, "I believe," besides declaring the inward assent of the mind, which is an internal act of faith, should also openly and with alacrity profess and proclaim what he inwardly and in his heart believes : for the faithful should be animated by the same spirit that spoke by the lips of the prophet, when he said : "I believe, and therefore did I speak,"[5] and should follow the example of the Apostles who replied to the princes of the earth : "We cannot but

Open profession of.

[1] Rom. iv. 18—21.   [2] 2 Cor. iv. 6.   [3] Ibid. v. 3.   [4] Rom. iii. 4.
[5] Ps. cxv. 1.

speak the things which we have seen and heard."[1] This spirit
should be excited within us by these admirable words of St. Paul:
" I am not ashamed of the Gospel, for it is the power of God unto
salvation, to every one that believeth ;"[2] sentiments which derive
additional force from these words of the same Apostle : " With
the heart we believe unto justice ; but with the mouth confession
is made unto salvation."[3]

" In God"] From these words we may learn, how exalted Christian
philosophy
are the dignity and excellence of Christian philosophy, and superior to
what a debt of gratitude we owe to the divine goodness ; we to human
whom it is given at once to soar on the wings of faith to the wisdom.
knowledge of a being surpassing in excellence and in whom all
our desires should be concentrated. For in this, Christian philosophy and human wisdom differ much ; that guided solely by the
light of nature, and having made gradual advances by reasoning
on sensible objects and effects, human wisdom, after long and
laborious investigation, at length reaches with difficulty the contemplation of the invisible things of God, discovers and understands the first cause and author of all things ; whilst on the contrary Christian philosophy so enlightens and enlarges the human
mind, that at once and without difficulty it pierces the heavens,
and illumined with the splendours of the divinity contemplates
first the eternal source of light, and in its radiance all created
things ; so that with the Apostle we experience with the most
exquisite pleasure, "and believing rejoice with joy unspeakable,"[4] that " we have been called out of darkness into his admirable light." [5] Justly, therefore, do the faithful profess first to
believe in God ; whose majesty, with the prophet Jeremiah, we
declare "incomprehensible,"[6] for, as the Apostle says, " He dwells
in light inaccessible, which no man hath seen or can see :"[7] and
speaking to Moses, he himself said " No man shall see my face
and live."[8] The mind, to be capable of rising to the contemplation of the Deity, whom nothing approaches in sublimity, must
be entirely disengaged from the senses ; and this the natural condition of man in the present life renders impossible.

" God," however, " left not himself without testimony ; doing Human
reason,
good from heaven ; giving rains and fruitful seasons, filling our however,
hearts with food and gladness."[9] Hence it is that philosophers capable
conceived no mean idea of the Divinity ; ascribed to him nothing of obtain-
corporeal, nothing gross, nothing compound ; considered him the ledge of
perfection and fulness of all good ; from whom, as from an eter- God from
nal, inexhaustible fountain of goodness and benignity, flows his works.
every perfect gift to all creatures ; called him the wise, the author
of truth, the loving, the just, the most beneficent; gave him, also,
many other appellations expressive of supreme and absolute perfection ; and said that his immensity filled every place, and his
omnipotence extended to every thing. This the Sacred Scriptures more clearly express, and more fully develope, as in the

[1] Acts. iv. 20 [2] Rom. i. 16. [3] Rom. x. 10. [4] 1 Pet. i. 8.
[5] 1 Pet. ii. 9. [6] Jerem. xxxii. 19. [7] 1 Tim. vi. 16. [8] Exod. xxxiii. 10.
[9] Acts xiv. 16.

following passages : " God is a spirit ;"[1] " Be ye perfect, even
as your Father, who is in heaven, is also perfect ;"[2] "all things are
naked and open to his eyes ;"[3] " Oh ! the depth of the riches of
the wisdom and of the knowledge of God ;"[4] " God is true ;"[5]
" I am the way, the truth and the life ;"[6] " Thy right hand is
full of justice ;"[7] " Thou openest thy hand, and fillest with blessing every living creature ;"[8] and finally : " Whither shall I go
from thy spirit, or whither shall I flee from thy face ? If I ascend into heaven, thou art there ; if I descend into hell thou art
there ; if I take wing in the morning, and dwell in the uttermost
parts of the sea ; even there also shall thy hand lead me, and thy
right hand shall hold me," &c.[9] and " Do I not fill heaven and
earth, saith the Lord ?"[10] These are great and sublime truths
regarding the nature of God ; and of these truths philosophers
attained a knowledge, which, whilst it accords with the authority
of the inspired volume, results from the investigation of created
things.

The know-
ledge de-
rived from
faith more
easy and
secure.

But we must, also, see the necessity of divine revelation, if
we reflect that not only does faith, as we have already observed,
make known at once to the rude and unlettered, those truths, a
knowledge of which philosophers could attain only by long and
laborious study ; but also impresses this knowledge with much
greater certainty and security against all error, than if it were the
result of philosophical inquiry. But how much more exalted
must not that knowledge of the Deity be considered, which cannot be acquired in common by all from the contemplation of nature, but is the peculiar privilege of those who are illumined by
the light of faith ?

This knowledge is contained in the articles of the Creed which
disclose to us the unity of the divine essence, and the distinction
of three persons ; and also that God is the ultimate end of our
being, from whom we are to expect the fruition of the eternal
happiness of heaven : for we have learned from St. Paul, that
" God is a rewarder of them that seek him." [11] The greatness
of these rewards, and whether they are such as that human
knowledge could aspire to their attainment, [12] we learn from these
words of Isaias uttered long before those of the Apostle ; " From
the beginning of the world they have not heard, nor perceived
with the ears : without thee, O God, the eye hath not seen what
things thou hast prepared for them that wait for thee." [13]

Unity of
God.

From what has been said, it must also be confessed that there
is but one God not many Gods ; for as we attribute to God supreme goodness and infinite perfection, it is impossible that what
is supreme and most perfect could be common to many. If a
being want any thing that constitutes this supreme perfection, it
is therefore imperfect, and cannot be endowed with the nature of
God. This is also proved from many passages of the Sacred

1 John iv. 24.   2 Matt. v. 48.   3 Heb. iv. 13.   4 Rom. xi. 33.
5 Rom. iii. 4.   6 John xiv. 6.   7 Ps. xlvii. 11.   8 Ps. cxliv. 16.
9 Ps. cxxxviii. 7, 8, 9, 10, &c.   10 Jer. xxiii. 24.   11 Heb. xi. 6.
12 1 Cor. ii. 9—14.   13 Isa. lxiv. 4.

Scripture; for it is written, " Hear, O Israel, the Lord our God, is one Lord ;"[1] again, " Thou shalt not have strange gods before me,"[2] is the command of God : and again he often admonishes us by the prophet, " I am the first, and I am the last, and besides me there is no God." [3] The Apostle also expressly declares ; " one Lord, one faith, one Baptism." [4] It should not, however, excite our surprise if the Sacred Scriptures sometimes give the name of God to creatures :[5] for when they call the prophets and judges gods, they do so not after the manner of the Gentiles; who, in their folly and impiety, formed to themselves many gods ; but in order to express, by a manner of speaking then not unusual, some eminent quality or function conferred on them by the divine munificence. Christian faith, therefore, believes and professes, as is declared in the Nicene Creed in confirmation of this truth, that God in his nature, substance and essence is one ; but soaring still higher, it so understands him to be one, that it adores unity in trinity and trinity in unity. Of this mystery we now proceed to speak, as it comes next in order in the Creed.

" THE FATHER"] As God is called " Father" for more rea- sons than one, we must first determine the strictly appropriated meaning of the word in the present instance. Some also on whom the light of faith never shone, conceived God to be an eternal substance from whom all things had their beginning, by whose providence they are governed and preserved in their order and state of existence. As, therefore, he, to whom a fa- mily owes its origin, and by whose wisdom and authority it is governed, is called a father ; so by analogy from things human, God was called Father, because acknowledged to be the crea- tor and governor of the universe. The Sacred Scriptures also use the same appellation, when, speaking of God, they declare that to him the creation of all things, power and admirable provi- dence, are to be ascribed : for we read, " Is not he thy Father that hath possessed thee, and made thee, and created thee ?"[6] And again, " Have we not all one Father ? Hath not one God created us ?"[7]

Propriety of the word " Father" as applied to God.

But God, particularly in the New Testament, is much more frequently, and in some sense peculiarly called the Father of Christians, who " have not received the spirit of bondage in fear, but have received the spirit of adoption of sons, whereby they cry abba Father;" [8] " for the Father hath bestowed on us that manner of charity, that we should be called, and be the sons of God ;" [9] " and if sons, heirs also, heirs, indeed, of God, and joint-heirs with Christ,"[10] " who is the first-born amongst many brethren, [11] for which cause he is not ashamed to call them bre- thren." [12] Whether, therefore, we look to the common title of crea- tion and conservation ; or to the special one of spiritual adoption,

God in a special manner the " Father" of Chris- tians.

[1] Deut. vi. 4. [2] Exod. xx. 3. [3] Is. xliv. 6; xlviii. 12. [4] Eph. iv. 5.
[5] Ps. lxxxi. 1. Exod. xxii. 28. 1 Cor. viii. 5. [6] Deut. xxxii. 6
[7] Mal. ii. 10. [8] Rom. viii. 15. [9] 1 John iii. 1. [10] Rom. viii. 17
[11] Rom. viii. 29. [12] Heb. ii. 11.

D

the term " Father," as applied to God by Christians, is alike appropriate.

The name of ' Father' implies plurality of persons

But the pastor will teach the faithful that, on hearing the word " Father," besides the ideas already unfolded, their minds should rise to the contemplation of more exalted mysteries. Under the name of " Father," the divine oracles begin to unveil to us a mysterious truth which is more abstruse, and more deeply hidden in that inaccessible light in which God dwells—a mysterious truth which human reason not only could not reach, but even conceive to exist. This name implies, that in the one essence of the Godhead is proposed to our belief, not only one person, but a distinction of persons: for in one Divine nature there are three persons; the Father, begotten of none; the Son, begotten of the Father before all ages; the Holy Ghost, proceeding from the Father and the Son from all eternity.

The Trinity.

The Father the first person.

But in the one substance of the Divinity the Father is the first person, who with his only begotten Son, and the Holy Ghost is one God and one Lord, not in the singularity of one person, but in the trinity of one substance. These three persons, (for it would be impiety to assert that they are unlike or unequal in any thing) are understood to be distinct only in their peculiar relations. The Father is unbegotten, the Son begotten of the Father, and the Holy Ghost proceeds from both; and we confess the essence of the three Persons, their substance to be so the same, that we believe that in the confession of the true and eternal God, we are piously and religiously to adore distinction in the Persons, unity in the essence, and equality in the Trinity. When we say that the Father is the first person, we are not to be understood to mean that in the Trinity there is any thing first or last, greater or less—let no Christian be guilty of such impiety, for Christianity proclaims the same eternity, the same majesty of glory in the three Persons—but the Father, because the beginning without a beginning, we truly and unhesitatingly affirm to be the first person, who, as he is distinct from the others by his peculiar relation of paternity, so of him alone is it true that he begot the Son from eternity : for, when in the Creed we pronounce together the words " God" and " Father," it intimates to us that he is God and Father from eternity.

Curiosity to be avoided in examining the mystery of the Trinity.

But as in nothing is a too curious inquiry more dangerous, or error more fatal, than in the knowledge and exposition of this, the most profound and difficult of mysteries, let the pastor instruct the people religiously to retain the terms used to express this mystery, and which are peculiar to essence and person ; and let the faithful know that unity belongs to essence, and distinction to Persons. But these are truths which should not be made matter of too subtile disquisition, when we recollect that " he, who is a searcher of majesty, shall be overwhelmed by glory."[1] We should be satisfied with the assurance which faith gives us that we have been taught these truths by God himself ; and to

<hr>

[1] Prov. xxv. 27.

dissent from his oracles is the extreme of folly and misery. He has said : " Teach ye all nations, baptising them in the name of the Father, and of the Son, and of the Holy Ghost ;"[1] and again, " there are three who give testimony in heaven ; the Father, the Word, and the Holy Ghost ; and these three are one."[2] Let him, however, who by the divine bounty believes these truths, constantly beseech and implore God, and the Father, who made all things out of nothing, and orders all things sweetly, who gave us power to become the sons of God, and who made known to us the mystery of the Trinity ; that admitted, one day, into the eternal tabernacles, he may be worthy to see how great is the fecundity of the Father, who contemplating and understanding himself, begot the Son like and equal to himself; how a love of charity in both, entirely the same and equal, which is the Holy Ghost, proceeding from the Father and the Son, connects the begetting and the begotten by an eternal and indissoluble bond ; and that thus the essence of the Trinity is one and the distinction of the three persons perfect.

"Almighty."] The Sacred Scriptures, in order to mark the piety and devotion with which the God of holiness is to be adored, usually express his supreme power and infinite majesty in a variety of ways; but the pastor should impress particularly on the minds of the faithful, that the attribute of *omnipotence* is that by which he is most frequently designated. Thus he says of himself, " I am the *Almighty* God ;"[3] and again, Jacob when sending his sons to Joseph thus prayed for them, " May my *Almighty* God make him favourable to you."[4] In the Apocalypse also it is written, " The Lord God, who is, who was, and who is to come, *the Almighty :*"[5] and in another place the last day is called " the day of *Almighty* God."[6] Sometimes the same attribute is expressed in many words ; thus : " no word shall be impossible with God :"[7] " Is the hand of the Lord unable ?"[8] " Thy power is at hand when thou wilt."[9] Many other passages of the same import might be adduced, all of which convey the same idea which is clearly comprehended under this single word " *Almighty*." By it we understand that there neither is, nor can be imagined any thing which God cannot do ; for he can not only annihilate all created things, and in a moment summon from nothing into existence many other worlds—an exercise of power, which, however great, comes in some degree within our comprehension—but he can do many things still greater, of which the human mind can form no conception. But though God can do all things, yet he cannot lie, or deceive, or be deceived ; he cannot sin, or be ignorant of any thing, or cease to exist. These things are compatible with those beings only whose actions are imperfect, and are entirely incompatible with the nature of God, whose acts are all-perfect. To be capable of these things is a proof of weakness,

Marginal notes:
Why the power and majesty of God are designated by many names, in the Sacred Scriptures.

That of Almighty most frequent.

Its meaning.

---

[1] Matt. xxviii. 19. [2] 1 John v. 7. [3] Gen. xvii. 1. [4] Gen. xliii. 14.
[5] Apoc. i. 8. [6] Apoc. xvi. 14. [7] Luke i. 37. [8] Num. xi. 23.
[9] Wisd. xii. 18.

not of supreme and infinite power, the peculiar attribute of God Thus, whilst we believe God to be omnipotent, we exclude from him whatever is not intimately connected, and entirely consistent with the perfection of his nature.

Omnipotence, why the only attribute of God mentioned in the Creed. But the pastor should point out the propriety and wisdom of having omitted all other names of God in the Creed, and of having proposed to us that alone of " *Almighty*" as the object of our belief; for by acknowledging God to be omnipotent, we also of necessity acknowledge him to be omniscient, and to hold all things in subjection to his supreme authority and dominion. When we doubt not that he is omnipotent, we must be also convinced of every thing else regarding him, the absence of which would render his omnipotence altogether unintelligible. Besides, nothing tends more to confirm our faith, and animate our hope, than a deep conviction that all things are possible to God: for whatever may be afterwards proposed as an object of faith, however great, however wonderful, however raised above the natural order, is easily and at once believed, when the mind is already imbued with the knowledge of the omnipotence of God. Nay more, the greater the truths which the divine oracles announce, the more willingly does the mind deem them worthy of belief; and should we expect any favour from heaven, we are not discouraged by the greatness of the desired boon, but are cheered and confirmed by frequently considering, that there is nothing which an omnipotent God cannot effect.

Necessity of faith in God 'Almighty' With this faith, then, we should be specially fortified whenever we are required to render any extraordinary service to our neighbour, or seek to obtain by prayer any favour from God. Its necessity in the one case, we learn from the Redeemer himself, who, when rebuking the incredulity of the Apostles, said to them, "If you have faith as a mustard-seed, you shall say to this mountain, remove from hence thither, and it shall remove; and nothing shall be impossible to you :"[1] and in the other, from these words of St. James, "Let him ask in faith, nothing wavering; for he that wavereth is like a wave of the sea, which is moved and carried about by the wind. Therefore, let not that man think that he shall receive any thing of the Lord."[2] This faith brings with it also many advantages. It forms us in the first place, to all humility and lowliness of mind, according to these words of the Prince of the Apostles: "Be you humbled, therefore, under the mighty hand of God."[3] It also teaches us not to fear where there is no cause of fear, but to fear God alone,[4] in whose power we ourselves and all that we have are placed ;[5] for our Saviour says, "I will show you whom you shall fear; fear ye him, who, after he hath killed, hath power to cast into hell."[6] This faith is, also, useful to enable us to know and exalt the infinite mercies of God towards us : he who reflects on the omnipotence of God, cannot be so

[1] Matt. xvii. 20.　　[2] James i. 6, 7.　　[3] 1 Pet. v. 6.　　[4] Ps. xxxii. 8. 33. 10.
[5] Wisd. vii. 16.　　[6] Luke xii. 5.

ungrateful as not frequently to exclaim, "He that is mighty hath done great things to me." [1]

When, however, in this article we call the Father "Almighty," Not three Almighties but one Almighty. let no person be led into the error of excluding, therefore, from its participation the Son and the Holy Ghost. As we say the Father is God, the Son is God, the Holy Ghost is God, and yet there are not three Gods, but one God, so, in like manner, we confess that the Father is Almighty, the Son Almighty, and the Holy Ghost Almighty, and, yet, there are not three Almighties, but one Almighty. The Father, in particular, we call Almighty, because he is the source of all origin; as we also attribute wisdom to the Son, because the eternal word of the Father; and goodness to the Holy Ghost, because the love of both. These, however, and such appellations, may be given indiscriminately to the three Persons, according to the rule of Catholic faith.

"CREATOR OF HEAVEN AND EARTH"] The necessity of having From what, how, and why, God made the world previously imparted to the faithful a knowledge of the omnipotence of God, will appear from what we are now about to explain with regard to the creation of the world. For when already convinced of the omnipotence of the Creator, we more readily believe the wondrous production of so stupendous a work. For God formed not the world from materials of any sort, but created it from nothing, and that not by constraint or necessity, but spontaneously, and of his own free will. Nor was he impelled to create by any other cause than a desire to communicate to creatures the riches of his bounty; for essentially happy in himself, he stands not in need of any thing; as David expresses it: "I said to the Lord, thou art my God, for of my goods thou hast no need." [2] But as, influenced by his own goodness, "he hath done all things whatsoever he would," [3] so in the work of the creation he followed no external form or model; but contemplating and, as it were, imitating the universal model contained in the divine intelligence, the supreme Architect, with infinite wisdom and power, attributes peculiar to the Divinity, created all things in the beginning: "he spoke and they were made, he commanded and they were created." [4] The words "heaven" and "earth" include all things which the heavens and the earth contain; for, besides the heavens, which the Prophet called "the work of his fingers," [5] he also gave to the sun its brilliancy, and to the moon and stars their beauty: and that they may be "for signs and for seasons, for days and for years," [6] he so ordered the celestial bodies in a certain and uniform course, that nothing varies more their continual revolution, yet nothing more fixed than that variety.

Moreover, he created from nothing spiritual nature, and angels Creation of Angels. innumerable to serve and minister to him: and these he replenished and adorned with the admirable gifts of his grace and power. That the devil and his associates, the rebel angels, were gifted at their creation with grace, clearly follows from these

---

[1] Luke i. 49. [2] Ps. xv. 2. [3] Ps. cxiii. 3. [4] Ps. xxxii. 9; cxlviii. 5
[5] Ps. viii. 4. [6] Gen. i. 14.

words of the Sacred Scriptures: "The devil stood not in the truth;"[1] on which subject St. Augustine says, "In creating the angels he endowed them with good will, that is, with pure love, by which they adhere to him, at once giving them existence, and adorning them with grace."[2] Hence we are to believe that the angels were never without "good will," that is, the love of God. As to their knowledge we have this testimony of Holy Scripture: "Thou, Lord, my King, art wise according to the wisdom of an Angel of God, to understand all things upon earth."[3] Finally, David ascribes power to them in these words; "mighty in strength, executing his word;"[4] and on this account, they are often called

Their fall in Scripture the "powers" and "the hosts of heaven." But although they were all endowed with celestial gifts, very many, however, having rebelled against God, their Father and Creator, were hurled from the mansions of bliss, and shut up in the dark dungeons of hell, there to suffer for eternity the punishment of their pride. Speaking of them the Prince of the Apostles says: "He spared not the angels that sinned; but delivered them, drawn down by infernal ropes, to the lower hell, into torments, to be reserved unto judgment."[5]

Creation of the earth. The earth, also, God commanded to stand in the midst of the world, rooted in its own foundation, and "made the mountains to ascend, and the plains to descend into the place which he had founded for them." That the waters should not inundate the earth, "he hath set a bound which they shall not pass over, neither shall they return to cover the earth."[6] He next not only clothed and adorned it with trees, and every variety of herb and flower, but filled it, as he had already filled the air and water, with innumerable sorts of living creatures.

Of Man. Lastly, he formed man from 'the slime of the earth, immortal and impassable, not, however, by the strength of nature, but by the bounty of God. His soul he created to his own image and likeness; gifted him with free will, and tempered all his motions and appetites, so as to subject them, at all times, to the dictate of reason. He then added the invaluable gift of original righteousness, and next gave him dominion over all other animals—By referring to the sacred history of Genesis the pastor will make himself familiar with these things for the instruction of the faithful.

God the Creator of all. What we have said, then, of the creation of the universe, is to be understood as conveyed by the words "heaven and earth," and is thus briefly set forth by the prophet: "Thine are the heavens, and thine is the earth: the world and the fulness thereof thou hast founded:"[7] and still more briefly by the Fathers of the Council of Nice, who added in their Creed these words, "of all things visible and invisible." Whatever exists in the universe, and was created by God, either falls under the senses, and is included in the word "visible," or is an object of perception to the mind, and is expressed by the word "invisible."

1 John viii. 44.   2 Aug. lib. 12. de Civit. Dei, cap. 9.   3 2 Kings nv. 20.
4 Ps. cii. 20.   5 2 Pet. ii. 4.   6 Ps. ciii. 8, 9.   7 Ps. lxxxviii. 12.

We are not, however, to understand that the works of God, The preserver and governor. when once created, could continue to exist unsupported by his omnipotence: as they derive existence from his supreme power, wisdom and goodness, so unless preserved continually by his superintending providence, and by the same power which produced them, they should instantly return into their original nothing. This the Scriptures declare, when they say, "How could any thing endure if thou wouldst not? or be preserved, if not called by thee?"[1] But not only does God protect and govern all things by his providence; but also by an internal virtue impels to motion and action whatever moves and acts, and this in such a manner, as that although he excludes not, he yet prevents the agency of secondary causes. His invisible influence extends to all things, and as the wise man says: "It reacheth from end to end, mighty, and ordereth all things sweetly."[2] This is the reason why the Apostle, announcing to the Athenians the God whom not knowing they adored, said; "He is not far from every one of us: for in him we live and move and have our being."[3]

Let thus much suffice for the explanation of the first article of the Creed: it may not, however, be unnecessary to add that the creation is the common work of the three Persons of the Holy and undivided Trinity—of the Father, whom, according to the doctrine of the Apostles, we here declare to be "Creator of heaven and earth;"—of the Son, of whom the Scripture says, "all things were made by him;"[4] and of the Holy Ghost, of whom it is written, "The Spirit of God moved over the waters:"[5] and again, "By the word of the Lord the heavens were established· and all the power of them by the Spirit of his mouth."[6]

Creation, the work of the three Persons.

ARTICLE II.

"AND IN JESUS CHRIST, HIS ONLY SON, OUR LORD."

THAT wonderful and superabundant are the blessings which flow to the human race, from the belief and profession of this article we learn from these words of St. John; "Whosoever shall confess that Jesus is the son of God, God abideth in him and he in God;"[7] and also from the words of Christ our Lord, proclaiming the Prince of the Apostles blessed for the confession of this truth; "Blessed art thou, Simon Bar-Jona: for flesh and blood have not revealed it to thee, but my Father who is in heaven."[8] This sublime truth is the most firm basis of our salvation and redemption.

The great blessings which flow from the belief and profession of this article.

But as the fruit of these admirable blessings is best known by considering the ruin brought on man, by his fall from that most

How we may learn

---

[1] Wisdom xi. 26. [2] Wisdom viii. 1. [3] Acts xvii. 27, 28. [4] John i. 3.
[5] Gen. i. 2. [6] Ps. xxxii. 6. [7] 1 John iv. 15. [8] Mat. xvi. 17.

to estimate their value. happy state in which God had placed our first parents, let the pastor be particularly careful to make known to the faithful, the cause of this common misery and universal calamity., When Adam had departed from the obedience due to God, and had violated the prohibition, "of every tree of Paradise thou shalt eat; but of the tree of knowledge of good and evil, thou shalt not eat, for in what day soever thou shalt eat it, thou shalt die the death ;"[1] he fell into the extreme misery of losing the sanctity and righteousness in which he was created ; and of becoming subject to all those other evils, which are detailed more at large by the holy Council of Trent.[2] The Pastor, therefore, will not omit to remind the faithful, that the guilt and punishment of original sin were not confined to Adam, but justly descended from him, as from their source and cause, to all posterity. The human race, having fallen from their elevated dignity, no power of men or angels could raise them from their fallen condition, and replace them in their primitive state. To remedy the evil, and repair the loss, it became necessary that the Son of God, whose merits are infinite, clothed in the weakness of our flesh, should remove the infinite weight of sin, and reconcile us to God in his blood.

Belief and profession of this article necessary to salvation. The belief and profession of this our redemption, as God declared from the beginning, are now, and always have been, necessary to salvation. In the sentence of condemnation, pronounced against the human race immediately after the sin of Adam, the hope of redemption was held out in these words, which denounced to the devil, the loss which he was to sustain by man's redemption: "I will put enmities between thee and the woman, and thy seed and her seed: she shall crush thy head, and thou shalt lie in wait for her heel."[3] The same promise he again often confirmed, and more distinctly signified his counsels to those chiefly whom he desired to make special objects of his predilection: amongst others to the patriarch Abraham, to whom he often declared this mystery, but then more explicitly when, in obedience to God's command, he was prepared to sacrifice his son Isaac : "Because," says he, "thou hast done this thing, and hast not spared thy only begotten son for my sake ; I will bless thee, and I will multiply thy seed as the stars of heaven, and as the sand that is by the sea shore. Thy seed shall possess the gates of their enemies, and in thy seed shall all the nations of the earth be blessed ; because thou hast obeyed my voice."[4] From these words it was easy to infer that he, who was to deliver mankind from the ruthless tyranny of Satan, was to be descended from Abraham ; and that, whilst he was the Son of God, he was to be born of the seed of Abraham according to the flesh. Not long after, to preserve the memory of this promise, he renewed the same covenant with Jacob, the grandson of Abraham. When in a vision Jacob saw a ladder standing on earth, and its top reaching to heaven, and the angels of God ascending and descending by it,[5] he also heard the Lord saying to him, as the Scripture

The promise of a Saviour.

Same promise renewed.

[1] Gen. ii. 16, 17.   [2] Sess. 5. Can. 1. & 2—Sess. 6. Can. 1. & 2.   [3] Gen. iii. 15
[4] Gen. xxii. 16, 17, 18.   [5] Gen. xxviii. 12.

testifies ; "I am the Lord God of Abraham thy father, and the God of Isaac ; the land, wherein thou sleepest, I will give to thee and to thy seed ; and thy seed shall be as the dust of the earth ; thou shalt spread abroad to the west and to the east, and to the north and to the south ; and in thee and thy seed all the nations of the earth shall be blessed."[1] Nor did God cease afterwards to excite in the posterity of Abraham, and in many others, the hope of a Saviour, by renewing the recollection of the same promise ; for, after the establishment of the Jewish republic and religion, it became better known to his people. Many types signified, and prophets foretold the numerous and invaluable blessings which our Redeemer, Christ Jesus, was to bring to mankind. And, indeed, the prophets, whose minds were illuminated with light from above, foretold the birth of the Son of God, the wondrous works which he wrought whilst on earth, his doctrine, manners, kindred, death, resurrection, and the other mysterious circumstances regarding him ;[2] and all these as graphically as if they were passing before their eyes. With the exception of the time only, we can discover no difference between the predictions of the prophets, and the preaching of the apostles, between the faith of the ancient patriarchs, and that of Christians—But, we are now to speak of the several parts of this Article.

"Jesus"]This is the proper name of the man-God, and signifies Saviour ; a name given him not accidentally, or by the judgment or will of man, but by the counsel and command of God. For the angel announced to Mary his mother : "Behold thou shalt conceive in thy womb and shalt bring forth a Son, and thou shalt call his name Jesus."[3] He afterwards not only commanded Joseph, who was espoused to the Virgin, to call the child by that name, but also declared the reason why he should be so called : "Joseph," says he, "Son of David, fear not to take Mary thy wife, for that which is born in her is of the Holy Ghost ; and she shall bring forth a Son, and thou shalt call his name Jesus, for he shall save his people from their sins,"[4] In the Sacred Scriptures we meet with many who were called by this name—the son of Nave, for instance, who succeeded Moses, and, by special privilege denied to Moses, conducted into the land of promise, the people whom Moses had delivered from Egypt ;[5] and Josedech, whose father was a priest.[6] But how much more appropriately shall we not deem this name given to him, who gave light and liberty and salvation, not to one people only, but to all men, of all ages—to men oppressed, not by famine, or Egyptian, or Babylonish bondage, but sitting in the shadow of death and fettered by sin, and riveted in the galling chains of the devil—to him who purchased for them a right to the inheritance of heaven, and reconciled them to God the

Meaning of the name Jesus, by whom and why given

[1] Gen. xxviii. 13, 14.   [2] Is. vii. 14 ; viii. 3 ; ix. 5 ; xi. 1—53 per totum. Jer. xxiii. 5 ; xxx. 9. Dan. vii. 13 ; ix. 21.   [3] Luke i. 31.   [4] Matt. i. 20, 21. [5] Eccl. xlvi. 1.   [6] Agg. i. 1.

E

Father. In those men, who were designated by the same name, we recognise so many types of Christ our Lord, by whom these blessings were accumulated on the human race. All other names, which were predicted to be given by divine appointment to the Son of God, are to be referred to this one name Jesus,[10] for whilst they partially glanced at the salvation which he was to purchase for us, this fully embraced the universal salvation of the human race.

The name Christ, why added to that of Jesus. "CHRIST"] To the name "Jesus" is also added that of "Christ," which signifies the "anointed;" a name expressive of honour and office, and not peculiar to one thing only, but common to many ; for, in the old law priests and kings, whom God, on account of the dignity of their office, commanded to be anointed, were called Christs ;[2]—Priests, because they commend the people to God by unceasing prayer, offer sacrifice to him and deprecate his wrath.—Kings, because they are entrusted with the government of the people, and to them principally belong the authority of the law, the protection of innocence, and the punishment of guilt. As, therefore, both seem to represent the majesty of God on earth, those who were appointed to the royal or sacerdotal office, were anointed with oil.[3] Prophets also were usually anointed, who, as the interpreters and ambassadors of the immortal God, unfolded to us the secrets of heaven, and by salutary precepts, and the prediction of future events, exhorted to amendment of life. When Jesus Christ our Saviour came into the world, he assumed these three characters of Prophet, Priest, and King, and is, therefore, called "Christ," having been anointed for the discharge of these functions, not by mortal hand, or with earthly ointment, but by the power of his heavenly Father, and with a spiritual oil ; for the plenitude of the Holy Spirit, and a more copious effusion of all gifts, than any created being is capable of receiving, were poured into his soul. This the prophet clearly indicates, when he addresses the Redeemer in these words. "Thou hast loved justice, and hatest iniquity . therefore God, thy God, hath anointed thee with the oil of gladness before thy fellows."[4] The same is also more explicitly declared by the prophet Isaiah: "The Spirit of the Lord," says he," is upon me, because the Lord hath anointed me ; he hath sent me to preach to the meek."[5] Jesus Christ, therefore, was the great prophet and teacher,[6] from whom we have learned the will of God, and by whom the world has been taught the knowledge of the Father; and the name of Prophet belongs to him pre-eminently, because all others who were dignified with that name were his disciples, sent principally to announce the coming of that Prophet who was to save all men. Christ was also a Priest, not, indeed of the tribe of Levi, as were the priests of the old law, but of that of which the prophet David sang:

[1] Is. vii. 14; viii. 8; ix. 6. Jer. xxiii. 6.   [2] 1 Kings xii. 3; xvi. 6; xxiv. 7.
[3] Lev. viii. 30.   3 Kings xix. 15, 16.   [4] Ps. xliv. 8.   [5] Is. lxi. 1.
[6] Deut. xviii. 15.

" Thou art a Priest for ever according to the order of Melchisedech."[1] This subject the Apostle fully and accurately developes in his epistle to the Hebrews.[2] Christ not only as·God, but as man, we also acknowledge to be a King: of him the angel testifies ; " He shall reign in the house of Jacob for ever, and of his kingdom there shall be no end."[3] This kingdom of Christ is spiritual and eternal, begun on earth, but perfected in heaven: and, indeed, he discharges by his admirable providence the duties of King towards his Church, governing and protecting her against the open violence and covert designs of her enemies, imparting to her not only holiness and righteousness, but also power and strength to persevere. But, although the good and the bad are contained within the limits of this kingdom, and thus all by right belong to it; yet· those, who, in conformity with his commands, lead unsullied and innocent lives, experience, beyond all others, the sovereign goodness and beneficence of our King. Although descended from the most illustrious race of kings, he obtained not this kingdom by hereditary or other human right, but because God bestowed on him as man all the power, dignity, and majesty of which human nature is susceptible. To him, therefore, God delivered the government of the whole world, and to this his sovereignty, which has already commenced, all things shall be made fully and entirely subject on the day of judgment.[4]

" His only Son"] In these words, mysteries more exalted with regard to Jesus are proposed to the faithful, as objects of their belief and contemplation—that he is the Son of God, and true God, as is the Father who begot him from eternity. We also confess that he is the second person of the Blessed Trinity, equal in all things to the Father and the Holy Ghost ; for, in the divine Persons nothing unequal or unlike should exist, or even be imagined to exist; whereas we acknowledge the essence, will and power of all to be one ; a truth clearly revealed in many of the oracles of inspiration, and sublimely announced in this testimony of St. John: " In the beginning was the Word, and the Word was God, and the Word was with God."[5] — *Christ, the Son of God and true God.*

But, when we are told that Jesus is the Son of God, we are not to understand any thing earthly or mortal of his birth; but are firmly to believe, and piously to adore that birth by which, from all eternity, the Father begot the Son ; a mystery which reason cannot fully conceive or comprehend, and at the contemplation of which, overwhelmed, as it were with admiration, we should exclaim with the prophet: " Who will declare his generation ?"[6] On this point, then, we are to believe that the Son is of the same nature, of the same power and wisdom with the Father ; as we more fully profess in these words of the Nicene Creed: " And in Jesus Christ, his only begotten Son, born of the Father before all ages, God of God, true God of true God, begotten, not made, consubstantial to the Father, by whom all — *His eternal generation incomprehensible.*

---

[1] Ps. cix. 4.   Heb. v. 5.   [2] Heb. v. & vii.   [3] Luke i. 33.   [4] 1 Cor. 15. 25—27.
[5] John i. 1.   [6] Is. liii. 8.

things were made." Amongst the different comparisons employed to elucidate the mode and manner of this eternal generation, that which is borrowed from thought seems to come nearest to its illustration; and hence St. John calls the Son " the word :"[1] for as the mind, in some sort looking into and understanding itself, forms an image of itself, which Theologians express by the term " word ;" so God, as far, however, as we may compare human things to divine, understanding himself, begets the eternal Word. Better, however, to contemplate what faith proposes, and, in the sincerity of our souls, believe and confess that Jesus Christ is true God and true man—as God, begotten of the Father before all ages—as man, born in time of Mary, his virgin mother. Whilst we thus acknowledge his twofold nativity, we believe him to be one Son, because his divine and human natures meet in one person. As to his divine generation

His unity of person. he has no brethren or coheirs ; being the only begotten Son of the Father, whilst we mortals are the work of his hands: but, if we consider his birth as man, he not only calls many by the name of brethren, but regards them as brethren—they are those who, by faith have received Christ the Lord, and who really, and by works of charity, approve the faith which they internally profess ; and hence it is that he is called by the Apostle: " the first born amongst many brethren."[2]

Why called by different names. " Our Lord"] Of our Saviour many things are recorded in Scripture, some of which clearly apply to him as God, and some as man ; because from his different natures he received the different properties which belong to each. Hence, we say with truth, that Christ is Almighty, Eternal, Infinite, and these attributes he has from his divine nature : again, we say of him that he suffered, died, and rose again, which manifestly are properties compatible only with his human nature.

Why called 'our Lord.' Besides these, there are others common to both natures ; as when in this article of the Creed, we say : " our Lord ;" a name strictly applicable to both. As he is eternal, as well as the Father, so is he Lord of all things equally with the Father ; and, as he and the Father are not, the one, one God, and the other, another God ; but one and the same God ; so likewise he and the Father are not, the one, one Lord, and the other, another Lord. As man, he is also, for many reasons, appropriately called " our Lord ;" and first, because he is our Redeemer, who delivered us from sin. This is the doctrine of St. Paul : " He humbled himself," says the Apostle, " becoming obedient unto death ; even to the death of the cross : for which cause God hath also exalted him, and hath given him a name, that is above all names, that at the name of Jesus every knee should bend of those that are in heaven, on earth and under the earth ; and that every tongue should confess that the Lord Jesus Christ is in the glory of God the Father."[3] And of himself he says, after his resurrection : " All power is given me in heaven, and on earth."[4]

[1] John i. 1. [2] Rom. viii. 29. [3] Phil. ii. 8—11. [4] Matt. xxviii. 18.

He is, also, called "Lord," because in one person both natures, the human and divine, are united; and though he had not died for us, he had yet deserved, by this admirable union, to be constituted common Lord of all created things, particularly of those who, in all the fervour of their souls, obey and serve him.

It remains, therefore, that the pastor exhort the faithful to the consideration of these his claims to the title of "our Lord;" that we, who, taking our name from him are called Christians, and who cannot be ignorant of the extent of his favours, particularly in having enabled us to understand all these things by faith, may know the strict obligation we, above all others, are under, of devoting and consecrating ourselves for ever, like faithful servants, to our Redeemer and our Lord. This we promised when, at the baptismal font, we were initiated and introduced into the Church of God; for we then declared that we renounced the devil and the world, and gave ourselves unreservedly to Jesus Christ. But if, to be enrolled as soldiers of Christ, we consecrated ourselves by so holy and solemn a profession to our Lord, what punishments should we not deserve were we, after our entrance into the Church, and after having known the will and laws of God, and received the grace of the sacraments, to form our lives upon the laws and maxims of the world and the devil; as if, when cleansed in the waters of baptism, we had pledged our fidelity to the world and to the devil, and not to Christ our Lord and Saviour! What heart so cold as not to be inflamed with love by the benevolence and beneficence exercised towards us by so great a Lord, who, though holding us in his power and dominion, as slaves ransomed by his blood, yet embraces us with such ardent love as to call us not servants, but friends and brethren?"[1] This, assuredly, supplies the most just and, perhaps, the strongest claim to induce us always to acknowledge, venerate and adore him as "our Lord."

Matter for exhortation supplied by this Article.

ARTICLE III.

"WHO WAS CONCEIVED OF THE HOLY GHOST, BORN OF THE VIRGIN MARY."

"WHO WAS CONCEIVED OF THE HOLY GHOST"] From what has been said in the preceding Article, the faithful are given to understand that, in delivering us from the relentless tyranny of Satan, God has conferred a singular and invaluable blessing on the human race: but, if we place before our eyes the economy of redemption, in it the goodness and beneficence of God shine forth with incomparable splendour and magnificence. The pastor, then, will enter on the exposition of this third Article, by

Incarnation of the Son of God.

[1] John xv. 14.

4

developing the grandeur of this mystery, which the Sacred Scriptures very frequently propose to our consideration as the principal source of our eternal salvation. Its meaning he will teach to be, that we believe and confess that the same Jesus Christ, our only Lord, the Son of God, when he assumed human flesh for us in the womb of the Virgin, was not conceived like other men, from the seed of man, but in a manner transcending the order of nature, that is, by the power of the Holy Ghost ;[1] so that the same person, remaining God as he was from eternity, became man,[2] what he was not before. That such is the meaning of these words is clear from the confession of the Holy Council of Constantinople, which says : " who for us men, and for our salvation, came down from heaven, and became incarnate by the Holy Ghost of the Virgin Mary, and WAS MADE MAN." The same truth we also find unfolded by St. John the Evangelist, who imbibed from the bosom of the Saviour himself, the knowledge of this most profound mystery. When he had thus declared the nature of the divine Word : " In the beginning was the Word, and the Word was with God, and the Word was God," he concludes, " And the Word was made flesh, and dwelt amongst us."[3] Thus, " the Word," which is a person of the divine nature, assumed human nature in such a manner that the person of both natures is one and the same : and hence this admirable union preserved the actions and properties of both natures, and, as we read in St. Leo, that great pontiff, " The lowliness of the inferior, was not consumed in the glory of the superior, nor did the assumption of the inferior diminish the glory of the superior."[4]

The work not of one, but of the three Persons of the Trinity. But as an explanation of the words, in which this Article is expressed, is not to be omitted, the pastor will teach that when we say that the Son of God was conceived by the power of the Holy Ghost, we do not mean that this Person alone of the Holy Trinity accomplished the mystery of the incarnation. Although the Son alone assumed human nature, yet all the Persons of the Trinity, the Father, the Son, and the Holy Ghost, were authors of this mystery. It is a principle of Christian faith, that whatever God does extrinsically, is common to the three Persons, and that one neither does more than, nor acts without another. But that one emanates from another cannot be common to all ; for the Son is begotten of the Father only, the Holy Ghost proceeds from the Father and the Son : but whatever proceeds from them extrinsically, is the work of the three Persons without difference of any sort, and of this latter description is the incarnation of the Son of God.

Why specially attributed to the Holy Ghost. Of those things, notwithstanding, that are common to all, the Sacred Scriptures often attribute some to one person, some to another : thus, to the Father they attribute power over all things : to the Son, wisdom ; to the Holy Ghost love ; and hence, as the mystery of the incarnation manifests the singular and boundless

---

[1] Matt. i. 20.   [2] John i. 14.   [3] John i. 1—14.   [4] Serm. i. de Nat.

love of God towards us, it is, therefore, in some sort peculiarly attributed to the Holy Ghost.

In this mystery we perceive that some things were done which *In what na-* transcend the order of nature, some by the power of nature: *tural, and* thus, in believing that the body of Christ was formed from the *in what su-* most pure blood of his Virgin Mother, we acknowledge the *pernatural.* operation of human nature, this being a law common to the formation of all human bodies. But what surpasses the order of nature and human comprehension is, that, as soon as the Blessed Virgin assented to the announcement of the angel in these words, " Behold the handmaid of the Lord, be it done unto me according to thy word,"[1] the most sacred body of Christ was immediately formed, and to it was united a rational soul ; and thus, in the same instant of time, he was perfect God and perfect man. That this was the astonishing and admirable work of the Holy Ghost cannot be doubted ; for according to the order of nature, nobody, unless after a certain period of time, can be animated with a human soul.

Again, and it should overwhelm us with astonishment; as *The Divi-* soon as the soul of Christ was united to his body, the Divinity *nity united* became united to both; and thus at the same time his body was *to the hu-* formed and animated, and the Divinity united to body and soul. *manity of* Hence, at the same instant, he was perfect God and perfect man, *Christ.* and the most Holy Virgin, having at the same moment, conceived God and man, is truly and properly, called Mother of God *The Virgin* and man. This, the Angel signified to her when he said : " Be- *truly mo-.* hold, thou shalt conceive in thy womb, and shalt bring forth a Son, *ther of God* and thou shalt call his name Jesus ; he shall be great, and shall be *and man.* called the Son of the Most High."[2] The event verified the prophecy of Isaiah : " Behold a Virgin shall conceive, and bring forth a Son."[3] Elizabeth also, when, filled with the Holy Ghost, she understood the conception of the Son of God, declared the same truth in these words: " Whence is this to me, that the Mother of my Lord should come to me ?"[4] But, as the body of Christ *The soul of* was formed of the pure blood of the immaculate Virgin without *Christ re-* the aid of man, as we have already said, and by the sole opera- *plenished* tion of the Holy Ghost; so also, at the moment of his concep- *from his* tion, his soul was replenished with an overflowing fulness of the *conception,* Spirit of God, and a superabundance of all graces ; for God gave *grace.* not to him, as to others adorned with graces and holiness, his Spirit by measure, as St. John testifies ;[5] but poured into his soul the plenitude of all graces so abundantly, that " of his fulness we have all received."[6]

Although possessing that Spirit by which holy men attained *Christ the* the adoption of sons of God, he cannot, however, be called the *Son of God* adopted Son of God ; for being the Son of God by nature, the *by nature,* grace, or name of adoption can, on no account, be deemed ap- *not by* plicable to him. *adoption.*

---

[1] Luke i. 38.   [2] Luke i. 31, 32.   [3] Isaiah vii. 14.   [4] Luke i. 43.
[5] John iii. 34.   [6] John i. 16.

These heads comprise the substance of what appeared to us to demand explanation regarding the admirable mystery of the conception. To reap from them abundant fruit of salvation, the faithful should particularly recall to their recollection, and frequently reflect, that it is God who assumed human flesh; but that the manner of its assumption transcends the limits of our comprehension, not to say, of our powers of expression; finally, that he vouchsafed to become man, in order that we mortals may be regenerated children of God. When to these subjects, they shall have given mature consideration, let them, in the humility of faith, believe and adore all the mysteries contained in this Article, nor indulge a curious inquisitiveness by investigating and scrutinizing them—an attempt scarcely ever unattended with danger.

How we are to reap fruit unto salvation from the belief of this Article.

BORN OF THE VIRGIN MARY"] These words comprise another part of this Article of the Creed, in the exposition of which the pastor should exercise considerable diligence; because the faithful are bound to believe, that Christ our Lord was not only conceived by the power of the Holy Ghost, but was also "born of the Virgin Mary." The words of the Angel, who first announced the happy tidings to the world, declare with what transports of joy, and emotions of delight, the belief of this mystery should be meditated by us: "Behold," says he, "I bring you good tidings of great joy, that shall be to all the people."[1] The song chanted by the heavenly host clearly conveys the same sentiments: "Glory," say they, to God in the highest: and on earth, peace to men of good-will."[2] Hence, also, began the fulfilment of the splendid promise made by Almighty God to Abraham, that in his seed all the nations of the earth should be blessed;[3] for Mary, whom we truly proclaim and venerate as Mother of God, because she brought forth him who is, at once, God and man, was descended from King David.[4] But as the conception itself transcends the order of nature, so also, the birth of the man-God presents to our contemplation nothing but what is divine.

Christ born of a Virgin.

Besides, a circumstance wonderful beyond expression or conception, he is born of his Mother without any diminution of her maternal virginity; and as he afterwards went forth from the sepulchre whilst it was closed and sealed, and entered the room in which his disciples were assembled, "the doors being shut;"[5] or, not to depart from natural events which we witness every day, as the rays of the sun penetrate, without breaking or injuring, in the least, the substance of glass; after a like, but more incomprehensible manner, did Jesus Christ come forth from his mother's womb without injury to her maternal virginity, which, immaculate and perpetual, forms the just theme of our eulogy. This was the work of the Holy Ghost, who, at the conception and birth of the Son, so favoured the Virgin Mother as to im-

Manner of his birth.

---

[1] Luke ii. 10.   [2] Luke ii. 14.   [3] Gen. xxii. 18.   [4] Matt. i. 1. 6.
[5] John xx. 19.

part to her fecundity, and yet preserve inviolate her perpetual virginity.

The Apostle, sometimes, called Jesus Christ the second Adam, and institutes a comparison between him and the first: for "as in the first all men die, so in the second all are made alive;"[1] and as in the natural order, Adam was the father of the human race; so, in the supernatural order, Christ is the author of grace and of glory. The Virgin Mother we may also compare to Eve, making the second Eve, that is Mary, correspond with the first; as we have already shown that the second Adam, that is, Christ, corresponds with the first Adam. By believing the serpent, Eve entailed malediction and death on mankind;[2] and Mary, by believing the Angel, became the instrument of the divine goodness in bringing life and benediction to the human race.[3] From Eve we are born children of wrath; from Mary we have received Jesus Christ, and through him are regenerated children of grace. To Eve it was said: "In sorrow shalt thou bring forth children:"[4] Mary was exempt from this law, for preserving her virginal integrity inviolate, she brought forth Jesus the Son of God, without experiencing, as we have already said, any sense of pain.

Christ compared to Adam, Mary to Eve.

The mysteries of this admirable conception and nativity being, therefore, so great and so numerous, it accorded with the views of Divine Providence to signify them by many types and prophesies. Hence the Holy Fathers understood many things which we meet in the Sacred Scriptures to relate to them, particularly that gate of the Sanctuary which Ezechiel saw closed;[5] the stone cut out of the mountain without hands, which became a great mountain and filled the universe;[6] the rod of Aaron, which alone budded of all the rods of the princes of Israel;[7] and the bush which Moses saw burn without being consumed.[8] The holy Evangelist describes in detail the history of the birth of Christ,[9] and, as the pastor can easily recur to the Sacred Volume, it is unnecessary for us to say more on the subject.

Types and figures of his conception and nativity.

But he should labour to impress deeply on the minds and hearts of the faithful these mysteries, "which were written for our instruction;"[10] first, that by the commemoration of so great a benefit they may make some return of gratitude to God, its author; and next, in order to place before their eyes, as a model for imitation, this striking and singular example of humility. What can be more useful, what better calculated to subdue the pride and haughtiness of the human heart, than to reflect, frequently, that God humbles himself in such a manner as to assume our frailty and weakness, in order to communicate to us his grace and glory—that God becomes man, and that he "at whose nod," to use the words of Scripture, "the pillars of heaven fear and tremble,"[11] bows his supreme and infinite majesty to minister to man—that he whom the angels adore in heaven

The lessons which this mystery conveys.

[1] I Cor. xv. 21, 22.   [2] Eccl. xxv. 33.   [3] Eph. i. 3.   [4] Gen. iii. 16.
[5] Ezech. xliv. 2.   [6] Dan. ii. 35.   [7] Num. xvii. 8.   [8] Exod. iii. 2.
[9] Luke ii.   [10] Rom. xv. 4.   [11] Job xxvi. 11.

4*   F

is born on earth!! When such is the goodness of God towards us, what, I ask, what should we not do to testify our obedience to his will? With what promptitude and alacrity should we not love, embrace, and perform all the duties of Christian humility? The faithful should also know the salutary lessons which Christ teaches at his birth, before he opens his divine lips;—he is born in poverty,—he is born a stranger under a roof not his own,—he is born in a lonely crib—he is born in the depth of winter! These circumstances, which attend the birth of the man-God, are thus recorded by St. Luke: " And it came to pass, that, when they were there, her days were accomplished that she should be delivered, and she brought forth her first-born son, and wrapped him up in swaddling clothes, and laid him in a manger, because there was no room for them in the inn."[1] Could the Evangelist comprehend under more humble terms the majesty and glory that filled the heavens and the earth? He does not say, there was no room in the inn, but " there was no room for *him* who says: mine is the earth and the fulness thereof ;"[2] and this destitution of the man-God another Evangelist records in these words; " He came unto his own, and his own received him not."[3]

The dignity which it confers on man.

When the faithful have placed these things before their eyes, let them also reflect, that God condescended to assume the lowliness and frailty of our flesh in order to exalt man to the highest degree of dignity; for this single reflection alone supplies sufficient proof of the exalted dignity of man conferred on him by the divine bounty—that he who is true and perfect God vouchsafed to become man; so that we may now glory that the Son of God is bone of our bone, and flesh of our flesh, a privilege not given to angels, " for no where," says the apostle, " doth he take hold of the angels: but of the seed of Abraham he taketh hold."[4]

The influence which it should have on his life.

We must also take care, that these singular blessings rise not in judgment against us; that, as at Bethlehem, the place of his nativity, he was denied a dwelling ; so also, now that he is no longer born in human flesh, he be not denied a dwelling in our hearts, in which he may be spiritually born: for, through an earnest desire for our salvation, this is the object of his most anxious solicitude. As then, by the power of the Holy Ghost, and in a manner superior to the order of nature, he was made man and was born, was holy and even holiness itself; so does it become our duty " to be born, not of blood nor of the will of flesh, but of God ;"[5] to walk, as new creatures in newness of spirit:[6] and to preserve that holiness and purity of soul that become men regenerated by the Spirit of God.[7] Thus shall we reflect some faint image of the holy conception and nativity of the Son of God, which are the objects of our firm faith, and believing which we revere and adore " in a mystery, wisdom of God which was hidden."[8]

1 Luke ii. 6, 7.   2 Ps. xlix. 12.   3 John i. 11.   4 Heb. ii. 16.
5 John i. 13.   6 Rom. vi. 4—7.   7 2 Cor. iii. 18.   8 1 Cor. ii. 7

ARTICLE IV.

"SUFFERED UNDER PONTIUS PILATE, WAS CRUCIFIED, DEAD, AND BURIED."

"SUFFERED UNDER PONTIUS PILATE, WAS CRUCIFIED"] How necessary the knowledge of this Article, and how assiduous the pastor should be in stirring up, in the minds of the faithful, the frequent recollection of our Lord's passion, we learn from the apostle when he says, that he knows nothing but Christ, and him crucified.[1] In illustrating this subject, therefore, the greatest care and pains should be taken by the pastor, that the faithful, excited by the remembrance of so great a benefit, may be entirely devoted to the contemplation of the goodness and love of God towards us. *Necessity of the knowledge and frequent exposition of this article.*

The first part of this Article (of the second we shall treat hereafter,) proposes to our belief, that when Pontius Pilate governed the province of Judea, under Tiberius Cæsar, Christ the Lord was nailed to a cross. Having been seized as a malefactor, mocked, outraged, and tortured, in various forms, he was finally crucified. Nor can it be matter of doubt that his soul, as to its inferior part, was not insensible to these torments; for as he really assumed human nature, it is a necessary consequence that he really, and in his soul, experienced a most acute sense of pain. Hence these words of the Saviour: "My soul is sorrowful, even unto death."[2] Although human nature was united to the divine person, he felt the bitterness of his passion as acutely as if no such union had existed; because in the one person of Jesus Christ were preserved the properties of both natures, human and divine; and, therefore, what was passible and mortal remained passible and mortal; and again, what was impassible and immortal, that is his divine nature, continued impassible and immortal. *What this part of the article proposes to our belief.*

But, if we find it here recorded with such historical minuteness, that Jesus Christ suffered when Pilate was procurator of Judea,[3] the pastor will explain the reason—it is, that by fixing the time, as the apostle does, in the sixth chapter of his first Epistle to Timothy, so important and so necessary an event may be ascertained by all with greater certainty; and to show that the event verified the prediction of the Saviour; "They shall deliver him to the Gentiles, to be mocked, and scourged, and crucified."[4] *Why the time of the passion is specially recorded.*

That he suffered the particular death of the cross is also to be traced to the economy of the divine councils, "that whence death came, thence life might arise." The serpent, which overcame our first parents by the fruit of the tree, was himself overcome by Christ on the wood of the cross. Many reasons, which the *Why Christ died on a cross.*

[1] 1 Cor. ii. 2. [2] Mat. xxvi. 38. Mark xiv. 34. [3] 1 Tim. vi. 13. [4] Mat. xx. 19.

Holy Fathers have evolved in detail, may be adduced to show
the congruity of the Saviour's having suffered the death of the
cross, rather than any other; but enough that the faithful be informed by the pastor, that that species of death, because confessedly the most ignominious and humiliating, was chosen by
the Saviour, as most consonant, and best suited to the plan of
redemption; for not only amongst the Gentiles was the death
of the cross deemed execrable and loaded with disgrace and infamy, but also amongst the Jews; for in the law of Moses, the
man is pronounced "accursed, who hangeth on a tree."[1]

Historical part of this article not to be omitted. But the historical part of this Article, which has been narrated
by the Holy Evangelists with the most minute exactness, is not
to be omitted by the pastor; in order that the faithful may be
familiarly acquainted with, at least, the principle heads of this
mystery, which are of more immediate necessity to confirm the
truth of our faith. For on this Article, as on a sort of foundation, rest the religion and faith of Christians, and on this foundation, when once laid, the superstructure rises with perfect
security. If any other truth of Christianity presents difficulties
to the mind of man, the mystery of the cross must, assuredly,
be considered to present still greater difficulties. We can scarcely be brought to think that our salvation depends on the cross, and
on him, who for us, was fastened to its wood. But in this, as the
apostle says, we may admire the supreme wisdom of divine
providence; "for seeing that in the wisdom of God, the world
by wisdom knew not God: it pleaseth God by the foolishness
of *our* preaching, to save them that believe."[2] We are not,
therefore, to be surprised, that the Prophets, before the coming
of Christ, and the apostles after his death and resurrection,
laboured so industriously to convince mankind that he was the
Redeemer of the world, and to bring them under the power and
obedience of him who was crucified.

Figures and prophe-cies of the passion and death of the Sa-viour. Knowing, therefore, that nothing is so far above the reach of
human reason as the mystery of the cross, Almighty God, im-
mediately from the fall of Adam, ceased not, both by figures and
by the oracles of the Prophets, to signify the death by which
his Son was to die. Not to dwell on these figures, Abel who
fell a victim to the envy of his brother,[3] Isaac who was commanded to be offered in sacrifice,[4] the lamb immolated by the
Jews on their departure from Egypt,[5] and also the brazen serpent lifted up by Moses in the desert,[6] were all figures of the
passion and death of Christ the Lord. That this event was foretold by many Prophets, is a fact too well known to require de-
velopement here. Not to speak of David, whose Psalms embrace the principal mysteries of redemption,[7] the oracles of
Isaias are so clear and graphic,[8] that he may be said rather to
have recorded a past, than predicted a future event.[9]

[1] Deut. xxi. 23. Gal. iii. 13.   [2] 1 Cor. i. 21.   [3] Gen. iv. 8.
[4] Gen. xxii. 6—8.   [5] Exod. xi. 5—7.   [6] Num. xxi. 8, 9. John iii. 14.
[7] Psalms ii. xxi. lxvi. cix.   [8] Isai. liii.   [9] Hier. Epist. ad Paulin. ante finem.

"Dead and buried"] When explaining these words, the pastor will propose to the belief of the faithful, that Jesus Christ, after his crucifixion, was really dead and buried. It is not without just reason that this is proposed as a separate and distinct object of belief; there were some who denied his death upon the cross. The apostles, therefore, were justly of opinion, that to such an error should be opposed the doctrine of faith contained in this Article of the Creed, the truth of which is placed beyond the possibilty of doubt, by the concurring testimony of all the Evangelists, who record that Jesus "yielded up the ghost."[1] Moreover, as Christ was true and perfect man, he of course, was, also, capable of dying, and death takes place by a separation of the soul from the body. When, therefore, we say that Jesus died, we mean that his soul was disunited from his body; not that his divinity was so separated. On the contrary, we firmly believe and profess that, when his soul was dissociated from his body, his divinity continued always united both to his body in the sepulchre, and to his soul in Limbo. It became the Son of God to die, "that through death he might destroy him who had the empire of death, that is to say, the devil; and might deliver them, who through fear of death, were all their lifetime subject to servitude."[2]

Christ really died

His divinity united to his soul and body whilst separated by death.

It was the peculiar privilege of the Redeemer to have died when he himself decreed to die, and to have died, not so much by external violence, as by internal assent; not only his death, but also its time and place were ordained by him, as we learn from these words of Isaias: "He was offered, because it was his own will."[3] The Redeemer, before his passion, declared the same of himself: "I lay down my life," says he, "that I may take it again. No man taketh it away from me; but I lay it down of myself, and I have power to lay it down; and I have power to take it again."[4] As to time and place, when Herod insidiously sought the life of the Saviour, he said: "Go, and tell that fox: behold I cast out devils, and perform cures this day and to-morrow, and the third day I am consummate. But yet I must walk this day, and to-morrow, and the day following, because it cannot be that a prophet perish out of Jerusalem."[5] He, therefore, offered himself not involuntarily or by external coaction; but of his own free will. Going to meet his enemies, he said, "I am he;[6] and all the punishments which injustice and cruelty inflicted on him he endured voluntarily.

His death voluntary,

When we meditate on the sufferings and torments of the Redeemer, nothing is better calculated to excite in our souls, sentiments of lively gratitude and love, than to reflect that he endured them voluntarily. Were any one to endure, by compulsion, every species of suffering, for our sake, we should deem his claims to our gratitude very doubtful; but were he to endure death freely, and for our sake only, having had it in his power

and, therefore, the stronger claim to our gratitude and love.

---

[1] Mat. xxvii. 50. Mark xv. 37. Luke xxiii. 46. John xix. 30.
[2] Heb. ii. 10. 14, 15.   [3] Isaias liii. 7.   [4] John x. 17, 18.   [5] Luke xiii. 32, 33.
[6] John xviii. 5.

to avoid it; this indeed is a favour so overwhelming, as to deprive even the most grateful heart, not only of the power of returning due thanks, but even of adequately feeling the extent of the obligation. We may hence form an idea of the transcendant and intense love of Jesus Christ towards us, and of his divine and boundless claims to our gratitude.

Why the word "buried' is mentioned in this article. But if, when we confess that he was buried, we make this, as it were, a distinct part of the Article, it is not because it presents any difficulty which is not implied in what we have said of his death; for believing, as we do, that Christ died, we can also easily believe that he was buried. The word "buried" was added in the creed, first, that his death may be rendered more certain, for the strongest proof of a person's death is the interment of his body; and, secondly, to render the miracle of his resurrection more authentic and illustrious. It is not, however, our belief, that the body of Christ was alone interred: these words propose, as the principal object of our belief, that *God was buried;* as, according to the rule of Catholic faith, we also say with the strictest truth, that *God* was born of a virgin, that *God* died; for, as the divinity was never separated from his body which was laid in the sepulchre, we truly confess that *God was buried.*

The body of Christ incorrupt in the sepulchre. As to the place and manner of his burial, what the Evangelists record on these subjects will be found sufficient for all the purposes of the pastor's instructions.[1] There are, however, two things which demand particular attention; the one, that the body of Christ was, in no degree, corrupted in the sepulchre, according to the prediction of the Prophet: "Thou wilt not give thy Holy One to see corruption;[2] the other, and it regards the several parts of this Article, that burial, passion, and also death, apply to Jesus Christ, not as God, but as man: to suffer and die are incidental to human nature only, although they are also attributed to God, because predicated with propriety of that *person* who is, at once, perfect God and perfect man.

Burial, passion, and death, refer to Christ as man, not as God.

Dignity of him who suffers. When the faithful have once attained the knowledge of these things, the pastor will next proceed to explain those particulars of the passion and death of Christ, which may enable them, if not to comprehend, at least to contemplate the infinitude of so stupendous a mystery. And, first, we are to consider who it is who suffers.—To declare, or even to conceive in thought, his dignity, is not given to man.—Of him, St. John says, that he is "the Word which was with God;"[3] and the apostle describes him in these sublime terms: "this is he, whom God hath appointed heir of all things, by whom also he made the world; who being the brightness of his glory, and the figure of his substance, and upholding all things by the word of his power, making purgation of sins, sitteth on the right hand of the majesty on high."[4] In a word, Jesus Christ, the man-God, suf-

---

[1] Mat. xxvii. 60. Mark xv. 46. Luke xxiii. 53. John xix. 38.
[2] Psalm xv. 10. Acts ii. 31.   [3] John i. 1, 2.   [4] Heb. i. 2, 3.

fers ! The Creator suffers for the creature—The Master for the servant—*He* suffers, by whom the elements, the heavens, men and angels were created, "of whom, by whom, and in whom, are all things."[1]

It cannot, therefore, be matter of surprise that, whilst he ago- *Reflection.* nized under such an accumulation of torments, the whole frame of the universe was convulsed, and, as the Scriptures inform us, "the earth trembled, and the rocks were rent, and the sun was darkened, and there was darkness all over the earth."[2] If, then, even mute and inanimate nature sympathized with the sufferings of her dying Lord, let the faithful conceive, if they can, with what torrents of tears they, "the living stones of the edifice,"[3] should evince their sorrow.

The reasons why the Saviour suffered are also to be explain- *Reasons* ed, that thus the greatness and intensity of the divine love to- *why he suf-* wards us, may the more fully appear. Should it then be asked *fered : firs* why the Son of God underwent the torments of his most bitter *love of us.* passion, we shall find the principal causes in the hereditary contagion of primeval guilt; in the vices and crimes which have been perpetrated from the beginning of the world to the present day; and in those which shall be perpetrated to the consummation of time. In his death and passion the Son of God contemplated the atonement of all the sins of all ages, with a view to efface them for ever, by offering for them to his Eternal Father, a superabundant satisfaction; and thus the principal cause of his passion will be found in his love of us.

Besides, to increase the dignity of this mystery, Christ not *Second* only suffered for sinners; but the very authors and ministers of *reason, to* all the torments he endured were sinners. Of this the apostle *original* reminds us in these words addressed to the Hebrews: "Think, *and actual* diligently, on him who endured such opposition from sinners *sin.* against himself; that you be not wearied, fainting in your minds."[4] In this guilt are involved all those who fall frequently into sin; for, as our sins consigned Christ our Lord to the death of the cross, most certainly, those who wallow in sin and iniquity, as far as depends on them, "crucify to themselves again the Son of God, and make a mockery of him."[5] This our guilt takes a deeper die of enormity when contrasted with that of the Jews: according to the testimony of the apostle, "if they had known it, they never would have crucified the Lord of Glory:"[6] whilst we, on the contrary, professing to know him, yet denying him by our actions, seem, in some sort, to lay violent hands on him.[7]

But that Christ the Lord was also delivered over to death by *Christ deli-* the Father and by himself, we learn from these words of Isaias: *vered over* "For the wickedness of my people have I struck him;"[8] and a *the Father* little before, when, filled with the Spirit of God, he sees the *and by* *himself.*

---

[1] Rom. xi. 36.   [2] Mat. xxvii. 51. Luke xxiii. 44, 45.   [3] 1 Peter ii. 5.
[4] Heb. xii. 3.   [5] Heb. vi. 6.   [6] 1 Cor. ii. 8.   [7] Tit. i. 16.
[8] Isaias liii. 8.

Lord covered with stripes and wounds, the same prophet says:
"We all, like sheep, have gone astray, every one hath turned
aside into his own way ; and the Lord hath laid on him the iniquities of us all."[1]   But of the Saviour it is written, "if he will
lay down his life for sin, he shall see a long-lived seed."[2] This
the apostle expresses in language still stronger when, on the
other hand, he wishes to show us how confidently we should
trust in the boundless mercy and goodness of God : " He that
spared not even his own Son," says the apostle, " but delivered
him up for us all, how hath he not also, with him, given us all
things ?"[3]

Bitterness
of his
passion.

The next subject of the pastor's instruction is the bitterness
of the Redeemer's passion. If, however, we bear in mind that
"his sweat became as drops of blood, trinkling down upon the

I.

ground ;"[4] and this, at the sole anticipation of the torments and
agony which he was soon after to endure, we must, at once,
perceive that his sorrows admitted of no increase ; for if, and
this sweat of blood proclaims it, the very idea of the impending
evils was so overwhelming, what are we to suppose their actual
endurance to have been?

II.

That our Lord suffered the most excruciating torments of mind
and body is but too well ascertained. In the first place, there was
no part of his body that did not experience the most agonising
torture—his hands and feet were fastened with nails to the cross—
his head was pierced with thorns and smitten with a reed—his
face was befouled with spittle and buffeted with blows—his

III.

whole body was covered with stripes—Men of all ranks and
conditions were also gathered together " against the Lord and
against his Christ."[5]—Jews and Gentiles were the advisers, the
authors, the ministers of his passion—Judas betrayed him[6]—
Peter denied him[7]—all the rest deserted him[8]—and, whilst he
hangs from the instrument of his execution, are we not at a
loss which to deplore, his agony or his ignominy—or both ?
Surely no death more shameful, none more cruel could have been
devised than that which was the ordinary punishment of guilty
and atrocious malefactors only—a death the tediousness of which
aggravated the protraction of its exquisite pain and excruciating

IV.

torture ! His agony was increased by the very constitution and
frame of his body. Formed by the power of the Holy Ghost,
it was more perfect and better organised than the bodies of other
men can be, and was, therefore, endowed with a superior suscep-
tibility of pain, and a keener sense of the torments which it

V.

endured : and as to his interior anguish of mind, that, too, was
no doubt extreme ; for those amongst the saints who had to endure torments and tortures, were not without consolation from
above, which enabled them not only to bear their violence patiently, but, in many instances, to feel, in the very midst of them,
elate with interior joy. "I rejoice," says the apostle, "in my

---

[1] Isaias liii. 6.   [2] Isaias liii. 10.   [3] Rom. viii. 32.   [4] Luke xxii. 44.
[5] Psalm ii. 2.   [6] Matt. xxvi. 47.   [7] Mark xiv. 68. 70, 71.   [8] Matt. xxvi. 56.

sufferings for you, and fill up those things that are wanting of the sufferings of Christ, in my flesh for his body, which is the Church;"[1] and in another place, "I am filled with comfort; I exceedingly abound with joy in all our tribulation."[2] Christ our Lord tempered with no admixture of sweetness the bitter chalice of his passion; but permitted his human nature to feel as acutely, every species of torment, as if he were only man, and not, also, God.

The blessings and advantages which flow to the human race, from the passion of Christ, alone remain to be explained. In the first place, then, the passion of our Lord was our deliverance from sin; for, as St. John says: "He hath loved us and washed us from our sins in his own blood;"[3] "He hath quickened you together with him;" says the Apostle, "forgiving you all offences, blotting out the hand writing of the decree that was against us, which was contrary to us, and he hath taken away the same, fastening it to the cross."[4] He has rescued us from the tyranny of the devil, for our Lord himself says; "Now is the judgment of the world; now shall the prince of this world be cast out; and I, if I be lifted up from the earth, will draw all things to myself."[5] He discharged the punishment due to our sins; and, as no sacrifice more grateful and acceptable could have been offered to God, he reconciled us to the Father,[6] appeased his wrath, and propitiated his justice. Finally, by atoning for our sins, he opened to us heaven, which was closed by the common sin of mankind, according to these words of the Apostle; "We have, therefore, brethren, a confidence in the entering into the Holies by the blood of Christ."[7]

The blessings of which it is the plenteous source. I. II. III. IV. V.

Nor are we without a type and figure of this mystery in the old law; those who were prohibited to return into their native country, before the death of the high-priest,[8] typified, that, until the supreme and eternal High-Priest, Christ Jesus, had died, and by dying opened heaven to those who, purified by the sacraments, and gifted with faith, hope, and charity, become partakers of his passion; no one, however just may have been his life, could gain admission into his celestial country.

Type and figure of the redemption.

The pastor will teach that all these inestimable and divine blessings flow to us from the passion of Christ; first, because the satisfaction which Jesus Christ has, in an admirable manner, made to his Eternal Father for our sins, is full and complete; and the price which he paid for our ransom not only equals but far exceeds the debts contracted by us. Again, the sacrifice was most acceptable to God, for when offered by his Son on the altar of the cross, it entirely appeased his wrath and indignation. This the Apostle teaches, when he says: "Christ loved us, and delivered himself for us, an oblation and a sacrifice to God for an odour of sweetness."[9] Of the redemption which he purchased the prince of the Apostles says: "You were not re-

Christ purchased our redemption.

[1] Coloss. i. 24. [2] 2 Cor. vii. 4. [3] Rev. i. 5. [4] Col. ii. 13, 14.
[5] John xii. 31. 32. [6] 2 Cor. v. 19. [7] Heb. x. 19. [8] Num. xxxv. 25,
[9] Eph. v. 2. 5 G

deemed with córruptible things, as gold and silver, from your vain conversations of the tradition of your fathers ; but with the precious blood of Christ, as of a lamb unspotted and undefiled."[1]

In his passion he has left us an example of every virtue.
Besides these inestimable blessings, we have also received another of the highest importance. In the passion alone, we have the most illustrious example of the exercise of every virtue. Patience, and humility, and exalted charity, and meekness, and obedience, and unshaken firmness of soul, not only in suffering for justice-sake, but also in meeting death, are so conspicuous in the suffering Saviour, that we may truly say, that, on the day of his passion alone, he offered, in his own person, a living exemplification of all the moral precepts, which he inculcated during the entire time of his public ministry. This exposition of the saving passion of Christ the Lord, we have given briefly— Would to God ! that these mysteries were always present to our minds, and that we learned to suffer, to die, and to be buried with Christ ; that, cleansed from the stains of sin, and rising with him to newness of life, we may at length, through his grace and mercy, be found worthy to be made partakers of the glory of his celestial kingdom.

ARTICLE V.

" HE DESCENDED INTO HELL, THE THIRD DAY HE AROSE AGAIN FROM THE DEAD."

Knowledge of this Article most important.
" HE DESCENDED INTO HELL"] To know the glory of the sepulture of our Lord Jesus Christ, of which we have last treated, is highly important; but of still higher importance is it to the faithful to know the splendid triumphs which he obtained, by having subdued the devil and despoiled the powers of hell. Of these triumphs, and, also, of his resurrection, we are now about to speak ; and, although the latter presents to us a subject which might with propriety, be treated under a separate and distinct head, yet, following the example of the holy Fathers, we have deemed it judicious to imbody it with his descent into hell.

What its first part proposes to our belief.
In the first part of this Article, then, we profess that, immediately after the death of Christ, his soul descended into hell, and dwelt there whilst his body remained in the grave : and also that the same *Person* of Christ was, at the same time, in hell and in the sepulchre. Nor should this excite our surprise ; for we have already, frequently said, that although his soul was separated from his body, his divinity was never separated from soul or body.

Meaning of the word " hell" in this Article.
But as the pastor, by explaining the meaning of the word hell, in this place, may throw considerable light on the exposition of this Article, it is to be observed, that by the word hell, is

[1] 1 Pet. i. 18. 19.

not here meant the sepulchre, as some have not less impiously than ignorantly, imagined ; for, in the preceding Article we learned that Christ was buried : and there was no reason why the Apostles, in delivering an article of faith, should repeat the same thing in other and more obscure terms.   Hell, then, here signifies those secret abodes in which are detained the souls that have not been admitted to the regions of bliss ; a sense in which the word is frequently used in Scripture.   Thus, the Apostle says, that, "at the name of Jesus, every knee should bend, of those that are in heaven, on earth and in hell ;"[1] and in the Acts of the Apostles, Peter says, that Christ the Lord was again risen, "having loosed the sorrows of hell."[2]

These abodes are not all of the same nature, for amongst them, is that most loathsome and dark prison in which the souls of the damned are buried with the unclean spirits, in eternal and inextinguishable fire.   This dread abode is called Gehenna, the bottomless pit, and, strictly speaking, means hell.   Amongst them is also the fire of purgatory, in which the souls of just men are cleansed by a temporary punishment, in order to be admitted into their eternal country, "into which nothing defiled entereth."[3]   The truth of this doctrine founded, as holy councils declare,[4] on Scripture, and confirmed by apostolical tradition, demands diligent and frequent exposition, proportioned to the circumstances of the times in which we live, when men endure not sound doctrine.   Lastly, the third kind of abode is that into which the souls of the just, who died before Christ, were received, and where, without experiencing any sort of pain, and supported by the blessed hope of redemption, they enjoyed peaceful repose.   To liberate these souls, who, in the bosom of Abraham, were expecting the Saviour, Christ the Lord descended into hell.

Its different meanings.

I.

II.

III.

But we are not to imagine that his power and virtue only, but we are also firmly to believe that his soul also, really and substantially descended into hell, according to this conclusive testimony of David : "Thou wilt not leave my soul in hell."[5]   But, although Christ descended into hell, his supreme power was still the same ; nor was the splendour of his sanctity in any degree obscured.   His descent served rather to prove, that whatever has been already said of his sanctity was true ; and that as he had previously demonstrated by so many miracles, he was truly the Son of God.

The soul of Christ really descended into hell.

This we shall easily understand by comparing the descent of Christ, in its causes and circumstances, with that of the just— They descended as captives :[6] He as free and victorious amongst the dead, to subdue those demons by whom, in consequence of primeval guilt, they were held in captivity—they descended, some to endure the most acute torments, others, though exempt from actual pain, yet deprived of the vision of God, and of the glory for which they sighed, and consigned to the torture of sus-

Difference between his descent and that of others.

[1] Philip. ii. 10.   [2] Acts ii. 24.   [3] Apoc. xxi. 27.   [4] Trid. Conc. Sess. 25.
[5] Ps. xv. 10.   [6] Ps. lxxxvii. 5, 6.

pense; Christ the Lord descended, not to suffer, but to liberate from suffering the holy and the just who were held in painful captivity, and to impart to them the fruit of his passion. His supreme dignity and power, therefore, suffered no diminution by his descent into hell.

Why he descended. I. Having explained these things, the pastor will, next, proceed to teach that the Son of God descended into hell, that, clothed with the spoils of the arch-enemy, he may conduct into heaven those holy fathers, and the other just souls, whose liberation from prison he had already purchased. This he accomplished in an admirable and glorious manner, for his august presence, at once shed a celestial lustre upon the captives; filled them with inconceivable joy; and imparted to them that supreme happiness which consists in the vision of God; thus verifying his promise to the thief on the cross: " Amen, I say to thee, this day thou shalt be with me in Paradise."[1] This, deliverance of the just was, long before, predicted by Ozeas, in these words: " O Death! I will be thy death, O Hell! I will be thy bite:"[2] and also by the prophet Zachary: " Thou, also, by the blood of thy testament, hast sent forth thy prisoners out of the pit wherein is no water,"[3] and lastly, the same is expressed by the Apostle in these words: " Despoiling the principalities and powers, he hath exposed them confidently, openly triumphing over them in himself."[4]

II. However, to comprehend still more clearly the efficacy of this mystery, we should frequently call to mind, that not only those who were born after the coming of the Saviour, but, also, those who preceded that event from the days of Adam, or shall succeed it to the consummation of time, are included in the redemption purchased by the death of Christ. Before his death and resurrection, heaven was closed against every child of Adam; the souls of the just, on their departure from this life, were borne to the bosom of Abraham; or, as is still the case with those who require to be freed from the stains of sin, or die indebted to the divine justice, were purified in the fire of purgatory.

III. Another reason, also, why Christ descended into hell is, that there, as well as in heaven and on earth he may proclaim his power and authority; and that " every knee of things in heaven, and on earth, and under the earth, should bend at his name."[5] And here, who is not filled with admiration and astonishment when he contemplates the infinite love of God to man! Not satisfied with having undergone for our sake a most cruel death, he penetrates the inmost recesses of the earth, to transport into bliss the souls whom he so dearly loved, and whose liberation from prison he had achieved at the price of his blood!

The second part of the Article. We now come to the second part of the Article, and how indefatigable should be the labours of the pastor in its exposition;

---

[1] Luke xxiii. 43.   [2] Oseas xiii. 14.   [3] Zach. ix. 11.   [4] Col. ii. 15
[5] Phil. ii. 10.

we learn from these words of the Apostle to Timothy; " **Be** mindful that the Lord Jesus Christ is risen again from the dead :"[1] words no doubt, addressed not only to Timothy, but to all who have care of souls. But the meaning of the Article is, that after Christ the Lord had expired on the cross, on the sixth day and ninth hour, and was buried on the evening of the same day by his disciples, who with the permission of the governor Pilate, laid the body of the Lord, when taken down from the cross, in a new tomb, in a garden near at hand ; his soul was reunited to his body, early on the morning of the third day after his death, that is on the Lord's-day ; and thus he, who was dead during those three days, returned to life, and rose from the embraces of the tomb.—By the word resurrection, however, we are not merely to understand that Christ was raised from the dead ; a privilege common with him to many others : but that he rose by his own power and virtue, a singular prerogative peculiar to him alone ; for it is incompatible with our nature, nor was it ever given to man to raise himself, by his own power, from death to life. This was an exercise of power reserved for the omnipotent hand of God, as these words of the Apostle declare ; " for, although he was crucified through weakness, yet he liveth by the power of God."[2] This divine power, having never been separated, either from his body whilst in the grave, or from his soul whilst disunited from his body, existed in both, and gave to both a capability of reuniting ; and thus did the Son of God, by his own power, return to life, and rise again from the dead. This David foretold, when, filled with the spirit of God, he prophesied in these words : " His right hand hath wrought for him salvation, and his arm is holy."[3] This we, also, have from the divine lips of the Redeemer himself: " I lay down my life," says he, " that I may take it again ; and I have power to lay it down, and power to take it again."[4] To the Jews he also said, in confirmation of his doctrine : " Destroy this temple, and in three days I will raise it up."[5] Although the Jews understood him to have spoken thus of the magnificent temple of Jerusalem, built of stone: yet, as the Scripture, testifies in the same place, " he spoke of the temple of his body."[6] We sometimes, it is true, read in Scripture, that he was raised by the Father;[7] but this refers to him as man ; as those passages, which, on the other hand, say that he rose by his own power, relate to him as God.[8]

It is also the peculiar privilege of Christ to have been the first who enjoyed this divine prerogative of rising from the dead, for he is called in Scripture " the first begotten of the dead :"[9] and also, " the first born from the dead ;"[10] the Apostle also says, " Christ is risen from the dead, the first fruits of them that sleep : for by a man came death, and by a man the resurrection

Marginal notes:
Its meaning.

Resurrection superior to the natural power of man.

Christ "the first begotten of the dead."

---

1 2 Tim. ii. 8.	2 2 Cor. xiii. 4.	3 Ps. xcvii. 2.	4 John x. 17, 18.
5 John ii. 19.	6 John ii. 21.	7 Acts ii. 24 ; iii. 15.	8 Rom. viii. 34.
	9 Apoc. i. 5.	10 Col. i. 18.	

5*

of the dead : and, as in Adam all die, so, also, in Christ all shall be made alive ; but every one in his own order ; the first fruits Christ, then they that are of Christ, who have believed in his coming."[1] These words of the Apostle are to be understood of a perfect resurrection, by which we are resuscitated to eternal life, being no longer subject to death. In this resurrection Christ the Lord holds the first place ; for, if we speak of resurrection, that is, of a return to life, subject to the necessity of again dying, many were thus raised from the dead before Christ ;[2] all of whom, however, were restored to life to die again ; but Christ the Lord, having conquered death, rose again to die no more, according to this clear testimony of the Apostle : " Christ rising again from the dead, dieth now no more, death shall no longer have dominion over him."[3]

Christ rose again on the third day.

" THE THIRD DAY"] In explanation of these additional words of the Article, the pastor will inform the people, that Christ did not remain in the grave during the entire of these three days, but, as he lay in the sepulchre during an entire natural day, during part of the preceding day, and part of the following, he is said, with strictest truth, to have lain in the grave for three days, and on the third day, to have risen again from the dead.

Why on the third day.

To declare his divinity, he deferred not his resurrection to the end of the world ; whilst at the same time, to prove his humanity, and the reality of his death, he rose not immediately, but on the third day after his death, a space of time sufficient to prove that he had really died.

'Accordinging to the Scriptures' why added to the creed.

Here the Fathers of the first Council of Constantinople added the words, " according to the Scriptures," which they received from Apostolical tradition, and imbodied with the creed, because the same Apostle teaches the absolute necessity of the mystery of the resurrection, when he says : " If Christ be not risen again, then is our preaching vain, and your faith is also vain, for you are yet in your sins."[4] Hence, admiring our belief of this Article, St. Augustine says : " It is of little moment to believe that Christ died ; this, the 'Pagans, Jews, and all the wicked believe ; in a word, all believe that Christ died ; but, that he rose from the dead is the belief of Christians ; to believe that he rose again, this we deem of great moment."[5] Hence it is, that our Lord very frequently spoke to his disciples of his resurrection ; and seldom or never of his passion without adverting to his resurrection. Thus, when he said : " The Son of Man shall be delivered to the Gentiles, and shall be mocked and scourged and spit upon ; and after they have scourged him, they will put him to death ;" he added ; "and the third day he shall rise again."[6] Also, when the Jews called upon him to give an attestation of the truth of his doctrine by some miraculous sign, he said : " A sign shall not be given them but the sign of Jonas the Prophet :' for as Jonas was three days and three nights in

[1] 1 Cor. xv. 20—23.   [2] 3 Kings xvii. 22.   4 Kings iv. 34.   [3] Rom. vi. 9.
[4] 1 Cor. xv. 14. 17.   [5] August in Ps. cxi. 4   [6] Luke xviii. 32, 33.   Matt. xvi. 21.

the whale's belly, so shall the Son of man be three days and three nights in the bosom of the earth."[1]

To understand, still better, the force and meaning of this Article, there are three things which demand attentive consideration: first, the necessity of the resurrection; secondly, its end and object; thirdly, the blessings and advantages of which it is to us the source. With regard to the first, it was necessary that he should rise again, in order to manifest the justice of God; for it was most congruous that he, who, through obedience to God, was degraded, and loaded with ignominy, should by him be exalted. This is a reason assigned by the Apostle in his Epistle to the Philippians: "He humbled himself," says he, "becoming obedient unto death; even unto the death of the cross; for which cause God, also, hath exalted him."[2] He rose, also, to confirm our faith, which is necessary to justification: the resurrection of Christ from the dead by his own power, affords an irrefragable proof of his divinity. It also nurtures and sustains our hope, for, as Christ rose again, we rest on an assured hope, that we too, shall rise again; the members must necessarily arrive at the condition of their head. This is the conclusion which St. Paul draws from the reasoning which he uses in his epistles to the Corinthians,[3] and Thessalonians;[4] and Peter, the prince of the Apostle, says: Blessed be God and the Father of our Lord Jesus Christ, who, according to his great mercy, hath regenerated us unto a lively hope, by the resurrection of Jesus Christ from the dead, unto the inheritance incorruptible."[5] Finally, the resurrection of our Lord, as the pastor will inculcate, was necessary to complete the mystery of our salvation and redemption: by his death, Christ liberated us from the thraldom of sin, and restored to us, by his resurrection, the most important of those privileges which we had forfeited by sin. Hence these words of the Apostle: "He was delivered up for our sins, and rose again for our justification."[6] That nothing, therefore, may be wanting to perfect the work of our salvation, it was necessary that, as he died, he should, also, rise again from the dead.

From what has been said we can perceive the important advantages which the resurrection of our Lord has conferred on the faithful; in his resurrection, we acknowledge him to be the immortal God, full of glory, the conqueror of death and hell; and this we are firmly to believe and openly to profess of Christ Jesus.

Again, the resurrection of Christ effectuates our resurrection, not only as its efficient cause, but also as its model. Thus with regard to the resurrection of the body, we have this testimony of the Apostle: "by a man came death, and by a man the resurrection of the dead."[7] To accomplish the mystery of our redemption in all its parts, God made use of the humanity of Christ as its efficient instrument, and hence, his resurrection is

Marginal notes:
Three things which are here to be explained.
I. Necessity of the resurrection.
II. Its end and object.
III. Its blessings and advantages.
L.
II.

---

[1] Luke xi. 29. Matt. xii. 39, 40.   [2] Philip. ii. 8, 9.   [3] 1 Cor. xv. 12.
[4] 1 Thes. iv. 14.   [5] 1 Peter i. 3, 4.   [6] Rom. iv. 25.   [7] 1 Cor. xv. 21.

the efficient cause of ours. It is also, the model: his resurrection was the most perfect of all ; and as his body, rising to immortal glory, was changed, so shall our bodies also, before frail and mortal, be restored and clothed with glory and immortality : in the language of the Apostle; "we look for the Saviour our Lord Jesus Christ, who will reform the body of our lowness, made like to the body of his glory."[1]

III. The same may be said of a soul dead in sin: how the resurrection of Christ is proposed to such a soul as the model of her resurrection, we learn from the same Apostle, when he says ; " Christ is risen from the dead by the glory of the Father, so we also may walk in newness of life ; for if we have been planted together in the likeness of his death, we shall be also in the likeness of his resurrection ;" and a little after, "knowing that Christ, rising from the dead, dieth no more, death shall no more have dominion over him ; for in that he died to sin, he died once: but in that he liveth, he liveth unto God. So do you also reckon, that you are dead to sin, but alive unto God in Christ Jesus our Lord."[2]

From the resurrection of Christ, therefore, we should derive two important lessons of instruction ; the one, that, after we have washed away the stains of sin, we should begin to lead a new life, distinguished by integrity, innocence, holiness, modesty, justice, beneficence, and humility ; the other, that we should so persevere in that newness of life, as never more, with the divine assistance, to stray from the paths of virtue on which we have once entered.

IV. Nor do the words of the Apostle prove only that the resurrection of Christ is proposed as the model of our resurrection ; they also, declare that it gives us power to rise again ; and imparts to us strength and courage to persevere in holiness and righteousness, and in the observance of the commandments of God. As his death not only furnishes us with an example, but also supplies us with strength to die to sin ; so also, his resurrection invigorates us to attain righteousness ; that worshipping God in piety and holiness, we may walk in the newness of life to which we have risen ; for the Redeemer achieved principally by his resurrection, that we, who before died with him to sin, and to the world, may rise, also, with him again to a new discipline and manner of life.

Principal proofs of a resurrection from sin. The principal proofs of this resurrection from sin which demand observation, are comprised in these words of the Apostle : " If you be risen with Christ, seek the things that are above, where Christ is sitting at the right hand of God."[3] Here, he distinctly tells us, that they, whose desire of life, honours, riches, and repose, are directed chiefly to the place in which Christ dwells, have truly risen with him : but when he adds : " Mind the things that are above, not the things that are on the earth ;"[4] he gives this, as it were, as another standard, by which we may

---

[1] Phil. iii. 20, 21. [2] Rom. vi. 4—6. 9—11. [3] Col. iii. 1. [4] Col. iii. 2.

ascertain if we have truly risen with Christ ; for as a relish for food indicates a healthy state of the body : so, with regard to the soul, if we relish " whatever is true, whatever is modest, whatever is just, whatever is holy,"[1] and experience within us a sense of the sweetness of heavenly things ; this we may consider a very strong proof, that with Christ we have risen to a new and spiritual life.

ARTICLE VI.

" HE ASCENDED INTO HEAVEN, SITTETH AT THE RIGHT HAND OF GOD THE FATHER ALMIGHTY."

" HE ASCENDED INTO HEAVEN"] Filled with the Spirit of God, and contemplating the blessed and glorious ascension of our Lord into heaven, the prophet David exhorts all to celebrate that splendid triumph, with the greatest joy and gladness : " Clap your hands," said he, " all ye nations, shout unto God with the voice of joy. God is ascended with jubilee, and the Lord with the sound of trumpet."[2] The pastor will hence learn the obligation imposed on him, of explaining this mystery with unremitting assiduity, and of taking especial care that the faithful not only see it with the light of faith, and of the understanding ; but still more, that, as far as it is in his power to accomplish, they make it their study, with the divine assistance, to reflect its image in their lives and actions. *Triumph of the ascension, how to be celebrated by Christians.*

With regard, then, to the exposition of this sixth Article, which has reference, principally, to the divine mystery of the ascension ; we shall begin with its first part, and point out its force and meaning. That Jesus Christ, having fully accomplished the work of redemption, ascended, as man, body and soul, into heaven, the faithful are unhesitatingly to believe ; for as God, he never forsook heaven, filling as he does all places with his divinity. *First part of the Article: What it teaches us to believe. I.*

The pastor is, also, to teach that he ascended by his own power, not by the power of another as did Elias, who was taken up into heaven in a fiery chariot ;[3] or, as the prophet Habacuc ;[4] or Philip, the deacon, who were borne through the air by the divine power, and traversed the distant regions of the earth.[5] Neither did he ascend into heaven, solely by the exercise of his supreme power as God, but also, by virtue of the power which he possessed as man ; although human power alone was insufficient to raise him from the dead, yet the virtue, with which the blessed soul of Christ was endowed, was capable of moving the body as it pleased, and his body, now glorified, readily obeyed its impulsive dominion. Hence, we believe that Christ ascended *II.* *III.*

---

[1] Phil. iv. 8.　　[2] Ps. xlvi. 1. 6.　　[3] 4 Kings ii. 11.　　[4] Dan. xiv. 35.
[5] Acts viii. 39.

H

into heaven as God and man, by his own power.—We now come to the second part of the Article.

Second part of the Article. A trope.

"SITTETH AT THE RIGHT HAND OF GOD THE FATHER ALMIGHTY"] In these words we observe a trope, that is, the changing of a word from its literal, to a figurative meaning, a thing not unfrequent in Scripture,[1] when, accommodating its language to human ideas, it attributes human affections and human members to God, who, spirit as he is, admits of nothing corporeal. But, as amongst men, he who sits at the right hand is considered to occupy the most honourable place, so, transferring the idea to celestial things, to express the glory which Christ, as man, enjoys above all others, we confess that he sits at the

What the word 'sitteth' means here.

right hand of his Eternal Father. This, however, does not imply position and figure of body: but declares the fixed and permanent possession of royal and supreme power and glory, which he received from the Father; as the Apostle says : " raising him up from the dead, and setting him on his right hand in the heavenly places, above all principality, and power, and virtue, and domination, and every name that is named, not only in this world, but also in that which is to come; and he hath subjected all things under his feet."[2] These words manifestly imply that this glory belongs to our Lord, in so special a manner, that it cannot consist with the nature of any other created being ; and hence, in another place, the Apostle asks : " To which of the angels said he at any time, sit on my right hand, 'till I make thine enemies thy footstool ?"[3]

History of the ascension.

But the pastor will explain the sense of the Article, more at large, by detailing the history of the ascension, of which the evangelist St. Luke has left us an admirable description, in the Acts of the

All other mysteries refer to it as to their end and completion.

Apostles.[4] In his exposition, he will observe, in the first place, that all other mysteries refer to the ascension, as to their end and completion ; as all the mysteries of religion commence with the Incarnation of our Lord, so his sojourn on earth terminates with

Tenor of the Saviour's life compared with his ascension.

his ascension into heaven. Moreover, the other Articles of the Creed, which regard Christ the Lord, show his great humility and lowliness : nothing can be conceived more humble, nothing more lowly, than that the Son of God assumed the frailty of our flesh, suffered and died for us ; but nothing more magnificently, nothing more admirably proclaims his sovereign glory and divine majesty, than what is contained in the present and preceding articles, in which we declare, that he rose from the dead, ascended into heaven, and now sits at the right hand of his Eternal Father.

Reasons of the ascension.

I.

When the pastor has accurately explained these truths, he will next inform the faithful, why our Lord ascended into heaven.— He ascended because the glorious kingdom of the highest heavens, not the obscure abode of this earth, presented a suitable dwelling-place to him whose glorified body, rising from the tomb,

II.

was clothed with immortality.—He ascended, not only to possess

---

[1] Dionys. Areop. Epist. ix.　　[2] Eph. i. 20—22. Athan. Serm. 1 contra Arian.
Basil. lib. de Spir. Sanct. c. vi.　　[3] Heb. i. 13.　　[4] Acts i.

the throne of glory, and the kingdom which he purchased at the price of his blood, but also to attend to whatever regards the salvation of his people.—He ascended, to prove thereby that " his kingdom is not of this world,"[1] for the kingdoms of this world are terrene and transient, and are based upon wealth and the power of the flesh; but the kingdom of Christ is not as the Jews expected, an earthly, but a spiritual and eternal kingdom. Its riches, too, are spiritual, as he shows by placing his throne in the heavens, where they, who seek most earnestly the things that are of God, abound most in riches and in abundance of all good things, according to these words of St. James : " Hath not God chosen the poor in this world, rich in faith and heirs of the kingdom which God hath promised to them that love him ?"[2]

III.

He also ascended into heaven, in order to teach us to follow him thither in mind and heart, for as, by his death and resurrection, he bequeathed to us an example of dying and rising again in spirit; so by his ascension he teaches us, though dwelling on earth, to raise ourselves in thought and desire to heaven, " confessing that we are pilgrims and strangers on the earth,[3] seeking a country ;" " fellow-citizens with the saints, and the domestics of God ;"[4] " for," says the same Apostle, " our conversation is in heaven."[5]

IV.

The extent and unspeakable greatness of the blessings, which the bounty of God has bestowed on us with a lavish hand, were, long before, as the Apostle interprets him, sung by David in these words: " He ascended on high, led captivity captive, and gave gifts to men."[6]   On the tenth day after his ascension, he sent down the Holy Ghost, with whose power and plenitude he filled the multitude of the faithful, then present, and fulfilled his splendid promise : " It is expedient for you that I go; for if I go not, the Paraclete will not come to you ; but, if I go, I will send him to you."[7]   He also ascended into heaven, according to the Apostle, " that he may appear in the presence of God for us,"[8] and discharge for us the office of advocate with the Father: " My, little children," says St. John, " these things I write to you, that you may not sin, but if any man sin, we have an advocate with the Father, Jesus Christ, the just, and he is the propitiation for our sins."[9]   There is nothing from which the faithful should derive greater joy than from the reflection that Jesus Christ is constituted our advocate and intercessor with the Father, with whom his influence and authority are supreme.

V

VI.

VII.

Finally, by his ascension, he has prepared for us a place, as he had promised, and has entered, as our head, in the name of us all, into the possession of the glory of heaven.[10]   Ascending into heaven, he threw open its gates, which had been closed by the sin of Adam ; and, as he foretold his disciples, at his last supper, secured to us a way by which we may arrive at eternal

VIII.

---

[1] John xviii. 36.   [2] James ii. 5.   [3] Heb. xi. 13, 14.   [4] Eph. ii. 19.
[5] Philip. iii. 20.   [6] Ps. lxvii. 19. Eph. iv. 8.   [7] John xvi. 7, 8. Acts i. 4, 5.
[8] Heb. ix. 24.   [9] 1 John ii. 1, 2.   [10] John xiv. 2.

happiness. In order to demonstrate this by the event, he introduced, with himself into the mansions of eternal bliss, the souls of the just whom he had liberated from prison.

Its other advantages. I. A series of important advantages followed in the train of this admirable profusion of celestial gifts : in the first place the merit of our faith was considerably augmented; because faith has for its object those things which fall not under the senses, and are far raised above the reach of human reason and intelligence. If, therefore, the Lord had not departed from us, the merit of our faith should not be the same, for Jesus Christ has said : " Blessed are they who have not seen and have believed."[1] In the next

II. place, it contributes much to confirm our hope : believing that Christ, as man, ascended into heaven, and placed our nature at the right hand of God the Father, we are animated with a strong hope that we, as members, shall also ascend thither, to be there united to our head, according to these words of our Lord himself : " Father, I will, that where I am, they, also, whom thou hast given me, may be with me."[2]

III. Another most important advantage, flowing from the ascension, is, that it elevates our affections to heaven, and inflames them with the Spirit of God; for, most truly has it been said, that, " where our treasure is, there, also, is our heart."[3] And, indeed, were Christ the Lord dwelling on earth, the contemplation of his person, and the enjoyment of his presence, must absorb all our thoughts, and we should view the author of such blessings only as man, and cherish towards him a sort of earthly affection : but, by his ascension into heaven, he has spiritualized our affection for him, and has made us venerate and love as God, him who, now absent, is the object of our thoughts, not of our senses. This we learn, in part, from the example of the Apostles, who, whilst our Lord was personally present with them, seemed to judge of him, in some measure, humanly ; and, in part, from these words of our Lord himself : " It is expedient for you that I go."[4] The affection, with which they loved him when present, was to be perfected by divine love, and that, by the coming of the Holy Ghost; and, therefore, he immediately subjoins : " If I go not, the Paraclete will not come to you."

IV. Besides, he thus enlarged his dwellingplace on earth, that is, his Church, which was to be governed by the power and guidance of the Holy Spirit; and left Peter the prince of the Apostles, as chief pastor, and supreme head upon earth, of the universal Church. " Some, also, he gave Apostles, some Prophets, and other some Evangelists, and other some Pastors and Doctors,"[5] and, thus, seated at the right hand of the Father, he continually bestows different gifts on different men ; according to the words of St. Paul : " To every one of us is given grace, according to the measure of the giving of Christ."[6]

V. Finally, what was already said of his death and resurrection

---

[1] John xx. 29. [2] John xvii. 24. [3] Matt. vi. 21. [4] John xvi. 7.
[5] Eph. iv. 11. [6] Eph. iv. 7.

the faithful will deem not less true of his ascension; for, although we owe our redemption and salvation to the passion of Christ, whose merits opened heaven to the just, yet his ascension is not only proposed to us as a model, which teaches us to look on high, and ascend in spirit into heaven : but also imparts to us a divine virtue which enables us to accomplish what it teaches.

ARTICLE VII.

" FROM THENCE HE SHALL COME TO JUDGE THE LIVING AND THE DEAD."

JESUS CHRIST is invested with three eminent offices and functions, those of Redeemer, Patron, and Judge. But as, in the preceding Articles, we have shown that the human race was redeemed by his passion and death ; and as, by his ascension into heaven, it is manifest that he has undertaken the perpetual advocacy and patronage of our cause; it next follows, that, in this Article, we set forth his character as judge. The scope and intent of the Article is to declare, that on the last day he will judge the whole human race: the Sacred Scriptures inform us, that there are two comings of Christ, the one, when he assumed human flesh, for our salvation, in the womb of a virgin ; the other, when he shall come, at the end of the world, to judge mankind. This coming is called, in Scripture, " The day of the Lord :" " The day of the Lord," says the Apostle, " shall come, as a thief in the night ;"[1] and our Lord himself says : " Of that day and hour nobody knoweth."[2] In proof of the last judgment, it is enough to adduce the authority of the Apostle: " We must all," says he, " appear before the judgment seat of Christ, that every one may receive the proper things of the body, according as he hath done, whether it be good or evil."[3] Sacred Scripture abounds in testimonies to the same effect, which the pastor will meet, everywhere, throughout the Inspired Volume,[4] and which not only establish the truth of the dogma, but also place it, in vivid colours, before the eyes of the faithful : that as, from the beginning, the day of the Lord, on which he was clothed with our flesh, was sighed for by all, as the foundation of their hope of deliverance ; so also, after the death and ascension of the Son of God, the second day of the Lord may be the object of our most earnest desires ; " looking for the blessed hope and coming of the glory of the great God."[5]

But, with a view to the better explanation of this subject, the pastor is to distinguish two distinct periods at which every one

The three offices of Christ.

Meaning of the Article. Last Judgment.

Two judgments.

[1] 1 Thess. v. 2.   [2] Matt. xxiv. 36.   Mark xiii. 32.   [3] 2 Cor. v. 10.
[4] 1 Kings ii. 10. Isaias ii. 12, 19; xiii. 9. Jerem. xxx. 23. Dan. vii. 9. Joel ii. 1.   [5] Tit. ii. 13.

6

must appear in the presence of God, to render an account of all his thoughts, words, and actions, and receive sentence according-

Particular. ly, from the mouth of his judge: the first, when each one departs this life; for he is instantly placed before the judgment seat of God, where all that he had ever done, or spoken, or thought, during life, shall be subjected to the most rigid scrutiny; and

General. this is called the particular judgment: the second, when, on the same day, and in the same place, all men shall stand together, before the tribunal of their judge, that, in the presence and hearing of a congregated world, each may know his final doom: an announcement which will constitute no small part of the pain and punishment of the wicked, and of the remuneration and re-wards of the just; when the tenor of each man's life shall appear

Why a ge- in its true colours. This is called the general judgment; and it *neral judg-* becomes an indispensable duty of the pastor to show why, be-*ment.* sides the particular judgment of each individual, a general one

I. should also be passed upon the assembled world. The first rea-son is founded on circumstances that must augment the rewards, or aggravate the punishments of the dead. Those who depart this life sometimes leave behind them children who imitate the conduct of their parents, dependants, followers; and others who admire and advocate the example, the language, the conduct of those on whom they depend, and whose example they follow; and as the good or bad influence of example, affecting as it does, the conduct of many, is to terminate only with this world; jus-tice demands that, in order to form a proper estimate of the good or bad actions of all, a general judgment should take place.

II. Moreover, as the character of the virtuous frequently suffers from misrepresentation, whilst that of the wicked obtains the commendation of virtue; the justice of God demands that the former recover, in the presence and with the suffrage of a con-gregated world, the good name of which they had been unjustly deprived before men.

III. Again, as the good and the bad perform their good and bad actions not without the co-operation of the body, these actions are common to the body as their instrument; and the body, there-fore, should participate with the soul in the eternal rewards of virtue, or the everlasting punishments of vice; and this can only be accomplished by means of a general resurrection and of a ge-neral judgment.

IV. Finally, it was important to prove, that in prosperity and ad-versity, which are sometimes the promiscuous lot of the good and of the bad, everything is ordered by an all-wise, all-just, and all-ruling Providence: it was therefore, necessary not only, that rewards and punishments should await us in the next life; but that they should be awarded by a public and general judgment; that thus they may be better known and rendered more conspicu-ous to all; and that, in atonement for the querulous murmur-ings, to which, on seeing the wicked abound in wealth and flourish in honours, even the Saints themselves, as men, have sometimes given expression ; a tribute of praise may be offered by all to the justice and providence of God. " My feet," says the Prophet, " were almost moved, my steps had well nigh slipt ; because I had a zeal on occasion of the wicked, seeing the prosperity of sinners :" and a little after : " Behold ! these are sinners, and yet abounding in the world, they have obtained riches ; and I said, then have I in vain justified my heart, and washed my hands among the innocent ; and I have been scourged all the day; and my chastisement hath been in the morning."[1] This has been the frequent complaint of many, and a general judgment is, therefore, necessary, lest, perhaps, men may be tempted to say that God, " walking about the poles of heaven,"[2] regards not the earth. Wisely, therefore, has this truth been made one of the twelve articles of the Christian creed, that should any be tempted to doubt for a moment, their faith may be confirmed by the satisfactory reasons which this doctrine presents to the mind. Besides, the just should be encouraged by the hope, the wicked appalled by the terror of a future judgment ; that knowing the justice of God, the former may not be disheartened, and, dreading his eternal judgments, the latter may be recalled from the paths of vice. Hence speaking of the last day, our Lord and Saviour declares, that a general judgment will, one day take place, and describes the signs of its approach ; that seeing them, we may know that the end of the world is at hand.[3] At his ascension also, to console his Apostles, overwhelmed with grief at his departure, he sent Angels, who said to them : " This Jesus who is taken up from you into heaven, shall so come as you have seen him going into heaven."[4]

That this judgment is ascribed to Christ our Lord, not only as God, but also as man, is expressly declared in Scripture : for although the power of judging is common to all the Persons of the blessed Trinity, yet it is specially attributed to the Son, because to him also in a special manner, is ascribed wisdom. But that as man, he will judge the world, is confirmed by the testimony of our Lord himself when he says: " As the Father hath life in himself; so he hath given to the Son also, to have life in himself; and he hath given him power to do judgment, because he is the Son of Man."[5] There is a peculiar propriety in Christ's sitting in judgment on this occasion ; that as sentence is to be pronounced on mankind, they may see their judge with their eyes, and hear him with their ears, and thus learn their final doom, through the medium of the senses. Most just is it also, that he who was most iniquitously condemned by the judgment of men, should himself be, afterwards seen by all men sitting in judgment on all. Hence the prince of the Apostles, when expounding, in the house of Cornelius, the principal dogmas of Christianity, and teaching that Christ was suspended from a cross, and put to death by the Jews, and rose the third day

Christ not only as God, but also as man universal judge.

Why as man ?

---

[1] Ps. lxxii. 2, 3. 12—14.   [2] Job xxii. 14.   [3] Matt. xxiv. 29.   [4] Acts i 11.
[5] John v 26, 27.

to life, added : "and he has commanded us to preach, and to testify to the people, that this is he, who was appointed of God to be the judge of the living and the dead."[1]

Signs which are to precede the general judgment. The Sacred Scriptures also inform us, that the general judgment shall be preceded by these three principal signs, the preaching of the Gospel throughout the world, a defection from the faith, and the coming of Antichrist. "This Gospel of the kingdom," says our Lord, " shall be preached in the whole world, for a testimony to all nations, and then shall come the consummation."[2] The apostle also admonishes us that we be not seduced by any one, "as if the day of the Lord were at hand ; for unless there come a revolt first, and the man of sin be revealed, the son of perdition,"[3] the judgment will not come.

The form and procedure of this judgment the pastor will easily learn from the oracles of Daniel,[4] the writings of the Evangelists and the doctrine of the Apostle. The sentence, also, to be pronounced by the judge, is here deserving of more than ordinary The last sentence.
The good. attention. Looking to the just standing on his right, with a countenance beaming with joy, the Redeemer will pronounce sentence on them, with the greatest benignity, in these words : " Come ye blessed of my Father, possess the kingdom prepared for you from the beginning of the world."[5] That nothing can be conceived, more delightful to the ear than these words, we shall comprehend, if we only compare them with the sentence of condemnation to be hurled against the wicked ; and call to mind, that by them the just are invited from labour to rest, from the vale of tears to the mansions of joy, from temporal misery to eternal happiness, the reward of their works of charity.

The bad. Turning next to those who shall stand on his left, he will pour out his justice on them in these words : " Depart from me, ye cursed, into everlasting fire, prepared for the devil and his angels."[6] These first words, " depart from me," express the heaviest punishment with which the wicked shall be visited—their eternal banishment from the sight of God, unrelieved by one consolatory hope of recovering so great a good. This divines call " the pain of loss," because in hell, the wicked shall be deprived of the light of the vision of God.[7] The words " ye cursed," which are added, must augment to an extreme degree, their wretched and calamitous condition. If when banished from the Divine presence, they could hope for blessing of any sort, it might be to them some source of consolation ; but deprived of every such expectation that could alleviate calamity, the divine justice, whose severity their crimes have provoked, pursues them with every species of malediction. The words, " into everlasting fire," which follow, express another sort of punishment, called by Divines " the pain of sense ; because, like other corporal punishments, amongst which, no doubt, fire produces the most

---

1 Acts x. 42.   2 Matt. xxiv. 14.   3 2 Thess. ii. 2, 3.   4 Dan. vii. 9.
5 Matt. xxv. 34.   6 Matt. xxv. 41.   7 Chrysost. in Matth. hom. 22. August. Serm. 181. de temp. Greg. lib. 9. moral. cap. 46.

intense pain, it is felt through the organs of sense. When, moreover, we reflect that this pain is to be eternal, we are at once satisfied that the punishment of the damned admits of no increase.

These are considerations, which the pastor should very frequently press upon the attention of the faithful; the truth which this Article announces, seen with the eyes of faith, is most efficacious in bridling the perverse propensities of the heart, and withdrawing souls from sin.[1] Hence we read in Ecclesiasticus: "Remember thy last end, and thou shalt never sin."[2] And indeed, it is almost impossible to find one so prone to vice, as not to be capable of being recalled to the pursuit of virtue, by the reflection—that the day will come when he shall have to render an account before a most rigorous judge, not only of all his words and actions, but even of his most secret thoughts, and shall suffer punishment according to his deserts. But the just man must be more and more excited to cultivate justice, and, although doomed to spend his life in want, and obloquy, and torments, he must be transported with the greatest joy, when he looks forward to that day on which, when the conflicts of this wretched life are over, he shall be declared victorious in the hearing of all men; and admitted into his heavenly country, shall be crowned with divine, and these, also, eternal honours. It becomes, therefore, the duty of the pastor to exhort the faithful to model their lives after the best manner, and exercise themselves in every practice of piety; that thus they may be enabled to look forward with greater security, to the great coming day of the Lord, and even as becomes children, desire it most earnestly.

The faithful to be frequently reminded of the last judgment.

ARTICLE VIII.

"I BELIEVE IN THE HOLY GHOST."

HITHERTO we have expounded, as far as the nature of the subject seemed to require, what regards the first and second Persons of the Holy Trinity. It now remains to explain what the Creed contains with regard to the third Person, the Holy Ghost. On this subject, also, the pastor will omit nothing that study and assiduity can effect; for on this, and the preceding Articles, error were alike unpardonable. Hence, the Apostle is careful to instruct some amongst the Ephesians, with regard to the Person of the Holy Ghost.[3] Having asked if they had received the Holy Ghost, and having received for answer, that they did not so much as know the existence of the Holy Spirit, he immediately subjoins: "In whom, therefore, were you baptised?"—

Necessity of Faith in the Holy Ghost.

[1] Aug. serm. 128. de temp. Greg. hom. 39. in Evang. Bernard. serm. 1. in festo omnium Sanctorum.   [2] Eccles. vii. 40.   [3] Acts xix. 2.

6*   I

to signify that a distinct knowledge of this Article is most necessary to the faithful. From it they derive this special fruit—considering, attentively, that whatever they possess, they possess through the bounty and beneficence of the Holy Spirit, they learn to think more modestly and humbly of themselves, and to place all their hopes in the protection of God, which is the first step towards consummate wisdom and supreme happiness.

Meaning of the words Holy Ghost. The exposition of this Article, therefore, should begin with the meaning here attached to the words, Holy Ghost; for, as this appellation is equally true when applied to the Father and the Son, (both are spirit, both holy,) and also includes angels, and the souls of the just; care must be taken that the faithful be not led into error by the ambiguity of the words. The pastor, then, will teach, in this Article, that by the words Holy Ghost, is understood the third Person of the blessed Trinity; a sense in which they are used, sometimes in the Old, and frequently in the New Testament. Thus David prays: " Take not thy Holy Spirit from me ;"[1] and in the Book of Wisdom, we read: " Who shall know thy thoughts, except thou give wisdom, and send thy Holy Spirit from above ?"[2] And in another place : " He created her in the Holy Ghost."[3] We are also commanded, in the New Testament, to be baptised, " in the name of the Father, and of the Son, and of the Holy Ghost :"[4] we read that the most holy Virgin conceived of the Holy Ghost;[5] and we are sent by St. John to Christ, " who baptiseth us in the Holy Ghost ;"[6] with a variety of other passages in which the words Holy Ghost occur.

Why the third Person of the holy Trinity has no proper name. Nor should it be deemed matter of surprise, that a proper name is not given to the third, as to the first and second Persons : the second Person is designated by a proper name, and called Son, because, as has been explained in the preceding Articles, his eternal birth from the Father is properly called generation. As, therefore, that birth is expressed by the word generation; so the Person, emanating from that generation, is properly called Son, and the Person, from whom he emanates, Father. But as the production of the third Person is characterised by no proper name, but is called spiration and procession ; the Person produced is, consequently, characterised by no proper name. As, however, we are obliged to borrow, from created objects, the names given to God, and know no other created means of communicating nature and essence than that of generation ; we cannot discover a proper name to express the manner in which God communicates himself entire, by the force of his love. Unable, therefore, to express the emanation of the third Person, by a proper, we have recourse to the common name of Holy Ghost; a name, however, peculiarly appropriate to him who infuses into us spiritual life, and without whose holy inspiration, we can do nothing meritorious of eternal life

---

[1] Ps. l. 12, 13.   [2] Wis. ix. 17.   [3] Eccles. i. 9.   [4] Matt. xxviii. 19.
[5] Matt. i. 20.   Luke i. 35.   [6] John i. 33.

But the people, when once acquainted with the import of the name, should, first of all, be taught that he is equally God with the Father and the Son, equally omnipotent, eternal, perfect, the supreme good, infinitely wise, and of the same nature with the Father and the Son. All this is, obviously enough, implied by the force of the word "in," when we say: "I believe in the Holy Ghost;" which, to mark the particularity of our faith, is prefixed to each Person of the Trinity; and is also clearly established by many passages of Scripture: when, in the Acts of the Apostles, St. Peter says: "Ananias! why hast thou conceived this thing in thy heart?" he immediately adds: "thou hast not lied to men but to God;"[1] calling him, to whom he had before given the name Holy Ghost, immediately after, God.

The Apostle, also, writing to the Corinthians, interprets what he says of God, as said of the Holy Ghost: "There are," says he, "diversities of operations, but the same God, who worketh all in all;" "but," continues he, "all these things one and the same spirit worketh, "dividing to every one according as he will."[2] In the Acts of the Apostles, also, what the prophets attribute to one God, St. Paul ascribes to the Holy Ghost; thus Isaias had said: "I heard the voice of the Lord, saying: Whom shall I send? and who shall go for us? and I said: Lo! here am I, send me. And he said: Go, and thou shalt say to this people: Blind the heart of this people, and make their ears heavy, and shut their eyes: lest they see with their eyes, and hear with their ears:"[3] Having cited these words, the Apostle adds: "Well did the Holy Ghost speak to our fathers, by Isaias the prophet."[4]

Again, the Sacred Scriptures, by annexing the Person of the Holy Ghost to those of the Father and the Son; as when baptism is commanded to be administered, "in the name of the Father, and of the Son, and of the Holy Ghost," leaves no room whatever to doubt the truth of this mystery: for if the Father is God, and the Son God, why not confess that the Holy Ghost, who is united with them in the same degree of honour, is also God? Besides, baptism administered in the name of any creature, can be of no effect: "Were you baptised in the name of Paul?"[5] says the Apostle, to show that such baptism could have availed them nothing to salvation. Having, therefore, been baptised in the name of the Holy Ghost, we must acknowledge the Holy Ghost to be God.

But this same order of the three Persons, which proves the divinity of the Holy Ghost, is observable in the epistle of St. John: "There are three who give testimony in heaven; the Father, the Word, and the Holy Ghost; and these three are one;"[6] and, also, in that noble eulogy, or form of praise to the Trinity: "Glory be to the Father, and to the Son, and to the Holy Ghost," which closes the psalms and divine praises.

Marginal notes:

The Holy Ghost equally God with the Father and the Son.

I.

II.

III.

IV.

V.

VI.

VII.

---

[1] Acts v. 3, 4.   [2] 1 Cor. xii. 6, 11.   [3] Isaias vi. 8—10.   [4] Acts xxviii. 25.
[5] 1 Cor. i. 14.   [6] 1 John v. 7.

VIII.   Finally, not to omit an argument which goes, most forcibly to establish this truth, the authority of Holy Scripture proves, that whatever faith attributes to God, belongs equally to the Holy Ghost: to him is ascribed, in Scripture, the honour of temples: "Know you not," says the Apostle, "that your members are the temple of "the Holy Ghost;"[1] and also sanctification,[2] vivification,[3] to search the depths of God,[4] to speak by the prophets,[5] and to be present in all places ;[6] all of which are attributed to God alone.

The Holy Ghost a distinct person from the Father and the Son.   The pastor will, also, accurately explain to the faithful, that the Holy Ghost is God, so as to be the third Person in the divine nature, distinct from the Father and the Son, and produced by their will. To say nothing of other testimonies of Scripture, the form of baptism, taught by the Redeemer,[7] furnishes an irrefragable proof that the Holy Ghost is the third Person, self-existent in the divine nature, and distinct from the other Persons: a doctrine taught, also, by the Apostle, when he says: "'The grace of our Lord Jesus Christ, and the charity of God, and the communication of the Holy Ghost, be with you all. Amen."[8] This same truth, is still more explicitly declared in the words which were here added by the Fathers of the first Council of Constantinople, to refute the impious folly of Macedonius: "And in the Holy Ghost the Lord and giver of life, who proceedeth from the Father, and the Son: who, together with the Father and the Son, is adored and glorified ; who spoke by the prophets." Thus, by confessing the Holy Ghost to be "Lord," they declare, how far he excels the angels, who are the perfection of created intelligence; for, "they are all," says the Apostle, "ministering spirits, sent to minister for them who shall receive the inheritance of salvation."[9]

Why called the "giver of life."   They, also, designate the Holy Ghost: "The giver of life," because the soul lives more by an union with God, than the body is nurtured and sustained by an union with the soul. As, then, the Sacred Scriptures ascribe to the Holy Ghost this union of the soul with God, with great propriety, is he denominated "the giver of life."

His procession from the Father and the Son.   With regard to the words immediately succeeding: "who proceedeth from the Father and the Son," the faithful are to be taught, that the Holy Ghost proceeds by eternal procession, from the Father and the Son, as from one principle: a truth propounded to us by an ecclesiastical rule, from which the least departure is unwarrantable, confirmed by the authority of the Sacred Scriptures, and defined by the Councils of the Church. Christ himself, speaking of the Holy Ghost, says: "He shall glorify me, because he shall receive of mine ;"[10] and we, also, find that the Holy Ghost is, sometimes, called, in Scripture, "the Spirit of Christ," sometimes, "the Spirit of the Father;" is, one time, said to be sent by the Father,[11] another time, by the

---

[1] 1 Cor. vi. 19.   [2] 2 Thess. ii. 13.   1 Petr. i. 2.   [3] John vi. 64.
[4] 2 Cor. iii. 6; 1 Cor. ii. 10.   [5] 2 Petr. i 21.   [6] Wis. i. 7.   [7] Matt. xxviii. 19.
[8] 2 Cor. xiii. 13.   [9] Heb. i. 14.   [10] John xvi. 14.   [11] John xiv. 26.

Son ;[1] thus signifying, in unequivocal terms, that he proceeds
alike from the Father and the Son. " He," says St. Paul,
" who has not the Spirit of Christ belongs not to him."[2] In
his epistle to the Galatians, he also calls the Holy Ghost the
Spirit of Christ : " God," says he, " hath sent the Spirit of
his Son into your hearts, crying : Abba, Father."[3] In the Gospel of St. Matthew, he is called the Spirit of the Father : " It
is not you that speak, but the Spirit of your Father that speaketh in you ;"[4] and our Lord himself said, at his last supper :
" When the Paraclate cometh, whom I will send you, the Spirit
of Truth, who proceedeth from the Father, he shall give testimony of me."[5] On another occasion, he declares, that he is
to be sent by the Father : " whom," says he, " the Father will
send in my name."[6] Understanding by these words, the procession of the Holy Ghost, we come to the inevitable conclusion,
that he proceeds from the Father and the Son. This exposition
embraces the doctrine to be taught with regard to the Person of
the Holy Ghost.

It is, also, the duty of the pastor to teach that there are certain admirable effects, certain exalted gifts of the Holy Ghost,
which are said to originate and emanate from him, as from a
perennial fountain of goodness. Although the extrinsic works
of the most Holy Trinity are common to the three Persons, yet
many of them are attributed, specially to the Holy Ghost ;
giving us to understand that they arise from the boundless love
of God towards us : for as the Holy Ghost proceeds from the
divine will, inflamed, as it were, with love, we can comprehend
that these effects which are referred, particularly, to the Holy
Ghost, are the result of the boundless love of God towards us.

The gifts of the Holy Ghost.

Hence it is, that the Holy Ghost is called A GIFT ; for by a
gift we understand that which is kindly and gratuitously bestowed, without reference to anticipated remuneration. Whatever gifts and graces, therefore, have been bestowed on us, by
Almighty God, and " what have we," says the Apostle, " that
we have not received from God ?"[7] we should piously and
gratefully acknowledge, as bestowed by the grace and gift of
the Holy Ghost.

These gifts are numerous : not to mention the creation of the
world, the propagation and government of all created beings, as
noticed in the first Article ; we proved, a little before, that the
giving of life is, particularly, attributed to the Holy Ghost, and
the propriety of this attribution is further confirmed by the testimony of the prophet Ezekiel : " I will give you spirit and
you shall live."[8] The prophet Isaias, however, enumerates the
effects peculiarly attributed to the Holy Ghost : " The spirit of
wisdom, and understanding, the spirit of counsel and fortitude,
the spirit of knowledge and piety, and the spirit of the fear of
the Lord :"[9] effects which are called the gifts of the Holy

---

1 John xv. 26.   2 Rom. viii. 9.   3 Gal. iv. 6.   4 Matth. x. 20.
5 John xv. 26.   6 John xiv. 26.   7 1 Cor. iv. 7.   8 Ezek. xxxvii. 6.
9 Isaias xi. 3.

Ghost, and, sometimes, the Holy Ghost. Wisely, therefore, does St. Augustine admonish us, whenever we meet the word Holy Ghost, in Scripture, to distinguish whether it means the third Person of the Trinity, or his gifts and operations:[1] they are as distinct as the Creator is from the creature. The diligence of the pastor, in expounding these truths, should be the greater, as it is from these gifts of the Holy Ghost that we derive rules of Christian life, and are enabled to know if the Holy Ghost dwells within us.

Justifying Grace, the transcendant gift of the Holy Ghost. But the grace of justification, "which signs us with the holy spirit of promise, who is the pledge of our inheritance,"[2] transcends his highest gifts: it unites us to God, in the closest bonds of love—lights up within us the sacred flame of piety—forms us to newness of life—renders us partakers of the divine nature—and enables us " to be called and really to be the sons of " God."[3] [4]

ARTICLE IX.

" I BELIEVE THE HOLY CATHOLIC CHURCH."

Why this Article is to be carefully explained. It will not be difficult to estimate the care with which the pastor should explain this ninth Article to the faithful,[5] if we attend to the following important considerations: that, as S. Augustine observes,[6] the prophets spoke more plainly and explicitly of the Church than of Christ, foreseeing that on this a much greater number may err and be deceived, than on the mystery of the incarnation: after ages were to behold wicked men, who, imitative as the ape, that would fain pass for one of the human species, arrogate to themselves exclusively the name of Catholic, and, with effrontery as unblushing as it is impious, assert that with them alone is to be found the Catholic Church— Secondly, that he, whose mind is deeply impressed with this truth, will experience little difficulty in avoiding the awful *Who is to be called a heretic.* danger of heresy; for a person is not to be called a heretic so soon as he errs in matters of faith: then only is he to be so called, when, in defiance of the authority of the Church, he maintains impious opinions, with unyielding pertinacity. As, therefore, so long as he holds what this Article proposes to be believed, no man can be infected with the contagion of heresy; the pastor should use every diligence, that the faithful, knowing this mystery, and prepared against the wiles of Satan, persevere in the true faith.

But this Article hinges upon the preceding one, for, having

---

[1] D. August. lib. 15. de Trinit. cap. xviii. 19.
[3] 1 John iii. 1. 2 Peter i. 4.
[5] 1 John iii. 1. 2 Peter i. 4.
[2] Eph. i. 13.
[4] Council Trid. Sess. 6.
[6] S. Aug. in Ps. xxx. 15

already established that the Holy Ghost is the source and giver of all holiness, we here confess our belief in the Church which he has endowed with sanctity.

As the word Ecclesia (church) which is borrowed from the Greek, has been applied, since the preaching of the Gospel, to sacred things, it becomes necessary to explain its meaning. The word Ecclesia (church) means a calling forth ; but writers afterwards used it to signify a council or assembly. Nor does it matter whether the word is used in reference to the professors of a true or a false religion : in the Acts of the Apostles it is said of the people of Ephesus, that, when the town-clerk had appeased a tumultuous assemblage, he said : " and if you inquire after any other matter, it may be decided in a lawful assembly" (Ecclesia) :[1] The Ephesians, who were worshippers of Diana, are thus called by the Apostle, " a lawful assembly" (Ecclesia) : Nor are the Gentiles only, who know not God, called a church or assembly, (Ecclesia) : the councils of wicked and impious men are also, sometimes, called by the same name : " I have hated the assembly (Ecclesiam) of the malignant," says the Psalmist, "and with the wicked I will not sit."[2] However, in ordinary Scripture-phrase, the word was afterwards used to designate the Christian commonwealth only, and the assemblies of the faithful ; that is of those who were called by faith to the light of truth, and the knowledge of God ; who, forsaking the darkness of ignorance and error, worship the living and true God in piety and holiness, and serve him from their whole hearts. In a word, " the Church," says S. Augustine, " consists of the faithful dispersed throughout the world."[3]

Under the word " Church" are comprehended no unimportant mysteries, for, in this "calling forth," which the word Ecclesia (church) signifies, we at once recognize the benignity and splendour of divine grace, and understand that the Church is very unlike all other commonwealths : they rest on human reason and human prudence ; this, on the wisdom and councils of God ; for he called us by the interior inspiration of the Holy Ghost, who, through the ministry and labour of his pastors, and preachers, penetrates into the hearts of men.

Moreover, from this calling we shall better understand the end which the Christian should propose to himself, that is, the knowledge and possession of things eternal, when we reflect why the faithful, living under the law, were of old, called a synagogue, that is, a congregation : as S. Augustine observes, " they were so called, because, like cattle which usually go together, they looked only to terrestrial and transitory things ;"[4] and hence the Christian people are called a church, not a synagogue, because, despising terrestrial and transitory things, they aspired only to things heavenly and eternal.

Many other names, replete with mysteries, are employed, by an easy deflection from their original meaning, to designate the

Marginal notes: Meaning of the word Ecclesia ; (church.) — Mysteries which the word comprises. — In what it differs from the Synagogue. — Other names of theChurch.

[1] Acts xix. 29. [2] Ps. xxv. 5. [3] S. Aug. in Ps. cxlix. [4] Aug. in Ps. lxxvii. lxxxi.

Christian commonwealth: by the Apostle it is called "the House and Edifice of God," when writing to Timothy, he says, "If I tarry long, that thou mayest know how thou oughtest to behave thyself in the house of God, which is the Church of the living God, the pillar and ground of truth."[1] It is called a house because it consists, as it were, of one family, governed by one Father, and enjoying a community of all spiritual goods. It is also called the flock of Christ, of which he is "the door and the shepherd."[2] It is called the spouse of Christ: "I have espoused you to one husband," says the Apostle to the Corinthians, "that I may present you a chaste virgin to Christ:"[3] and writing to the Ephesians, he says: "Husbands, love your wives, as Christ, also, loved the Church, and delivered himself up for it:"[4] and, also, speaking of marriage, he says: "This is a great sacrament, but I speak in Christ and in the Church."[5] Finally, the Church is called the body of Christ, as may be seen in the epistles of St. Paul to the Ephesians,[6] and Colossians:[7] appellations each of which has considerable influence in exciting the faithful to prove themselves worthy the boundless clemency and goodness of God, who chose them to be his people.

(margin notes: I. II. III. IV.)

The Church triumphant and militant;

Having explained these things, it will be necessary to enumerate the several component parts of the Church, and point out their difference, in order that the faithful may the better comprehend the nature, properties, gifts, and graces of the Church, the object of God's special predilection; and unceasingly offer to the divine majesty the homage of their grateful praise. The Church consists principally of two parts, the one called the Church triumphant, the other, the Church militant.[8]

Triumphant;

The Church triumphant is that most glorious and happy assemblage of blessed spirits, and of those souls who have triumphed over the world, the flesh, and the devil, and, now exempt from the troubles of this life, are blessed with the fruition of everlasting bliss.

Militant.

The Church militant is the society of all the faithful still dwelling on earth, and is called militant, because it wages eternal war with those implacable enemies, the world, the flesh and the devil. We are not, however, hence to infer that there are two Churches: they are two constituent parts of one Church; one part gone before, and now in the possession of its heavenly country; the other, following every day, until, at length, united to its invisible head, it shall repose in the fruition of endless felicity.[9]

Composed of the good and the bad.

The Church militant is composed of two classes of persons, the good and the bad, both professing the same faith and partaking of the same sacraments; yet differing in their manner of life and morality. The good are those who are linked together not only by the profession of the same faith, and the par-

[1] 1 Tim. iii. 15.   [2] Ezek. xxxiv. 5. John x. 7.   [3] 2 Cor. xi. 2.   [4] Eph. v. 25.
[5] Eph. v. 32.   [6] Eph. i. 23.   [7] Colos. i. 24.   [8] Aug. Ench. c. 10.
                    [9] Aug. lib. ii. de Civ. Dei, c. 2.

ticipation of the same sacraments; but also by the spirit of grace, and the bond of charity: of whom St. Paul says: " The Lord knoweth who are his."[1] Who they are that compose this class we, also, may remotely conjecture; pronounce with certainty we cannot.[2] Of this part of his Church, therefore, our Lord does not speak, when he refers us to the Church, and commands us to hear and to obey her:[3] unknown as is that portion of the Church, how ascertain with certainty, whose decision to recur to, whose authority to obey ? The Church, therefore, as the Sacred Scriptures, and the writings of the holy men who are gone before us, testify, includes within her fold the good and the bad : and this interpretation is sustained by the Apostle, when he says: " There is one body and one spirit."[4] Thus *Figures* understood, the Church is known, and is compared to a city built *and comparisons* on a mountain, and seen from every side.[5] As all must yield *of the* obedience to her authority, it is necessary that she may be *Church.* known by all. That the Church is composed of the good and the bad we learn from many parables contained in the Gospel: thus, the kingdom of heaven, that is, the Church militant, is compared to a net cast into the sea,[6] to a field in which tares were sown with the good grain,[7] to a threshing floor on which the grain is mixed up with the chaff,[8] and, also, to ten virgins, five of whom were wise, and five foolish ;[9] and, long before, we trace a figure and striking resemblance of the Church in the ark of Noah, which contained not only clean, but also unclean animals.[10] But, although the Catholic faith uniformly and truly teaches that the good and the bad belong to the Church, yet the same faith declares that the condition of both is very different : the wicked are contained in the Church, as the chaff is mingled with the grain on the threshing floor, or as dead members, sometimes, remain attached to a living body.

Hence, there are but three classes of persons excluded from *Those who* her pale, infidels, heretics and schismatics, and excommunicated *are excluded from her* persons ; infidels, because they never belonged to, and never *pale.* knew the Church, and were never made partakers of any of her sacraments ; heretics and schismatics, because they have separated from the Church, and belong to her, only as deserters belong to the army from which they have deserted. It is not, however, to be denied, that they are still subject to the jurisdiction of the Church, inasmuch as they are liable to have judgment passed on their opinions, to be visited with spiritual punishments, and denounced with anathema. Finally, excommunicated persons, because excluded by her sentence from the number of her children, belong not to her communion until restored by repentance. But with regard to the rest; however wicked and flagitious, it is certain that they still belong to the Church; and of this the faithful are frequently to be reminded, in order to be convinced that, were even the lives of her ministers de-

---

[1] 2 Tim. ii. 19.   [2] Conc. Trid. Sess. 6. c. 12.   [3] Matt. xviii. 17.   [4] Eph. iv. 4.
[5] Matt. v. 15.   [6] Matt. xiii. 47.   [7] Matt. xiii. 24.   [8] Luke iii. 17.
     [9] Matt. xxv. 1, 2.   [10] Gen. vii. 2. 1 Pet. iii. 20.

based by crime, they are still within her pale, and, therefore, lose no part of the power, with which her ministry invests them.

Other applications of the word Church. But portions of the Universal Church are, also, usually called a Church, as when the Apostle mentions the Church at Corinth,[1] at Galatia,[2] at Laodicea,[3] at Thessalonica.[4] The private houses of the faithful, he, also, calls Churches: the Church in the house of Priscilla and Aquila he commands to be saluted:[5] and in another place, he says: " Aquila and Priscilla, with their domestic Church, salute you much."[6] Writing to Philemon, he makes use of the same word, in the same sense.[7] Sometimes, also, the word Church is used to signify the prelates and pastors of the Church: " If he will not hear thee," says our Lord, " tell it to the Church."[8] Here the word Church means the authorities of the Church. The place in which the faithful assemble to hear the word of God, or for other religious purposes is, also, called a Church;[9] but, in this Article, the word is specially used to signify the good and the bad, the governing and the governed.

Distinctive marks of the Church. The distinctive marks of this Church are also to be made known to the faithful, that thus they may be enabled to estimate the extent of the blessing, conferred by God on those who have had the happiness to be born and educated within her pale. The first mark of the true Church is described in the Creed of the Fathers, and consists in unity : " My dove is one, my beautiful one is one."[10] So vast a multitude, scattered far and wide, is called one, for the reasons mentioned by St. Paul in his epistle to the Ephesians: " One Lord, one faith, one baptism."[11] This Church has, also, but one ruler and one governor, the invisible one, Christ, whom the Eternal Father " hath made head over all the Church, which is his body ;"[12] the visible one, him, who, as legitimate successor of Peter the prince of the Apostles, fills the apostolic chair.

I. Unity.

A visible head necessary to preserve unity. That this visible head is necessary to establish and preserve unity in the Church is the unanimous accord of the Fathers ; and on this, the sentiments of St. Jerome, in his work against Jovinian, are as clearly conceived as they are happily expressed: " One," says he, " is chosen, that, by the appointment of a head, all occasion of schism may be removed ;"[13] and to Damascus, " Let envy cease, let the pride of Roman ambition be humbled: I speak to the successor of the fisherman, and to the disciple of the cross. Following no chief but Christ, I am united in communion with your Holiness, that is, with the chair of Peter. I know that on that rock is built the Church. Whoever will eat the lamb outside this house is profane : whoever is not in the ark of Noah shall perish in the flood." The

[1] 2 Cor. i. 1.   [2] Gal. i. 2.   [3] Colos. iv. 16.   [4] 1 Thess. i. 1.
[5] Rom. xvi. 3–5.   [6] 1 Cor. xvi. 19.   [7] Phil. i. 2.   [8] Mat. xviii. 17.
[9] 1 Cor. xi. 18.   [10] Cant. vi. 8.   [11] Eph. iv. 5.   [12] Eph. i. 22, 23.
[13] S. Hyeron. lib. 1. contr. Jovin. in med. et epist. 57.

same doctrine was, long before, established by S. S. Irenæus,[1] and Cyprian :[2] the latter, speaking of the unity of the Church, observes : " The Lord said to Peter, ' I say to thee Peter! thou art Peter : and upon this rock I will build my Church :'[3] he builds his Church on one ; and although, after his resurrection, he gave equal power to all his Apostles, saying, ' As the Father hath sent me, I also send you. Receive ye the Holy Ghost ;'[4] yet, to display unity, he disposed, by his own authority, the origin of this unity, which had its beginning with one, &c." Again, Optatus of Milevis says : " It cannot be ascribed to ignorance on your part, knowing, as you do, that the episcopal chair, in which, as head of all the Apostles, Peter sat, was, first, fixed by him in the city of Rome ; that in him alone may be preserved the unity of the Church ; and that the other Apostles may not claim each a chair for himself ; so that, now, he, who erects another, in opposition to this single chair, is a schismatic and a prevaricator."[5] In the next place, S. Basil has these words : " Peter is made the foundation, because he says : ' Thou art Christ, the Son of the living God:' and hears in reply that he is a rock ; but although a rock, he is not such a rock as Christ, for in himself Christ is, truly, an immoveable rock, but Peter, only by virtue of that rock ; for God bestows his dignities on others : He is a priest, and he makes priests ; a rock, and he makes a rock : what belongs to himself, he bestows on his servants."[6] Lastly, S. Ambrose says : " Should any one object, that the Church is content with one head and one spouse, Jesus Christ, and requires no other ; the answer is obvious ; for, as we deem Christ not only the author of all the Sacraments, but, also, their invisible minister ; (he it is who baptises, he it is who absolves, although men are appointed by him the external ministers of the sacraments) so has he placed over his Church, which he governs by his invisible spirit, a man to be his vicar, and the minister of his power : a visible Church requires a visible head, and, therefore, does the Saviour appoint Peter head and pastor of all the faithful, when, in the most ample terms, he commits to his care the feeding of all his sheep ;[7] desiring that he, who was to succeed him, should be invested with the very same power of ruling and governing the entire Church."

The Apostle, moreover, writing to the Corinthians, tells them, that there is but one and the same Spirit who imparts grace to the faithful, as the soul communicates life to the members of the body.[8] Exhorting the Ephesians to preserve this unity, he says, " Be careful to keep the unity of the Spirit in the bond of peace."[9] As the human body consists of many members, animated by one soul, which gives sight to the eyes,

Unity of the faithful how to be preserved.

1.

---

[1] Iren. lib. 3. contr. hæres. cap. 3.   [2] B. Cyprian. de simp. præel. in principio fere.   [3] Matt. xvi. 18.   [4] John xx. 21, 22.
[5] Optat. Initio lib. 2. ad Parmen.   [6] Basil. hom. 29. quæ est de pænit.
[7] John xxi. 15.   [8] 1 Cor. xii 11, 12.   [9] Eph. iv. 3.

hearing to the ears, and to the other senses, the power of discharging their respective functions; so, the mystical body of Christ, which is the Church, is composed of many faithful. The hope, to which we are called, is, also, one, as the Apostle tells us in the same place :[1] we all hope for the same consummation, eternal life. Finally, the faith, which all are bound to believe and to profess, is one : " Let there be no schisms amongst you ;"[2] and baptism, which is the seal of our solemn initiation into the Christian faith, is, also, one.[3]

II.
Holiness.
Another distinctive mark of the Church is holiness, as we learn from these words of the prince of the apostles : " You are a chosen generation, a holy nation."[4] The Church is called holy, because she is consecrated and dedicated to God ;[5] as other things, such as vessels, vestments, altars, when appropriated and dedicated to the worship of God, although material, are called holy ; and, in the same sense, the first-born, who were dedicated to the Most High God, were, also, called holy.[6]

It should not be deemed matter of surprise, that the Church, although numbering amongst her children many sinners, is called holy ; for as those who profess any art, although they should depart from its rules, are called artists ; so the faithful, although offending in many things, and violating the engagements, to the observance of which they had solemnly pledged themselves, are called holy, because they are made the people of God, and are consecrated to Christ, by baptism and faith. Hence, S. Paul calls the Corinthians sanctified and holy, although it is certain that amongst them there were some, whom he severely rebuked as carnal, and, also, charged with grosser crimes.[7] She is, also, to be called holy, because, as the body, she is united to her head, Christ Jesus,[8] the fountain of all holiness, from whom flow the graces of the Holy Spirit, and the riches of the divine bounty. S. Augustine interpreting these words of the prophet : " Preserve my soul because I am holy,"[9] thus admirably expresses himself : " Let the body of Christ boldly say, let also, that one man, exclaiming from the ends of the earth, boldly say, with Christ his head, and under Christ his head ; I am holy : for he received the grace of holiness, the grace of baptism and of remission of sins :" and a little after : " If all Christians and all the faithful, having been baptized in Christ, have put him on, according to these words of the Apostle : ' as many of you as have been baptized in Christ, have put on Christ :'[10] if they are made members of his body, and yet say they are not holy, they do an injury to their head, whose members are holy."[11] [12] Moreover, the Church alone has the legitimate worship of sacrifice, and the salutary use of the sacraments, by which, as the efficacious instruments of divine grace, God establishes us in true holiness ; so that to possess true holiness we must belong

---

[1] Eph. iv. 4.   [2] 1 Cor. i. 10.   [3] Eph. iv. 5.   [4] 1 Pet. ii. 9.
[5] Levit. xxvii. 28. 30.   [6] Exod. xiii. 12.   [7] 1 Cor. i. 2. 1 Cor. iii. 3.
[8] Eph. iv. 15, 16.   [9] Ps. lxxxv. 2.   [10] Gal. iii. 27.
[11] Eph. v. 26, 27. 30.   [12] St. Aug. in Psalm lxxxv. 2.

to this Church. The Church, therefore, it is clear, is holy,[1] and holy, because she is the body of Christ, by whom she is sanctified, and in whose blood she is washed.[2][3]

The third mark of the Church is, that she is Catholic, that is, universal; and justly is she called Catholic, because, as S. Augustine says: "She is diffused by the splendour of one faith from the rising to the setting sun."[4] Unlike republics of human institution, or the conventicles of heretics, she is not circumscribed within the limits of any one kingdom, nor confined to the members of any one society of men; but embraces, within the amplitude of her love, all mankind, whether barbarians or Scythians, slaves or freemen, male or female. Therefore it is written, " Thou hast redeemed us to God in thy blood, out of every tribe, and tongue, and people, and nation, and hast made us to our God, a kingdom."[5] Speaking of the Church, David says: "Ask of me, and I will give thee the Gentiles for thy inheritance, and the utmost parts of the earth for thy possession:"[6] and also, "I will be mindful of Rahab and of Babylon knowing me:"[7] and " *This* man and *that* man is born in her:"[8] To this Church, "built on the foundation of the Apostles and Prophets,"[9] belong all the faithful who have existed from Adam to the present day, or who shall exist, in the profession of the true faith, to the end of time; all of whom are founded and raised upon the one corner stone, Christ, who made both one, and announced peace to them that are near, and to them that are afar. She is, also, called universal, because all who desire eternal salvation must cling to and embrace her, like those who entered the ark, to escape perishing in the flood.[10] This, therefore, is to be taught as a most just criterion, to distinguish the true from a false Church.

The true Church is, also, to be known from her origin, which she derives under the law of grace, from the Apostles; for her doctrines are neither novel nor of recent origin, but were delivered, of old, by the Apostles, and disseminated throughout the world. Hence, no one can, for a moment, doubt that the impious opinions which heresy invents, opposed, as they are, to the doctrines taught by the Church from the days of the Apostles to the present time, are very different from the faith of the true Church. That all, therefore, may know the true Catholic Church, the Fathers, guided by the Spirit of God, added to the Creed the word "APOSTOLIC;"[11] for the Holy Ghost, who presides over the Church, governs her by no other than Apostolic men; and this Spirit, first imparted to the Apostles, has, by the infinite goodness of God, always continued in the Church. But

III. Catholicity.

IV. Apostolicity.

---

[1] Eph. i. 1—4.   [2] Eph. i. 7. 13; v. 26.
[3] De sanctitate Ecclesiæ vide Justin. Mart. in utraque Apol. Tert. in Apol. Aug. contr. Fulg. c. 17. Gregor. Moral. L. 37. c. 7.
[4] S. Aug. serm. 131 & 181. de temp.   [5] Apoc. v. 9, 10.   [6] Ps. ii. 8.
[7] Ps. lxxxvi. 4.   [8] Ps. lxxxvi. 5.   [9] Eph. ii. 20.   [10] Gen. vii. 7.
[11] De vera. Ecclesiæ notis vide Aug. contra epist. fundamenti, cap. 4. Tertul. lib eto de præscript.

as this one Church, because governed by the Holy Ghost, cannot err in faith or morals, it necessarily follows, that all other societies arrogating to themselves the name of Church, because guided by the spirit of darkness, are sunk in the most pernicious errors both doctrinal and moral.

Figures of theChurch. But as the figures of the Old Testament have considerable influence in exciting the minds of the faithful, and recalling to their recollection these most salutary truths, and are, principally on this account, mentioned by the Apostle, the pastor will not pass by so copious a source of instruction. Amongst these figures the ark of Noah holds a conspicuous place. It was

I constructed by the command of God,[1] in order, no doubt, to signify the Church, which God has so constituted, as that whoever enters her, through baptism, may be safe from all danger of eternal death, while such as are not within her, like those who were not in the ark, are overwhelmed by their own crimes.

II. Another figure presents itself in the great city of Jerusalem,[2] which, in Scripture, often means the Church. In Jerusalem only was it lawful to offer sacrifice to God, and in the Church of God only are to be found the true worship and true sacrifice which can, at all, be acceptable to God. Finally, with regard

The Church to be believed, and how? to the Church, the pastor will teach how to believe the Church can constitute an article of faith. Reason, it is true, and the senses are competent to ascertain the existence of the Church, that is, of a society of men devoted and consecrated to Jesus Christ; nor does faith seem necessary in order to understand a truth which is acknowledged by Jews and Turks: but it is from the light of faith only, not from the deductions of reason, that the mind can comprehend the mysteries, which, as has been already glanced at, and as shall be, hereafter, more fully developed, when we come to treat of the Sacrament of Orders, are contained in the Church of God. As, therefore, this Article, as well as the others, is placed above the reach, and defies the strength, of the human understanding, most justly do we confess, that human reason cannot arrive at a knowledge of the origin, privileges and dignity of the Church; these we can contemplate only with the eyes of faith.

The Church by whom founded. This Church was founded not by man, but by the immortal God himself, who built her upon a most solid rock: " The Highest Himself," says the Prophet, " hath founded her."[3] Hence, she is called " The inheritance of God,"[4] " The people of God,"[5] and the power, which she possesses, is not from man but from God. As this power, therefore, cannot be of human origin, divine faith can alone enable us to understand that the keys of the kingdom of Heaven are deposited with the Church,[6] that to her has been confided the power of remitting sins;[7] of denouncing excommunication;[8] and of consecrating

---

[1] Gen. vi. 14.   [2] Gal. iv. 26. Heb. xii. 22. Deut. xii. 11—14. 18. 21.
[3] Ps. lxxxvi. 5.   [4] Ps. ii. 8.   [5] Osee. ii. 1.   [6] Matt. xvi. 19.
[7] John xx. 23.   [8] Matt. xviii. 17.

the real body of Christ ;[1] and that her children have not here a permanent dwelling, but look for one above.[2]

We are, therefore, bound to believe that there is one Holy Catholic Church ; but, with regard to the three Persons of the Holy Trinity, the Father, the Son, and the Holy Ghost, we not only believe them, but, also, believe IN them ; and hence, when speaking of each dogma, we make use of a different form of expression, professing to believe the holy, not IN the Holy Catholic Church ;[3] by this difference of expression, distinguishing God, the author of all things, from his works, and acknowledging ourselves debtors to the divine goodness for all these exalted benefits bestowed on the Church.

We believe theChurch, not in the Church.

"THE COMMUNION OF SAINTS."

THE Evangelist St. John, writing to the faithful on the divine mysteries, tells them, that he undertook to instruct them on the subject; " that you," says he, " may have fellowship with us, and our fellowship be with the Father and with his Son Jesus Christ."[4] This " fellowship" consists in the Communion of Saints, the subject of the present Article. Would, that, in its exposition, pastors imitated the zeal of St. Paul and of the other Apostles ![5] for not only does it serve as an interpretation of the preceding Article, and is a point of doctrine productive of abundant fruit ; but it also teaches the use to be made of the mysteries contained in the Creed ; because the great end, to which all our researches and knowledge are to be directed, is our admission into this most august and blessed society of the saints, and our steady perseverance therein, " giving thanks, with joy, to God the Father who hath made us worthy to be partakers of the lot of the saints in light."[6]

This Article to be carefully explained.

The faithful, therefore, in the first place, are to be informed that this Article is, as it were, a sort of explanation of the preceding one, which regards the unity, sanctity, and catholicity of the Church : for the unity of the Spirit, by which she is governed, establishes among all her members a community of spiritual blessings, whereas the fruit of all the Sacraments is common to all the faithful, and these Sacraments, particularly baptism, the door, as it were, by which we are admitted into the Church,[7] are so many connecting links which bind and unite them to Jesus Christ. That this Communion of Saints implies a communion of Sacraments, the Fathers declare in these words of the Creed: " I confess one baptism."[8] After baptism, the Eucharist holds the first place in reference to this communion ; and after the Eucharist, the other Sacraments ; for, although

In what " the Communion of Saints" consists.

---

[1] Heb. xiii. 10. [2] Heo. xiii. 14. [3] Aug. serm. 131. de. temp. [4] John i. 3.
[5] Aug. in Joan. Tract. 32. [6] Col. i. 12. [7] Aug. l. 19, contr. Faustum. c. 11.
[8] Damasc. lib. 4. de fide orthodox. cap. 12. 1 Cor. 13.

common to all the Sacraments, because all unite us to God, and render us partakers of him whose grace they communicate to us, this communion belongs, in a peculiar manner, to the Eucharist, by which it is directly accomplished.[1]

But there is, also, another communion in the Church, which demands attention : every pious and holy action, done by one, belongs to and becomes profitable to all, through charity, " which seeks not her own."[2] In this we are fortified by the concurrent testimony of St. Ambrose, who explaining these words of the Psalmist ; " I am a partaker with all them that fear thee," observes : " As we say that a member is partaker of the entire body, so are we partakers with all that fear God."[3] Therefore, has Christ taught us to say, "*our*," not "*my*" bread ;[4] and the other petitions of that admirable prayer are equally general, not confined to ourselves alone, but directed, also, to the general interest, and salvation of all. This communication of goods is often, very appositely illustrated in Scripture by a comparison borrowed from the members of the human body : in the human body there are many members, but though many, they, yet, constitute but one body, in which each performs its own, not all, the same functions. All do not enjoy equal dignity, or discharge functions alike useful or honourable ; nor does one propose to itself its own exclusive advantage, but that of the entire body.[5] Besides, they are so well organised and knit together, that if one suffers, the rest naturally sympathise with it, and if, on the contrary, one enjoys health, the feeling of pleasure is common to all. The same may be observed of the Church ; although composed of various members ; of different nations, of Jews, Gentiles, freemen and slaves, of rich and poor ; yet all, initiated by faith, constitute one body with Christ, who is their head. To each member of the Church, is, also, assigned its own peculiar office ; and as some are appointed apostles, some teachers, but all for the common good ; so to some it belongs to govern and teach, to others to be subject and to obey.

A scriptural illustration of this communion:

This communion how far common to the wicked.

But, the advantages of so many and such exalted blessings, bestowed by Almighty God, are pre-eminently enjoyed by those who lead a Christian life in charity, and are just and beloved of God ; whilst the dead members, that is, those who are bound in thraldom of sin, and estranged from the grace of God, although not deprived of these advantages, so as to cease to be members of this body, are yet, as dead members, deprived of the vivifying principle which is communicated to the just and pious Christian. However, as they are in the Church, they are assisted in recovering lost grace and life by those who are animated by the Spirit of God, and are in the enjoyment of those fruits which are no doubt, denied to such as are, entirely, cut off from the communion of the Church.[6]

[1] 1 Cor. x. 16.   [2] 1 Cor. xiii. 5.   [3] S. Ambr. in Ps. cxviii. serm. 8. v. 63.
[4] Matt. vi. 11.   [5] 1 Cor. xii. 14.   [6] Aug. in Ps. 70. serm. 2.

But the gifts, which justify and endear us to God, are not alone common : "graces gratuitously granted," such as knowledge, prophecy, the gifts of tongues and of miracles, and others of the same sort,[1] are common, also, and are granted even to the wicked; not, however, for their own, but for the general good; for the building up of the Church of God. Thus, the gift of healing is given, not for the sake of him who heals, but for the sake of him who is healed. In fine, every true Christian possesses nothing which he should not consider common to all others with himself, and should, therefore, be prepared promptly to relieve an indigent fellow-creature ; for he that is blessed with worldly goods, and sees his brother in want, and will not assist him, is at once convicted of not having the love of God within him.[2] Those, therefore, who belong to this holy communion, it is manifest, enjoy a sort of happiness here below, and may truly say with the Psalmist : " How lovely are thy tabernacles, O Lord of hosts ! my soul longeth and fainteth for the courts of the Lord. Blessed are they who dwell in thy house, O Lord !"[3]

[Margin note: "Graces gratuitously granted" common to them with the good.]

ARTICLE X.

" THE FORGIVENESS OF SINS."

THE enumeration of this amongst the other Articles of the Creed, is alone sufficient to satisfy us, that it conveys a truth, which is not only in itself a divine mystery, but also a mystery very necessary to salvation. We have already said that, without a firm belief of all the Articles of the Creed, Christian piety is wholly unattainable. However, should a truth, which ought to bring intrinsic evidence to every mind, seem to require any other authority in its support; enough that the Redeemer, a short time previous to his ascension into heaven, " when opening the understanding of his disciples, that they might understand the Scriptures," bore testimony to this Article of the Creed, in these words: " It behoved Christ to suffer, and to rise again from the dead the third day, and that penance and remission of sins, should be preached, in his name, unto all nations, beginning at Jerusalem."[4] Let the pastor but weigh well these words, and he will readily perceive, that the Lord has laid him under a most sacred obligation, not only of making known to the faithful, whatever regards religion in general, but also of explaining, with particular care, this article of the Creed. On this point of doctrine, then, it is the bounden duty of the pastor to teach that, not only is " forgiveness of sins" to be found in the Catholic Church, as Isaias had foretold in these words : " The

[Margin note: The belief of this Article necessary to salvation.]

[Margin note: Obligation of the pastor to explain it to the people.]

---

[1] 1 Cor. xii. 2.   [2] 1 John iii. 17.   [3] Ps. lxxxiii. 2. 3.   [4] Luke xxiv. 46, 47.

L

people that dwell therein shall have their iniquity taken away from them;"[1] but, also, that in her resides the power of forgiving sins ;[2] which power, if exercised duly, and according to the laws prescribed by our Lord, is, we are bound to believe, such as, truly to pardon and remit sins.

Baptism remits all sins and the punishments due to them.   But, when we first make a profession of faith at the baptismal font, and are cleansed in its purifying waters, we receive this pardon entire and unqualified ; so that no sin, original or actual, of commission or omission, remains to be expiated, no punishment to be endured. The grace of baptism, however, does not give exemption from all the infirmities of nature : on the contrary, contending, as we each of us have to contend, against the motions of concupiscence, which ever tempts us to the commission of sin, there is scarcely one to be found amongst us, who opposes so vigorous a resistance to its assaults, or who guards his salvation so vigilantly, as to escape all the snares of Satan.[3]

The power of the keys given to the Church.   It being necessary, therefore, that a power of forgiving sins, distinct from that of baptism, should exist in the Church, to her were entrusted the keys of the kingdom of heaven, by which each one, if penitent, may obtain the remission of his sins, even though he were a sinner to the last day of his life. This truth is vouched by the most unquestionable authority of the Sacred Scriptures : in St. Matthew, the Lord says to Peter : " I will give to thee the keys of the kingdom of heaven ; and whatever thou shalt bind on earth shall be bound also in heaven ; and whatever thou shalt loose on earth, shall be loosed also in heaven :"[4] and again, " whatever you shall bind on earth shall be bound also in heaven ; and whatever you shall loose on earth, shall be loosed also in heaven."[5] Again, the testimony of St. John assures us that the Lord, breathing on the Apostles, said . " Receive ye the Holy Ghost, whose sins you shall forgive, they are forgiven them ; and whose sins you shall retain, they are retained."[6]

This power extends to all sins.   Nor is the exercise of this power restricted to particular sins, for no crime, however heinous, can be committed, which the Church has not power to forgive : as, also, there is no sinner, however abandoned, none, however depraved, who should not confidently hope for pardon, provided he sincerely repent of his past transgressions.[7] Neither is the exercise of this power restricted to particular times ; for whenever the sinner turns from his evil ways, he is not to be rejected, as we learn from the reply of our Lord to the prince of the Apostles, asking how often we should pardon an offending brother, whether seven times : " Not only seven times," says the Redeemer, " but even seventy times seven."[8]

But is confined to bishops and priests.   But if we look to its ministers, or to the manner in which it is to be exercised, the extent of this power will not appear so great ; for it is a power not given to all, but to bishops and

---

[1] Isaias xxxiii. 24.   [2] Aug. homil. 49. cap. 3.   [3] Trident, Sess. v. can. 5. Aug. 1, 2, de peccat. merit. c. 28.   [4] Matt. xvi. 19.   [5] Matt. xviii. 18.   [6] John xx. 23. [7] Ambros. lib. 1. de pœnit. c. 1, 2. Aug. in Enoh. c. 93.   [8] Matt. xviii. 21, 22.

priests only; and sins can be forgiven only through the Sacraments, when duly administered. The Church has received no power otherwise to remit sin.[1]

But to raise the admiration of the faithful, for this heavenly gift, bestowed on the Church by the singular mercy of God towards us, and to make them approach its use with the more lively sentiments of devotion; the pastor will endeavour to point out the dignity and the extent of the grace which it imparts. If there be any one means better calculated than another to accomplish this end, it is, carefully to show how great must be the efficacy of that which absolves from sin, and restores the unjust to a state of justification. This is, manifestly, an effect of the infinite power of God, of that same power which we believe to have been necessary to raise the dead to life, and to summon creation into existence.[2] But if it be true, as the authority of St. Augustine assures us it is,[3] that, to recall a sinner from the state of sin to that of righteousness, is even a greater work than to create the heavens and the earth from nothing, though their creation can be no other than the effect of infinite power; it follows, that we have still stronger reason to consider the remission of sins, as an effect proceeding from the exercise of this same infinite power. With great truth, therefore, have the ancient Fathers declared, that God alone can forgive sins, and that to his infinite goodness and power alone is so wonderful a work to be referred: " I am he," says the Lord himself, by the mouth of his prophet, " I am he, who blotteth out your iniquities."[4] The remission of sins seems to bear an exact analogy to the cancelling of a pecuniary debt: as, therefore, none but the creditor can forgive a pecuniary debt, so the debt of sin, which we owe to God alone, (and our daily prayer is : " forgive us our debts,"[5]) can, it is clear, be forgiven by him alone, and by none else.

Its inestimable value.

But this wonderful gift, this emanation of the divine bounty, was never communicated to creatures, until God became man. Christ our Lord, although true God, was the first who, as man, received this high prerogative from his heavenly Father : " That you may know," says he to the paralytic, " that the Son of Man hath power on earth to forgive sins, rise, take up thy bed, and go into thy house."[6] As, therefore, he became man, in order to bestow on man this forgiveness of sins, he communicated this power to bishops and priests in the Church, previously to his ascension into heaven, there to sit for ever at the right hand of God. Christ, however, as we have already said, remits sin by virtue of his own authority; all others by virtue of his authority delegated to them as his ministers.

First given to Christ as man.

If, therefore, whatever is the effect of infinite power claims our highest admiration, and commands our profoundest reve-

The greatest of his gifts.

[1] Trid. Sess. 14. c. 6. Hier. epist. 1. post med. Ambr. de Cain et Abel, c. 4.
[2] Trid. Sess. 6. c. 7. & Sess. 14. 1, 2. &c. tract. 7. 2. in Joan.
[3] Aug. lib. 1. de pecc. merit. c. 23. 1. 50. hom. 23. Ambr. de Abel, cap. 4.
[4] Isaias xliii. 25. [5] Matt. vi. 11. [6] Matt. ix. 6. Mark ii. 9, 10.

rence; we must readily perceive that this gift, bestowed on the Church by the bounteous hand of Christ our Lord, is one of inestimable value. The manner, too, in which God, in the fullness of his paternal clemency, resolved to cancel the sins of the world, must powerfully excite the faithful to the contemplation of this great blessing: it was his will that our offences should be expiated in the blood of his only begotten Son, that he should voluntarily assume the imputability of our sins, and suffer a most cruel death; the just for the unjust, the innocent for the guilty.[1] When, therefore, we reflect, that " we were not redeemed with corruptible things, as gold or silver, but with the precious blood of Christ, as of a lamb unspotted and undefiled;"[2] we are naturally led to conclude that we could have received no gift more salutary than this power of forgiving sins, which proclaims the ineffable providence of God, and the excess of his love towards us.

Mortal sin, how great an evil. This reflection must produce, in all, the most abundant spiritual fruit; for whoever offends God, even by one mortal sin, instantly forfeits whatever merits he may have previously acquired through the sufferings and death of Christ, and is entirely shut out from the gate of heaven, which, when already closed, was thrown open to all by the Redeemer's passion. And, indeed, when this reflection enters into the mind, impossible not to feel impressed with the most anxious solicitude, and contemplating the picture of human misery which it presents to our view. But if we turn our attention to this admirable power with which God has invested his Church; and, in the firm belief of this Article, feel convinced that to every sinner is offered the means of recovering, with the assistance of divine grace, his former dignity; we can no longer resist sentiments of exceeding joy, and gladness, and exultation, and must offer immortal thanks to God. If, when labouring under some severe malady, the medicines prepared for us by the art and industry of the physician, generally become grateful and agreeable to us; how much more grateful and agreeable should those remedies prove, which the wisdom of God has established to heal our spiritual maladies, and restore us to the life of grace; remedies which, unlike the medicines used for the recovery of bodily health, bring with them, not, indeed, uncertain hope of recovery, but certain health to such as desire to be cured.

The faithful should have recourse to the exercise of this power. The faithful, therefore, having formed a just conception of the dignity of so excellent and exalted a blessing, should be exhorted to study, religiously, to turn it, also, to good account: for he who makes no use of what is really useful and necessary, affords a strong presumption that he despises it; particularly as, in communicating to the Church the power of forgiving sins, the Lord did so with the view, that all should have recourse to this healing remedy; for, as without baptism, no man can be cleansed from original sin, so, without the sacrament of penance,

---

[1] 1 Pet. iii. 18. [2] 1 Pet. i. 18, 19.

which is another means instituted by God to cleanse from sin, he who desires to recover the grace of baptism, forfeited by actual mortal guilt, cannot recover lost innocence.

But here the faithful are to be admonished to guard against the danger of becoming more propense to sin, or slow to re- pentance, from a presumption that they can have recourse to this plenary power of forgiving sins, which, as we have already said, is unrestricted by time ; for as such a propensity to sin, must, manifestly, convict them of acting injuriously and contu- maciously to this divine power, and must, therefore render them unworthy of the divine mercy ; so, this slowness to repentance must afford great reason to apprehend, lest overtaken by death, they may, in vain, confess their belief in the remission of sins, which their tardiness and procrastination have, deservedly, for- feited.[1] *Danger of its abuse to be avoided.*

ARTICLE XI.

"THE RESURRECTION OF THE BODY."

THAT this Article supplies a convincing proof of the truth of our faith, is evinced by the circumstance of its not only being proposed, in the Sacred Scriptures, to the belief of the faithful, but also fortified by numerous arguments. This we scarcely find to be the case with regard to the other Articles : a circum- stance which justifies the inference that on it, as on its most solid basis, rests our hope of salvation ; for according to the reasoning of the Apostle, "If there be no resurrection of the dead, then Christ is not risen again ; and if Christ be not risen again, then is our preaching vain, and your faith is also vain."[2] The zeal and assiduity, therefore, of the pastor in its exposition should not be inferior to the labour which impiety has expended in fruitless efforts to overturn its truth. That eminently im- portant advantages flow to the faithful from the knowledge of this Article will appear from the sequel. *Importance of this Ar- ticle.*

And, first, that in this Article the resurrection of mankind is called "the resurrection of the body," is a circumstance which deserves attention. The Apostles had for object, (for it is not without its object,) thus to convey an important truth, the im- mortality of the soul. Lest, therefore, contrary to the Sacred Scriptures, which, in many places, teach the soul to be immor- tal,[3] any one may imagine that it dies with the body, and that both are to be resuscitated, the Creed speaks only of "the re- surrection of the body." The word, "caro," which is used *The resur- rection of mankind why called " the resur- rection of the body."*

[1] Aug. in Joan. Tract. 23. et lib. 50. homil. 41. Ambros. lib. 2. de poenit. c. 1, 2, & 11. [2] 1 Cor. xv. 13, 14. [3] Wis. ii. 23; iii. 4. Matt. x. 28; xxii. 31, 32.

in the symbol, translated literally, means "flesh:" a word, which, though of frequent occurrence in Scripture to signify the whole man, soul and body, as in Isaias, "All flesh is grass;"[1] and in St. John, "The Word was made flesh;"[2] is, however used, here, to express the body only; thus giving us to understand, that of the two constituent parts of man, one only, that is the body, is corrupted, and returns to its original dust; whilst the soul remains incorrupt and immortal. As then, without dying, a man cannot be said to return to life; so the soul, which never dies, could not, with propriety, be said to rise again. The word body, is, also, mentioned, in order to confute the heresy of Hymeneus and Philetus, who during the life-time of the Apostle, asserted, that, whenever the Scriptures speak of the resurrection, they are to be understood to mean not the resurrection of the body, but that of the soul, by which it rises from the death of sin to the life of grace.[3] The words of this Article, therefore, clearly confute the error, and establish a real resurrection of the body.

Proofs of the resurrection of the body. But it will be the duty of the pastor to illustrate this truth by examples taken from the Old and New Testaments, and from all ecclesiastical history. In the Old Testament, some were restored to life by Elias,[4] and Elizeus;[5] and in the New, besides those who were raised to life by our Lord,[6] many were resuscitated by the Apostles, and by others.[7] Their resurrection confirms the doctrine conveyed by this Article, for believing that many were recalled from death to life, we are also naturally led to believe the general resurrection of all; and the principal fruit which we should derive from these miracles is to yield to this Article our most unhesitating belief. To pastors, ordinarily conversant with the Sacred Volumes, many Scripture proofs will, at once, present themselves; but, in the Old Testament, the most conspicuous are those afforded by Job, when he says, "that in his flesh he shall see God;"[8] and by Daniel when, speaking of those "who sleep in the dust of the earth," he says, "some shall awake to eternal life, others to eternal reproach."[9] In the New Testament the principal passages are those of St. Matthew, which record the disputation which our Lord held with the Sadducees;[10] and those of the Evangelists which relate to the last judgment.[11] To these we may also add, the accurate reasoning of the Apostle, on the subject, in his epistles to the Corinthians,[12] and Thessalonians.[13]

Illustrated by comparisons. But, incontrovertibly as is this truth established by faith, it will, notwithstanding, be of material advantage to show from analogy and reason, that what faith proposes to our belief, nature acknowledges to accord with her laws, and reason with her dictate. To one, asking how the dead should rise again, the Apostle answers; "Foolish man! that which thou sowest is

---

[1] Isaias xl. 6. [2] John i. 14. [3] 2 Tim. ii. 17. [4] 3 Kings xvii. 21, 22.
[5] 4 Kings iv. 34; xiii. 21. [6] Matt. ix. 25. Luke vii. 14, 15. John xi. 43, 44.
[7] Acts ix. 40; xx. 10. [8] Job xix. 26. [9] Dan. xii. 2. [10] Matt. xxii. 31.
[11] John v. 25; xxviii. 29. [12] 1 Cor. xv. [13] 1 Thess. iv. 13.

not quickened, except it die first; and that which thou sowest, thou sowest not the body that shall be; but bare grain as of wheat, or of some of the rest; but God giveth it a body as he will:" and a little after, " It is sown in corruption, it shall rise in incorruption."[1] St. Gregory, calls our attention to many other arguments of analogy tending to the same effect: " The sun," says he, "is every day withdrawn from our eyes, as it were, by dying, and is again recalled, as it were, by rising again : trees lose, and again, as it were, by a resurrection, resume their verdure : seeds die by putrefaction, and rise again by germination."[2]

The reasons, also, adduced by ecclesiastical writers, are well calculated to establish this truth.   In the first place, as the soul is immortal, and has, as part of man, a natural propensity to be united to the body, its perpetual separation from it must be considered contrary to nature.   But as that which is contrary to nature, and offers violence to her laws, cannot be permanent, it appears congruous that the soul should be reunited to the body; and, of course, that the body should rise again.   This argument, our Saviour himself employed, when, in his disputation with the Sadducees, he deduced the resurrection of the body from the immortality of the soul.[3]

[margin: Proved by arguments from reason.]

In the next place, as an all-just God holds out punishments to the wicked, and rewards to the good, and as very many of the former depart this life unpunished for their crimes, and of the latter unrewarded for their virtues ; the soul should be reunited to the body, in order, as the partner of her crimes, or the companion of her virtues, to become a sharer in her punishments or her rewards.[4]   This view of the subject has been admirably treated by St. Chrysostom in his homily to the people of Antioch.[5] To this effect, the Apostle speaking of the resurrection, says, " If in this life only, we have hope in Christ, we are of all men the most miserable."[6] These words of St. Paul cannot be supposed to refer to the misery of the soul, which, because immortal, is capable of enjoying happiness in a future life, were the body not to rise; but to the whole man; for, unless the body receive the due rewards of its labours, those, who, like the Apostles, endured so many afflictions and calamities in this life, should necessarily be " the most miserable of men."   On this subject the Apostle is much more explicit in his epistle to the Thessalonians : " We glory in you," says he, " in the Churches of God, that you may be counted worthy of the kingdom of God, for which, also, you suffer: seeing it is a just thing with God to repay tribulation to them that trouble you; and to you who are troubled, rest with us, when the Lord Jesus shall be revealed from heaven with the angels of his power; in a flame of fire, yielding vengeance to them who know not God, and who obey not the Gospel of our Lord Jesus Christ."[7]

[1] 1 Cor. xv. 36—42.   [2] S. Gregor. lib. 14. moral. c. 28—30.
[3] Matt. xxii. 23.   [4] Damasc. lib. 4. de fide orthod. cap. 28. Ambros. lib.
de fide resurr.   [5] S. Chrysostom, homil. 49 and 50.   [6] 1 Cor. xv. 19.
[7] 2 Thess. i. 4.

Again, whilst the soul is separated from the body, man cannot enjoy the consummation of happiness, replete with every good; for as a part, separated from the whole, is imperfect, the soul separated from the body must be imperfect; and, therefore, that nothing may be wanting to fill up the measure of its happiness, the resurrection of the body is necessary. By these, and similar arguments, the pastor will be able to instruct the faithful in this Article.

The resurrection of all not the same. He should also, carefully explain, from the Apostle, who are to be raised to life. Writing to the Corinthians, St. Paul says, " as in Adam all die, so, also, in Christ all should be made alive."[1] Good and bad, then, without distinction, shall all rise from the dead, although the condition of all shall not be the same—those who have done good, shall rise to the resurrection of life; and those who have done evil, to the resurrection of judgment.

All shall die to rise again. When we say " all," we mean those who shall have died before the day of judgment, as well as those who shall then die. That the Church acquiesces in the opinion which asserts that all, without distinction, shall die, and that this opinion is more consonant to truth, is recorded by the pen of St. Jerome,[2] whose authority is fortified by that of St. Augustine.[3] Nor does the Apostle, in his epistle to the Thessalonians, dissent from this doctrine, when he says; " The dead who are in Christ shall rise first, then we who are alive, who are left, shall be taken up together with them in the clouds to meet Christ, into the air."[4] St. Ambrose explaining these words says, " In that very taking up, death shall anticipate, as it were by a deep sleep, and the soul, having gone forth from the body, shall instantly return; for those who are alive, when taken up, shall die, that, coming to the Lord, they may receive their souls from his presence; because in his presence they cannot be dead."[5] This opinion is fortified by the authority of St. Augustine in his book on the City of God.[6]

All shall rise in their own bodies. But as it is of vital importance to be fully convinced that the identical body, which belongs to each one of us during life, shall, though corrupt, and dissolved into its original dust, be raised up again to life; this, too, is a subject which demands accurate explanation from the pastor. It is a truth conveyed by the Apostle in these words; " This corruptible must put on incorruption;"[7] emphatically designating by the word " this," the identity of our bodies. It is also, evident from the prophecy of Job, than which nothing can be more express: " I shall see my God," says he, " whom I myself shall see, and mine eyes behold, and not another."[8] Finally, if we only consider the very definition of resurrection, we cannot, reasonably, entertain a shadow of doubt on the subject; for resurrection, as Damas-

---

[1] 1 Cor. xv. 22.   [2] S. Hieron. epist. 152.   [3] August. de Civit. Dei. lib. xx. c. 20.
[4] 1 Thess. iv. 15, 16.   [5] In 1. epist. ad Thess. c. 4.   [6] Lib. xx. c. 20.
[7] 1 Cor. xv. 53.   [8] Job xix. 26, 27.

cene defines it, is "a return to the state from which one has fallen."[1] Finally, if we consider the arguments by which we have already established a future resurrection, every doubt on the subject must, at once, disappear. We have said that the body is to rise again, that "every one may receive the proper things of the body, according as he hath done, whether it be good or evil."[2] Man is, therefore, to rise again, in the same body with which he served God, or was a slave to the devil; that in the same body he may experience rewards, and a crown of victory, or endure the severest punishments, and never ending torments.

Not only will the body rise, but it will rise endowed with whatever constitutes the reality of its nature, and adorns and ornaments man: according to these admirable words of St. Augustine: "There shall, then, be no deformity of body; if some have been overburdened with flesh, they shall not resume its entire weight; whatever shall exceed the proper habit shall be deemed superfluous. On the other hand, should the body be wasted by the malignity of disease, or the debility of old age, or be emaciated from any other cause, it shall be recruited by the divine power of Jesus Christ, who will not only restore the body, but repair whatever it shall have lost through the wretchedness of this life."[3] In another place he says; "Man shall not resume his former hair, but shall be adorned with such as will become him, according to these words of the Redeemer, ' The very hairs of your head are all numbered:'[4] God will restore them according to his wisdom."[5]

In what state the bodies shall rise.

The members, because essential to the integrity of human nature, shall all be restored: the blind from nature or disease, the lame, the maimed, and the paralysed shall rise again with perfect bodies: otherwise the desires of the soul, which so strongly incline it to a union with the body, should be far from satisfied; and yet we are convinced, that in the resurrection, these desires shall be fully realized. Besides, the resurrection, like the creation, is clearly to be numbered amongst the principal works of God. As, therefore, at the creation, all things came perfect from the hand of God; so, at the resurrection shall all things be perfectly restored by the same omnipotent hand.

None shall rise maimed.

These observations are not to be restricted to the bodies of the martyrs; of whom St. Augustine says: "As the mutilation which they suffered should prove a deformity, they shall rise with all their members; otherwise those who were beheaded should rise without a head. The scars, however, which they received, shall remain, shining like the wounds of Christ, with a brilliancy far more resplendent than that of gold and of precious stones."[6] The wicked too, shall rise with all their members, although they should have been lost through their own

The scars of the martyrs shall remain to their glory: the members of the wicked shall be restored, to increase their punishment.

---

[1] Damasc. lib. iv. de fid. orthod. 28. [2] 2 Cor. v. 10. [3] S. Aug. l. xxii. de Civit. Dei, c. 19—21. & Ench. c. 86—89. Hierm. Epist. 59. 61.
[4] Luke xii. 7. [5] S. Aug Ench. c. lxxxvi. [6] Lib. xxii. de Civ. Dei, c. 20.

fault: for the greater the number of members which they shall have, the greater shall be their torments; and, therefore, this restoration of members, will serve to increase, not their happiness, but their misery. Merit or demerit is ascribed not to the members, but to the person to whose body they are united: to those, therefore, who shall have done penance, they shall be restored as sources of reward; and to those who shall have contemned it, as instruments of punishment. If the pastor bestow mature consideration on these things, he can never want words or ideas to move the hearts of the faithful, and enkindle in them the flame of piety; that, considering the troubles of this life, they may look forward, with eager expectation, to that blessed glory of the resurrection which awaits the just.

The bodies of the good and of the bad shall rise immortal. It now remains to explain to the faithful, in an intelligible manner, how the body, when raised from the dead, although substantially the same, shall be different in many respects. To omit other points, the great difference between the state of all bodies when risen from the dead, and what they had previously been, is, that, before the resurrection, they were subject to dissolution; but, when reanimated, they shall all, without distinction of good and bad, be invested with immortality. This admirable restoration of nature is the result of the glorious victory of Christ over death; as it is written, "He shall cast death down headlong for ever;"[1] and, "O Death! I will be thy death;"[2] words which the Apostle thus explains, "and the enemy death shall be destroyed last;"[3] and St. John, also, says, "Death shall be no more."[4] There is a peculiar congruity in the superiority of the merits of Christ, by which the power of death is overthrown,[5] to the fatal effects of the sin of Adam; and, it is consonant to the divine justice, that the good enjoy endless felicity; whilst the wicked, condemned to everlasting torments, "shall seek death, and shall not find it; shall desire to die, and death shall fly from them."[6] Immortality, therefore, will be common to the good and to the bad.

This, the result of the victory of Christ over death.

The qualities of a glorified body. Moreover, the bodies of the saints when resuscitated, shall be distinguished by certain transcendant endowments, which will ennoble them far beyond their former condition. Amongst these endowments, four are specially mentioned by the Fathers, which they infer from the doctrine of St. Paul, and which are called "qualities."[7]

Impassibility. The first is "impassibility," which shall place them beyond the reach of pain or inconvenience of any sort. Neither the piercing severity of cold, nor the glowing intensity of heat can affect them, nor can the impetuosity of waters hurt them. "It is sown," says the Apostle, "in corruption, it shall rise in incorruption."[8] This quality, the schoolmen call impassibility, not incorruption: in order to distinguish it as a property peculiar to

---

[1] Isa. xxv. 8.   [2] Osee xiii. 14.   [3] 1 Cor. xv. 26.   [4] Apoc. xi. 4.
[5] Heb. ii. 14.   [6] Apoc. ix. 6.   [7] De his Aug. Serm. 99. de temp. Ambr. in com. in 1. ad Cor. c. 15.   [8] 1 Cor. xv. 42.

a glorified body. The bodies of the damned, though incorruptible, shall not be impassible : they shall be capable of experiencing heat and cold, and of feeling pain.

The next quality is " brightness," by which the bodies of the **Brightness.** saints shall shine like the sun ; according to the words of our Lord recorded in the Gospel of St. Matthew : " The just shall shine as the sun, in the kingdom of their Father."[1] To remove the possibility of doubt on the subject, he left us a splendid exemplification of this glorious quality in his transfiguration.[2] This quality the Apostle sometimes calls glory, sometimes brightness ; " He will reform the body of our lowness, made like to the body of his glory :"[3] and again, " It is sown in dishonour, it shall rise in glory."[4] Of this glory the Israelites beheld some image in the desert ; when the face of Moses, after he had been in the presence of, and had conversed with God, shone with such resplendent lustre that they could not look on it.[5] This brightness is a sort of refulgence reflected from the supreme happiness of the soul—an emanation of the bliss which it enjoys, and which beams through the body. Its communication is analogous to the manner in which the soul itself is rendered happy, by a participation of the happiness of God.' Unlike the former, this quality is not common to all in the same degree. All the bodies of the saints shall, it is true, be equally impassible : but the brightness of all shall not be the same : for, according to the Apostle ; " One is the glory of the sun, another the glory of the moon, and another the glory of the stars, for star differeth from star in glory : so also, is the resurrection of the dead."[6]

To this quality is united that of " agility," as it is called, by **Agility.** which the body shall be freed from the burden that now presses it down ; and shall require a capability of moving with the utmost facility and celerity, wherever the soul pleases, as St. Augustine teaches in his book on the City of God,[7] and St. Jerome on Isaias.[8] Hence these words of the Apostle ; " It is sown in weakness, it shall rise in power."[9]

Another quality is that of " subtilty ;" a quality which sub- **Subtilty.** jects the body to the absolute dominion of the soul, and to an entire obedience to her control : as we infer from these words of the Apostle ; " It is sown a natural body, it shall rise a spiritual body."[10] These are the principal points on which the pastor will dwell in the exposition of this Article.

But in order that the faithful may know what fruit they are **Advantages of deep meditation on this Article.** to reap from a knowledge of so many and such exalted mysteries ; the pastor will proclaim, in the first place, that to God, who has hidden these things from the wise, and made them known to little ones, we owe a debt of boundless gratitude! How many men, eminent for wisdom and learning, who never

L

---

[1] Matt. xiii. 43.   [2] Matt. xvii. 2.   [3] Philip. iii. 21.   [4] 1 Cor. xv. 43.
[5] Exod. xxxiv. 29.   2 Cor. iii. 7.   [6] 1 Cor. xv. 41, 42.   [7] Aug. de Civ. Dei,
lib. xiii. c. 18. 20, et lib. xxii. c. 11.   [8] Hieron. in Isaiam, cap. 40.
[9] 1 Cor. xv. 43.   [10] 1 Cor. xv. 44

arrived at a knowledge of this truth? Aware, then, of his special predilection towards us, in making known to us this sublime truth—to us who could never aspire to such knowledge—it becomes our duty to pour forth our gratitude in unceasing praises of his goodness and clemency.

II. Another important advantage to be derived from deep reflection on this Article is, that in it we shall experience a balm, to heal the wounded spirit, when we mourn the loss of those who were endeared to us by friendship or connected with us by blood; a balm which the Apostle himself administered to the Thessalonians when writing to them "concerning those who slept."[1]

III. But in all our afflictions and calamities, the thought of a future resurrection must bring relief to the troubled heart; as we learn from the example of Job, who supported himself under an accumulation of afflictions and of sorrows, solely by the hope of, one day, rising from the grave, and beholding the Lord his God.[2]

IV. It must also, prove a powerful incentive to the faithful to use every exertion to lead lives of rectitude and integrity, unsullied by the defilement of sin; for, if they reflect, that those riches of inconceivable value, which God will bestow on his faithful servants after the resurrection, are now proposed to them as rewards; they must find in the reflection the strongest inducement

V to lead virtuous and holy lives. On the other hand, nothing will have greater effect in subduing the passions, and withdrawing souls from sin, than frequently to remind the sinner of the miseries and torments with which the justice of God will visit the reprobate, who, on the last day, shall rise to the resurrection of judgment.[3]

ARTICLE XII.

"LIFE EVERLASTING."

Why the last Article of the Creed. THE wisdom of the Apostles, our guides in religion, suggested to them the propriety of giving this Article the last place in the Creed, which is the summary of our faith; first, because, after the resurrection of the body, the only object of the Christian's hope, is the reward of everlasting life; and secondly, in order that perfect happiness, embracing as it does, the fulness of all good, may be ever present to our minds, and absorb all our thoughts and affections. In his instructions to the faithful, the pastor, therefore, will unceasingly endeavour to light up in their souls, an ardent desire of the proposed rewards of eternal life; that thus they may look upon whatever difficulties they

[1] 1 Thess. iv. 13.   [2] Job xix. 26.   [3] John v. 29.

may experience in the practice of religion, as light, and even agreeable, and may yield a more willing and an entire obedience to God.

But as many mysteries lie concealed under the words, which *Its mean* are here used, to declare the happiness reserved for us ; they *ing.* are to be explained in such a manner as to make them intelligible to all, as far as their respective capacities will allow. The faithful, therefore, are to be informed, that the words, "life everlasting," signify not only that continuity of existence, to which the devils and the wicked are consigned, but also, that perpetuity of happiness which is to satisfy the desires of the blessed. In this sense they were understood by the "ruler," mentioned in the Gospel, when he asked the Redeemer: "Lord! what shall I do to possess everlasting life?"[1] As if he had said, what shall I do, in order to arrive at the enjoyment of everlasting happiness? In this sense they are understood in the Sacred Volumes, as is clear from a reference to many passages of Scripture.[2] The supreme happiness of the blessed is thus designated, principally to exclude the notion that it consists in corporeal and transitory things, which cannot be everlasting.[3]

The word "blessedness" is insufficient to express the idea, *Why call-* particularly as there have not been wanting men, who, inflated *ed life* with the vain opinions of a false philosophy, would place the *everlast-* supreme good in sensible things; but these grow old and perish, *ing* whilst supreme happiness is defined by no limits of time. Nay, more, so far is the enjoyment of the goods of this life from conferring real happiness, that, on the contrary, he who is captivated by a love of the world, is farthest removed from true happiness: for it is written: "Love not the world, nor the things that are in the world; if any one love the world, the love of the Father is not in him:"[4] and a little after, "The world passeth away and the concupiscence thereof."[5] The pastor, therefore, will be careful to impress these truths on the minds of the faithful, that they may learn to despise earthly things, and to know that, in this world, in which we are not citizens, but sojourners,[6] happiness is not to be found. Yet, even here below, we may be said, with truth, to be happy in hope; "if denying ungodliness and worldly desires, we live soberly, and justly, and godly in this world; looking for the blessed hope and coming of the great God, and our Saviour Jesus Christ."[7] Many "who seemed to themselves wise,"[8] not understanding these things, and imagining that happiness was to be sought in this life, became fools and the victims of the most deplorable calamities.

These words, "Life everlasting," also teach us that, contrary *True hap-* to the false notions of some, happiness once attained can never *piness*

---

[1] Luke xviii. 18. [2] Matt. xix. 29; xxv. 46. Rom. vi. 22.
[3] Aug. de Civ. Dei, lib. 19. c. 11. [4] 1 John ii. 15. [5] 1 John ii. 17.
[6] 1 Pet. ii. 11. [7] Tit. ii. 11. 13. [8] Rom. i. 22.

must be everlasting. be lost. Happiness is an accumulation of good without admixture of evil, which, as it fills up the measure of man's desires, must be eternal. He who is blessed with its enjoyment must earnestly desire its continuance, and, were it transient and uncertain, should necessarily experience the torture of continual apprehension.[1]

The happiness of the just, intense and incomprehensible: The intensity of the happiness which the just enjoy in their celestial country, and its utter incomprehensibility to all but to themselves alone, are sufficiently conveyed by the very words which are here used to express that happiness. When, to express any idea, we make use of a word common to many others, we do so, because we have no proper term by which to express it clearly and fully. When, therefore, to express happiness, we adopt words which are equally applicable to all who are to live for ever, as to the blessed; we are led to infer that the idea presents to the mind something too great, too exalted, to be expressed fully by a proper term. True, the happiness of heaven is expressed in Scripture by a variety of other words, such as, the "Kingdom of God,"[2] " of Christ,"[3] " of heaven,"[4] " Paradise,"[5] " the Holy City," " the New Jerusalem,"[6] "my Father's house ;"[7] yet it is clear that none of these appellations is sufficient to convey an adequate idea of its greatness.

a powerful incentive to virtue. The pastor, therefore, will not neglect the opportunity which this Article affords, of inviting the faithful to the practice of piety, of justice, and of all the other virtues, by holding out to them such ample rewards as are announced in the words "life everlasting." Amongst the blessings which we instinctively desire, life is, confessedly, esteemed one of the greatest: by it principally, when we say " life everlasting," do we express the happiness of the just. If then, during this short and chequered period of our existence, which is subject to so many and such various vicissitudes, that it may be called death rather than life, there is nothing to which we so fondly cling, nothing which we love so dearly as life; with what ardour of soul, with what earnestness of purpose, should we not seek that eternal happiness, which, without alloy of any sort, presents to us the pure and unmixed enjoyment of every good? The happiness of eternal life is, as defined by the Fathers, "an exemption from all evil, and an enjoyment of all good."[8] That it is an exemption from all evil, the Scriptures declare in the most explicit terms: " they shall no more hunger and thirst," says St. John, " neither shall the sun fall on them, nor any heat ;"[9] and again, " God shall wipe away all tears from their eyes : and death shall be no more, nor mourning, nor crying, nor sorrow, shall be any more, for the former things are passed away."[10] But the glory of

[1] Vid. Aug. de Civ. Dei, lib. 12. cap. 20. lib. 22. c. 29, & 30. de libero arbit. cap. 25. de verb. Domini, serm. 64, & serm. 37, de Sanctis.

[2] Acts xiv. 22.   [3] 2 Pet. i. 11.   [4] Matt. v. 3. 20.

[5] Luke xxiii. 43.   [6] Apoc. xxi. 10.   [7] John xiv. 2.

[8] Chrysost. in 30. cap. ad Theod. lapsum. Aug. de Civ. Dei, lib. 22. cap. 30. Anselm. epist 2. et de similit. c. 47. et seq.

[9] Apoc. vii. 16.   [10] Apoc. xxi. 4.

the blessed shall be without measure, and their solid joys and pleasures without number. The mind is incapable of comprehending or conceiving the greatness of this glory: it can be known only by its fruition, that is, by entering into the joy of the Lord, and thus satisfying fully the desires of the human heart. Although, as St. Augustine observes, it would seem easier to enumerate the evils from which we shall be exempt, than the goods and the pleasures which we shall enjoy;[1] yet we must endeavour to explain, briefly and clearly, these things which are calculated to inflame the faithful with a desire of arriving at the enjoyment of this supreme felicity.

Before we proceed to this explanation, we shall make use of a distinction, which has been sanctioned by the most eminent writers on religion; it is, that there are two sorts of goods, one an ingredient, another an accompaniment of happiness. The former, therefore, for the sake of perspicuity, they have called essential; the latter, accessory. Solid happiness, which we may designate by the common appellation, "essential," consists in the vision of God, and the enjoyment of his eternal beauty who is the source and principle of all goodness and perfection : "This," says our Lord, "is eternal life, that they may know thee, the only true God, and Jesus Christ whom thou hast sent."[2] These sentiments St. John seems to interpret, when he says; "Dearly beloved! We are now the sons of God; and it hath not yet appeared what we shall be. We know that when he shall appear, we shall be like to him : because we shall see him, as he is."[3] These words inform us that the happiness of heaven consists of two things: to see God such as he is in his own nature and substance, and to be made like unto him. *(marginal: Happiness two-fold, essential and accessory.)*

Those who enjoy the beatific vision, whilst they retain their own nature, shall assume a certain admirable and almost divine form, so as to seem gods rather than men; and why they assume this form, becomes at once intelligible, if we only reflect that every thing is known from its essence, or from its resemblance and external appearance: but as nothing resembles God, so as to afford, by that resemblance, a perfect knowledge of him, no creature can behold his divine nature and essence, unless admitted by the Deity to a sort of union with himself; according to these words of St. Paul : "We now see through a glass in a dark manner, but then face to face."[4] The words, "in a dark manner," St. Augustine understands to mean that we see him in a resemblance calculated to convey to us some faint notion of the Deity.[5] This, St. Denis clearly shows, when he says : "The things above cannot be known by comparison with the things below; for, 'the essence and substance of any thing incorporeal must be known, through the medium of that which is corporeal : particularly as a resemblance must be less gross *(marginal: Effect of the beatific vision on the blessed)* *(marginal: How communicated to them.)*

[1] Serm. vi. 4. de verb. Domini et de Symb. ad Catech. lib. 3. [2] John xvii. 3.
[3] 1 John iii.   [4] 1 Cor. xiii. 12.   [5] Aug. lib. 15. de Civ. Dei, c. 9.

and more spiritual, than that which it represents, as we know, from universal experience. Since, therefore, we can find nothing created, equally pure and spiritual with God, no resemblance can enable us, perfectly to comprehend the divine essence."[1] Moreover, all created things are circumscribed within certain limits of perfection ; but God is circumscribed by no limits, and therefore nothing created can reflect his immensity. The only means, therefore, of arriving at a knowledge of the divine essence, is that God unite himself in some sort to us ; and after an incomprehensible manner, elevate our minds to a higher degree of perfection, and thus render us capable of contemplating the beauty of his nature. This the light of his glory will accomplish: illumined by its splendour, we shall see God, the true light, in his own light.[2] The blessed always see God present, and by this greatest and most exalted of gifts, "being made partakers of the divine nature,"[3] they enjoy true and solid happiness. Our belief of this truth should therefore be animated by an assured hope of one day arriving, through the divine goodness, at the same happy term ; according to these words of the Nicene Creed : "I expect the resurrection of the dead, and the life of the world to come." These are divine truths which defy the powers of human language, and mock the limits of human comprehension. We may, however, trace some resemblance of this happy change in sensible objects, for as iron, when acted on by fire, becomes ignited, and, whilst it is substantially the same, seems changed into fire, which is a different substance; so the blessed, who are admitted into the glory of heaven, and who burn with a love of God, although they cease not to be the same, are yet affected in such a manner, as that they may be said with truth to differ more from the inhabitants of this earth, than iron, when ignited, differs from itself when cold.

An illustration of this truth.

To say all in a few words : supreme and absolute happiness, which we call essential, consists in the possession of God ; for what can *he* want to consummate his happiness, who possesses God, the fountain of all good, the fulness of all perfection ?

In what essential happiness consists.

To this happiness, however, are appended certain gifts which are common to all the blessed, and which, because more within the reach of human comprehension, are generally found more effectual in exciting the mind and inflaming the heart.[4] These the Apostle seems to have in view, when, in his epistle to the Romans, he says : "Glory, and honour, and peace, to every one that worketh good."[5] The blessed shall enjoy glory, not only that glory which we have already shown to constitute essential happiness, or to be its inseparable accompaniment ; but also that glory which consists in the clear and comprehensive knowledge, which each of the blessed shall have of the singular and exalted dignity of his companions in glory.

The accessories of happiness.

[1] Dionys. Areop. de. divin. nom. c. 1.   [2] Ps. xxxv. 10.   [3] 2 Pet. i. 4.
[4] Aug. de Civ. Dei, lib. xxii. c. 30.   [5] Rom. ii. 10.

But how distinguished must not that honour be which is con- The first. ferred by God himself, who no longer calls them servants, but friends,[1] brethren,[2] and sons of God![3] Hence the Redeemer will address his elect in these words, which at once breathe infinite love, and bespeak the highest honour: " Come, ye blessed of my Father, possess you the kingdom prepared for you."[4] Justly, then, may we exclaim with the psalmist: " Thy friends, O God! are made exceedingly honourable."[5] They shall also receive the highest praise from Christ the Lord, in presence of his Heavenly Father, and before the assembled hosts of heaven. And, if nature has interwoven in the human heart, the desire of The second. honour, particularly when conferred by men eminent for wis- dom, who are, therefore, the most authoritative vouchers of merit; what an accession of glory to the blessed, to evince to- wards each other the highest veneration ?

To enumerate all the delights with which the souls of the The third blessed shall be inebriated, would be an endless task: we can- not even conceive them in idea: with this truth, however, the minds of the faithful should be deeply impressed, that the hap- piness of the saints is full to overflowing, of all those pleasures which can be enjoyed or even desired in this life, whether they regard the powers of the mind or the perfection of the body: a consummation more exalted in the manner of its accomplish- ment, than, to use the words of the Apostle, " eye hath seen, ear heard, or the heart of man conceived."[6]—The body, which The fourth. was before gross and material, having put off mortality, and now refined and spiritualized, shall no longer stand in need of corpo- ral nutriment: whilst the soul shall be satiated with that eternal The fifth. food of glory, which the master of that great feast will minister, in person, to all.[7] Who will desire rich apparel or royal robes, The sixth. where these appendages of human grandeur shall be superse- ded; and all shall be clothed with immortality and splendour, and adorned with a crown of imperishable glory! And, if the The se- possession of a spacious and magnificent mansion forms an in- venth gredient in human happiness, what more spacious, what more magnificent, can imagination picture, than the mansion of heaven, illumined, as it is throughout, with the blaze of glory which encircles the Godhead! Hence, the prophet, contem- plating the beauty of this dwelling-place, and burning with the desire of reaching those mansions of bliss, exclaims: " How lovely are thy tabernacles, O Lord of hosts! my soul longeth and fainteth for the courts of the Lord: my heart and my flesh have rejoiced in the living God."[8] That the faithful may be all filled with the same sentiments, and utter the same language, should be the object of the pastor's most earnest desires; as it should be of his zealous labours. " In my Father's house," says our Lord, " there are many mansions,"[9] in which shall be distributed rewards of greater and of less value, according to

[1] John xv. 14.　[2] Matt. xii. 49.　[3] Rom. viii. 15, 16.　[4] Matt. xxv. 34.
[5] Ps. cxxxviii. 17.　[6] 1 Cor. ii. 9.　[7] Luke xii. 37.　[8] Ps. lxxxiii. 1, 2.
[9] John xiv. 2.

9　　N

each one's deserts: for " He who soweth sparingly, shall reap sparingly: and he who soweth in blessings, shall also reap of blessings."[1]

How to arrive at the enjoyment of this happiness.

The pastor, therefore, will not only move the faithful to a desire of arriving at this happiness; but will frequently remind them that, infallibly to attain it, they must possess the virtues of faith and charity; they must persevere in the exercise of prayer, and the salutary use of the sacraments, and in a faithful discharge of all the good offices which spring from fraternal charity. Thus, through the mercy of God, who has prepared that blessed glory for those who serve him, shall be one day fulfilled the words of the prophet: " My people shall sit in the beauty of peace, and in the tabernacles of confidence and of wealthy rest."[2]

[1] 2 Cor. ix. 6.   [2] Isaias xxxii. 18.

CATECHISM

OF

THE COUNCIL OF TRENT.

PART II.

ON THE SACRAMENTS.

IF the exposition of every part of the doctrines of Christianity demands knowledge and assiduity on the part of the pastor, that of the Sacraments, which, by the ordinance of God, are a necessary means of salvation, and a plenteous source of spiritual advantage, demands, in a special manner, the application of his combined talents and industry.[1] Thus, by accurate and frequent instruction, shall the faithful be enabled to approach worthily and with salutary effect, these inestimable and most holy institutions ; and the pastor will not depart from the rule laid down in the divine prohibition : " Give not that which is holy to dogs : neither cast ye your pearls before swine."[2]

As then we are about to treat of the Sacraments in general, it is proper to begin, in the first place, by explaining the force and meaning of the word " Sacrament," and removing all ambiguity as to its signification, in order the more easily to comprehend the sense in which it is here used. The faithful, therefore, are to be informed that the word Sacrament is differently understood by sacred and profane writers ; and to point out its different acceptations will be found pertinent to our present purpose. By some it has been used to express the obligation which arises from an oath, pledging to the performance of some service ; and hence, the oath by which soldiers promise military service to the state, has been called a military Sacrament. Amongst profane writers, this seems to have been the most ordinary meaning of the word. But, by the Latin Fathers, who have written on theological subjects, the word Sacrament is used to signify a sacred thing which lies concealed. The Greeks, to express the same idea, made use of the word " Mystery." This, we understand to be the meaning of the word, when, in

Side notes: A knowledge of the Sacraments particularly necessary.

Different meanings of the word "Sacrament."

L

II

---

[1] Vid. Concil. Trid. Sess. 17. [2] Matt. vii. 6.

the epistle to the Ephesians, it is said: "that he might make known to us the mystery (sacramentum) of his will ;"[1] and to Timothy, "great is the mystery (sacramentum) of godliness ;"[2] and in the book of Wisdom: "They knew not the secrets (sacramenta) of God.[3] In these and many other passages the word Sacrament, it will be perceived, signifies nothing more than a holy thing that lies concealed. The Latin Fathers, therefore, deemed the word no inappropriate term to express a sensible sign, which at once, communicates grace to the soul of the receiver, and declares, and, as it were, places before the eyes the grace which it communicates. St. Gregory, however, is of opinion that it is called a Sacrament, because through its instrumentality, the divine power secretly operates our salvation, under the veil of sensible things.[4]

III.

Sacrament, a word of ancient ecclesiastical usage.

Let it not, however, be supposed that the word Sacrament is of recent ecclesiastical usage. Whoever peruses the writings of S. S. Jerome,[5] and Augustine,[6] will at once perceive, that ancient ecclesiastical writers made frequent use of the word "Sacrament," and sometimes also of the word "symbol," or "mystical or sacred sign," to designate that of which we here speak. Thus much will suffice in explanation of the word Sacrament : and indeed, what we have said applies equally to the Sacraments of the old law : but superseded, as they have been, by the gospel law and grace, instruction regarding them were superfluous.

Definition of a Sacrament.

Besides the meaning of the word, which alone has hitherto engaged our attention, the nature and efficacy of that which it expresses demand our particular inquiry ; and the faithful must be taught what constitutes a Sacrament. That the Sacraments are amongst the means of attaining righteousness and salvation, cannot be questioned : but of the many definitions, each of them sufficiently appropriate, which may serve to explain the nature of a Sacrament, there is none more comprehensive, none more perspicuous, than that of St. Augustine : a definition which has since been adopted by all scholastic writers : "A Sacrament," says he, "is a sign of a sacred thing ;" or in other words of the same import; "A Sacrament is a visible sign of an invisible grace, instituted for our justification."[7]

Definition explained.

The more fully to develope this definition, the pastor will explain it in all its parts. He will first observe, that sensible objects are of two sorts: some invented as signs, others not invented as signs, but existing absolutely and in themselves. To the latter class, almost every object in nature may be said to belong ; to the former, spoken and written languages, military standards, images, trumpets, and a multiplicity of other things of the same sort, too numerous to be mentioned. Thus, with regard to words ; take away their power of expressing ideas,

---

[1] Eph. i. 9. [2] 1 Tim. iii. 16. [3] Wisd. ii. 22. [4] D. Greg. in 1. Reg. cap. 16. vers. 13. [5] Vid. Hieron. in Amos, c. 1, v. i. & Iren. c. i. v. 15.
[6] Aug. in Joan. Tract. 80. in fine, et contra Faust. lib. 19. c. 11. Cypr. epist. 15, et bh de bapt. Christ. [7] D. Aug. lib. 10. de Civ. Dei, c. 5. & epist. 2.

and you seem to take away the only reason for their invention. They are, therefore, properly called signs : for, according to St. Augustine, a sign, besides what it presents to the senses, is a medium through which we arrive at the knowledge of something else : from a footstep, for instance, which we see traced on the ground, we instantly infer that some one whose footstep appears has passed.[1]

A Sacrament, therefore, is clearly to be numbered amongst those things which have been instituted as signs : it makes known to us by external resemblance, that which God, by his invisible power, accomplishes in our souls.[2] To illustrate what we have said by an example ; baptism, for instance, which is administered by external ablution, accompanied with certain solemn words, signifies that by the power of the Holy Ghost, all the interior stains and defilements of sin are washed away, and that the soul is enriched and adorned with the admirable gift of heavenly justification ; whilst, at the same time, the baptismal ablution, as we shall hereafter explain in its proper place, accomplishes in the soul, that of which it is externally significant. That a Sacrament is to be numbered amongst signs is clearly inferred from Scripture. Speaking of circumcision, a Sacrament of the old law which was given to Abraham, the father of all believers,[3] the Apostle, in his epistle to the Corinthians, says ; " and he received the sign of circumcision, a seal of the justice of the faith which he had ;"[4] and in another place ; " All we," says he, " who are baptized in Christ Jesus, are baptized in his death :"[5] words which justify the inference that baptism signifies, to use the words of the same Apostle, that " we are buried together with him by baptism into death."[6] To know that the Sacraments are signs, is important to the faithful. This knowledge will lead them more readily to believe, that what they signify, contain, and effectuate, is holy and august ; and recognising their sanctity, they will be more disposed to venerate and adore the beneficence of God displayed towards us in their institution.

A Sacrament proved to be "a sign."

We now come to explain the words, " sacred thing," which constitute the second part of the definition. To render this explanation satisfactory we must enter somewhat more minutely into the accurate and acute reasoning of St. Augustine on the variety of signs.[7]

Also, " a sacred thing."

Of signs some are called natural, which besides making themselves known to us, also convey a knowledge of something else ; an effect, as we have already said, common to all signs. Smoke, for instance, is a natural sign from which we immediately infer the existence of fire. It is called a natural sign, because it implies the existence of fire, not by arbitrary institution, but by its

Of signs, some are natural ;

---

[1] Aug. lib. 2. de doct. Christ. c. 1.
[2] Aug. de doct. Christ. lib. 3. c. 9. et epist. 23. et de Catch. erud. c. 26. potest videri Tertul. de resur. carnis. c. 8. et Greg. in 1. Reg. lib. 6. c. 3. post init.
[3] Gen. xvii. 10.   [4] Rom. iv. 11.   [5] Rom. vi. 3.   [6] Rom. vi. 4
[7] Lib. 1. de doctr. Christ. c. 1.

9*

intimate connexion with that element: when smoke appears we are at once convinced of the existence of latent fire.[1]

some conventional.

Other signs are not natural, but conventional, invented and instituted by men to enable them to commune one with another, mutually to convey their sentiments and communicate their counsels. The variety and multiplicity of such signs may be inferred from the circumstance, that some belong to the eyes, some to the ears, some to each of the other senses. When we intimate any thing by a sensible sign, for instance, by removing a military standard, it is obvious that such intimation can reach us only through the medium of the eyes; and it is equally obvious that the sound of the trumpet, of the lute, and of the lyre, instruments which are not only sources of pleasure, but frequently signs of ideas, is addressed to the ear. Through the latter sense, are also conveyed words, which are the best medium of communicating our inmost thoughts.

Signs instituted by God: some significant only: others significant and efficient.

Besides those signs of which we have hitherto spoken, and which are conventional; there are others, and confessedly of more sorts than one, which are of divine appointment. Some were instituted by God, solely to indicate something, or recall its recollection: such were the purifications of the law, the showbread, and many other things which belonged to the Mosaic worship;[2] others not only to signify, but, also, to accomplish what they signify. Among the latter, are manifestly to be numbered the Sacraments of the New Law. They are signs instituted by God, not invented by man, which we believe, with an unhesitating faith, to carry with them that sacred efficacy of which they are the signs. Having, therefore, shown that signs present a variety of appearances; the "sacred thing" which they contain, must also exist under a variety of forms.

Meaning of the words "sacred thing."

With regard to the proposed definition of a Sacrament, divines prove, that by the words "sacred thing," is to be understood the grace of God, which sanctifies the soul and adorns it with every virtue; and of this grace they consider the words "sacred thing," an appropriate appellation, because by its salutary influence the soul is consecrated and united to God.

A fuller explanation of a Sacrament.

In order, therefore, to explain more fully the nature of a Sacrament, the pastor will teach that it is a thing subject to the senses; and, possessing by divine institution, at once the power of signifying sanctity and justice, and of imparting both to the receiver. Hence, it is easy to perceive, that the images of the saints, crosses, and the like, although signs of sacred things, cannot be called Sacraments. That such is the nature of a Sacrament is easily proved by applying to each of the Sacraments what has been already said of baptism, viz. that the solemn ablution of the body not only signifies, but has power to effect a sacred thing which is wrought in the soul by the invisible operation of the Holy Ghost.

[1] Aug. de doct. Christ. lib. 2. c. 1. et seq.
[2] Aug. de doct. Christ. lib. 3. c. 9. Exod. xii. 15. Concil. Trid. Sess. 7. de Sacr.

It is also pre-eminently, the property of these mystical signs, instituted by Almighty God, to signify, by divine appointment, more than one thing, and this applies to all the Sacraments. All declare not only our sanctity and justification, but also two other things most intimately connected with both—the passion of our Lord, which is the source of our sanctification, and eternal life to which, as to its end, our sanctification should be referred. Such, then, being the nature of all the Sacraments, the doctors of the Church justly hold, that each of them has a threefold significancy ; reminding us of something passed, indicating something present, foretelling something future. When we say that this is an opinion, held by the Doctors of the Church, let it not be imagined that it is unsupported by Scriptural authority. When the Apostle says : " All we who are baptized in Christ Jesus, are baptized in his death ;"[1] he gives us clearly to understand that baptism is called a sign, because it reminds us of the death and passion of our Lord. When he says : " We are buried together with him by baptism into death, that as Christ is risen from the dead by the glory of the Father, so, we also, may walk in newness of life ;"[2] he also clearly shows, that baptism is a sign which indicates the infusion of divine grace into the soul, enables us by its efficacy to form our lives anew, and renders the performance of all the duties of true piety at once easy and inviting. Finally, when he adds : " If we have been planted together in the likeness of his death, we shall be also in the likeness of his resurrection ;"[3] he teaches that baptism gives no obscure intimation of eternal life also, which we are to reach through its efficacy.

Every Sacrament signifies three things.

Besides the different significations already evolved, the Sacraments also not unfrequently indicate and mark the presence of more than one thing. The holy Eucharist, for instance, at once signifies the presence of the real body and blood of Christ, and the grace which it imparts to the worthy receiver. What has been said, therefore, cannot fail to supply the pastor with arguments to prove, how much the power of God is displayed— how many hidden miracles are contained in the Sacraments ; that thus all may know and feel their obligation to reverence them with the most profound veneration, and to receive them with the most ardent devotion.

A Sacrament sometimes signifies the presence of more than one thing.

But, of all the means employed to make known the proper use of the Sacraments, there is none more effectual than a careful exposition of the reasons of their institution. Amongst these reasons, for there are many, the first is the imbecility of the human mind : we are so constituted by nature, that no one can aspire to mental and intellectual knowledge, unless through the medium of sensible objects. Impelled, therefore, by his goodness towards us, and guided by his wisdom, the Sovereign Creator of the universe, in order to bring the mysterious effects of his divine power more immediately within the sphere of our com-

The Sacraments, why instituted. First.

[1] Rom. vi. 3   [2] Rom. vi. 4   [3] Rom. vi. 5

prehension, has ordained that it should be manifested to us, through the intervention of certain sensible signs. As St. Chrysostom happily expresses it: " If man were not clothed with a material body, these good things would have been presented to him unveiled by sensible forms ; but, as he is composed of body and soul, it was absolutely necessary to employ sensible signs, in order to assist in making them understood."[1]

Second.

Another reason is, because the mind yields a reluctant assent to promises ; and hence, God, from the beginning of the world, very frequently, and in express terms points our attention to the .promises which he had made; and when designing to execute something, the magnitude of which might weaken a belief in its accomplishment, he confirms his promise by signs, which sometimes appear miraculous. When, for instance, God sends Moses to deliver the people of Israel ; and Moses commissioned as he was by God, and shielded by his protecting arm, still hesitates, fearing his incompetency to the task imposed on him, or the incredulous rejection of the divine oracles on the part of the people, the Almighty confirms his promise by many signs.[2] As, then, in the old law, God ordained that every important promise should be confirmed by certain signs ; so, in the new, our divine Redeemer, when he promises pardon of sin, divine grace, the communication of the Holy Spirit, has instituted certain sensible signs which are so many pledges of the inviolability of his word—pledges which we are well assured he will not fail to redeem.[3]

Third.

A third reason is, that the Sacraments bring, to use the words of St. Ambrose, the healing remedies and medicines, as it were, of the Samaritan mentioned in the Gospel. God wishes us to have recourse to them in order to preserve or recover the health of the soul ;[4] for, through the Sacraments as through its proper channel, should flow into the soul the efficacy of the passion of Christ, that is the grace which he purchased for us on the altar of the cross, and without which we cannot hope for salvation. Hence, our most merciful Redeemer has bequeathed to his Church, Sacraments stamped with the sanction of his word, and sealed with the security of his promise, through which, provided we make pious and devout use of these sovereign remedies, we firmly believe that the fruit of his passion is really conveyed to our souls.

Fourth.

A fourth reason why the institution of the Sacraments may seem necessary is, that there may be certain marks and symbols to distinguish the faithful; particularly as, to use the words of St. Augustine, " no society of men, professing a true or a false religion, can, as it were, be incorporated, unless united and held together by some federal bond of sensible signs."[5] Both these objects, the Sacraments of the new law accomplish ; distinguish-

<hr/>

[1] Chrys. hom. 83. in Matt. & hom. 60. ad Pop. Antioch.   [2] Exod. iii. 10, 11. Ibid. iv. 2.   [3] Aug. lib. 4. de baptis. contra Donatist. cap. 24.   [4] Ambr. lib. 5. de Sacr. c. 4.   [5] D. Aug. lib. 19. contra Faust. c. 11 & de vera rel. c. 17. Basil. in orb. ad bapt.

ing the Christian from the infidel, and connecting the faithful by a sort of sacred bond.

Again, the Apostle says : " With the heart we believe unto justice ; but with the mouth confession is made unto salvation."[1] These words, also, afford another very just reason for the institution of the Sacraments—by approaching them, we make a public profession of our faith in the face of all men. Thus, when we stand before the baptismal font, we openly profess our belief in its efficacy, and declare that, by virtue of its salutary waters, in which we are washed, the soul is spiritually cleansed and regenerated. The Sacraments have also great influence, not only in exciting and exercising our faith, but also in inflaming that charity with which we should love one another ; recollecting that, by participating of these mysteries in common, we are knit together in the closest bonds of union, and are made members of one body. *[Fifth.]*

Finally, and the consideration is of the highest importance in the study of Christian piety, the Sacraments repress and subdue the pride of the human heart, and exercise the Christian in the practice of humility, by obliging him to a subjection to sensible elements ; that thus, in atonement for his criminal defections from God to serve the elements of this world, he may yield to the Almighty the tribute of his obedience. These are principally what appeared to us necessary for the instruction of the faithful, in the name, nature, and institution of a Sacrament. When they shall have been accurately expounded by the pastor, his next duty will be to explain the constituent parts of each Sacrament, and the rites and ceremonies used in its administration. *[Sixth.]*

In the first place, then, the pastor will inform the faithful, that the " sensible thing" which enters into the definition of a Sacrament as already given, although constituting but one sign, is of a twofold nature : every Sacrament consists of two things ; " matter," which is called the element, and " form," which is commonly called " the word." This is the doctrine of the Fathers of the Church, upon which the testimony of St Augustine is familiar to all : " The word," says he, " is joined to the element, and it becomes a Sacrament."[2] By the words " sensible thing," therefore, the Fathers understand not only the matter or element, such as water in baptism, chrism in confirmation, and oil in extreme-unction, all of which fall under the eye ; but also the words which constitute the form, and which are addressed to the ear. Both are clearly pointed out by the Apostle, when he says : " Christ loved the Church, and delivered himself up for it, that he might sanctify it, cleansing it by the laver of water in the word of life."[3] Here the matter and form of the Sacrament are expressly mentioned. But in order to explain, more fully and clearly, the particular efficacy of each, the words which compose the form were to be added to the matter ; for *[Every Sacrament consists of matter and form]*

---

[1] Rom. x. 10.   [2] Aug. in Joan, tract. 80.   [3] Eph. v. 25

O

of all signs, words are evidently the most significant, and without them it would be difficult to comprehend what the matter of the Sacraments may designate and declare. Water, for instance, has the quality of cooling as well as of cleansing, and may be symbolic of either. In baptism, therefore, unless the words were added, it might be matter of conjecture, of certainty it could not, which was signified; but when the words which compose the form are added, we are no longer at a loss to understand, that baptism possesses and signifies the power of cleansing.[1]

The Sacraments of the New Law, excel those of the Old. In this, the Sacraments of the New Law excel those of the Old, that there was no definite form, known to us, of administering those of the Old, a circumstance which rendered them uncertain and obscure, whilst, in those of the new, the form is so definite, that any, even a casual, deviation from it renders the Sacrament null; and it is therefore expressed in the clearest terms, and such as exclude the possibility of doubt. These then are the parts which belong to the nature and substance of the Sacraments, and of which every Sacrament is necessarily composed.

Sacraments administered with certain ceremonies; and why. To these are added certain ceremonies, which although not to be omitted without sin, unless in case of necessity, yet, if at any time omitted, because not essential to its existence, do not invalidate the Sacrament. It is not without good reason, that the administration of the Sacraments has been, at all times, from the earliest ages of the Church, accompanied with certain solemn ceremonies.

First reason. There is, in the first place, an obvious propriety in manifesting such a religious reverence to the sacred mysteries, as to appear to handle holy things holily.

Second. These ceremonies also serve to display more fully, and place as it were before our eyes, the effects of the Sacraments, and to impress more deeply on the minds of the faithful the sanctity of these sacred institutions.

Third. They also elevate to sublime contemplation, the minds of those who behold them with respectful and religious attention; and excite within them the virtues of faith and of charity. To enable the faithful therefore to know, and understand clearly, the meaning of the ceremonies made use of in the administration of each Sacrament, should be an object of special care and attention to the pastor.

Number of the Sacraments, useful to be known. We now come to explain the number of the Sacraments; a knowledge of which is attended with this advantage, that the greater the number of supernatural aids to salvation which the faithful shall understand to have been provided by the divine goodness, the more ardent the piety with which they will direct all the powers of their souls to praise and proclaim the singular beneficence of God.

Their number, seven. The Sacraments then of the Catholic Church are seven, as is proved from Scripture, from the unbroken tradition of the Fathers, and from the authoritative definitions of councils.[2] Why

---

[1] Aug. de doct. Christi, lib. ii. c. 3.   [2] Trid. sess. 7. can
1 de sac. in gen. Conc. Flo. in dec. ad Arm. D. Th. p. 3. q. 63. art. 1.

they are neither more nor less, may be shown, at least with some degree of probability, even from the analogy that exists between natural and spiritual life. In order to exist, to preserve existence, and to contribute to his own and to the public good, seven things seem necessary to man—to be born—to grow—to be nurtured—to be cured when sick—when weak to be strengthened—as far as regards the public weal, to have magistrates invested with authority to govern—and, finally, to perpetuate himself and his species by legitimate offspring. Analogous then as all these things obviously are, to that life by which the soul lives to God, we discover in them a reason to account for the number of the Sacraments. Amongst them, the first is Baptism, the gate, as it were, to all the other Sacraments, by which we are born again to Christ. The next is Confirmation, by which we grow up, and are strengthened in the grace of God : for, as St. Augustine observes, " to the Apostles who have already received baptism, the Redeemer said : ' stay you in the city till you be indued with power from on high.' "[1] The third is the Eucharist, that true bread from heaven which nourishes our souls to eternal life, according to these words of the Saviour ; " My flesh is meat indeed, and my blood is drink indeed."[2] The fourth is Penance, by which the soul, which has caught the contagion of sin, is restored to spiritual health. The fifth is Extreme Unction, which obliterates the traces of sin, and invigorates the powers of the soul ; of which St. James says : " if he be in sins, they shall be forgiven him."[3] The sixth is Holy Orders, which gives power to perpetuate in the Church the public administration of the Sacraments, and the exercise of all the sacred functions of the ministry.[4] The seventh and last is Matrimony, a Sacrament instituted for the legitimate and holy union of man and woman, for the conservation of the human race, and the education of children, in the knowledge of religion, and the love and fear of God.

Explained by analogy.

Baptism.

Confirmation.

Eucharist.

Penance.

Extreme Unction.

Holy Orders.

Matrimony.

All and each of the Sacraments, it is true, possess an admirable efficacy given them by God : but it is well worthy of remark, that all are not of equal necessity or of equal dignity, nor is the signification of all the same. Amongst them three are of paramount necessity, a necessity, however, which arises from different causes. The universal and absolute necessity of baptism, these words of the Redeemer unequivocally declare :— " Unless a man be born again of water and the Holy Ghost, he cannot enter into the kingdom of God."[5] The necessity of Penance is relative : Penance is necessary for those only who have stained their baptismal innocence, by mortal guilt : without sincere repentance, their eternal ruin is inevitable. Orders, too, although not necessary to each of the faithful, are of absolute general necessity to the Church.[6] But, the dignity of the Sa-

All the Sacraments not equally necessary.

[1] D. Aug. ep. 108. et Luke xxiv. 49.   [2] John vi. 55.   [3] James v. 15.
[4] Luke v. 14.   [5] John iii. 5.   [6] Trid. 1. Sess. 7, can. 3, 4. de Sacr. in germ.
D. Th. p. 3. q. 65. art. 4.

The Eucharist excels all the others in dignity.

craments considered, the Eucharist, for holiness, and for the number and greatness of its mysteries, is eminently superior to all the rest. These, however, are matters which will be more easily understood, when we come to explain, in its proper place, what regards each of the Sacraments.[1]

Christ, the author of the Sacraments.

We come, in the next place, to ask from whom we have received these sacred and divine mysteries: any boon, however excellent in itself, receives no doubt an increased value and dignity from him by whose bounty it is bestowed. The question, however, is not one of difficult solution: justification comes from God; the Sacraments are the wonderful instruments of justification; one, and the same God in Christ, must, therefore, be the author of justification, and of the Sacraments.[2] The Sacraments, moreover, contain a power and efficacy which reach the inmost recesses of the soul; and as God alone has power to enter into the sanctuary of the heart, he alone, through Christ, is manifestly the author of the Sacraments. That they are interiorly dispensed by him, is also matter of faith; according to these words of St. John: "He who sent me to baptize with water, said to me; he upon whom thou shalt see the Spirit descending, and remaining upon him, he it is that baptizeth with the Holy Ghost."[3]

Men, their ministers.

But God, although the author and dispenser of the Sacraments, would have them administered in his Church by men, not by angels: and to constitute a Sacrament, as constant tradition testifies, matter and form are not more necessary than is the ministry of men.

The unworthiness of the minister does not affect the validity of the Sacraments.

But, representing as he does, in the discharge of his sacred functions, not his own, but the person of Christ, the minister of the Sacraments, be he good or bad, validly consecrates and confers the Sacraments; provided he make use of the matter and form instituted by Christ, and always observed in the Catholic Church, and intends to do what the Church does in their administration. Unless, therefore, Christians will deprive themselves of so great a good, and resist the Holy Ghost, nothing can prevent them from receiving, through the Sacraments, the fruit of grace.[4] That this was, at all times, a fixed and well defined doctrine of the Church, is established beyond all doubt by St. Augustine, in his disputations against the Donatists;[5] and should we desire Scriptural proof also, we have it in the words of St. Paul; "I have planted, Apollo watered; but God gave the increase."[6] Neither he that plants, therefore, nor he that waters, is any thing, but God who gives "the increase." As, therefore, in planting trees, the vices of the planter do not impede the growth of the vine, so, and the comparison is suffi-

---

[1] Dionys. lib. de Eccles. Hier. c. 3.
[2] Ambr. lib. 4. de Sacr. cap. 6. D. Tho. p. 3. q. 62. Trid. Sess. 7. can. 1 de Sacr. in gen. lib. de Eccles. dog. & Cassian. collat. 7. 18.   [3] John i 33.
[4] Trid. Sess. 7. de Sac. in gen. c. 11 & 12. Greg. Naz. in Orat. in S. bapt. Ambr. de his qui myst. init. cap. 5. Chrysost. hom. 8. in 1 Cor.
[5] Aug. contra Crescen. lib. 4. c. 20. contra Donat. lib. 1. c. 4. & lib. 2. contra lit Petil. c. 47.   [6] 1 Cor. iii. 6.

eiently intelligible, those who were planted in Christ by the ministry of bad men, sustain no injury from guilt which is not their own. Judas Iscariot, as the Holy Fathers infer from the Gospel of St. John,[1] conferred baptism on many ; and yet none of those whom he baptized are recorded to have been baptized again. To use the memorable words of St. Augustine : "Judas baptized, and yet after him none were rebaptized : John baptized, and after John they were rebaptized, because the baptism administered by Judas was the baptism of Christ, but that administered by John was the baptism of John :[2] not that we prefer Judas to John, but that we justly prefer the baptism of Christ, although administered by Judas, to the baptism of John although administered by the hands of John."[3]

But, let not the pastor, or other minister of the Sacraments, hence infer that he fully acquits himself of his duty, if, disregarding integrity of life and purity of morals, he attend only to the administration of the Sacraments in the manner prescribed. True, the manner of administering them is a matter of the highest importance ; but it is no less true, that it does not constitute all that enters into the worthy discharge of this duty. It should never be forgotten, that the Sacraments, although they cannot lose the divine efficacy inherent in them, bring eternal death and everlasting perdition on him who dares to administer them with hands stained with the defilement of sin. Holy things, and the observation cannot be too often repeated, should be treated holily, and with due reverence :[4] "To the sinner," says the prophet, "God has said : why dost thou declare my justices, and take my covenant in thy mouth, seeing that thou hast hated discipline ?"[5] If then, for him who is defiled by sin it is unlawful to speak on divine things, how enormous the guilt of that man, who, with conscious guilt, dreads not to consecrate with polluted lips these holy mysteries—to take them—to touch them —nay more, with sacrilegious hands, to administer them to others ?[6] The symbols, (so he calls the Sacraments) "the wicked," says St. Denis, "are not allowed to touch."[7] It therefore becomes the first, the most important duty of the minister of these holy things, to aspire to holiness of life, to approach with purity the administration of the Sacraments, and so to exercise himself in the practice of piety, that, from their frequent administration and use, they may every day receive, with the divine assistance, a more abundant effusion of grace.

When these important matters have been explained, the effects of the Sacraments present to the pastor the next subject of instruction ; a subject, it is hoped, which will throw considerable light on the definition of a Sacrament as already given.

The principal effects of the Sacraments are two ; sanctifying grace, and the character which they impress. The former, that is, the grace which we, in common with the doctors of the

Side notes: To administer the Sacraments in a state of sin is a grievous crime

The effects of the Sacraments.

Justifying grace.

---

[1] John iv. 2.   [2] Acts xix. 3—5.   [3] Aug. in Joan.
[4] Aug. in Joan. tract. 5. & contra Cresc. lib. 3. c. 6. D. Thom. p. 3. q. 93. art. 4.
[5] Ps. xlix. 16.   [6] Conc. Trid. can. 6.   [7] S. Dion. de Eccl. Hier. c. 1.

Church, call sanctifying grace, deservedly holds the first place. That this is an effect produced by the Sacraments, we know from these words of the Apostle: " Christ," says he, " loved the Church, and delivered himself up for it; that he might sanctify it, cleansing it by the laver of water in the word of life."[1] But how so great and so admirable an effect is produced by the Sacraments, that, to use the words of St. Augustine, " water cleanses the body, and reaches the heart:"[2] this, indeed, the mind of man, aided by the light of reason alone, is unequal to comprehend. It ought to be an established law, that nothing sensible can, of its own nature, reach the soul; but we know by the light of faith, that in the Sacraments exists the power of the Omnipotent, effectuating that which the natural elements cannot of themselves accomplish.[3]

The grace of the Sacraments, why, of old, proved by miracles.
. That on this subject no doubt may exist in the minds of the faithful, God, in the abundance of his mercy, was pleased, from the moment of their institution, to manifest by exterior miracles, the effects which they operate interiorly in the soul: this he did, in order that we may always believe that the same interior effects, although inaccessible to the senses, are still produced by them. To say nothing of that which the Scripture records—that, at the baptism of the Redeemer in the Jordan, " The heavens were opened, and the Holy Ghost appeared in the form of a dove;"[4] to teach us, that when we are washed in the sacred font, his grace is infused into our souls—to omit these splendid miracles which have reference rather to the consecration of baptism, than to the administration of the Sacraments— do we not read, that on the day of Pentecost, when the Apostles received the Holy Ghost, and were, thenceforward, inspired with greater courage and firmer resolution to preach the faith, and brave danger of every sort for the glory of Christ, " there came suddenly a sound from heaven, as of a mighty wind coming, and it filled the whole house where they were sitting, and there appeared to them parted tongues, as it were of fire."[5] These visible effects give us to understand that, in the Sacrament of Confirmation, the same spirit is given us, and the same strength imparted, which enable us resolutely to encounter, and with fortitude to resist, our implacable enemies, the world, the flesh, and the devil.[6] As often as these Sacraments were administered by the Apostles, so often, during the infancy of the Church, did the same miraculous effects follow ; and they ceased not to be visible until the faith had acquired maturity and strength.

The Sacraments of the new law superi-
From what has been said of sanctifying grace, the first effect of the Sacraments, it also clearly follows, that there resides in the Sacraments of the New Law, a virtue far more exalted and

---

[1] Eph. v. 25, 26.   [2] S. Aug. in Joan. tract. 80.
[3] De hoc effectu sacramen. vid. Trid. Sess. 7, can. 6, 7, 8. de sacr. Aug. tract. 26 in Joan. & contr. Faust. c. 16 & 17, & in Ps. lxxvii. 15, 16.
[4] Matt. iii. 16.   Mark i. 10.   Luke iii. 22.   [5] Acts i. 2, 3.
[6] Aug. lib. quaest. Vet. & Nov. Test. q. 93.

efficacious than that of the Sacraments of the Old,[1] which, as or to those " weak and needy elements,[2] sanctified such as were defiled to of the old. the cleansing of the flesh,"[3] but not of the spirit. They were, therefore, instituted as signs only of those things, which were to be accomplished by the Sacraments of the new law—Sacraments which flowing from the side of Christ, " who, by the Holy Ghost, offered himself unspotted unto God, cleanse our consciences from dead works, to serve the living God,"[4] and thus work in us, through the blood of Christ, the grace which they signify. Comparing them, therefore, with the Sacraments of the old law, we shall find that not only are they more efficacious, but, also, more exuberant of spiritual advantages, and stamped with the characters of superior dignity and holiness.[5]

The other effect of the Sacraments, an effect, however, not Three of common to all, but peculiar to three, Baptism, Confirmation, and the Sacra- Holy Orders, is the character which they impress on the soul. ments im-
press a cha- When the Apostle says : " God hath anointed us, who also hath racter. sealed us, and given the pledge of the Spirit in our hearts,"[6] he clearly designates by the word " sealed," this sacramental character, the property of which is to impress a seal and mark on the soul. This character is, as it were, a distinctive and indelible impression stamped on the soul ;[7] of which St. Augustine says : " Shall the Christian Sacraments accomplish less than the bodily mark impressed on the soldier ? That mark is not stamped on his person anew, as often as he resumes the military service which he had relinquished ; but the old one is recognised and approved."[8]

This character has a two-fold effect, it qualifies us to receive Its effect or perform something sacred, and distinguishes us one from an- two-fold. other. In the character impressed by Baptism, both effects are exemplified : by it we are qualified to receive the other Sacraments ; and the Christian is distinguished from those who profess not the name of Christ. The same illustration is afforded by the characters impressed by Confirmation and Holy Orders : by the one we are armed and arrayed as soldiers of Christ, publicly to profess and defend his name, to fight against our domestic enemy, and against the spiritual powers of wickedness in the high places, and are also distinguished from those who, being newly baptized, are, as it were, new-born infants : the other combines the power of consecrating and administering the Sacraments, and also distinguishes those who are invested with this power, from the rest of the faithful. The rule of the Catholic Church is, therefore, inviolably to be observed : it teaches that these three Sacraments impress a character and are never to be reiterated.

---

[1] Aug. lib. 19. contr. Faust. c. 13, & in Ps. lxxxiii. Ambr. lib. de Sacr. c. 4.
[2] Gal. iv. 9.   [3] Heb. ix. 13.   [4] Heb. ix. 14.
[5] Aug. lib. 2. de Simb. c. 6, & in Joan. Tract. 15, & lib. 15. de Civit. Dei, c. 26
[6] 2 Cor. i. 21.   [7] Trid. ib. can.
[8] De hoc charact. vide Aug. lib. 2. contr. ep Parm. c. 33, & ep. 50, circa. medium, & tract 6, in Joan. & lect. 1. contr. Crescen. c. 30. item D. Thom. p. 3. q. 63.

Two things to be kept in view by the Pastor, in his explanation of the Sacraments.

On the subject of the Sacraments in general, these are the matters of instruction which we proposed to deliver. In communicating them to the faithful, the pastor will keep in view, principally, two things : the one, to impress on the minds of the faithful a deep sense of the honour, respect and veneration, due to these divine and celestial gifts ; the other, to urge on all the necessity of having recourse, piously and religiously, to those sacred institutions established by the God of infinite mercy, for the common salvation of all ; and of being so inflamed with the desire of attaining Christian perfection, as to deem it a deplorable loss to be, for any time, deprived of the salutary use, particularly, of Penance, and of the Holy Eucharist. These important objects the pastor will find little difficulty in accomplishing, if he press frequently on the attention of the faithful, what we have already said on the august dignity and salutary efficacy of the Sacraments—that they were instituted by the Lord Jesus, from whom nothing imperfect can emanate—that when administered, the most powerful influence of the Holy Ghost is present, pervading the inmost sanctuary of the soul—that they possess an admirable and unfailing virtue to cure our spiritual maladies, and communicate to us the inexhaustible riches of the passion of our Lord—in fine, that the whole edifice of Christian piety, although resting on the most firm foundation of the corner stone, unless supported on every side by the preaching of the divine word, and by the use of the Sacraments, must, it is greatly to be apprehended, having partially yielded, ultimately fall to the ground ; for as we are ushered into spiritual life by means of the Sacraments ; so, by the same means, are we nurtured and preserved, and grow to spiritual increase.

ON THE SACRAMENT OF BAPTISM.

Importance of the knowledge of the Sacraments in particular.

Of Baptism.

FROM what has been hitherto said on the Sacraments in general, we may judge how necessary it is, to a proper understanding of the doctrines of the Christian faith, and to the practice of Christian piety, to know what the Catholic Church proposes to our belief on the Sacraments in particular. That a perfect knowledge of Baptism is particularly necessary to the faithful, an attentive perusal of the epistles of St. Paul, will force upon the mind. The Apostle, not only frequently, but also in language the most energetic, in language full of the Spirit of God, renews the recollection of this mystery, exalts its transcendant dignity, and in it places before us the death, burial, and resurrection of our Lord, as objects of our contemplation and imitation.[1] The pastor, therefore, can never think that he has be-

[1] Rom. vi. 3. Colos. ii. 12, 13.

stowed sufficient labour and attention on the exposition of this Sacrament. Besides the great festivals of Easter and Pentecost, festivals on which the Church celebrated this Sacrament with the greatest solemnity and devotion, and on which particularly, according to ancient practice, its divine mysteries are to be explained; the pastor should, also, take occasion, at other times, to make it the subject matter of his instructions.[1]

For this purpose, a most convenient opportunity would seem to present itself, whenever the pastor, when about to administer this Sacrament, finds himself surrounded by a considerale number of the faithful: on such occasions, it is true, his exposition cannot embrace every thing that regards baptism; but he can develope one or two points with greater facility, whilst the faithful see them expressed, and contemplate them with devout attention, in the sacred ceremonies which he is performing. Thus each person, reading a lesson of admonition in the person of him who is receiving baptism, calls to mind the promises by which he had bound himself to the service of God when initiated by baptism, and reflects whether his life and morals evince that fidelity to which every one pledges himself, by professing the name of Christian. *When most conveniently explained.*

To render what we have to say, on this subject, perspicuous, we shall explain the nature and substance of the Sacrament; premising, however, an explication of the word Baptism. The word Baptism, as is well known, is of Greek derivation. Although used in Scripture to express not only that ablution which forms part of the Sacrament, but also every species of ablution,[2] and sometimes, figuratively, to express sufferings; yet it is employed, by ecclesiastical writers, to designate not every sort of ablution, but that which forms part of the Sacrament, and is administered with the prescribed sacramental form. In this sense, the Apostles very frequently make use of the word, in accordance with the institution of Christ.[3] *Meaning of the word "Baptism."*

This Sacrament, the Holy Fathers designate also by other names. St. Augustine informs us that it was sometimes called the Sacrament of Faith; because, by receiving it, we profess our faith in all the doctrines of Christianity:[4] by others it was denominated "Illumination," because by the faith which we profess in baptism, the heart is illumined: "Call to mind," says the Apostle, alluding to the time of baptism, "the former days, wherein being illumined, you endured a great fight of afflictions."[5] St. Chrysostom, in his sermon to the baptized, calls it a purgation, through which "we purge away the old leaven, that we may become a new paste:"[6] he, also, calls it a burial, a planting, and the cross of Jesus Christ:[7] the reasons for all these appellations may be gathered from the epistle of St. Paul *Other names of.*

---

[1] De hoc usu antiquo vid. Tertul. lib. de Baptis. c. 19. Basil. in exhort. ad bapt. Amb. lib. de myst. Paschæ.   [2] Mark vii. 4.
[3] Rom. vi. 3. 1 Pet. iii. 21. Octo baptismi geneva vid. Damasc. lib. 4. de fide orthod. 10.   [4] D. Aug. epist. 25. in fin.   [5] Heb. x. 32.   [6] 1 Cor. v. 7.
[7] S. Chrysost. x. 5.

to the Romans.[1] St. Denis calls it the beginning of the most holy commandments, for this obvious reason, that baptism is, as it were, the gate through which we enter into the fellowship of Christian life, and begin thenceforward, to obey the commandments.[2] This exposition of the different names of the Sacrament of baptism, the pastor will briefly communicate to the people.[3]

Definition of.
With regard to its definition, although sacred writers give many, to us that which may be collected from the words of our Lord, recorded in the Gospel of St. John, and of the Apostle, in his epistle to the Ephesians, appears the most appropriate : " Unless," says our Lord, a man be born again of water and the Holy Ghost, he cannot enter into the kingdom of God ;"[4] and, speaking of the Church, the Apostle says : " cleansing it by the laver of water in the word of life."[5] From these words, Baptism may be accurately and appropriately defined : " The Sacrament of regeneration by water in the word." By nature, we are born from Adam, children of wrath ; but by baptism we are regenerated in Christ, children of mercy ; for, " He gave power to men to be made the sons of God, to them that believe in his name, who are born not of blood, nor of the will of flesh, nor of the will of man, but of God."[6]

In what the Sacrament consists.
But, define Baptism as we may, the faithful are to be informed that this Sacrament consists of ablution, accompanied, necessarily, according to the institution of our Lord, by certain solemn words.[7] This is the uniform doctrine of the Holy Fathers ; a doctrine proved by the authority of St. Augustine : " The word," says he, " is joined to the element, and it becomes a Sacrament." That these are the constituents of Baptism, it becomes more necessary to impress on the minds of the faithful, that they may not fall into the vulgar error of thinking, that the baptismal water, preserved in the sacred font, constitutes the Sacrament. Then only is it to be called the Sacrament of Baptism, when it is really used in the way of ablution, accompanied with the words appointed by our Lord.[8]

Its matter.
But, as we first said, when treating of the Sacraments in general, that every Sacrament consists of matter and form ; it is therefore, necessary to point out what constitutes each of these in the Sacrament of Baptism. The matter then, or element of this Sacrament, is any sort of natural water, which is, simply, and without addition of any kind, commonly called water ; be it sea-water, river-water, water from a pond, well, or fountain : our Lord has declared that, " Unless a man be born again of water and the Holy Ghost, he cannot enter into the kingdom of God."[9] The Apostle also says, that the Church was cleansed

---

[1] Rom. vi. 3.   [2] S. Dion. de Eccl. Hier. c. 2.
[3] De variis baptis. nom. vid. Gregor. Nazianz. orat. in sancta lumina. et Clem. Alex. lib. 1. Poedag. cap. 6.   [4] John iii. 5.   [5] Eph. v. 26.
[6] John i. 12, 13.   [7] Matt. xxviii. 19.
[8] Hac de re vid. Chrysost. hom. 24. in Joan. Aug. lib. 6. contra. Donatist. c. 25. Conc. Florent. et Trid. item August. tract. 80 in Joan.   [9] John iii. 5.

"by the laver of water;"[1] and in the epistle of St. John, we read these words :—" There are three that give testimony on earth ; the spirit, and the water, and the blood."[2] The Scripture affords other proofs which establish the same proof. When, however, the baptist says that the Lord will come, " who will baptise in the Holy Ghost, and in fire ;"[3] he is not to be understood to speak of the matter, but of the effect of baptism, produced in the soul by the interior operation of the Holy Ghost; or, if not, of the miracle performed on the day of Pentecost, when the Holy Ghost descended on the Apostles, in the form of fire,[4] as was foretold by our Lord, in these words; " John, indeed, baptized with water, but you shall be baptized with the Holy Ghost, not many days hence."[5]

That water is the matter of Baptism, the Almighty signified both by figures and by prophecies, as we know from holy Scripture: According to the prince of the Apostles, in his first epistle, the deluge which swept the world, because " the wickedness of men was great on the earth, and all the thoughts of their hearts were bent upon evil,"[6] was a figure of the waters of Baptism.[7] To omit the cleansing of Naaman the Syrian,[8] and the admirable virtue of the pool of Bethsaida,[9] and many similar types, manifestly symbolic of this mystery ; the passage through the Red Sea, according to St. Paul, in his epistle to the Corinthians, was typical of the waters of Baptism.[10] With regard to the oracles of the prophets, the waters to which the prophet Isaias so freely invites all that thirst,[11] and those which Ezekiel saw in spirit, issue from the temple,[12] and also, " the fountain " which Zachary foresaw, " open to the house of David, and to the inhabitants of Jerusalem, for the washing of the sinner and of the unclean woman,"[13] were, no doubt, so many types which prefigured the salutary effects of the waters of Baptism. *Figure and prophecies of.*

The propriety of constituting water the matter of baptism, of the nature and efficacy of which it is at once expressive, St. Jerome, in his epistle to Oceanus, proves by many arguments.[14] Upon this subject, however, the pastor will teach, that water, which is always at hand, and within the reach of all, was the fittest matter of a Sacrament which is essentially necessary to all ; and, also, that water is best adapted to signify the effect of baptism. It washes away uncleanness, and is, therefore, strikingly illustrative of the virtue and efficacy of baptism, which washes away the stains of sin. We may also add that, like water which cools the body, baptism in a great measure extinguishes the fire of concupiscence in the soul.[15] *Water, why the matter of baptism.*

But, although, in case of necessity, simple water unmixed *Chrism,*

1 Eph. v. 26.   2 1 John v. 8.   3 Matt. iii. 11.   4 Acts ii. 3
5 Acts i. 5.   6 Gen. vi. 5.   7 1 Pet. iii. 20, 21.   8 4 Kings v. 14.
9 John v. 2.   10 1 Cor. x. 1, 2.   11 Isaias lv. 1.   12 Ezek. xlvii. 1.
13 Zach. xiii. 1.   14 D. Hieronymus epist. 85.
15 De materia bapt. vid. Conc. Florent. et Trid. sess. 7, can. 2, & de consecrat. dist. 4, item D. Thom. p. 3. q. 56, art. 5.

why used
in baptism.
with any other ingredient, is sufficient for the matter of baptism; yet, when administered in public with solemn ceremonies, the Catholic Church guided by apostolic tradition, the more fully to express its efficacy, has uniformly observed the practice of adding holy chrism.[1] And, although it may be doubted whether this or that water be genuine, such as the Sacrament requires, it can never be matter of doubt that the proper and the only matter of baptism is natural water.

Form of
baptism to
be care-
fully ex-
plained.
Having carefully explained the matter, which is one of the two parts of which the Sacrament consists, the pastor will evince equal diligence in explaining the second, that is the form, which is equally necessary with the first. In the explication of this Sacrament, a necessity of increased care and study arises, as the pastor will perceive, from the circumstance that the knowledge of so holy a mystery, is not only in itself a source of pleasure to the faithful, as is generally the case with regard to religious knowledge, but, also, very desirable for almost daily practical use. This Sacrament, as we shall explain in its proper place, is frequently administered by the laity, and most frequently, by women; and it, therefore, becomes necessary to make all the faithful indiscriminately, well acquainted with whatever regards its substance.

In what it
consists,
and when
instituted.
The pastor, therefore, will teach, in clear, unambiguous language intelligible to every capacity, that the true and essential form of baptism is: "I BAPTIZE THEE IN THE NAME OF THE FATHER, AND OF THE SON, AND OF THE HOLY GHOST:" a form delivered by our Lord and Saviour when, as we read in St. Matthew, he gave to his Apostles the command: "Going teach all nations, baptizing them in the name of the Father, and of the Son, and of the Holy Ghost."[2] By the word "baptizing," the Catholic Church, instructed from above, most justly understands that the form of the Sacrament should express the action of the minister, and this takes place when he pronounces the words: "I baptize thee." Besides the minister of the Sacrament, the person to be baptized and the principal efficient cause of baptism should be mentioned. The pronoun "thee," and the names of the Divine Persons are, therefore, distinctly added; and, thus, the absolute form of the Sacrament is expressed in the words already mentioned: "I baptize thee in the name of the Father, and of the Son, and of the Holy Ghost." Baptism is the work not of the Son alone, of whom St. John says: "This is he who baptizeth;"[3] but of the three Persons of the blessed Trinity. By saying, however, "in the name," not names, we distinctly declare that in the Trinity there is but one nature and Godhead. The word "name" is here referred not to the persons, but to the divine essence, virtue and power, which are one and the same in the three Persons.[4]

What es-
It is however to be observed, that of the words contained in

[1] Ambr. lib. 1. sacr. c. 2. et Innoc. lib. 1. decr. tit. 1. c. 3.
[2] Matt. xxviii. 19.　　　　[3] John i. 33.
[4] Vid. Aug. contra Donatist. lib. 6. c. 25. D. Thom. p. 3. q. 66. art. 5.

this form, which we have shown to be the true and essential one, some are absolutely necessary, the omission of them rendering the valid administration of the Sacrament impossible; whilst others, on the contrary, are not so essential as to affect its validity. Of the latter kind is, in the Latin form, the word "ego," (I) the force of which is included in the word "baptizo," (I baptize.) Nay more, the Greek Church, adopting a different manner of expressing the form, and being of opinion that it is unnecessary to make mention of the minister, omits the pronoun altogether. The form universally used in the Greek Church is : " Let this servant of Christ be baptized in the name of the Father, and of the Son, and of the Holy Ghost." It appears, however, from the opinion and definition of the Council of Florence, that the Greek form is valid, because the words of which it consists, sufficiently express what is essential to the validity of baptism, that is, the ablution which then takes place. *sential, what not essential, to it.*

If at any time the Apostles baptized in the name of the Lord Jesus Christ only,[1] they did so, no doubt, by the inspiration of the Holy Ghost, in order, in the infancy of the Church, to render their preaching in the name of the Lord Jesus Christ more illustrious, and to proclaim more effectually his divine and infinite power. If, however, we examine the matter more closely, we shall find that the Greek form omits nothing which the Saviour himself commands to be observed ; for the name of Jesus Christ implies the Person of the Father by whom, and that of the Holy Ghost in whom he was anointed. However, the use of this form by the Apostles becomes, perhaps, matter of doubt, if we yield to the opinions of Ambrose[2] and Basil,[3] Holy Fathers eminent for sanctity and of paramount authority, who interpret " baptism in the name of Jesus Christ" as contradistinguished to " baptism in the name of John," and who say that the Apostles did not depart from the ordinary and usual form which comprises the distinct names of the three Persons. Paul, also, in his epistle to the Galatians, seems to have expressed himself in a similar manner : " As many of you," says he, " as have been baptized in Christ, have put on Christ :"[4] meaning that they were baptized in the faith of Christ, and with no other form than that commanded by him to be observed. *Baptism in the name of Christ only.*

What has been said on the principal points which regard the matter and form of the Sacrament will be found sufficient for the instruction of the faithful : but, as in the administration of the Sacrament, the legitimate ablution should also be observed, on this point too the pastor will explain the doctrine of the Church. He will briefly inform the faithful that, according to the common practice of the Church, baptism may be administered by immersion, infusion, or aspersion ; and that administered in either of these forms it is equally valid. In baptism water is used to signify the spiritual ablution which it accomplishes, and *Baptism may be administered by immersion, infusion, or aspersion*

---

[1] Act ii. 38 ; viii. 16 ; x. 48 ; xix. 5. [2] Ambr. lib. 1. de Spiritu Sancto, c. 3.
[3] Basil. lib. 1. de Spiritu Sancto, c. 12. [4] Gal. iii. 27.

on this account baptism is called by the Apostle, a "laver."[1] This ablution takes place as effectually by immersion, which was for a considerable time the practice in the early ages of the Church, as by infusion, which is now the general practice, or by aspersion, which was the manner in which Peter baptized, when he converted and gave baptism to about three thousand souls."[2]   It is also matter of indifference to the validity of the Sacrament, whether the ablution is performed once or thrice; we learn from the epistle of St. Gregory the great to Leander, that baptism was formerly and may still be validly administered in the Church in either way.[3]   The faithful, however, will follow the practice of the particular Church to which they belong.

Two important matters to be observed in its administration.   The pastor will be particularly careful to observe, that the baptismal ablution is not to be applied indifferently to any part of the body, but principally to the head, which is pre-eminently the seat of all the internal and external senses; and also that he who baptizes is to pronounce the words which constitute the form of baptism, not before or after, but when performing the ablution.

Baptism when instituted.   When these things have been explained, it will also be expedient to remind the faithful that, in common with the other Sacraments, baptism was instituted by Christ. On this subject, the pastor will frequently point out two different periods of time which relate to baptism—the one the period of its institution by the Redeemer—the other, the establishment of the law which renders it obligatory. With regard to the former, it is clear that this Sacrament was instituted by our Lord, when, being baptized by John, he gave to the water the power of sanctifying. St. Gregory Nazianzen[4] and St. Augustine testify that to the water was then imparted the power of regenerating to spiritual life. In another place St. Augustine says: "From the moment that Christ is immersed in water, water washes away all sins:"[5] and again the Lord is baptized, not because he had occasion to be cleansed, but by the contact of his pure flesh to purify the waters, and impart to them the power of cleansing." The circumstances which attended the event afford a very strong argument to prove that baptism was then instituted by our Lord. The three persons of the most Holy Trinity, in whose name baptism is conferred, manifest their august presence—the voice of the Father is heard—the Person of the Son is present—the Holy Ghost descends in form of a dove—and the heavens, into which we are enabled to enter by baptism, are thrown open.[6]

Water consecrated to the use of baptism, when Christ was baptized.   Should we, however, ask how our Lord has endowed water with a virtue so great, so divine; this indeed is an inquiry which transcends the power of the human understanding. That when our Lord was baptized, water was consecrated to the salutary use of baptism, deriving, although instituted before the

[1] Eph. v. 26.   [2] Acts ii. 41.   [3] Greg. lib. i. regist. epist. 41.
[4] Greg. orat. in nat. Salvat. circa finem.   [5] Aug. serm. 29. 36, 37. de temp.
[6] Matt. iii. 16, 17.   Mark i. 10, 11.   Luke ii. 21, 22.

passion, all its virtue and efficacy from the passion, which is the
consummation, as it were, of all the actions of Christ—this, indeed, we sufficiently comprehend.[1]

The second period to be distinguished, that is, when the law The law of
of baptism was promulgated, also admits of no doubt. The baptism,
Holy Fathers are unanimous in saying, that after the resurrec- mulgated.
tion of our Lord, when he gave to his Apostles the command:
" Go, and teach all nations, baptizing them in the name of the
Father, and of the Son, and of the Holy Ghost;"[2] the law of
baptism became obligatory, on all, who were to be saved. This
is to be inferred from these words of St. Peter: " who hath regenerated us unto a lively hope, by the resurrection of Jesus
Christ, from the dead ;"[3] and also from the words of St Paul;
" He delivered himself up for it :" (he speaks of the Church)
that he might sanctify it, cleansing it by the laver of water in
the word of life."[4] In both passages, the obligation of baptism
is referred to the time, which followed the death of our Lord.
These words of our Lord: " Unless a man be born again of
water and the Holy Ghost, he cannot enter into the kingdom
of God,"[5] refer also, no doubt, to the time subsequent to his
passion. If then the pastor use all diligence in explaining these
truths accurately to the faithful, impossible that they should not
fully appreciate the high dignity of this Sacrament, and entertain towards it the most profound veneration ; a veneration which
will be heightened by the reflection, that the Holy Ghost, by
his invisible agency, still infuses into the heart, at the moment
of baptism, those blessings of incomparable excellence, and of
inestimable value, which were so strikingly manifested, by miracles, at the baptism of Christ our Lord. Were our eyes, like
those of the servant of Eliseus,[6] opened to see these heavenly
things, who so insensible as not to be lost in rapturous admiration of the divine mysteries, which baptism would then present
to the astonished view ! when, therefore, the riches of this Sacrament are unfolded to the faithful by the pastor, so as to enable
them to behold them, if not with the eyes of the body, with
those of the soul illumined with the light of faith, is it not reasonable to anticipate similar results ?

In the next place, it appears not only expedient but necessary, The minis-
to say who are ministers of this Sacrament; in order that those ters of the
to whom this office is specially confided, may study to perform ment.
its functions, religiously and holily ; and that no one, outstep-
ping as it were, his proper limits, may unseasonably take possession of, or arrogantly assume, what belongs to another ; for,
as the Apostle teaches, order is to be observed in all things.[7]

The faithful, therefore, are to be informed that of those who Bishops
administer baptism there are three gradations : bishops and and priests
priests hold the first place ; to them belongs the administration office:

---

[1] Vid. Hieron. in com. in. 3. cap. Matt. Aug. serm. 36. de temp.
[2] Mark xvi. 15. Matt. xxviii. 19.   [3] 1 Pet. i. 3.   [4] Eph. v. 25, 26.
[5] John iii. 5.   [6] 4 Kings vi. 17.   [7] 1 Cor. xiv. 40.

of this Sacrament, not by any extraordinary concession of power, but by right of office ; for to them, in the persons of the Apostles, was addressed the command : " Go, baptize."[1] Bishops, it is true, not to neglect the more weighty charge of instructing the faithful, generally leave its administration to priests ; but the authority of the Fathers,[2] and the usage of the Church, prove that priests exercise this function of the ministry by a right inherent in the priestly order, a right which authorises them to baptize even in presence of the bishop. Ordained to consecrate the Holy Eucharist, the Sacrament of peace and unity,[3] it is necessary that they be invested with power to administer all those things, which are required to enable others to participate of that peace and unity. If, therefore, the Fathers have at any time said, that without the leave of the bishop, the priest has not power to baptize ; they are to be understood to speak of that baptism only, which was administered on certain days of the year with solemn ceremonies.

Deacons by permission. Next to bishops and priests, are deacons, for whom, as numerous decrees of the holy Fathers attest, it is not lawful, without the permission of the bishop or priest to administer baptism.[4]

All persons in case of necessity ; but without its solemn ceremonies. Those who may administer baptism, in case of necessity, but without its solemn ceremonies, hold the third and last place ; and in this class are included all, even the laity, men and women, to whatever sect they may belong. This power extends, in case of necessity, even to Jews, infidels, and heretics ; provided, however, they intend to do what the Catholic Church does in that act of her ministry. Already established by the decrees of the ancient Fathers and Councils, these things have been again confirmed by the Council of Trent, which denounces anathema against those who presume to say, " that baptism, even when administered by heretics, in the name of the Father, and of the Son, and of the Holy Ghost, with the intention of doing what the Church does, is not true baptism."[5]

In this, the goodness and wisdom of God to be admired. And here let us admire the supreme goodness and wisdom of our Lord, who, seeing the necessity of this Sacrament for all, not only instituted water, than which nothing can be more common, as its matter ; but also placed its administration within the jurisdiction of all. In its administration, however, as we have already observed, all are not allowed to use the solemn ceremonies ; not that rites and ceremonies are of higher dignity, but because they are of inferior necessity to the Sacrament.

Order to be observed by the ministers of baptism. Let not the faithful, however, imagine that this office is given promiscuously to all, so as to supersede the propriety of observing a certain order amongst those who administer baptism : when a man is present, a woman ; when a clerk, a layman ;

---

[1] Matt. xxviii. 19.   [2] Isid. lib. 2. de offic. Eccles. cap. 4.
[3] 1 Cor. x. 17.   [4] Distinct. 93. cap. 13.
[5] Trid. sess. 7. can. de consec. dist. 4. cap. 24. Aug. lib. 7. contra Donatist. cap. 51. et ibid. lib. 3. cap. 10. et lib. 2. contra Parmen. et Councit. Lat. cap. 1. et Conc. Florent. in decr. Eugenii.

when a priest, a simple clerk, should not administer this Sacrament. Midwives, however, when accustomed to its administration, are not to be found fault with, if sometimes, when a man is present, who is unacquainted with the manner of its administration, they perform what may otherwise appear to belong more properly to men.

To those who, as we have hitherto explained, administer baptism, another class of persons is to be added, who, according to the most ancient practice of the Church, assist at the baptismal font; and, who, although formerly called by sacred writers by the common name of sponsors or sureties, are now called Godfathers and God-mothers.[1] As this is an office common almost to all the laity, the pastor will teach its principal duties, with care and accuracy. He will, in the first instance, explain why at baptism, besides those who administer the Sacrament, Godfathers and God-mothers are also required. The propriety of the practice will at once appear, if we keep in view the nature of baptism, that it is a spiritual regeneration, by which we are born children of God; of which St. Peter says: "As newborn infants desire the rational milk without guile."[2] As, therefore, every one, after his birth, requires a nurse and instructor, by whose assistance and assiduity he is brought up, and formed to learning and morality; so those, who, by the efficacy of the regenerating waters of baptism, are born to spiritual life, should be intrusted to the fidelity and prudence of some one, from whom they may imbibe the precepts of the Christian religion, and the spirit of Christian piety; and thus grow up gradually in Christ, until, with the divine assistance, they at length arrive at the full growth of perfect manhood. This necessity must appear still more imperious, if we recollect, that the pastor, who is charged with the public care of his parish, has not sufficient time to undertake the private instruction of children in the rudiments of faith. For this very ancient practice, we have this illustrious testimony of St. Denis: "It occurred," says he, "to our divine leaders," (so he calls the Apostles,) "and they in their wisdom ordained, that infants should be introduced into the Church, in this holy manner—that their natural parents should deliver them to the care of some one well skilled in divine things, as to a master under whom, as a spiritual father and guardian of his salvation in holiness, the child may lead the remainder of his life."[3] The same doctrine is confirmed by the authority of Higinus.[4]

The Church, therefore, in her wisdom, has ordained that not only the person who baptizes, contracts a spiritual affinity with the person baptized, but also the sponsor with the God-child and its parents: so that marriage cannot be lawfully contracted by them, and if contracted, it is null and void.

Sponsors, of ancient institution, why instituted

Affinity contracted in baptism, what and between whom

---

[1] Tert. 1. de bapt. c. 18. et de coron. milit. cap. 3.   [2] 1 Pet. ii. 2.
[3] Dionys. de Eccl. Hier. c. 7. parte 3.
[4] Habetur de consec. dist. 5. cap. 100. et Leo, pp. ib. c. 101. et Conc. Mogunt. ib. cap. 101. et 30. q. 1.

The faithful are also to be taught the duty of sponsors; for such is the negligence with which the office of sponsor is treated in the Church, that its name only remains ; whilst few, if any, have the least idea of its sanctity. Let all sponsors then, at all times recollect that they are strictly bound to exercise a constant vigilance over their spiritual children, and carefully to instruct them in the maxims of a Christian life ; that they may approve themselves through life, such as their sponsors promised they should be, by the solemn ceremony of becoming sponsors. On this subject, the words of St. Denis demand attention : Speaking in the person of the sponsor, he says : " I promise, by my constant exhortations to induce this child, when he comes to a knowledge of religion, to renounce every thing opposed to his Christian calling, and to profess and perform the sacred promises, which he made at the baptismal font."[1] St. Augustine also says : " I most earnestly admonish you, men and women, who have become sponsors, to consider that you stood as sureties before God, for those whose sponsors you have undertaken to become."[2] And, indeed, it is the paramount duty of every man, who undertakes any office, to be indefatigable in the discharge of the duties which it imposes ; and he, who solemnly professed to be the teacher and guardian of another, should not abandon to destitution him whom he once received under his care and protection, as long as he should have occasion for either. Speaking of the duties of sponsors, St. Augustine comprises, in a few words, the lessons of instruction which they are bound to inculcate upon the minds of their spiritual children: " They ought," says he, " to admonish them to observe chastity, love justice, cherish charity ; and, above all, they should teach them the Creed, the Lord's prayer, the ten commandments, and the rudiments of the Christian religion."[3]

Hence, it is not difficult to decide, who are inadmissible as sponsors. To those, who are unwilling to discharge its duties with fidelity, or who cannot do so with care and accuracy, this sacred trust, no doubt, should not be confided. Besides, therefore, the natural parents, who, to mark the great difference that exists between this spiritual and the carnal bringing up of youth, are not permitted to undertake this charge, heretics, Jews particularly, and infidels, are on no account to be admitted to the office of sponsor. The thoughts and cares of these enemies of the Catholic Church, are, continually, employed in darkening, by falsehood, the true faith, and subverting all Christian piety.[4]

The number of sponsors is also limited by the Council of Trent, to one male or female ; or at most, to one male and one female ; because a number of teachers may confuse the order of discipline and instruction ; and also to prevent the multiplica-

[1] Loco sup. cit. 64.   [2] D. Aug. serm. 163. de temp. et ser. 215.
[3] Serm. 165, de temp. de cons. dist. 4. c. 120.
[4] 30 q. 1 cap. 1 D. Thom. p. 3. q. 67. art. 8. ad 2. ex Mogunt. Concil. de consec. dist. 4. cap. 104.

tion of affinities, which must impede a wider diffusion of society by means of lawful marriage.[1]

If the knowledge of what has been hitherto explained, be, as it is, of importance to the faithful, it is no less important to them to know, that the law of baptism, as established by our Lord, extends to all, in so much, that unless they are regenerated through the grace of baptism, be their parents Christians or infidels, they are born to eternal misery and everlasting destruction. The duty of the pastor, therefore, demands of him a frequent exposition of these words of the Gospel : " Unless a man be born again of water and the Holy Ghost, he cannot enter into the kingdom of God."[2] *The law ot baptism extends to all.*

That this law extends, not only to adults, but also to infants, and that the Church has received this its interpretation from Apostolic tradition, is confirmed by the authority and strengthened by the concurrent testimony of the Fathers. Besides, it is not to be supposed, that Christ our Lord, would have withheld the Sacrament of baptism, and the grace which it imparts from children, of whom he said : " Suffer the little children, and stay them not from coming unto me ; for the kingdom of heaven is for such"[3]—from children whom he embraced—upon whom he imposed hands—whom he blessed.[4] Moreover, when we read that an entire family was baptized by St. Paul,[5] children, who are included in their number, must, it is obvious, have also been cleansed in the purifying waters of baptism. Circumcision, too, which was a figure of baptism, affords a strong argument in proof of this primitive practice. That children were circumcised on the eighth day is universally known.[6] If, then, circumcision, " made by hand, in despoiling of the body of the flesh,"[7] was profitable to children, shall not baptism, which is the circumcision of Christ, not " made by hand," be also profitable to them ? Finally, to use the words of the Apostle, " if by one man's offence, death reigned through one ; much more they who receive abundance of grace, and of the gift, and of justice, shall reign in life through one, Jesus Christ."[8] If, then, through the transgression of Adam, children inherit the stain of primeval guilt, is there not still stronger reason to conclude, that the efficacious merits of Christ the Lord must impart to them that justice and those graces, which will give them a title to reign in eternal life ? This happy consummation baptism alone can accomplish.[9] The pastor, therefore, will inculcate the absolute necessity of administering baptism to infants, and of gra- *Infant Baptism proved.* I. II. III. IV. V. *Moral reflection.*

---

[1] De conc. dist. 4. c. 101. et Concil. Trid. sess. 14. c. 10. de refor. Matrim.

[2] John iii. 5. De his vide Clem. pp. epist. 4. in med. Aug. in Joan. tract. 13. et de Eccles. dogm. cap. 24. Amb. de iis qui myst. initiantur, c. 4. Concil Lateran. c. 1. Trid. sess. 7. can. 51. [3] Matt. xix. 14. [4] Mark x. 16.

[5] 1 Cor. i. 16. Acts xvi. 33. [6] Gen. xxi. 4. Lev. xii. 3. Luke i. 59 ; ii. 21

[7] Coloss. ii. 11. [8] Rom. v. 17.

[9] Conc. Trid. sess. 5. decret. de peccato Origin. et sess. 7. de baptism. cap. 12—14. Dionys. de Eccles. Hier. cap. 7. Cyprian. ep. 59. Aug. epist. 28. et lib. de 1. peccat. merit. c. 23. Chrys. hom. de Adamo de Evâ. Conc. Milevit. c. 2. et de consec. dist. 4. passim.

dually forming their tender minds to piety, by Christian precept; according to these admirable words of the Wiseman: "A young man according to his way, even when he is old, he will not depart from it."[1]

That when baptized they receive the mysterious gifts of faith cannot be matter of doubt; not that they believe by the formal assent of the mind, but because their incapacity is supplied by the faith of their parents, if the parents profess the true faith, if not, (to use the words of St. Augustine) "by that of the universal society of the saints;"[2] for they are said with propriety to be presented for baptism by all those, to whom their initiation in that sacred rite was a source of joy, and by whose charity they are united to the communion of the Holy Ghost.

The faithful are earnestly to be exhorted, to take care that their children be brought to the church, as soon as it can be done with safety, to receive solemn baptism: infants, unless baptized, cannot enter heaven, and hence we may well conceive how deep the enormity of their guilt, who, through negligence, suffer them to remain without the grace of the sacrament, longer than necessity may require; particularly at an age so tender as to be exposed to numberless dangers of death.[3]

With regard to adults who enjoy the perfect use of reason, persons, for instance, born of infidel parents, the practice of the primitive Church points out a different manner of proceeding: to them the Christian faith is to be proposed; and they are earnestly to be exhorted, allured, and invited to embrace it. If converted to the Lord God, they are then to be admonished, not to defer baptism beyond the time prescribed by the Church: it is written, "delay not to be converted to the Lord, and defer it not from day to day;"[4] and they are to be taught, that in their regard perfect conversion consists in regeneration by baptism.

Besides, the longer they defer baptism, the longer are they deprived of the use and graces of the other Sacraments, which fortify in the practice of the Christian religion, and which are

accessible through baptism only. They are also deprived of the inestimable graces of baptism, the salutary waters of which not only wash away all the stains of past sins, but also enrich the soul with divine grace, which enables the Christian to avoid sin for the future, and preserve the invaluable treasures of righteousness and innocence: effects which, confessedly, constitute a perfect epitome of a Christian life.[5]

On this class of persons, however, the Church does not confer this Sacrament hastily: she will have it deferred for a certain time; nor is the delay attended with the same danger as in the case of infants, which we have already mentioned: and should any unforeseen accident deprive adults of baptism, their

---

[1] Prov. xxii. 6.   [2] Ep. 23 ad Bon.
[3] Aug. lib. 3 de orig. anim. c. 9. et lib. 1. de pecc. merit. c. 2, et ep. 28.
[4] Eccl. v. 8.
[5] Tertul. lib. de pœnit. cap. 6. et de præscript. cap. 41. Cypr. epist. 13. de consec. dist. 4. c. 64. et 65. Aug. lib. de fide et operib. c. 9.

intention of receiving it, and their repentance for past sins, will
avail them to grace and righteousness. Nay, this delay seems   II.
to be attended with·some advantages.—The Church must take
particular care, that none approach this Sacrament, whose hearts
are vitiated by hypocrisy and dissimulation ; and, by the intervention of some delay, the intentions of such as solicit baptism,
are better·ascertained. In this wise precaution originated a decree, passed by the ancient councils, the purport of which was,
that Jewish converts, before admission to baptism, should spend
some months in the ranks of the Catechumens.· The candidate   III.
for baptism is, also, thus better instructed in the faith which he
is to profess, and in the morality which he is to practise ; and
the Sacrament, when administered with solemn ceremonies, on   IV
the appointed days of Easter and Pentecost only, is treated
with more religious respect

Sometimes, however, when there exists a just cause to ex- When not
clude delay, as in the case of imminent danger of death, its ad- to be defer-
ministration is not to be deferred ; particularly, if the person to red.
be baptized is well instructed in the mysteries of faith. This
we find to have been done by Philip, and by the prince of the
Apostles, when, without the intervention of any delay, the one
baptized the Eunuch of queen Candaces, the other, Cornelius,
as soon as they professed a willingness to embrace the faith
of Christ.' The faithful are, also, to be instructed in the necessary dispositions for baptism, that, in the first place, they
must desire and purpose to receive it ; for, as in baptism we die
- to sin and engage to live a new life, it is fit that it be administered to those, only, who receive it of their own free will and
accord, and is to be forced upon none. Hence, we learn from
holy tradition, that it has been the invariable practice of the
Church, to administer baptism to no individual, without previously asking him if he be willing to receive it.² This disposition even infants are presumed not to want—the will of the
Church, when answering·for them, is declared in the most explicit terms.

Insane persons, who are favoured with lucid intervals, and, Insane per-
during these lucid intervals, express no wish to be baptized, are sons, when
not to be admitted to baptism, unless in extreme cases when tized and
death is apprehended. In such cases, if, previously to their·in- when not.
sanity, they give intimation of a wish to be baptized, the Sa-
. crament is to be administered ; without such indication previously given, they are not to be admitted to baptism ;³ and the
same rule is to be followed with regard to persons in a state of
lethargy. But if they never enjoyed the use of reason, the authority and practice of the Church decide, that they are to be
baptized in the faith of the Church, on the same principle that
children are baptized, before they come to the use of reason.

---

¹ Acts viii. 36, and x. 48.
² Aug. lib. de pœn. medi. c. 2. D. Thom. 3. p. q. 63. § 7.
· ³ D. Thom. 3. p. q. 86. ar. 12.
  11*

Three conditions required in adults, faith, compunction, and a firm purpose of avoiding sin.

Besides a wish to be baptized, in order to obtain the grace of the Sacrament, faith, for the same reason, is also necessary: our Lord has said: " he that believes and is baptized shall be saved."[1] Another necessary condition is compunction for past sins, and a fixed determination to refrain from their future commission: should any one dare to approach the baptismal font, a slave to vicious habits, he should be instantly repelled, for what so obstructive to the grace and virtue of baptism, as the obdurate impenitence of those who are resolved to persevere in the indulgence of their unhallowed passions? Baptism should be sought with a view to put on Christ and to be united to him; and it is, therefore, manifest that he who purposes to persevere in sin, should be repelled from the sacred font, particularly if we recollect that none of those things which belong to Christ and his Church, are to be received in vain, and that, as far as regards sanctifying and saving grace, baptism is received in vain by him who purposes to live according to the flesh, and not according to the spirit.[2] As far, however, as regards the validity of the Sacrament, if, when about to be baptized, the adult intends to receive what the Church administers, he no doubt, validly receives the Sacrament. Hence, to the vast multitude, who, as the Scripture says, " being compunct in heart," asked him and the other Apostles what they should do, Peter answered : " Do penance and be baptized, every one of you ;"[3] and in another place : " Repent ye, therefore, and be converted, that your sins may be blotted out."[4] Writing to the Romans, St. Paul also clearly shows, that he who is baptized should entirely die to sin; and he therefore admonishes us, " not to yield our members as instruments of iniquity unto sin; but present ourselves to God, as those that are alive from the dead."[5]

Reflections
I.

Frequent reflection upon these truths cannot fail, in the first place, to fill the minds of the faithful with admiration of the infinite goodness of God, who, uninfluenced by any other consideration than that of his own tender mercy, gratuitously bestowed upon us, undeserving as we are, a blessing such as baptism

II.

—a blessing so extraordinary, so divine ! If, in the next place, they consider how spotless should be the lives of those, who have been made the objects of such singular munificence, they cannot fail to be convinced of the imperative obligation imposed upon them, to spend each day of their lives in such sanctity and religious fervour, as if it were that on which they had received the sacrament and were ennobled by the grace of baptism. To inflame their minds, however, with a zeal for true piety, the pastor will find no means more efficacious than an accurate exposition of the effects of baptism.

Effects of Baptism.

As, then, these effects are to afford matter of frequent instruction, that the faithful may be rendered more sensible of the high dignity to which they are raised by baptism, and may never suffer themselves to be degraded from its elevation by the

[1] Mark xvi. 14. [2] Rom. viii. 1. [3] Acts ii. 38. [4] Acts iii. 19. [5] Rom. vi. 13.

disguised artifices or open assaults of Satan, they are to be taught, in the first place, that such is the admirable efficacy of this sacrament as to remit original sin, and actual guilt however enormous. This its transcendant efficacy was foretold long before by Ezekiel, through whom God said: " I will pour upon you clean water, and you shall be cleansed from all your filthiness."[1] The Apostle also, writing to the Corinthians, after having enumerated a long catalogue of crimes, adds: " such you were, but you are washed, but you are sanctified."[2] That such was, at all times, the doctrine of the Catholic Church, is not matter of doubtful inquiry: " By the generation of the flesh," says St. Augustine, in his book on the baptism of infants, " we contract original sin only ; by the regeneration of the Spirit, we obtain forgiveness not only of original, but also of actual guilt."[3] St. Jerome, also, writing to Oceanus, says: " All sins are forgiven in baptism."[4] To obviate the possibility of doubt upon the subject, the Council of Trent, to the definitions of former Councils, has added its own distinct declaration, by pronouncing anathema against those, who should presume to think otherwise, or should dare to assert " that although sin is forgiven in baptism, it is not entirely removed, or totally eradicated ; but is cut away in such a manner, as to leave its roots still firmly fixed in the soul."[5] To use the words of the same holy Council: " God hates nothing in those who are regenerated, for in those who are truly buried with Christ, by baptism, unto death,[6] ' who walk not according to the flesh,' there is no condemnation :[7] putting off the old man, and putting on the new, which is created according to God,[8] they become innocent, spotless, innoxious, and beloved of God."

    That concupiscence, however, or the fuel of sin, still remains, as the Council declares in the same place, must be acknowledged :[9] but concupiscence does not constitute sin, for, as St. Augustine observes, " in children, who have been baptized, the guilt of concupiscence is removed, the concupiscence itself remains for our probation ;" and in another place: " the guilt of concupiscence is pardoned in baptism, but its infirmity remains."[10] Concupiscence is the effect of sin, and is nothing more than an appetite of the soul, in itself repugnant to reason. If unaccompanied with the consent of the will, or unattended with neglect on our part, it differs essentially from the nature of sin. This doctrine does not dissent from these words of St. Paul: " I did not know concupiscence, if the law did not say : ' thou shalt not covet.' "[11] The apostle speaks not of the importunity of concupiscence, but of the sinfulness of the interior

Marginal notes: first effect. — Concupiscence which remains after baptism, no sin.

---

[1] Ezek. xxxvi 25. [2] 1 Cor. vi. 11.
[3] Lib. 1. de pec. merit. et remiss. c. 15. [4] Epist. 85. ante medium.
[5] Sess. 5. can. 5. [6] Rom. vi. 4.
[7] Rom. viii. 1. [8] Eph. iv. 22. 24.
[9] De hoc effectu baptismi vide insuper Aug. lib. 1. contra duas ep. Pelag. c. 13. et l. 3. c. 5. in Enchir. c. 64. et lib. 1. de nupt. et concup. c. 25. item Greg. lib. 9 ep. 39. Concil Vienn. et Flor in mater. de Sacrament.
[10] Aug. l. 2. de pec. mer. remiss. c. 4. [11] Rom. vii. 7.

act of the will, in assenting to its solicitations. The same doctrine is taught by St. Gregory, when he says: "If there are any who assert that, in baptism, sin is but superficially effaced, what can savour more of infidelity than the assertion? By the Sacrament of Baptism sin is utterly eradicated, and the soul adheres entirely to God."[1] In proof of this doctrine he has recourse to the testimony of our Lord himself, who says in St. John: "He that is washed, needeth not but to wash his feet, but he is wholly clean."[2]

Figure of baptism illustrative of its first effect.

But should illustration be desired, an express figure and image of the efficacy of baptism will be found in the history of the leprosy of Naaman the Syrian, of whom the Scriptures inform us, that when he had washed seven times in the waters of the Jordan, he was so cleansed from his leprosy, that his flesh became "like the flesh of a child."[3] The remission of all sin, original and actual, is therefore the peculiar effect of baptism. That this was the object of its institution by our Lord and Saviour, is a truth clearly deduced from the testimony of St. Peter, to say nothing of the array of evidence that might be adduced from other sources: "Do penance," says he, "and be baptized every one of you, in the name of Jesus Christ, for the remission of your sins."[4]

Second effect of baptism.

But in baptism, not only is sin forgiven, but with it all the punishment due to sin is remitted by a merciful God. To communicate the virtue of the passion of Christ is an effect common to all the Sacraments; but of baptism alone does the Apostle say, that "by it we die and are buried together with Christ."[5] Hence the Church has uniformly taught, that to impose those offices of piety, usually called by the Fathers works of satisfaction, on him, who is to be cleansed in the salutary waters of baptism, would be derogatory in the highest degree to the dignity of this Sacrament.[6]

This doctrine not inconsistent with the practice of the primitive Church.

Nor is there any discrepancy between the doctrine here delivered and the practice of the primitive Church, which of old commanded the Jews, when preparing for baptism, to observe a fast of forty days. The fast thus imposed was not enjoined as a work of satisfaction: it was a practical lesson of instruction to those who were to receive the Sacrament; and one well calculated to impress upon their minds a deeper sense of the august dignity of a rite, of which they were not admitted to be participators, without devoting some time to the uninterrupted exercise of fasting and prayer.

Baptism gives no

But, although the remission by baptism of the punishments due to sin cannot be questioned, we are not hence to infer that

[1] L. 9. Reg. epist. 39.   [2] John xiii. 10.   [3] 4 Kings v. 14.
[4] Acts ii. 38. De concupiscentia remanente in baptizatis vide Aug. lib 1. de pec. merit. et remiss. c. 39. item lib. 1. contra duas Epist. Pelag. c. 13. lib. 3. c. 3. in medio, et lib. 1. de nupt. et concup. c. 23. et 25. item lib. 6. contra Julian. q. 5. et de verb. Apost. serm. 6.
[5] Rom. vi. 3, 4. Col. ii. 12.
[6] Quod poenæ peccatis debitæ remittantur in baptismo, vide Ambros. in c. 11. ad Rom. Aug. l. 1. de nupt. et concupis. c. 33. et in Ench. c. 4. D. Thom. p. 3. q. 69. art. 2. unde nec ulla est imponenda poenitentia. Greg. l. 7. regist. Epist. 24. et habetur de consecrat. distinct. 4. cap. ne quod absit. D. Thom. 3. p q. 68. art. 5.

it gives the offender an exemption from undergoing the punish- *exemption* ments awarded by the civil laws to public delinquency—that, *from the* for instance, it rescues from the hand of justice the man who is *of the civil* legally condemned to forfeit his life to the violated laws of his *law.* country. We cannot, however, too highly commend the religion and piety of those princes, who, on some occasions, remit the sentence of the law, that the glory of God may be the more strikingly displayed in his Sacraments. Baptism also remits all the punishment due to original sin in the next life, and this it does through the merits of our Lord Jesus Christ. By baptism, as we have already said, we die with Christ, "for if," says the Apostle, "we have been planted together in the likeness of his death, we shall be also in the likeness of his resurrection."[1]

Should it be asked why, after baptism, we are not exempt in *These in-* this life from these inconveniences, which flow from original *convenien-* sin, and restored by the influence of this Sacrament to that state *ginal sin,* of perfection, in which Adam, the father of the human race, *why not* was placed before his fall; for this two principal reasons are *removed* assigned: the first, that we, who by baptism are united to, and *by baptism.* become members of Christ's body, may not be more honoured than our head. As, therefore, Christ, our Lord, although clothed from his birth with the plenitude of grace and truth, was not divested of human infirmity, until, having suffered and died, he rose to the glory of immortality; it cannot appear extraordinary, if the faithful, even after they have received the grace of justification by baptism, are clothed with frail and perishable bodies; that after having undergone many labours for the sake of Christ, and having closed their earthly career, they may be recalled to life, and found worthy to enjoy with him an eternity of bliss.

The second reason why corporal infirmity, disease, sense of pain, and motions of concupiscence, remain after baptism, is, that in them we may have the germs of virtue from which we shall hereafter receive a more abundant harvest of glory, and treasure up to ourselves more ample rewards. When, with patient resignation, we bear up against the trials of this life, and aided by the divine assistance, subject to the dominion of reason the rebellious desires of the heart, we may and ought to cherish an assured hope, that the time will come when, if with the Apostle we shall have "fought a good fight, finished the course, and kept the faith, the Lord, the just judge, will render to us, on that day, a crown of justice, which is laid up for us."[2] Such seems to have been the divine economy with regard to *An illus-* the children of Israel: God delivered them from the bondage *tration.* of Egypt, having drowned Pharaoh and his host in the sea;[3] yet he did not conduct them immediately into the happy land of promise. He first tried them by a variety and multiplicity of sufferings; and when he afterwards placed them in possession of the promised land, he expelled from their native terri-

[1] Rom. vi. 5. [2] Tim. iv. 7. [3] Exod. xiv. 27

R

tories, the other inhabitants; whilst a few other nations, whom they could not exterminate, remained, that the people of God might never want occasions to exercise their warlike fortitude and valour.[1]

III.   To these we may add another consideration, which is, that if to the heavenly gifts with which the soul is adorned in baptism, were appended temporal advantages, we should have good reason to doubt whether many might not approach the baptismal font, with a view to obtain such advantages in this life, rather than the glory to be hoped for in the next; whereas the Christian should always propose to himself, not the delusive and uncertain things of this world, " which are seen," but the solid and eternal enjoyments of the next, " which are not seen."[3]

Baptism, the source of happiness to the Christian, even in this life.   This life, however, although full of misery, does not want its pleasures and joys. To us, who by baptism are engrafted as branches on Christ,[3] what source of purer pleasure, what object of nobler ambition, than, taking up our cross, to follow him as our leader, fatigued by no labour, retarded by no danger in pursuit of the rewards of our high vocation; some to receive the laurel of virginity, others the crown of doctors and confessors, some the palm of martyrdom, others the honours appropriated to their respective virtues? These splendid titles of exalted dignity none of us should receive, had we not contended in the race, and stood unconquered in the conflict.

Third effect of baptism.   But to return to the effects of baptism, the pastor will teach that, by virtue of this Sacrament, we are not only delivered from what are justly deemed the greatest of all evils, but are also enriched with invaluable goods. Our souls are replenished with divine grace, by which, rendered just and children of God, we are made coheirs to the inheritance of eternal life; for it is written, " he that believeth and is baptized, shall be saved;"[4] and the Apostle testifies, that the Church is cleansed, " by the laver of water, in the word of life."[5] But grace, according to the definition of the Council of Trent, a definition to which, under pain of anathema, we are bound to defer, not only remits sin, but is also a divine quality inherent in the soul, and, as it were a brilliant light that effaces all those stains which obscure the lustre of the soul, and invests it with increased brightness and beauty.[6] This is also a clear inference from the words of Scripture when it says, that grace is " poured forth,"[7] and also when it calls grace, " the pledge" of the holy Ghost.[8]

Fourth effect of baptism   The progress of grace in the soul is also accompanied by a most splendid train of virtues; and hence, when writing to Titus, the Apostle says: " He saved us by the laver of regeneration, and renovation of the Holy Ghost, whom he hath poured

---

[1] Judges iii. 1, 2.   [2] 2 Cor. iv. 17, 18.   [3] John xv. 2.
[4] Mark xvi. 16.   [5] Ephes. v. 26.
[6] Sess. 6, 7, de justifie.   [7] Tit. iii. 6.
[8] Eph. i. 14—2 Cor. i. 22, et v. 5.—Quid sit gratia de qua hic vide August. lib. 1. de peccat. merit. et remiss. c. 10, item de spiritu et litera, c. 28, versus finem. Bernard, serm. 1. in coena domini.

forth upon us abundantly, through Jesus Christ our Saviour;"[1] St. Augustine, in explanation of the words, "poured forth on us abundantly," says, "that is, for the remission of sins, and for abundance of virtues."[2]

By baptism we are also united to Christ, as members to their head: as, therefore, from the head proceeds the power by which the different members of the body are impelled to the proper performance of their peculiar functions; so from the fulness of Christ the Lord, are diffused divine grace and virtue through all those who are justified, qualifying them for the performance of all the offices of Christian piety.[3] *Fifth effect of baptism.*

We are, it is true, supported by a powerful array of virtues. It should not, however, excite our surprise if we cannot, without much labour and difficulty undertake, or, at least, perform acts of piety, and of moral virtue. If this is so, it is not because the goodness of God has not bestowed on us the virtues from which these actions emanate; but because there remains, after baptism, a severe conflict of the flesh against the spirit,[4] in which, however, it would not become a Christian to be dispirited or grow faint. Relying on the divine goodness, we should confidently hope, that by a constant habit of leading a holy life, the time will arrive, when "whatever things are modest, whatever just, whatever holy,"[5] will also prove easy and agreeable. Be these the subjects of our fond consideration; be these the objects of our cheerful practice; that "the God of peace may be with us."[6] *Difficulty of practising virtue even after baptism, whence it arises, how to be combated.*

By baptism, moreover, we are sealed with a character that can never be effaced from the soul, of which, however, it were here superfluous to speak at large, as in what we have already said on the subject, when treating of the Sacraments in general, the pastor will find sufficient matter on the subject, to which he may refer.[7] *Sixth effect of baptism.*

But as from the nature and efficacy of this character, it has been defined by the Church, that this Sacrament is on no account to be reiterated, the pastor should frequently and diligently admonish the faithful on this subject, lest at any time they may err on a matter of such moment. The doctrine which prohibits the reiteration of baptism, is that of the Apostle, when he says: "One Lord, one faith, one baptism."[8] Again, when exhorting the Romans, that dead in Christ by baptism, they lose not the life which they received from him, he says: "In *Baptism not to be repeated, and why.*

[1] Tit. iii. 5, 6.
[2] De hoc effectu baptismi vide Chrysost. hom. ad Neoph. et baptis. Damas. lib. 2, de fide Orthod. c. 36. Lactant. lib. 3, Divin. Instit. c. 25. Aug. Epist 23, ad Bonifac. item lib. 1, de peccat. merit. et remiss. c. 29, Prosp. l. 2, de vocat. Gent. c. 9.
[3] Quod per baptismum Christi capiti ut membra connectamur, vide August. epist. 23, item lib. 1, de pec. meritis et remiss. c. 16. Prosp. de voc. Gent. l. 1, c. 9. Bernard. serm. 1. in Cœna Dom. D. Thom. 3. p. q. 69. art. 5.
[4] Gal. v. 17.   [5] Philip. iv. 8.
[6] 2 Cor. xiii. 11.—Vide hæc de re Aug. lib. v. contra Julian. c. 2, et 5. item de peccat. merit. et remiss. lib. 1. c. 3.
[7] Vide Aug. lib. 6, contra Donatist. cap. 1. et in epist. Joan. tract. 5. Trid. sess. 7.
[8] Eph. iv. 5.

that Christ died to sin, he died once;"[1] he seems clearly to signify that as Christ cannot die again, neither can we die again by baptism. Hence the Church openly professes that she believes " one baptism ;" and that this accords with the nature and object of the Sacrament appears from the very idea of baptism, which is a spiritual regeneration. As then, according to the laws of nature, we are born but once, and " our birth," as St. Augustine observes, " cannot be repeated,"[2] so, in the supernatural order, there is but one spiritual regeneration, and, therefore, baptism can never be administered a second time.[3]

Not repeated, even when administered conditionally. Nor let it be supposed, that this Sacrament is repeated by the Church, when she admits to the baptismal font those of whose previous baptism reasonable doubts are entertained, making use of this form : " if thou art already baptized, I baptize thee not again ; but if thou are not already baptized, I baptize thee in name of the Father, and of the Son, and of the Holy Ghost :" in such cases baptism is not to be considered as repeated (its repetition would be an impiety), but as holily, because conditionally administered.

When to to be administered conditionally. In this, however, the pastor should use particular precaution, in order to avoid certain abuses which are of almost daily occurrence, to the no small irreverence of this Sacrament. There are those who think that they commit no sin by the indiscriminate administration of conditional baptism : if a child is brought before them, they imagine that inquiry as to its previous baptism is unnecessary, and accordingly proceed, without delay, to administer the Sacrament. Nay more, having ascertained that the child received private baptism, they hesitate not to repeat its administration conditionally, making use, at the same time, of the solemn ceremonies of the Church ! Such temerity incurs the guilt of sacrilege, and involves the minister in what theologians call an " irregularity." It has been authoritatively decided by pope Alexander, that the conditional form of baptism is to be used only when, after due inquiry, doubts are entertained of the validity of the previous baptism ;[4] and in no other case can it ever be lawful to administer baptism a second time, even conditionally.[5]

Seventh effect of baptism. Besides the many other advantages which accrue to us from baptism, we may look upon it as the last, to which all the rest seem to be referred, that it opens to us the portals of Heaven, which sin had closed against our admission. All these effects, which are wrought in us by virtue of this Sacrament, are distinctly marked by the circumstances which, as the Gospel relates, accompanied the baptism of our Saviour. The heavens

[1] Rom. vi. 10.   [2] In Joan. tract. 11.
[3] Hæc de re vide Trid. Sess. 7. de baptismo, can. 11. et 13. item Concil. Cartha. can. 1, Vien. ut habetur in Clem. 1. lib. de sum. Trinit. D. August. tract. 11. in Joan. Beda in capite 3, Joan. Leo Mag. epist. 37, et 39, D. Thom. 3. p. q. 66, a. 9.
[4] Lib. 1. Decretal. tit. de baptismo. c. de quidem.
[5] De irregularitate cujus hic est mentio, vid. apostat. et reit. baptism. c. ex litterarum, et de Consecr. dist. 4. c. eos qui. et lib. 3. decretal. de baptismo et ejus effectu. c. de quibus.

were opened and the Holy Ghost appeared descending upon Christ our Lord, in form of a dove;[1] by which we are given to understand, that to those who are baptized are imparted the gifts of the Holy Spirit, that to them are unfolded the gates of Heaven, opening to them an entrance into glory; not, it is true, immediately after baptism, but in due season, when freed from the miseries of this life, which are incompatible with a state of bliss, they shall exchange a mortal for an immortal life.

These are the fruits of baptism, which, as far as regards the efficacy of the Sacrament, are, no doubt, common to all; but as far as regards the dispositions with which it is received, it is no less certain that all do not participate equally of these heavenly gifts and graces. Efficacy of the Sacrament common to all. not so its gifts and graces.

It now remains to explain, clearly and concisely, what regards the prayers, rites, and ceremonies of this Sacrament. To rites and ceremonies may, in some measure, be applied what the Apostle says of the gift of tongues, that it is unprofitable to speak, unless he who hears understands.[2] They present an image, and convey the signification of the things that are done in the Sacrament; but if the people understand not their force and significancy, they can be of very little advantage to them. To make them understood, therefore, and to impress the minds of the faithful with a conviction that, although not of absolute necessity, they are of very great importance, and challenge great veneration, are matters which solicit the zeal and industry of the pastor. This, the authority of those by whom they were instituted, who were, no doubt, the Apostles, and also the object of their institution, sufficiently prove. That ceremonies contribute to the more religious and holy administration of the Sacraments, serve to exhibit to the eyes of the beholder a lively picture of the exalted and inestimable gifts which they contain, and impress on the minds of the faithful a deeper sense of the boundless beneficence of God, are truths as obvious as they are unquestionable.[3] The prayers, rites, and ceremonies of baptism, to be explained.

But that in his expositions the pastor may follow a certain order, and that the people may find it easier to recollect his instructions, all the ceremonies and prayers which the Church uses in the administration of baptism, are to be reduced to three heads. The first comprehends such as are observed before coming to the baptismal font—the second, such as are used at the font—the third, those that immediately follow the administration of the Sacrament. Reduced to three heads

In the first place, then, the water to be used in baptism should be previously prepared: the baptismal water is consecrated with the oil of mystic unction; and this cannot be done at all times, but, according to ancient usage, on the vigils of certain festivals, which are justly deemed the greatest and the most holy solem- I. The water, consecration of.

[1] Matth. iii. 16. [2] 1 Cor. xiv. 2.
[3] De eis ritibus vide Dion. cap. 2. de Eccles. Hier. Clem. Epist. 3. Tertul. lib. de corona milit. et de baptism. passim. Origen. hom. 12. in num. Cypr. Epist. 70. item vide de consecr. dist. 4.

12

nities in the year, and on which alone, except in cases of necessity, it was the practice of the ancient Church to administer baptism.[1]   But although the Church, on account of the dangers to which life is continually exposed, has deemed it expedient to change her discipline in this respect, she still observes with the greatest solemnity the festivals of Easter and Pentecost, on which the baptismal water is to be consecrated.

The person to be baptized stands at the church door.   After the consecration of the water, the other ceremonies that precede baptism, are next to be explained.   The person to be baptized is brought or conducted to the door of the church, and is forbidden to enter, as unworthy to be admitted into the house of God, until he has cast off the yoke of the most degrading servitude of Satan, devoted himself unreservedly to Christ, and pledged his fidelity to the just sovereignty of the Lord Jesus.[2]

Catechetical instruction.   The priest then asks what he demands of the Church of God; and having received the answer, he first instructs him catechetically, in the doctrines of the Christian faith, of which a profession is to be made in baptism.[3]   This practice of thus communicating instruction originated, no doubt, in the precept of our Lord, addressed to his Apostles: " Go ye into the whole world, and teach all nations, baptizing them in the name of the Father, and of the Son, and of the Holy Ghost, teaching them to observe all things whatsoever I have commanded you ;"[4] words from which we may learn that baptism is not to be administered until, at least, the principal truths of religion are explained. But as the catechetical form consists of question and answer; if the person to be instructed be an adult, he himself answers the interrogatories; if an infant, the sponsor answers according to the prescribed form, and enters into a solemn engagement for the child.

The exorcism.   The exorcism comes next in order: it consists of words of sacred and religious import, and of prayers; and is used to expel the devil, to weaken and crush his power. To the exorcism are added other ceremonies, each of which, being mystical, has its clear and proper signification.[5] **The salt.** When, for instance, salt is put into the mouth of the person to be baptized, it evidently imports, that by the doctrines of faith, and by the gift of grace, he shall be delivered from the corruption of sin, shall experience a relish for good works, and shall be nurtured with the food of divine wisdom.[6] **The sign of the cross.** Again, his forehead, eyes, breast, shoulders, ears, are signed with the sign of the cross, to declare, that by the mystery of baptism, the senses of the person baptized are opened and strengthened, to enable him to

---

[1] Cypr. epist. 70. item Basil. de Spiritu S. c. 27. et de consec. dist. 4. c. in Sabbato.
[2] Tertul. de corona milit. c. 3. Cyril. Hierosol. Catech. 8,
[3] Clem. Rom. epist. 3. Aug. de fide et oper. c. 9.
[4] Mark xvi. 15.   Matth. xxviii. 19, 20.
[5] De exorcismis vide Tertul. de præscript. c. 41. Cypr. epist. 2. Aug. lib. 2. de gratia Dei et peccat. orig. cap. 40. et lib. 2. de Nupt. et concupis. cap. 26. optat. lib. 4. contra Parmenianum.
[6] Bed. in lib. Esdræ, c. 9. Isid. lib. 2. de offic. eccl. c. 20. et Aug. lib. 1. contom. c. 11

receive God, and to understand and observe his commandments.[1]
His nostrils and ears are next touched with spittle, and he is
then immediately admitted to the baptismal font: by this ceremony we understand that, as sight was given to the blind man,
mentioned in the Gospel, whom the Lord, having spread clay
on his eyes, commanded to wash them in the waters of Siloe;[2]
so by the efficacy of holy baptism, a light is let in on the mind,
which enables it to discern heavenly truth.[3] *The spittle.*

After the performance of these ceremonies, the person to be
baptized approaches the baptismal font, at which are performed
other rites and ceremonies, which present a summary of the
obligations imposed by the Christian religion. In three distinct
interrogatories, he is formally asked by the minister of religion,
" dost thou renounce Satan ?" " and all his works ?" " and all
his pomps ?"—to each of which he, or the sponsor in his name,
replies in the affirmative. Whoever, then, purposes to enlist
under the standard of Christ, must, first of all, enter into a sacred and solemn engagement to renounce the devil and the
world, and, as his worst enemies, to hold them in utter detestation.[4] *II. The renunciation.*

He is next anointed with the oil of catechumens on the
breast and between the shoulders—on the breast, that by
the gift of the Holy Ghost he may lay aside error and ignorance, and receive the true faith ; for " the just man liveth by
faith"[5]—on the shoulders, that by the grace of the Holy Spirit
he may be enabled to shake off negligence and torpor, and engage actively in the performance of good works ; for " faith
without works is dead."[6] *The oil of catechumens.*

Next, standing at the baptismal font, he is interrogated by
the minister of religion in these words : " Dost thou believe
in God, the Father Almighty ?" to which is answered ; " I believe ;" a like interrogatory is proposed with regard to the other
articles of the creed, successively ; and thus is made a solemn
profession of faith. These two engagements, the renunciation
of Satan and all his works and pomps, and the belief of all the
articles of the creed, including, as they do, both faith and practice, constitute, it is clear, the whole force and discipline of the
law of Christ.[7] *The profession of faith.*

When baptism is now about to be administered, the priest
asks him if he will be baptized ; to which an answer in the affirmative being given by him, or, if an infant, by the sponsor, the
priest performs the ablution, " in the name of the Father, and
of the Son, and of the Holy Ghost." As man, by yielding the
assent of his will to the wicked suggestions of Satan, fell under
a just sentence of condemnation ; so God will have none en- *The will of the person to be baptized asked, and when ascertained, baptism is administered.*

[1] De signo crucis vide Tertul. lib. de resurr. carn. Basil. lib. de spiritu Sancto
Chrys. contra gentes et alios.   [2] John ix. 7.
[3] De saliva Am. lib. 1. de sacram. 1. et de iis qui myst. init. c. 1. et de consecr
distinct. 4. c. postea.
[4] Tertul. lib. de coron. mil. c. 13. et de spectac. c. 4. et de Idol. c. 6. Cypr. epist. 7. 54.
[5] Gal. iii. 11.   [6] James ii. 26.
[7] Cyril. Hier. Catech. 2 et 3.

rolled in the number of his soldiers, but those whose service is voluntary; that by a willing obedience to his commands they may obtain eternal salvation.

III. The oil of chrism.
After the person has been baptized, the priest anoints with chrism the crown of his head, thus giving him to understand, that from the moment of his baptism, he is united as a member to Christ, his head, and ingrafted on his body; and that he is, therefore, called a Christian, from Christ, as Christ is so called from Chrism. What the Chrism signifies, the prayers offered by the priest, as St. Ambrose observes, sufficiently explain.[1]

The white garment.
On the person baptized the priest then puts a white garment, saying, "receive this white garment, which mayest thou carry unstained before the judgment-seat of our Lord Jesus Christ; that thou mayest have eternal life. Amen." Instead of a white garment, infants because not formally dressed, receive a white kerchief, accompanied with the same words. According to the doctrine of the Holy Fathers this symbol signifies the glory of the resurrection to which we are born by baptism, the brightness and beauty with which the soul, when purified from the stains of sin, is invested, and the innocence and integrity which the person who has received baptism, should preserve through life.[2]

The burning light.
To signify that faith received in baptism, and inflamed by charity, is to be fed and augmented by the exercise of good works, a burning light is next put into his hand.

The name, its utility, its selection.
Finally, a name is given, which should be taken from some person, whose eminent sanctity has given him a place in the catalogue of the Saints: this similarity of name will stimulate to the imitation of his virtues and the attainment of his holiness; and we should hope and pray that he who is the model of our imitation, may also, by his advocacy, become the guardian of our safety and salvation. Hence we cannot mark in terms too strong, our disapprobation of the conduct of those who, with a perverse industry, search for, and whose delight it is to distinguish their children by, the names of heathens; and what is still worse, of monsters of iniquity, who, by their profligate lives, have earned an infamous notoriety. By such conduct they practically prove, how little they regard a zeal for Christian piety, who so fondly cherish the memory of impious men, as to wish to have their profane names continually echo in the ears of the faithful.

Recapitulation.
This exposition of baptism, if given by the pastor, will be found to embrace, almost every thing of importance, which regards this Sacrament. We have explained the meaning of the word "baptism," its nature and substance, and also the parts of which it is composed—we have said by whom it was instituted

---

[1] Lib. 1. de Sacram. Dionys. Eccl. Hierar. c. 3. Cyril. Hieros. Catech. 3. Basil lib. de Spiritu Sancto, c. 27.

[2] Dionys. loco citato. Amb. de iis qui myst. init. c. 8.

[3] De hoc cereo vide Gregor. Nazian. serm. de bapt. Gregor. Turon. lib. 5. cap 11. Niceph. hist. Eccle. lic. 3. c. 12.

—who are the ministers necessary to its administration—who should be, as it were, the tutors, whose instructions should sustain the weakness of the person baptized—to whom baptism should be administered, and how they should be disposed—what are the virtue and efficacy of the Sacrament. Finally, we have developed, at sufficient length for our purpose, the rites and ceremonies that should accompany its administration. The pastor will recollect that all these instructions have principally for object, to induce the faithful to direct their constant attention and solicitude to the fulfilment of the sacred and inviolable engagements into which they entered at the baptismal font, and to lead lives not unworthy the sanctity of the name and profession of Christian.

ON THE SACRAMENT OF CONFIRMATION.

If ever there was a time that demanded the assiduity of the pastor in explaining the Sacrament of Confirmation, it is doubtless the present, when there are found in the Church of God many by whom it is altogether omitted; whilst very few study to derive from it the fruit of divine grace, which its worthy reception imparts. That this divine blessing, therefore, may not seem through their fault, and to the serious injury of their immortal souls, to have been conferred in vain, the faithful are to be instructed, on Whitsunday, and on such other days as the pastor shall deem convenient, in the nature, efficacy, and dignity of this Sacrament; so as to make them sensible that not only is it not to be neglected, but that it is to be approached with the greatest reverence and devotion. *(margin: Urgent necessity of explaining the Sacrament of confirmation in these days.)*

To begin therefore with its name, the pastor will inform the faithful that this Sacrament is called Confirmation, because, if no obstacle is opposed to its efficacy, the person who receives it, when anointed with the sacred chrism by the hand of the bishop, who accompanies the unction with these words: "I sign thee with the sign of the cross, and confirm thee with the chrism of salvation, in the name of the Father, and of the Son, and of the Holy Ghost," is confirmed in strength by receiving new virtue, and becomes a perfect soldier of Christ.[1] *(margin: Why called confirmation.)*

That confirmation has all the conditions of a true Sacrament has been at all times, the doctrine of the Catholic Church, as Pope Melchiades,[2] and many other very holy and ancient pontiffs expressly declare. The truth of this doctrine St. Clement could not have confirmed in stronger terms than when he says. "All should hasten, without delay to be born again to God, and then to be sealed by the bishop, that is, to receive the seven-fold *(margin: Confirmation a Sacrament.)*

[1] Conc. Aur. c. 3, item Flor.
[2] Epist. ad Episcop. Hispan. c 2. ep. 4, ante finem.

gift of the Holy Ghost; for, as we have learned from St. Peter, and as the other Apostles taught in obedience to the command of our Lord, he who contumeliously and not from necessity, but voluntarily neglects to receive this Sacrament, cannot possibly become a perfect Christian."[1] This same doctrine has been confirmed, as may be seen in their decrees, by the Urbans, the Fabians, the Eusebius's, pontiffs who, animated with the same spirit, shed their blood for the name of Christ. It is also fortified by the unanimous testimony of the Fathers, amongst whom Denis the Areopagite, bishop of Athens, teaching how to consecrate and make use of the holy ointment, says: " The priest clothes the person baptized with a garment emblematic of his purity, in order to conduct him to the bishop; and the bishop signing him with the holy and divine ointment, makes him partaker of the most holy communion."[2] Of such importance does Eusebius of Cæsarea deem this Sacrament, that he hesitates not to say, that the heretic Novatus could not receive the Holy Ghost, because, having received baptism, he was not, when visited by severe illness, sealed with the sign of chrism.[3] On this subject we might adduce testimonies the most conclusive from St. Ambrose in his book on the Initiated,[4] and from St. Augustine in his works against the epistles of the Donatist Petilian: so convinced were they, that no doubt could exist as to the reality of this Sacrament, that they not only taught the doctrine, but confirmed its truth by many passages of Scripture, the one applying to it these words of the Apostle: " Grieve not the Holy Spirit of God, whereby you are sealed unto the day of redemption,"[5] the other, these words of the Psalmist: " like the precious ointment on the head, that ran down upon the beard of Aaron,"[6] and also these words of the same Apostle, " The charity of God is poured forth in our hearts by the Holy Ghost who is given to us."[7]

Confirmation, although said by Melchiades to have a most intimate connexion with baptism,[8] is yet an entirely different Sacrament: the diversity of the grace which each Sacrament confers, and the diversity of the external sign employed to signify that grace, obviously constitute them different Sacraments. As by the grace of baptism we are begotten to newness of life, and by that of confirmation grow to full maturity, " having put away the things of a child,"[9] we can hence sufficiently comprehend that the same difference which exists in the natural order between birth and growth, exists also in the supernatural, be-

Confirmation entirely different from baptism. I.

---

[1] Habes decreta horum Pontificum de consecrat. dist. 5.
[2] S. Dionysius de Eccles. Hierar. c. 2.   [3] Lib. 6. histor. cap. 43.
[4] Lib. de iis qui myst. initiantur. c. 7, lib. 2, c. 104.
[5] Eph. iv. 30.   [6] Psalm cxxxii. 2.
[7] Rom. v. 5.—Confirmationem esse sacramentum habes insuper ex Ambros. de Sacr. lib. 3, c. 2, lib. de Spiritu Sancto, c. 6 et 7, item Aug. de Trinit. lib. 15, c. 26, et in epist. Joan tract. 3 et 6, et in Psalmis 26, et ante hos omnes —Tertul. lib. de Resurr. car. Cypr. epist. 7.—Origen, hom. 9, in Levit. Hieron. contr. Lucif. Cyril. Hieros. Catech. 3.
[8] Epist. ad Episc. Hisp. in med.   [9] 1 Cor. xii. 11

tween baptism which regenerates, and confirmation which imparts full growth and perfect spiritual strength.

Again, if the new difficulties which the soul has to encounter, demand the aid of a new and distinct Sacrament, it is obvious that as we have occasion for the grace of baptism to stamp upon the soul the impress of the true faith, so it is of the utmost advantage that a new grace fortify us with such intrepidity of soul, that no danger, no dread of pains, tortures, death, have power to deter us from the profession of the true faith. Hence, Pope Melchiades marks the difference between them with minute accuracy in these terms: "In baptism," says he, "the Christian is enlisted into the service, in confirmation he is equipped for battle; at the baptismal font the Holy Ghost imparts the plenitude of innocence, in confirmation the perfection of grace; in baptism we are regenerated to life, after baptism we are fortified for the combat; in baptism we are cleansed, in confirmation we are strengthened; regeneration saves by its own efficacy those who receive baptism in peace, confirmation arms and prepares for the conflict."[1] These are truths not only recorded by other Councils, but specially defined by the Council of Trent, and we are therefore no longer at liberty not only to dissent from, but even to entertain the least doubt regarding them.[2]

But, to impress the faithful with a deeper sense of the sanctity of this Sacrament, the pastor will make known to them by whom it was instituted; a knowledge the importance of which with regard to all the Sacraments, we have already pointed out. He will, accordingly, inform them that not only was it instituted by our Lord Jesus Christ, but as St. Fabian Bishop of Rome testifies, the chrism and the words used in its administration were also appointed by him: a fact of easy proof to those who believe confirmation to be a Sacrament, for all the sacred mysteries are beyond the power of man, and could have been instituted by God alone.[3]

Of the component parts of the Sacrament, and, first, of its matter, we now come to treat. The matter of confirmation is chrism, a word borrowed from the Greek language, and which, although used by profane writers to designate any sort of ointment, is appropriated, by ecclesiastical usage, to signify ointment composed of oil and balsam, and solemnly consecrated by the episcopal benediction. A mixture of oil and balsam, therefore, constitutes the matter of confirmation; and this mixture of different elements at once expresses the manifold graces of the Holy Ghost, and the excellence of this sacrament. That such is its matter the Church and her councils have uniformly taught; and the same doctrine has been handed down to us by St. Denis, and by many other fathers of authority too great to be questioned, particularly by Pope Fabian,[4] who testifies that the Apostles received the composition of chrism from our Lord, and

II.

Instituted by Christ.

Its matter, Chrism.

---

[1] Loco citato.
[2] Laod. can. 48, Meld. c. 6. Florent. et Constant. Trid. sess. 7.
[3] Epist. 2, initio.   [4] Epist. 3. ad Episc. Orient.

Propriety of Chrism as its matter.

transmitted it to us.[1] To declare the effects of Confirmation, no sacramental matter could have been more appropriate than chrism: oil, by its nature unctuous and fluid, expresses the plenitude of divine grace which flows from Christ the head, through the Holy Ghost, and is poured out, "like the precious ointment on the head, that ran down upon the beard of Aaron, to the skirt of his garment;"[2] for "God anointed him with the oil of gladness, above his fellows,"[3] and "of his fulness we all have received."[4] Balsam, too, the odour of which is most grateful, signifies that the faithful, made perfect by the grace of Confirmation, diffuse around them, by reason of their many virtues, such a sweet odour that they may truly say with the Apostle: "We are the good odour of Christ unto God."[5] Balsam has also the quality of preserving incorrupt whatever it embalms; a quality well adapted to express the virtue of this Sacrament; prepared by the heavenly grace infused in Confirmation, the souls of the faithful may be easily preserved from the corruption of sin.

Chrism, why consecrated, and by bishops only.

The chrism is consecrated with solemn ceremonies, by the bishop. That this its solemn consecration is in accordance with the instructions of our Lord, when at his last supper he committed to his Apostles the manner of making chrism, we learn from Pope Fabian, a man eminently distinguished by his sanctity, and by the glory of martyrdom.[6] Indeed, reason alone demonstrates the propriety of this consecration; for in most of the other sacraments, Christ so instituted the matter as to impart to it holiness; it was not only his will that water should constitute the matter of the Sacrament of Baptism, when he said: "Unless a man be born again of water and the Holy Ghost, he cannot enter the kingdom of God;"[7] but he also, at his own baptism, imparted to it the power of sanctifying; "The water of baptism," says St. Chrysostome, "had it not been sanctified by contact with the body of our Lord, could not cleanse the sins of believers."[8] As, therefore, our Lord did not consecrate by using the matter of confirmation, it becomes necessary to consecrate it by holy and devout prayer, which is the exclusive prerogative of bishops, who are constituted the ordinary ministers of this Sacrament.

Form of the Sacrament of Confirmation.

The other component part of this Sacrament, that is to say, its form, comes next to be explained. The faithful are to be admonished that when receiving Confirmation, they are, on hearing the words pronounced by the bishop, earnestly to excite themselves to sentiments of piety, faith, and devotion, that on their part no obstacle may be opposed to the heavenly grace of the Sacrament. The form of Confirmation consists of these words: "I SIGN THEE WITH THE SIGN OF THE CROSS, AND I

[1] Vid. Aug. in Ps. 44. vers. 9. et lib. 13. de Trinit. cap. 26. Greg. in 1. cap. can. Conc. Laod. cap. 48. et Carth. 2 c. 2. et 3. c. 39. Dionys. de Eccl.-Hierar. c. 2. et 4. De oleo vide Ambr. in Ps. 118 et lib. de Spiritu Sancto, cap. 3. Cyprian Epist. 70.
[2] Ps. cxxxii. 2.　　[3] Ps. xliv. 8.　　[4] John i. 16.　　[5] 2 Cor. ii. 15.
[6] S. Fab. papa, uti supra.　　[7] John iii. 5.
[8] Hom. 4. oper. imperf. et habetur de consec. dist. 4. c. Nunquid.

CONFIRM THEE WITH THE CHRISM OF SALVATION, IN THE NAME OF THE FATHER, AND OF THE SON, AND OF THE HOLY GHOST." Were we to acknowledge the incompetency of reason to establish the truth and strict propriety of this form, the authority of the Catholic Church, by which it has been at all times taught and recognised, would alone be sufficient to dispel all doubt on the subject: judging of it, however, by the standard of reason, we arrive at the same conclusion. The form of the Sacrament should embrace whatever is necessary to explain its nature and substance; with regard to the nature and substance of Confirmation, there are three things that demand particular attention, the divine power, which, as a primary cause, operates in the Sacrament; the spiritual strength which it imparts to the faithful unto salvation; and lastly, the sign impressed on him who is to engage in the warfare of Christ. The words " in the name of the Father, and of the Son, and of the Holy Ghost," with which the form closes, sufficiently declare the first; the second is comprised in the words, "I confirm thee with the chrism of salvation; and the words, " I sign thee with the sign of the cross," with which the form opens, convey the third.

To whom principally, is intrusted the administration of this Sacrament, is a matter to which the pastor will also call the attention of the faithful. There are many, according to the prophet, who run and yet are not sent; and hence the necessity of informing the faithful who are its true and legitimate ministers, in order that they may really receive the Sacrament and grace of Confirmation.[1] That bishops alone are the ordinary ministers of this sacrament, is the doctrine of Scripture; we read in the Acts of the Apostles, that when Samaria had received the Gospel, Peter and John were sent to them and prayed for them, that they might receive the Holy Ghost; " for he was not yet come upon any of them, but they were only baptized, in the name of the Lord Jesus."[2] Here we find that he who administered baptism, having only attained the degree of deacon, had no power to administer confirmation; its administration was reserved to a more elevated order of the ministry, that is, to the Apostles alone. Whenever the sacred Scriptures speak of this Sacrament, they convey to us the same truth. We have also the clearest testimony of the Fathers, and, as may be seen in the decrees of their Popes, of Urban, of Eusebius, of Damasus, of Innocent, and of Leo. In confirmation of the same doctrine, we may also add that St. Augustine loudly complains of the corrupt practice which prevailed in the Churches of Egypt and Alexandria in his day, a practice according to which priests presumed to administer the Sacrament of Confirmation."[3]

The bishop its ordinary minister.

---

[1] Trid. Sess. 23. c. 4. et can. 7.   [2] Acts viii. 14. 16.
[3] Episcopum ministrum esse ordinarium Confirmationis tradunt Urbanus Papa Epist. ad omnes Christianos in fine; Eusebius Papa Epist. 3. ad Episcop. Tusciæ et Campaniæ Damasus Papa, Epist. 4. ad Pros. et cæteros Episc. Orthod. circa med. Innocentius Papa Epist. 1. ad Veren. c. 3. Leo Papa Epist. 88. ad Germanæ et Galliæ. Episc. Melchiades Papa, Epist. ad Episc. Hispaniæ. Clemens item Papa,

Propriety of restricting Confirmation to bishops.

To illustrate the propriety of restricting the exercise of this function to the episcopal office, the following comparison may be found not inappropriate. As in the construction of an edifice, the artisans, who are inferior agents, prepare and dispose mortar, lime, timber, and the other materials; whilst, however, the completion of the work belongs to the architect; so in like manner should Confirmation, which is as it were the completion of the spiritual edifice, be administered by no other than episcopal hands.

A sponsor required, and why.

In Confirmation, as in Baptism, a sponsor is required. If the gladiator who presents himself as a combatant, has occasion for the skill and address of a master, to direct him by what thrusts and passes he may, without endangering his own safety, despatch his antagonist, how much more necessary to the faithful is a guide and instructer, when, sheathed as it were in the panoply of this sacrament, they engage in the spiritual conflict, in which eternal salvation is to reward the success of the victor. Sponsors therefore are, with great propriety, required in the administration of this Sacrament also; and the same affinity

Consequent affinity.

which, as we have already shown, is contracted in Baptism, impeding the lawful marriage of the parties, is also contracted in Confirmation.[1]

The faithful to be instructed in the age and dispositions for Confirmation.

To pass over in silence those who have arrived at such a degree of impiety, as to have the hardihood to contemn and despise this Sacrament; since in receiving Confirmation it frequently happens, that the faithful betray inconsiderate precipitation or unpardonable neglect, it is the duty of the pastor to make known the age and dispositions which its sanctity demands.

Confirmation instituted for the use of all the faithful.

They are, in the first place, to be informed that this Sacrament is not essential to salvation; but that although not essential, it is not therefore to be omitted: on the contrary, in a matter so holy, through which the gifts of God are so liberally bestowed, the greatest care should be taken to avoid all neglect; and what God proposed for the common sanctification of all, all should desire with intense earnestness.[2] Describing this admirable effusion of the Holy Spirit, St. Luke says: "And suddenly there came a sound from heaven, as of a mighty wind coming, and it filled the whole house, where they were sitting:" and a little after, "and they were all filled with the Holy Ghost."[3] From these words we may infer, that as the house in which they were assembled, was a type and figure of the church, the Sacrament of Confirmation, which had its existence for the first time on that day, is intended for the use of all the faithful. This is also an easy inference from the nature of the Sacrament: Confir-

Epist 4. Concil Wormaciense, c. 8. et Florent de Sacram. Horum summorum Pontificum Epist. habentur in tomis Conciliorum fere omnes in primo juxta cujusque ætatem. Vide insuper August. in quæst. novi Testam. quæst. 42.
[1] Trid. Sess. 24. c. 2. de reform. matrim.
[2] De consec. dist. 5. c. 2. et 3. item Conc. Aurel. c. 3. Hugo de sanct. Vict. de Sacram. lib. 2. p. 7. c. 39. [3] Acts ii. 2. 4.

mation is necessary for those who have occasion for spiritual increase, and hope to arrive at religious perfection; but to this all should aspire, for as Nature intends that all her children should grow up and reach full maturity, although her wishes are not always realized; so it is the earnest desire of the Catholic Church, the common mother of all, that those whom she has regenerated by Baptism, may be brought to perfect maturity in Christ. This happy consummation can be accomplished only through the mystic unction of Confirmation; and hence it is clear, that this Sacrament is equally intended for all the faithful.

It is to be observed, that the Sacrament of Confirmation may be administered to all, as soon as they have been baptized; but, until children shall have reached the use of reason, its administration is inexpedient. If not postponed to the age of twelve, it should therefore be deferred until at least that of seven. Confirmation has not been instituted as necessary to salvation; but to enable us to be armed and prepared, whenever we may be called upon, to fight for the faith of Christ; and for this conflict no one will consider children, not yet arrived at the use of reason, fit subjects. *The proper age for its reception.*

From what has been said, it follows, that persons of mature years who are to be confirmed, must, if they hope to receive the grace of this Sacrament, not only bring with them faith and devotion, but also be pierced with heartfelt compunction for the grievous sins into which they may have had the misfortune to fall. The pastor, therefore, will labour to induce them to have previous recourse to the tribunal of penance, will endeavour to excite them to fasting and other exercises of devotion, and will exhort them to the revival of that laudable practice of the ancient Church, of receiving the Sacrament of confirmation fasting.[1] To induce the faithful to enter into these dispositions would appear no difficult task, if they but learn to appreciate the blessings and extraordinary effects which flow from this Sacrament. *Dispositions for receiving it worthily.*

The pastor therefore will teach, that in common with the other sacraments, Confirmation, unless some obstacle be opposed by the receiver, imparts new grace. We have already shown, that it is the property of these sacred and mystic signs, at once to indicate and produce grace; and as we cannot imagine grace and sin to coexist in the soul, it follows, as a necessary consequence, that it also remits sin. *Effects of confirmation. I.*

Besides these properties, common alike to this and the other Sacraments, it is the peculiar characteristic of confirmation to perfect the grace of baptism: those who are initiated into the Christian religion, share, as it were, the tenderness and infirmity of new-born infants; but they afterwards gather strength from the Sacrament of chrism, to combat the assaults of the world, the flesh, and the devil, and are confirmed in faith to confess and glorify the name of our Lord Jesus Christ. From this last *II*

[1] D. Th. p. 3. q. 72. a. ad. 2 Conc. Aur. c. 2.

An error
refuted.

mentioned circumstance it arose, no doubt, that the Sacrament was distinguished by the name of confirmation. This its name is not, as some with equal ignorance and impiety have imagined, derived from the supposed circumstance of baptized persons, when grown to maturity, formerly presenting themselves before the bishop to confirm their adherence to the faith of Christ, which they had embraced in baptism; an opinion, according to which, confirmation would not seem to differ from catechetical instruction. Of such a practice no proof can be adduced, no vestige traced; and this sacrament is called Confirmation, because by virtue of it, God confirms in us what was commenced in baptism, and conducts to the perfection of solid Christian virtue.[1]

III.

Not only does this Sacrament confirm; it also increases divine grace in the soul : " The Holy Ghost," says Melchiades, " who descends with salutary influence on the waters of baptism, imparts the plenitude of grace to innocence : in confirmation, the same Holy Ghost gives an increase of divine grace, and not only an increase, but an increase after a wonderful manner.[2] This extraordinary efficacy of confirmation, the Scriptures beautifully express by a metaphor : " stay you in the city," says our Lord speaking of this Sacrament, " until you be indued with power from on high."[3]

Its efficacy
illustrated.

To show the divine efficacy of this Sacrament, (and this, no doubt, will have great influence on the minds of the faithful) the pastor has only occasion to explain the effects which it produced on the Apostles themselves. Before, and even at the very time of the passion, so weak and listless were they, that no sooner was our Lord apprehended, than they all fled ;[4] and Peter, who was destined to be the rock and foundation of the Church, and who had displayed an unshaken constancy, and an intrepid spirit to be dismayed by the appearance of no danger,[5] was so terrified at the voice of one weak woman, as to deny once, and again, and a third time, that he was a disciple of Jesus Christ.[6] Even after the resurrection they remained, through fear of the Jews, shut up in a house, the doors being closed.[7] But how extraordinary the revolution ! On the day of Pentecost, filled with the grace of the Holy Ghost, they fearlessly, and in defiance of all danger, proclaim the Gospel, not only through Judea, but throughout the world ;[8] they deem it the greatest happiness, to be thought worthy to suffer contumely, chains, tortures, and crucifixion itself, for the name of Christ.[9]

IV.

Confirmation has also the effect of impressing a character ; and hence, as we said before, with regard to baptism, and as will be more fully explained in its proper place, with regard to

---

[1] Trid. Sess. 7. can. 1 de confir.
[2] De cons. dist. 5. c. Spiritus. Euseb. Emis. hom. in die Pent.
[3] Luke xxiv. 49.   [4] Matth. xxvi. 56.
[5] Matth. xvi. 18—26. 51.   [6] Matth. xxvi. 70. 72. 74.
[7] John xx. 19.   [8] Acts ii. 1.
[9] Acts v. 41.

orders, it is on no account to be administered a second time.
If these things are frequently and accurately explained, it is almost impossible that the faithful, knowing the utility and dignity of this Sacrament, should not use every exertion to receive
it with piety and devotion.[1]

The rites and ceremonies used in the administration of this
Sacrament, now remain lightly to be glanced at: the advantages of
this explanation the pastor will at once see, by reverting to what
we have already said on this subject, in its proper place. The
forehead of the person to be confirmed is anointed with sacred
chrism; for in this Sacrament the Holy Spirit pours himself
into the souls of the faithful, and imparts to them increased
strength and courage, to enable them in the spiritual contest, to
fight manfully, and to resist successfully their most implacable
foes. They are therefore told, that henceforward, they are not
to be deterred by fear or shame, feelings of which the countenance is the principal index, from the open confession of the
name of Christ.[2] Besides, the mark by which the Christian is
distinguished from all others, as the soldier is distinguished by
his peculiar military badges, should be impressed on the fore-
head, the most dignified and conspicuous part of the human
form.

Its rites and ceremonies explained.

Unction of the fore-head.

Sign of the cross.

The festival of Pentecost was also chosen for its solemn administration, because the Apostles were then strengthened and
confirmed by the power of the Holy Ghost;[3] and also to remind
the faithful, by the recollection of that supernatural event, of
the number and magnitude of the mysteries contained in that
sacred unction.

Why admi-nistered at Pentecost.

The person, when confirmed, receives a gentle slap on the
cheek from the hand of the bishop, to remind him, that as a
courageous champion, he should be prepared to brave with unconquered resolution, all adversities for the name of Christ.

The gentle slap on the cheek.

Finally, he receives the kiss of peace, to give him to understand that he has been blessed with the fulness of divine grace,
and with that "peace which surpasseth all understanding."[4]
These things will be found to contain a summary of the exposition to be given by the pastor on the Sacrament of confirmation; but let them be delivered, not so much in the cold language
of formal instruction, as in the burning accents of fervent piety;
so as to penetrate into the minds, and inflame the hearts of the
faithful.

The kiss of peace.

[1] Confirmationem non esse iterandam, vide de Consec. dist. 5. c. dictum est, ut cap. de hom. D. Thom. p. 3. q. 72. art. 5.
[2] Rhaban. lib. 1. de instit. cleric. c. 30. et habetur de consec. dist. 5, c. novies. Aug. in Ps. 141, D. Thom. 3. p. q. 71. art. 9.
[3] Acts ii. 2.
[4] Phil. iv. 7.

ON THE SACRAMENT OF THE EUCHARIST.

Dignity of the Eucharist, matter of frequent exposition, to deter from its abuse.

OF all the sacred mysteries bequeathed to us by our Lord, as unfailing sources of grace, there is none that can be compared to the most holy Sacrament of the Eucharist; for no crime, therefore, is there reserved by God a more terrible vengeance than for the sacrilegious abuse of this adorable Sacrament, which is replete with holiness itself.[1] The Apostle, illumined with wisdom from above, clearly saw and emphatically announced these awful consequences, when having declared the enormity of their guilt, "who discern not the body of the Lord," he immediately added, "therefore are there many infirm and weak among you, and many sleep."[2] That the faithful, therefore, deeply impressed with the divine honour due to this heavenly Sacrament, may derive from its participation, abundant fruit of grace, and escape the just anger of God, the pastor will explain with indefatigable diligence, all those things which seem best calculated to display its majesty.

Its institution.

Following the example of St. Paul, who declares to the Corinthians what he had received from the Lord, the pastor will begin by explaining to the faithful the circumstances of its institution: these he will find thus clearly recorded by the Evangelist—our Lord, who "having loved his own, loved them to the end,"[3] to give them some admirable and divine pledge of this his love, aware that the hour was come when he should pass out of this world to the Father, by an effect of wisdom which transcends the order of nature, devised a means of being always present with his own. Having celebrated the feast of the paschal lamb with his disciples, that the figure might give way to the reality, the shadow to the substance, "Jesus took bread, and giving thanks to God, blessed and brake, and gave to his disciples, and said, take ye and eat: This is my body, which shall be delivered for you: this do for the commemoration of me: and taking the chalice also after he had supped, he said, this chalice is the New Testament in my blood: this do, as often as you shall drink it in commemoration of me."[4]

Why called "the Eucharist."

Satisfied that language could supply no one word sufficiently comprehensive to give full expression to the dignity and excellence of this Sacrament, sacred writers have endeavoured to express it by a variety of appellations. It is sometimes called "The Eucharist," a word which may be translated, "the good grace," or "the thanksgiving:" the propriety of the one appears from two considerations: the Eucharist gives a foretaste of eter-

---

[1] Dionys. de Eccl. Hier. c. 6. et de consec. dist. c. 2. nihil in.
[2] 1 Cor. xi. 30.　　　　[3] John xiii. 1.
[4] Matth. xxvi. 26.　Mark xiv. 22.　Luke xxii. 19.　1 Cor. xi. 24.　De Euch. institutione vide Trid. Sess. 13, c. 2, de Euch. Leo serm. 7, de Pasc. c. 3, Euseb. Emiss. hom. 4, et habetur de consec. dist. 2. 1. quin corpus.

nal life, of which it is written: " The grace of God is life everlasting :"[1] it also contains Christ our Lord, the true grace, and
the source of all heavenly gifts. The other translation is no less
appropriate, for when we offer this most spotless victim, we
render to God a homage of infinite value, in return for all the
benefits which we have received from his bounty, particularly for the inestimable treasure of grace bestowed on us
in this Sacrament. The word " thanksgiving," also accords
with the conduct of our Lord, when instituting this mystery:
" Taking bread, he brake it, and *gave thanks*."[2] David too,
contemplating the grandeur of this mystery, says, " He hath
made a remembrance of his wonderful works, being a merciful
and gracious Lord : he hath given food to them that fear him ;"[3]
but he had premised these words of *thanksgiving* : " His work
is praise and magnificence."[4]

It is also frequently called "The Sacrifice," of which we
shall treat more at large in the subsequent part of this exposition. It is also called " Communion," a word borrowed from
the Apostle, when he says : " The chalice of benediction which
we bless, is it not the communion of the blood of Christ ?
And the bread which we break, is it not the participation of the
body of the Lord ?"[5] " This Sacrament," to use the words of
Damascene, " unites us to Christ, and renders us partakers of
his flesh, and of his divinity, reconciles us to each other in the
same Christ, and consolidates us as it were into one body."[6]
Hence it is also called the Sacrament of peace and charity ;
giving us to understand how unworthy the name of Christians
are they who indulge in enmity ; and that hatred, discord, and
strife are to be banished the society of the faithful, as their
worst enemies ; an obligation which becomes still more imperative when we reflect that in the daily oblation of the sacred
mysteries, we profess to study with watchful solicitude, to preserve peace and charity inviolate. Sacred writers also frequently
call it " The Viaticum," as well because it is the spiritual food
by which we are supported during our mortal pilgrimage : as
also, because it prepares for us a passage to eternal happiness
and everlasting glory. Hence, in accordance with the ancient
practice of the Church, none of the faithful are suffered to depart this life without being previously fortified with this living
bread from heaven. The name of " The Supper," has also
been sometimes given to this Sacrament by the most ancient
Fathers, in imitation of the Apostle,[7] because it was instituted

The Eucharist designated by other appellations: " sacrifice," " communion."

"The Sacrament of peace and charity."

" Viaticum."

"The Supper."

[1] Rom. vi. 23.
[2] Mark xxvi. 26. xiv. 22. Luke xxii. 19. 1 Cor. xi. 24.
[3] Psalm cx. 4, 5.
[4] Psalm cx. 3. Chrysost. hom. 24 in 1 ad Cor. ad hæc verba, Calix benedic-
tionis. Cypr. lib. de lapsis. Ambr. lib. 5. de Sacr. c. 3. D. Th. p. 3, q. 73, a. 4.
[5] 1 Cor. x. 16.
[6] Damasc. lib. 4. de fid. orthod. c. 4. Vid. Iren. lib. 5, c. 7, Chrys. hom. 44 et 45
in Joan. Cyrill. in lib. 7. in Joan. c. 13. Cyrill. Hier. Catech. 4, Aug. Tract. 26, in
Joan. Trid. sess. 13. de Euchar. in præf. Concil. Nicœn. 21, Cart. 4, c. 77 et 26, q
6, passim.   [7] 1 Cor. xi. 20.

The Eucharist to be consecrated and received, fasting.

by our Lord at the saving mystery of The Last Supper.[1] This circumstance, which regards the time of its institution, does not however, justify the inference that the Eucharist is to be consecrated or received by persons not fasting: the salutary practice of consecrating and receiving it fasting, introduced, as ancient writers record, by the Apostles, has always been observed in the Church.[2]

A Sacrament.

Having thus premised an explanation of the names by which this Sacrament is distinguished, the pastor will teach that it has all the qualities of a true Sacrament, and is one of the seven which have been at all times recognised and revered by the Catholic Church. Immediately after the consecration of the chalice, it is called "a mystery of faith;" and to omit an almost innumerable host of sacred writers, vouchers of the same doctrine, that the holy Eucharist is a Sacrament is demonstrated by the very nature of a Sacrament. It has sensible and outward signs: it signifies and produces grace in the soul; and all doubt as to its institution by Christ is removed by the Apostle and the Evangelists. These circumstances, combining as they do to establish the truth of the Sacrament, supersede the necessity of pressing the matter by further argument.[3]

The name of Sacrament, given to many things in the Eucharist, strictly applies to the species only.

That in the Eucharist there are many things to which sacred writers have occasionally given the name of Sacrament, the pastor will particularly observe: sometimes its consecration, sometimes its reception, frequently the body and blood of our Lord which are contained in it, are called the Sacrament; because, as St. Augustine observes, this Sacrament consists of two things, the visible species of the elements, and the invisible flesh and blood of our Lord Jesus Christ.[4] We also say that this Sacrament is to be adored,[5] meaning of course, the body and blood of our Lord. But all these, it is obvious, obtain the name of Sacrament in its less strict sense: the species of bread and wine, strictly speaking, constitute the Sacrament.

The Eucharist differs from the other Sacraments.

I.

II.

The great points of difference between this and the other Sacraments are easily understood; the other Sacraments are perfected by the use of their matter, that is, by their administration; baptism, for instance, becomes a Sacrament when the ablution has been performed: the Eucharist is constituted a Sacrament by the sole consecration of the elements, and when preserved in a pyxis, or deposited in a tabernacle, under either species, it ceases not to be a Sacrament. In the material elements of which the other Sacraments are composed, no change takes place; in baptism, for instance, the water, in confirmation, the chrism, lose not in their administration, the nature of water and of oil; whilst in the Eucharist, that which before

[1] Cypr. de cœna. Domini.   [2] Aug. Epist. 188, c. 6.
[3] Aug. lib. 3. de Trinit. cap. 4, et 1. 20, contra Faust. cap. 13, Ambr. lib. 1. de sacram. cap. 2. Trid. sess. 13. de Euch. c. 5. D. Thom. 3. p. q. 73. art. 1.
[4] De Catec. erud. lib. 5. c. 16. August. hic ad sensum potius quam ad verba citatus; sed lege hac de materia librum Lanfranci contra Berengarium: constat. 23, tantum capitibus: vide de consecr. dist. 2. fere tota.
[5] Trid. sess. 15, de Euch. cap. 5. et can. 6.

consecration was bread and wine, becomes, after consecration, really and substantially the body and blood of our Lord.

But although in the Eucharist the sacramental matter consists of two elements, that is, of bread and wine, yet, guided by the authority of the Church, we profess that they are elements, not of two, but of one Sacrament. This is proved by the very number of the Sacraments, which, according to the doctrine of apostolic tradition, and the definitions of the Councils of Lateran,[1] Florence,[2] and Trent,[3] is confined to seven. It also follows from the nature of the Holy Eucharist; the grace which it imparts renders us one mystic body; and to accord with what it accomplishes, the Eucharist must constitute but one Sacrament—one, not by consisting of one element, but by signifying one thing. Of this the analogy which exists between this our spiritual food, and the food of the body, furnishes an illustration. Meat and drink, although two different things, are used only for one object, the sustenance of the body; so should the two different species of the Sacrament, to signify the food of the soul, be significant of one thing only, and constitute therefore but one Sacrament. The justness of this analogy is sustained by these words of our Lord: "My flesh is meat indeed, and my blood is drink indeed."[4]

The Sacramental matter composed of two elements, but constitutive of one Sacrament.

What the Sacrament of the Eucharist signifies, the pastor will also carefully explain, that on beholding the sacred mysteries, the faithful may also, at the same time, feed their souls on the contemplation of heavenly things. This Sacrament, then, is significant of three things—the passion of Christ, a thing past—divine grace, a thing present—and eternal glory, a thing future. It is significant of the passion of Christ: "This do," says our Lord, "for a commemoration of me."[5] "As often," says the Apostle, "as you shall eat this bread, and drink the chalice, you shall show the death of the Lord, until he come."[6]

The Eucharist signifies three things.

I.

It is significant of divine grace, which is infused, on receiving this sacrament, to nurture and preserve the soul.[7] As by Baptism, we are begotten to newness of life, and by Confirmation, are strengthened to resist Satan, and to profess openly the name of Christ; so, by the Sacrament of the Eucharist, are we spiritually nurtured and supported. It is also significant of eternal glory, which, according to the divine promises, is reserved for us in our celestial country. These three things, distinguished as they are by different times, past, present, and future, the Holy Eucharist, although consisting of different species, marks as significantly as if they were but one.

II.

III.

To consecrate the Sacrament validly, to instruct the faithful in that of which it is the symbol, and to kindle in their souls an ardent desire of possessing the invaluable treasure which it signifies, it is of vital importance that the pastor make himself

The matter of this Sacrament.

---

[1] Ex Conciliis citatis Lateranense generale sub Innocent II.—Non numerat qui lem distincte septem Sacramenta, sed ex variis Canonib. satis clare colliguntur.
[2] Florent. in doct. de sacrem.   [3] Trid. sess 7, can. 1.   [4] John vi. 56.
[5] Luke xxii. 19.   [6] 1 Cor. xi. 26.   [7] Tertul. de Resur. carnis, c. 8.

acquainted with its matter. The matter of this Sacrament is
two-fold, consisting of wheaten bread, and of wine pressed from
the grape, mixed with a little water. The first element, then,
(of the latter we shall treat hereafter) is bread: as the Evangelists, Matthew,[1] Mark,[2] and Luke,[3] testify : "Christ our Lord,"
say they, "took bread into his hands, blessed, and brake it,
saying, THIS IS MY BODY ;" and according to St. John, he denominated himself bread in these words : "I am the living bread
that came down from heaven."[4]

**The sacra-
mental
bread,
wheaten.**
As, however, there are different sorts of bread, composed of
different materials, such as wheat, barley, pease, or made in different manners, such as leavened and unleavened ; it is to be
observed that, with regard to the former, the sacramental matter, according to the words of our Lord, should consist of
wheaten bread ; for when we simply say bread, we mean, according to common usage, "wheaten bread."[5] This is also distinctly declared by a figure of the Holy Eucharist in the Old
Testament: the Lord commanded that the loaves of proposition,
which prefigured this Sacrament, should be made of "fine
flour."[6]

**Also, un-
leavened.**
As, therefore, wheaten bread alone is the proper matter of
this Sacrament, a doctrine handed down by Apostolic tradition,
and confirmed by the authority of the Catholic Church ; it may
also be inferred from the circumstances in which the Eucharist
was instituted, that this wheaten bread should be unleavened.
It was consecrated and instituted by our Lord, on the first day
of unleavened bread, a time when the Jews were prohibited by
**Objection
answered.**
the law, to have leavened bread in their houses.[7] Should the
words of the Evangelist St. John, who says that all this was
done before the Passover, be objected, the objection is one of
easy solution : by "the day before the Pasch,"[8] St. John understands the same day, which the other Evangelists designate
"the first day of unleavened bread." He had for object, principally, to mark the *natural* day, which does not commence
until sunrise ; and the first *natural* day of the Pasch, therefore,
being Friday, "the day before the Pasch" means Thursday,
on the evening of which the festival of unleavened bread began, and on which our Lord celebrated the Pasch and instituted the Holy Eucharist. Hence, St. Chrysostome understands
the first day of unleavened bread to be the day, on the evening of
which the unleavened bread was to be eaten.[9] The peculiar
propriety of the consecration of unleavened bread, to express
that integrity and purity of heart, with which the faithful should
approach this Sacrament, we learn from these words of the

---

[1] Matt. xxvi. 26.   [2] Mark xiv. 22.   [3] Luke xxii. 19.
[4] John vi. 41. Vide de consecr. dist. 2. c. 1. et 2. et 55. ubi habes de hac materia
decreta Alexandr. Pap. in 1. Epist. ad omnes Orthodoxos et Cypr. lib. 2. Epist. 3. et
Ambr. l. 4. de Sacram. c. 4. vide etiam Iren. l. 4. c. 34. et l. 5. c. 2.
[5] D. Th. 3 p. 9. 74. c. 3.   [6] Lev. xxiv. 5.
[7] Matt. xxvi. 17. Mark xiv. 12. Luke xxii. 7. Vide l. 3. decretal. tit. de cele-
brat Missarum, c. ult. ubi habes auctoritatam Honorii Pap. 3.
[8] John xiii. 1.   [9] In Math. hom. 83.

Apostle : "Purge out the old leaven, that you may be a new paste, as you are unleavened ; for Christ our Pasch is sacrificed. Therefore, let us feast not with the old leaven, not with the leaven of malice and wickedness, but with the unleavened bread of sincerity and truth."[1]

This property of the bread, however, is not to be considered so essential as that its absence must render the Sacrament null : both sorts, leavened and unleavened, are called by the common name, and have each the nature and properties, of bread.[2] No one, however, should on his own individual authority, have the temerity to depart from the laudable rite, observed in the Church to which he belongs ; and such departure is the less warrantable in priests of the Latin Church, commanded, as they are, by authority of the supreme Pontiff, to celebrate the sacred mysteries with unleavened bread only.[3] With regard to the first element of this Sacrament, this exposition will be found sufficiently comprehensive. We may, however, observe in addition, that the quantity of bread to be used is not determined, depending as it does upon the number of communicants, a matter which cannot be defined.

We come next to treat of the second element of this Sacrament, which forms part of its matter, and consists of wine, pressed from the grape, mingled with a little water. That our Lord made use of wine, in the institution of this Sacrament, has been at all times the doctrine of the Catholic Church. He himself said : "I will not drink, henceforth, of this fruit of the vine, until that day."[4] On these words of our Lord, St. Chrysostome observes : "Of the fruit of the vine, which certainly produces wine, not water ; as if he had it in view, even at so early a period, to crush by the evidence of these words, the heresy which asserted that water alone is to be used in these mysteries."[5] With the wine used in the sacred mysteries, the Church of God, however, has always mingled water, because, as we know on the authority of councils and the testimony of St. Cyprian, our Lord himself did so ;[6] and also because this admixture renews the recollection of the blood and water which issued from his sacred side. The word water we also find used in the Apocalypse, to signify the people,[7] and, therefore, water mixed with wine signifies the union of the faithful with Christ their head. This rite, derived from apostolic tradition, the Catholic Church has at all times observed. The propriety of mingling water with the wine rests, it is true, on authority so grave, that to omit the practice would be to incur the guilt of mortal sin ; however, its sole omission would be insufficient to render the Sacrament null. But care must be taken not only to mingle water with the wine, but also to mingle it in small quan-

Margin notes:
Unleavened bread not essential.

The second element, wine of the grape, mingled with a little water.

---

[1] 1 Cor. v. 7, 8.   [2] Concil Florent. sess. ult.
[3] Lib. 2. decret. de celebr. miss. c. final.   [4] Matt. xxvi. 29. Mark xiv. 25.
[5] Hom. 83. in Matth.
[6] Cyp. lib. 1. epist. 3. Trid. sess. 22. de sacrif. miss. c. 7. et can. 9.
[7] Apoc. xvii. 15.

tity; for in the opinion of ecclesiastical writers, the water is changed into wine. Hence, these words of Pope Honorius: "A pernicious abuse has prevailed, for a long time, amongst you, of using in the holy sacrifice a greater quantity of water than of wine; whereas in accordance with the rational practice of the Universal Church, the wine should be used in much greater quantity than the water."[1] We have now treated of the only two elements of this Sacrament; and although some dared to do otherwise, many decrees of the Church justly enact that no celebrant offer any thing but bread and wine.[2]

Peculiar aptitude of these elements.
I.

We now come to consider the aptitude of these two elements to declare those things of which they are the sensible signs. In the first place, they signify Christ, the true life of the world; for our Lord himself has said: " My flesh is meat indeed, and my blood is drink indeed."[3] As, therefore, the body of our Lord Jesus Christ nourishes to eternal life those who receive it with purity and holiness, with great propriety is this Sacrament composed principally of those elements which sustain life; thus giving the faithful to understand that the soul is nurtured with grace by a participation of the precious body and blood of

II.

Christ. These elements serve also to prove the dogma of the real presence. Seeing, as we do, that bread and wine are every day changed by the power of nature, into human flesh and blood, we are, by the obvious analogy of the fact, the more readily induced to believe that the substance of the bread and wine is changed, by the celestial benediction, into the real body

III.

and blood of Christ.[4] This admirable change also contributes to illustrate what takes place in the soul. As the bread and wine, although invisibly, are really and substantially changed into the body and blood of Christ, so are we, although interiorly and invisibly, yet really renewed to life, receiving in the Sacrament of the Eucharist, the true life. Moreover, the body

IV.

of the Church, although one, and undivided, consists of the union of many members, and of this mysterious union nothing is more strikingly illustrative than bread and wine. Bread is made from many grains, wine is pressed from many grapes, and thus are we too, although many, closely united by this mysterious bond of union, and made as it were one body.

The form to be used in the consecration of the bread, proved from Scripture;

The form to be used in the consecration of the bread, we now come to explain; not, however, with a view that the faithful should be taught these mysteries, unless necessity require it, (a knowledge of them is obligatory on ecclesiastics alone) but to obviate the possibility of mistakes on the part of the celebrant, through ignorance of the form; mistakes, were they to occur, as discreditable to the minister, as derogatory to the dignity of the divine mysteries. From the Evangelists Matthew and Luke, and also from the Apostle, we learn that the form of

---

[1] Habetur l. 3. Decretal, de cel. miss. c. 13.
[2] Vid. de consecr. dist. 2. c. 1. 2. et seq.   [3] John vi. 56.
[4] Damas. l. 4. de fid. orthod. c. 14.

the Sacrament consists in these words: "THIS IS MY BODY." We read that when they had supped, "Jesus took bread, and blessed and brake and gave to his disciples, saying: take and eat, THIS IS MY BODY;"[1] and this form of consecration, made from the use of by Jesus Christ, has been uniformly and inviolably ob- Fathers served in the Catholic Church. The testimonies of the Fathers and Councils; in proof of its legitimacy, may be here omitted; to enumerate them would prove an endless task. The decree of the Council of Florence to the same effect, because of easy access to all, it is also unnecessary to cite. The necessity of every other proof is superseded by these words of the Saviour: "This do for a commemoration of me."[2] This command of our Lord embraces not only what he did, but also what he said, and has more immediate reference to his own words uttered not less for the purpose of effecting, than of signifying what they effected.[3]

That these words constitute the form is easily proved from from rea- reason alone. The form of a Sacrament is that which signifies son. what is accomplished in the Sacrament: what is accomplished in the Eucharist, that is the conversion of the bread into the true body of our Lord, the words "this is my body," signify and declare; they therefore constitute the form. The words of the Evangelist, "he blessed," go to support this reasoning. They are equivalent to saying: "taking bread, he blessed it, saying, this is my body."[4] The words, "take and eat," it is true, precede the words "this is my body," but they evidently express the use, not the consecration of the matter, and cannot, therefore constitute the form. But although not necessary to the consecration of the Sacrament, they are not, however, on any account, to be omitted. The conjunction "for," has also a place amongst the words of consecration; otherwise it would follow that if the Sacrament were not to be administered to any one, it should not, or even could not be consecrated; whereas, that the priest by pronouncing the words of our Lord, according to the institution and practice of the Church, truly consecrates the proper matter of the Sacrament, although it should after-wards happen never to be administered, admits not the least shadow of doubt.

The form of the consecration of the wine, the other element The form of this Sacrament, is, for the reasons assigned with regard to the to be used bread, necessary to be accurately known, and clearly understood in the con- secration of by the priest. It is firmly to be believed that the form of con- the wine, secrating the chalice is comprehended in these words: "THIS proved IS THE CHALICE OF MY BLOOD OF THE NEW AND ETERNAL TESTA- from Scrip- ture; MENT: THE MYSTERY OF FAITH: WHICH SHALL BE SHED FOR YOU, AND FOR MANY TO THE REMISSION OF SINS."[5] These words

---

[1] Matt. xxvi. 26. Mark xiv. 22. Luke xxii. 19. 1 Cor. xi. 24.
[2] Luke xxii. 19. In decret. de sacram. item Trid. sess. 13. c. 1.
[3] Quod ad Patres attinet, vid. Amb. l. 4. de sacram. c. 4. et 5. Chrys. hom. de prodit. Judæ. Aug. l. 3. de Trinit. c. 4. Iren. l. 4. contr. hær. c. 34. Orig. lib. 8. contr. Celsum. Hesich. l. 6. in Levit. c. 22. Cyril. Alex. epist. ad Calosorum episcop. Tertul. l. 4. contr. Marc. in Hiear. epist. l.
[4] Matt. xxvi. 26.   [5] Decretal. l. 3. de celeb. miss. c. 6.

are for the most part taken from Scripture. Some of them, however, have been preserved in the Church by apostolic tradition. The words "this is the chalice" are taken from St. Luke,[1] and are also mentioned by the Apostle.[2] The words that immediately follow, "of my blood, or my blood of the new testament, which shall be shed for you, and for many to the remission of sins," are taken in part from St. Luke,[3] and in part from St. Matthew.[4] The words "and eternal," and also the words "the mystery of faith," have been transmitted to us by holy tradition, the interpreter and guardian of Catholic unity. Of the legitimacy of this form we cannot entertain a shadow of doubt, if we attend to what has been already said of the form used in the consecration of the bread. The form to be used in the consecration of this element, should, confessedly, consist of words signifying that the substance of the wine is changed into the blood of our Lord: this the words already cited clearly declare; and therefore, they alone exclusively constitute the form.

from tradition,

from reason.

They also express certain admirable fruits produced by the blood of Christ, which was shed on Calvary, fruits which belong in a special manner to this Sacrament. Of these one is admission into the eternal inheritance to which we have acquired a right by "the new and everlasting testament:"[5] another is admission to righteousness by "the mystery of faith," for "God hath proposed" Jesus "to be a propitiation through faith in his blood, to the showing of his justice, that he himself may be just, and the justifier of him, who is of the faith of Jesus Christ:"[6] a third is the remission of sin.[7]

Expresses three effects of the blood of the Saviour.
I.

II.

III.

But as the words of consecration are replete with mysteries, and are most appropriate in their application to our present subject, they demand a more minute consideration. When, therefore, it is said: "This is the chalice of my blood,"[8] these words are to be understood to mean: "This is my blood which is contained in this chalice." The mention of "the chalice," at the moment of its consecration, to be the drink of the faithful, is peculiarly appropriate: without its mention as the vessel in which it is contained, the words: "This is my blood," would not seem sufficiently to designate this supernatural species of drink. Next follow the words: "of the New Testament;" they are added to give us to understand, that the blood of the Saviour is not now given figuratively, as in the Old Law, of which we read in the Apostle, that without blood a Testament is not dedicated;[9] but really and truly given, a prerogative peculiar to the New Testament. Hence the Apostle says: "Therefore, Christ is the mediator of the New Testament, that by means of his death, they who are called may receive the promise of eternal inheritance."[10] The word "eternal" refers to

The form of consecrating the wine, explained.

[1] Luke xxii. 20.　　[2] 1 Cor. xi. 25.　　[3] Luke xxii. 20.
[4] Matt. xxvi. 28.　　[5] Heb. x. 20. xiii. 20.　　[6] Rom. iii. 25, 26.
[7] Heb. ix. 12.　　[8] Decret. l. 3. de cel. Miss. c. 8.
[9] Heb. ix. 18.　　[10] Heb. ix. 15.

the eternal inheritance, our title to which has been purchased by Christ the Lord, the eternal Testator. The words "mystery of faith," which are added, exclude not the reality, but signify that what lies concealed under the veil of mystery, and is far removed from the ken of mortal eye, is to be believed with the certainty of faith. Here, however, these words bear an import entirely different from that which they have when applied to baptism. Here, the mystery of faith consists in this, that we see by faith the blood of Christ, veiled under the species of wine; but baptism is properly called by us "the Sacrament," by the Greeks, "the mystery of faith," because it comprises the entire profession of the faith of Christ. There is also another reason why the blood of our Lord is called "the mystery of faith." In its belief human reason experiences the greatest difficulties, because faith proposes to us to believe that the Son of God, God and man, suffered death for our redemption, a death signified by the Sacrament of his blood. His passion, therefore, is more appropriately commemorated here, in the words, "which shall be shed for the remission of sins," than at the consecration of his body. The separate consecration of the blood places before our eyes, in more vivid colours, his passion, crucifixion, and death. The additional words, "for you and for many," are taken, some from St. Matthew,[1] some from St. Luke,[2] and under the guidance of the Spirit of God, combined together by the Catholic Church. They serve emphatically to designate the fruit and advantages of his passion. Looking to the efficacy of the passion, we believe that the Redeemer shed his blood for the salvation of all men; but looking to the advantages, which mankind derive from its efficacy, we find, at once, that they are not extended to the whole, but to a large proportion of the human race. When, therefore, our Lord said: "for you," he meant either those who were present, or those whom he had chosen from amongst the Jews, amongst whom were, with the exception of Judas, all his disciples with whom he then conversed; but when he adds, "for many," he would include the remainder of the elect from amongst the Jews and Gentiles. With great propriety therefore, were the words, *for all*, omitted, because here the fruit of the passion is alone spoken of, and to the elect only did his passion bring the fruit of salvation. This the words of the Apostle declare, when he says, that Christ was offered once, to take away the sins of many;[3] and the same truth is conveyed in these words of our Lord recorded by St. John: "I pray for them, I pray not for the world; but for them whom thou hast given me, because they are thine."[4] The words of consecration also convey many other truths; truths, however, which the pastor by the daily meditation and study of divine things, and aided by grace from above, will not find it difficult to discover.

[1] Matt. xxvi. 28.   [2] Luke xxii. 20.
[3] Heb. ix. 26   [4] John xvii. 9.

This sublime mystery to be judged of by faith, not by the senses.

To return to those things, of which the faithful are on no account to be suffered to remain ignorant, the pastor, aware of the awful denunciation of the Apostle against those who discern not the body of the Lord,[1] will, first of all, impress on the minds of the faithful, the necessity of detaching, as much as possible, their minds and understandings from the dominion of the senses, for were they, with regard to this sublime mystery, to constitute the senses the only tribunal to which they are to appeal, the awful consequence must be, their precipitation into the extreme of impiety. Consulting the sight, the touch, the smell, the taste, and finding nothing but the appearances of bread and wine, the senses must naturally lead them to think, that this Sacrament contains nothing more than bread and wine. Their minds, therefore, are as much as possible to be withdrawn from subjection to the senses, and excited to the contemplation of the stupendous power of God.

The words of consecration effect three things.
I.

II.

III.

The Catholic Church, then, firmly believes, and openly professes that in this Sacrament, the words of consecration accomplish three things ; first, that the true and real body of Christ, the same that was born of the Virgin, and is now seated at the right hand of the Father in heaven, is rendered present in the Holy Eucharist;[2] secondly, that however repugnant it may appear to the dictate of the senses, no substance of the elements remains in the Sacrament;[3] and thirdly, a natural consequence from the two preceding, and one which the words of consecration also express, that the accidents which present themselves to the eyes, or other senses, exist in a wonderful and ineffable manner without a subject. The accidents of bread and wine we see; but they inhere in no substance, and exist independently of any. The substance of the bread and wine is so changed into the body and blood of our Lord, that they, altogether, cease to be the substance of bread and wine.

The real presence proved from Scripture.

To proceed in order, the pastor will begin with the first, and give his best attention to show, how clear and explicit are the words of our Saviour, which establish the real presence of his body in the Sacrament of the Eucharist. When our Lord says: "'This is my body, this is my blood,"[4] no man however ignorant, unless he labours under some obliquity of intellect, can mistake his meaning: particularly if he recollect, that the words "body" and "blood" refer to his human nature, the real assumption of which by the Son of God no Catholic can doubt. To use the admirable words of St. Hilary, a man not less eminent for piety than learning: "When our Lord himself declares, as our faith teaches us, that his flesh is meat indeed, what room can remain for doubt?"[5] The pastor will also ad-

---

[1] 1 Cor. xi. 29.
[2] Vide Dionys. de Eccl. Hierarch. c. 3, Ignat. Epist. ad Smyr. Just. Apol. 2, Iren. l. 4, c. 34, et l. 5. c. 2. Trid. Sess. 13, c. 1, de Euch.
[3] Cypr. de cœna domini Euse. Emiss. hom. 5. de Pasch. Cyril. Hyeros. Catech. l. 3 et 4, Ambr. l. 4, de Sacram. c. 4, Chrysost. hom. 83. in Matt. et 60, ad pop. Antioch.
[4] Matt. xxvi. 28. Mark xiv. 22, 24. Luke xxii. 19.
[5] S. Hilar. l. 8, de Trinitat. super illa verba velut unum.

duce another passage from Scripture in proof of this sublime truth : having recorded the consecration of bread and wine by our Lord, and also the administration of the sacred mysteries to the Apostles, by the hands of the Saviour, the Apostle adds : " But let a man prove himself, and so eat of that bread and drink of the chalice, for he that eateth and drinketh unworthily, eateth and drinketh judgment to himself, not discerning the body of the Lord."[1] If, as heresy asserts, the Sacrament presents nothing to our veneration but a memorial and sign of the passion of Christ, why exhort the faithful, in language so energetic to prove themselves ? The answer is obvious : by the heavy denunciation contained in the words "judgment," the Apostle marks the enormity of his guilt, who receives unworthily and distinguishes not from common food the body of the Lord, concealed beneath the eucharistic veil. The preceding words of the Apostle develope more fully his meaning : " The chalice of benediction," says he, " which we bless, is it not the communion of the blood of Christ ? and the bread which we break, is it not the participation of the body of the Lord ?"[2] words which prove to demonstration the real presence of Jesus Christ in the holy Sacrament of the Eucharist.

These passages of Scripture, are, therefore, to be expounded by the pastor, and he will emphatically press upon the attention of the faithful, that their meaning, in itself obvious, is placed beyond all doubt by the uniform interpretation and authority of the Holy Catholic Church. That such has been at all times the doctrine of the Church, may be ascertained in a two-fold manner ; by consulting the Fathers who flourished in the early ages of the Church and in each succeeding century, who are the most unexceptionable witnesses of her doctrine, and all of whom teach in the clearest terms, and with the most entire unanimity, the dogma of the real presence ; and also by appealing to the Councils of the Church, convened on this important subject. To adduce the individual testimony of each Father would prove an endless task—enough, that we cite, or rather point out a few, whose testimony will afford a sufficient criterion by which to judge of the rest. Let St. Ambrose first declare his faith : in his book on " the Initiated" he says, that the same true body of our Lord, which was assumed of the Virgin, is received in this Sacrament ; a truth which he declares is to be believed with the certainty of faith ; and in another place he distinctly tells us, that before consecration it is bread, but after consecration it is the flesh of Christ.[3] St. Chrysostome, another witness of equal fidelity and weight, professes and proclaims this mysterious truth, particularly in his sixtieth homily on those who receive the sacred mysteries unworthily ; and also in his fortyfourth and forty-fifth homilies on St. John : " Let us," says he, "obey, not contradict God, although what he says may

From tradition.

[1] 1 Cor. xi. 28, 29. [2] 1 Cor. x. 16.
[3] Lib. 4, de Sacr. c. 4, et de iis qui myster. init. c. 9. vide et de consec. dist. 2 plurim. in locis.

14

seem contrary to our reason and our sight: his words cannot deceive, our senses are easily deceived."[1] With the doctrine thus taught by St. Chrysostome, that uniformly taught by St. Augustine fully accords, particularly when in his explanation of the thirty-third Psalm, he says: "To carry himself in his own hands, is impossible to man, and peculiar to Christ alone; he was carried in his own hands, when giving his body to be eaten, he said, This is my body."[2] To pass by Justin and Irenæus, St. Cyril, in his fourth book on St. John, declares in such express terms, that the body of our Lord is contained in this Sacrament, that no sophistry can distort, no captious interpretations obscure his meaning. Should the pastor wish for additional testimonies of the Fathers, he will find it easy to add the Hilaries, the Jeromes, the Denises, the Damascenes, and a host of other illustrious names, whose sentiments on this most important subject he will find collected by the labour and industry of men eminent for piety and learning.[3]

From Councils.   Another means of ascertaining the belief of the Church on matters of faith, is the condemnation of the contrary doctrine. That the belief of the real presence was that of the universal Church of God, unanimously professed by all her children, is demonstrated by a well authenticated fact. When in the eleventh century, Berengarius presumed to deny this dogma, asserting that the Eucharist was only a sign, the innovation was immediately condemned by the unanimous voice of the Christian world. The Council of Vercelli, convened by authority of Leo IX., denounced the heresy, and Berengarius himself retracted and anathematized his error. Relapsing, however, into the same infatuation and impiety, he was condemned by three different Councils, convened, one at Tours, the other two at Rome: of the two latter, one was summoned by Nicholas II., the other by Gregory VII. The general Council of Lateran held under Innocent III., further ratified the sentence; and the faith of the Catholic Church, on this point of doctrine, was more fully declared and more firmly established in the Councils of Florence and Trent.

And confirmed by reason.   If, then, the pastor carefully explain these particulars, his labours will be blessed with the effect of strengthening the weak, and administering joy and consolation to the pious; (of those who, blinded by error, hate nothing more than the light of truth, we waive all mention) and this two-fold effect will be more securely attained, as the faithful cannot doubt that this

I.   dogma is numbered amongst the articles of faith. Believing and confessing as they do, that the power of God is supreme,

---

[1] St. Chrys. ad popul. Antioch. homil. 60 et 61.
[2] Divus Augustinus in Psalm xxxiii. Conc. 1, a medio ad finem usque. Cyril. lib. 4, in Joan. c. 33, et 14, et lib. 1, c. 13. Inst. Apolog. 2, sub finem ad Antonium Pium.
[3] Iren. lib. 5, contra heretic. et lib. 5, in Joan. c. 34. Dionys. Eccles. Hier. c. 3, Hilar. lib. 8. de Trinit. Hieron. epist. ad Damascen. Damas. lib. 4, de orthod. fid. c. 14.

they must also believe that his omnipotence can accomplish the great work which we admire and adore in the Sacrament of the Eucharist; and again, believing as they do, the Holy Catholic Church, they must necessarily believe that the doctrine expounded by us, is that which was revealed by the Son of God.

But nothing contributes more to light up in the pious soul that spiritual joy, of which we have spoken; nothing is more fertile of spiritual fruit, than the contemplation of the exalted dignity of this most august Sacrament. From it we learn how great must be the perfection of the gospel dispensation, under which we enjoy the reality of that, which under the Mosaic Law was only shadowed by types and figures. Hence St. Denis, with a wisdom more than human, says that our Church is a mean between the synagogue and the heavenly Jerusalem, and participates of the nature of both.[1] The perfection of the Holy Catholic Church, and her exalted glory, removed only by one degree from heaven, the faithful cannot sufficiently admire. In common with the inhabitants of heaven, we, too, possess Christ, God and man, present with us; but they, and in this they are raised a degree above us, are admitted to the actual enjoyment of the beatific vision; whilst we, with a firm and unwavering faith, offer the tribute of our homage to the Divine Majesty present with us, not, it is true, in a manner visible to mortal eye, but hidden by a miracle of power, under the veil of the sacred mysteries. How admirably does not this Sacrament, also, display to us the infinite love of Jesus Christ to man! It became the goodness of the Saviour not to withdraw from us that nature which he assumed for our sake, but to desire, as far as possible, to dwell permanently amongst us, at all times strictly verifying the words: "My delight is to be with the children of men."[2]

Here the pastor will also explain to the faithful, that in this Sacrament are contained not only the true body of Christ, and all the constituents of a true body, but also Christ whole and entire—that the word Christ designates the man-God, that is to say, one Person in whom are united the divine and human natures—that the holy Eucharist, therefore, contains both, and whatever is included in the idea of both, the divinity and humanity whole and entire, the soul, the body and blood of Christ with all their component parts—all of which faith teaches us are contained in the Sacrament. In heaven the whole humanity is united to the divinity in one hypostasis, or person, and it were impious, therefore, to suppose that the body of Christ, which is contained in the Sacrament, is separated from his divinity.[3]

The pastor, however, will not fail to observe, that in the Sacrament all are not contained after the same manner, or by the same efficacy: some things, we say, the efficacy of consecra-

Marginal notes:
II.

The dignity conferred on the Church by the institution of this Sacrament.

Christ whole and entire, present in this Sacrament.

In this Sacrament, some things ef-

---

[1] De Eccl. Hierar. c. 3. p. 1.   [2] Prov. viii. 31.
[3] Vide de consec. dist. 2, multis in locis, item Amb. de iis qui myst. init. c. 9, D. T. p. 3. q. 76, art. 1.

fected by
the words
of conse-
cration,
some by
concomi-
tance.
tion accomplishes; for as the words of consecration effectuate
what they signify, sacred writers usually say, that whatever the
form expresses, is contained in the Sacrament by virtue of the
Sacrament; and hence, could we suppose any one thing to be
entirely separated from the rest, the Sacrament, in their opinion,
would be found to contain solely what the form expresses. But,
some things are contained in the Sacrament, because united to
those which are expressed in the form; for instance, the words
"This is my body," which comprise the form used to consecrate the bread, signify the body of the Lord, and hence, the
body of the Lord is contained in the Eucharist, by virtue of the
Sacrament. As, however, to the body are united his blood, his
soul, his divinity, they too must be found to coexist in the Sacrament; not, however, by virtue of the consecration, but by virtue
of the union that subsists between them and his body; and this
theologians express by the word "concomitance." Hence it is
clear that Christ, whole and entire, is contained in the Sacrament; for when two things are actually united, where one is,
the other must also be. Hence it also follows, that Christ,
whole and entire, is contained under either species, so that as
under the species of bread, are contained not only the body, but
also the blood and Christ entire, so in like manner, under the
species of wine are contained not only the blood, but also the
The ele-
ments,
why sepa-
rately con-
secrated.
body and Christ entire. These are matters on which the faithful
cannot entertain a doubt. Wisely, however, was it ordained
that two distinct consecrations should take place: they represent in a more lively manner, the passion of our Lord, in which
his blood was separated from his body; and hence, in the form
of consecration we commemorate the effusion of his blood.
The sacrament is to be used by us as the food and nourish-
ment of our souls; and it was most accordant with this its use,
that it should be instituted as meat and drink, which obviously
constitute the proper food of man.

Christ,
whole and
entire in
each parti-
cle of
either spe-
cies.
The pastor will also inform the faithful, that Christ, whole
and entire, is contained not only under either species, but also
in each particle of either species: "Each," says St. Augustine,
"receives Christ the Lord entire in each particle: he is not
diminished by being given to many, but gives himself whole
and entire to each."[1] This is also an obvious inference from
the narrative of the Evangelists: it is not to be supposed that
the bread used at the Last Supper was consecrated by our Lord
in separate parts, applying the form particularly to each, but
that all the sacramental bread then used, was consecrated in
sufficient quantity to be distributed amongst the Apostles, at the
same time and with the same form. That the consecration of
the chalice also, was performed in the same manner, is obvious
from these words of the Saviour: "Take and divide it amongst
you."[2]

Transub-
stantiation
What has hitherto been said is intended to enable the pastor

[1] August. de consec. dist. 2. c. singulis.   [2] Luke xxii. 17.

to show, that the body and blood of Christ are really and truly proved
from rea-
son. contained in the Sacrament of the Eucharist. That the substance of the bread and wine does not continue to exist in the Sacrament after consecration, is the next subject of instruction which is to engage his attention; a truth which, although well calculated to excite our profound admiration, is yet a necessary consequence from what has been already established. If, after consecration, the body of Christ is really and truly present under the species of bread and wine, not having been there before, it must have become so by change of place—by creation —or by transubstantiation. It cannot be rendered present by change of place, because it would then cease to be in heaven, for whatever is moved must necessarily cease to occupy the place from which it is moved. Still less can we suppose it to be rendered present by creation, an idea which the mind instantly rejects. In order that the body of our Lord be present in the Sacrament, it remains, therefore, that it be rendered present by transubstantiation, and of course, that the substance of the bread entirely cease to exist. Hence our predecessors in From the the faith, the Fathers of the general Council of Laterân,[1] and Councils of Florence,[2] confirmed by solemn decrees the truth of this Church. Article. In the Council of Trent it was still more fully defined in these words: " If any one shall say, that in the holy Sacrament of the Eucharist the substance of the bread and wine remains, together with the body and blood of our Lord Jesus Christ, let him be anathema."[3] The doctrine thus defined is a From natural inference from the words of Scripture. When insti- Scripture. tuting this Sacrament, our Lord himself said: " this is my body:"[4] the word "*this*," expresses the entire substance of the thing present; and therefore, if the substance of the bread remained, our Lord could not have said: " *This* is my body." In St. John he also says: " The bread that I will give is my flesh, for the life of the world:"[5] the bread which he promises to give, he here declares to be " his flesh." A little after he adds: " Unless you eat the flesh of the Son of Man, and drink his blood, you shall not have life in you:"[6] and again, " My flesh is meat indeed, and my blood is drink indeed."[7] When, therefore, in terms so clear and so explicit, he thus calls his flesh " meat indeed," and his blood " drink indeed," he gives us sufficiently to understand, that the substance of the bread and wine no longer exists in the Sacrament. Whoever turns over the From the pages of the Holy Fathers will easily perceive, that, on the concurrent doctrine of Transubstantiation, they have been at all times una- of the Fa- nimous. St. Ambrose says: " You say, perhaps, ' this bread is thers. no other than what is used for common food:' before consecration it is indeed bread; but, no sooner are the words of conse-

[1] Lateran. Concil. c. 1.
[2] Flor. in epist. Eugenii IV. data ad Arm, et a Concilio approbata.
[3] Trid. sess, 13, can. 4.
[4] Matt. xxvi. 26. Mark xiv 22. Luke xxi. 18. 1 Cor. xi. 24.
[5] John vi. 52.   [6] John vi. 54.   [7] John vi. 56.
14*   X

cration pronounced, than from bread it becomes the flesh of Christ."[1] To prove this position more clearly, he elucidates it by a variety of comparisons and examples. In another place, when explaining these words of the Psalmist: "Whatsoever the Lord pleased he hath done in heaven and on earth,"[2] he says: "Although the species of bread and wine are visible, yet faith tells us that after consecration, the body and blood of Christ are alone there."[3] Explaining the same doctrine almost in the same words, St. Hilary says, that although externally it appear bread and wine, yet in reality it is the body and blood of the Lord.[4]

The Eucharist, why called bread after consecration. Here the pastor will not omit to observe to the faithful, that we should not at all be surprised, if even after consecration, the Eucharist is sometimes called bread: it is so called because it has the appearance and still retains the natural quality of bread, which is to support and nourish the body. That such phraseology is in perfect accordance with the style of the Holy Scriptures, which call things by what they appear to be, is evident from the words of Genesis, which say, that Abraham saw three men, when, in reality, he saw three angels;[5] and the two angels also, who appeared to the Apostles after the ascension of our Lord, are called not angels, but men.[6]

The manner in which this conversion is to be explained to the people. To explain this mystery in a proper manner is extremely difficult. On the manner of this admirable conversion, the pastor, however, will endeavour to instruct those who are more advanced in the knowledge and contemplation of divine things: those who are yet weak may, it were to be apprehended, be overwhelmed by its greatness. This conversion, then, is so effectuated that the whole substance of the bread and wine is changed by the power of God, into the whole substance of the body of Christ, and the whole substance of the wine, into the whole substance of his blood, and this, without any change in our Lord himself: he is neither begotten, nor changed, nor increased, but remains entirely and substantially the same. This sublime mystery St. Ambrose thus declares: "You see how efficacious are the words of Christ; if, then, the word of the Lord Jesus is so powerful as to summon creation into existence, shall it not require a less exercise of power, to make that subsist, which already has existence, and to change it into another thing?"[7] Many other Fathers, whose authority is too grave to be questioned, have written to the same effect: "We faithfully confess," says St. Augustine, "that before consecration it is bread and wine, the produce of nature; but after consecration it is the body and blood of Christ, consecrated by the blessing."[8] "The body," says Damascene, "is truly united to the divinity, the body assumed of the virgin; not that the body thus assumed

---

[1] Lib. 4, de sacr. c. 4. et c. 5, c. 4.   [2] Ps. cxxxiv. 6.
[3] De consec. dist. 2. c. omnia.
[4] Hilar. de Trin. lib 8, et de consec. dist. 2. cap. 28.   [5] Gen. xviii. 2.
[6] Acts i. 10. vid. D. Thom. 3, p. q. 75, art. 3 et 4.   [7] D. Ambr. lib 4. de sacr. c. 4.
[8] Citatur de consec. dist. 2, can. Nos. autem.

descends from heaven, but that the bread and wine are changed into the body and blood of Christ."[1] This admirable change, as the Council of Trent teaches, the Catholic Church most appropriately expresses by the word "transubstantiation."[2] When, in the natural order, the form of a being is changed, that change may be properly termed "a transformation;" in like manner, when, in the Sacrament of the Eucharist, the whole substance of one thing passes into the whole substance of another, the change our predecessors in the faith wisely and appropriately called "transubstantiation." But according to the admonition so frequently repeated by the Holy Fathers, the faithful are to be admonished against the danger of gratifying a prurient curiosity, by searching into the manner in which this change is effected. It mocks the powers of conception, nor can we find any example of it in natural transmutations, nor even in the wide range of creation. The change itself is the object not of our comprehension, but of our humble faith; and the manner of that change forbids the temerity of a too curious inquiry.[3]

This conversion appropriately called transubstantiation.

A mystery not to be curiously searched into.

The same salutary caution should also be observed by the pastor, with regard to the mysterious manner in which the body of our Lord is contained whole and entire under the least particle of the bread.[4] Such inscrutable mysteries should scarcely ever become matter of disquisition. Should Christian charity, however, require a departure from this salutary rule, the pastor will recollect first to prepare and fortify his hearers, by reminding them, that "no word shall be impossible with God."[5]

The same salutary caution again necessary.

The pastor will next teach, that our Lord is not in the Sacrament as in a place: place regards things, only inasmuch as they have magnitude; and we do not say that Christ is in the Sacrament inasmuch as he is great or small, terms which belong to quantity, but inasmuch as he is a substance. The substance of the bread is changed into the substance of Christ, not into magnitude or quantity; and substance, it will be acknowledged, is contained in a small as well as in a large space. The substance of air, for instance, whether in a large or in a small quantity, and that of water whether confined in a vessel, or flowing in a river, must necessarily be the same. As, then, the body of our Lord succeeds to the substance of the bread, we must confess it to be in the Sacrament after the same manner, as the bread was before consecration: whether the substance of the bread was present in greater or less quantity is a matter of entire indifference.

The body of our Lord present in the Sacrament, not as in a place.

We now come to the third effect produced by the words of consecration, the existence of the species of bread and wine in the Sacrament without a subject, an effect as stupendous as it is admirable. What has been said in explanation of the two preceding points, must facilitate the exposition of this mysterious

The accidents remain in the Eucharist without a subject.

---

[1] Lib. 4, de orthod. fid. c. 14.
[2] Trid. sess. 13, c. 4, et can. 2, et de consec. distinct. 2, c. panis.   [3] Eccl. iii. 22.
[4] D. Thom. 3, p. q. 76, Trid. sess. 13, c. 3, et can. 3, et Florent. in decret. Eugen.
[5] Luke i. 37.

truth. We have already proved that the body and blood of our Lord are really and truly contained in the Sacrament, to the entire exclusion of the substance of the bread and wine: the accidents cannot inhere in the body and blood of Christ: they must, therefore, contrary to the physical laws, subsist of themselves, inhering in no subject. This has been, at all times, the doctrine of the Catholic Church; and the same authorities by which we have already proved, that the substance of the bread and wine ceases to exist in the Eucharist, go to establish its truth.[1]

Duties of piety towards this Sacrament.

But it becomes the piety of the faithful, omitting subtle disquisitions, to revere and adore in the simplicity of faith, the majesty of this august Sacrament; and with sentiments of gratitude and admiration, to recognise the wisdom of God in the institution of the holy mysteries, under the species of bread and wine.

The Eucharist, why instituted under the forms of bread and wine.

To eat human flesh, or to drink human blood, is most revolting to human nature, and, therefore, has God in his infinite wisdom, established the administration of the body and blood of Christ, under the forms of bread and wine, the ordinary and agreeable food of man. From its administration under these forms, also flow two other important advantages: it obviates the calumnious reproaches of the unbeliever, to which a manducation of the body and blood of our Lord, under human form, must be exposed; whilst, by receiving him under a form in which he is impervious to the senses, our faith is augmented, " which," as St. Gregory observes, " has no merit in those things, which fall under the jurisdiction of reason."[2] But what has been hitherto said on this subject, demands much prudent precaution in its exposition; and in this the pastor will be guided by the capacity of his hearers, by times and circumstances.

The salutary effects of the Eucharist to be fully explained to all, and how.

With regard to the salutary effects of this Sacrament, these, because most necessary to be known by all, the pastor will expound to all, indiscriminately and without reserve.[3] What we have said at such length on this subject, is to be made known to the faithful, principally with a view to make them sensible of the advantages which flow from its participation, advantages too numerous and important to be expressed in words, and amongst which the pastor must be content to select one or two points for explanation, to show the superabundant graces

I.

with which the holy mysteries abound. To this end it will be found conducive, to premise an explanation of the nature and efficacy of the other Sacraments, and then compare the Eucharist to the living fountain, the other Sacraments to so many rivulets. With great truth is the Holy Eucharist called the fountain of all grace, containing as it does, after an admi-

[1] Vid. de consecr. dist. 2, c. Nos autem et Decretal. lib. 1, tit. de celeb. Miss. c. cum Matt. et D. Th. 3, p. q. 75, a. 3, et q. 77, a. 1.

[2] Hom. 26, super Evangelia, vid. Cyrill. lib. 4, in Joan. c. 22, Cypr. de Cœna Domini. Ambr. de Sacram. lib. 4, c. 4, Aug. Tract. 27, in Joan. D. Thom. p. 3, q. 74, a. 1, et q. 75, a. 1.

[3] Trid. sess. 13, c. 3, et can. 5, Iren. lib. 4, c. 14, Cyril. lib. 4. in Joan. c. 11 et 14. Chrysost. hom. 45, in Joan. D. Thom. 3, p. q. 79.

rable manner, the source of all gifts and graces, the author of all the Sacraments, Christ our Lord, from whom as from their source, they derive all their goodness and perfection. This comparison, therefore, serves to show how great are the treasures of grace, which are derived from this Sacrament.

It will also be found expedient to consider attentively the nature of bread and wine, the symbols of this sacrament: what bread and wine are to the body, the Eucharist is, in a superior order, to the health and joy of the soul. It is not, like bread and wine, changed into our substance; but, in some measure, changes us into its own nature, and to it we may apply these words of St. Augustine: "I am the food of the grown; grow and thou shalt partake of this food; nor shalt thou change me into thee, as thou dost thy corporal food, but thou shalt be changed into me."[1] If then "grace and truth come by Jesus Christ,"[2] these spiritual treasures must be poured into that soul, which receives with purity and holiness, him who says of himself: "He that eateth my flesh and drinketh my blood, abideth in me and I in him."[3] Those who piously and religiously receive this Sacrament, receive, no doubt, the Son of God into their souls, and are united, as living members, to his body; for it is written: "He that eateth me, the same also shall live by me;"[4] and also: "The bread that I will give is my flesh, for the life of the world."[5] Explaining these words of the Saviour, St. Cyril says: "The Eternal Word, uniting himself to his own flesh, imparted to it a vivifying power; it became him, therefore, to unite himself to us after a wonderful manner, through his sacred flesh and precious blood, which we receive in the bread and wine, consecrated by his vivifying benediction."[6]

But when it is said, that this Sacrament imparts grace, it is not intended to mean that, to receive this Sacrament with advantage, it is unnecessary to be previously in the state of grace. Natural food can be of no use to a person who is already dead, and in like manner the sacred mysteries can avail him nothing, who lives not in Spirit. Hence this Sacrament has been instituted under the forms of bread and wine, to signify, that the object of its institution is not to recall to life a dead soul, but to preserve life to a living one. We say that this Sacrament imparts grace, because even the *first* grace, which all should have before they presume to approach this Sacrament, least they "eat and drink judgment to themselves,"[7] is given to none unless they desire to receive the Holy Eucharist, which is the end of all the Sacraments, the symbol of ecclesiastical unity, to which he who does not belong, cannot receive divine grace. Again, as the body is not only supported but increased by natural food, from which we derive new pleasure every day; so also the life of the soul is not only sustained but invigorated by

Marginal notes:
II.

1. It imparts grace.

To communicate worthily we must be in the state of grace.

[1] Lib. 7. Conf. c. 10. Vid. Ambr. lib. 5. de sacr. c. 4 et Crys. hom. 45. in Joan.
[2] John i. 17. [3] John vi. 57. [4] John vi. 58. [5] John vi. 52.
[6] Lib. 4. in Joan, c. 12, 14, et ep. 10. ad Nestor. [7] 1 Cor. xi. 29.

feasting on the Eucharistic banquet, which imparts to it an increasing zest for heavenly things. With strictest truth and propriety, therefore, do we say that this Sacrament, which may be well compared to manna, "having in it all that is delicious, and the sweetness of every taste," imparts grace to the soul.[1]

II.
The Eucharist remits venial sins.

That the Holy Eucharist remits lighter offences, or, as they are commonly called, venial sins, cannot be matter of doubt. Whatever losses the soul sustains by falling into some slight offences, through the violence of passion, these the Eucharist, which cancels lesser sins, repairs in the same manner, not to depart from the illustration already adduced, that natural food, as we know from experience, gradually repairs the daily waste caused by the vital heat of the system. Of this heavenly Sacrament justly, therefore, has St. Ambrose said: "This daily bread is taken as a remedy for daily infirmity."[2] This, however, is to be understood of venial imperfections only.

III.
Is an antidote against the contagion of sins.

The Holy Eucharist is also an antidote against the contagion of sin, and a shield against the violent assaults of temptation.[3] It is, as it were, a heavenly medicine, which secures the soul against the easy approach of virulent and deadly infection. St. Cyprian records that when, in the early ages of the Church, Christians were hurried in multitudes by tyrants, to torments and death, because they professed the name of Christ, they received from the hand of the bishop, the Sacrament of the body and blood of our Lord, lest, perhaps overcome by excess of torments, they should yield in the saving conflict.[4] It also re-

IV.
Represses concupiscence.

presses the licentious desires of the flesh, and keeps them in due subjection to the spirit: in proportion as it inflames the soul with the fire of charity, in the same proportion does it necessarily extinguish the fire of concupiscence. Finally, to nar-

V.
Facilitates the attainment of eternal life.

row within the compass of a few words all the advantages and blessings which emanate from this Sacrament, the Holy Eucharist facilitates to an extraordinary degree, the attainment of eternal life: "He that eateth my flesh, and drinketh my blood," says the Redeemer, "hath everlasting life, and I will raise him up on the last day."[5] The grace which it imparts, brings peace and tranquillity to the soul; and when the hour shall have arrived in which he is to take his departure from this mortal life, like another Elias, who in the strength of his miraculous repast, walked to Horeb the mount of God,[6] the Christian, invigorated by the strengthening influence of this heavenly food, shall wing his way to the mansions of everlasting glory and

These effects ex-

never-ending bliss. All these important particulars the pastor will be able fully to expound to the faithful, if he but dilate on

---

[1] Wisd. xvi. 20.
[2] Lib. 4. de Sacram. c. 6. et lib. c. 4. Innocent. III lib. 4. de myst. Miss. c. 44. Cyrill. lib. 4. in Joan, c. 17. et lib. 3. c. 36. Inter opera D. Bernardi habetur cujusdam sermo domini, qui incipit: PANEM ANGELORUM, et singularis est de Euchar. videatur, et D. Thom. 3. p. q. 79.
[3] Aug. tract. 26. in Joan.   [4] Lib. 1. Epist. 2. ad Cornel.
[5] John vi. 55. Vid. Chrys. de sacerdotio, dial. o. D. Thom. 3. p. q. 79. art. 2.
[6] 3 Kings xix. 8.

the sixth chapter of St. John, in which are developed the mani- plained
fold effects of this Sacrament; or if, glancing through the life and illus-
and actions of our Lord, he shows that if they who received trated.
him beneath their roof during his mortal life,[1] or were restored
to health by touching his vesture, or even the hem of his garment,[2] were justly deemed happy, how much more happy we,
into whose souls, resplendent as he is with unfading glory, he
disdains not to enter, to heal all our spiritual wounds, to enrich
us with his choicest gifts, and to unite us to himself!

But to excite the faithful to emulate better gifts,[3] the pastor The man-
will also point out who they are who derive these inestimable ner of com-
blessings from a participation of the holy mysteries, reminding municating
them that Christians may communicate differently and with dif- threefold:
ferent effects.   Hence our predecessors in the faith, as we read
in the Council of Trent,[4] distinguished three classes of communicants—Some receive the Sacrament only: such are those sin- Sacramen
ners who dread not to approach the holy mysteries with pol- tally.
luted lips and depraved hearts, who, as the Apostle says, " eat
and drink unworthily."[5]   Of this class of communicants St.
Augustine says : " He who dwells not in Christ, and in whom
Christ does not dwell, most certainly eats not spiritually his
flesh, although carnally and visibly he press with his teeth the
Sacrament of his flesh and blood."[6]   Not only, therefore, do
those who receive the Holy Eucharist with these dispositions,
obtain no fruit from its participation, but, as the Apostle says,
" they eat and drink judgment to themselves."[7]   Others are Spiritually.
said to receive the Holy Eucharist in spirit only : they are those
who, inflamed with a lively " faith that worketh by charity,"[8]
participate in desire, of this celestial food, from which they receive, if not the entire, at least very considerable fruit.   Lastly, Sacramen-
there are some who receive the Holy Eucharist both spiritually tally, and
and sacramentally, those who, according to the advice of the spiritually.
Apostle, having first proved themselves,[9] approach this divine
banquet, adorned with the nuptial garment,[10] and derive from it
all those superabundant graces which we have already mentioned.
Those, therefore, who, having it in their power to receive, with
due preparation, the Sacrament of the body and blood of the
Lord, are yet satisfied with a spiritual communion only, manifestly
deprive themselves of a heavenly treasure of inestimable value.

We now come to point out the manner in which the faithful
should be previously prepared for sacramental communion.   To Necessity
demonstrate the necessity of this previous preparation, the ex- of previous
ample of the Saviour is to be proposed to the faithful.   Before prepara-
he gave to his Apostles the Sacrament of his body and blood, tion.
although they were already clean, he washed their feet, to declare that we must use extreme diligence to bring with us to its
participation the greatest integrity and innocence of soul.   In

---

[1] Luke xix. 9.   [2] Matt. xiv. 36 and ix. 20.   [3] 1 Cor. xii. 31.
[4] De consecr. dist. 2. can. 46 sess. 13. cap. 8.   [5] 1 Cor. xi. 29.
[6] In Joan. tract. 16. et contra Donat. lib. 5. c. 8.   [7] 1 Cor. xi. 29.
[8] Gal. v. 6.   [9] 1 Cor. xi. 28.   [10] Matt. xxii. 11.

the next place, the faithful are to understand that as he who approaches thus prepared and disposed, is adorned with the most ample gifts of heavenly grace, so on the contrary, he who approaches without this preparation and without these dispositions, not only derives from it no advantage, but plunges his own soul into the most unutterable misery. It is the property of the best and most salutary medicine, if seasonably applied, to be productive of the greatest benefit, but if unseasonably, to prove most pernicious and destructive. It cannot, therefore, excite our surprise, that the great and exalted gifts of God, when received into a soul properly predisposed, are of the greatest assistance towards the attainment of salvation ; whilst to those who receive them without these necessary dispositions, they

Illustration. bring with them eternal death. Of this, the Ark of the Lord affords a convincing illustration : the people of Israel possessed nothing more precious ; it was to them the source of innumerable blessings from God ; but, when borne off by the Philistines, it brought on them a most destructive plague and the heaviest calamities, heightened, as they were, by eternal disgrace.[1] Food when received into a healthy stomach nourishes and supports the body ; but the same food, when received into a stomach replete with peccant humours, generates malignant disease.[2]

First preparation ; The first preparation, then, which the faithful should make, is to distinguish table from table, this sacred table from profane tables,[3] this celestial bread from common bread. This we do when we firmly believe, that the Eucharist really and truly contains the body and blood of the Lord, of him whom the angels adore in heaven, "at whose nod the pillars of heaven fear and tremble,"[4] of whose glory the heavens and the earth are full.[5] This is to discern the body of the Lord, in accordance with the admonition of the Apostle,[6] venerating rather, the greatness of the mystery, than too curiously investigating its truth by idle

Second, disquisition. Another very necessary preparation is to ask ourselves, if we are at peace with, if we sincerely and from the heart love our neighbour. "If, therefore, thou offerest thy gift at the altar, and there rememberest, that thy brother hath aught against thee, leave there thy offering before the altar, and go first to be reconciled to thy brother, and then coming thou

Third shalt offer thy gift."[7] We should in the next place, carefully examine our consciences, lest perhaps they be defiled by mortal guilt, which sincere repentance alone can efface. This severe scrutiny is necessary in order to cleanse the soul from its defilement, by applying to it the salutary medicine of contrition and confession. The Council of Trent has defined, that no one

---

[1] 1 Kings v. toto.
[2] De præparatione ad Euch. requisita vide Trid. sess. 13. c. 7. et can. 11. Basil. q. 172. regul. brev. et serm. 2. de bapt. Cyprian. toto fere lib. de Lapsis, agendo de Pœnit. Aug. serm. 1. de Temp. Chrys. hom. 44, 45, 46. in Joan. et in Matt. hom. 83.
[3] 1 Cor. x. 21.　　　[4] Job xxvi. 11.　　　[5] Isa. vi. 3.
[6] 1 Cor. xi. 29.　　　[7] Matt. v. 24, 25.

conscious of mortal sin, and having an opportunity of recurring to a confessor, however contrite he may deem himself, is to approach the Holy Eucharist, until he has been purified by sacramental confession.[1] We should also reflect in the silence of our own hearts, how unworthy we are that God should bestow on us this divine gift, and with the Centurion, of whom our Lord declared, that he found not "so great a faith in Israel," we should exclaim: "Lord, I am not worthy that thou shouldst enter under my roof."[2] We should also put the question to ourselves, whether we can truly say with Peter: "Lord, thou knowest that I love thee;"[3] and should recollect, that he who sat down at the marriage feast without a nuptial garment, was cast into exterior darkness, and condemned to eternal torments.[4]

Fourth,

Fifth,

Our preparation should not, however, be confined to the soul: it should also extend to the body. We are to approach the Holy Eucharist fasting, having neither eaten nor drunk, at least from the preceding midnight.[5] The dignity of so great a Sacrament also demands, that married persons abstain from the marriage-debt, for some days previous to communion, an observance recommended by the example of David, who, when about to receive the show-bread from the hands of the priest, declared, that he and his servants had been "clean from women for three days."[6] These particulars contain a summary of the principal things to be observed by the faithful, preparatory to receiving the sacred mysteries; and to these heads may be reduced, whatever other preparations piety will suggest to the devout communicant.[7]

Sixth.

But that none may be deterred by the difficulty of the preparation from approaching the Holy Eucharist, the faithful are frequently to be reminded that they are all bound to receive this Sacrament; and that the Church has decreed that whoever neglects to approach the holy communion once a year, at Easter, subjects himself to sentence of excommunication.[8] However, let not the faithful imagine that it is enough to receive the body of the Lord once a year only, in obedience to the decree of the Church: they should approach oftener; but whether monthly, weekly, or daily, cannot be decided by any fixed universal rule. St. Augustine, however, lays down a most certain rule applicable to all—"Live," says he, "in such a manner as to be able to receive every day."[9] It will therefore be the duty of the pastor frequently to admonish the faithful, that as they deem it necessary to afford daily nutriment to the body, they should also feel

All bound to communicate once a year, at Easter.

Importance of frequent communion.

<hr>

[1] Sess. 13. can. 11. Chrys. hom. 30, in Genes. et 20. in Matth. Cypr. in lib. de Lapsis.
[2] Matt. viii. 8. 10.   [3] John xxi. 15.   [4] Matt. xxii. 12, 13.
[5] Vid. Aug. epist. 118. e. 6. et lib. 1. ad inquis. Januarii c. 6.
[6] 1 Kings xxi. 3 4, 5.
[7] Greg. in responsione 10. ad interrog. Aug. et hab. 23. q. 4, c. 7. Aug. serm. 2. de temp. et 2, 4.
[8] Concil. Lat. c. 28. et habetur lib. 5. Decret. tit. de Pœnit. et remiss. cap. omnis utriusque sexus. Trid. sess. 13, 9.
[9] St. Aug. de verbis Domini, ser. 28. qui desumptus est ex. Amb. lib. 5. de sacram. c. 4.

15   Y

solicitous to feed and nourish the soul every day with this heavenly food. The soul stands not less in need of spiritual, than the body of corporal food. Here it will be found most useful to recapitulate the inestimable advantages which, as we have already shown, flow from sacramental communion, and the manna also which was a figure of this Sacrament, and of which the Israelites had occasion to partake every day, may be used as a further illustration.[1] The Fathers, who earnestly recommended the frequent participation of this Sacrament, may be adduced as additional authority to enforce the necessity of frequent communion ; and the words, "thou sinnest daily, receive daily," convey the sentiments not alone of St. Augustine, but of all the Fathers who have written on the subject.[2]

Daily communion, the practice of the ancient Church.   That there was a time when the faithful approached the Holy Communion every day, we learn from the Acts of the Apostles. All who then professed the faith of Christ, burned with such pure and ardent charity, that devoting themselves, as they did unceasingly, to prayer and other works of piety,[3] they were found prepared to communicate daily. This devout practice, which seems to have been interrupted for a time, was again partially revived by Pope Anacletus, a most holy martyr, who commanded, that all the ministers who assisted at the holy sacrifice, should communicate, an ordinance, as the Pontiff declares, of Apostolic institution.[4] It was also for a long time the practice of the Church, that, as soon as the sacrifice was ended, the priest, turning to the congregation, invited the faithful to the holy table in these words : "Come, brethren, and receive the communion ;" and those who were prepared, advanced to receive the holy mysteries with hearts animated by the most fervent devotion.[5] But subsequently, when charity and devotion declined amongst Christians, and the faithful very seldom approached the holy communion, it was decreed by Pope Fabian, that all should communicate thrice every year, at Christmas, at Easter, and at Pentecost, a decree which was afterwards confirmed by many Councils, particularly by the first of Agath.[6]

Thrice a year, subsequently decreed.

Finally, once a year.   Such, at length, was the decay of piety, that not only was this holy and salutary practice unobserved, but communion was deferred for years. The Council of Lateran, therefore, decreed that all the faithful should communicate, at least, once a year, at Easter, and that the omission should be chastised by exclu-

---

[1] Exod. xvi. 21, 22.
[2] Ad frequentem communionem hortantur Augustin. de verbis Domini serm. 28. sed hic sermo cum non sit August. sed Ambr. lib. 5. de sacram c. 4. rejectus est in appendicem tomi 10. item vide eundem Aug. Epist. 118. c. 3. item, Ignat. ad Ephes. satis ante finem. Basil. Epist. ad Cæsar. patr. Ambr. lib. 3. de sacr. c. 4. Chrysost. hom. 61. ad pop. Antioch. Cypr. de Ora. Dominica ad hæc verba, panem nostram quot Hieron. Epist. 28, ad Lucin. vers. finem. Cyril. c. 3. in Joan. c. 37. vide etiam de consecr. dist. 2. per multa capita hac de re.
[3] Acts ii. 42. 46.   [4] De consec. dist. 2, c. 10.
[5] De quotidiana communione vide Dionys. de Eccles. Hierarch. c. 3, parte 2, Hieron. Epist. 28, ad Lucin. Greg. lib. 2, dialog. c. 23. Item vide lib. de Eccl dogmat. c. 53, et citatur de consec. dist. 2, c. 13.
[6] Fab. decret. habes de cons. dist. 2. c. 16. et ib. citatur Concil. Agathense c. 18. c. seculares.

sion from the society of the faithful.[1] But although this law, sanctioned, as it is, by the authority of God and of his Church, regards all the faithful, the pastor, however, will teach that it does not extend to persons who have not arrived at the years of discretion, because they are incapable of discerning the Holy Eucharist from common food, and cannot bring with them to this Sacrament, the piety and devotion which it demands. To extend the precept to them would appear inconsistent with the institution of this Sacrament by our Lord: "Take," says he, "and eat,"[2] words which cannot apply to infants, who are evidently incapable of taking and eating. In some places, it is true, an ancient practice prevailed of giving the Holy Eucharist even to infants;[3] but, for the reasons already assigned, and for other reasons most consonant to Christian piety, this practice has been long discontinued by authority of the same Church. With regard to the age at which children should be admitted to communion, this the parents and confessor can best determine: to them it belongs to ascertain whether the children have acquired a competent knowledge of this admirable Sacrament, and desire to taste this bread of angels.

To whom the obligation of this law extends.

The Eucharist anciently given to infants,

From persons labouring under actual insanity the Sacrament should also be withheld. However, according to the decree of the Council of Carthage, it may be administered to them at the close of life, provided they had evinced, previously to their insanity, a sincerely pious desire of being admitted to its participation, and if no danger arising from the state of the stomach or other inconvenience or indignity, is to be apprehended.[4]

When to be given, when not to be given to insane persons.

As to the rite to be observed in the administration of this Sacrament, the pastor will teach that the law of the Church interdicts its administration under both kinds to any but to the officiating priest, unless by special permission of the Church. Christ, it is true, as has been explained by the Council of Trent,[5] instituted and administered to his Apostles, at his last supper, this great Sacrament under both kinds; but it does not follow of necessity, that by doing so he established a law rendering its administration to the faithful under both species imperative. Speaking of this sacrament he himself frequently mentions it under one kind only: "If," says he, "any man eat of this bread, he shall live for ever, and the bread that I will give is my flesh for the life of the world," and, "He that eateth this bread shall live for ever."[6] The Church, no doubt, was influenced by numerous and cogent reasons, not only to approve but confirm by solemn decree, the general practice of communicating under one species. In the first place, the greatest caution

To be received under both kinds by the officiating priest only, and why.

I.

---

[1] Citat. lib. 5. decr. tit. de pœn. et remiss. c. omnes utriusque serus.
[2] Matt. xxvi. 26.   [3] Cypr. de Lapsis post med.   [4] Conc. Cath. 4. 76.
[5] Sess. 21. decem. sub utraque specie can. 1. 2. 3.
[6] John vi. 52. 59. Unius tantum speciei usum sufficere ad perfectam communionem colliges ex Tertull. lib. 2. ad uxorem. Cypr. de Lapsis. Orig. hom. 13. in Exod. Basil. epist. ad Cæsar. patr. Aug. ep. 86. Hier. in Apol. ad Pammach. Chrysost. hom. 41. operis imperf. in Matth.

was necessary to avoid accident or indignity, which must become almost inevitable, if the chalice were administered in a

II.   crowded assemblage. In the next place, the Holy Eucharist
should be at all times in readiness for the sick, and if the species of wine remained long unconsumed, it were to be appre-

III.   hended that it may become vapid. Besides, there are many
who cannot bear the taste or smell of wine; lest, therefore,
what is intended for the nutriment of the soul should prove noxious to the health of the body, the Church, in her wisdom, has
sanctioned its administration under the species of bread alone.

IV.   We may also observe that in many places wine is extremely
scarce, nor can it be brought from distant countries without incurring very heavy expense, and encountering very tedious and

V.   difficult journeys. Finally, a circumstance which principally
influenced the Church in establishing this practice, means were
to be devised to crush the heresy which denied that Christ,
whole and entire, is contained under either species, and asserted
that the body is contained under the species of bread without
the blood, and the blood under the species of wine without the
body. This object was attained by communion under the species of bread alone, which places, as it were, sensibly before
our eyes, the truth of the Catholic faith. Those who have written expressly on this subject, will, if it appear necessary, furnish the pastor with additional reasons for the practice of the
Catholic Church in the administration of the Holy Eucharist.

Priests   To omit nothing doctrinal on so important a subject, we now
alone, the   come to speak of the minister of the sacrament, a point, how-
ministers   ever, on which scarcely any one is ignorant. The pastor then
of the Eu-   will teach, that to priests alone has been given power to con-
charist.   secrate and administer the Holy Eucharist. That the unvarying practice of the Church has also been, that the faithful receive the Sacrament from the hand of the priest, and that the
priest communicate himself, has been explained by the Council
of Trent;[1] and the same holy Council has shown that this
practice is always to be scrupulously adhered to, stamped, as it
is, with the authoritative impress of Apostolic tradition, and
sanctioned by the illustrious example of our Lord himself, who,
with his own hands, consecrated and gave to his disciples, his
most sacred body.[2]

The laity   To consult as much as possible, for the dignity of this so au-
prohibited   gust a Sacrament, not only is its administration confined exclu-
to touch   sively to the priestly order, but the Church has also, by an ex-
the sacred   press law, prohibited any but those who are consecrated to re-
vessels,   ligion, unless in case of necessity, to touch the sacred vessels,
&c.   the linen, or other immediate necessaries for consecration.
Priests and people may hence learn what piety and holiness
Efficacy of   they should possess who consecrate, administer, or receive the
the Eucha-   Holy of Holies. The Eucharist, however, as was observed
rist not af-   with regard to the other Sacraments, whether administered by
fected by

---

[1] Sess. 13, c. 10.   [2] Matt. xxvi. 26. Matt. xiv. 23

holy or unholy hands, is equally valid. It is of faith that the the merit efficacy of the Sacraments does not depend on the merit of the or demerit minister, but on the virtue and power of our Lord Jesus Christ. nister.

With regard to the Eucharist as a Sacrament, these are the The Eu-principal points which demanded explanation. Its nature as a charist a sacrifice we now come to explain, that pastors may know what are the principal instructions to be communicated to the faithful regarding this mystery, on Sundays and holidays, in compliance with the decree of the Council of Trent.[1] Not only is this Sacrament a treasure of heavenly riches, which if we turn to good account will purchase for us the favour and friendship of heaven ; but it also possesses the peculiar and extraordinary value, that in it we are enabled to make some suitable return to God for the inestimable benefits bestowed on us by his bounty. If duly and legitimately offered, this victim is most grateful and most acceptable to God. If the sacrifices of the old law, of which it is written: " Sacrifices and oblations thou wouldst not :"[2] and also, " If thou hadst desired sacrifice, I would, indeed, have given it: with burnt-offering thou wilt not be delighted,"[3] were so acceptable in his sight that, as the Scripture testifies, from them " he smelt a sweet savour,"[4] that is to say, they were grateful and acceptable to him ; what have we not to hope from the efficacy of a sacrifice in which is immolated and offered no less a victim than he, of whom a voice from heaven twice proclaimed : " This is my beloved Son, in whom I am well pleased."[5] This mystery, therefore, the pastor will carefully explain to the people, that when assembled at its celebration, they may learn to make it the subject of attentive and devout meditation.

He will teach, in the first place, that the Eucharist was insti- Instituted tuted by our Lord for two great purposes, to be the celestial for two great ends food of the soul, preserving and supporting spiritual life, and to give to the Church a perpetual sacrifice, by which sin may be expiated, and our heavenly Father, whom our crimes have often grievously offended, may be turned from wrath to mercy, from the severity of just vengeance to the exercise of benignant clemency. Of this the paschal lamb, which was offered and eaten by the Israelites as a sacrament and sacrifice, was a lively figure.[6] Nor could our divine Lord, when about to offer him- Reflection self to his eternal Father on the altar of the cross, have given a more illustrious proof of his unbounded love for us, than by bequeathing to us a visible sacrifice, by which the bloody sacrifice, which, a little after, was to be offered once on the cross, was to be renewed, and its memory celebrated daily throughout the universal Church even to the consummation of time, to the great advantage of her children.

The difference between the Eucharist as a sacrament and The diffe-sacrifice is very great, and is two-fold: as a sacrament it is per- rence be-tween the

Sess. 22. princip. c. 8.   [2] Ps. xxxix. 7.   [3] Ps. l. 18.   [4] Gen. viii. 21.
[5] Matt. iii. 17.   [6] Deut. 16.

15*

Eucharist as a sacrament and sacrifice, two-fold.

fected by consecration, as a sacrifice all its efficacy consists in its oblation. When deposited in a tabernacle, or borne to the sick, it is, therefore, a sacrament, not a sacrifice. As a sacrament, it is also to the worthy receiver a source of merit, and brings with it all those advantages which we have already mentioned ; as a sacrifice it is not only a source of merit, but also of satisfaction. As, in his passion, our Lord merited and satisfied for us, so in the oblation of this sacrifice, which is a bond of Christian unity, Christians merit the fruit of his passion, and satisfy for sin.

This sacrifice when, and by whom instituted.

With regard to the institution of this sacrifice, the Council of Trent has obviated all doubt on the subject, by declaring that it was instituted by our Lord at his last supper, whilst it denounces anathema against all who assert that in it is not offered to God a true and proper sacrifice ; or that *to offer* means nothing more than that Christ gives himself to be our spiritual food.[1] That sacrifice is due to God alone, the holy Council

Sacrifice due to God alone.

also states in the clearest terms.[2] The solemn sacrifice of the Mass is, it is true, sometimes offered to honour the memory of the Saints ; but it is never offered to them, but to Him alone who has crowned them with unfading glory. Never does the officiating minister say : " I offer sacrifice to thee, Peter, or to thee, Paul ;" but whilst he offers sacrifice to God alone, he renders him thanks for the signal victories won by the martyrs, and implores their patronage, " that they whose memory we celebrate on earth, may vouchsafe to intercede for us in heaven."[3] The doctrine of the Catholic Church with regard to this sacrifice, she received from our Lord, when at his last supper, committing to his Apostles the sacred mysteries, he said : " This do, for a commemoration of me."[4] He then, as the holy Synod has defined, ordained them priests, and commanded them and their successors in the ministry, to immolate and offer in sacrifice his precious body and blood.[5] Of this the words of the Apostle to the Corinthians also afford sufficient evidence : " You cannot," says he, " drink the chalice of the Lord, and the chalice of devils : you cannot be partakers of the table of the Lord, and of the table of devils."[6] As then, by the " table of devils," we understand the altar upon which sacrifice was offered to them; so by " the table of the Lord," to bring the words of the Apostle to an apposite conclusion, should be understood the altar on which sacrifice was offered to the Lord.

Figures and prophecies of this sacrifice.

Should we look for figures and prophecies of this sacrifice in the Old Testament, we find, in the first place, that its institution was clearly foretold by Malachy in these words : " From the rising of the sun, even to the going down thereof, my name

---

[1] Vid. Trid. de Sacrif. Missæ c. 1. 3. Dionys. lib. 17. de Eccles. c. 3. Ignat. epist ad Smyrn. Tert. lib. de Orat. Iren. lib. 4. c. 32. Aug. lib. 10. de Civit. Dei, c. 10. et lib. 17. c. 20. et lib. 18. c. 35. et lib. 10. c. 13. et lib. 22. c. 8. et alibi passim. Vide etiam. Sess. 22. de sacrific. Missæ, c. 1. et can. 1 and 2.
[2] Trid. Synod. sess. 21. c. 3.   [3] Aug. contra Faust. lib. 20. c. 21.
[4] Luke xxii. 19. 1 Cor. xi. 24.   [5] Conc. Trid. sess. 22. c. 1.   [6] 1 Cor. x. 21.

is great among the Gentiles, and in every place there is sacrifice, and there is offered to my name a clean oblation: for my name is great among the Gentiles, saith the Lord of hosts."[1] This saving victim was also foretold, as well before as after the promulgation of the Mosaic law, by a variety of sacrifices; for this alone, as the perfection and completion of all, comprises all the advantages which were typified by the other sacrifices. In none of the sacrifices of the old law, however, do we discover a more lively image of the Eucharistic sacrifice than in that of Melchisedech.[2] Our Lord himself, at his last Supper, offered to his Eternal father his precious body and blood under the appearances of bread and wine, at the same time declaring himself, "a priest for ever according to the order of Melchisedech."[3]

We, therefore, confess that the sacrifice of the Mass is one and the same sacrifice with that of the cross: the victim is one and the same, Christ Jesus, who offered himself, once only, a bloody sacrifice on the altar of the cross. The bloody and unbloody victim is still one and the same, and the oblation of the cross is daily renewed in the eucharistic sacrifice, in obedience to the command of our Lord: "This do, for a commemoration of me."[4] The priest is also the same, Christ our Lord: the ministers who offer this sacrifice, consecrate the holy mysteries not in their own but in the person of Christ. This the words of consecration declare: the priest does not say: "This is the body of Christ," but, "This is my body;" and thus invested with the character of Christ, he changes the substance of the bread and wine into the substance of his real body and blood.[5] That the holy sacrifice of the Mass, therefore, is not only a sacrifice of praise and thanksgiving, or a commemoration of the sacrifice of the cross; but also a sacrifice of propitiation, by which God is appeased and rendered propitious, the pastor will teach as a dogma defined by the unerring authority of a general Council of the Church.[6] If, therefore, with pure hearts and a lively faith, and with a sincere sorrow for past transgressions, we immolate and offer in sacrifice this most holy victim, we shall, no doubt, receive from the Lord "mercy and grace in seasonable aid."[7] So acceptable to God is the sweet odour of this sacrifice, that through its oblation he pardons our sins, bestowing on us the gifts of grace and of repentance. This is the solemn prayer of the Church: as often as the commemoration of this victim is celebrated, so often is the work of our salvation promoted, and the plenteous fruits of that bloody victim flow in upon us abundantly, through this unbloody sacrifice.

The pastor will also teach, that such is the efficacy of this sacrifice, that its benefits extend not only to the celebrant and

The sacrifice of the Mass the same with that of the cross.

The Mass, a sacrifice of praise, thanksgiving, and propitiation.

Available to the liv-

[1] Malach. i. 11.   [2] Gen. xiv. 18.   [3] Heb. vii. 17. Ps. cix. 4.
[4] Luke xxii. 19. 1 Cor. xi. 24.
[5] Chrys. hom. 2. in 2. ad Timoth. et hom. de prod. Judæ. Ambr. lib. 4. de Sacram. c. 4.   [6] Trident. sess. 22. de sacrif. Missæ, c. 2. et can. 3.
[7] Hebr. iv. 16.

ing and the communicant, but also to all the faithful whether living or num-
dead : bered amongst those who have died in the Lord, but whose sins
have not yet been fully expiated. According to apostolic tradition the most authentic, it is not less available when offered
for them than when offered in atonement for the sins, in alle-
viation of the punishments, the satisfactions, the calamities, or
Common to for the relief of the necessities, of the living.[1] It is hence easy
all the to perceive, that the mass, whenever and wherever offered, be-
faithful. cause conducive to the common interests and salvation of all, is
to be considered common to all the faithful.
Its rites and This great sacrifice is celebrated with many solemn rites and
ceremo- ceremonies : of these rites and ceremonies let none be deemed
nies. useless or superfluous : all on the contrary tend to display the
majesty of this august sacrifice, and to excite the faithful, by the
celebration of these saving mysteries, to the contemplation of
the divine things which lie concealed in the eucharistic sacrifice.
On these rites and ceremonies we shall not enter at large : they
require a more lengthened exposition than is compatible with
the nature of the present work ; and the pastor has it in his
power to consult on the subject, a variety of treatises composed
by men eminent alike for piety and learning. What has been
said will, with the divine assistance, be found sufficient to explain the principal things which regard the Holy Eucharist both
as a sacrament and sacrifice.

ON THE SACRAMENT OF PENANCE.

Necessity As the frailty and weakness of human nature are universally
of the sa- known and felt, no one can be ignorant of the paramount ne-
crament of cessity of the Sacrament of Penance. If, therefore, in the ex-
Penance. position of the different matters of instruction, we are to measure the assiduity of the pastor by the weight and importance
of the subject, we must come to the conclusion that, in expounding this Sacrament, he can never be sufficiently assiduous.
Its exposition demands an accuracy superior to that of baptism.
Baptism is administered but once, and cannot be repeated ;
penance may be administered and becomes necessary, as often
as we may have sinned after baptism, according to the definition of the Fathers of Trent. " For those who fall into sin
after baptism," say they, " the sacrament of penance is as necessary to salvation, as is baptism for those who have not
been already baptized."[2] On this subject the words of St. Jerome, which say, that penance is "a second plank,"[3] are universally known, and highly commended by all who have written

[1] Trid. Synod. sess. 22. cap. 206.
[2] Sess. 6. de Just. cap. 14. et Sess. 14. de pœnit. cap. 3. in 3 cap.
[3] Hieron. ad hæc verba, Ruit Hierusalem, et epistola 8.

on this Sacrament. As he who suffers shipwreck has no hope of safety, unless, perchance, he seize on some plank from the wreck; so he that suffers the shipwreck of baptismal innocence, unless he cling to the saving plank of penance, may abandon all hope of salvation. These instructions, however, are intended not only for the benefit of the pastor, but also for that of the faithful at large, whose attention they may awaken, lest they be found culpably negligent in a matter of all others the most important. Impressed with a just sense of the frailty of human nature, their first and most earnest desire should be, to advance, with the divine assistance, in the ways of God, flying sin of every sort. But should they, at any time, prove so unfortunate as to fall, then, looking at the infinite goodness of God, who like the good shepherd binds up and heals the wounds of his sheep, they should have immediate recourse to the sacrament of penance, that by its salutary and medicinal efficacy their wounds may be healed.[1]

But to enter more immediately on the subject, and to avoid all error to which the ambiguity of the word may give rise, its different meanings are first to be explained. By penance some understand satisfaction; whilst others, who wander far from the doctrine of the Catholic faith, supposing penance to have no reference to the past, define it to be nothing more than newness of life. The pastor, therefore, will teach that the word (pœnitentia) has a variety of meanings. In the first place, it is used to express a change of mind; as when, without taking into account the nature of the object, whether good or bad, what was before pleasing, is now become displeasing to us. In this sense the Apostle makes use of the word, when he applies it to those, "whose sorrow is according to the world, not according to God; and therefore, worketh not salvation, but death."[2] In the second place, it is used to express that sorrow which the sinner conceives for sin, not however for sake of God, but for his own sake. A third meaning is when we experience interior sorrow of heart, or give exterior indication of such sorrow, not only on account of the sins which we have committed, but also for sake of God alone whom they offend. To all these sorts of sorrow the word (pœnitentia) properly applies.

Different meanings of the word penance.

I

II.

III.

When the Sacred Scriptures say that God repented,[3] the expression is evidently figurative: when we repent of any thing, we are anxious to change it; and thus, when God is said to repent.

In what sense God is said to repent.

---

[1] Ezech. xxxiv. 16. De Pœnitentia e patribus antiquis scripserunt Tertul. librum unum. Cypr. epistolas plures et unum lib. de Lapsis, Pacianus lib. unum et duas epistolas ad Symproniam, ac de pœnit. et confession. seu paran. ad pœnit. Ambros. libros duos pœnit. Chrysost. Homilias 10. et sermon. de pœnit. Ephrem. lib. et sermon. de pœnit. Fulgentius lib. 2. de remission. peccatorum ad Euthymium, et seqq. 14. de pœnit. cap. 3. Greg. Nyssenus orationem de pœnit. Basil. homil. unam quæ est postrema variarum, Augustin. denique lib. unum de vera et falsa pœnitentia, et librum insignem de pœnitentiæ medicina. His adde Marcum Eremitam cujus extat de pœnitent. liber unus, sed caute legendus: de eo vide Bellarmin. de Script. Eccles. Qui non habet Patres supra citatos, videat in Decreta Gratiani de pœnitent. 7. distinctiones.

[2] 2 Cor. vii. 10. [3] Gen. vi. 6. 1 Kings xv. 11. Ps. cv. 45. Jer. xxvi. 3.

Z

change any thing, the Scriptures, accommodating their language to our ideas, say that he repents. Thus we read that "it repented him that he had made man,"[1] and also that it repented him to have made Saul king.[2]

Meaning of penance here.
But an important distinction is to be made between these different significations of the word: to repent, in its first meaning, argues imperfection—in its second, the agitation of a disturbed mind—in the third, penance is a virtue and a sacrament, the sense in which it is here used.

Penance as a virtue.
We shall first treat of penance as a virtue, not only because it is the bounden duty of the pastor to form the faithful, with whose instruction he is charged, to the practice of every virtue; but also, because the acts which proceed from penance as a virtue, constitute the matter, as it were, of penance as a sacrament; and if ignorant of it in this latter sense, impossible not to be ignorant also of its efficacy as a sacrament. The faithful, therefore, are first to be admonished and exhorted to labour strenuously to attain this interior penance of the heart, which we call a virtue, and without which exterior penance can avail them very little.[3] This virtue consists in turning to God sincerely and from the heart, and in hating and detesting our past transgressions, with a firm resolution of amendment of life, hoping to obtain pardon through the mercy of God. It is accompanied with a sincere sorrow, which is an agitation and affection of the mind, and is called by many a passion, and if accompanied with

Supposes faith.
detestation, is, as it were, the companion of sin. It must, however, be preceded by faith, for without faith no man can turn to God. Faith, therefore, cannot on any account be called a part

Proved to be a virtue. I.
of penance.[4] That this inward affection of the soul is, as we have already said, a virtue, the various precepts which enforce its necessity prove; for precepts regard those actions only, the

II.
performance of which implies virtue. Besides, to experience a sense of sorrow at the time, in the manner, and to the extent which are consonant to reason and religion, is no doubt an exercise of virtue: and this sorrow is regulated by the virtue of penance. Some conceive a sorrow which bears no proportion to the enormity of their crimes: "There are some," says Solomon, "who are glad when they have done evil;"[5] whilst others, on the contrary, consign themselves to such morbid melancholy and to such a deluge of grief, as utterly to abandon all hope of salvation. Such perhaps was the condition of Cain when he exclaimed: "My iniquity is greater than that I may deserve pardon:"[6] such certainly was the condition of Judas, who, "repenting," hanged himself in despair, and thus sacrificed soul and body.[7] Penance, therefore, considered as a

---

[1] Gen. vi. 6.   [2] 1 Kings xv. 11.
[3] Vide Amb. in sermone de pœn. et citatur. de pœnit. dist. 3. cap. pœnitentia. Aug. lib. de vera et falsa pœn. c. 8. et habetur de pœn. 3. c. 4. Greg. hom. 34. in Evang. et lib. 9. Regist. Epist. 39.
[4] Trid. Sess. 14. de pœn. c. 3. can. 4.
[5] Prov. ii. 14.   [6] Gen. iv. 13.   [7] Matt. xxvii. 3.

virtue, assists us in restraining within the bounds of moderation our sense of sorrow.

III. That penance is a virtue may also be inferred from the ends which the penitent proposes to himself. The first is to destroy sin and efface from the soul its every spot and stain; the second, to make satisfaction to God for the sins which he has committed, and this is an act of justice towards God. Between God and man, it is true, no relation of strict justice can exist, so great is the distance between the Creator and the creature; yet between both there is evidently a sort of justice, such as exists between a father and his children, between a master and his servants. The third end is, to rein-state himself in the favour and friendship of God whom he has offended, and whose hatred he has earned by the turpitude of sin. That penance is a virtue, these three ends which the penitent proposes to himself, sufficiently prove.

We must also point out the steps, by which we may ascend to this divine virtue. The mercy of God first prevents us and converts our hearts to him; this was the object of the prophet's prayer: "Convert us, O Lord! and we shall be converted."[1]—Illumined by this celestial light the soul next tends to God by faith: "He that cometh to God," says the Apostle, "must believe that he is, and is a rewarder to them that seek him."[2] A salutary fear of God's judgments follows, and the soul, contemplating the punishments that await sin, is recalled from the paths of vice: "As a woman with child," says Isaias, "when she draweth near the time of her delivery, is in pain and crieth out in her pangs; so are we become in thy presence, O Lord!"[3]—We are also animated with a hope of obtaining mercy from God, and cheered by this hope we resolve on a change of life.—Lastly, our hearts are inflamed by charity; and hence we conceive that filial fear which a dutiful and ingenuous child experiences towards a parent. Thus, dreading only to offend the majesty of God in any thing, we entirely abandon the ways of sin. These are, as it were, the steps by which we ascend to this most exalted virtue, a virtue altogether heavenly and divine, to which the Sacred Scriptures promise the inheritance of heaven: "Do penance," says the Redeemer, "for the kingdom of heaven is at hand:"[4] "If," says the prophet Ezekiel, "the wicked do penance for all his sins which he hath committed, and keep all my commandments, and do judgment and justice, living he shall live, and shall not die:"[5] "I desire not, saith the Lord, the death of the wicked, but that the wicked turn from his way and live;"[6] words which are evidently understood of eternal life.

The degrees by which we attain this virtue.

I.

II.

III

IV.

V.

Heaven the reward of penance.

With regard to external penance, the pastor will teach that it is that which constitutes the sacrament of penance: it consists of certain sensible things significant of that which passes inte-

Penance as a sacrament.

---

[1] Jerem. xxxi. 18.   [2] Heb. xi. 6.   [3] Isn. xxvi. 17.
[4] Matt. iv. 17.   [5] Ezek. xviii. 21.   [6] Ezek. xxxiii. 11.

Why insti-
tuted by
our Lord.
I.

riorly in the soul; and the faithful are to be informed, in the first place, why the Redeemer was pleased to give it a place among the Sacraments. His object was, no doubt, to remove, in a great measure, all uncertainty as to the pardon of sin promised by our Lord when he said : "If the wicked do penance for all his sins, which he hath committed, and keep all my commandments, and do judgment and justice, living he shall live, and shall not die."[1] Pronouncing upon his own actions, every man has reason to question the accuracy of his own judgment, and hence, on the sincerity of interior penance the mind must be held in anxious suspense. To calm this our solicitude, the Redeemer instituted the sacrament of penance, in which we cherish a well founded hope, that our sins are forgiven us by the absolution of the priest, and the faith which we justly have in the efficacy of the Sacraments, has much influence in tranquillizing the troubled conscience and giving peace to the soul. The voice of the priest, who is legitimately constituted a minister for the remission of sins, is to be heard as that of Christ himself, who said to the lame man : "Son, be of good cheer, thy sins are forgiven thee."[2]

II.

Moreover, as salvation is unattainable but through Christ and the merits of his passion, the institution of this sacrament was in itself accordant to the views of divine wisdom, and pregnant with blessings to the Christian. Penance is the channel through which the blood of Christ flows into the soul, washes away the stains contracted after baptism, and calls forth from us the grateful acknowledgment, that to the Saviour alone we are indebted for the blessing of a reconciliation with God.

Penance
proved to
be a sacra-
ment.

That penance is a sacrament the pastor will not find it difficult to establish : baptism is a sacrament because it washes away all, particularly original sin : penance also washes away all sins of thought or deed committed after baptism; on the same principle, therefore, penance is a sacrament. Again, and the argument is conclusive, a sacrament is the sign of a sacred thing, and what is done externally, by the priest and penitent, is a sign of what takes place, internally, in the soul : the penitent unequivocally expresses, by words and actions, that he has turned away from sin : the priest, too, by words and actions, gives us easily to understand, that the mercy of God is exercised in the remission of sin : this is, also, clearly evinced by these words of the Saviour : " I will give to thee the keys of the kingdom of heaven, whatever sins you loose on earth, shall be loosed, also, in heaven."[3] The absolution of the priest, which is expressed in words, seals, therefore, the remission of sins, which it accomplishes in the soul, and thus is penance invested with all the necessary conditions of a sacrament, and is, therefore, truly a sacrament.

That penance is not only to be numbered amongst the sacra-

[1] Ezek. xviii. 21.
[2] Matt. ix. 2. Vid. Conc. Trid. sess. xiv. c. 1. in noc. 1. Epist. 91 inter epist. Aug.
[3] Matt. xvi. 19.

ments, but also amongst the sacraments that may be repeated, The sacrament of penance may be repeated. the faithful are next to be taught. To Peter, asking if sin may be forgiven seven times, our Lord replies: "I say, not seven times, but seventy times seven."[1] Whenever, therefore, the ministry of the priest is to be exercised towards those who seem to diffide in the infinite goodness and mercy of God, the zealous pastor will seek to inspire them with confidence, and to reanimate their hopes of obtaining the grace of God. This he will find it easy to accomplish by expounding the preceding words of our Lord, by adducing other texts of the same import, which are to be found numerously scattered throughout the Sacred Volume; and by adopting those reasons and arguments which are supplied by St. Chrysostome in his book " on the fallen," and by St. Ambrose in his treatise on penance.[2]

As, then, amongst the sacraments there is none on which the Its matter. faithful should be better informed, they are to be taught, that it differs from the other sacraments in this: the matter of the other sacraments is some production of nature or art; but the acts of the penitent, contrition, confession, and satisfaction, constitute, as has been defined by the Council of Trent, the matter as it were (quasi materia) of the sacrament of penance.[3] They are called parts of penance, because required in the penitent, by divine institution for the integrity of the Sacrament and the full and entire remission of sin. When the holy synod says, that they are "the matter as it were," it is not because they are not the real matter, but because they are not, like water in baptism and chrism in confirmation, matter that may be applied externally. With regard to the opinion of some, who hold that the Sins in what sense its matter. sins themselves constitute the matter of this sacrament, if well weighed, it will not be found to differ from what has been already laid down: we say that wood which is consumed by fire, is the matter of fire; and sins which are destroyed by penance, may also be called, with propriety, the matter of penance.

The form, also, because well calculated to excite the faithful, Its form. to receive with fervent devotion the grace of this sacrament, the pastor will not omit to explain. The words that compose the form are: " I ABSOLVE THEE," as may be inferred not only from these words of the Redeemer: " Whatsoever you shall bind upon earth, shall be bound also in heaven;"[4] but also from the same doctrine of Jesus Christ, as recorded by the Apostles. That this is the perfect form of the sacrament of penance, the very nature of the form of a sacrament proves. The form of a sacrament signifies what the sacrament accomplishes: these words " I absolve thee" signify the accomplishment of absolution from sin through the instrumentality of this sacrament; they therefore constitute its form. Sins are, as it were, the chains by

---

[1] Matt. xviii. 22.
[2] Chrys. l. 5. lib. de laps. repar. et habetur de pœnit. dist. 3. c. talis. Amb. de pœnit. lib. 1. c, 1. et 2. vid. et Aug. lib. de vera et falsa pœnit. c. 5. citatur de pœnit. dist. c. 3. adhuc instant.
[3] Sess. 24. de pœnit. c. 3. et can. 4.   [4] Matt. xviii. 18.

16

which the soul is fettered, and from the bondage of which it is
"loosed" by the sacrament of penance. This form is not less
true, when pronounced by the priest over him, who by means
of perfect contrition, has already obtained the pardon of his sins.
Perfect contrition, it is true, reconciles the sinner to God, but
his justification is not to be ascribed to perfect contrition alone,
independently of the desire which it includes of receiving the
sacrament of penance. Many prayers accompany the form,
not because they are deemed necessary, but in order to remove
every obstacle, which the unworthiness of the penitent may oppose to the efficacy of the sacrament. Let then the sinner pour
out his heart in fervent thanks to God, who has invested the
ministers of his Church with such ample powers! Unlike the
authority given to the priests of the Old Law, to declare the
leper cleansed from his leprosy,[1] the power with which the
priests of the New Law are invested, is not simply to declare
that sins are forgiven, but, as the ministers of God, really to
absolve from sin; a power which God himself, the author and
source of grace and justification, exercises through their ministry.

*Why ac-
companied
with pray-
ers.*

Reflection.

The rites used in the administration of this sacrament, also
demand the serious attention of the faithful. They will enable
them to form a more just estimate of the blessings which it bestows, recollecting that as servants, they are reconciled to the
best of masters, or rather, as children, to the tenderest of fathers. They will, also, serve to place in a clearer point of
view, the duty of those who desire, and desire every one should,
to evince their grateful recollection of so inestimable a favour.
Humbled in spirit, the sincere penitent casts himself down at
the feet of the priest, to testify, by this his humble demeanour,
that he acknowledges the necessity of eradicating pride, the
root of all those enormities which he now deplores. In the
minister of God, who sits in the tribunal of penance as his
legitimate judge, he venerates the power and person of our Lord
Jesus Christ; for in the administration of this, as in that of the
other sacraments, the priest represents the character and discharges the functions of Jesus Christ. Acknowledging himself deserving of the severest chastisements, and imploring the
pardon of his guilt, the penitent next proceeds to the confession
of his sins. To the antiquity of all these rites St. Denis bears
the most authentic testimony.[2]

*The rites
to be ob-
served in
receiving
this sacra-
ment.*

To the faithful, however, nothing will be found more advantageous, nothing better calculated to animate them to frequent
the sacrament of penance with alacrity, than the frequent exposition of the inestimable advantages which it confers. They
will then see, that of penance it may be truly said: that "its
root is bitter, but its fruit sweet." The great efficacy of penance
is, therefore, that it restores us to the favour of God, and unites

*Its advan-
tages.*

[1] Levit. xiii. 9. et xiv. 2.
[2] In epist. ad Demoph. Vid. et Tertul. lib. de pœnit. c. 9.

us to him in the closest bonds of friendship.[1] From this recon-   **II.**
ciliation with God, the devout soul, who approaches the sacrament with deep sentiments of piety and religion, sometimes experiences the greatest tranquillity and peace of conscience, a
tranquillity and peace accompanied with the sweetest spiritual   **III.**
joy. There is no sin, however grievous, no crime however   **IV.**
enormous or however frequently repeated, which penance does
not remit: "If," says the Almighty, by the mouth of his prophet, "the wicked do penance for all his sins, which he hath
committed, and keep all my commandments, and do judgment
and justice, living he shall live and shall not die; I will not remember all his iniquities which he hath done."[2] "If," says
St. John, "we confess our sins, he is faithful and just to forgive
us our sins;"[3] and a little after he adds: "If any man sin, we
have an advocate with the Father, Jesus Christ, the just; and
he is the propitiation for our sins; and not for ours only, but
also for those of the whole world."[4] If, therefore, we read in   Note.
the pages of inspiration, of some who earnestly implored the
mercy of God, but implored it in vain, it is because they did not
repent sincerely and from their hearts.[5] When we also meet
in the Sacred Scriptures and in the writings of the Fathers, passages which seem to say, that some sins are irremissible, we
are to understand such passages to mean, that it is very difficult
to obtain the pardon of them. A disease may be said to be
incurable, when the patient loathes the medicine that would accomplish his cure; and, in the same sense, some sins may be
said to be irremissible, when the sinner rejects the grace of God,
the proper medicine of salvation. To this effect St. Augustine
says: "When, after having arrived at a knowledge of God,
through the grace of Jesus Christ, any one opposes the fellowship of the faith, and maliciously resists the grace of Jesus
Christ, so great is the enormity of his crime, that, although his
guilty conscience obliges him to acknowledge and declare his
guilt, he cannot submit to the humiliation of imploring pardon."[6]

To return to penance, to it belongs, in so special a manner, Penance
the efficacy of remitting actual guilt, that without its interven- necessary
tion we cannot obtain or even hope for pardon. It is written: to obtain
"Unless you do penance, you shall all perish."[7] These words of sin.
of our Lord are to be understood of grievous and deadly sins,
although, as St. Augustine observes, venial sins also require
some penance: "If," says he, "without penance, venial sin
could be remitted, the daily penance, performed for them by the
Church, would be nugatory."[8]

But as, on matters which, in any degree, affect moral actions, The three
it is not enough to convey instruction in general terms, the pas- integral

---

[1] Conc. Trid. sess. 14. can. 3, &c. 1. de pœnitent.   [2] Ezek. xviii. 21, 22.
[3] 1 John i. 9.   [4] 1 John ii. 1, 2.   [5] 2 Mach. ix. 13.
[6] Lib. 1. de sermon. Domini in monte, c. 42. et 44. et retract. lib. c. 8, 19. Aug.
serm. 1. de verbis Domini, et epist. 50. ad Bonif.   [7] Luke xiii. 3, 5.
[8] Aug. lib. 50. hom. 50. item epist. 168. et Ench. cap. 71.

parts of
penance.

tor will be careful to expound, severally, all those particulars which may give the faithful a knowledge of that penance, which is unto salvation. To this sacrament, then, it is peculiar that, besides matter and form, which are common to all the sacraments, it has, also, as we said before, what are called integral parts of penance, and these integral parts are contrition, confession, and satisfaction. "Penance," says St. Chrysostome, "induces the sinner cheerfully to undergo every rigour; his heart is pierced with contrition; his lips utter the confession of his guilt; and his actions breathe humility, and are accepted by

Their nature.

God as a satisfaction."[1] These component parts of penance are such as we say are necessary to constitute a whole. The human form, for instance, is composed of many members, of hands, of feet, of eyes, &c. of which, if any are wanting, man is justly deemed imperfect, and if not, perfect. Analogous to this, penance consists of the three parts which we have already enumerated; and although, as far as regards the nature of penance, contrition and confession are sufficient for justification, yet, if unaccompanied with satisfaction, something is still wanting to

Their connexion.

its integrity. So connected then are these parts one with the other, that contrition and a disposition to satisfaction precede confession, and contrition and confession precede satisfaction.

Why integral parts.

Why these are integral parts of penance may be thus explained —We sin against God by thought, word, and deed: when recurring to the power of the keys, we should, therefore, endeavour to appease his wrath, and obtain the pardon of our sins, by the very same means, by which we offended his supreme majesty. In further explanation we may also add, that penance is, as it were, a compensation for offences, which proceed from the free will of the person offending, and is appointed by the will of God, to whom the offence has been offered. On the part of the penitent, therefore, a willingness to make this compensation is required, and in this willingness chiefly consists contrition. The penitent must also submit himself to the judgment of the priest, who is the vicegerent of God, to enable him to award a punishment proportioned to his guilt; and, hence, are clearly understood the nature and necessity of confession and satisfaction.

Contrition
defined
and explained.

But as the faithful require instruction on the nature and efficacy of these parts of penance, we shall begin with contrition, a subject which demands to be explained with more than ordinary care; for as often as we call to mind our past transgressions, or offend God anew, so often should our hearts be pierced with contrition. By the Fathers of the Council of Trent, contrition is defined: "A sorrow and detestation of past sin, with a purpose of sinning no more."[2] Speaking of the motion of the will to contrition, the Council, a little after, adds: "if joined with a confidence in the mercy of God, and an earnest desire

[1] Hom. 11. quæ est de pœnit. Vid. conc. Trid. 14. de pœnit. cap. 3. et can. 4. Item. conc. Flor. in doctrin. de Sacram.
[2] Ead. sess. 14.

of performing whatever is necessary to the proper reception of the Sacrament, it thus, at length, prepares us for the remission of sin." From this definition, therefore, the faithful will perceive that contrition does not simply consist in ceasing to sin, purposing to enter, or having actually entered, on a new life: it supposes, first of all, a hatred of sin, and a desire of atoning for past transgressions. This, the cries of the holy Fathers of antiquity, which are poured out in the pages of inspiration, sufficiently prove:[1] "I have laboured in my groaning;" says David, "every night I will wash my bed;" and again, "The Lord hath heard the voice of my weeping."[2] "I will recount to thee all my years," says the prophet Isaias, "in the bitterness of my soul."[3] These and many other expressions of the same import, were called forth by an intense hatred and a lively detestation of past transgressions.

But, although contrition is defined "a sorrow," the faithful are not thence to conclude, that this sorrow consists in sensible feeling: contrition is an act of the will, and as St. Augustine observes, sorrow is not penance, but the accompaniment of penance.[4] By "sorrow" the Fathers of Trent understood a hatred and detestation of sin; because, in this sense, the Sacred Scriptures frequently make use of the word: "How long," says David, "shall I take counsels in my soul, sorrow in my heart all the day?"[5] and also because from contrition arises sorrow in the inferior part of the soul, which, in the language of the schools, is called the seat of concupiscence. With propriety, therefore, is contrition defined a "sorrow," because it produces sorrow, a sorrow so intense that in other days, penitents, to express its intensity, changed their garments, a practice to which our Lord alludes when he says; "Wo to thee, Corozain; wo to thee, Bethsaida: for if in Tyre and Sidon had been wrought the miracles that have been wrought in thee, they had done penance, long since, in sackcloth and ashes."[6] To signify the intensity of this sorrow, the "detestation of sin," of which we speak, is properly expressed by the word "contrition," a word which, literally understood, means the breaking into small parts by means of some harder substance, and which is here used metaphorically, to signify that our hearts, hardened by pride, are subdued and reduced by penance. Hence no other sorrow, not even that which is felt for the death of parents, or children, or for any other visitation however calamitous, is called contrition: the word is exclusively employed to express the sorrow with which we are overwhelmed by the forfeiture of the grace of God and of our own innocence. It is, however, often designated by other names: sometimes it is called "contrition of heart," because the word "heart" is frequently used in Scripture to express the will, for as the heart is the principle, which originates the motion of the human system; so, the will

The sorrow which contrition requires explained.

Propriety of the word "contrition."

Sometimes called by other names.

---

[1] Vid. de poenit. dist. 1. c. et venit, et ibid. dist. c. totam.   [2] Ps. vi. 7—9.
[3] Isa. xxxviii. 15.   [4] Homil. 50.   [5] Ps. xii. 2.   [6] Matt xi. 21.

is the faculty which governs and controls the other powers of
the soul. By the holy Fathers it is also called " compunction
of heart," and hence the works written by them on contrition
they prefer inscribing, treatises on " compunction of heart;"[1]
for, as imposthumes are cut with a lancet in order to open a
passage to the virulent matter accumulated within; so the heart
of the sinner is, as it were, pierced with contrition, to enable it
to emit the deadly poison of sin which rankles within it.
Hence, contrition is called by the Prophet Joel, a rending of
the heart: " Be converted to me," says he, " with all your
hearts in fasting, in weeping, in mourning, and rend your
hearts."[2]

This sor-
row should
be su-
preme in
degree.
I.

That for past transgressions the sinner should experience the
deepest sorrow, a sorrow not to be exceeded, will easily appear
from the following considerations. Perfect contrition is an act
of charity, emanating from what is called filial fear: the measure of contrition and charity should, therefore, it is obvious,
be the same: but the charity which we cherish towards God,[3] is
the most perfect love; and, therefore, the sorrow which contrition inspires, should also be the most perfect. God is to be loved
above all things; and whatever separates us from God is, therefore, to be hated above all things. It is, also, worthy of observation, that to charity and contrition the language of Scripture assigns the same extent: of charity it is said: " Thou
shall love the Lord thy God with thy *whole* heart:"[4] of contri-

II.

trition: " Be converted with thy *whole* heart."[5] Besides, if it
is true, that of all objects which solicit our love, God is the supreme good, and no less true, that of all objects which deserve
our execration sin is the supreme evil; the same principle
which prompts us to confess that God is to be loved above all
things, obliges us also of necessity to acknowledge that sin is
to be hated above all things. That God is to be loved above
all things, so that we should be prepared to sacrifice our lives
rather than offend him, these words of the Redeemer declare:
" He that loveth father or mother more than me, is not worthy

III.

of me:"[6] " He that will save his life shall lose it."[7] As charity, it is the observation of St. Bernard, recognises neither
measure nor limit, or to use his own words, as " the measure

And also
in inten-
sity.

of loving God is to love him without measure,"[8] so the measure
of hating sin should be, to hate sin without measure. Besides,
our contrition should be supreme not only in degree, but also
in intensity, and thus perfect, excluding all apathy and indifference, according to these words of Deuteronomy: " When thou
shalt seek the Lord thy God, thou shalt find him: yet so if thou
seek him with all thy heart, and all the affliction of thy soul;"[9]
and of the prophet Jeremiah: " thou shalt seek me and shalt
find me, when thou shalt seek me with all thy heart; and I

---

[1] Chrysost. de compunct. cordis. Triden. de summo bono, lib. 2. c. 12.
[2] Joel ii. 12.   [3] 1 John iv. 7.   [4] Deut. vi. 5.   [5] Joel ii. 12.
[6] Matt. x. 37.   [7] Matt. xvi. 25. Mark vii. 35.
[8] Lib. de diligendo Deo circa med.   [9] Deut. iv. 29.

will be found by thee, saith the Lord."[1] If, however, our con- Imperfect
trition be not perfect, it may, nevertheless, be true and efficacious; contrition
for as things which fall under the senses frequently touch the $\frac{may\ be}{true\ and}$
heart more sensibly than things purely spiritual, it will some- efficacious.
times happen that persons feel more intense sorrow for the
death of their children, than for the grievousness of their sins.
Our contrition may also be true and efficacious, although unac- Tears de-
companied with tears. That sorrow for his sins bathe the of- sirable, but
fender in tears, is, however, much to be desired and com- $\frac{not\ neces-}{sary.}$
mended. On this subject the words of St. Augustine are admi-
rable : " The spirit of Christian charity," says he, " lives not
within you, if you lament the body from which the soul has departed, but lament not the soul from which God has departed."[2]
To the same effect are the words of the Redeemer above cited :
" Wo to thee, Corozain, wo to thee, Bethsaida, for if in Tyre
and Sidon had been wrought the miracles that have been
wrought in thee, they had long since done penance, in sackcloth and ashes."[3] Of this, however, we have abundant illustration in the well known examples of the Ninevites,[4] of David,[5]
of the woman caught in adultery,[6] and of the Prince of the
Apostles,[7] all of whom obtained the pardon of their sins, imploring the mercy of God with abundance of tears.

The faithful are most earnestly to be exhorted to study to di- Contrition
rect their contrition specially to each mortal sin into which $\frac{should\ ex-}{tend\ to\ all}$
they may have had the misfortune to fall : " I will recount to thee," mortal sins.
says Isaias, " all my years in the bitterness of my soul :"[8] as
if he had said, " I will count over all my sins severally, that
my heart may be pierced with sorrow for them all." In Ezekiel, also, we read : " If the wicked do penance for all his sins,
he shall live."[9] In this spirit, St. Augustine says : " Let the
sinner consider the quality of his sins, as affected by time,
place, variety, person."[10] In the work of conversion, however, Note.
the sinner should not despair of the infinite goodness and mercy
of God : he is most desirous of our salvation ; and, therefore,
refuses not to pardon, but embraces, with a father's fondness, the
prodigal child, the moment he returns to a sense of his duty,
and is converted to the Lord, detesting his sins, which he will
afterwards, if possible, recall, severally, to his recollection, and
abhor from his inmost soul. The Almighty himself, by the
mouth of his prophet, commands us to hope, when he says :
" The wickedness of the wicked shall not hurt him, in what
day soever he shall turn from his wickedness."[11]

To convey a knowledge of the most important qualities of The quali
true contrition, what has been said will be found sufficiently $\frac{ties\ of\ true}{contrition.}$
comprehensive. In these the faithful are to be accurately in-
structed, that each may know the means of attaining, and may
have a fixed standard by which to determine how far he may be

[1] Jer. xxix. 13.   [2] Ser. 41. de sanctis.   [3] Matt. xi. 21.
[4] Jonas iii. 6.   [5] Ps. 6 and 50.   [6] Luke vii. 37. 48. 51.
[7] Luke xxii. 62.   [8] Isa. xxxviii. 15.   [9] Ezek. xviii. 21.
[10] Lib. de vera et falsa relig. cap. 14.   [11] Ezek. xxxiii. 12.

I. removed from the perfection of this virtue. We must, then, in the first place, detest and deplore all our sins : if our sorrow and detestation extend only to some, our repentance cannot be sincere or salutary : " Whosoever shall keep the whole law," says St. James, " but offend in one point, is become guilty of

II. all."[1] In the next place, our contrition must be accompanied with a desire of confessing and satisfying for our sins : dispo-

III. sitions of which we shall treat in their proper place. Thirdly, the penitent must form a fixed and firm purpose of amendment of life, according to these words of the prophet : " If the wicked do penance for all his sins which he hath committed, and keep all my commandments, and do judgment and justice, living he shall live, and shall not die : I will not remember all his iniquities which he hath done ;" and a little after ; " Be converted, and do penance for all your iniquities, and iniquity shall not be your ruin. Cast away from you all your transgressions, by which you have transgressed, and make your-

Illustrations. selves a new heart."[2] To the woman caught in adultery the Redeemer himself imparts the same lesson of instruction : " Go thy way, and sin no more,"[3] and also to the lame man whom he cured at the pool of Bethsaida : " Behold, thou art made whole, sin no more."[4] That a sorrow for sin, and a firm purpose of avoiding sin for the future, are indispensable to contrition, is the dictate of unassisted reason. He who would be reconciled to a friend, must regret to have injured or offended him ; and the tone and tenor of his conduct must be such that the charge of violating the duties of friendship cannot, in future, justly attach to his character. These are principles to which man is bound to yield obedience ; the law to which man is subject, be it natural, divine, or human, he is bound to obey. If, therefore, by force or fraud, the penitent has injured his neighbour in his property, he is bound to restitution : if, by word or deed he has injured his honour or reputation, he is under an obligation of repairing the injury, according to the well known maxim of St. Augustine : " the sin is not forgiven unless what has been taken

IV. away is restored."[5] In the fourth and last place, and the condition is no less important, true contrition must be accompanied with forgiveness of the injuries which we may have sustained from others. This our Lord emphatically declares and energetically inculcates, when he says : " If you will forgive men their offences, your heavenly Father will forgive you also your offences ; but if you will not forgive men, neither will your Father forgive you your offences."[6] These are the conditions which true contrition requires. There are other accompaniments which, although not essential, contribute to render contrition more perfect in its kind, and which will reward, without fatiguing the industry of the pastor.

Efficacy and import- It will conduce in an eminent degree, to the spiritual interests

[1] James ii. 10.   [2] Ezek. xviii. 21, 22.   [3] John viii. 11
[4] John v. 14.   [5] Epist. v. 4.   [6] Matt. vi. 14.

of the faithful, if the pastor press frequently upon their attention, ance of the efficacy and importance of contrition. To make known the truths of salvation should not be deemed a full discharge of the duty of the pastor: his zeal should be exerted to persuade them to the adoption of these truths as their rule of conduct through life, as the governing principle of all their actions. Other pious exercises, such as alms, fasting, prayer, and the like, in themselves holy and commendable, are sometimes, through human infirmity, rejected by Almighty God ; but contrition can never be rejected by him, never prove unacceptable to him : " A contrite and humbled heart, O God !" exclaims the prophet, " thou wilt not despise."[1] Nay more, the same prophet declares that, as soon as we have conceived this contrition in our hearts, our sins are forgiven: " I said, I will confess my injustice to the Lord, and thou hast forgiven the wickedness of my sin."[2] Of this we have a figure in the ten lepers, who, when sent by our Lord to the priests, were cured of their leprosy, before they had reached them ;[3] to give us to understand, that such is the efficacy of true contrition, of which we have spoken above, that through it we obtain from God the immediate pardon of our sins.

To excite the faithful to contrition, it will be found very salutary if the pastor point out the spiritual exercises conducive to contrition. This is to be accomplished by admonishing them, frequently to examine their consciences, in order to ascertain if they have been faithful in the observance of those things which God and his Church require ; and should any one be conscious of crime, he should immediately accuse himself, humbly solicit pardon from God, and implore time to confess, and satisfy for his sins. Above all, let him supplicate the aid of divine grace, by which he may be fortified against a relapse into those crimes, the commission of which he now penitently deplores. The faithful are also to be excited to a hatred of sin, arising from the consideration of its baseness and turpitude, and of the evils and calamities of which it is the poisoned source, estranging us, as it does, from the friendship of God, to whom we are already indebted for so many invaluable blessings, and from whom we might have expected to receive gifts of still higher value, and consigning us to eternal death, to be the unhappy victims of the most excruciating torments.

Having said thus much on contrition, we now come to confession, which is another part of penance. The care and exactness which its exposition demands, must be at once obvious, if we only reflect, that whatever of piety, of holiness, of religion, has been preserved to our times in the Church of God, is, in the general opinion of the truly pious, to be ascribed in a great measure, under divine Providence, to the influence of Confession. It cannot, therefore, be matter of surprise, that the enemy of the human race, in his efforts to level to its foundation the

Marginalia: ance of contrition. Spiritual exercises conducive to contrition. I. II. III. IV V Confession, its importance. I.

fabric of Catholicity, should, through the agency of the ministers of his wicked designs, have assailed, with all his might,
this bulwark of Christian virtue. The pastor, therefore, will
teach, in the first place, that the institution of confession is most
useful and even necessary.

II.
Contrition, it is true, blots out sin; but who is ignorant, that
to effect this, it must be so intense, so ardent, so vehement, as
to bear a proportion to the magnitude of the crimes which it
effaces? This is a degree of contrition which few reach, and
hence, through perfect contrition alone, very few indeed could
hope to obtain the pardon of their sins. It, therefore, became
necessary, that the Almighty, in his mercy, should afford a less
precarious and less difficult means of reconciliation, and of salvation; and this he has done, in his admirable wisdom, by
giving to his Church the keys of the kingdom of heaven. According to the doctrine of the Catholic Church, a doctrine firmly
to be believed and professed by all her children, if the sinner
have recourse to the tribunal of penance with a sincere sorrow
for his sins, and a firm resolution of avoiding them in future,
although he bring not with him that contrition which may be
sufficient of itself to obtain the pardon of sin; his sins are forgiven by the minister of religion, through the power of the keys.
Justly, then, do the Holy Fathers proclaim, that by the keys
of the Church, the gate of heaven is thrown open;[1] a truth
which the decree of the Council of Florence, declaring that the
effect of penance is absolution from sin, renders it imperative
on all, unhesitatingly to believe.[2]

III.
To appreciate the advantages of confession, we should not
lose sight of an argument which has the sanction of experience.
To those who have led immoral lives, nothing is found so useful towards a reformation of morals, as sometimes to disclose
their secret thoughts, their words, their actions, to a prudent
and faithful friend, who can guide them by his advice, and assist
them by his co-operation. On the same principle must it prove
most salutary to those, whose minds are agitated by the consciousness of guilt, to make known the diseases and wounds of their
souls to the priest, as the vicegerent of Jesus Christ, bound to
eternal secrecy by every law human and divine. In the tribunal of penance they will find immediate remedies, the healing
qualities of which will not only remove the present malady, but
also prove of such lasting efficacy as to be, in future, an antidote against the easy approach of the same moral disease.

IV
Another advantage, derivable from confession, is too important to be omitted: confession contributes powerfully to the
preservation of social order. Abolish sacramental confession,
and, that moment, you deluge society with all sorts of secret
crimes—crimes too, and others of still greater enormity, which
men, once that they have been depraved by vicious habits, will

[1] Ambr. serm. 1, de quadrag. citatur de pœnit. dist. 1. c. ecce nunc. August. lib.
[2] de adul. conjug. 59. Chrysost. de sacerdot. lib. 3.
[3] Flor. Conc. in decreto Eugenii. IV. de pœnit. dist. 6. c. sacerdos.

not dread to commit in open day. The salutary shame that attends confession, restrains licentiousness, bridles desire, and coerces the evil propensities of corrupt nature.

Having explained the advantages of confession, the pastor will next unfold its nature and efficacy. Confession, then, is defined " A sacramental accusation of one's self, made to obtain pardon by virtue of the keys." It is properly called " an accusation," because sins are not to be told as if the sinner boasted of his crimes, as they do, " who are glad when they have done evil ;"[1] nor are they to be related as idle stories or passing occurrences, to amuse : they are to be confessed as matters of self-accusation, with a desire, as it were, to avenge them on ourselves. But we confess our sins with a view to obtain the pardon of them ; and, in this respect, the tribunal of penance differs from other tribunals, which take cognizance of capital offences, and before which a confession of guilt is sometimes made, not to secure acquittal but to justify the sentence of the law. The definition of confession by the Holy Fathers,[2] although different in words, is substantially the same : " Confession," says St. Augustine, " is the disclosure of a secret disease, with the hope of obtaining a cure ;"[3] and St. Gregory ; " confession is a detestation of sins :"[4] both of which accord with, and are contained in the preceding definition.

Nature and efficacy of confession.

The pastor will next teach, with all the decision due to a revealed truth, a truth of paramount importance, that this Sacrament owes its institution to the singular goodness and mercy of our Lord Jesus Christ, who ordered all things well, and solely with a view to our salvation.[5] After his resurrection, he breathed on the assembled Apostles, saying : " Receive ye the Holy Ghost, whose sins you shall forgive, they are forgiven ; and whose sins you shall retain, they are retained."[6] By investing the sacerdotal character with power to retain as well as to remit sins, he thus, it is manifest, constitutes them judges in the causes on which this discretionary power is to be exercised. This he seems to have signified when, having raised Lazarus from the dead, he commanded his Apostles to loose him from the bands in which he was bound.[7] This is the interpretation of St. Augustine : " they," says he, " the priests, can now do more : they can exercise greater clemency towards those who confess, and whose sins they forgive. The Lord by the hands of his Apostles delivered Lazarus, whom he had already raised from the dead, to be loosed by the hands of his disciples ; thus giving us to understand that to priests was given the power of loosing."[8] To this, also, refers the command given by our Lord to the lepers cured on the way, to show themselves

Instituted by Christ.
I.

II.

---

[1] Prov. ii. 14.   [2] Chrysost. 20, in Genes.
[3] Aug. ser. 4, de verbis Domini.   [4] Greg. hom. 40. in Evangel.
[5] Vid. Trid. sess. 14. de poenit c. 5. et can. 6. Aug. lib. 50. hom. homil. 64, et citatur de poenit. dist. 1. c. agite. Orig. hom. 1. in Psal. 37. Chrysost. de sacerd. lib. 3.
[6] John xx. 22, 23.   [7] John xi. 44.
[8] De vera et falsa poenit. c. 16. et serm. 8. de verbis Domini.

to the priests, and subject themselves to their judgment.[1] Invested, then, as they are, by our Lord with power to remit and retain sins, priests are, evidently, appointed judges of the matter on which they are to pronounce; and as, according to the wise admonition of the Council of Trent, we cannot form an accurate judgment on any matter, or award to crime a just proportion of punishment, without having previously examined, and made ourselves well acquainted with the cause; hence arises a necessity, on the part of the penitent, of making known to the priest, through the medium of confession, each and every sin.[2] This doctrine, a doctrine defined by the holy synod of Trent, the uniform doctrine of the Catholic Church, the pastor

III.   will teach. An attentive perusal of the Holy Fathers will present innumerable passages throughout their works, proving in the clearest terms that this Sacrament was instituted by our Lord, and that the law of sacramental confession, which, from the Greek, they call "exomologesis," and "exagoreusis," is to be received as evangelical. That the different sorts of sacrifices, which were offered by the priests for the expiation of different sorts of sins, seem, beyond all doubt, to have reference to sacramental confession, an examination of the figures of the Old Testament will also evince.

Rites and ceremonies used at confession.   Not only are the faithful to be taught that confession was instituted by our Lord; but they are also to be reminded that, by authority of the Church, have been added certain rites and solemn ceremonies, which, although not essential to the Sacrament, serve to place its dignity more fully before the eyes of the penitent, and to prepare his soul, now kindled into devotion, the more easily to receive the grace of the Sacrament. When, with uncovered head, and bended knees, with eyes fixed on the earth, and hands raised in supplication to heaven, and with other indications of Christian humility not essential to the Sacrament, we confess our sins, our minds are thus deeply impressed with a clear conviction of the heavenly virtue of the Sacraments, and also of the necessity of humbly imploring and of earnestly importuning the mercy of God.

Confession necessary.   Nor let it be supposed that confession, although instituted by our Lord, is not declared by him necessary for the remission of sin: the faithful must be impressed with the conviction, that he who is dead in sin, is to be recalled to spiritual life by means of sacramental confession, a truth clearly conveyed by our Lord himself, when, by a most beautiful metaphor, he calls the power of administering this sacrament, "the keys of the kingdom of heaven."[3] To obtain admittance into any place, the concurrence of him to whom the keys have been committed is necessary, and therefore, as the metaphor implies, to gain admission

---

[1] Luke xvii. 14.
[2] Sess. 14. c. 5. et can. 7. de pœnit. Sacerdotes esse peccatorum judices docent August. lib. 20. de civit. Dei, c. 9. Hieron. epist. 1. ad Heliod. Chrysost. lib. 3. de Sacerd. et hom. 5. de verbis Isaiæ. Greg. hom. 26. in Evang. Ambr. lib. 2. de Cain, cap. 4. Trid. sess. 14. de pœnit. c. 5. can. 7.   [3] Matt. xvi. 19.

into heaven, its gates must be opened to us by the power of the keys, confided by Almighty God to the care of his Church. This power should otherwise be nugatory: if heaven can be entered without the power of the keys, in vain shall they to whose fidelity they have been intrusted, assume the prerogative of prohibiting indiscriminate entrance within its portals. This doctrine was familiar to the mind of St. Augustine : " Let no man," says he, " say within himself ; ' I repent in secret with God ; God, who has power to pardon me, knows the inmost sentiments of my heart :' was there no reason for saying : ' whatsoever you loose on earth, shall be loosed in heaven ;'[1] no reason why the keys were given to the Church of God ?"[2] The same doctrine is recorded by the pen of St. Ambrose, in his treatise on penance, when refuting the heresy of the Novatians, who asserted that the power of forgiving sins belonged solely to God : " Who," says he, " yields greater reverence to God, he who obeys or he who resists his commands ? God commands us to obey his ministers ; and by obeying them, we honour God alone."[3]

As the law of confession was, no doubt, enacted and established by our Lord himself, it is our duty to ascertain, on whom, at what age, and at what period of the year, it becomes obligatory. . According to the canon of the Council of Lateran, which begins : " Omnis utriusque sexus," no person is bound by the law of confession until he has arrived at the use of reason, a time determinable by no fixed number of years.[4] It may, however, be laid down as a general principle, that children are bound to go to confession, as soon as they are able to discern good from evil, and are capable of malice ; for, when arrived at an age to attend to the work of salvation, every one is bound to have recourse to the tribunal of penance, without which the sinner cannot hope for salvation. In the same canon the Church has defined the period, within which we are bound to discharge the duty of confession : it commands all the faithful to confess their sins at least once a year.[5] If, however, we consult for our eternal interests, we will certainly not neglect to have recourse to confession as often, at least, as we are in danger of death, or undertake to perform any act incompatible with the state of sin, such as to administer or receive the sacraments. The same rule should be strictly followed when we are apprehensive of forgetting some sin, into which we may have had the misfortune to fall : to confess our sins, we must recollect them ; and the remission of them we can only obtain through the sacrament of penance, of which confession is a part.

But as, in confession, many things are to be observed, some of which are essential, some not essential to the sacrament, the faithful are to be carefully instructed on all these matters ; and the pastor can have access to works, from which such instructions

Marginal notes:
Confession obligatory, at what age.

At what time.

Integrity essential to a good confession, in what it consists.

[1] Lib. 50. hom. 49. [2] Matt. xviii. 18. [3] Lib. 1. de pœn. 2.
[4] Lat. conc. cap. 22. [5] Lat. conc. cap. 21.
17   2 B

may easily be drawn. Amongst these matters, he will, on *no*
account, omit to inform the faithful, that to a good confession
integrity is essential. All mortal sins must be revealed to the
minister of religion: venial sins, which do not separate us from
the grace of God, and into which we frequently fall, although
as the experience of the pious proves, proper and profitable to
be confessed, may be omitted without sin, and expiated by a
variety of other means.[1] Mortal sins, as we have already said,
although buried in the darkest secrecy, and also sins of desire
only, such as are forbidden by the ninth and tenth commandments, are all and each of them to be made matter of confession. Such secret sins often inflict deeper wounds on the soul,
than those which are committed openly and publicly. It is,
however, a point of doctrine defined by the Council of Trent;[2]
and as the holy Fathers testify, the uniform and universal doctrine of the Catholic Church : " Without the confession of his
sin," says St. Ambrose, "no man can be justified from his
sin."[3] In confirmation of the same doctrine, St. Jerome, on
Ecclesiastes, says ; " If the serpent, the devil, has secretly and
without the knowledge of a third person, bitten any one, and
has infused into him the poison of sin; if unwilling to disclose
his wound to his brother or master, he is silent and will not do
penance, his master who has power to cure him, can render
him no service." The same doctrine we find in St. Cyprian,
in his sermon on the lapsed: " Although guiltless," says he,
" of the heinous crime of sacrificing to idols, or of having purchased certificates to that effect ; yet, as they entertained the
thought of doing so, they should confess it with grief, to the
priest of God."[4] In fine, such is the unanimous voice, such
the unvarying accord of all the Doctors of the Church.[5]

Aggrava-
ting cir-
cumstan-
ces when
necessary
to be men-
tioned in
confession.

In confession we should employ all that care and exactness
which we usually bestow upon worldly concerns of the greatest
moment, and all our efforts should be directed to effect the cure
of our spiritual maladies and to eradicate sin from the soul.
With the bare enumeration of our mortal sins, we should not
be satisfied ; that enumeration we should accompany with the
relation of such circumstances as considerably aggravate or extenuate their malice. Some circumstances are such, as of themselves to constitute mortal guilt; on no account or occasion
whatever, therefore, are such circumstances to be omitted. Has
any one imbrued his hands in the blood of his fellow man ?
He must state whether his victim was a layman or an ecclesiastic. Has he had criminal intercourse with any one ? He

---

[1] Quomodo venialia dimittantur vide Aug. in Ench. cap. 71. citatur de pœnit.
dist. 3. c, de quotidianis, et in Conc. Tolet. 4. cap. 9.
[2] Sess. 14. de pœnit. c. 5. et can. 7.
[3] Lib. de Paradiso, c. 4. c. 1. super illud : si mordeat serpens.
[4] Circa finem.
[5] Singula peccata mortalia confiteri oportere docent August. lib. de vera et
falsa pœnit. cap. 10. Gregor. homil. 10. super Ezekiel. Ambr. lib. de parad. cap. 14.
Hieron. in Ecclesiast. c. 10. Cypr. de lapsis circa finem. Vid. et de pœnit. dist. 3.
cap. sunt plures, &c. pluit et ibid. dist. 1. c. quem pœn. et ibid. pass.

must state whether the female was married or unmarried, a relative or a person consecrated to God by vow. These are circumstances which alter the species of the sins : the first is called simple fornication ; the second adultery ; the third incest ; and the fourth sacrilege. Again, theft is numbered in the catalogue of sins ; but if a person has stolen a guinea, his sin is less grievous than if he had stolen one or two hundred guineas, or a considerable sum ; and if the stolen money were sacred, the sin would be still aggravated. To time and place the same observation equally applies ; but the instances in which these circumstances alter the complexion of an act, are so familiar and are enumerated by so many writers, as to supersede the necessity of a lengthened detail. Circumstances such as these are, therefore, to be mentioned ; but those, which do not considerably aggravate, may be lawfully omitted. When unnecessary.

So important, as we have already said, is integrity to confession, that if the penitent wilfully neglect to accuse himself of some sins which should be confessed, and suppress others, he not only does not obtain the pardon of his sins, but involves himself in deeper guilt. Such an enumeration cannot be called sacramental confession : on the contrary, the penitent must repeat his confession, not omitting to accuse himself of having, under the semblance of confession, profaned the sanctity of the sacrament. But should the confession seem defective, either because the penitent forgot some grievous sins, or because although intent on confessing all his sins, he did not explore the recesses of his conscience with extraordinary minuteness, he is not bound to repeat his confession : it will be sufficient, when he recollects the sins which he had forgotten, to confess them to a priest on a future occasion. We are not, however, to examine our consciences with careless indifference, or evince such negligence in recalling our sins to our recollection, as if we were unwilling to remember them ; and should this have been the case, the confession must be reiterated. Concealment of a sin in confession a grievous crime : the confession to be repeated. Omission of a sin through forgetfulness does not render it necessary to repeat the confession.

Our confession should also be plain, simple, and undisguised, not clothed in that artificial language with which some invest it, who seem more disposed to give an outline of their general manner of living, than to confess their sins. Our confession should be such as to reflect a true image of our lives, such as we ourselves know them to be, exhibiting as doubtful that which is doubtful, and as certain that which is certain. If, then, we neglect to enumerate our sins, or introduce extraneous matter, our confession, it is clear, wants this quality. Confession should be plain, simple, undisguised,

Prudence and modesty in explaining matters of confession are also much to be commended, and a superfluity of words is to be carefully avoided : whatever is necessary to make known the nature of every sin, is to be explained briefly and modestly. prudent, and modest.

Secrecy should be strictly observed as well by penitent as priest, and, hence, because in such circumstances secrecy must be insecure, no one can, on any account, confess by messenger or letter. Secrecy to be observed by priest and penitent.

Frequent
confession.

But above all, the faithful should be most careful to cleanse their consciences from sin by frequent confession: when oppressed by mortal guilt, nothing can be more salutary, so precarious is human life, than to have immediate recourse to the tribunal of penance; but could we even promise ourselves length of days, yet should not we who are so particular in whatever relates to cleanliness of dress or person, blush to evince less concern in preserving the lustre of the soul pure and unsullied from the foul stains of sin.

The minister of the sacrament of penance.

We now come to treat of the minister of this sacrament—That the minister of the sacrament of penance must be a priest possessing ordinary or delegated jurisdiction, the laws of the Church sufficiently declare: whoever discharges this sacred function must be invested, not only with the power of orders, but also with that of jurisdiction. Of this ministry we have an illustrious proof in these words of the Redeemer, recorded by St. John: " Whose sins you shall forgive, they are forgiven, and whose sins you shall retain they are retained;"[1] words addressed not to all but to the Apostles only, to whom, in this function of the ministry, priests succeed. This admirably accords with the economy of religion, for as the grace imparted by this sacrament emanates from Christ the head, and is diffused through his members, they who alone have power to consecrate his true body, should alone have power to administer this sacrament to his mystical body, the faithful; particularly as they are qualified and disposed by means of the sacrament of penance, to receive the Holy Eucharist. The scrupulous care which, in the primitive ages of the Church, guarded the right of the ordinary priest, is very intelligible from the ancient decrees of the Fathers, which provided, "that no bishop or priest, except in case of necessity, presume to exercise any function in the parish of another without the authority of the ordinary;" a law which derives its sanction from the Apostle, when he commanded Titus to ordain priests in every city,[2] to administer to the faithful

Any priest, the minister in an extreme case.

the heavenly food of doctrine and of the sacraments. But in case of imminent danger of death, when recourse cannot be had to the proper priest, that none may perish, the Council of Trent teaches that, according to the ancient practice of the Church of God, it is then lawful for any priest, not only to remit all sorts of sins, whatever faculties they might otherwise require, but also to absolve from excommunication.[3]

Qualifications of the minister.

Knowledge.

Besides the power of orders and of jurisdiction, which are of absolute necessity, the minister of this sacrament, holding as he does, the place at once of judge and physician, should also be gifted with knowledge and prudence. As judge, his knowledge, it is evident, should be more than ordinary, for by it he is to examine into the nature of sins, and, amongst the various sorts of sins, to judge which are grievous and which are not, keeping in view the rank and condition of the person. As physician,

[1] John xx. 23.   [2] Tit. i. 5.   [3] Sess. 14. c. 6. de pœnit.

he has also occasion for consummate prudence, for to him it Prudence. belongs to administer to the distempered soul those sanative medicines, which will not only effect the cure of her present malady, but prove preservatives against its future contagion.[1] The faithful, therefore, will perceive the great importance to be attached to the choice of a confessor, and will use their best endeavours to choose one who is recommended by integrity of Integrity of life, by learning and prudence, who is deeply impressed with life. the awful weight and responsibility of the station which he holds, who understands well the punishment due to every sin, and can also discern who are to be loosed and who to be bound.

But as all are anxious, that their sins should be buried in The seal of eternal secrecy, the faithful are to be admonished that there is confession. no reason whatever to apprehend, that what is made known in confession will ever be revealed by any priest, or that by it the penitent can, at any time, be brought into danger or difficulty of any sort. All laws human and divine guard the inviolability of the seal of confession, and against its sacrilegious infraction the Church denounces her heaviest chastisements.[2] "Let the priest," says the great Council of Lateran, "take especial care, neither by word nor sign, nor by any other means whatever, to betray, in the least degree, the sacred trust confided to him by the sinner."[3]

Having treated of the minister of this sacrament, the order Negli-of our matter requires, that we next proceed to explain some gence of general heads, which are of considerable practical import-sinners. ance with regard to confession. Many, to whom, in general, no time seems to pass so slowly as that which is appointed by the laws of the Church for the duty of confession, so far from giving due attention to those other matters, which are obviously most efficacious in conciliating the favour and friendship of God, are placed at such a distance from Christian perfection, as scarcely to recollect the sins, which are to be the matter of their confession. As, therefore, nothing is to be omitted, which can The con assist the faithful in the important work of salvation, the priest fessor will will be careful to observe, if the penitent be truly contrite for observe if his sins, and deliberately and firmly resolved to avoid sin for tent be tru the future. If the sinner is found to be thus disposed, he is to ly contrite be admonished and earnestly exhorted, to pour out his heart in treated if gratitude to God for this invaluable blessing, and supplicate un-contrite: ceasingly the aid of divine grace, shielded by which he may securely combat the evil propensities of corrupt nature. He should also be taught, not to suffer a day to pass, without devoting a portion of it to meditation on some mystery of the passion, in order to excite himself to an imitation of his great model, and inflame his heart with ardent love for his Redeemer. The fruit of such meditation will be, to fortify him more and more, every day, against all the assaults of the devil ; for, what

[1] Ex Basil. in reg. brevibus, q. ii. 29.   [2] Ex Leonis Papæ epist. 80.
[3] Cap. 21.
    17*

other reason is there, why our courage sinks, and our strength fails, the moment the enemy makes even the slightest attack on us, but that we neglect by pious meditation, to kindle within us the fire of divine love, which animates and invigorates the soul? But, should the priest perceive, that the penitent gives equivocal indications of true contrition, he will endeavour to inspire him with an anxious desire for it, inflamed by which he may resolve to ask and implore this heavenly gift from the mercy of God.

If not contrite:

The pride of some, who seek by vain excuses to justify or extenuate their offences, is carefully to be repressed. If, for instance, a penitent confesses that he was wrought up to anger, and immediately transfers the blame of the excitement to another, who, he complains, was the aggressor; he is to be reminded, that such apologies are indications of a proud spirit, and of a man who either thinks lightly of, or is unacquainted with the enormity of ·his sin, whilst they serve rather to aggravate than extenuate his guilt. He, who thus labours to justify his conduct, seems to say, that then only will he exercise patience, when no one injures or offends him, a disposition than which nothing can be more unworthy of a Christian. A Christian should lament the state of him who inflicted the injury, and, yet, regardless of the grievousness of the sin, he is angry with his brother: having had an opportunity of honouring God by his exemplary patience, and of correcting a brother by his Christian meekness, he converts the very means of salvation into the means of injuring his own soul.

If fond of justifying or extenuating his guilt:

Still more pernicious is the conduct of those, who yielding to a foolish bashfulness, cannot induce themselves to confess their sins. Such persons are to be encouraged by exhortation, and to be reminded, that there is no reason whatever why they should yield to such false delicacy; that to no one can it appear surprising, if persons fall into sin, the common malady of the human race, and the natural appendage of human infirmity.

If under the influence of a false shame:

There are others who, either because they seldom approach the tribunal of penance, or because they have bestowed no care or attention on the examination of their consciences, know not well how to begin or end their confession. Such persons deserve to be severely rebuked, and are to be taught that before any one approaches the tribunal of penance, he should employ every diligence to excite himself to contrition for his sins, and that this he cannot do without endeavouring to know and recollect them severally. Should then the confessor meet persons of this class, entirely unprepared for confession, he should dismiss them without harshness, exhorting them in the kindest terms, to take some time to reflect on their sins, and then return; but, should they declare that they have already done every thing in their power to prepare, as there is reason to apprehend, that, if sent away, they may not return, their confession is to be heard, particularly if they manifest some disposition to amend their lives, and can be induced to accuse their own negligence, and promise

If indolent or negligent.

to atone for it at another time, by a diligent and accurate scrutiny of conscience. In such cases, however, the confessor will proceed with caution. If, after having heard the confession, he is of opinion that the penitent did not want diligence in examining his conscience, or sorrow in detesting his sins, he may absolve him; but if he has found him deficient in both, he will, as we have already said, admonish him to use greater care in his examination of conscience, and will dismiss him in the kindest manner.

But as it sometimes happens, that females, who may have forgotten some sin in a former confession, cannot bring themselves to return to the confessor, dreading to expose themselves to the suspicion of having been guilty of something grievous, or of looking for the praise of extraordinary piety, the pastor will frequently remind the faithful, both publicly and privately, that no one is gifted with so tenacious a memory, as to be able to recollect all his thoughts, words, and actions, that the faithful, therefore, should they call to mind any thing grievous, which they had previously forgotten, should not be deterred from returning to the priest. These and many other matters of the same nature, demand the particular attention of the confessor in the tribunal of penance. *A remedy for false modesty on the part of the penitent.*

We now come to the third part of penance, which is called satisfaction. We shall begin by explaining its nature and efficacy, because the enemies of the Catholic Church have hence taken ample occasion, to sow discord and division amongst Christians, to the no small injury of the Christian Commonwealth. Satisfaction, then, is the full payment of a debt, for when satisfaction is made, nothing remains to be supplied. Hence, when we speak of reconciliation by grace, to satisfy is the same as to do that which may be sufficient to atone to the angered mind for an injury offered; and thus, satisfaction is nothing more than " compensation for an injury done to another." Hence theologians make use of the word " satisfaction," to signify the compensation made by man to God, by doing something in atonement for the sins which he has committed. *Satisfaction.*

This sort of satisfaction, embracing, as it does, many degrees, admits of many acceptations. The first degree of satisfaction, and that which stands pre-eminently above all the rest, is that by which whatever is due by us to God, on account of our sins, is paid abundantly, although he should deal with us according to the strictest rigour of his justice. This, we say, has appeased God and rendered him propitious to us, and for it we are indebted to Christ alone, who, having paid the price of our sins on the cross, offered to his Eternal Father a superabundant satisfaction. No created being could have paid so heavy a debt for us: " He is the propitiation for our sins," says St. John, " and not for ours only, but also for those of the whole world."[1] This satisfaction, therefore, is full and superabundant, commen- *Its different degrees. I.*

---

[1] 1 John ii. 2.

surate to all sorts of sins perpetrated by the human race: it gives to man's actions merit before God; without it they could avail him nothing to eternal life. This David seems to have had in view, when, having asked himself, " what shall I render to the Lord, for all the things that he hath rendered to me ?"[1] and finding nothing worthy of such blessings but this satisfaction, which he expressed by the word " chalice," he replies: " I will take the chalice of salvation, and I will call upon the name of the Lord."[2]

II.   There is another sort of satisfaction, which is called canonical, and is performed within a certain fixed period of time. Hence, according to the most ancient practice of the Church, when penitents are absolved from their sins, some penance is imposed, the performance of which is commonly called " satisfaction."

III.   Any sort of punishment endured for sin, although not imposed by the priest, but spontaneously undertaken by the sinner, is also called by the same name: it belongs not, however, to penance as a sacrament: the satisfaction which constitutes part of the sacrament is, as we have already said, that which is imposed by the priest, and which must be accompanied with a deliberate and firm purpose carefully to avoid sin for the future. To satisfy, as some define it, is to pay due honour to God, and this, it is evident, no person can do, who is not resolved to avoid sin. To satisfy is also to cut off all occasions of sin, and to close every avenue of the heart against its suggestions. In accordance with this idea of satisfaction, some have considered it a cleansing, which effaces whatever defilement may remain in the soul from the stains of sin, and which exempts us from the temporal chastisements due to sin.

Necessity of satisfaction.   Such being the nature of satisfaction, it will not be found difficult to convince the faithful of the necessity imposed on the penitent, of satisfying for his sins: they are to be taught that sin carries in its train two evils, the stain which it affixes, and the punishment which it entails. The punishment of eternal death is, it is true, forgiven with the sin to which it was due, yet, as the Council of Trent declares, the stain is not always entirely effaced, nor is the temporal punishment always remitted.[3] Of this the Scriptures afford many evident examples, as we find in the third chapter of Genesis,[4] in the twelfth and twenty-second of Numbers,[5] and in many other places. That of David, however, is the most conspicuous and illustrious.— Already had Nathan announced to him: " The Lord also hath taken away thy sin, thou shalt not die;"[6] yet the royal penitent voluntarily subjected himself to the most severe penance, imploring, night and day, the mercy of God, in these words: " Wash me yet more from my iniquity, and cleanse me from my sin, for I know my iniquity and my sin is always before

[1] Ps. cxv. 12.   [2] cxv. 13.   [3] Sess. 14. c. 8. can. 12 et 14.
[4] Gen. iii. 17.   [5] Num. xii. 14. 22. 23. 34.   [6] 2 Kings xii. 13.

me."[1] Thus did he beseech God to pardon not only the crime, but also the punishment due to it, and to restore him, cleansed from the stains of sin, to his former state of purity and integrity. This is the object of his most earnest supplications to the throne of God, and yet the Almighty punishes his transgression with the death of his adulterous offspring, the rebellion and death of his beloved son Absalom, and with the other heavy chastisements with which his vengeance had already threatened him. In Exodus too the Almighty, although yielding to the importunity of Moses, he had spared the idolatrous Israelites, threatens the enormity of their crime with heavy chastisement;[2] and Moses himself declares, that the Lord will take vengeance on it, even to the third and fourth generation. That such was at all times the doctrine of the Fathers, a reference to their writings will place beyond the possibility of doubt.[3]

Why in the sacrament of penance, as in that of baptism, the punishment due to sin is not entirely remitted, is admirably explained in these words of the Council of Trent: " Divine justice seems to require, that they who through ignorance sinned before baptism, should recover the friendship of God in a different manner from those, who, freed from the thraldom of sin and the slavery of the devil, and having received the gifts of the Holy Ghost, dread not knowingly to violate the temple of God and grieve the Holy Spirit. It also consists with the divine mercy not to remit our sins without satisfaction, lest, taking occasion hence, and imagining our sins less grievous than they are, injurious, as it were, and contumelious to the Holy Ghost, we fall into greater enormities, treasuring up to ourselves wrath against the day of wrath. These satisfactory penances have, no doubt, great influence in restraining from sin, in bridling, as it were, the passions, and rendering the sinner more vigilant and cautious for the future."[4] Another advantage resulting from them is, that they serve as public testimonies of our sorrow for sin, and atone to the Church who is grievously insulted by the crimes of her children: " God," says St. Augustine, " despises not a contrite and humble heart, but, as heartfelt grief is generally concealed from others, and is not communicated by words or other signs, wisely, therefore, are penitential times appointed by those who preside over the Church, in order to atone to the Church, in which sins are forgiven." Besides, the example presented by our penitential practices, serves as a lesson to others, how to regulate their lives, and practise piety: seeing the punishments inflicted on sin, they must feel the necessity of using the greatest circumspection through life, and of correcting their former evil habits. The Church, therefore, with great wisdom

Margin notes:
The punishment due to sin, why not remitted by penance as by baptism.

Advantages of canonical penance.
I.
II.

III.

[1] Ps. I. 4, 5.   [2] Exod. xxxii. 8, 9.
[3] Vide Aug. lib. 2. de peccat. merit. et remiss. cap. 34. et contra Faust. lib. 22. cap. 66. et praesertim in Joan. tractat. 124. paulo ante med. Greg. lib. 9. moral. cap. 24. Chrysost. hom. 8. ad pop. Antioch. Interam. Aug. Euch. cap. 30. Ambr. de poen. lib. 2. cap. 5. vide item canones poenitentiales apud Anton. Aug. vel in actis Eccl. Mediolan.
[4] Sess. 14. de paenit. cap. 8.

Wisely instituted by the Church. ordained, that those who by their scandalous disorders may have given public disedification, should atone for them by public penance, that others may be thus deterred from their commission. This has sometimes been observed even with regard to secret sins, when marked by peculiar malignity.[1] But with regard to public sinners, they, as we have already said, were never absolved until they had performed public penance. Meanwhile, the pastor poured out his prayers to God for their salvation, and ceased not to exhort them to do the same. This salutary practice gave active employment to the zeal and solicitude of St. Ambrose; many, who came to the tribunal of penance hardened in sin, were by his tears softened into true contrition.[2] But in process of time the severity of ancient discipline was so relaxed, and charity waxed so cold, that in our days many seem to think inward sorrow of soul and grief of heart unnecessary, and deem the semblance of sorrow sufficient.

By penance we are made like unto Christ. Again, by undergoing these penances we are made like unto the image of Jesus Christ our head, inasmuch as he himself suffered and was tempted,[3] and, as St. Bernard observes, "nothing can appear so unseemly as a delicate member under a head crowned with thorns."[4] To use the words of the Apostle, "we are joint-heirs with Christ, yet so if we suffer with him;"[5] and again: "If we be dead with him, we shall live also with him; if we suffer, we shall also reign with him."[6]

Two effects produced in the soul by sin, removed by penance. St. Bernard also observes, that sin produces two effects in the soul; the one, the stain which it imparts, the other, the wound which it inflicts; that the turpitude of sin is removed through the mercy of God, whilst to heal the wound inflicted, the medicinal care applied by penance is most necessary; for as after a wound has been healed, some scars remain which demand attention, so with regard to the soul, after the guilt of sin is forgiven, some of its effects remain, from which the soul requires to be cleansed. St. Chrysostome also fully confirms the same doctrine, when he says: "Not enough that the arrow has been extracted from the body, the wound which it inflicted must also be healed: so with regard to the soul, not enough that sin has been pardoned, the wound which it has left, must also be healed by penance."[7] St. Augustine, also, frequently teaches that penance exhibits at once the mercy and the justice of God, his mercy by which he pardons sin, and the eternal punishment due to sin, his justice by which he exacts temporary punishment from the sinner.[8]

Penance disarms the Finally, the punishment which the sinner endures, disarms the vengeance of God, and prevents the punishments decreed

---

[1] Vide Aug. lib. 5, de civit. Dei cap. 26. et ep. 54. et lib. 50. hom. 49. et de vera et falsa pœn. passim. Ambr. lib. 2. de pœnit. c. 10. et citatur de pœn. dist. 3. cap. reperiuntur. Cypr. de lapsis multis in locis. Conc. Agath. cap. 35. et citatur. dist. 50. cap. pœnitentes.
[2] Paulinus et ejus vita. [3] Heb. ii. 17. [4] Serm. 5. de omn. sanct.
[5] Rom. viii. 17. [6] 2 Tim. ii. 11, 12.
[7] Serm. 1. in cœna Domini. Hom. 80. ad Pop. Antioch.
[8] In Ps. l. ad hæc verba, ECCE ENIM VENIT.

against us, according to these words of the Apostle: "If we would judge ourselves, we should not be judged; but whilst we are judged, we are chastised by the Lord, that we be not condemned with this world."[1] These matters, if explained to the faithful, must have considerable influence in exciting them to penance. Divine vengeance.

Of the great efficacy of penance we may form some idea, if we reflect that it arises entirely from the merits of the passion of our Lord Jesus Christ: it is his passion that imparts to our good actions the two-fold quality of meriting the rewards of eternal life, so that a cup of cold water given in his name shall not be without its reward,[2] and, also, of satisfying for our sins.[3] Nor does this derogate from the most perfect and superabundant satisfaction of Christ, but, on the contrary, renders it still more conspicuous and illustrious; the grace of Jesus Christ appears to abound more, inasmuch as it communicates to us not only what he alone merited, but also what, as head, he merited and paid in his members, that is, in holy and just men. This it is that imparts such weight and dignity to the good actions of the pious Christian; for our Lord Jesus Christ continually infuses his grace into the devout soul united to him by charity, as the head to the members, or as the vine through the branches, and this grace always precedes, accompanies, and follows our good works: without it we can have no merit, nor can we at all satisfy God. Hence it is that nothing seems wanting to the just: by their works done by the power of God, they fulfil the divine law, as far as is compatible with our present condition, and can merit eternal life, to the fruition of which they shall be admitted, if they depart this life adorned with divine grace: "He," says the Redeemer, "that shall drink of the water that I will give him, shall not thirst for ever; but the water that I will give him shall become in him a fountain of water, springing up into life everlasting."[4] The efficacy of penance arises entirely from the passion of Christ

In satisfaction two things are particularly required; the one, that he who satisfies be in a state of grace, the friend of God: works done without faith and charity cannot be acceptable to God: the other, that the works performed be such as are of their own nature painful or laborious. They are a compensation for past sins, and, to use the words of St. Cyprian, "the redeemers, as it were, of sins,"[5] and must, therefore, be such as we have described. It does not, however, always follow that they are painful or laborious to those who undergo them: the influence of habit or the intensity of divine love frequently renders the soul insensible to things the most difficult to be endured. Such works, however, do not, therefore, cease to be satisfactory: it is the privilege of the children of God to be so inflamed with his love, that whilst undergoing the most cruel tortures for his sake, they are either entirely insensible to them, Two things particularly necessary in satisfaction. Note.

---

[1] 1 Cor. xi. 31, 32. [2] Matt. x. 42.
[3] Vid. de pœnit. sess 14. cap. 8. et can. 13. 14. et sess. 6. de justific. c. 18.
[4] John iv. 14. [5] Lib. 1. Epist. 3. post. med.

or at least bear them not only with fortitude but with the greatest joy.

The pastor will teach that every species of satisfaction is included under these three heads, prayer, fasting, and alms-deeds, which correspond with these three sorts of goods, those of the soul, of the body, and what are called external goods, all of which are the gifts of God. Than these three sorts of satisfaction, nothing can be more effectual in eradicating sin from the soul. Whatever is in the world is the lust of the flesh, the " lust of the eyes, or pride of life,"[1] and fasting, alms-deeds, and prayer are, it is obvious, most judiciously employed as antidotes to neutralize the operation of these three causes of spiritual disease ; to the first is opposed fasting ; to the second, alms-deeds ; to the third, prayer. If, moreover, we consider those whom our sins injure, we shall easily perceive why all satisfaction is referred principally to God, to our neighbour, and to ourselves ; God we appease by prayer, our neighbour we satisfy by alms, and ourselves we chastise by fasting.

But, as this life is checkered by many and various afflictions, the faithful are to be particularly reminded, that afflictions coming from the hand of God, if borne with patience, are an abundant source of satisfaction and of merit ; but, if borne with reluctant impatience, far from being the means of atoning for past sins, they are rather the instruments of the divine wrath, taking just vengeance on the sinner.

But in this the mercy and goodness of God shine conspicuous, and demand our grateful acknowledgments, that he has granted to our frailty the privilege that one may satisfy for another. This, however, is a privilege which is confined to the satisfactory part of penance alone, and extends not to contrition and confession : no man can be contrite or confess for another ; whilst those who are gifted with divine grace may pay through others what is due to the divine justice, and thus we may be said in some measure to bear each other's burdens.[2] This is a doctrine on which the faithful cannot for a moment entertain a doubt, professing, as we do, in the Apostle's Creed, our belief in the " Communion of Saints." Regenerated, as we all are, to Christ in the same cleansing waters of baptism, partakers of the same sacraments, and, above all, of the same heavenly food, the body and blood of our Lord Jesus Christ, we are all, it is

manifest, members of the same mystical body. As then the foot does not perform its functions solely for itself, but also for sake of the other members, and as the other members perform their respective functions, not only for their own, but also for the common good ; so works of satisfaction are common to all

the members of the Church. This, however, is not universally true in reference to all the advantages to be derived from works of satisfaction : of these works some are also medicinal, and are so many specific remedies prescribed to the penitent, to heal

---

[1] 1 John ii. 16.   [2] Gal. vi. 2.

the depraved affections of the heart; a fruit which, it is evident, they alone can derive from them, who satisfy for themselves. Of these particulars touching the three parts of penance, contrition, confession, and satisfaction, it is the duty of the pastor to give an ample and clear exposition.

The confessor, however, will be scrupulously careful, before he absolves the penitent whose confession he has heard, to insist that if he has been really guilty of having injured his neighbour in property or character, he make reparation for the injury: no person is to be absolved until he has first faithfully promised to repair fully the injury done; and, as there are many who, although free to make large promises to comply with their duty in this respect, are yet deliberately determined not to fulfil them, they should be obliged to make restitution, and the words of the Apostle are to be strongly and frequently pressed upon upon their minds: "He that stole, let him now steal no more; but rather let him labour working with his hands the thing which is good, that he may have something to give to him that suffereth need."[1]

No person to be absolved, until he has promised faithfully to repair the injury done.

But, in imposing penance, the confessor will do nothing arbitrarily; he will be guided solely by justice, prudence, and piety; and in order to follow this rule, and also to impress more deeply on the mind of the penitent the enormity of sin, he will find it expedient to remind him of the severe punishments inflicted by the ancient penitential canons, as they are called, for certain sins. The nature of the sin, therefore, will regulate the extent of the satisfaction: but no satisfaction can be more salutary than to require of the penitent to devote, for a certain number of days, a certain portion of time to prayer, not omitting to supplicate the divine mercy in behalf of all mankind, and particularly for those who have departed this life in the Lord. Penitents should, also, be exhorted to undertake of their own accord, the frequent performance of the penances usually imposed by the confessor, and so to order the tenor of their future lives that, having faithfully complied with every thing which the sacrament of Penance demands, they may never cease studiously to practise the virtue of penance. But, should it be deemed proper sometimes to visit public crimes with public penance, and should the penitent express great reluctance to submit to its performance, his importunity is not to be readily yielded to: he should be persuaded to embrace with cheerfulness that which is so salutary to himself and to others. These things, which regard the sacrament of Penance and its several parts, the pastor will teach in such a manner as to enable the faithful not only to understand them perfectly, but, also, with the Divine assistance, piously and religiously to reduce them to practice.

Penance how to be imposed.

Public crimes to be visited with public penance.

---

[1] Ephes. iv. 28.

18

ON THE SACRAMENT OF EXTREME UNCTION.

This Sacra-
ment
should be
the subject
of frequent
instruction

"In all thy works," says Ecclesiasticus, "remember thy
last end, and thou shalt never sin ;"[1] words which convey to
the pastor a silent admonition, to omit no opportunity of exhorting the faithful to constant meditation on their last end. The
sacrament of Extreme Unction, because inseparably associated
with this awful recollection, should, it is obvious, form a subject of frequent instruction, not only inasmuch as it is eminently
useful to develope the mysteries of salvation, but also because
death, the inevitable doom of all men, when frequently recalled
to the minds of the faithful, represses the licentiousness of depraved passion. Thus shall they be less appalled by the terrors of approaching dissolution, and will pour forth their gratitude in endless praises to God, whose goodness has not only
opened to us the way to true life in the sacrament of Baptism,
but has also instituted that of Extreme Unction, to afford us,
when departing this mortal life, an easier access to heaven.

This Sacra-
ment why
called Ex-
treme Unc-
tion.

In order, therefore, to follow, in a great measure, the same
order observed in the exposition of the other sacraments, we
will first show that this sacrament is called "Extreme Unction,"
because amongst the other unctions prescribed by our Lord to
his Church, this is the last to be administered. It was hence
called by our predecessors in the faith, "the sacrament of the
anointing of the sick," and also, "the sacrament of dying persons," names which naturally lead the minds of the faithful to
the remembrance of that last awful hour.[2]

Proved to
be a Sacra-
ment.
I.

That Extreme Unction is, strictly speaking, a sacrament, is
first to be explained ; and this the words of St. James, promul-
gating the law of this sacrament, clearly establish : " Is any
man," says he, " sick amongst you ? Let him bring in the
priests of the Church, and let them pray over him, anointing
him with oil in the name of the Lord : and the prayer of faith
shall save the sick man ; and the Lord shall raise him up ; and
if he be in sins, they shall be forgiven him."[3] When the
Apostle says : " if he be in sins, they shall be forgiven him,"
he ascribes to Extreme Unction, at once the nature and efficacy

II.

of a sacrament. That such has been at all times the doctrine
of the Catholic Church, many Councils testify, and the Council of Trent denounces anathema against all who presume to
teach or think otherwise.[4] Innocent III., also, recommends
this sacrament with great earnestness to the attention of the

Note.

faithful.[5] The pastor, therefore, will teach that extreme Unc-

---

[1] Eccles. vii. 40.
[2] Vid. Hugon. de Sacr. part. 15. c. 2. Pet. Dam. serm. 1. de dedicat. Eccles.
[3] James v. 14.   [4] Sess. 43. de Extrem. Unc. c. 1. et can. 3.
[5] Innoc. ep. 1. ad Decent. c. 8. et citatur dist. 95. c. illud superfluum : tera
Conc. Cabilon. c. 48. Wormaciense c. 72. Constan. et Floren.

tion is a true sacrament, and that, although administered with many unctions, performed each with a peculiar prayer, and under a peculiar form, it constitutes but one sacrament—one, not by the inseparable continuity of its parts, but, like every thing composed of parts, by the perfection of the whole. As an edifice which consists of a great variety of parts, derives its perfection from one form, so is this sacrament, although composed of many and different things, but one sign, and its efficacy is that of one thing of which it is the sign.

The pastor will also teach what are the component parts of this Sacrament, its matter and form : these St. James does not omit, and each is replete with its own peculiar mysteries.[1] Its element, then, or matter, as defined by many Councils, particularly by the Council of Trent, consists of oil of olives, consecrated by episcopal hands. No other sort of oil can be the matter of this Sacrament; and this its matter is most significant of its efficacy. Oil is very efficacious in soothing bodily pain, and this Sacrament sooths and alleviates the pain and anguish of the soul. Oil also contributes to restore health and spirits, serves to give light, and refreshes fatigue ; and these effects correspond with and are expressive of those produced, through the divine power, on the sick, by the administration of this Sacrament. These few words will suffice in explanation of the matter.

Its matter

With regard to the form, it consists of the following words, which contain a solemn prayer, and are used at each anointing, according to the sense to which the unction is applied : " BY THIS HOLY UNCTION, AND THROUGH HIS GREAT MERCY, MAY GOD INDULGE THEE WHATEVER SINS THOU HAST COMMITTED BY SIGHT, SMELL, TOUCH, &c. &c." That this is the true form of this Sacrament, we learn from these words of St. James : " Let them pray over him, and the prayer of faith shall save the sick man ;"[2] words which intimate that the form is to be applied by way of prayer, although the Apostle does not say of what particular words that prayer is to consist. But this form has been handed down to us by apostolic tradition, and is universally retained, as observed by the Church of Rome, the mother and mistress of all churches. Some, it is true, alter a few words, as when for " God indulge thee," they say, " God remit," or " spare," and sometimes, " heal whatever thou hast committed ;" but the sense is evidently the same, and, of course, the form observed by all is strictly the same. Nor should it excite our surprise that, whilst the form of each of the other Sacraments either absolutely signifies what it expresses, such as, " I baptise thee," or " I sign thee with the sign of the cross," or is pronounced, as it were, by way of a command, as in administering Holy Orders, " Receive power," the form of Extreme Unction alone is expressed by way of prayer. The propriety of this difference will at once appear, if we reflect, that this Sacrament

Its form.

Expressed by way of prayer and why.

[1] James v. 14.　　　[2] James v. 14.

is administered not only for the health of the soul, but also for that of the body ; and as it does not please Divine Providence, at all times, to restore health to the sick, the form consists of a prayer, by which we beg of the divine bounty that which is not a constant and uniform effect of the Sacrament.

Administration of this Sacrament, why accompanied with many prayers.

In the administration of this Sacrament, peculiar rites are also used ; but they consist principally of prayers, offered by the priest for the recovery of the sick person. There is no Sacrament the administration of which is accompanied with more numerous prayers ; and with good reason, for then, in a special manner, the faithful require the assistance of pious prayers. Not only the pastor, in the first place, but, also, all who may be present, should pour out their fervent aspirations to the throne of grace, in behalf of the sick person, earnestly recommending him, soul and body, to the divine mercy.

This Sacrament instituted by Christ.

Note.

Having thus shown that Extreme Unction is to be numbered amongst the Sacraments, we infer, and the inference is just, that it owes its institution to our Lord Jesus Christ, and was subsequently made known and promulgated to the faithful, by the Apostle St. James. Our Lord himself, would, however, seem to have given some indication of it, when he sent his disciples, two and two, before him ; for the Evangelist informs us that " going forth, they preached that all should do penance ; and they cast out many devils, and anointed with oil many who were sick, and healed them."[1] This anointing cannot be supposed to have been invented by the Apostles : it was commanded by our Lord. Nor did its efficacy arise from any natural virtue peculiar to oil ; its efficacy is mystical, having been instituted to heal the maladies of the soul, rather than to cure the diseases of the body. This is the doctrine taught by the Fathers of the Church, by the Denises, the Ambroses, the Chrysostomes, by Gregory the Great ; and Extreme Unction is to be recognised and venerated as one of the Sacraments of the Catholic Church.

Extreme Unction, to whom and when to be administered.

But although instituted for the use of all, Extreme Unction is not to be administered indiscriminately to all. In the first place, it is not to be administered to persons in sound health, according to these words of St. James : " Is any one sick amongst you ?"[2] and, as reason also proves, it was instituted as a remedy not only for the diseases of the soul, but also for those of the body : this can apply to the sick only, and therefore, this Sacrament is to be administered to those only, whose malady is such as to excite apprehensions of approaching dissolution. It is, however, a very grievous sin to defer the Holy Unction until, all hope of recovery now lost, life begins to ebb, and the sick person is fast verging into a state of insensibility. It is obvious that, if administered whilst the mental faculties are yet unimpaired, whilst reason still exercises her dominion, and the mind is capable eliciting acts of faith, and of directing the will

[1] Mark vi. 12, 13.   [2] James v. 14

to sentiments of piety, the Sacrament must contribute to a more abundant participation of the graces which it imparts. This heavenly medicine, therefore, in itself at all times salutary, the pastor will be careful to apply, when its efficacy can be aided by the piety and devotion of the sick person. Extreme Unction, then, can be administered only to the sick, and not to persons in health, although engaged in any thing however dangerous, such as a perilous voyage, or the fatal dangers of battle. It cannot be administered even to persons condemned to death, and already ordered for execution. Its participation is also denied to insane persons, and to children incapable of committing sin, who, therefore, do not require to be purified from its stains, and also to those who labour under the awful visitation of madness, unless they give indications, in their lucid intervals, of a disposition to piety, and express a desire to be anointed. To persons insane from their birth, this Sacrament is not to be administered; but if a sick person, whilst in the possession of his faculties, expressed a wish to receive Extreme Unction, and afterwards becomes delirious, he is to be anointed.

The Sacred Unction is to be applied not to the entire body, but to the organs of sense only—to the eyes the organs of sight, to the ears of hearing, to the nostrils of smelling, to the mouth of taste and speech, to the hands of touch. The sense of touch, it is true, is diffused throughout the entire body, yet the hands are its peculiar seat. This manner of administering Extreme Unction is observed throughout the universal Church, and accords with the medicinal nature of this Sacrament. As in corporal disease, although it affects the entire body, yet the cure is applied to that part only which is the seat of the disease, so in spiritual malady, this Sacrament is applied not to the entire body, but to those members which are properly the organs of sense, and also to the loins, which are, as it were, the seat of concupiscence, and to the feet, by which we move from one place to another. *How to be administered.*

Here it is to be observed, that, during the same illness, and whilst the danger of dying continues the same, the sick person is to be anointed but once; should he, however, recover after he has been anointed, he may receive the aid of this Sacrament, as often as he shall have relapsed into the same danger. This Sacrament, therefore, is evidently to be numbered amongst those which may be repeated. *It may be repeated, and when.*

But as every obstacle which may impede its efficacy should be removed with the greatest care, and as nothing is more opposed to it than a state of mortal guilt, the pastor will follow the uniform practice of the Catholic Church, and not administer Extreme Unction, until the penitent has confessed and received. He will then earnestly exhort the sick person, to receive this Sacrament with the same sentiments of faith which animated the primitive Christians, who presented themselves to the Apostles to be healed by them. The health of the soul is to be the first object of the sick man's prayers, the second, that of the *Preparation for receiving it worthily.*

body, should it tend to his eternal interests. The faithful should be convinced, that the solemn and holy prayers, which are offered by the priest, not in his own name, but in that of the Church and of its divine Founder, are heard by Almighty God; and they cannot be too earnestly exhorted, to be careful to accompany the administration of the Sacrament, with all the sanctity and religious fervour that become that awful hour, when the dying Christian is about to engage in the last conflict, and the energies of the mind as well as of the body seem to be enfeebled.

The minister of this Sacrament. With regard to the minister of Extreme Unction, this too we learn from St. James, when he says: " Let him bring in the priests:"[1] by the word "priests," as the Council of Trent has defined,[2] he does not mean elders or persons advanced in years, or of elevated rank, but priests duly ordained by bishops with the imposition of hands. The administration of this Sacrament, therefore, is committed to priests, not however to every priest, in accordance with the decree of the Church; but to the proper priest, who has jurisdiction, or to another authorized by him.

Note. In this, as in the other Sacraments, it is also to be distinctly recollected, that the priest is the representative of Jesus Christ and of his Church.

Its advantages. The advantages, which flow from this Sacrament, are also to be explained more minutely, that if the sick are influenced by no other consideration, they may, at least, yield to this, for we are disposed to measure every thing by its utility. The pastor,

I. therefore, will teach, that the grace of this Sacrament remits sins, especially lighter offences, or, as they are commonly called, venial sins. Its primary object is not to remit mortal sins. For this the Sacrament of penance was instituted, as was that of baptism

II. for the remission of original sin. Another advantage arising from Extreme Unction is, that it removes the languor and infirmity entailed by sin, with all its other inconveniences. The time most seasonable for the application of this cure is, when we are visited by some severe malady, which threatens to prove fatal; for nature dreads no earthly visitation so much as death, and this dread is considerably augmented by the recollection of our past sins, particularly if the mind is harrowed up by the poignant reproaches of conscience; as it is written: " They shall come with fear at the thought of their sins, and their iniquities shall stand against them to convict them."[3] A source of alarm still more distressing is the awful reflection, that, in a few moments, we shall stand before the judgment-seat of God, whose justice will award that sentence, which our lives may have deserved. The terror inspired by these considerations frequently agitates the soul with the most awful apprehensions; and to calm this terror nothing can be so efficacious as the Sacrament of Extreme Unction. It quiets our fear, illumines the gloom in which the soul is enveloped, fills it with pious and

---

[1] James v. 14.   [2] Sess. 14, c. 3.   [3] Wisdom iv. 20.

holy joy, and enables us to wait with cheerfulness the coming of the Lord, prepared to yield up all that we have received from his bounty, whenever he is pleased to summon us from this world of wo. Another, and the most important advantage de- | IV.
rived from Extreme Unction, is, that it fortifies us against the violent assaults of Satan. The enemy of mankind never ceases to seek our ruin : but to complete our destruction, and, if possi-ble, deprive us of all hope of mercy, he more than ever increases his efforts, when he sees us approach our last end. This Sa-crament, therefore, arms and strengthens the faithful against the violence of his assaults, and enables them to fight resolutely and successfully against him. Tranquillized and encouraged by the hope of the divine mercy, the soul bears up with fortitude against every difficulty, experiences an alleviation of the burden of sickness, and eludes with greater ease, the artifice and cun-ning of the enemy, who lies in wait for her. Finally, the re- | V.
covery of health, if advantageous to the sick person, is another effect of this Sacrament. However, should this effect not follow, it arises not from any defect in the Sacrament, but from weak-ness of faith on the part of him by whom it is received, or of him by whom it is administered ; for the Evangelist informs us, that our Lord wrought not many miracles amongst his country-men, because of their incredulity.[1] It may, however, be pro- | Note.
per to observe, that Christianity, now that it has taken deep root in the minds of men, stands less in need of the aid of such miracles in our days, than in the early ages of the Church. Nevertheless, our faith is here to be strongly excited, and what-ever it may please God in his wisdom to do with regard to the health of the body, the faithful should be animated with an as-sured hope of receiving from it spiritual health and strength, and of experiencing, at the hour of their dissolution, the truth of these consoling words : "Blessed are the dead who die in the Lord."[2]

We have thus briefly explained the sacrament of Extreme Unction. If the heads of the matter be developed by the pas-tor more at large, with the diligence which their importance de-mands, the faithful, no doubt, will derive from their exposition abundant fruit of piety.

ON THE SACRAMENT OF ORDERS.

FROM an attentive consideration of the nature of the other | The Sacra-
Sacraments we shall find little difficulty in perceiving, that, so | ment of
dependent are they all on that of orders, that without its inter- | Orders,
vention some could not exist, or be administered, whilst others | why to be explained

---

[1] Matt. xiii. 58.   [2] Apoc. xiv. 13.

to the peo-
ple.

I.

II.

III.

IV.

should be stripped of the religious rites and solemn ceremonies and of that exterior respect which should accompany their ad ministration. The pastor, therefore, following up his exposi tion of the sacraments, will deem it a duty to bestow, also, on the Sacrament of Orders, an attention proportioned to its im portance. This exposition cannot fail to prove salutary, in the first place, to the pastor himself, in the next place, to those who may have embraced the ecclesiastical state, and finally to the faithful at large—to the pastor himself, because, whilst explain ing this Sacrament to others, he himself is excited to stir up within him the grace which he received at his ordination—to others whom the Lord has called to his sanctuary, by inspiring them with the same love of piety, and imparting to them a knowledge of those things which will qualify them the more easily to advance to higher orders—to the faithful at large, by making known to them the respect due to the ministers of reli gion. It also not unfrequently occurs, that, amongst the faith ful there are many who intend their children for the ministry whilst yet young, and some who are themselves candidates for that holy state ; and it is proper that such persons should not be entirely unacquainted with its nature and obligations.[1]

Dignity of
this Sacra-
ment.
I.

The faithful then are to be made acquainted with the exalted dignity and excellence of this sacrament in its highest degree, which is the priesthood. Priests and bishops are, as it were, the interpreters and heralds of God, commissioned in his name to teach mankind the law of God, and the precepts of a Chris tian life—they are the representatives of God upon earth. Im possible, therefore, to conceive a more exalted dignity, or func tions more sacred. Justly, therefore, are they called not only angels,[2] but gods,[3] holding, as they do, the place and power and authority of God on earth. But the priesthood, at all times an elevated office, transcends in the New Law all others in dignity. The power of consecrating and offering the body and blood of our Lord and of remitting sin, with which the priesthood of the New Law is invested, is such as cannot be comprehended by the human mind, still less is it equalled by, or assimilated to, any thing on earth. Again, as Christ was sent by the Father,[4] the Apostles and Disciples by Christ,[5] even so are priests invested with the same power, and sent "for the perfecting of the saints, for the work of the ministry, and the edification of the body of Christ."[6]

Those who
are to re-

'This office, therefore, is not to be rashly imposed on any one: to those only it is to be intrusted, who, by the sanctity

---

[1] Qui spectat ad mores eorum qui in aliquo ordine ecclesiastico sunt, videndum est, immo sciendum Conc. Trid. in posteriore parte cujusque sessionis. quæ est de reformatione ; quod vero attinet a ordinem ut est sacramentum, vide idem Conc. sess. 13. et de singulis ordinationibus vide Conc. Carthag. IV. sub Anastasio Ponti fice. anno 398.
[2] Mal. ii. 7.   [3] Ps. lxxxi. 6.   [4] John viii. 36.   [5] Matt. xxviii. 19.
[6] Ephes. iv. 12.—De sacerdotii dignitate vide Ignat. epist. ad Smyrn. Amb. lib. 5. epist. 32. et lib. 10. ep. 82. Chrysost. hom. 60. ad pop. Antioch, et in Matt. hom. 83. Nazian. orat. 17. ad suos cives.

of their lives, by their knowledge, their faith, and their prudence, are capable of sustaining its weight: " Nor let any one
take this honour to himself," says the Apostle, " but he that is
called by God as Aaron was."[1]   This call from God we recognise, in that of the lawful ministers of his Church. Of those,
who would arrogantly obtrude themselves into the sanctuary,
the Lord has said: " I sent not the prophets, and yet they ran :"[2]
such sacrilegious intruders bring the greatest misery on themselves, and the heaviest calamities on the Church of God.[3] But
as in every undertaking the end proposed is of the highest importance, (when the end is good, every thing proceeds well)
the candidate for the ministry should first of all be admonished
to propose to himself no motive unworthy of so exalted a station ; an admonition which demands particular attention in these
our days, when the faithful are but too unmindful of its spirit:
there are those who aspire to the priesthood with a view to
secure to themselves a livelihood, who, like worldlings in matters of trade or commerce, look to nothing but sordid pelf.
True, the natural and divine law command, that to use the
words of the Apostle, " he that serves the altar, should live by
the altar;"[4] but to approach the altar for gain, this indeed were
a sacrilege of the blackest die. Others there are whom a love
of honours, and a spirit of ambition conduct to the altar ; others
whom the gold of the sanctuary attracts ; and of this we require
no other proof than that they have no idea of embracing the
ecclesiastical state unless preferred to some rich ecclesiastical
benefice. These are they whom the Lord denounces as " hire-
lings,"[5] who, to use the words of Ezekiel, " feed themselves,
and not the sheep."[6] Their turpitude and profligacy have not
only tarnished the lustre and degraded the dignity of the sacerdotal character in the eyes of the faithful, but the priesthood
brings to them in its train the same rewards which the Apostle-
ship brought to Judas—eternal perdition.

But they who, in obedience to the legitimate call of God, undertake the priestly office, solely with a view to promote his
glory, are truly said " to enter by the door." The obligation
of promoting his glory is not confined to them alone ; for this
were all men created—this the faithful in particular, consecrated,
as they have been, by baptism to God, should promote with
their whole hearts, their whole souls, and with all their strength.
Not enough, therefore, that the candidate for holy orders propose
to himself to seek in all things the glory of God, a duty common alike to all men, and particularly incumbent on the faithful :
he must also be resolved to serve God in holiness and righteousness, in the particular sphere in which his ministry is to
be exercised. As in an army, all obey the command of the
general, whilst amongst them some hold the place of colonel,
some of captain, and others, stations of subordinate rank: so in

[1] Heb. v. 4.　[2] Jerem. xxiii. 21.　[3] Vid. dist. 23. multis in capitibus.
[4] 1 Cor. ix. 13.　[5] John x. 12.　[6] Ezek. xxxiv. 1.

the Church, whilst all without distinction should be earnest in the pursuit of piety and innocence, the principal means of rendering homage to God; to those, however, who are initiated in the Sacrament of Orders, special offices belong, on them special functions devolve—to offer sacrifice for themselves, and for all the people—to instruct others in the law of God—to exhort and form them to a faithful and ready compliance with its injunctions—and to administer the Sacraments, the sources of grace. In a word, set apart from the rest of the people, they are engaged in a ministry the most sacred and the most exalted.

The power conferred by the Sacrament of Orders, two-fold, of jurisdiction, and of orders. Having explained these matters to the faithful, the pastor will next proceed to expound those things which are peculiar to this Sacrament, that thus the candidate for orders may be enabled to form a just estimate of the nature of the office to which he aspires, and to know the extent of the power conferred by Almighty God on his Church and her ministers. This power is two-fold, of jurisdiction, and of orders: the power of orders has reference to the body of our Lord Jesus Christ in the Holy Eucharist, that of jurisdiction to his mystical body, the Church; for to this latter belong the government of his spiritual kingdom on earth, and the direction of the faithful in the way of salvation. In the power of Orders is included not only that of consecrating the Holy Eucharist, but also of preparing the soul for its worthy reception, and whatever else has reference to the sacred mysteries. Of this the Scriptures afford numerous attestations, amongst which the most striking and weighty are contained in the words recorded by St. John and St. Matthew on this subject: "As the Father hath sent me," says the Redeemer, "I send you: Receive ye the Holy Ghost: whose sins you shall forgive, they are forgiven them, and whose sins you shall retain, they are retained;"[1] and again, "Amen, I say unto you, whatever you shall bind on earth, shall be bound also in heaven; and whatever you shall loose on earth, shall be loosed also in heaven."[2] These passages, if expounded by the pastor from the doctrine, and on the authority of the Fathers, will shed considerable light on this important subject.

Greatness of this power. This power far transcends that which was given to those, who, under the law of nature, exercised a special superintendence over sacred things.[3] The age anterior to the written law must have had its priesthood, a priesthood invested with spiritual power: that it had a law cannot be questioned: and so intimately interwoven are these two things with one another, that, take away one, you of necessity remove the other.[4] As then, prompted by the dictate of the instinctive feelings of his nature, man recognises the worship of God as a duty, it follows as a necessary consequence, that, under every form of government, some persons must have been constituted the official guardians

---

[1] John xx. 21, 22, 23.   [2] Matt. xviii. 18.

[3] Vid. de consecr. dist. 2. cap. nihil in sacrificiis, Conc. Trid. sess. 22. cap. 1. Iren. lib. 4. c. 34. Aug. lib. 19. de civit. Dei, cap. 23.

[4] Heb. vii. 12.

of sacred things, the legitimate ministers of the divine worship; and of such persons the power might, in a certain sense, be called spiritual.

With this power the priesthood of the Old Law was also invested; but, although superior in dignity to that exercised under the law of nature, it was far inferior to the spiritual power enjoyed under the Gospel dispensation. The power, with which the Christian priesthood is clothed, is a heavenly power, raised above that of angels: it has its source not in the Levitical priesthood, but in Christ the Lord, who was a priest not according to Aaron, but according to the order of Melchisedech.[1] He it is who, endowed with supreme authority to grant pardon and grace, has bequeathed this power to his Church, a power limited, however, in its extent, and attached to the sacraments.

To exercise this power, therefore, ministers are appointed and solemnly consecrated, and this solemn consecration is denominated "Ordination," or "the Sacrament of Orders." To designate this Sacrament, the word "Orders" has been made use of by the Holy Fathers, because its signification is very comprehensive, and, therefore, well adapted to convey an idea of the dignity and excellence of the ministers of God. Understood in its strict and proper acceptation, order is the disposition of superior and subordinate parts, which, when united, present a combination so harmonious as to stand in mutual and accordant relations. Comprising then, as the ministry does, many gradations and various functions, and disposed, as all these gradations and functions are, with the greatest regularity, this Sacrament is very appropriately called "the Sacrament of Orders." *Name of this Sacrament.*

That Holy Orders are to be numbered amongst the Sacraments of the Church, the Council of Trent establishes on the same principle to which we have so often referred in proving the other Sacraments. A Sacrament is a sensible sign of an invisible grace, and with these characters Holy Orders are invested: their external forms are a sensible sign of the grace and power which they confer on the receiver: Holy Orders, therefore, are really and truly a Sacrament.[2] Hence the bishop, handing to the candidate for priest's orders, a chalice which contains wine and water, and a patena with bread, says: "Receive the power of offering Sacrifice," &c., words which, according to the uniform interpretation of the Church, impart power, when the proper matter is supplied, of consecrating the Holy Eucharist, and impress a character on the soul. To this power is annexed grace duly and lawfully to discharge the priestly office, according to these words of the Apostle: "I admonish thee, that thou stir up the grace of God which is in *Orders, a Sacrament.*

[1] Heb. vii. 11.
[2] Sess. 23. de ordine. ordinem esse sacramentum vid. Trid. sess. 23. de ordine. c. 1. et 3. et can. 3, 4, 5. Conc. Florent. in decret. de sacr. Aug. lib. 2. contr. epist. Parmen. cap. 13. de bono conjug. cap. 24. et lib. 1. de bapt. contra Donat. c. 1. Leo. epist. 18. Greg. in c. 10. libr. 1. Reg.

thee, by the imposition of my hands; for God hath not given us the spirit of fear, but of power, and of love, and of sobriety."[1]

Number of Orders.

With regard to the number of orders, to use the words of the Council of Trent, "As the ministry of so exalted a priesthood is a divine thing, it was meet, in order to surround it with the greater dignity and veneration, that in the admirable economy of the Church there should be several distinct orders of ministers, intended by their office to serve the priesthood, and so disposed, as that, beginning with the clerical tonsure, they may ascend gradually through the lesser to the greater orders." Their number, according to the uniform and universal doctrine of the Catholic Church, is seven, Porter, Reader, Exorcist, Acolyte, Sub-deacon, Deacon, and Priest.[2] That these compose the number of ministers in the Church may be proved from the functions necessary to the solemn celebration of Mass, and to the consecration and administration of the Holy Eucharist, for which they were principally instituted. Of these some are greater, which are also called "Holy," some lesser, which are called "Minor Orders." The greater or Holy Orders are Subdeaconship, Deaconship, and Priesthood; the lesser or Minor Orders are Porter, Reader, Exorcist, and Acolyte. To facilitate the duty of the pastor, particularly when conveying instruction to those who are about to be initiated in any of the orders, it is necessary to say a few words on each.

Tonsure, its form, origin, and import.

We shall begin with the tonsure, which is a sort of preparation for receiving orders: As persons are prepared for baptism by exorcisms, and for marriage by espousals, so those who are consecrated to God by tonsure, are prepared for admission to the Sacrament of Orders. Tonsure declares what manner of person he should be, who desires to receive orders: the name of "Clerk," (clericus) which he receives then for the first time, implies[3] that thenceforward he has taken the Lord for his inheritance, like those who, in the Old Law, were consecrated to the service of God, and to whom the Lord forbade that any portion of the ground should be distributed in the land of promise, saying, "I am thy portion and thy inheritance."[4] This, although true of all Christians, applies in a special manner to those who have been consecrated to the ministry.[5] In tonsure the hair of the head is cut in form of a crown, and should be worn in that form, enlarging the crown according as the ecclesiastic advances in Orders. This form of the Tonsure the Church teaches to be of Apostolic origin: it is mentioned by the most ancient and venerable Fathers, by St. Denis the Areopagite,[6]

---

[1] Tim. i. 6.
[2] Horum ordinum meminerunt Dionys. lib. Eccl. Hier. cap. 3. Cornel. Papa in epist ad Fab. episcop. Antioch. extat apud Euseb. Hist. Eccles. lib. 6. cap. 35. Conc. Carth. 4. can. 4. et seq. Ignat. epist. ad Antioch.
[3] κληρος, sors. a lot. T.   [4] Num. xviii. 20.
[5] Vid. Hieron. epist. 2. ad Nepot. et citatur 12. q. 1. c. clericus.
[6] Dionys. de Eccles. Hier. c. 6. part. 2.

by St. Augustine,[1] and by St. Jerome.[2] According to these venerable personages the Tonsure was first introduced by the prince of the Apostles, in honour of the crown of thorns which was pressed upon the head of the Redeemer; that the instrument devised by the impiety of the Jews for the ignominy and torture of Christ may be worn by his Apostles as their ornament and glory. It was also intended to signify that the ministers of religion are, in all things, so to comport themselves, as to carry about them the figure and the likeness of Christ. Some, however, assert that tonsure is an emblem of the royal dignity, which belongs peculiarly to those who are specially called to the inheritance of God: for to the ministers of the Church belongs, in a peculiar manner, what the Apostle Peter says of all Christians: "You are a chosen generation, a royal priesthood, a holy nation."[3] Others are of opinion that tonsure, which is cut in form of a circle, the most perfect of all figures, is emblematic of the superior perfection of the ecclesiastical state; or that, as it consists of cutting off hair, which is a sort of superfluity, it implies a contempt of worldly things, and a detachment from all earthly cares and concerns.

The order of Porter follows Tonsure: its duty consists in taking care of the keys and door of the Church, and in suffering none to enter to whom entrance is prohibited. The Porter also assisted at the Holy Sacrifice, and took care that no one should approach too near the altar or interrupt the celebrant. To the order of Porter also belonged other functions, as is clear from the forms used at his consecration: taking the keys from the altar and handing them to him, the bishop says: "CONDUCT YOURSELF AS HAVING TO RENDER AN ACCOUNT TO GOD FOR THOSE THINGS WHICH ARE KEPT UNDER THESE KEYS." That in the ancient Church this office was one of considerable dignity may be inferred from still existing ecclesiastical observances; for to the Porter belonged the office of treasurer of the Church, to which was also attached that of guardian of the sacristy; stations the duties of which are still numbered amongst the most honourable functions of the ecclesiastic.[4] *Porter.*

The second amongst the Minor Orders is that of Reader: to him it belongs to read to the people, in a clear and distinct voice, the sacred Scriptures, particularly the Nocturnal Psalmody; and on him also devolves the task of instructing the faithful in the rudiments of the faith. Hence the bishop, in presence of the people, handing him a book which contains what belongs to the exercise of this function, says: " RECEIVE (THIS BOOK,) AND BE YOU A REHEARSER OF THE WORD OF GOD, DESTINED, IF YOU APPROVE YOURSELF FAITHFUL AND USEFUL IN THE DISCHARGE *Reader.*

[1] Aug. serm. 17. ad Fratres in Eremo.
[2] Hier. in cap. 44. Ezek. vid. Rhaban. Maur. lib. de institut. cleric. Bed. lib. hist. 5. Angl. c. 22.
[3] 1 Pet. ii. 9.
[4] De Ostiario vid. Trid. sess. 23. de reform. c. 17. Conc. Tolet. c. 6. et citatur. dist. 25. Ostiar. Isid. lib. de Eccl. c. 14. et dist. 25. c. perlectis, et apud Baron. Annal. Eccl. an. 34. num. 287. et an. 44. num. 78. et num. 80

OF YOUR OFFICE, TO HAVE A PART WITH THOSE WHO FROM THE BEGINNING, HAVE ACQUITTED THEMSELVES WELL IN THE MINISTRY OF THE DIVINE WORD."[1]

Exorcist. The third order is that of Exorcist: to him is given power to invoke the name of the Lord over persons possessed by unclean spirits. Hence the bishop, when initiating the Exorcist, hands him a book containing the exorcisms, and says: "TAKE THIS AND COMMIT IT TO MEMORY, AND HAVE POWER TO IMPOSE HANDS ON PERSONS POSSESSED, BE THEY BAPTIZED OR CATECHUMENS."[2]

Acolyte. The fourth and last amongst the Minor Orders is that of Acolyte: the duty of the Acolyte is to attend and serve those in holy orders, Deacons and Sub-deacons, in the ministry of the altar. The Acolyte also attends to the lights used at the celebration of the Holy Sacrifice, particularly whilst the Gospel is read. At his ordination, therefore, the bishop, having carefully admonished him of the nature of the office which he is about to assume, places in his hand a light, with these words: "RECEIVE THIS WAX-LIGHT, AND KNOW THAT HENCEFORWARD YOU ARE DEVOTED TO LIGHT THE CHURCH, IN THE NAME OF THE LORD." He then hands him empty cruits, intended to supply wine and water for the sacrifice, saying: "RECEIVE THESE CRUITS, WHICH ARE TO SUPPLY WINE AND WATER FOR THE EUCHARIST OF THE BLOOD OF CHRIST, IN THE NAME OF THE LORD."[3]

Sub-deacon. Minor Orders, which do not come under the denomination of Holy, and which have hitherto formed the subject-matter of our exposition, are, as it were, the vestibule through which we ascend to holy orders. Amongst the latter the first is that of Sub-deacon: his office, as the name implies, is to serve the Deacon in the ministry of the altar: to him it belongs to prepare the altar-linen, the sacred vessels, the bread and wine necessary for the Holy Sacrifice, to minister water to the Priest or Bishop at the washing of the hands at Mass, to read the Epistle, a function which was formerly discharged by the Deacon, to assist at Mass in the capacity of a witness, and see that the Priest be not disturbed by any one during its celebration. These functions, which appertain to the ministry of the Sub-deacon, may be learned from the solemn ceremonies used at his consecration. In the first place, the bishop admonishes him that by his ordination he assumes the solemn obligation of perpetual continence, and proclaims aloud that he alone is eligible to this office, who is prepared freely to embrace this law. In the next place, when the solemn prayer of the Litanies has been recited, the Bishop enumerates and explains the duties and functions of the Sub-deacon. This done, each of the candidates for

[1] Vid. Cypr. epist. 33. et Tertull. de praescript. c. 61. et apud Baron. Annal. Eccl. anno. 34. num. 287. et an. 54. 78, 79. an. 153. num. 93. an. 456. num. 20.
[2] De Exorcist. vid. supra cit. auctores et apud Baron. Annal. Eccl. an. 34. num. 287. an. 44. num. 78. et num. 80. an. 237. num. 89. an. 56. num. 5. et num. 8. 9. 10. 11. 12.
[3] De Acolytis vid. etiam Cypr. epist. 55. et apud Baron. Annal. Eccl. an. 44. num. 39. et num. 80.

ordination receives from the Bishop a chalice and consecrated patena, and from the Archdeacon, cruits filled with wine and water, and a basin and towel for washing and drying the hands, to remind him that he is to serve the Deacon. These ceremonies the bishop accompanies with this solemn admonition: "SEE WHAT SORT OF MINISTRY IS CONFIDED TO YOU: I ADMONISH YOU THEREFORE SO TO COMPORT YOURSELVES AS TO BE PLEASING IN THE SIGHT OF GOD." Additional prayers are then recited, and when, finally, the bishop has clothed the Sub-deacon with the sacred vestments, on putting on each of which he makes use of appropriate words and ceremonies, he then hands him the book of the Epistles, saying: "RECEIVE THE BOOK OF THE EPISTLES, AND HAVE POWER TO READ THEM IN THE CHURCH OF GOD, BOTH FOR THE LIVING AND THE DEAD."[1]

The second amongst the Holy Orders is that of Deacon: his ministry is more comprehensive, and has been always deemed more holy: to him it belongs constantly to accompany the bishop, to attend him when preaching, to assist him and the priest also during the celebration of the Holy Mysteries, and at the administration of the Sacraments, and to read the Gospel at the Sacrifice of the Mass. In the primitive ages of the Church, he not unfrequently exhorted the faithful to attend to the divine worship, and administered the chalice in those Churches, in which the faithful received the Holy Eucharist under both kinds In order to administer to the wants of the necessitous, to him was also committed the distribution of the goods of the Church. To the Deacon also, as the eye of the bishop, it belongs to in quire and ascertain who within his diocess lead lives of piety and edification, and who do not; who attend the Holy Sacrifice of the Mass and the instructions of their pastors, and who do not; that thus the bishop, made acquainted by him with these matters, may be enabled to admonish each offender privately, or, should he deem it more conducive to their reformation, to rebuke and correct them publicly. He also calls over the names of catechumens, and presents to the bishop those who are to be promoted to orders. In the absence of the bishop and priest, he is also authorized to expound the Gospel to the people, not however from an elevated place, to make it understood that this is not one of his ordinary functions. That the greatest care should be taken, that no unworthy person be advanced to the office of Deacon, is evinced by the emphasis with which the Apostle, writing to Timothy, dwells on the morals, the virtue, the integrity which should mark the lives of those who are invested with this sacred character.[2] The rites and ceremonies used at his ordination also sufficiently convey the same lesson of instruction. The prayers used at the ordination

Deacon.

[1] De Subdiaconis præter auctores supra citatos vide Cypr. epist. 24. et epist. 42. dist. 17. c. presbyteris, Can. Apost. can. 25. Conc. Carthag. 4. can. 5. Arelat. 2. can. 2. Aurel. 3. cap. 2. Eliber. can. 33. Leo l. Epist. 82. item apud Baron. Annal. Eccl. an 44 num. 79. et 80. an. 253. num. 72. num. 97. an. 239. num. 21. an. 324. nnm. 126. an. 566. num. 48. an. 589. num. 6. an. 1057. num. 32.   [2] 1 Tim. iii. 8.

of a Deacon are more numerous and solemn than at that of a Sub-deacon: his person is also invested with the sacred stole: of his ordination as of that of the first Deacons who were ordained by the Apostles,[1] the imposition of hands also forms a part; and, finally, the book of the Gospels is handed to him by the bishop with these words: "RECEIVE POWER TO READ THE GOSPEL IN THE CHURCH OF GOD, AS WELL FOR THE LIVING AS FOR THE DEAD, IN THE NAME OF THE LORD."[2]

Priest. The third and highest degree of all Holy Orders is the Priesthood. Persons raised to the Priesthood the Holy Fathers distinguish by two names: they are called "Presbyters," which in Greek signifies elders, and which was given them, not only to express the mature years required by the Priesthood, but still more, the gravity of their manners, their knowledge and prudence: "Venerable old age is not that of long time, nor counted by the number of years; but the understanding of a man is grey hairs:"[3] they are also called "Priests," (Sacerdotes) because they are consecrated to God, and to them it belongs to administer the sacraments and to handle sacred things.

The Priesthood, two-fold; But as the Priesthood is described in the Sacred Scriptures as two-fold, internal and external, a line of distinction must be drawn between them, that the pastor may have it in his power to explain to the faithful the Priesthood which is here meant.

Internal, The internal Priesthood extends to all the faithful, who have been baptized, particularly to the just, who are anointed by the Spirit of God, and by the divine grace are made living members of the High-priest Christ Jesus. Through faith inflamed by charity, they offer spiritual sacrifices to God on the altar of their hearts, and in the number of these sacrifices are to be reckoned good and virtuous actions, referred to the glory of God. Hence we read in the Apocalypse: "Christ hath washed us from our sins in his own blood, and had made us a kingdom and priests to God and his Father."[4] The doctrine of St. Peter to the same effect we find recorded in these words: "Be you also as living stones, built up, a spiritual house, a holy priesthood, to offer up spiritual sacrifices acceptable to God by Jesus Christ."[5] The Apostle also exhorts us, "to present our bodies a living sacrifice, holy, pleasing unto God, our reasonable service;"[6] and David had said long before: "A sacrifice to God is an afflicted spirit; a contrite and humble heart, O God! thou wilt not despise."[7] That all these authorities regard the internal Priesthood, it requires little discernment to discover.

and external. The external Priesthood does not extend indiscriminately to

1 Acts vi. 6.
2 De Diaconis præter citatos supra vid. Clem. Rom. Constit. Apostol. lib. 2. c. 6 Cypr. de lapsis. Amb. lib. 1. offic. c. 41. Leo 1. serm. de S. Laurent. Clem. Rom. epist. 1. ad Jacob. Fratrem Domini, Hier. epist. 48. et apud Baron. Annal. Eccl. an. 33. num. 41. an. 34. num. 283. an. 285 et 287. an. 34. num. 316. an. 44. num. 78 et 80. an. 57. num. 31 et num. 195. an. 58. num. 102, an. 112. num. 7. 8. 9. an. 316. num. 48. an. 324. num. 325. an. 325. num. 152. an. 401. num. 44 et 47. an. 508. num. 15. an. 741. num. 12   3 Wisd. 4. 8.
4 Apoc. i. 5, 6   5 1 Pet. ii. 5.   6 Rom. xii. 1.   7 Ps. l. 19.

the great body of the faithful; it is appropriated to a certain class of persons; who, being invested with this august character, and consecrated to God by the lawful imposition of hands and the solemn ceremonies of the Church, are devoted to some particular office in the sacred ministry.

This distinction of Priesthood is observable even in the Old Law. We have already seen that David spoke of the internal Priesthood; and with regard to the external, the numerous commands delivered by God to Moses and Aaron in reference to it, are too well known to require special mention. Moreover, the Almighty appointed the tribe of Levi to the ministry of the temple, and forbade by an express law that any member of a different tribe should assume that function; and Osias, stricken by God with leprosy for having usurped the sacerdotal office, was visited with the heaviest chastisement for his arrogant and sacrilegious intrusion.[1] As, then, we find this same distinction of internal and external Priesthood in the New Law, the faithful are to be informed that we here speak of the external only, for that alone belongs to the Sacrament of Holy Orders.

This distinction observable in the Old Law.

We here speak of the external priesthood.

The office of the Priest is then, as the rites used at his consecration declare, to offer sacrifice to God, and to administer the Sacraments of the Church: the bishop, and after him the priests who may be present, impose hands on the candidate for priesthood; then placing a stole on his shoulders, he adjusts it in form of a cross, to signify that the priest receives strength from above, to enable him to carry the cross of Jesus Christ, to bear the sweet yoke of his divine law, and to enforce this law, not by word only, but also by the eloquent example of a holy life. He next anoints his hands with sacred oil, reaches him a chalice containing wine and a patena with bread, saying: "RECEIVE POWER TO OFFER SACRIFICE TO GOD, AND TO CELEBRATE MASS AS WELL FOR THE LIVING AS FOR THE DEAD." By these words and ceremonies he is constituted an interpreter and mediator between God and man, the principal function of the Priesthood. Finally, placing his hands on the head of the person to be ordained, the bishop says: "RECEIVE YE THE HOLY GHOST; WHOSE SINS YOU SHALL FORGIVE, THEY ARE FORGIVEN THEM: AND WHOSE SINS YOU SHALL RETAIN, THEY ARE RETAINED;"[2] thus investing him with that divine power of forgiving and retaining sins, which was conferred by our Lord on his disciples—These are the principal and peculiar functions of the Priesthood.

Its office proved from the rites by which it is conferred.
I.
II.

III.

IV.

The Order of Priesthood, although essentially one, has different degrees of dignity and power. The first is confined to those who are simply called Priests, and whose functions we have now explained. The second is that of Bishops, who are placed over their respective Sees, to govern not only the other

The priesthood, although one, has different degrees of dignity and power

[1] Amb. lib. 4. de sacram. cap. 1. August. lib. 10. de civ. Dei, c. 6 et 10. Leo. serm. 3. de Annivers. Pontific. 2 Par. 26, 18, 19.
[2] John iii xx. 22, 23

19*

I.
II.

ministers of the Church, but also the faithful; and, with sleepless vigilance and unwearied care, to watch over and promote their salvation. Hence the Sacred Scriptures frequently call them "the pastors of the sheep;" and their office, and the duties which it imposes, are developed by Paul in his sermon to the Thessalonians, recorded in the Acts of the Apostles.[1] Peter also has left for the guidance of Bishops a divine rule; and if their lives harmonize with its spirit, they will no doubt be esteemed, and will really be, good pastors.[2] But Bishops

III.

are also called "Pontiffs," a name borrowed from the ancient Romans, and used to designate their Chief-priests. The third degree is that of Archbishop: he presides over several Bishops, and is also called "Metropolitan," because he is placed over the Metropolis of the Province. Archbishops, therefore, (although their ordination is the same,) enjoy more ample power,

IV.

and a more exalted station than bishops. Patriarchs hold the fourth place, and are, as the name implies, the first and supreme Fathers in the Episcopal order. Formerly, besides the Sovereign Pontiff, there were but four Patriarchs in the Church: their dignity was not the same; the Patriarch of Constantinople, although last in the order of time, was first in rank—an honour conceded to him as Bishop of Constantinople, the capital of the imperial world. Next to the Patriarchate of Constantinople, is that of Alexandria, a see founded by the Evangelist St. Mark by command of the prince of the Apostles. The third is the Patriarchate of Antioch, founded by St. Peter, and the first seat of the Apostolic See; the fourth and last, the Patriarchate of Jerusalem, founded by St. James, the brother of our Lord.

V.

Superior to all these is the Sovereign Pontiff, whom Cyril, Archbishop of Alexandria, denominated in the Council of Ephesus, "the Father and Patriarch of the whole world." Sitting in that chair in which Peter the prince of the Apostles sat to the close of life, the Catholic Church recognises in his person the most exalted degree of dignity, and the full amplitude of jurisdiction; a dignity and a jurisdiction not based on synodal, or other human constitutions, but emanating from no less an authority than God himself. As the successor of St. Peter, and the true and legitimate vicar of Jesus Christ, he, therefore, presides over the Universal Church, the Father and Governor of all the faithful, of Bishops, also, and of all other prelates, be their station, rank, or power what they may.[3]

Instruction to the faithful on this Sacrament.

From what has been said, the pastor will take occasion to inform the faithful what are the principal offices and functions of Ecclesiastical Orders, and their degrees, and, also, who is the minister of this Sacrament.

[1] Acts xx. 28.   [2] 1 Pet. v. 2.
[3] De primatu Summi Pontificis vid. Anacl. epist. 3. c. 3. et citatur dist. 22. c. Sacrosancta. Greg. lib. 7. epist. 64 et 65. Nicol. Pap. epist. ad Mediolanens. et citat dist. 22. c. omnes, vid. item eadem dist. c. Constantin. Conc. Chalced. in ep. ad Leonem.

That to the Bishop belongs exclusively the administration of this Sacrament is matter of certainty, and is easily proved by the authority of Scripture, by traditional evidence the most unequivocal, by the unanimous attestation of all the Holy Fathers, by the decrees of Councils, and by the practice of the Universal Church. Some Abbots, it is true, were occasionally permitted to confer Minor Orders : all, however, admit that even this is the proper office of the Bishop, to whom, and to whom alone, it is lawful to confer the other Orders: Sub-deacons, Deacons, and Priests are ordained by one Bishop only, but according to Apostolic tradition, a tradition which has always been preserved in the Church, he himself is consecrated by three Bishops. *The minister of the Sacrament of Orders, a Bishop.*

We now come to explain the qualifications necessary in the candidate for Orders, particularly for Priesthood. From what we shall have said on this subject, it will not be difficult to decide what should also be the qualifications of those who are to be initiated in other Orders, according to their respective offices and comparative dignities. That too much precaution cannot be used in promoting to Orders is obvious from this consideration alone : the other Sacraments impart grace for the sanctification and salvation of those who receive them—Holy Orders for the good of the Church, and therefore for the salvation of all her children. Hence it is that Orders are conferred on certain appointed days only, days on which, according to the most ancient practice of the Church, a solemn fast is observed, to obtain from God by holy and devout prayer, ministers not unworthy of their high calling, qualified to exercise the transcendant power with which they are to be invested, with propriety and to the edification of his Church. *Necessity of extreme caution in promoting to Orders.*

In the candidate for priesthood, therefore, integrity of life is a first and essential qualification, not only because to procure, or even to permit his ordination, whilst his conscience is burdened with the weight of mortal sin, is to aggravate his former guilt, by an additional crime of the deepest enormity ; but, also, because it is his to enlighten the darkness of others by the lustre of his virtue, and the bright example of innocence of life. The lessons addressed by the Apostle to Titus and to Timothy[1] should, therefore, supply the pastor with matter for instruction ; nor should he omit to observe, that whilst by the command of God bodily defects disqualified for the ministry of the altar in the Old Law, in the Christian dispensation such exclusion rests principally on the deformities of the mind. The candidate for Orders, therefore, in accordance with the holy practice of the Catholic Church, will first study diligently to purify his conscience from sin in the Sacrament of Penance. *Qualifications for the priesthood. I.*

In the Priest we also look not merely for that portion of knowledge which is necessary to the proper administration of the Sacraments : more is expected—an intimate acquaintance *II.*

[1] Tit. i. and 1 Tim. iii.

with the science of the Sacred Volume should fit him to instruct the faithful in the mysteries of religion, and in the precepts of the Gospel, to reclaim from sin, and excite to piety and virtue. The due consecration and administration of the Sacraments, and the instruction of those who are committed to his care in the way of salvation, constitute two important duties of the pastor. "The lips of the priest," says Malachy, "shall keep knowledge, and they shall seek the law at his mouth; because he is the angel of the Lord of Hosts."[1] To a due consecration and administration of the Sacraments, a moderate share of knowledge suffices; but to instruct the faithful in all the truths and duties of religion, demands considerable ability, and extensive

Note. knowledge. In all priests, however, recondite learning is not demanded: it is sufficient that each possess competent knowledge to discharge the duties of his own particular office in the ministry.

On whom Orders are not to be conferred. The Sacrament of Orders is not to be conferred on very young, or on insane persons, because they do not enjoy the use of reason: if administered, however, it no doubt impresses a character. The age required for the reception of the different Orders may be easily known by consulting the decrees of the Council of Trent. Persons obligated to render certain stipulated services to others, and therefore not at their own disposal, are inadmissible to Orders; persons accustomed to shed blood, and homicides, are also excluded from the ecclesiastical state by an ecclesiastical law, and are irregular. The same law excludes those whose admission into the ministry may and must bring contempt on religion; and hence illegitimate children, and all who are born out of lawful wedlock, are disqualified for the sacred ministry. Finally, persons who are maimed, or who labour under any remarkable personal deformity, are also excluded; such defects offend the eye, and frequently incapacitate for the discharge of the duties of the ministry.

Effects of the Sacrament of Orders. I. Having explained these matters, it remains that the pastor unfold the effects of this Sacrament. It is clear, as we have already said, that the Sacrament of Orders, although primarily instituted for the advantage and edification of the Church, imparts grace to him who receives it with the proper dispositions, which qualifies and enables him to discharge with fidelity the duties which it imposes, and amongst which is to be numbered the administration of the Sacraments. As baptism qualifies for

II. their reception, so Orders qualify for their administration. Orders also confer another grace, which is a special power in reference to the Holy Eucharist; a power full and perfect in the priest, who alone can consecrate the body and blood of our Lord, but in the subordinate ministers, greater or less in proportion to their approximation to the sacred mysteries of the altar.

III. This power is also denominated a spiritual character, which, by a certain interior mark impressed on the soul, distinguishes the

[1] Malach. ii. 7.

ecclesiastic from the rest of the faithful, and devotes them specially to the divine service. This the Apostle seems to have had in view, when he thus addressed Timothy : " Neglect not the grace that is in thee, which was given thee by prophecy, with the imposition of the hands of the priesthood ;"[1] and again, " I admonish thee, that thou stir up the grace of God, which is in thee by the imposition of my hands."[2]

On the Sacrament of Orders let thus much suffice. Our purpose has been to lay before the pastor the most important particulars upon the subject, in order to supply him with matter upon which he may draw for the instruction of the faithful, and their advancement in Christian piety.

ON THE SACRAMENT OF MATRIMONY.

As it is the duty of the pastor to propose to himself the holiness and perfection of the faithful, his earnest desires must be in full accordance with those of the Apostle, when, writing to the Corinthians, he says : " I would that all men were even as myself ;"[3] that is, that all embraced the virtue of continence. If there be any one blessing superior to every other, it surely falls to the lot of him who, unfettered by the distracting cares of the world, the turbulence of passion tranquillized, the unruly desires of the flesh extinguished, reposes in the practice of piety and the contemplation of heavenly things. But as, according to the same Apostle, " every one hath his proper gift from God, one after this manner, and another after that,"[4] and marriage is gifted with many divine blessings, holding, as it does, a place amongst the Sacraments of the Church, and honoured, as it was, by the presence of our Lord himself,[5] it becomes the obvious duty of the pastor to expound its doctrine ; particularly when we find that St. Paul, and the prince of the Apostles, have, in many places, minutely described to us not only the dignity but also the duties of the married state. Filled with the Spirit of God, they well understood the numerous and important advantages which must flow to Christian society from a knowledge of the sanctity and an inviolable observance of the obligations of marriage ; whilst they saw that from an ignorance of the former, and a disregard of the latter, marriage must prove the fertile source of the greatest evils, and the heaviest calamities to the Church of God.

The nature and import of marriage are, therefore, to be first explained ; for as vice not unfrequently assumes the semblance of virtue, care must be taken that the faithful be not deceived

A life of continence to be desired by all.

The sanctity of marriage.

Nature and import of marriage to be first explained.

---

[1] 1 Tim. iv. 14. [2] 2 Tim. i. 6. [3] 1 Cor. vii. 7.
[4] 1 Cor. vii. 7. [5] John ii. 2.

by a false appearance of marriage, and thus stain their souls with the turpitude and defilement of wicked lusts. To give them competent and correct information on this important subject, we

Meaning of the word "matrimony."

shall begin with the meaning of the word "Matrimony." It is called "Matrimony," because the principal object which a female should propose to herself in marriage is to become a mother ; (matrem) or because to a mother it belongs to conceive, bring forth, and train up her offspring. It is also called "wed-

"Wedlock."

"Marriage."

lock," (conjugium) from the conjugal union of man and wife ; (a conjugendo) because a lawful wife is united to her husband, as it were, by a common yoke. It is called "marriage," (nuptiæ) because, as St. Ambrose observes, the bride veiled her face (se obnuberent) through modesty, a reverential observance which would also seem to imply that she was to be subject to her husband.[1]

Definition of matrimony, explanation of.

Matrimony, in the general opinion of divines, is defined "The conjugal and legitimate union of man and woman, which is to last during life." In order that the different parts of this definition may be better understood, the pastor will teach that, although a perfect marriage has all these conditions, viz. internal consent, external assent expressed by words, the obligation and tie which arise from the contract, and the marriage debt by which it is consummated; yet the obligation and tie expressed by the word "union," alone have the force and nature of marriage. The peculiar character of this union is marked by the word "conjugal," distinguishing it from other contracts by which persons unite to promote their common interests, engage to render some service for a stipulated time, or enter into an agreement for some other purpose, contracts all of which differ essentially from this "conjugal union." Next follows the word "legitimate ;" for persons excluded by law cannot contract marriage, and if they do their marriage is invalid. Persons, for instance, within the fourth degree of kindred, a boy before his fourteenth year, and a female before her twelfth, the ages established by the laws,[2] cannot contract marriage. The words "which is to last during life," express the indissolubility of the tie, which binds husband and wife.

In what marriage consists.

Hence, it is evident, that in that tie consists marriage. Some eminent divines, it is true, say that it consists in the consent, as when they define it : "The consent of the man and woman ;" but we are to understand them to mean that the consent is the efficient cause of marriage, which is the doctrine of the Fathers of the Council of Florence ; because, without the consent and contract, the obligation and tie cannot possibly exist. But it is of absolute necessity that the consent be expressed in words which designate the present time. Marriage is not a simple

[1] De his nomin. vid. Aug. lib. 19. contr. Faust. c. 26. Ambr. lib. 1. de Abraham c. 9. in fine. item vid. 30. q. 5. c. fœmina, et 33. q. 5. c. Mulier. Isidor. lib. de Eccl. officiis c. 19.

[2] Such laws, the reader will perceive, are of a local nature, and vary in different countries.—T.

donation, but a mutual contract; and therefore the consent of one of the parties is insufficient, that of both necessary to its validity; and to declare this consent, words are obviously the medium to be employed. If the internal consent alone, without any external indication, were sufficient, it would then seem to follow as a necessary consequence, that were two persons, living in the most separate and distant countries, to consent to marry, they should contract a true and indissoluble marriage, even before they had mutually signified to each other their consent by letter or messenger; a consequence as repugnant to reason as it is opposed to the decrees and established usage of the Church.

It has been wisely provided that the consent of the parties to the marriage contract be expressed in words which have reference to the present time. Words which signify a future time promise, but do not actually unite in marriage: it is evident that what is to be done has no present existence: what does not exist can have little or no firmness or stability: a promise of marriage, therefore, does not give a title to the rights of marriage. Such promises are, it is true, obligatory; and their violation involves the offending party in a breach of faith: but although entered into they have not been actually fulfilled, and cannot therefore constitute marriage. But he who has once entered into the matrimonial alliance, regret it as he afterwards may, cannot possibly change, or invalidate, or undo the compact. As then the marriage contract is not a mere promise, but a transfer of right, by which the man yields the dominion of his person to the woman, the woman the dominion of her person to the man, it must therefore be made in words which designate the present time, the force of which words abides with undiminished efficacy from the moment of their utterance, and binds the husband and wife by a tie which can never be dissolved, but by death of one of the parties. *The consent of the parties to be expressed in words which have reference to the present time.*

Instead of words, however, it may be sufficient for the validity of the marriage contract to substitute a nod or other unequivocal sign of tacit consent: even silence, when the result of female modesty, may be sufficient, provided the parents answer for their daughter. Hence the pastor will teach the faithful that the nature and force of marriage consists in the tie and obligation; and that, without consummation, the consent of the parties, expressed in the manner already explained, is sufficient to constitute a true marriage. It is certain that our first parents before their fall, when, according to the Holy Fathers, no consummation took place, were really united in marriage.[1] The holy Fathers, therefore, say that marriage consists not in its consummation, but in the consent of the contracting parties; a doctrine repeated by St. Ambrose in his book on virginity.[2] *A nod or other unequivocal sign may be sufficient. Consummation not necessary.*

Having explained these matters, the pastor will proceed to teach that matrimony is to be considered in two points of view, *Marriage two-fold.*

[1] Gen. ii. 22.   [2] De instit. virgin. cap. 6.

natural and sacramental.

either as a natural union, (marriage was invented not by man but by nature) or as a sacrament, the efficacy of which transcends the order of nature; and as grace perfects nature, (" That was not first which is spiritual, but that which is natural; afterwards that which is spiritual,")[1] the order of our matter requires that we first treat of matrimony as a natural contract, and next as a sacrament.

Natural marriage instituted by God.

The faithful, therefore, are to be taught, in the first place, that marriage was instituted by God. We read in Genesis, that " God created them male and female, and blessed them saying: 'Increase and multiply:'" and also: "It is not good for a man to be alone: let us make him a help like unto himself. Then the Lord God cast a deep sleep upon Adam; and when he was fast asleep, he took one of his ribs, and filled up flesh for it. And the Lord God built the rib which he took from Adam into a woman, and brought her to Adam; and Adam said: this is now bone of my bones, and flesh of my flesh: she shall be called woman, because she was taken out of man: wherefore a man shall leave father and mother, and shall cleave to his wife; and they shall be two in one flesh.'"[2] These words, according to the authority of our Lord himself as we read in St. Matthew, establish the divine institution of Matrimony.[3]

Indissoluble.

Not only did God institute marriage; he also, as the Council of Trent declares, rendered it perpetual and indissoluble:[4] " what God hath joined together," says our Lord, "let not man separate."[5] As a natural contract, it accords with the duties of marriage that it be indissoluble; yet its indissolubility arises principally from its nature as a sacrament; and this it is that, in all its natural relations, elevates it to the highest perfection. Its dissolubility, however, is at once opposed to the proper education of children, and to the other important ends of marriage.

Marriage not obligatory on all.

But the words "increase and multiply," which were uttered by Almighty God, do not impose on every individual an obligation to marry: they declare the object of the institution of marriage; and now that the human race is widely diffused, not only is there no law rendering marriage obligatory, but, on the contrary, virginity is highly exalted and strongly recommended in Scripture as superior to marriage, as a state of greater perfection and holiness. On this subject the doctrine taught by our Lord himself is contained in these words: "He that can take it, let him take it;"[6] and the Apostle says: "Concerning virgins I have no commandment from the Lord; but I give counsel as having obtained mercy from the Lord to be faithful."[7]

Marriage why instituted.
I.

But why marriage was instituted is a subject which demands exposition—The first reason of its institution is because nature instinctively tends to such a union; and under the vicissitudes

---

[1] 1 Cor. xv 46.   [2] Gen. i. 27, 28.   Gen. ii. 18. 21, 22. 23, 24.
[3] Matt. xix. 6.   [4] Sess. 24. init.   [5] Matt. xix. 6.
[6] Matt. xix. 12.   [7] 1 Cor. vii. 25.

of life and the infirmities of old age, this union is a source of
mutual assistance and support. Another is the desire of family,   II.
not so much, however, with a view to leave after us heirs to
inherit our property and fortune, as to bring up children in the
true faith and in the service of God. That such was the principal object of the Holy Patriarchs when they engaged in the married state, we learn from the Sacred Volumes ; and hence the
angel, when informing Tobias of the means of repelling the violent assaults of the evil demon, says : "I will show thee who
they are over whom the devil can prevail ; for they who in
such manner receive matrimony, as to shut out God from themselves and from their mind, and to give themselves to their lust,
as the horse and mules which have not understanding, over
them the devil hath power." He then adds : "thou shalt
take the virgin with the fear of the Lord, moved rather for love
of children than for lust, that in the seed of Abraham thou
mayest obtain a blessing in children."[1] This was also amongst Note.
the reasons why God instituted marriage from the beginning ;
and therefore married persons who, to prevent conception or
procure abortion, have recourse to medicine, are guilty of a
most heinous crime—nothing less than premeditated murder.
The third reason is one which is to be numbered amongst the   III.
consequences of primeval transgressions : stript of original innocence, human appetite began to rise in rebellion against right
season ; and man, conscious of his own frailty, and unwilling
to fight the battles of the flesh, is supplied by marriage with an
antidote against the licentiousness of corrupt desire. "For
fear of fornication," says the Apostle, "let every man have his
own wife, and let every woman have her own husband ;" and
a little after, having recommended to married persons a temporary abstinence from the marriage debt, "to give themselves to
prayer," he adds : "Return together again, lest Satan tempt
you for your incontinency."[2]

These are ends, some one of which, those who desire to con- Note
tract marriage piously and religiously, as becomes the children
of the Saints, should propose to themselves. If to these we
add other concurring causes which induce to contract marriage,
such as the desire of leaving an heir, wealth, beauty, illustrious
descent, congeniality of disposition, such motives, because not
inconsistent with the holiness of marriage, are not to be condemned : we do not find that the Sacred Scriptures condemn
the patriarch Jacob for having chosen Rachel for her beauty, in
preference to Lia.[3]

These are the instructions which the pastor will communi- Matrimony
cate to the faithful on the subject of marriage, as a natural con- as a Sacra-
tract : as a sacrament he will show that marriage is raised to a perior to
superior order, and referred to a more exalted end. The ori- the natural
ginal institution of marriage, as a natural contract, had for object contract.
the propagation of the human race : its subsequent elevation to

[1] Tob. vi. 16, 17, 18. 22.   [2] I Cor. vii. 2.   [3] Gen. xxix.

the dignity of a sacrament is intended for the procreation and education of a people in the religion and worship of the true God, and of our Lord Jesus Christ. When the Redeemer would exemplify the close union that subsists between him and his Church, and his boundless love towards us, he declares this divine mystery principally by alluding to the holy union of man and wife; and the aptitude of the illustration is evinced by this, that of all human relations no one is so binding as that of marriage, and those who stand in that relation are united in the closest bonds of affection and love. Hence the Sacred Scriptures, by assimilating it to marriage, frequently place before us this divine union of Christ with his Church.

Exemplifies the union of Christ and his Church.

That marriage is a sacrament has been at all times held by the Church as a certain and well ascertained truth; and in this she is supported by the authority of the Apostle in his Epistle to the Ephesians: "Husbands," says he, "should love their wives, as their own bodies: he who loveth his wife, loveth himself, for no one ever hated his own flesh, but nourisheth and cherisheth it, even as Christ doth the Church, for we are members of his body, of his flesh, and of his bones. For this cause shall a man leave his father and mother, and shall cleave to his wife, and they shall be two in one flesh. This is a great sacrament, but I speak in Christ, and in the Church."[1] When the Apostle says: "This is a great sacrament," he means, no doubt, to designate marriage;[2] as if he had said: The conjugal union between man and wife, of which God is the author, is a sacrament, that is, a sacred sign of the holy union that subsists between Christ and his Church. That this is the true meaning of his words is shown by the Holy Fathers who have interpreted the passage; and the Council of Trent has given to it the same interpretation.[3] The husband therefore is evidently compared by the Apostle to Christ, the wife to the Church;[4] "the man is head of the woman, as Christ is of the Church;"[5] and hence the husband should love his wife, and again, the wife should love and respect her husband, for "Christ loved his Church, and gave himself for her;" and the Church, as the same Apostle teaches, is subject to Christ.

Marriage a Sacrament.

That this sacrament signifies and confers grace, and in this the nature of a sacrament principally consists, we learn from these words of the Council of Trent: "The grace which perfects that natural love, and confirms that indissoluble union, Christ himself, the author and finisher of the sacraments, has merited for us by his passion."[6] The faithful are, therefore, to be taught, that, united in the bonds of mutual love, the husband and wife are enabled, by the grace of this sacrament, to repose in each other's affections; to reject every criminal attachment; to repel every inclination to unlawful intercourse; and,

It signifies and confers grace

[1] Eph. v. 28.
[2] Tertull. lib. de Monog. Aug. de fide et oper. c. 7. lib. de nupt. et concup. c. 10. et 12.　　　[3] Sess. 24.　　　　[4] Ambr. in epist. ad Ephes.
[5] Eph. v. 23.　　　[6] Sess. 24. de matrim.

in every thing to preserve " marriage honourable, and the bed undefiled."[1]

·The great superiority of the sacrament of matrimony to those Its supe- marriages which took place before or after the Law, we may riority to
Gentile learn from the following considerations—The Gentiles, it is and Jewish true, looked upon marriage as something sacred, and therefore marriage. considered promiscuous intercourse to be inconsistent with the law of nature: they also held that fornication, adultery, and other licentious excesses should be repressed by legal sanctions; but their marriages had nothing whatever of the nature of a sacrament. Amongst the Jews the laws of marriage were observed with more religious fidelity, and their marriages, no doubt, were more holy. Having received the promise that in the seed of Abraham all nations should be blessed,[2] it was justly deemed a matter of great piety amongst them to beget children, the offspring of a chosen people, from whom, as to his human nature, Christ our Lord and Saviour was to descend; but their marriage also wanted the true nature of a Sacrament. Of this it is a further confirmation, that whether we consider the law of nature after the fall of Adam, or the law given to Moses, we at once perceive that marriage had fallen from its primitive excellence and sanctity. Under the Law of Moses we find that many of the Patriarchs had several wives at the same time, and, should a cause exist, it was subsequently permitted to dismiss one's wife, having given her a bill of divorce;[3] both of which abuses have been removed by the Gospel dispensation, and marriage restored to its primitive state.

That polygamy is opposed to the nature of marriage is shown Polygamy by our Lord in these words: "For this cause a man shall opposed to
the nature leave father and mother, and cleave to his wife, and they two of mar- shall be in one flesh. Therefore," continues the Redeemer, riage. "now they are not two but one flesh."[4] The Patriarchs, who, by the permission of God, had a plurality of wives, are not on that account to be condemned: the words of the Redeemer, ·however, clearly show that marriage was instituted by God as the union of two only; and this he again expressly declares when he says: "Whoever shall dismiss his wife, and shall marry another, doth commit adultery, and he that shall marry her that is dismissed, committeth adultery."[5] If a plurality of wives be lawful, we can discover no more reason why he who marries a second wife whilst he retains the first should be said to be guilty of adultery, than he who, having dismissed the first, takes to himself a second. Hence, if an infidel, in accordance with the laws and customs of his country, has married several wives, the Church commands him, when converted to the faith, to look upon the first alone as his lawful wife, and to separate from the others.

That marriage cannot be dissolved by divorce is easily proved Marriage from the same testimony of our Lord: if by a bill of divorce indissolu-
ble.

---

[1] Heb. xiii. 4. [2] Gen. xxii. 18, [3] Deut. xxiv. 1. Matt. xix. 7.
[4] Matt. xix. 9. [5] Matt. xix. 9.

the matrimonial link were dissolved, the wife might lawfully, and without the guilt of adultery, take another husband ; yet our Lord expressly declares, that " whoever shall dismiss his wife, and marry another, committeth adultery."[1] The bond of marriage, therefore, can be dissolved by death alone, and this the Apostle confirms when he says : " A woman is bound by the law, as long as her husband liveth ; but if her husband die, she is at liberty : let her marry whom she will, only in the Lord." and again : " To them that are married, not I, but the Lord commandeth, that the wife depart not from her husband, and if she depart, that she remain unmarried or be reconciled to her husband."[2] Thus to her who has separated from her husband, even for a just cause, the only alternative left by the Apostle is to remain unmarried or be reconciled to her ·husband : the Church, unless influenced by very weighty causes, does not sanction the separation of husband and wife.

Beneficial consequences of its indissolubility.
I.

That this the law of marriage may not appear too rigorous, its beneficial consequences are to be presented to the consideration of the faithful. In the first place, they should know that the choice of a companion for life should be influenced by virtue and congeniality of disposition, rather than by wealth or beauty ; a consideration which confessedly is of the highest practical importance to the interests of society. Besides, if marriage were dissoluble by divorce, married persons could scarcely ever want causes of dissension, which the inveterate enemy of peace and virtue would never fail to supply ; whereas, when the faithful reflect that, although separated as to bed and board, they are still bound by the tie of marriage, and that all hope of a second marriage is cut off, they are more slow to anger and more averse to dissension ; and if sometimes separated, feeling the many inconveniencies that attend their separation, their reconciliation is easily accomplished through the intervention of friends. Here, the salutary admonition of St. Augustine is also not to be omitted by the pastor : to convince the faithful that they should not deem it a hardship to be reconciled to their penitent wives, whom they may have put away for adultery. " Why," says he, " should not the Christian husband receive his wife, whom the Church receives ? Why should not the wife pardon her adulterous but penitent husband, whom Christ has pardoned ? When the Scriptures call him who keeps an adultress ' a fool,'[3] it means an adultress who after her delinquency refuses to repent, and perseveres in the career of turpitude which she had commenced."[4] In perfection and dignity, it is clear therefore, from what has been said, that marriage amongst the Jews and Gentiles is far inferior to Christian marriage.

II.

III.

IV.

V.

Three advantages arising from marriage.

The faithful are also to be informed that there are three advantages which arise from marriage, offspring, faith, and the sacrament ; advantages which alleviate those evils which the

---

[1] Matt. xix. 8. Luke xiv. 18.   [2] 1 Cor. vii. 39.   [3] Prov. xviii. 21
[4] Lib. de adult. conjug. c. 6. et 9.

Apostle points out when he says : " Such shall have tribulation of the flesh ;"[1] and which render that intercourse, which without marriage should be deservedly reprobated, an honourable union.[2] The first advantage, then, is that of legitimate offspring ; an advantage so highly appreciated by the Apostle, that he says : " The woman shall be saved through child-bearing."[3] These words of the Apostle are not, however, to be understood to refer solely to the procreation of children : they also refer to the discipline and education by which children are reared to piety ; for the Apostle immediately adds : " If she continue in faith." " Hast thou children," says Ecclesiasticus, " instruct them and bow down their neck from their childhood :"[4] the same important lesson is inculcated by the Apostle ; and of such an education the Scripture affords the most beautiful illustrations in the persons of Tobias, Job, and of other characters eminent for sanctity. But the further development of the duties of parents and children we reserve for the exposition of the Fourth Commandment.

The next advantage is faith, not the habitual faith infused in baptism, but the fidelity which the husband plights to the wife and the wife to the husband, to deliver to each other the mutual dominion of their persons, and to preserve inviolate the sacred engagements of marriage. This is an obvious inference from the words of Adam on receiving his consort Eve, which, as the Gospel informs us, the Redeemer has sanctioned by his approbation : " Wherefore," says our protoparent, " a man shall leave father and mother, and shall cleave to his wife ; and they shall be two in one flesh."[5] Nor are the words of the Apostle less explicit : " The wife," says he, " hath not power of her own body ; but the husband."[6] Hence against adultery, because it violates this conjugal faith, the Almighty justly decreed in the Old Law the heaviest chastisements.[7] This matrimonial faith also demands, on the part of husband and wife, a singular, holy, and pure love, a love not such as that of adulterers, but such as that which Christ cherishes towards his Church. This is the model of conjugal love proposed by the Apostle when he says : " Men, love your wives, as Christ also loved the Church."[8] The love of Christ for his church was great, not an interested love, but a love which proposed to itself the sole happiness of his spouse.

The third advantage is called the sacrament, that is the indissoluble tie of marriage : " The Lord," says the Apostle, " hath commanded that the wife depart not from her husband, and if she depart, that she remain unmarried, or be reconciled to her husband ; and that the husband dismiss not his wife."[9] If, as a sacrament, marriage is significant of the union of Christ with his Church, it follows that as Christ never separates himself

I

Note.

II

III

---

[1] 1 Cor. vii. 28. [2] Vid. Aug. lib. 5. contr. Tul. cap. 5. [3] 1 Tim. ii. 15.
[4] Eccl. vii. 25. [5] Gen. ii. 24. Matt. xix. 5. [6] 1 Cor. vii. 4.
[7] Num. v. 12. [8] Ephes. v. 25. [9] 1 Cor. vii. 10.

20*   2 G

from his Church, so a wife, as far as regards the tie of marriage, can never be separated from her husband.

Duties of a husband.
I.

The more easily to preserve the happiness of this holy union undisturbed by domestic broils, the pastor will instruct the faithful in the duties of husband and wife, as inculcated by St. Paul and by the prince of the Apostles.[1] It is then the duty of the husband to treat his wife liberally and honourably: it should not be forgotten that Eve was called by Adam "his companion:" "The woman," says he, "whom thou gavest me as a companion." Hence it was, according to the opinion of some of the Holy Fathers, that she was formed not from the feet but from the side of man; as, on the other hand, she was not formed from his head, in order to give her to understand that it was not hers to command but to obey her husband.

The husband should also be constantly occupied in some honest pursuit, with a view as well to provide necessaries for his family, as to avoid the languor of idleness, the root of almost

III.

every vice. He is also to keep all his family in order, to correct their morals, fix their respective employments, and see that they

Duties of a wife.
I.

discharge them with fidelity. On the other hand, the duties of a wife are thus summed up by the prince of the Apostles: "Let wives be subject to their husbands; that if any believe not the word, they may be won without the word, by the conversation of the wives; considering your chaste conversation with fear: whose adorning let it not be the outward plaiting of the hair, or the wearing of gold, or the putting on of apparel, but the hidden man of the heart in the incorruptibility of a quiet and meek spirit, which is rich in the sight of God. For after this manner, heretofore, the holy women also, who trusted in God, adorned themselves, being in subjection to their own husbands,

II.

as Sarah obeyed Abraham, calling him Lord."[2] To train up their children in the practice of virtue, and to pay particular attention to their domestic concerns, should also be especial ob-

III.

jects of their attention and study. Unless compelled by necessity to go abroad, they should also cheerfully remain at home; and should never leave home without the permission of their

IV.

husbands. Again, and in this the conjugal union chiefly consists, let them never forget that, next to God, they are to love their husbands, to esteem them above all others, yielding to them, in all things not inconsistent with Christian piety, a willing and obsequious obedience.

Rites observed in the administration of marriage.

Having explained these matters, the pastor will next proceed to instruct his people in the rites to be observed in the administration of marriage. Here, however, it is not to be supposed that we give in detail the laws that regulate marriage: these have been accurately fixed, and are detailed at large in the decree of the Council of Trent on marriage, a decree with which the pastor cannot be unacquainted. Here, therefore, it will suf-

---

[1] Vid. Aug. lib. 1. de adult. conjug. c. 21 et 22. et de bono conjug. car. 7. et concupia. lib. 1. c. 10.   [2] 1 Pet. iii. 1, 2.

fice to admonish him to study to make himself acquainted, from the doctrine of the Council, with what regards this subject, and to make it a matter of assiduous exposition to the faithful.[1]

But above all, lest young persons, and youth is a period of life marked by extreme weakness and indiscretion, deceived by the specious but misapplied name of marriage, may rush into hasty engagements, the result of criminal passion; the pastor cannot too frequently remind them that, without the presence of the parish-priest, or of some other priest commissioned by him or by the ordinary, and that of two or three witnesses, there can be no marriage.

Youth to be admonished on the subject of marriage.

The impediments of marriage are also to be explained, a subject so minutely and accurately treated by many writers on morality, of grave authority and profound erudition, as to render it an easy task to the pastor to draw upon their labours, particularly as he has occasion to have such works continually in his hands. The instructions, therefore, which they contain, and also the decrees of the Council with regard to the impediments arising from "spiritual affinity," from "the justice of public honesty," and from "fornication," the pastor will peruse with attention and expound with care and accuracy.

The impediments of marriage.

The faithful may hence learn the dispositions with which they should approach the sacrament of marriage: they should consider themselves as about to engage, not in a human work, but in a divine ordinance; and the example of the Fathers of the Old Law, by whom marriage, although not raised to the dignity of a sacrament, was deemed a most holy and religious rite, evinces the singular purity of soul and sentiments of piety, with which Christians should approach so holy a sacrament.

The dispositions with which the sacrament of marriage is to be approached.

But, amongst many other matters there is one which demands the zealous exhortation of the pastor, it is, that children pay it as a tribute of respect due to their parents, or to those under whose guardianship and authority they are placed, not to engage in marriage without their knowledge, still less in defiance of their express wishes. In the Old Law children were uniformly given in marriage by their parents; and that the will of the parent is always to have very great influence on the choice of the child, is clear from these words of the Apostle: "He that giveth his virgin in marriage doth well; and he that giveth her not, doth better."[2]

Clandestine marriage.

Finally, with regard to the use of marriage, this is a subject which the pastor will approach with becoming delicacy, avoiding the use of any expression that may be unfit to meet the ears of the faithful, that may be calculated to offend the piety of some, or excite the laughter of others. "The words of the Lord are chaste words;"[3] and the teachers of a Christian people should make use of no language that is not characterized by gravity, and that does not breathe purity of soul. Two les-

Two lessons of instruction which regard the use of marriage.

[1] Sess. 24. decret. de reformat. matrimon.   [2] 1 Cor. vii. 38.   [3] Ps. xi. 7.

sons of instruction are, then, to be specially pressed upon the
I.   attention of the faithful: the first, that marriage is not to be
sought from motives of sensuality, but that its use is to be re-
strained within those limits, which, as we have already shown,
are fixed by God.   They should be mindful of the exhortation
of the Apostle: "'They," says he, " that have wives, let them
be as though they had them not."[1]   The words of St. Jerome
are also worthy of attention: " the love," says he, " which a
wise man cherishes towards his wife, is the result of judgment,
not the impulse of passion : he governs the impetuosity of desire, and is not hurried into indulgence.   What greater turpitude than that a husband should love his wife, as the seducer
II.   loves the adulteress."[2]   But as every blessing is to be obtained
from God by holy prayer, the faithful are also to be taught
sometimes to abstain from the marriage debt, in order to devote
themselves to prayer.   This religion continence, according to
the proper and pious injunction of our predecessors in the faith,
is particularly to be observed for at least three days previous to
communion, and for a longer time during the solemn and penitential season of Lent.   Thus will the faithful experience the
blessings of the holy state of marriage by a constantly increasing
accumulation of divine grace ; and living in the pursuit and
practice of piety, they will not only spend this mortal life in
peace and tranquillity, but will also repose in the true and firm
hope, " which confoundeth not,"[3] of arriving one day, through
the divine goodness, at the fruition of that life which is eternal.[4]

[1] 1 Cor. vii. 29.   [2] S. Hier. lib. 1. contra. Iovian. in fine.   [3] Rom. v. 5.
[4] Vid. 33. q. 4. per totan et de consecr. dist. 2. cap. omnis homo. Hier. in apol.
pro libris contra Iovian. post medium inter epist. num. 50. et in c. 12. Zach. super.
illud: " In die planctus magnus erit fructus thori immaculati."

THE

CATECHISM

OF

THE COUNCIL OF TRENT.

PART III.

ON THE DECALOGUE.

●

THAT the Decalogue is an epitome of the entire law of God The Deca is the recorded opinion of St. Augustine.[1] The Lord, it is true, logue an had uttered many things for the instruction and guidance of his epitome of the entire people; yet two tables only were given to Moses. They were law of God. made of stone, and were called "the tables of the testimony," and were to be deposited in the ark; and on them, if minutely examined and well understood, will be found to hinge whatever else is commanded by God. Again, these ten commandments are reducible to two, the love of God and of our neighbour, on which "depend the whole Law and the Prophets."[2]

Imbodying then, as the Decalogue does, the whole Law, it To be care- is the imperative duty of the pastor to give his days and nights fully stu- to its consideration; and to this he should be prompted by a died and explained desire not only to regulate his own life by its precepts, but also by the pas- to instruct in the law of God the people committed to his care. tor. "The lips of the priest," says Malachy, "shall keep knowledge, and they shall seek the law at his mouth, because he is the angel of the Lord of Hosts."[3] To the priests of the New Law this injunction applies in a special manner; they are nearer to God, and should be "transformed from glory to glory as by the Spirit of the Lord."[4] Christ our Lord has said that they are "the light of the world:"[5] they should, therefore, be "a light to them that are in darkness, the instructers of the foolish, the teachers of infants;"[6] and "if a man be overtaken in any fault, those who are spiritual should instruct such a one."[7] In the tribunal of penance the priest holds the place of a judge, and pronounces sentence according to the nature of the offence. Unless, therefore, he is desirous that his ignorance

[1] Quæstio 140. super Exod. [2] Matt. xxii. 40. [3] Mal. ii. 7. [4] 2 Cor. iii. 18
[5] Matt. v. 14. [6] Rom. ii. 19, 20. [7] Gal. vi. 1

should prove an injury to himself, and an injustice to others, he must bring with him to the discharge of this duty, the greatest vigilance, and the most intimate and practised acquaintance with the interpretation of the Law, in order to be able to pronounce according to this divine rule on every omission and commission; and that, as the Apostle says, he teach sound doctrine,[1] doctrine free from error, and heal the diseases of the soul, which are the sins of the people, that they may be "acceptable to God, pursuers of good works."[2]

Motives for its observance. In the discharge of this duty of instruction, the pastor will propose to himself and to others such considerations, as may be best calculated to impress upon the mind the conviction, that obedience to the law of God is the duty of every man; and if in the Law there are many motives to stimulate to its observance, there is one which of all others is powerfully impressive—it is, that God is its author. True, it is said to have been delivered by angels,[3] but its author, we repeat, is God. Thus, not only the words of the Legislator himself, which we shall subsequently explain, but also, innumerable other passages of Scripture, which the memory of the pastor will readily supply, bear ample testimony. Who is not conscious that a law is inscribed on his heart by the finger of God, teaching him to distinguish good from evil, vice from virtue, justice from injustice? The force and import of this unwritten law do not conflict with that which is written. How unreasonable then to deny that God is the author of the written, as he is of the unwritten law.

The written law, why given. But, lest the people, aware of the abrogation of the Mosaic Law, may imagine that the precepts of the Decalogue are no longer obligatory, the pastor will inform them, that these precepts were not delivered as new laws, but rather as a renewal nd development of the law of nature: its divine light, which was obscured and almost extinguished by the crimes and the perversity of man, shines forth in this celestial code with increased **Note.** and renovated splendour. The Ten Commandments, however, we are not bound to obey because delivered by Moses, but because they are so many precepts of the natural law, and have been explained and confirmed by our Lord Jesus Christ.

Considerations calculated to enforce its observance. I. But it must prove a most powerful and persuasive argument for enforcing its observance, to reflect that the founder of the Law is no less a person than God himself—that God whose wisdom and justice we mortals cannot question—whose power and might we cannot elude. Hence, we find that when by his prophet, he commands the Law to be observed, he proclaims that he is "the Lord God." The Decalogue, also, opens with the same solemn admonition: "I am the Lord thy God;"[4] and in Malachy we read the indignant interrogatory: "If I am a master, where is my fear!"[5] That God has vouchsafed to give us a transcript of his holy will, on which depends our eternal

D

[1] 2 Tim. iv. 3.   [2] Tit. ii. 14.   [3] Gal. iii. 19.   [4] Exod. xx. 2.   [5] Malach. i. 6.

salvation, is a consideration which, besides animating the faithful to the observance of his commandments, must call forth the expression of their grateful homage in return for his beneficent condescension. Hence the Sacred Scriptures, in more passages than one, setting forth this invaluable blessing, admonish us to know our own dignity, and to appreciate the divine bounty : "This," says Moses, "is your wisdom and understanding in the sight of nations, that hearing all these precepts they may say: 'behold a wise and understanding people, a great nation;'"[1] "He hath not done in like manner to every nation;" says the royal psalmist, "and his judgments he hath not made manifest to them."[2]

The circumstances which accompanied the promulgation of the Law, as recorded in the Sacred Volumes, also demand the attention of the pastor; they are well calculated to convey to the minds of the faithful an idea of the piety and humility with which they should receive and reverence a Law delivered by God himself.—Three days previous to its promulgation, was announced to the people the divine command, to wash their garments, to abstain from conjugal intercourse, in order that they may be more holy and better prepared to receive the Law, and on the third day to be in readiness to hear its awful announcement. When they had reached the mountain from which the Lord was to deliver the Law by Moses, Moses alone was commanded to ascend; and the Lord descending from on high with great majesty, filling the mount with thunder and lightning, with fire and dense clouds; spoke to Moses, and delivered to him the Law.[3] In this the divine wisdom had solely for object to admonish us to receive his Law with pure and humble minds, and to impress the salutary truth, that over the neglect of his commands impend the heaviest chastisements of the divine justice. *The circumstances which attended its promulgation. Note.*

The pastor will also teach that the commandments of God are not difficult of observance, as these words of St. Augustine are alone sufficient to show: "How, I ask, is it said to be impossible for man to love—to love, I say, a beneficent Creator, a most loving Father, and also, in the persons of his brethren, to love his own flesh? Yet,[4] 'he who loveth has fulfilled the Law.'"[5] Hence, the Apostle St. John expressly says, that "the commandments of God are not heavy?"[6] for, as St. Bernard observes, "no duty more just could be exacted from man, none that could confer on him a more exalted dignity, none that could contribute more largely to his own interests."[7] Hence in this pious effusion addressed to the Deity himself, St. Augustine expresses his admiration of his infinite bounty: "What," says he, "is man thou wouldst be loved by him? And if he loves thee not, thou threatenest him with heavy punishment—Is it not punishment enough that I love thee not?" *Its observance, easy.*

[1] Deut. iv. 6.   [2] Ps. cxlvii. 20.   [3] Exod. xix. 10. et seq.
[4] Aug. serm. 47. de temp.   [5] Rom. xiii. 8.   [6] 1 John v. 3.
[7] Lib. de diligendo Deo, lib. 1. Confess. c. 5.

Human infirmity no plea for its non-observance. But should any one plead human infirmity to exculpate himself from not loving God, it is not to be forgotten that he who demands our love " pours into our hearts by the Holy Ghost" the fervour of his love,[1] " and this good Spirit our Heavenly Father gives to those that ask him."[2] " Give what thou commandest," says St. Augustine, " and command what thou pleasest."[3] As then, God is ever ready by his divine assistance to sustain our weakness, especially since the death of Christ the Lord, by which the prince of this world was cast out ; there is no reason why we should be disheartened by the difficulty of the undertaking ; to him who loves, nothing is difficult.[4]

All bound to obey its injunctions. To show that we are all laid under the necessity of obeying the Law is a consideration, which must possess additional weight in the enforcement of its observance ; and it becomes the more necessary to dwell on this particular in these our days, when there are not wanting those who, to the serious injury of their own souls, have the impious hardihood to assert that the observance of the Law, whether easy or difficult, is by no means necessary to salvation. This wicked and impious error the pastor will refute from Scripture, by the authority of which they endeavour to defend their impious doctrine. What then are the words of the Apostle? " Circumcision is nothing, and uncircumcision is nothing, but the keeping of the commandments of God."[5] Again, inculcating the same doctrine, he says : " A new creature, in Christ, alone avails ;"[6] by a " new creature," evidently meaning him who observes the commandments of God ; for, as our Lord himself testifies in St. John, he who observes the commandments of God loves God : " If any one love me," says the Redeemer, " he will keep my word."[7]

Note. A man, it is true, may be justified, and from wicked may become righteous, before he has fulfilled by external acts each of the divine commandments ; but no one who has arrived at the use of reason, unless sincerely disposed to observe them all, can be justified.

Fruits of its observance. Finally, to leave nothing unsaid that may be calculated to induce to an observance of the Law, the pastor will point out how abundant and sweet are its fruits. This he will easily accomplish by referring to the eighteenth psalm, which celebrates the praises of the divine Law, amongst which its highest eulogy is, that it proclaims more eloquently the glory and the majesty of God than even the celestial orbs, which by their beauty and order, excite the admiration of the most barbarous nations, and compel them to acknowledge and proclaim the glory, the wisdom, and the power of the Creator and Architect of the universe. " The Law of the Lord" also " converts souls :" knowing the ways of God and his holy will through the medium of his Law, we learn to walk in the way of the Lord. It

---

[1] Rom. v. 5.   [2] Luke ii. 13.
[3] Lib. 10. confess. c. 29. 31 et 37. Item de bono persever. c. 20.
[4] Aug. in Ps. lii. Bern. Serm. de Dom. in ramis palm. item in serm. de Magdal.
[5] 1 Cor. vii. 19.   [6] Gal. vi. 15.   [7] John xiv. 21. 23.

also, " gives wisdom to little ones :"[1] they alone who fear God are truly wise. Hence, the observers of the Law of God are filled with a profusion of pure delights, are enlightened by the knowledge of the divine mysteries, and are blessed with an accumulation of pleasures and rewards as well in this life, as in the life to come.

In our observance of the Law, however, we should not be actuated so much by a sense of our own advantage as by a regard for the holy will of God, unfolded to man by the promulgation of his Law : if the irrational part of creation is obedient to this his sovereign will, how much more reasonable that man should live in subjection to its dictate ? *To be observed for sake of God.*

A further consideration which cannot fail to arrest our attention, is, that God has pre-eminently displayed his clemency and the riches of his bounty in this, that whilst he might have commanded our service without a reward, he has, notwithstanding, deigned to identify his own glory with our advantage, thus rendering what tends to his honour, conducive to our interests. This is a consideration of the highest importance, and one which proclaims aloud the goodness of God. The pastor then will not fail to impress on the minds of the faithful this salutary truth, telling them in the language of the prophet whom we have last quoted, that " in keeping the commandments of God there is a great reward."[2] Not only are we promised those blessings which seem to have reference to earthly happiness, to be " blessed in the city, and blessed in the field ;"[3] but we are also promised " a very great reward in heaven,"[4] " good measure, pressed down, shaken together, and running over,"[5] which, aided by the divine mercy, we merit by our actions when recommended by piety and justice. *A great reward awaits its observance.*

THE FIRST COMMANDMENT.

"I AM THE LORD THY GOD, WHO BROUGHT THEE OUT OF THE LAND OF EGYPT, OUT OF THE HOUSE OF BONDAGE : THOU SHALT NOT HAVE STRANGE GODS BEFORE ME : THOU SHALT NOT MAKE TO THYSELF A GRAVEN THING, &c."[6]

THE law announced in the Decalogue, although delivered to the Jews by the Lord from the summit of Sinai, was originally written by the finger of nature on the heart of man,[7] and was therefore rendered obligatory on mankind at all times by the Author of nature. It will, however, be found very salutary to explain with minute attention the words in which it was pro- *The words of the law and the history of the people of Israel to be explained.*

---

1 Ps. xviii. 8.　2 Ps. xviii. 12.　3 Deut. xxviii. 3.　4 Matt. v. 12.
5 Luke vi. 38.　6 Exod. xx. 2.　7 Rom. i. 19, 20.

claimed to the people of Israel by Moses, its minister and interpreter, and to present to the faithful an epitome of the mysterious economy of Providence towards that people.

An epitome of their history. The pastor will first show, that from amongst the nations of the earth, God chose one which descended from Abraham; that it was the divine will that Abraham should be a stranger in the land of Canaan, the possession of which he had promised him; and that, although for more than forty years he and his posterity were wanderers, before they obtained possession of the land, God withdrew not from them his protecting care. "They passed from nation to nation and from *one* kingdom to another people; he suffered no man to hurt them, and he reproved kings for their sakes."[1] Before they went down into Egypt, he sent before them one by whose prudence they and the people of Egypt were rescued from famine. In Egypt such was his paternal kindness towards them, that although opposed by the power of Pharaoh who sought their destruction, they increased to an extraordinary degree; and when severely harassed and cruelly treated as slaves, he raised up Moses as a leader to conduct them from bondage with a strong hand—This their deliverance is particularly referred to in these opening words of the Law; "I am the Lord thy God who brought thee out of the land of Egypt, out of the house of bondage."

The people of Israel, why chosen by God. Having premised this brief sketch of the history of the people of Israel, the pastor will not omit to observe, that from amongst the nations of the earth one was chosen by Almighty God whom he called "his people," and by whom he would be known and worshipped;[2] not that they were superior to other nations in justice or in numbers, and of this God himself reminds them, but because, by the multiplication and aggrandizement of an inconsiderable and impoverished nation, he would display to mankind the extent of his power and the riches of his goodness. Such having been the circumstances of the Jewish nation, "He was closely joined to them, and loved them,"[3] and Lord of heaven and earth as he was, he disdained not to be called "their God." The other nations were thus to be excited to a holy emulation, that seeing the superior happiness of the Israelites, mankind might embrace the worship of the true God; as St. Paul says that by placing before them the happiness of the Gentiles and the knowledge of the true God, "he provoked to emulation those who were his own flesh."[4]

The Israelites why consigned to such trials. The pastor will next inform the faithful that God suffered the Hebrew Fathers to wander for so long a time, and their posterity to be oppressed and harassed by a galling servitude, in order to teach us, that to be friends of God we must be enemies of the world, and pilgrims in this vale of tears; that an entire detachment from the world gives us an easier access to the friendship of God; and that admitted to his friendship we

[1] Ps. civ. 11.   [2] Deut. vii. 6, 7.   [3] Deut. x. 15.   [4] Rom. xi. 14.

may experience the superior happiness enjoyed by those who serve God rather than the world. This is the solemn admonition of God himself: "yet they shall serve him, that they may know the difference between my service and the service of a kingdom of the earth."[1]

The pastor will also remind the faithful that God delayed the fulfilment of his promise until after the lapse of more than four hundred years, in order that the Israelites might be sustained by faith and hope; for, as we shall show more particularly when we come to explain the First Commandment, God will have his children centre all their hopes and repose all their confidence in his goodness. *The fulfilment of the divine promises why so long deferred.*

Finally, the time and place, when and where the people of Israel received this law, deserve particular attention. They received it when, having been delivered from the bondage of Egypt, they had come into the wilderness; in order, that impressed with a lively sense of gratitude for a blessing still fresh in their recollection, and awed by the dreariness of the wild waste in which they journeyed, they might be the better disposed to receive the law. To those whose bounty we have experienced we are bound by ties of reciprocity; and when man has lost all hope of assistance from his fellow man, he then seeks refuge in the protection of God. We are hence given to understand, that the more detached the faithful are from the allurements of the world, and the pleasures of sense, the more disposed are they to lend a willing ear to the doctrines of salvation: "whom shall he teach knowledge," says Isaias, "and whom shall he make to understand the hearing? Them that are weaned from the milk, that are drawn away from the breasts."[2] *The time and place in which the law was delivered why chosen.* *Note.*

The pastor, then, will use his best endeavours to induce the faithful to keep continually in view these words, "I am the Lord thy God." From them they will learn that he who is their Creator and conservator, by whom they were made, and are preserved, is also their legislator, and that they may truly say with the Psalmist: "He is the Lord our God, and we are the people of his pasture and the sheep of his hand."[3] The frequent and earnest inculcation of these words will also serve to induce the faithful to a more willing observance of the law, and a more cautious abstinence from sin. *Opening words of the Decalogue.*

The words, "who brought thee out of the land of Egypt and the house of bondage," come next in order; and, whilst they seem to relate solely to the Jews liberated from the bondage of Egypt, are, if considered in their implicit reference to universal salvation, still more applicable to Christians, who are liberated, not from the bondage of Egypt, but from the slavery of sin, and "the power of darkness, and are translated into the kingdom of his beloved Son."[4] Contemplating in the vision of prophecy the magnitude of this favour, the prophet Jere- *A strong incentive to the love of God.*

---

[1] 2 Par. xii. 8.   [2] Isa. xxviii. 9.   [3] Ps. xciv. 7.   [4] Col. i. 13.

miah exclaims: " behold the days come, saith the Lord, when
it shall be said no more: the Lord liveth that brought forth the
children of Israel out of the land of Egypt; but the Lord liveth
that brought the children of Israel out of the land of the North
and out of all the lands to which I cast them out; and I will
bring them again into their land which I gave to their Fathers.
Behold, I will send many fishes, saith the Lord, and they shall
fish them, &c."[1]   Our most indulgent Father has "gathered
together" through his beloved Son, his "children that were
dispersed,"[2] that, " being made free from sin and made the servants of justice,"[3] " we may serve before him in holiness and
justice all our days."[4]   Against every temptation, therefore,
the faithful should arm themselves with these words of the
Apostle as with a shield: " shall we who are dead to sin live
any longer therein?"[5]   We are no longer our own: we are
his who died and rose again for us: he is the Lord our God
who has purchased us for himself at the price of his blood.
Shall we then be any longer capable of sinning against the
Lord our God, and crucifying him again?   Being made truly
free, and with that liberty wherewith Christ has made us free,
let us, as we heretofore yielded our members to serve injustice,
henceforward yield them to serve justice to sanctification.

Division of
the Deca-
logue.

" THOU SHALT NOT HAVE STRANGE GODS BEFORE ME."[6]] The
Decalogue naturally divides itself into two parts, the first embracing what regards God, the second what regards our neighbour; the duties which we discharge towards our neighbour
are referred to God; then only do we fulfil the divine precept
which commands us to love our neighbour, when we love him
in God.   This division of the Decalogue the pastor will make
known to the faithful; and he will add that the commandments
which regard God, are those which were inscribed on the first
table of the law.

This pre-
cept com-
mands and
prohibits:
what it
commands.

He will next show that the words which form the subject
matter of the present exposition contain a two-fold precept;
the one mandatory, the other prohibitory   When it is said;
" Thou shalt not have strange gods before me," it is equivalent to saying; "thou shalt worship me the true God: thou
shalt not worship strange gods."   The former contains a precept of faith, hope, and charity—of faith, for, acknowledging
God to be immoveable, immutable, always the same, faithful,
we acknowledge an eternal truth in the recognition of these his
attributes: assenting therefore to his oracles, we necessarily
yield to him all faith and authority—of hope, for who can contemplate his omnipotence, his clemency, his beneficence, and
not repose in him all his hopes?—of charity, for who can
behold the riches of his goodness and love, which he lavishes
on us with so bounteous a hand, and not love him? with this

---

[1] Jerem. xvi. 14, et seq.   [2] John xi. 52.   [3] Rom. vi. 18.
[4] Luke i. 74, 75.   [5] Rom. vi. 2.   [6] Exod. xx. 3.

exalted claim upon our obedience therefore commence, with this conclude all his commandments: " I am the Lord."

The negative part of the precept is comprised in these words: What it prohibits. " thou shalt not have strange gods before me." This our divine legislator subjoins, not because it is not implied in the positive part of the precept, which says equivalently: " thou shalt worship me the only God," for if he is God, he is the only God; but on account of the blindness of many, who of old professed to worship the true God, and yet adored a multitude of gods. Of these there were many even amongst the Israelites, whom Elias reproached with having " halted between two sides,"[1] and also amongst the Samaritans, who worshipped the God of Israel and the gods of the nations.[2]

Having thus explained the precept in its two-fold import, the This first commandment of superior importance to the rest. pastor will observe that this is the first and principal commandment, not only in order, but also in its nature, dignity, and excellence. God is entitled to infinitely greater love and to higher authority with regard to his creatures than the masters or monarchs of the earth. He created us, He governs us, He nurtured us even in the womb, brought us into existence, and still supplies us by his provident care with all the necessaries of life. Against this commandment therefore transgress all who How violated. have not faith, hope, and charity; a numerous class, amongst whom are those who fall into heresy, who reject what the church of God teaches; those who give credit to dreams, divination, fortunetelling, and such superstitious illusions; those who despairing of salvation trust not in the goodness of God; and also those who place their happiness solely in the wealth of this world, in health and strength, in personal attractions, or mental endowments. But these are matters which the pastor will find developed more at large in treatises on morality.[3]

ON THE HONOUR AND INVOCATION OF THE SAINTS.

In the exposition of this precept, the faithful are also to be ac- The honour and invocation of the saints not prohibited by this commandment curately taught that the veneration and invocation of angels and saints, who enjoy the glory of heaven, and the honour which the Catholic Church has always paid even to the bodies and ashes of the saints, are not forbidden by this commandment.[4] Were a king to prohibit by proclamation any individual to as-

---

[1] 3 Kings xviii. 21.   [2] 4 Kings xvii. 33.
[3] De variis istis peccatis vide dist. 24. q. 2. multis in capitibus. Aug. in lib. de divinat. dæmon. cap. 5. et citatur 26. q. 4. a. secundum. Origen. hom. 5. in Joshue et habet 26. q. 2. c. sed et illud Aug. lib. 2. de doct. Christian. cap. 19. and 20. et citatur eodem cap. illud quod est. Conc. Carth. 4. cap. 19. vid. plura 26. q. 2, 3 et 5.
[4] Vid. Trid. sess. 17. de Sacrif. Missæ. c. 3. et sess. 25. sub princip. cap. de invocat. Sanctorum. Item vid. Synod. 7. act. 6. in fine. item Aug. lib. 8. de civit. Dei. c. 27. et lib. 10. c. 1. et lib. 21. contra Faust. c. 21. Basil. Hom. 20. in 40. Mar. et 26. de Mar. Mamman : item Nazian. orat. in laud. S. Cyprian.

sume the regal character, or accept the honours due to the royal person, how unreasonable to infer from such an edict a prohibition that suitable honour and respect should be paid to his magistrates? Of this nature is the relative honour paid by the Catholic Church to angels and saints. When, walking in the footsteps of those exalted characters, whose names are recorded in the Old Testament, she is said "to adore the angels of God," she venerates them as the special friends and servants of God, but gives not to them that supreme honour which is due to God alone.

Angels refused to be worshipped by men, on what occasions. To be honoured,

True, we sometimes read that angels refused to be worshipped by men;[1] but the worship which they refused to accept was the supreme honour due to God alone: the Holy Spirit who says: "Honour and glory to God alone,"[2] commands us also to honour our parents and elders;[3] and the holy men who adored one God only, are also said in Scripture to have "adored," that is supplicated and venerated, kings. If then kings, by whose agency God governs the world, are so highly honoured,[4] shall it be deemed unlawful to honour those angelic spirits, whom God has been pleased to constitute his ministers, whose services he makes use of not only in the government of his Church, but also of the Universe, by whose invisible aid we are every day delivered from the greatest dangers of soul and body? Are they not, rather, to be honoured with a veneration greater, in proportion as the dignity of these blessed spirits exceeds that of kings? Another claim on our veneration is their love of us, which, as the Scripture informs us,[5] prompts them to pour out their prayers for those countries over which they are placed by Providence, and for us whose guardians they are, and whose prayers and tears they present before the throne of God.[6] Hence our Lord admonishes us in the Gospel not to offend the little ones, "because their angels in heaven always see the face of their Father who is in heaven."[7]

and invoked.

Their intercession, therefore, we invoke, because they always see the face of God, and are constituted by him the willing advocates of our salvation. To this their invocation the Scriptures bear testimony—Jacob invoked, nay compelled, the angel with whom he wrestled, to bless him,[8] declaring that he would not let him go until he had blessed him; and not only did he invoke the blessing of the angel whom he saw, but also of him whom he saw not: "The angel," says he, "who delivered me out of all evil, bless these children."[9]

To honour the saints does not detract from, but

From these attestations we are justified in concluding, that to honour the saints "who sleep in the Lord," to invoke their intercession, and to venerate their sacred relics and ashes, far from diminishing, tends considerably to increase the glory of

---

[1] Apoc. xix. 10. Apoc. xxii. 9.   [2] 1 Tim. i. 17. Exod. xx. 3. Levit. xix. 11.
[3] Deut. v. 16.   [4] Gen. xxiii. 7. 2 Kings xxiv. 20. 1 Par. 29. 20.
[5] Dan. x. 13.   [6] Tob. xii. 12. Apoc. viii. 3.
[7] Matt. xviii. 10.   [8] Gen. xxxii. 26. Osee vii. 4.
[9] Gen. xlviii. 16

God, in proportion as the Christian's hope is thus animated and adds to the honour due to God. fortified, and he himself excited to the imitation of their virtues. This is a doctrine which is also supported by the authority of the second Council of Nice,[1] the Council of Gangre,[2] and of The Councils. Trent,[3] and by the testimony of the Holy Fathers.[4] In order The fathers. however that the pastor may be the better prepared to meet the objections of those who impugn this doctrine, he will consult particularly St. Jerome against Vigilantius, and the fourth book, sixteenth chapter of Damascene on the orthodox faith;[5] and Apostolic tradition. what, if possible, is still more conclusive, he will appeal to the uniform practice of Christians, as handed down by the Apostles and faithfully preserved in the Church of God.[6] But what ar- Scripture. gument more convincing, than that which is supplied by the admirable praises given in Scripture to the saints of God! If the inspired Volume celebrates the praises of particular saints, why question for a moment the propriety of paying them the same tribute of praise and veneration?[7] Another claim which The saints assist us by their prayers. the saints have to be honoured and invoked is, that they earnestly importune God for our salvation, and obtain for us by their intercession many favours and blessings. If there is joy in heaven for the conversion of one sinner,[8] can the citizens of heaven be indifferent to his conversion, or neglect to assist him by their prayers? When their interposition is solicited by the penitent, will they not rather implore the pardon of his sins, and the grace of his conversion? Should it be said that their patron- Objection. age is unnecessary, because God hears our prayers without the intervention of a mediator, the objection is at once met by the observation of St. Augustine: " There are many things," says Answer. he, " which God does not grant without a mediator and interces- sor:"[9] an observation the justness of which is confirmed by two illustrious examples—Abimelech and the friends of Job were par- doned but through the prayers of Abraham and of Job.[10] Should it be alleged, that to recur to the patronage and intercession of the saints argues want or weakness of faith, the answer of the Cen- turion refutes the allegation: his faith was highly eulogized by our Lord himself; and yet he sent to the Redeemer " the An- cients of the Jews," to intercede with him to heal his servant.[11]

True, there is but one Mediator, Christ the Lord, who alone Objection. has reconciled us through his blood,[12] and who, having accom- plished our redemption, and having once entered into the Holy of Holies, ceases not to intercede for us ;[13] but it by no means Answer.

---

[1] Nicæn. Conc. 2. act. 6.
[2] Gangr. Can. xx. et citatur dist. 30. cap. si quis per superbiam.
[3] Trid. sess. 25. item Conc. Chalced. sub finem et in 6. Synod. General. c. 7. et Conc. Geron. c. 3. Aurel. 1. c. 29.
[4] Damasc. de orth. fid. lib. 4. c. 6.   [5] Lib. 4. de orth. fid. c. 16.
[6] Dionys. c. 7. Hier. Eccles. Ireo. lib. 5. contra hæres. c. 19. Athan. serm. in Evangel. de sancta Deip. Euseb. lib. 13. præpar. Evang. c. 7. Cornel. pap. epist. 1. Hilar. in Ps. 126. Ambr. in lib. de viduis.
[7] Eccl. xliv. xlv. xlvi. xlvii. xlviii. xlix. lib. Hebr. xi.   [8] Luke xv. 7. 10.
[9] Aug. quæst. 149 super Exod. serm. 2. et 4. de St. Steph.
[10] Gen. xx.   [11] Matt. viii. 5. Luke vii. 3.   [12] 1 Tim. ii. 5.
[13] Heb. ix. 12 et 7. 25.

follows, that it is therefore unlawful to have recourse to the intercession of the saints. If, because we have one mediator Christ Jesus, it were unlawful to ask the intercession of the saints, the Apostle would not have recommended himself with so much earnestness to the prayers of his brethren on earth.[1] In his capacity as Mediator, the prayers of the living should derogate from the glory and dignity of Christ not less than the interces sion of the saints in heaven.

The invocation of saints proved by the miracles wrought at their tombs,

But what incredulity so obstinate but must yield to the evidence in support of the honour and invocation of the saints, which the wonders wrought at their tombs flash upon the mind? The blind see, the lame walk, the paralyzed are invigorated, the dead raised to life, and evil demons are expelled from the bodies of men! These are authentic facts, attested not, as frequently happens, by very grave persons who have heard them from others; they are facts which rest on the ocular attestation of witnesses, whose veracity is beyond all question, of an Ambrose,[2]

and confirmed by the efficacy of relics.

and an Augustine.[3] But why multiply proofs on this head? If the clothes, the kerchiefs,[4] and even the very shadows of the saints, whilst yet on earth, banished disease and restored health and vigour, who will have the hardihood to deny that God can still work the same wonders by the holy ashes, tho bones and other relics of his saints who are in glory? Of this we have a proof in the resuscitation of the dead body which was let down into the grave of Eliseus, and which, on touching the body of the prophet, was instantly restored to life.[5]

"Thou shalt not make to thyself a graven thing, nor the likeness of any thing that is in heaven above, or in the earth beneath, nor of those things that are in the waters under the earth: thou shalt not adore them nor serve them."[6]

These words do not contain a distinct precept.

Some, supposing these words to constitute a distinct precept, reduce the ninth and tenth commandments into one. St. Augustine holds a different opinion: considering the two last to be distinct, he refers these words to the first commandment;[7] and this division, because well known and much approved in the Catholic church, we willingly adopt. As a very strong argument in its favour, we may, however, add the propriety of annexing to the first commandment its sanction, the rewards or punishments attached to its observance or violation; a propriety which can be preserved in the arrangement alone which we have chosen.

Do not prohibit the use of images.

· This commandment does not prohibit the arts of painting or sculpture; the Scriptures inform us that God himself commanded images of Cherubim,[8] and also the brazen serpent[9] to be made;

[1] Rom. xv. 30. Heb. xiii. 18.   [2] Ambr. epist. 85. et serm. 95.
[3] Aug. de civit. Dei, lib. 22. c. 8. et epist. 137.
[4] Acts v. xix. 12 et 5. 15.   [5] 4 Kings xiii. 21.   [6] Exod. xx. 4.
[7] Vid. Aug. super Exod. quaest. 71. and in Ps. 32. serm. 2. Sententia D. Aug. de praeceptorum distinctione magis placet Ecclesiae Vid. D. Thom. i. 2. quaest. 100. art. 4.
[8] Exod. xxv. 18. 3 Kings vi. 27.   [9] Num. xxi. 8, 9.

and the conclusion, therefore, at which we must arrive, is that images are prohibited only in as much as they may be the means of transferring the worship of God to inanimate objects, as though the adoration offered them were given to so many Gods.

By the violation of this commandment the majesty of God is Prohibit two things. grievously offended in a two-fold manner: the one, by worshipping idols and images as gods, or believing that they possess any divinity or virtue entitling them to our worship, by praying to, or reposing confidence in them, as the Gentiles did, who placed their hopes in idols, and whose idolatry the Scriptures universally reprobate: the other, by attempting to form a representation of the Deity, as if he were visible to mortal eyes, or could be represented by the pencil of the painter or the chisel of the statuary. "Who," says Damascene, "can represent God, invisible, as he is, incorporeal, uncircumscribed by limits, and incapable of being described under any figure or form?"[1] This subject, however, the pastor will find treated more at large in the second Council of Nice.[2] Speaking of the Gentiles, the Apostle has these admirable words: "They changed the glory of the incorruptible God into a likeness of the image of a corruptible man, and of birds, and of four-footed beasts, and of creeping things."[3] Hence the Israelites, when they exclaimed before the molten calf: "These are thy Gods, O Israel, that have brought thee out of the land of Egypt,"[4] are denounced as idolaters; because they "changed their glory into the likeness of a calf that eateth grass."[5]

When, therefore, the Almighty forbids the worship of strange Their meaning. gods, with a view to the utter extinction of all idolatry, he also prohibits the formation of an image of the Deity from brass or other materials, as Isaias declares when he asks: "To whom then have you likened God, or what image will you make for him?"[6] That this is the meaning of the prohibitory part of the precept is proved, not only from the writings of the Holy Fathers, who, as may be seen in the seventh General Council, give to it this interpretation; but also from these words of Deuteronomy, by which Moses sought to withdraw the Israelites from the worship of idols: "You saw not," says he, "any similitude in the day that the Lord God spoke to you in Horeb, from the midst of the fire."[7] These words this wisest of legislators addressed to the people of Israel, lest through error of any sort, they should make an image of the Deity, and transfer to any thing created, the honour due to God alone.

To represent the Persons of the Holy Trinity by certain To represent any of the Persons of the Trinity under certain forms, not prohibited. forms, under which, as we read in the Old and New Testaments, they deigned to appear, is not to be deemed contrary to religion, or the Law of God. Who so ignorant as to believe that such forms are express images of the Deity?—forms, as

---

[1] Damas. lib. 4. de ortrod. fid. c. 17.
[2] Conc. Nicæn. 2 act. 3
[3] Rom. i. 23.   [4] Exod. xxxii. 4.
[5] Ps. cv. 20.
[6] Isa. xl. 18. Acts vii. 40.
[7] Deut. iv. 15, 16.

the pastor will teach, which only express some attribute or action ascribed to God. Thus, Daniel describes "The Ancient of Days, seated on a throne, and before him the books opened;" to signify his eternity and wisdom, by which he sees and judges all the thoughts and actions of men.[1] Angels, also, are represented under human form and winged, to give us to understand that they are actuated by benevolent feelings towards us, and are always prepared to execute the ministry of God to man: "they are all ministering spirits, sent to minister for them who shall receive the inheritance of salvation."[2] That attributes of the Holy Ghost are represented under the forms of a dove, and of tongues of fire, as we read in the Gospel[3] and in the Acts of the Apostles,[4] is a matter too well known to require lengthened exposition.

But to make and honour the images of our Lord, of his holy and virginal Mother, and of the Saints, all of whom appeared in human form, is not only not forbidden by this commandment, but has always been deemed a holy practice, and the surest indication of a mind deeply impressed with gratitude towards them. This position derives confirmation from the monuments of the Apostolic age, the General Councils of the Church, and the writings of so many amongst the Fathers, eminent alike for sanctity and learning, all of whom are of one accord upon the subject. But the pastor will not content himself with showing the lawfulness of the use of images in churches, and of paying them religious respect, when this respect is referred to their prototypes—he will do more—he will show that the uninterrupted observance of this practice up to the present time has been attended with great advantage to the faithful; as may be seen in the work of Damascene, on images,[5] and in the seventh General Council, which is the second of Nice.[6]

But as the enemy of mankind, by his wiles and deceits, seeks to pervert even the most holy institutions, should the faithful happen at all to offend in this particular, the pastor, in accordance with the decree of the Council of Trent,[7] will use every exertion in his power to correct such an abuse, and, if necessary, explain the decree itself to the people. He will also inform the unlettered, and those who may be ignorant of the proper use of images, that they are intended to instruct in the history of the Old and New Testaments, and to revive the recollection of the events which they record; that thus excited to the contemplation of heavenly things we may be the more ardently inflamed to adore and love God. He will, also, inform the faithful that the images of the Saints are placed in churches, not only to be honoured, but that, also, admonished by their example we may imitate their lives and emulate their virtues.[8]

Marginal notes:
The same doctrine true with regard to angels;

Forms which represent the Holy Ghost;

the Saints, and also the Redeemer.

The lawful use of images.

[1] Dan. vii. 13.   [2] Heb. i. 14.   [3] Mat. iii. 16. Mark i. 10. Luke iii. 22.
John i. 32.   [4] Acts ii. 3.   [5] Lib. 4. de fid. orthod. cap. 17.
[6] Nic. Syn. passim.   [7] Trid. Con. Sess. 25.
[8] De cultu et usu imaginum vid. Concil. Nicaen. 1. act 7. Histor. tripart. lib. 6.

"I AM THE LORD THY GOD, MIGHTY, JEALOUS, VISITING THE INIQUITY OF THE FATHERS UPON THE CHILDREN TO THE THIRD AND FOURTH GENERATION OF THEM THAT HATE ME, AND SHOWING MERCY UNTO THOUSANDS OF THEM THAT LOVE ME, AND KEEP MY COMMANDMENTS."] In this concluding clause of the first commandment, two things occur which demand exposition. The first is, that whilst, on account of the enormous guilt incurred by the violation of the first commandment, and the propensity of man towards its violation, the punishment is here properly proposed: it is also appended to all the other commandments. Every law enforces its observance by some sanction, by rewards and punishments; and hence the frequent and numerous promises of God, which are recorded in Scripture. To omit those that we meet almost in every page of the Old Testament, we read in the Gospel: "If thou wilt enter into life, keep the commandments;"[1] and again: "He that doth the will of my Father who is in heaven, he shall enter heaven;"[2] and also; "Every tree that doth not yield good fruit shall be cut down and cast into the fire;"[3] "Whosoever is angry with his brother shall be guilty of the judgment;"[4] "If you will not forgive men, neither will your Father forgive you your offences."[5] The other observation is, that this divine sanction is to be proposed in a very different manner to the spiritual and to the carnal Christian: to the spiritual who is animated by the Spirit of God,[6] and who yields to him a willing and cheerful obedience, it is, in some sort, glad tidings, and a strong proof of the divine goodness: in it he recognises the parental care of a most loving God, who, now by rewards, again by punishments, almost compels his creatures to adore and worship him. The spiritual man acknowledges the infinite goodness of God in vouchsafing to issue his commands to him, and to make use of his service to the glory of the divine name; and not only does he acknowledge the divine goodness, he also cherishes a strong hope that, when God commands what he pleases, he will also give strength to fulfil what he commands. But to the carnal man, who is not yet disenthralled from the spirit of servitude, and who abstains from sin more through fear of punishment than love of virtue, this sanction of the divine Law, which closes each of the commandments, is burdensome and severe. He is, therefore, to be supported by pious exhortation, and to be led, as it were, by the hand, in the path pointed out by the Law of God. These two classes of persons the pastor, there-

In these concluding words, two things demand explanation.

I.

II.

c. 41. Eus. lib. 8. Hist. Eccl. c. 14. Cyril. lib. 6. contr. Jul. Aug. lib. 1. de consensu Evang. c. 10. vid. item. sextam Synod. can. 82. et Conc. Rom. sub. Greg. III. et Conc. Gentiliac. Item et aliud Rom. sub Stephano III. Vid. etiam lib. de Rom. Pontif. in vita Sylvestri. Item Lactant. carm. de pass. Dom. Basil orat. in S. Barlaham, Greg. Nyss. orat. in Theod. Prud. Hym. de S. Cas. et hym. de S. Hippolyt. Item apud Baron. Annal. Eccles. an 57. num. 116. et deinceps. vid. interum Aug. contra Faust. lib. 22. c. 73.

[1] Matt. xix. 17. [2] Matt. vii. 21. [3] Matt. iii. 10. and vii. 19.
[4] Matt. v. 22. [5] Matt. vi. 15. [6] Rom. viii. 14.

fore, will keep in view, as often as he has occasion to explain any of the commandments.

They also contain two arguments for the observance of the Law.
I.
The carnal and spiritual are, however, to be excited by two considerations, which are contained in this concluding clause, and are well calculated to enforce obedience to the divine Law. The one is, that when God is called "The Strong," the force of that appellation requires to be fully expounded to the faithful; because, unappalled by the terrors of the divine menaces, the flesh frequently indulges in the delusive expectation of escaping, in a variety of ways, the wrath of God and his menaced judgments. But when deeply impressed with the awful conviction that God is "The Strong," the sinner will exclaim with David: "Whither shall I go from thy spirit? or whither shall I flee from thy face?"[1] The flesh, also, distrusting the promises of God, sometimes magnifies the power of the enemy to such an extent, as to believe itself unable to withstand his assaults; whilst on the contrary, a firm and unshaken faith, which relies confidently on the strength and power of God, animates and confirms the hopes of man: it exclaims with the Psalmist: "The Lord is my light and my salvation; whom shall I fear?"[2]

II.
The second consideration is the jealousy of God. Man is sometimes tempted to think that God, indifferent whether we contemn or observe his Law, takes no concern in human affairs, an error which is the source of the greatest disorders; but when we believe that God is a jealous God, the reflection tends powerfully to restrain us within the limits of our duty towards him. The jealousy attributed to God does not, however, imply agitation of mind: it is that divine love and charity by which God will suffer no human creature to resist his sovereign will with impunity, and which "destroys all those who are disloyal to him."[3] The jealousy of God, therefore, is the most impartial justice, the calmness of which is undisturbed by the least commotion, a justice which repudiates as an adulteress the soul which is corrupted by erroneous opinions and criminal passions; and in this jealousy of God, evincing as it does his boundless and incomprehensible goodness towards us, we recognise at once a source of pure and unmixed pleasure. It declares that the soul is his spouse, and what stronger tie of affection, or closer bond of union can bind him to us? God, therefore, when frequently comparing himself to a spouse or husband, he calls himself a jealous God, demonstrates the excess of his love towards us.

Zeal in the service of God.
The pastor, therefore, will here exhort the faithful, that they should be so warmly interested in promoting the worship and honour of God, as to be said with more propriety to be jealous of, rather than to love him; imitating the example of Elias, who says of himself: "With zeal have I been zealous for the

[1] Ps. cxxxviii. 7.   [2] Ps. xxvi. 1.   [3] Ps. lxxii. 27.

Lord God of Hosts;"[1] or rather of Jesus Christ himself, who says : " The zeal of thy house hath eaten me up."[2]

The pastor should also set forth the terrors denounced in the menaces of God's judgments—menaces which declare that he will not suffer sinners to run their iniquitous career with impunity ; but will chastise them with the fondness of a parent, or punish them with the rigour of a judge ; and which, on another occasion, are thus expressed by Moses : " Thou shalt know that the Lord thy God is a strong and faithful God, keeping his covenant and mercy to them that love him, and to them that keep his commandments, unto a thousand genera-' tions ; and repaying forthwith them that hate him, so as to destroy them without further delay, immediately rendering to them what they deserve."[3] " You will not," says Josue, " be able to serve the Lord ; for he is a holy God, and mighty and jealous, and will not forgive your wickedness and sins. If you leave the Lord and serve strange gods, he will turn and will afflict you, and will destroy you."[4] The faithful are also to be taught, that the punishments here threatened await the third and fourth generation of the impious and wicked ; not that the children are always visited with the chastisements due to the delinquency of their parents, but that, although they and their children may go unpunished, their posterity shall not all escape the wrath and vengeance of the Almighty. Of this we have an illustration in the life of king Josias : God had spared him for his singular piety, and allowed him to be gathered to the tomb of his fathers in peace, that his eyes might not behold the evils of the times that were to befall Judah and Jerusalem, on account of the wickedness of his father Manasseh ; yet, after his decease, the divine vengeance so overtook his posterity, that even the children of Josias were not spared.[5]

The words of this commandment may perhaps seem to be at variance with the sentence pronounced by the prophet: " The soul that sins shall die ;"[6] but the authority of St. Gregory, supported by the concurrent testimony of all the ancient fathers, satisfactorily reconciles this apparent contradiction: " Whoever," says he,- " follows the bad example of a wicked father is also bound by his sins ; but he, who does not follow the example of a wicked father, shall not at all suffer for the sins of the father. Hence it follows that a wicked son, who dreads not to superadd his own malice to the vices of his father, by which he knows the divine wrath to have been excited, is burdened not only with his own additional sins, but also with those of his wicked father.—It is just that he who dreads not to walk in the footsteps of a wicked father, in presence of a rigorous judge, should be subjected in the present life to the punishment invoked by the crimes of his wicked parent."[7]

The Law not to be violated with impunity.

Note.

An apparent contradiction reconciled

---

[1] 3 Kings xix. 10. [2] Ps. lxviii. 10. John ii. 17. [3] Deut. vii. 9, 10.
[4] Josue xxiv. 19, 20. [5] 2 Par. 36. iii. 6. 4 Kings xxii. 20. [6] Ezech. xviii. 4.
[7] Extat locus Greg. lib. 15. moral. c. 31. Vid. Aug. epist. 75. D. Thom. 1. 2. q. 87 art. 8.

The mercy of God exceeds his justice. That the goodness and mercy of God far exceed his justice is another observation, which the pastor will not fail to make to the faithful: he is angry to the third and fourth generation; but he bestows his mercy on thousands.

The wicked hate God. The words: "Of them that hate me" display the grievousness of sin: what more wicked? what more detestable than to hate God, the supreme goodness and sovereign truth? This,

The good are influenced by love in the observance of his Law. however, is the crime of all sinners: for as he who observes the commandments of God, loves God,[1] so he who despises his Law, and violates his commandments, is justly said to hate God. The concluding words: "And them that love me," point out the manner and motive of observing the Law of God: those who observe the divine Law should be influenced in its observance by the same love and charity which they bear to God; a principle which applies with equal force and truth to the exposition and observance of all the other commandments.

THE SECOND COMMANDMENT.

"THOU SHALT NOT TAKE THE NAME OF THE LORD THY GOD IN VAIN."[2]

This commandment, why distinct from the first. THIS precept is necessarily comprised in the former, which commands us to worship God in piety and holiness: He who is to be honoured must also be spoken of with reverence and must forbid the contrary, according to these words of Malachy: "The son honoureth the father, and the servant his master: if then I be a father, where is my honour?"[3] Yet, on account of the importance of the obligation which it imposes, God would make this law, which commands his name to be honoured, a distinct precept; and this he does in the clearest and simplest terms. This observation must have much influence in convincing the pastor, that on this point it is not enough to speak in general terms: that its importance is such as to require to be dwelt upon at considerable length, and to be explained to the faithful in all its bearings with distinctness, clearness, and accuracy.[4]

Demands assiduous exposition. This assiduity on the part of the pastor cannot be deemed superfluous: there are not wanting those who are so blinded by the darkness of error as not to dread to blaspheme his name, whom the angels glorify; and who are not deterred by the divine commandment from shamefully and daringly outraging his divine majesty every day, or rather every hour and moment of

---

[1] John xiv. 21. [2] Exod. xx. 7. [3] Malach. i. 6.
[4] De hoc præcepto vid. D. Thom. 2. 2. q. 122. art. 3. item et 1. 2. q. 100, art. 5.

the day. Who is ignorant that every assertion is accompanied with an oath? that every conversation teems with curses and imprecations? To such lengths has this impiety been carried, that one scarcely buys, or sells, or transacts ordinary business of any sort, without interposing the solemn pledge of an oath, and even in matters the most unimportant and trivial, thousands of times rashly appealing to the most holy name of God! It therefore becomes more imperative on the pastor, not to neglect, carefully and frequently, to admonish the faithful of the grievousness and horror of this detestable crime.

But in the exposition of this commandment, the pastor will *Contains a* show, that, besides a negative, it also contains a positive precept *negative* commanding the performance of a duty, and will give to each a *tive pre-* separate exposition.—In the first place, to facilitate the explana- *cept.* tion of these matters, it is necessary to know what the precept commands, and what it prohibits. It commands us to honour the name of God, and when solemnly appealing to him by an oath, fo do so with due reverence: it prohibits us to contemn the divine name, to take it in vain, or swear by it falsely, un- necessarily, or rashly. When therefore we are commanded to *Note.* honour the name of God, the command, as the pastor will show, is not directed to the letters or syllables of which that name is composed, or in any respect to the mere name; but to the im- port of a word used to express the Omnipotent and Eternal Majesty of the Godhead, Trinity in unity. Hence we at once perceive the superstition of those amongst the Jews who, whilst they hesitated not to write, dared not to pronounce the name of God, as if the divine power consisted in the letters of which it is composed, and not in their signification.

In the annunciation of the divine precept, the word "name," *The com-* although occurring in the singular number, "Thou shalt not *mandment* take the name of God," is not to be understood to refer to any *every name* one name in particular: it extends to every name by which *by which* God is generally designated. He is called by many names, *signated.* such as "the Lord," "the Almighty," "the Lord of Hosts," "the King of Kings," "the Strong," and by others of similar import, which we meet in Scripture; all of which are entitled to the same veneration.

The pastor will also teach how the name of God is to be ho- *The name* noured. Christians, whose tongues should every day celebrate the *of God,* divine praises, are not to be ignorant of a matter so important, *noured.* indeed so necessary to salvation. The name of God may be honoured in a variety of ways; but all seem to be included under the following heads.—His name is honoured, when we *I* openly and confidently confess him to be our Lord and our God; and not only acknowledge but proclaim Christ to be the author of our salvation. It is also honoured when we pay a re- *II.* ligious attention to his Word, which announces to us his sove- reign will; make it the subject of our daily meditation; and by reading or hearing it, study, according to our respective capa- cities and conditions of life, to become acquainted with its

III. saving truths. Again, we honour and venerate the name of God, when from a sense of religious duty we celebrate his praises, and under all circumstances, whether prosperous or adverse, return him unbounded thanks; saying in the language of the prophet: " Bless the Lord, O my soul, and never forget all he hath done for thee."[1] Amongst the Psalms of David we have many, in which, animated with singular piety towards God, the Psalmist chants in sweetest strains the divine praises. We have also the admirable example of Job, who, when visited with the heaviest and most appalling calamities, never ceased, with lofty and unconquered soul, to give praise to God. When, therefore, we labour under affliction of mind or body; when oppressed by misery and misfortune; let us instantly direct all our thoughts, and all the powers of our souls, to the praises of God, saying with Job: " Blessed be the name of the Lord."[2]

IV. The name of God is not less honoured when we confidently invoke his assistance, either to relieve us from our afflictions, or to give us constancy and strength to endure them with fortitude. This is in accordance with his own wishes : " Call upon me," says he, " in the day of trouble : I will deliver thee, and thou shalt glorify me ;"[3] and we have illustrious examples of such supplications in the sixteenth, forty-third, and one hundred and eighteenth Psalms, and also in many other parts of Scripture.—

V. Finally, we honour the name of God, when we solemnly call upon him to witness the truth of what we assert; and this solemn appeal differs much from the means of honouring the divine name already enumerated. Those means are in their own nature so good, so desirable, that our lives, day and night, could not be more happily or more holily spent than in such practices of piety : " I will bless the Lord," says David, " at all times, his praise shall be always in my mouth :"[4] but with regard to oaths, although in themselves lawful, they should seldom be used. The reason of this difference is, that oaths are constituted as remedies to human frailty, and a necessary means of establishing the truth of what we advance. As it is inexpedient to have recourse to medicine, unless when it becomes necessary, and as its frequent use is most pernicious; so, with regard to oaths, we should never recur to them, unless when there is weighty and just cause; and a frequent recurrence to them, far from being advantageous, is on the contrary highly prejudicial. Hence the excellent observation of St. Chrysostome : " Oaths were introduced amongst men, not at the beginning of the world, but long after; when vice had overspread the earth ; when the moral world was convulsed to its centre, and universal confusion reigned throughout ; when, to complete the picture of human depravity, man debased the dignity of his nature by prostrating himself in degrading servitude to idols : then it was that God was appealed to as a witness of the truth, when, considering to what a height perfidy and wickedness had

Oaths should seldom be taken.

---

[1] Ps. cii. 1. [2] Job i. 21. [3] Ps. xlix. 15. [4] Ps. xxxiii. 2.

risen, it was with difficulty that man could be induced to credit the assertion of his fellow-man."[1]

But as in explaining this part of the commandment our chief object is, to teach the faithful the conditions necessary to render an oath reverential and holy, it is first to be observed, that to swear, whatever the form of the oath may be, is nothing else than to call God to witness: to say "God is my witness," and to swear by his holy name, are exactly the same. To swear by creatures, in order to gain credit for what we say, is an oath: to swear by the holy Gospels, by the cross, by the names or relics of the saints, and all such solemn attestations, are also oaths. Of themselves, it is true, such objects give no weight or authority to an oath: its derives its obligation from God, whose divine majesty shines forth in them: and hence to swear by the Gospel is to swear by God himself, whose revealed word it is. This holds equally true with regard to those who swear by the saints, who are the temples of God, who believed the truth of his Gospel, were faithful to its dictates, and diffused its doctrines amongst the remotest nations of the earth. This is also true of oaths uttered by way of execration, such as that of St. Paul: "I call God to witness upon my soul:"[2] by this form of oath we subject ourselves to God as the avenger of falsehood. We do not, however, deny that some of these forms may be used without constituting an oath; but even in such cases it will be found useful to observe what has been said with regard to an oath, and to direct and regulate such forms by the same rule and standard.

Oaths are of two kinds, affirmatory and promissory: an oath is affirmatory when, under its solemn sanction, we affirm any thing, past, present, or to come; such as the affirmation of the Apostle in his Epistle to the Galatians: "Behold! before God, I lie not."[3] An oath is promissory when we promise the certain performance of any thing; such as that of David, who swore to Bethsabee his wife, by the Lord his God, that Solomon should be heir to his kingdom and successor to his throne;[4] and this class of oaths also includes comminations.

But although to constitute an oath it is sufficient to call God to witness, yet to constitute a holy and just oath many other conditions are required; and these it is the duty of the pastor carefully to explain. The other conditions, as St. Jerome observes,[5] are briefly enumerated in these words of the prophet Jeremiah: "Thou shalt swear: as the Lord liveth, in truth and in judgment, and in justice;"[6] words which briefly sum up all the conditions, which constitute the perfection of an oath —truth, judgment, justice.

Truth, then, holds the first place in an oath: what we swear must be true; that is, he who swears must believe what he swears to be true, founding his conviction not upon rash grounds

Marginal notes: Different sorts of oaths. I. II. III. — Oaths are affirmatory and promissory. — Conditions of a lawful oath. — Truth.

---

[1] Ad. pop. Antioch. hom. 26.
[2] 2 Cor. i. 23.
[3] Gal. i. 20.
[4] 3 Kings i. 17.
[5] St. Hieron in hunc locum.
[6] Jerem. iv. 2.

or vain conjecture, but upon motives of undoubted credibility. Truth is a condition not less necessary, as is obvious, in a promissory than in an affirmatory oath : he who promises must be disposed to perform and fulfil his promise at the appointed time. As no conscientious man will promise to do what he considers to be a violation of the commandments, and in opposition to the will of God ; so, having promised and sworn to do what is lawful, he will adhere with fidelity to the sacred and solemn engagement ; unless, perhaps, change of circumstances should so alter the complexion of the case, that he could not stand to his promise without incurring the displeasure and enmity of God. That truth is necessary to a lawful oath David also declares, when, having asked who is worthy to sit in the tabernacle of the Most High, he answers : " He that sweareth to his neighbour, and deceiveth not."[1]

Judgment.   The second condition is judgment : an oath is not to be taken rashly and inconsiderately, but after mature deliberation and calm reflection. When about to take an oath, therefore, we should first consider whether it be or be not necessary, and whether the case, if well weighed in all its circumstances, be of sufficient importance to demand an oath. Many other circumstances of time, place, &c. are also to be taken into consideration ; and in taking an oath we should never be influenced by love or hatred, or any other passion, but by the nature and necessity of the case. Without this calm and dispassionate consideration, an oath must be rash and hasty ; and of this character are the irreligious affirmations of those, who, on the most unimportant and trifling occasions, swear from the influence of bad habit alone. This criminal abuse is but too prevalent amongst buyers and sellers, of whom the latter, to sell at the highest price, the former to purchase at the cheapest rate, make no scruple to strengthen with an oath, their praise or dispraise of the goods in question. Judgment and prudence therefore are necessary, and hence Pope Gelasius, a pontiff of eminent piety, decreed that an oath should not be administered to children before their fourteenth year, because before that period their tender age is incompetent to perceive so acutely, and to balance so accurately, the nice distinctions of things.

Justice.   The third and last condition of an oath is justice ; a condition which in promissory oaths demands particular attention. Hence, if a person swear to do what is unjust or unlawful, he sins by taking the oath, and adds sin to sin by executing his promise. Of this the Gospel supplies an example. Herod bound himself by oath to grant the request of Herodias, as a reward for the pleasure which she afforded him by dancing : she demanded the head of John the baptist ; and Herod criminally adhered to the rash oath which he had sworn.[2] Such was also the oath taken by the Jews, who, as we read in the Acts of the Apostles, bound themselves by oath not to eat, until they had shed the blood of Paul.[3]

[1] Ps. xiv. 4.   [2] Matt. xiv. 7.   [3] Acts xxiii. 12.

An oath therefore accompanied, and guarded as it were by these conditions, is no doubt lawful, a position which is easily and satisfactorily established. The law of God, the purity and sanctity of which will not be questioned,[1] not only permits but commands such an oath to be taken: " Thou shalt fear the Lord thy God," says Moses, " and shalt serve him only, and thou shalt swear by his name :"[2] " All they," says David, " shall be praised that swear by him."[3] The inspired Volume also informs us, that the Apostles, whose bright example it cannot be unlawful for Christians to follow, sometimes made use of oaths : they are recorded in the Epistles of St. Paul.[4] Even the angels have sometimes sworn : " The angel," says St. John in his Apocalypse, " swore by him who lives for ever."[5] In fine, God himself, the Lord of angels, has sworn, and, as we read in many passages of the Old Testament, has confirmed his promises with an oath. This he did to Abraham and to David ;[6] and of the oath sworn by the Almighty David says : " The Lord hath sworn, and he will not repent : thou art a priest for ever according to the order of Melchisedech."[7]

To him who considers the matter attentively and in all its bearings, its origin and its end, it can be no difficult matter to explain the reasons why the taking of an oath is not only lawful but even laudable. An oath has its origin in faith, by which we believe God to be the author of all truth, who cannot deceive or be deceived, " to whose eyes all things are naked and open,"[8] who, in fine, superintends in an admirable manner all human affairs, whose providence governs the world : imbued with this faith we appeal to God as a witness of the truth, to whom it were wicked and impious not to yield implicit belief. With regard to the end of an oath, its scope and intent is to establish the justice and innocence of man, and to terminate disputes and contests : this is the doctrine of St. Paul in his Epistle to the Hebrews.[9] Nor does this doctrine at all clash with these words of the Redeemer, recorded in St. Matthew : " You have heard that it was said of old ; thou shalt not commit perjury, but thou shalt perform thy oaths to the Lord : but I say to you not to swear at all ; neither by heaven, because it is the throne of God ; neither by the earth, because it is the footstool of his feet ; neither by Jerusalem, because it is the city of the great king : neither shalt thou swear by thy head, because thou canst not make one hair white or black. Let your talk be yea, yea ; no, no ; and that which is over and above these is of evil."[10] It cannot be asserted that these words condemn oaths universally and under all circumstances : we have already seen that the Apostles and even our Lord himself swore frequently : the object of the Redeemer was rather to reprove the perverse opinion of the Jews, which taught them to think that to justify the

Margin notes:
An oath accompanied with these conditions, lawful
I.
II.
III.
IV
V.
VI.
Objection.
Its solution.

---

[1] Ps. xviii. 8.   [2] Deut. vi. 13.   [3] Ps. lxii. 12.
[4] 2 Cor. i. 23. Philem. i. 8. 1 Thess. ii. 10.   [5] Apoc. x. 6.
[6] Heb. vi. 17. Gen. xxii. 16. Exod. xxxiii. 1.   [7] Ps. cix. 4.
[8] Heb. iv. 13.   [9] Heb. vi. 16.   [10] Matt. v. 34—37.

taking of an oath, its truth alone was sufficient. Hence even on the most trivial occasions they did not hesitate to make frequent use of oaths, and to exact them from others. This practice the Redeemer condemns and reprobates; teaching that an oath is never to be taken, unless necessity require so solemn a pledge. Oaths have been instituted as remedies for human frailty; and bespeaking, as it does, the inconstancy of him who takes, or the contumacy of him who exacts it, and who refuses to yield his assent without it, an oath has its source in the corruption of our nature, and can therefore be justified by necessity alone.

Explana-
tion of the
words of
the Re-
deemer.

But to explain the words of the Redeemer—When our Lord says: " Let your speech be yea, yea; no, no,"[1] he evidently forbids the habit of swearing in familiar conversation and on trivial matters: he therefore admonishes us particularly against an habitual propensity to swearing; and this admonition the pastor will impress deeply and repeatedly on the minds of the faithful. That countless evils grow out of the unrestrained habit of swearing is a melancholy truth supported by the evidence of Scripture, and the testimony of the Holy Fathers. Thus we read in Ecclesiasticus: " Let not thy mouth be accustomed to swearing; for in it there are many falls;"[2] and again: " A man that sweareth much shall be filled with iniquity, and a scourge shall not depart from his house."[3] In the works of St. Basil, and also in the treatise of St. Augustine against lying, the pastor will find abundant matter on this subject.[4]

Negative
part of the
command-
ment.

Having hitherto explained the positive, we now come to explain the negative part of the commandment. By it we are forbidden to take the name of God in vain; and he who, not guided by prudent deliberation, but hurried on by rashness, dares to take an oath, is guilty of a grievous sin. This the very words of the commandment declare: " Thou shalt not take the name of the Lord thy God in vain." In these words the Almighty would seem to assign the reason why a rash oath is so grievous a crime:—It derogates from the majesty of him whom we profess to recognise as our Lord and our God. This commandment, therefore, forbids to swear falsely, because he who does not hesitate to appeal to God to witness falsehood, offers a grievous injury to the divine Majesty, charging him either with ignorance, as though the truth could be concealed from his all-seeing eye, or with injustice and depravity, as though the Eternal Truth could bear testimony to falsehood.

How vio-
lated.
I. & II.

Amongst false swearers are to be numbered not only those who affirm as true what they know to be false, but also those who swear to what is really true, believing it to be false.[5] The essence of a lie consists in speaking contrary to one's conviction; and such persons, therefore, as swear to what they believe to be false, are evidently guilty of a lie, and therefore of

III.

perjury. On the same principle, he who swears to that which

---

[1] Matt. v. 37.   [2] Eccl. xiii. 9.   [3] Eccl. xxiii. 12.
[4] Basil. in Psal. 14. ad haec verba: qui jurat proximo suo, et Aug. lib. de mendac c. 14. Vid. 12. q. 2. c. primum est.   [5] Lev. xix. 12.

he thinks to be true, but which, although he swears according to his conviction, is really false, also incurs the guilt of perjury; unless he has used moral diligence to arrive at the truth. He who binds himself by oath to the performance of any thing, not intending to fulfil his promise, or having had the intention neglects its performance, is also guilty of perjury; and this equally applies to those who, having bound themselves to God by vow, neglect its fulfilment.

This commandment is also violated, if justice, which is one of the three conditions of an oath, be wanting; and hence he who swears to commit a mortal sin, to perpetrate murder, for instance, violates this commandment, although he should have really intended to commit the crime, and his oath should have possessed what we before pointed out as a necessary condition of every oath, that is, truth. To these are to be added oaths sworn through a sort of contempt; such as an oath not to observe the Evangelical counsels of celibacy and poverty. None, it is true, are obliged to embrace these counsels, but by swearing to their non-observance, they are contemned and violated. This commandment is also sinned against, and the second condition of an oath, which is "judgment," is violated by swearing on slight grounds and mere conjecture, although what is sworn be true, and believed to be so by him who swears; because, notwithstanding its truth, it still involves a sort of falsehood; for he who swears with such indifference exposes himself to extreme danger of perjury. To swear by false gods is likewise to swear falsely: what more opposed to truth than to appeal to lying and false deities as to the true God?[1]

But as the Scripture, when it prohibits perjury, adds: "Thou shalt not profane the name of thy God,"[2] it therefore prohibits all irreverence not only to his name, but also to those things to which, in accordance with this commandment, reverence is due; such as the Word of God, the majesty of which has been recognised and revered not only by the pious, but also sometimes by the impious, as we read in Judges of Eglon, king of the Moabites.[3] But he who, to support heresy and impiety, wrests the Sacred Scriptures from their genuine and true meaning, is guilty of the most flagrant irreverence towards the Divine Word; and of this we are admonished by these words of the prince of the Apostles: "There are some things hard to be understood, which the unlearned and unstable wrest, as they do also the other Scriptures, to their own destruction."[4] It is also a shameful irreverence of the Scripture, to pervert the words and sentences which it contains, and which should be mentioned with due reverence, to some profane purpose, such as scurrility, fable, vanity, flattery, detraction, superstition, satire, and the like. Such profanation of the Divine Word the Council of Trent commands to be severely reprehended.[5] In

IV.

Note.

V

VI.

VII.

VIII.

IX

X.

---

[1] Vid. Aug. epist. 54.   [2] Lev. xix. 12.   [3] Judges iii. 20.
[4] Pet. iii. 16.   [5] Sess. 4. in fine.

XI.   the next place, as they who under severe affliction implore the assistance of God, so they, who invoke not his aid, deny him due honour; and these David rebukes when he says: "They have not called upon the Lord, they trembled for fear where there was no fear."[1] Still more enormous is the guilt of those

XII.   who, with impure and impious lips, dare to curse or blaspheme the holy name of God, that name which is to be blessed and praised above measure by all his creatures, or even the names of the Saints who reign with him in glory. Shuddering, as it were, at its very mention, the Sacred Scriptures sometimes express the crime of which they are guilty, by the word "benediction."[2]

Sanction of this precept.   As, however, the dread of punishment has often a powerful effect in checking the licentiousness of crime, the pastor, in order the more effectually to excite, and the more easily to induce to an observance of this commandment, will diligently explain the remaining words, which are, as it were, its appendix, and which run thus; "FOR THE LORD WILL NOT HOLD HIM GUILTLESS THAT SHALL TAKE THE NAME OF THE LORD HIS GOD IN VAIN."[3]

Its wisdom to be developed by the pastor.
I.   In the first place the pastor will teach, that in the annexation of threats to the violation of this commandment reason discovers the wisest ends: it demonstrates at once the grievousness of sin and the goodness displayed in our regard by a beneficent God, who, far from desiring the death of the sinner, deters by these salutary threats from incurring his severity, doubtless in order that we may experience his kindness rather than his anger. The pastor will urge this consideration, a consideration to be dwelt on with indefatigable earnestness, in order that the faithful may be made sensible of the grievousness of the crime, may detest it still more, and may employ increased care and caution to avoid its commission.

II.   He will also observe how prone Christians are to this sin, since God has not only issued a command for its prevention, but has also enforced this command by so severe a sanction. The advantages to be derived from this consideration are indeed incredible: as nothing is more injurious than a listless security, so the knowledge of our own weakness is attended with the

III.   most salutary consequences. He will next observe that the punishment, which awaits the violation of this commandment, is not fixed and determinate; the threat is general: it declares that he who is guilty of the violation shall not escape unpunished. The chastisements, therefore, with which we are every day visited, should impress upon our minds the enormity of this crime. They admonish us, in language the most intelligible, that the violation of this commandment cannot pass with impunity; that the heaviest punishments will overtake him who profanes the name of God; a consideration which it is hoped must excite to future vigilance.

Ps. xiii. 5. et liii. 26.   [2] 3 Kings xxi. 13.   Joh i. 11. et ii. 9.   [3] Exod. xx. 7.

Deterred therefore by a holy and salutary dread, the faithful should use every exertion to avoid the violation of this commandment: if "for every idle word that men shall speak, they shall render an account on the day of judgment;"[1] how severe the account which they shall have to render, whose crime involves the awful guilt of contemning the name of the Eternal God ! *Practical conclusion.*

THE THIRD COMMANDMENT.

"REMEMBER THAT THOU KEEP HOLY THE SABBATH DAY. SIX DAYS SHALT THOU LABOUR AND SHALT DO ALL THY WORKS; BUT ON THE SEVENTH DAY IS THE SABBATH OF THE LORD THY GOD: THOU SHALT DO NO WORK ON IT, THOU NOR THY SON, NOR THY DAUGHTER, NOR THY MAN-SERVANT, NOR THY MAID-SERVANT, NOR THY BEAST, NOR THE STRANGER THAT IS WITHIN THY GATES: FOR IN SIX DAYS THE LORD MADE HEAVEN AND EARTH, AND THE SEA, AND ALL THINGS THAT ARE IN THEM, AND RESTED ON THE SEVENTH DAY: THEREFORE THE LORD BLESSED THE SEVENTH DAY: AND SANCTIFIED IT."[2]

THIS commandment, as is required by the natural order, prescribes the external worship which is due to God, and is, as it were, a consectary of the preceding commandment. If we sincerely and devoutly yield internal worship to God, guided by the faith and hope we have in him, we cannot but honour him with external worship and thanksgiving:[3] this duty we cannot easily discharge whilst occupied in worldly affairs ; and hence the necessity of appointing a fixed time for its performance. As, therefore, this commandment, if duly observed, is productive of much fruit, it is of the highest importance that the pastor use the utmost diligence in its exposition. The word " Remember," with which the commandment commences, must animate him to the zealous performance of this duty: if the faithful are commanded to " remember" this commandment, it becomes the duty of the pastor to recall it frequently to their recollection. *What this commandment prescribes.* *Importance of its exposition,*

The importance of its observance may be inferred from the consideration, that a faithful compliance with its injunctions facilitates the observance of all the other commandments. Amongst the other works of piety by which the Sabbath is to be sanctified, the faithful are bound to assemble in the Church *and observance.*

------

[1] Matt. xii. 36.   [2] Exod. xx. 8.
[3] Vid. Trid. decret. de ciborum delectu et festis diebus, sess. ult. sub finem. Item D. Thom. 2. 2. q. 122. art. 4. item de consecrat. dist. 3. multis capitib.

to hear the divine word: when they have thus learned the justifications of the Lord, they will be prompted to the faithful and willing observance of his holy Law. Hence the sanctification of the Sabbath is very often enforced in Scripture, as may be seen in Exodus,[1] Leviticus,[2] Deuteronomy,[3] and in the prophecies of Isaias,[4] Jeremiah,[5] and Ezekiel,[6] all of which contain this precept which commands the observance of the Sabbath.[7]

Princes and magistrates are to be admonished and exhorted to lend the sanction and support of their authority to the pastors of the Church, particularly in upholding and extending the worship of God, and in commanding obedience to the spiritual injunctions of the pastor.

With regard to the exposition of this commandment, the faithful are to be carefully taught in what it accords with, and in what it differs from the others, in order that they may understand why Christians observe not the Sabbath, but the Lord's-day. The point of difference is evident: the other commandments of the Decalogue are precepts of the natural law, obligatory at all times and unalterable, and hence, after the abrogation of the Law of Moses, all the commandments contained in the two tables are observed by Christians, not however because their observance is commanded by Moses, but because they accord with the law of nature and are enforced by its dictate: whereas this commandment, if considered as to the time of its fulfilment, is not fixed and unalterable, but is susceptible of change, and belongs not to the moral but ceremonial Law. Neither is it a principle of the natural law: we are not instructed by the natural law to worship God on the Sabbath, rather than on any other day. The Sabbath was kept holy from the time of the liberation of the people of Israel from the bondage of Pharaoh: the obligation was to cease with the abrogation of the Jewish worship, of which it formed a part; and it therefore was no longer obligatory after the death of Christ. Having been, as it were, images which shadowed the light and the truth, these ceremonies were to disappear at the coming of that light and truth, which is Christ Jesus. Hence St. Paul, in his Epistle to the Galatians, when reproving the observers of the Mosaic rites, says: " you observe days and months and times and years; I am afraid of you lest perhaps I have laboured in vain amongst you;"[8] sentiments which are also to be found in his Epistle to the Colossians.[9] On the difference between this and the other commandments these observations will suffice.

As to their accordance, it consists not in rites and ceremonies, but in as much as this commandment, in common with the others, expresses a moral obligation, founded on the law of nature. The worship of God and the practice of religion,

[1] Exod. xvi. 20. 31.   [2] Lev. xvi. 19. 23. 26.   [3] Deut. v.
[4] Isa. lvi. 58. 66.   [5] Jerem. 17.   [6] Ezek. xx. 22, 23. 46.
[7] De præd. verb. Dei, vid. Trid. sess. 5. c. 2. vide et singulare hac de re libellum
S Caroli Borrom in actis Eccles. Mediol. vide etiam acta eccles. Bononiens.
[8] Galat. iv. 10.   [9] Col. ii. 16.

which it comprises, have the natural law for their basis: the unbidden impulse of nature prompts us to give some time to the worship of God; and this is a truth demonstrated by the unanimous consent of all nations, who, accordingly, consecrated festivals to the public solemnities of religion. As nature requires some time to be given to necessary relaxation, to sleep, and to the repose and refreshment of the body; so she also requires, that some time be devoted to the mind, to refresh and invigorate its energies by heavenly contemplation. Hence the necessity of consecrating some time to the worship of the Deity and to the practice of religion, duties which, doubtless, form part of the moral law. The Apostles therefore resolved to consecrate the first day of the week to the divine worship, and called it "the Lord's-day:" St. John in his Apocalypse makes mention of "the Lord's-day;"[1] and the Apostle commands collections to be made "on the first day of the week,"[2] that is, according to the interpretation of St. Chrysostome, on the Lord's-day; and thus we are given to understand that even then the Lord's-day was kept holy in the church.

An illustration.

The Jewish Sabbath when and by whom changed to the "Lord's day."

In order that the faithful may know what they are to do, what to avoid, on the Lord's-day, it will not be found foreign to his purpose, if the pastor, dividing the commandment into four parts, explain each part with minute accuracy. In the first place, then, he will explain generally the meaning of these words: "Remember that thou keep holy the Sabbath day." The word "remember" is appropriately made use of at the beginning of the commandment, to signify that the sanctification of that particular day belonged to the ceremonial law. Of this it would seem to have been necessary to admonish the people, for, although the law of nature commands us to give religious worship to God, it fixes no particular day for the performance of that duty. They are also to be taught, that from these words we may learn how we should employ our time during the week; that we are to keep constantly in view the Lord's-day, on which we are, as it were, to render an account to God for the manner in which we have spent the week: and that therefore our occupations and conduct should be such as not to be unacceptable in the sight of God, or, as it is written, be to us "an occasion of grief, and a scruple of heart."[3] Finally, we are taught, and the instruction demands our serious attention, that there are but too many circumstances which may lead to a forgetfulness of this commandment, such as the evil example of others who neglect its observance, and an inordinate love of amusements, which frequently withdraw from the holy and religious observance of the Lord's-day.

This commandment divided into four parts.

I.

II.

III.

We now come to the meaning of the word "Sabbath."

---

[1] Apoc. i. 10.
[2] Chrysost. hom. 13. in Corinth. Amb. item et Theophylact. vid. etiam. Can. Apost. c. 67. Ignat. Epist. ad Magnes. Just. apol. 2. Tertul. in apol. c. 16. et de Coron. milit. c. 3. et de idol. c. 14. et Cyp. epist. 33. Clement. Alex. lib. 5. Strom. satis ante finem. Orig. hom. 7. in Exod.   [3] 1 Kings xxv. 31.

23   2 L

Meaning of the word "Sabbath." Sabbath is a Hebrew word: it signifies cessation; to keep the Sabbath, therefore, means to cease from labour; and in this sense the seventh day was called the "Sabbath," (it is so called by God in Exodus) because, having finished the creation of the world, God rested from all the work which he had done.[1] Not only the seventh day, but, in honour of that day, the entire week was subsequently called "the Sabbath;" and in this meaning of the word, the Pharisee says in St. Luke: "I fast twice in a Sabbath."[3] Thus much will suffice with regard to the signification of the word "Sabbath."

Sanctification of the Sabbath. In the words of the commandment, the sanctification of the Sabbath is a cessation from bodily labour and worldly business, as is clear from the following words: "Thou shalt do no work on it." This alone, however, does not comprise the meaning of the commandment: if it did, it would have been sufficient to say in Deuteronomy, "observe the day of the Sabbath;"[3] but it is added, "and sanctify it;" and these additional words prove that the Sabbath is a day sacred to religion, set apart for works of piety and exercises of devotion. The Sabbath, therefore, we sanctify by devoting it to duties of piety and religion; and this is evidently the Sabbath, which Isaias calls "delightful;"[4] when thus spent, it is the delight of God and of his faithful servants. If then to this religious and holy observance of the Sabbath we add works of mercy, the rewards proposed to our piety in the same chapter are numerous and most important.[5]

The true meaning of the precept. The true and proper meaning, therefore, of this commandment tends to this, that we take special care to set apart some fixed time, when, disengaged from bodily labour, and undisturbed by worldly cares, we may devote our whole being, soul and body, to the religious worship of God.

Second part of the commandment: its meaning. The other part of the precept declares that the seventh day was consecrated by Almighty God to his worship: "Six days," says he, "shalt thou labour, and do all thy works;" but on "the seventh day is the Sabbath of the Lord thy God;" that is to say, the Sabbath is consecrated to the Lord, and on that day we are to render him the duties of religion, and to know that the seventh day is a sign of his rest. The Sabbath was consecrated to the worship of God, because it must have proved inconvenient to leave to a rude people the choice of a time of worship, lest, perhaps, they may be led to imitate the idolatrous rites of Egypt. The seventh day was, therefore, chosen for the worship of God, and its dedication to that end is replete with mystery.

The Sabbath why fixed for the divine worship.

Its mystic meaning.
I.

II Hence in Exodus,[6] and in Ezekiel[7] the Lord calls it "a sign:" "I gave them," says he, "my Sabbaths to be a sign between me and them; and that they might know that I am the Lord that sanctify them."[8] It was a sign that man should dedicate and consecrate himself to God, whereas even the very day is dedicated and consecrated to him: it is

<hr>

[1] Gen. ii. 3. Exod. xx. 21. Deut. v. 12.   [3] Luke xviii. 12.   [3] Deut. v. 12.
[4] Isa. lviii. 13.   [5] Isa. lviii. 6.   [6] Exod. xxxi. 13.
[7] Ezek. xx. 12.   [8] Deut. v. 15.

holy because devoted in a special manner to holiness and to religion. It was also a sign, and, as it were, a memorial, of the stupendous work of the creation. To the Jews it was also a traditional sign, reminding them that they had been delivered by the hand of God from the galling yoke of Egyptian bondage. This the Almighty himself declares in these words: "Remember that thou also didst serve in Egypt, and the Lord thy God brought thee out from thence with a strong hand and a stretched out arm. Therefore hath he commanded thee that thou shouldst observe the Sabbath day."

It is also a sign of the spiritual and celestial Sabbath. The spiritual Sabbath consists in a holy and mystical rest, wherein the old man, being buried with Christ, is renewed to life, and studies to act in accordance with the spirit of Christian piety: "you were, therefore, darkness," says the Apostle, "but now light in the Lord. Walk then as children of the light; for the fruit of the light is in all goodness, and justice and truth, having no fellowship with the unfruitful works of darkness."[1] The celestial Sabbath, as St. Cyril observes on these words of the Apostle, "There remaineth therefore a day of rest for the people of God,"[2][3] is that life which we shall enjoy with Christ, in the fruition of all good, when sin shall be no more, according to these words of Isaias: "No lion shall be there, nor shall any mischievous beast go it, nor be found there; but a path and a way shall be there, and it shall be called the holy way;"[4] for the souls of the saints enjoy the plenitude of happiness in the vision of God. The pastor therefore will exhort and animate the faithful in the words of the Apostle: "Let us hasten therefore to enter into that rest."[5]

Besides the Sabbath, the Jews observed other festivals which were instituted by the divine law, and the end and aim of which was to awaken in the people the recollection of the principal favours conferred on them by the Almighty. On these festivals the pastor will see Leviticus,[6] Numbers,[7] and Deuteronomy;[8] and on the moral objects contemplated in the institution of such festivals, he may also consult St. Cyril,[9] and St. Thomas.[10]

But the Church of God has in her wisdom ordained that the celebration of the Sabbath should be transferred to "the Lord's-day:" as on that day light first shone on the world, so by the resurrection of our Lord on the same day, by whom was thrown open to us the gate to eternal life, we were called out of darkness into light; and hence the Apostle would have it called "the Lord's-day." We also learn from the sacred Volume that the first day of the week was held sacred for other reasons: on that day the work of the creation commenced, and on that day the Holy Ghost descended upon the Apostles. From the

The spiritual Sabbath; its meaning.

The celestial Sabbath; its meaning.

Other festivals observed by the Jews.

The Sabbath why changed to "the Lord's-day."

II.

---

[1] Eph. v. 8. [2] St. Cyril. Lat. lib. 4. in Joan. c. 51. [3] Heb. iv. 2.
[4] Isa. xxxv. 9. [5] Heb. iv. 11. [6] Levit. xxiii
[7] Num. xxix. [8] Deut. vi.
[9] Cyril. de adoratione in spiritu et verit. lib. 17.
[10] D. Thom. 1. 2. q. 102. art. 4. ad 10.

Other festivals why instituted: their order.

very infancy of the church other days were also appointed by the Apostles, and by their successors in after-times, to be kept holy, in order to commemorate the special gifts bestowed on us Christians. Amongst these days the most conspicuous are those which were instituted to honour the mysteries of our redemption, and next to them, those which are dedicated to the most blessed Virgin Mother, to the Apostles, Martyrs and other Saints who reign with Christ, and in the celebration of whose victories the divine power and goodness, which triumphed in them are praised, due honour is paid to their memories, and the faithful are excited to the imitation of their virtues.

Sloth and indolence condemned: no servile work to be deferred to the Lord's-day.

And as the observance of the precept is very strongly enforced in these words: "Six days shalt thou labour, and shalt do all thy works; but on the seventh day is the Sabbath of the Lord thy God;" the pastor should therefore carefully explain them to the people. They implicitly admonish him that the faithful are to be exhorted not to waste their lives in indolence and sloth, but mindful of the words of the Apostle, and in accordance with his command, "do their own business, and work with their own hands."[1] These words also enjoin as a duty that "in six days we do all our works," and admonish us not to defer to the Sunday or holiday what should have been done during the other days of the week, and what if deferred must withdraw our attention from the sanctification of the Sabbath.

The third part of the commandment, what it prohibits.

The third part of the commandment comes next to be explained. It points out, to a certain extent, the manner in which we are to keep holy the Sabbath day, and explains particularly what is prohibited to be done on that day: "Thou shalt do no work on it," says the Lord, "thou, nor thy son, nor thy daughter, nor thy man-servant, nor thy maid-servant, nor thy

I.

beast, nor the stranger that is within thy gates." These words teach us, in the first place, to avoid whatever may interfere with the worship of God on the Sabbath day; and hence it is not difficult to perceive that all servile works are forbidden, not because they are improper or evil in themselves, but because they withdraw from the worship of God, which is the great end of

II.

the commandment. The faithful should be still more careful not to profane the Sabbath by sin, which not only withdraws the mind from the contemplation of divine things, but entirely alienates us from the love of God.[2] But whatever regards the

What it permits.
I

celebration of divine worship, such as the decoration of the altar or church on occasion of some festival, and the like, although servile works, are not prohibited; and hence our Lord himself says: "The priests in the temple break the Sabbath, and are

II.

without blame."[3] Neither are we to suppose that this commandment forbids attention to those things on the Sabbath, which if neglected on that day perish to the proprietor. Their preservation is no violation of the commandment, and is ex-

[1] 1 Thess. iv. 11.
[2] Vid. Aug. tract. 3. in Joan. et in Ps. xxxi. serm. 1. et lib. de decem chordis c. 3.
[3] Matt. xii. 5.

pressly permitted by the sacred canons. There are many other things which our Lord declares lawful to be done on Sundays and holydays, and which may be seen by the pastor in St. Matthew and St. John.

But to omit nothing that may interfere with the sanctification of the Sabbath, cattle are mentioned in the commandment, because their use must prevent its due observance. If cattle be employed on the Sabbath, human labour also becomes necessary: they do not labour alone, but assist the labours of man. The prohibition of the employment of cattle is therefore a consequence of the prohibition of human labour; they are correllative; one supposes the other. If then God commands the exemption of cattle from labour on the Sabbath, still more imperative is the obligation to avoid all acts of inhumanity towards servants, or others whose labour and industry we employ in our service.

Cattle not to be employed on the Sabbath; and why.

The pastor should also not omit to inform the faithful how they are to sanctify Sundays and holydays; and amongst other means he will not forget to mention the obligation of visiting the temple of God, and there, with heartfelt piety and devotion, assisting at the celebration of the holy sacrifice of the Mass;[1] and also the duty of approaching frequently the sacraments of the Church, instituted for our sanctification and salvation, to heal our spiritual maladies.[2] Nothing can be more seasonable or salutary than frequent recourse to the tribunal of penance; and to this the pastor will be enabled to exhort the faithful by recurring to what we have already said in its proper place on the sacrament of penance. But not only will he excite his people to have recourse to the sacrament of penance—he will also zealously exhort them again and again, to approach frequently the holy sacrament of the Eucharist. Sermons are also in those days to be heard by the faithful with attention and reverence—nothing is more intolerable, nothing more unworthy of a Christian than to despise the words of Christ, or hear them with indifference.[3] Devout prayer and the praises of God should also frequently exercise the piety of the faithful on Sundays and holydays; and an object of their special attention should be to attend particularly to catechetical instruction, in order to learn those things which form to a Christian life; and to practise with assiduity these duties of Christian piety, viz. giving alms to the poor, visiting the sick, administering consolation to the afflicted. "Religion clear and undefiled before God and the Father is this," says St. James, "to visit the fatherless and widows in their tribulation."[4]

Sundays and holydays how to be sanctified.
I.

II.

III.

IV.

V.

VI.

VII
VIII

IX.

From what has been said it is easy to perceive, how this commandment may be violated: but the pastor will also deem

Reason ableness of

---

[1] Conc. Agath. c. 47. Aurel. c. 8. Tribur. c. 35. Vide de cons. dist. 1. cap. Missas. et cum ad celebrandas, et omnes fideles.

[2] Aug. de Eccl. dogm. c. 53. et citatur de cons. dist. 2. c. quotidien.

[3] Justin. Apol. 2. et ex Act. Apost. c. 20. 7. Aug. lib. 50. hom. 26. et cit. 1. q. lib. cap. interroga.

[4] James i. 27. Sic faciebant veteres Christiani, test. Just. Apol. 2. Tertull. in Apol. et iu lib. ad martyres et in lib. 2. ad uxorem prope finem.

23*

this commandment

it a duty to impress on the minds of the faithful the conviction, that this commandment is to be observed with pious zeal and the greatest exactitude. To the attainment of this end it will materially conduce, if he make them understand and see clearly, how just and reasonable it is to devote certain days, exclusively, to the worship of God, to acknowledge, adore, and venerate him from whom we have received such innumerable and inestimable blessings.

Note.

Had God commanded us to offer him, on each day of our lives, the tribute of religious worship, would it not be our duty, in return for the inestimable and infinite benefits which his bounty has showered on us, to endeavour to obey the command with promptitude and alacrity? But now that the days specially consecrated to his service are but few in number, is it not as unreasonable as it is criminal to neglect so sacred a duty, or to discharge it with reluctance?[1]

Importance of its observance.
I.

The pastor will next point out the importance of a faithful compliance with this precept. Those who are faithful in its observance are admitted, as it were, into the divine presence, to commune freely with God; for in prayer we contemplate the increated majesty, and hold free converse with the Deity; in hearing religious instruction, we hear the voice of God, which reaches us through that of his pious and zealous minister; and at the Holy Sacrifice of the Mass, we adore Christ the Lord, present on our altars. These are amongst the spiritual advantages, of which a faithful compliance with this commandment

II.

is the pure and plenteous source. But those, who altogether neglect its fulfilment, resist God and his Church: they are enemies of God and of his holy laws; and the facility with which the commandment may be fulfilled is at once a proof and an aggravation of their guilt. We should, it is true, be prepared to undergo the severest labour for sake of God; but in this commandment he imposes on us no labour; he only commands us to disengage ourselves from worldly cares on those days which are to be kept holy. To refuse obedience to this commandment is, therefore, a proof of extreme temerity; and the punishments with which its infraction has been visited should be a salutary admonition to Christians.[2]

Note

In order, therefore, to avoid this guilt and these punishments, we should frequently ponder this word: "Remember," and place before us the important advantages, which, as we have already seen, flow from the religious observance of Sundays and holydays, and also numerous other considerations of the same tendency, which the good and zealous pastor will develope at large to his people as circumstances may require.

[1] Vid. de consecr. dist. 1. et in decret. Titul. de feriis et Conc. Matisc. 2. c. 1. et 37. Tribur. c. 35. Ignat. in p. ad Philip. Leon. serm. 3. de quadrag. Aug. serm. 151. de temp. [2] Num. xv. 32. et seq.

THE FOURTH COMMANDMENT.

"HONOUR THY FATHER AND THY MOTHER, THAT THOU MAYEST BE
LONG-LIVED UPON THE LAND WHICH THE LORD THY GOD WILL
GIVE THEE."[1]

THE preceding commandments, having God as their imme- *Accord-diate* end, take precedence in order as well as in dignity and *ance of this with the* importance; but those which follow, although ultimately referred *preceding* to God as the end contemplated in the love of our neighbour, *command-* have for their immediate object to instruct us in the duty of *ments.* loving our neighbour, and, therefore, deservedly hold the next place. Hence our Lord himself has declared, that these two commandments, which inculcate the love of God and of our neighbour, are like unto each other.[2] The advantages arising from a faithful observance of this commandment can scarcely be expressed in words, bringing with it, as it does, not only its own fruit, and that in the richest abundance and of superior excellence, but also affording a test of the sincerity of our love for God: "He that loveth not his brother whom he seeth," says St. John, "how can he love God whom he seeth not?"[3] In like manner, if we do not honour and reverence our parents whom we see, how can we honour or reverence God, the supreme and best of parents, whom we see not? and hence the obvious analogy and accordance of both commandments.

The application of this commandment is of very great lati- *Extent of* tude: besides our natural parents, there are many others whose *its applica-* power, rank, usefulness, exalted functions, or office, entitle *tion.* them to parental honour. It also lightens the labour of parents and superiors: amongst the duties which devolve on them, the principal one is to mould the lives of those who are placed under their care, according to the maxims of the divine law, and the performance of this duty must be considerably facilitated, if it be universally felt, that to honour parents is an obligation, sanctioned and commanded by no less an authority than that of God himself. To impress the mind with this truth, it will be found useful to distinguish the commandments of the first from those of the second table. This distinction, therefore, the pastor will first explain, and will accordingly teach that the divine precepts of the Decalogue were written on two tables, one of which, in the opinion of the Holy Fathers, contained the three preceding, the other the remain-

[1] Exod. xx. 12.
[2] Matt. xxii. 39. Mark xii. 31. Vid. Aug. in Ps. xxxii. serm. 1. item lib. 3. de doctrin. Christ. c. 10. et lib. 50. hom. 36. D. Thom. 2. 2. quaest. 17. art. 6.
[3] 1 John iv. 20.

Note.

ing seven commandments of the Decalogue.[1] This order of the commandments is very apposite, for by it their nature and object are also distinguished: whatever is commanded or prohibited in Scripture by the divine law springs from one of two principles, the love of God or of our neighbour: and in the discharge of every duty we must be actuated by this love. The three preceding commandments teach us the love which we owe to God, and the other seven, the duties which we owe to domestic and public society. The distinction, therefore, which refers some to the first, others to the second table, is not without good ground: in the three first, God, the supreme good, is, as it were, the subject matter, in the others, the good of our neighbour: the first propose the supreme, the others the proximate object of our love: the first regard the ultimate end, the others those duties which refer to that end.[2]

Difference between the commandments of the first and second tables.

I.

Again, the love of God terminates in God himself, for God is to be loved above all things for his own sake; but the love of our neighbour originates in, and is to be referred to, the love of God. If we love our parents, obey our masters, respect our superiors, our ruling principle in doing so should be, that God is their Creator, and wishes to give pre-eminence to those by whose co-operation he governs and protects all others; and as he requires that we yield a dutiful respect to such persons, we should do so, because he deems them worthy of this honour. If then we honour our parents, the tribute is paid to God rather than to man; and accordingly we read in the tenth chapter of St. Matthew, which, amongst other matters, treats also of duty to superiors; "He that receiveth you, receiveth me;"[3] and the Apostle in his Epistle to the Ephesians, giving instruction to servants, says: "Servants, be obedient to them that are your lords according to the flesh, with fear and trembling, in the simplicity of your heart, as to Christ: not serving to the eye, as it were pleasing men, but as the servants of Christ, doing the will of God from the heart."[4]

II.

Moreover, no honour, no piety, no devotion can be rendered to God, worthy of him towards whom love admits of infinite increase, and hence our charity should become every day more fervent towards him, who commands us to love him "with our

Note.

whole heart, our whole soul, and with all our strength:"[5] but the love of our neighbour has its limits, for we are commanded to love our neighbour as ourselves; and to outstep these limits, by loving him as we love God, were a crime of the blackest enormity. "If any man come to me," says our Lord, "and hate not his father and mother, and wife and children, and

---

[1] Vid. Clem. Alexan. lib. 6. Strom. satis ante finem, Aug. in Exod. q. 71. D. Thom. 1. 2. q. 100. art. 4.

[2] Vid Aug. in Ps. xxxii. serm. 1. D. Thom. 2. 2. q. 122. art. 1 et 2. et in opusc. 7. cap. de primo præcepto.   [3] Matt. x. 40.

[4] Ephes. vi. 5, 6. Vid. Aug. lib. 3. de doct. Christ. c. 12. et lib. 4. Conf. c. 9—12. Prosper. lib. 3. de vita contempl. c. 13. Bernard. de diligendo Deo.

[5] Deut. vi. 5.   Luke x 27.   Matt. xxii. 37—39.

brethren and sisters, yea, and his own life also ; he cannot be my disciple."[1] To him who would first attend the burial of his father, and then follow Christ, our Lord says, to the same effect ; " Let the dead bury their dead ;"[2] and the same lesson of instruction is more clearly conveyed in these words of St. Matthew : " He that loveth father or mother more than me, is not worthy of me."[3] Parents, no doubt, are to be affectionately loved, and highly respected ; but religion requires that supreme honour and homage be given to him alone, who is the sovereign Creator, and universal Father, and that our love for our parents be referred to our eternal Father who is in heaven. Should, however, the injunctions of parents be at any time opposed to the commandments of God, children, are, of course, to prefer the will of God to the desires of their parents, always keeping in view the divine maxim : " We ought to obey God rather than men."[4]

Note.

Having premised this exposition, the pastor will proceed to explain the words of the commandment, beginning with " honour." To " honour" is to think respectfully of any one, and, in every relation in which he may be considered, to hold him in the highest estimation. It includes love, respect, obedience, and reverence, and is here used with great propriety in preference to the word " fear" or " love ;" although parents are also to be much loved and feared. Respect and reverence are not always the accompaniments of love, neither is love the inseparable companion of fear ; but honour, when proceeding from the heart, combines both fear and love.

To " honour," meaning of.

The pastor will next explain who they are, whom the commandment designates as fathers: for although it refers primarily to our natural fathers, yet the word has a secondary meaning ; and, a matter at which we have already glanced, includes, as we know from numerous passages of Scripture, many others who are also entitled to due honour. In the first place, the prelates of the Church, her pastors and clergy, are called fathers, after the example of the Apostle : " I write not these things," says he, " to confound you ; but I admonish you as my dearest children: for if you have ten thousand instructers in Christ ; yet not many fathers; for in Christ Jesus by the Gospel I have begotten you."[5] We also read in Ecclesiasticus : " Let us praise men of renown, and our fathers in their generation."[6] Those who govern the state, to whom are intrusted power, magistracy, or empire, are also called fathers : thus Naaman was called father by his servants.[7] To those, to whose care, fidelity, probity and wisdom, others are committed, such as pastors, instructers, masters, and guardians, is also given the name of father ; and hence the sons of the prophets called Elias[8] and Eliseus[9] by this name. Finally, aged men, whose years entitle them to our respect, we also call fathers. In the

Whom the commandment designates as Fathers.

I.

II.

III.

IV.

V.

1 Luke xiv. 26.   2 Luke ix. 60.   3 Matt. x. 37.   4 Act v. 29.
5 1 Cor. iv. 14—16.   6 Eccl. xliv. 1.   7 4 Kings v. 13   8 4 Kings ii. 12.
9 4 Kings xiii. 14.

Note.

instructions of the pastor, however, it will not be forgotten to enforce particularly the obligation we are under, of honouring all who are entitled to be denominated fathers, especially our natural fathers, of whom the divine commandment particularly speaks. They are, as it were, representatives of the one, great, immortal, and universal Father: in them we behold the image of our own origin: from them we have received existence: them God made use of to impart to us the soul with all its faculties: by them we have been conducted to the sacraments, formed to society, blessed with education, and instructed in purity and holiness of life.[1]

Mothers to be loved and honoured.

The pastor will teach that the name of "mother" is also mentioned in this commandment, and with good reason, awakening in us, as it does, a grateful recollection of the benefits which we have received from her; of the claims which she has to our dutiful affection; of the care and solicitude with which she bore us, the pain and travail with which she brought us forth, and the labour and anxiety with which she watched over our infant years.

Nature of the honour due to parents.

I.

Moreover, the honour which children are commanded to pay to their parents should be the spontaneous offering of sincere and dutiful love. This respectful regard they challenge upon the strongest titles—they who, for love of us, decline no labour, spare no exertion, shrink from no danger; whose highest pleasure it is to indulge in the reflection that they are beloved by their children, the dear objects of their parental solicitude and affection. Joseph, when next to majesty, he enjoyed in Egypt the highest station, and the most ample power, received his father with honour, when he went down into Egypt;[2] Solomon rose to meet his mother as she approached; and having paid her the tribute of filial respect, placed her on a royal throne on his right hand.[3]

II.

We also owe to our parents other duties of respect, such as to supplicate God in their behalf, that they may lead prosperous and happy lives, beloved and esteemed by all who know them,

III.

and most pleasing in the sight of God and of his saints. We also honour them by submission to their wishes and inclinations: "My son," says Solomon, "hear the instruction of thy father, and forsake not the law of thy mother; that grace may be added to thy head, and a chain of gold to thy neck."[4] "Children," says St. Paul, "obey your parents in the Lord, for this is just;"[5] and also, "children, obey your parents in all things, for this is well-pleasing to the Lord."[6] This doctrine is confirmed by the example of those who were most eminent for sanctity: Isaac, when bound for sacrifice by his father, meekly obeyed;[7] and the Rechabites, not to depart from the counsel of

IV.

their fathers, always abstained from wine.[8] We also honour

[1] De officiis filiorum erga parentes vid. Antonium Augustinum lib. 10. tit. 19.
[2] Gen. xlvi.　　[3] 3 Kings ii. 19.　　[4] Proverbs i. 8, 9.
[5] Ephes. vi. 1.　　[6] Col. iii. 20.　　[7] Gen. xxii. 9.
[8] Jerem. xxxv. 6.

our parents by the imitation of their good example: to study the life of another, as a model for imitation, is the highest mark of esteem. We honour them when we not only ask but follow their counsels; and also when we relieve their necessities, supplying them with necessary food and raiment, according to these words of the Redeemer: "why do you also transgress the commandments of God for your tradition? For God said: 'Honour father and mother;' and 'he that shall curse father or mother dying let him die.' But you say; whosoever shall say to father or mother, the gift whatsoever proceedeth from me, shall profit thee; and shalt not honour his father or his mother; and you have made frustrate the commandment of God for your own tradition."[1]

V.
VI.

But if at all times it is our duty to honour our parents, this duty becomes still more imperative, when they are visited by severe illness: we should then pay particular attention to what regards their eternal salvation, taking especial care that they duly receive the last sacraments, consoling them with the frequent conversation of pious and religious persons, who may strengthen their weakness, assist them by their counsel, and animate them to the hope of a glorious immortality; that having risen above the concerns of this world, they may fix their thoughts and affections entirely on God. Thus blessed with the sublime virtues of faith, hope, and charity, and fortified by the sacraments of the Church, they will not only look at death without dismay, for death is the lot of all men; but will hail it as the bright opening to a blessed immortality.

VII.

Finally, we honour our parents when, after they have been summoned from this world, we discharge the last offices of filial piety towards them, giving them an honourable interment, attending to the celebration of their obsequies, their anniversaries, the oblation of the holy sacrifice for the repose of their souls, and faithfully executing their last wills.

VIII.

But we are bound to honour not only our natural parents, but also those who are entitled to be called fathers, such as bishops and priests, kings, princes, and magistrates, tutors, guardians and masters, teachers, aged persons and the like, all of whom are entitled, some in a greater, some in a less degree, to share our love, our obedience, our assistance. Of bishops and other pastors St. Paul says: "Let the priests that rule well be esteemed worthy of double honour, especially they who labour in the word and doctrine."[2] What proofs of ardent love for the Apostle the Galatians must have given may be inferred from the illustrious testimony in which he has recorded their benevolence: "I bear you witness," says he, "that if it could be done, you would have plucked out your own eyes, and would have given them to me."[3] The priest is also entitled to receive

Others who are entitled to the name of father to be honoured.

Bishops and priests how to be honoured.

I.

II.

[1] Matt. xv. 3—6. Subveniendum esse parentibus, vid. Basil. hom. de honore parentum et in Hexam. hom. 9. Amb. lib. 5. Hexam. c. 16. Conc. Gangr. can. 6. Vid. item dist. 86. multis in locis Hier. lib. 2. Commentar. in Matt. Aug. lib. 1. quæst. Evang. cap. 14. [2] 1 Tim. v. 17. [3] Gal. iv. 15

whatever is necessary for his support: "Who," says St. Paul, "serveth as a soldier at his own charges?"[1] "Give honour to the priests," says Ecclesiasticus, "and purify thyself with thy arms; give them their portion, as it is commanded thee, of the first fruits and of purifications."[2] The Apostle also teaches that they are entitled to obedience: "Obey your prelates, and be subject to them; for they watch as being to render an account of your souls."[3] Nay, more, Christ himself commands obedience even to wicked pastors: "Upon the chair of Moses have sitten the Scribes and Pharisees: all things, therefore, whatsoever they shall say to you, observe ye and do ye; but according to their works do ye not, for they say and do not."[4]

The same rule is to regulate our conduct towards princes and magistrates, and all others to whose authority we are subject; and the honour and obedience due to them are explained at large by the Apostle in his Epistle to the Romans:[5] He also commands us to pray for them;[6] and St. Peter says: "Be ye subject therefore to every human creature for God's sake: whether it be to the king as excelling, or to governors as sent by him."[7] The honour which we render them is referred to God: it is paid to their exalted dignity, which is derived from and emblematic of the divine power; and in which we recognise a superintending Providence, who has committed to them the administration of the State, and who makes use of them as the ministers of his power.[8] It is not that we respect the profligacy or wickedness of the man, should such moral turpitude debase the lives of public functionaries—no; we revere the authority of God with which they are invested. Therefore it is, and it may appear to some matter of surprise, that, be their sentiments towards us the most inimical, be their hostility the most immitigable, their personal enmity and hostility do not, however, afford a just cause to release us from the duty of submissive respect to their persons and authority. Thus the Scriptures record the important services rendered by David to Saul, at a time when David was the innocent object of his hatred: "With them that hated peace," says he, "I was peaceable."[9] But should they issue a wicked or unjust mandate, they are on no account to be obeyed: such a mandate is not the legitimate exercise of power, but an act of perverse injustice.

Having expounded these matters severally, the pastor will next consider the nature of the reward promised to the observance of this commandment, and its accordance with the duty of filial piety. It consists principally in length of days: they who always preserve the grateful recollection of a benefit

Side notes:

III.

Note.

Princes and public functionaries to be honoured.

Note.

Princes, when to be obeyed.

When not to be obeyed.

Reward promised to the observance of this commandment.

[1] 1 Cor. ix. 7.
[2] Eccl. vii. 33, 34. Decimas solvendas esse vid. Conc. Aurel. 1. c. 17. Matiscon. 2. c. 5. Forojul. c. ultim. Lat. Magn. c. 36. Trid. sess. 25. c. 13. vid. item multa capita 16. q. 1 et 7. et Tit. decimis in decr. D. Th. 2. 2. q. 87.   [3] Heb. xiii. 17.
[4] Matt. xxiii. 2, 3.   [5] Rom. xiii.   [6] 1 Tim. ii. 2.
[7] 1 Pet. ii. 13, 14.   Vid. Tertull. in Apol. 6. 30 et 32. et ad Scap. c. 2.
[8] Vid. Aug. lib. 5. de civit Dei, c. 10, 11. 14, 15.   [9] Ps. cxix. 7.

deserve to be blessed with its lengthened enjoyment; and this children do, who honour their parents. To those from whom they received existence they gratefully acknowledge the obligation, and are therefore deservedly rewarded with the protracted enjoyment of that existence to an advanced age. The nature of the divine promise also demands explanation: it includes not only the eternal life of the blessed, but also the term of our mortal existence, according to these words of the Apostle: "Godliness is profitable to all things, having promise of the life that now is, and of that which is to come."[1] Many very holy men, it is true, Job,[2] David,[3] Paul,[4] desired to die, and a long life is burdensome to the wretched;[5] but the reward which is here promised is, notwithstanding, neither inconsiderable, nor to be despised. The additional words, "which the Lord thy God will give thee," promise not only length of days, but also repose, tranquillity, security, which render life happy; for in Deuteronomy it is not only said, "that thou mayest live a long time;" but it is also added, "and that it may be well with thee;"[6] words which the Apostle repeats in his Epistle to the Ephesians.[7]

These blessings, we say, are conferred on those only, on whose piety God really deems it a reward to bestow them, otherwise the divine promises would not be fulfilled. The more dutiful child is sometimes the more short-lived; either because his interests are best consulted by summoning him from this world, before he has strayed from the path of virtue and of duty, according to these words of the Wise man: "He was taken away lest wickedness should alter his understanding, or deceit beguile his soul;"[8] or because, when the gathering storm threatens to burst upon society, carrying anarchy and ruin in its desolating career, he is called from the troubled scene, in order to escape the universal calamity. Thus, when God avenges the crimes of mortals, his virtue and salvation are secured against the dangers to which they might otherwise have been exposed; or else, he is spared the bitter anguish of witnessing the calamities of which, in such melancholy times, his friends and relations might become the victims. "The just man," says the Prophet, "is taken away from before the face of evil."[9] The premature death of the good, therefore, gives just reason to apprehend the approach of calamitous days.

But, if Almighty God holds forth rewards to remunerate filial dutifulness, he also reserves the heaviest chastisements to punish filial ingratitude and impiety: it is written: "He that curseth his father or mother shall die the death:"[10] "he that afflicteth his father and chaseth away his mother, is infamous and unhappy:"[11] "he that curseth his father and mother, his lamp shall be put out in the midst of darkness;"[12] "the eye that mocketh at his father, and that despiseth the labour of his mother

[margin notes:]
This reward not always conferred on dutiful children, and why.
I.
II.
III.
Note.
Punishment of its violation.

---

[1] 1 Tim. iv. 8. [2] Job iii.   [3] Ps. cxix. 5.   [4] Phil. ii. 17.
[5] 2 Cor. v. 2.   [6] Deut. v. 16.   [7] Eph. vi. 3.   [8] Wisd. iv. 10, 11.
[9] Isa. lvii. 1.   [10] Exod. xxi. 17. Lev. xx. 9.   [11] Prov. xix. 26.   [12] Prov. xx. 20.

24

in bearing him, let the ravens of the brooks pick it out, and the young eagles eat it."[1] There are on record many instances of undutiful children, who were made the signal objects of the divine vengeance. The disobedience of Absalom to his father

David did not go unpunished: he perished miserably: three lances transfixed his body.[2] But of those who resist the spiritual authority of the priest it is written: "He that will be proud, and refuse to obey the commandment of the priest who ministereth at that time to the Lord thy God, by the decree of the judge that man shall die."[3]

Duties of parents towards their children.
As, then, the law of God commands children to honour their parents and render them an obsequious obedience, so are there reciprocal duties which parents owe to their children, to bring them up in the knowledge and the practice of religion, and to give them the best precepts for the regulation of their lives; that instructed in the truths of religion, and prepared to make these truths the guiding principles of their conduct through life, they may preserve inviolate their fidelity to God, and serve him in holiness. This duty of parents is beautifully illustrated in the conduct of the parents of the chaste Susanna.[4] The pastor, therefore, will admonish parents to be to their children models of the virtues, which it is their duty to inculcate, of justice, chastity, modesty, and, in a word, of every Christian virtue.

Three things to be avoided by parents.
I.
He will also admonish them to guard particularly against three things, in which they but too often transgress.—In the first place, they are not by words or actions to exercise too much harshness towards their children: this is the instruction of St. Paul in his Epistle to the Colossians: "Fathers," says he, "provoke not your children to indignation, lest they be discouraged."[5] Parental severity may, it is to be apprehended, break the spirit of the child, and render him abject and timid, afraid of every thing, and is therefore to be deprecated: instead of indulging intemperate passion, the parent should reprove in the spirit of parental correction, not of revenge.

II.
Should a fault be committed which requires reproof and chastisement, the parent should not, on the other hand, by an unseasonable indulgence, overlook its correction: children often become depraved by too much lenity and indulgence; and the pastor, therefore, will deter from such criminal weakness, by the warning example of Heli, who, in the misguided fondness of a father's feelings, forgot his duty to religion, and was in consequence visited with the heaviest chastisements.[6]

III.
Finally, in the instruction and education of their children, let them not follow the pernicious example of many parents, whose sole concern it is to leave their children wealth, riches, an ample and splendid fortune; who stimulate them not to piety and religion, or to honourable and virtuous pursuits, but to avarice, and an increase of wealth;

---

[1] Prov. xxx. 17.   [2] Kings xviii. 14.
[3] Deut. xvii. 12.—Vid. Clem. epist. 3. sub init. item ep. 1. etiam sub init. Ambr lib. 1. 2. offic. c. 24. Hieron. epist 1. post med. vid. item 11. q. 3. c. 11—13.
[4] Dan. xiii. 3.   [5] Col. iii. 21.   [6] 1 Kings ii. 3, 4.

and who, provided their children are rich and wealthy, are regardless of those qualities which would render them truly estimable, and secure their eternal salvation. Language cannot express, nor can thought conceive, any thing to exceed in turpitude the criminal conduct of such parents, of whom it is true to say, that instead of bequeathing wealth to their children, they leave them rather their own wickedness and crimes for an inheritance; and instead of conducting them to heaven, lead them to perdition. The pastor therefore will impress on the minds of parents salutary principles for the guidance of their conduct, and will excite them to imitate the virtuous example of Tobias;[1] that having thus trained up their children to the service of God, and to holiness of life, they may, in turn, experience at their hands abundant fruit of filial affection, respect, and obedience.

THE FIFTH COMMANDMENT.

"THOU SHALT NOT KILL."[2]

THE great happiness proposed to the peacemakers, of being called "the children of God," should prove a powerful excitement to animate the zeal of the pastor in explaining with diligent accuracy the obligations imposed by this commandment. No means more efficacious can be adopted to promote peace and harmony amongst mankind, than the due and holy and universal observance of the law announced by this commandment, if properly explained. Then might we hope that, united in the strictest bonds of union, mankind would live in perfect peace and concord. The necessity of explaining this commandment to the faithful is evinced by two considerations. Immediately after the earth was overwhelmed in universal deluge, the first prohibition issued by the Almighty was, that man should not imbrue his hands in the blood of his fellow man: "I will require the blood of your lives," says he, "at the hand of every beast, and at the hand of man."[3] In the next place, amongst the precepts of the Old Law expounded by our Lord, this commandment holds the first place, as may be seen by consulting the fifth chapter of St. Matthew, where the Redeemer says: "It has been said thou shalt not kill," &c.[4] The faithful should also hear with willing attention the exposition of a commandment, the observance of which must be the security of their own lives: these words, "Thou shalt not kill," emphatically forbid the shedding of human blood; and they

Utility and necessity of explaining this commandment.

Note.

---

[1] Tob. iv. [2] Exod. xx. 13. [3] Gen ix. 5. [4] Matt. v. 21.

should be heard by all with the same pleasure as if God, expressly naming each individual, were to prohibit injury to be offered him under a threat of the divine anger, and the heaviest chastisement of the divine wrath. As, then, the announcement of this commandment must be heard with pleasure, so should its observance be to us a pleasing duty.

Its obligation twofold; prohibitory, and mandatory.

In its development our Lord himself points out its twofold obligation; the one forbidding to kill, the other commanding us to cherish sentiments of charity, concord, and friendship towards our enemies, to have peace with all men, and finally, to endure with patience every inconvenience which the unjust aggression of others may inflict. With regard to the prohibitory part of the commandment, the pastor will first point out the limits which restrict the prohibition. - In the first place, we are not prohibited to kill those animals which are intended to be the food of man: if so intended by Almighty God, it must be lawful for us to exercise this jurisdiction over them. "When," says St. Augustine, "we hear the words ' thou shalt not kill,' we are not to understand the prohibition to extend to the fruits of the earth which are insensible, nor to irrational animals, which form no part of the great society of mankind."[1]

Exceptions to the first.
I.

II.

Again, this prohibition does not apply to the civil magistrate, to whom is intrusted power of life and death, by the legal and judicious exercise of which he punishes the guilty and protects the innocent. The use of the civil sword, when wielded by the hand of justice, far from involving the crime of murder, is an act of paramount obedience to this commandment which prohibits murder. The end of the commandment is the preservation and security of human life, and to the attainment of this end the punishments inflicted by the civil magistrate, who is the legitimate avenger of crime, naturally tend, giving security to life by repressing outrage and violence. Hence these words of David: "In the morning I put to death all the wicked of the land; that I might cut off all the workers of iniquity from the city of the Lord."[2] In like manner, the soldier is guiltless who, actuated not by motives of ambition or cruelty, but by a pure desire of serving the interests of his country, takes away the life of an enemy in a just war.[3] There are on record instances of carnage executed by the special command of God himself: the sons of Levi, who had put to death so many thousands in one day, were guilty of no sin: when the slaughter had ceased, they were addressed by Moses in these words: "you have consecrated your hands this day to the Lord."[4]

III.

IV.

V.

Death, when caused by accident, not by intent or design, is not murder: "He that killed his neighbour ignorantly," says

---

[1] De civit. Dei. lib. 1. c. 20. item de morib. Manich. lib. 2. c. 13—15.

[2] Ps. c. 8. Aug. epist. 154. et citat. 23. q. 5. cap. de occidendis. item epist. 54 et citatur ibid. cap. non est iniquitatis. Vide adhuc ibid. alia capita et D. Thom. 2. 2. q. 64. a. 2. et q. 108. a. 3.

[3] Aug. de civit. Dei.-c. 26. citatus 23. q. 5. cap. miles. Vide item de bello D. Thom. 2. 2. q. 40. per 4. art.　　　　[4] Exod. xxxii. 29.

the book of Deuteronomy, " and who is proved to have had no hatred against him yesterday, and the day before, but to have gone with him to the wood, to hew wood, and in cutting down the tree, the axe slipt out of his hand, and the iron slipping from the handle struck his friend and killed him, shall live."[1] Such accidental deaths, because inflicted without intent or design, involve no guilt whatever, and in this we are fortified by the opinion of St. Augustine : " God forbid," says he, " that what we do for a good or lawful end should be imputed to us, if, contrary to our intention, evil accrue to any one."[2] There are, however, two cases in which guilt attaches to accidental death : the one, when it is the consequence of an unlawful act ; when, for instance, a person strikes a woman in a state of pregnancy, and abortion follows. The consequence, it is true, may not have been intended, but this does not exculpate the offender, because the act was in itself unlawful. The other case is, when death is caused by negligence, incaution, or want of due circumspection.

Two cases in which guilt attaches to accidental death.

If a man kill another in self-defence, having used every precaution consistent with his own safety to avoid the infliction of death, he evidently does not violate this commandment.

VI.

These are the instances in which human blood may be shed without the guilt of murder ; and with these exceptions the precept binds universally with regard to the person who kills, the person killed, and the means used to kill. As to the person who kills, the commandment recognises no exception whatever, be he rich or powerful, master or parent : all, without exception of person or distinction of rank, are forbidden to kill. With regard to the person killed, the obligation of the law is equally extensive, embracing every human creature ; there is no individual, however humble or lowly his condition, whose life is not shielded by this law. It also forbids suicide. No man possesses such absolute jurisdiction over himself as to be at liberty to put a period to his own existence ; and hence we find that the commandment does not say, " thou shalt not kill another," but simply, " Thou shalt not kill." Finally, if we consider the numerous means by which murder may be committed, the law admits of no exception : not only does it forbid to take away the life of another by laying violent hands on him, by means of a sword, a dagger, a stone, a stick, a halter, or by administering poison ; but also strictly prohibits the accomplishment of the death of another by counsel, assistance, or any other means of co-operation.

With these exceptions, the prohibitory part, universal in its obligation, with regard to the person who kills, the person killed, and the means used to kill. Note.

The Jews, with singular dulness of apprehension, thought that to abstain from shedding human blood was enough to satisfy the obligation imposed by this commandment. But the Christian, who, instructed by the interpretation of Jesus Christ, has learned that the precept is spiritual, and that it commands

Prohibits not only murder but anger.

[1] Deut. xix.
[2] Vide Aug. epist. 154. et citatur 23. q. 5. c. de occidendis. Item vide multa capita dist. 5. D. Thom. 2. 2. q. 64. a. 8. Trid. Sess. 14. de reform. c. 7.

us not only to keep our hands unstained, but our hearts pure and undefiled, will not deem such a compliance sufficient: him the Gospel has taught, that it is unlawful even to be angry with a brother: " But I say to you that whosoever is angry with his brother shall be in danger of judgment; and whosoever shall say to his brother, Raca, shall be in danger of a council; and whosoever shall say, thou fool, shall be guilty of the hell of fire."[1] From these words it clearly follows that he who is angry with his brother, although he may conceal his resentment, is not exempt from sin; that he who gives indication of that anger sins grievously; and that he who dreads not to treat his brother with harshness, and to utter contumelious reproaches against him, sins still more grievously.[2]

Anger, when lawful. This, however, is to be understood of cases in which no just cause of anger exists. To animadvert on those who are placed under our authority, when they commit a fault, is an occasion of anger, which God and his laws permit; but even in these circumstances the anger of a Christian should be the dictate of duty, not the impulse of passion, for we should be temples of the Holy Ghost, in which Jesus Christ may dwell.[3] Our Lord has left us many other lessons of instruction which regard the perfect observance of this law, such as " not to resist evil; but if one strike thee on thy right cheek, turn to him also the other; and to him that will contend with thee in judgment, and take away thy coat, let go thy cloak also unto him; and whosoever will free thee one mile, go with him other two."[4]

Remedies against the violation of this commandment. From what has been already said, it is easy to perceive how propense man is to those sins which are prohibited by this commandment, and how many are guilty of murder, if not in fact, at least in desire. As then the sacred Scriptures prescribe remedies for so dangerous a disease, to spare no pains in making them known to the faithful becomes an obvious duty of the pastor. Of these remedies the most efficacious is to form a just conception of the wickedness of him who imbrues his hands in the blood of his fellow-man. The enormity of this sin is set forth by attestations of Holy Scripture as strong as they are numerous. In the inspired Volume God pours out the deepest execrations against the murderer, declares that of the very beast of the field he will exact vengeance for the life of man, commanding the beast that sheds human blood to be put to death.[5]

I.

Note.

II. And if the Almighty commanded man to abstain from the use of blood, he did so for no other reason than to impress on his mind the obligation of entirely refraining, both in act and desire, from the enormity of shedding human blood. The murderer is the worst enemy of his species, and consequently of nature: to the utmost of his power, he destroys the universal work

[1] Matt. v. 22.—De ira vide Basil. hom. 10. Chrysost. hom. 29. ad pop. Antioch. D. Thom. 22. quaest. 108. per totam.
[2] Vide Aug. de serm. Dom. in monte, lib. 1. D. Thom. 2. 2. q. 158. a. 3.
[3] 1 Cor. vi. 19.
[4] Matt. v. 39. Vide Aug. epist. 5. ad Mar. et de serm. Domini in monte, lib. 2. c. 20.   [5] Gen. ix. 5, 6.

of God by the destruction of man, for whose sake God declares that he created all things: nay, as it is prohibited in Genesis to take away human life, because God created man to his own image and likeness, he, therefore, who destroys his image offers great injury to God, and seems, as it were, to lay violent hands on God himself! David, with a mind illumined from above, deeply impressed with the enormity of such guilt, characterizes the sanguinary in these words: "Their feet are swift to shed blood."[1] He does not simply say, "they kill," but, "they shed blood;" words which serve to set that execrable crime in its true light, and to mark emphatically the barbarous cruelty of the murderer. With a view also to describe energetically how the murderer is precipitated by the impulse of the devil into the commission of such an enormity, he says: "Their feet are swift." *Note.*

But the tendency of the injunctions of Christ our Lord, regarding the observance of this commandment, is, that we have peace with all men. Interpreting the commandment he says: "If therefore thou offer thy gift at the altar, and there thou rememember that thy brother hath aught against thee; leave there thy offering, and go first to be reconciled to thy brother; and then coming thou shalt offer thy gift," &c.[2] In unfolding the spirit of this admonition, the pastor will show that it inculcates the duty of cherishing charitable feelings towards all without exception, feelings to which, in his exposition of this commandment, he will exhort with the most earnest solicitude, evincing, as they do most effectually, the virtue of fraternal charity. It will not be doubted that hatred is forbidden by this commandment, for, "whosoever hateth his brother is a murderer;"[3] from this principle it follows as an evident consequence, that the commandment also inculcates charity and love; and inculcating charity and love it must also enjoin all those duties and good offices which follow in their train. "Charity is patient," says St. Paul;[4] we are therefore commanded patience, in which, as the Redeemer teaches, "we shall possess our souls."[5] "Charity is kind;"[6] beneficence is, therefore, her companion and hand-maid. The virtue of beneficence is one of very great latitude: its principal offices are to relieve the wants of the poor, to feed the hungry, to give drink to the thirsty, to clothe the naked; and in all these acts of beneficence we should proportion our liberality to the wants and necessities of their objects. *Mandatory part of the commandment, inculcates charity to all men.*

And also the duties of charity.

I.

II

These works of beneficence and goodness, in themselves exalted, become still more illustrious when done towards an enemy, in accordance with the command of the Saviour: "Love your enemies, do good to them that hate you:"[7] "If thine enemy be hungry," says St. Paul, "give him to eat: if he thirst, give him to drink; for doing this, thou shalt heap coals of fire on his head. Be not overcome by evil, but overcome *III.*

[1] Ps. xiii. 5.   [2] Matt. v. 24.   [3] 1 John iii. 15.
[4] 1 Cor. xiii. 4.   [5] Luke xxi. 19.   [6] 1 Cor. xiii. 4.
[7] Matt. v. 44.

evil by good."[1] Finally, if we consider the law of charity,
which is " kind," we shall be convinced that to practise the
good offices of mildness, clemency, and other kindred virtues,
is a duty prescribed by that law.

But a duty of pre-eminent excellence, and that, too, which
is the fullest expression of charity, and to the practice of which
we should most habituate ourselves, is to pardon and forgive
from the heart the injuries which we may have received from
others. To a full and faithful compliance with this duty the
Sacred Scriptures, as we have already observed, frequently
admonish and exhort, not only pronouncing those who do so
"blessed," but also declaring that, whilst to the sinner, who
neglects or refuses to comply with this precept, pardon is
denied by the Almighty, it is extended to him who discharges
this duty of charity towards an offending brother.[2] But, as
the desire of revenge is almost natural to fallen man, it becomes necessary for the pastor to exert his utmost diligence
not only to instruct but also earnestly to persuade the faithful,
that a Christian should forget and forgive injuries ; and as this
is a duty frequently inculcated by theological writers, he will
consult them on the subject, and furnish himself with the
cogent and appropriate arguments urged by them, in order to
be enabled to subdue the pertinacity of those, whose minds are
obstinately bent on revenge.[3]

Three con-
siderations
to enforce
forgiveness
of injuries.
I.

The three following considerations, however, demand particular attention and exposition.—First, to use every effort to
persuade him, who conceives himself injured, that the man of
whom he desires to be revenged, was not the principal cause
of the loss sustained or of the injury inflicted. This is exemplified in the conduct of that admirable man, Job: when
violently assailed by men and demons, by the Labeans, the
Chaldeans, and by Satan, without at all directing his attention
to them, as a righteous and holy man he exclaimed with no
less truth than piety: " The Lord gave, the Lord hath taken
away."[4] The words and the example of that man of patience
should, therefore, convince Christians, and the conviction is
most just, that whatever chastisements we endure in this life
come from the hand of God, the fountain of all justice and
mercy. He chastises us not as enemies, but, in his infinite
goodness, corrects us as children. To view the matter in its
true light, men, in these cases, are nothing more than the ministers and agents of God. One man, it is true, may foster the
worst feelings towards another: he may harbour the most
malignant hatred against him ; but, without the permission of
God, he can do him no injury. Hence Joseph patiently endured the wicked counsels of his brethren,[5] and David the

---

[1] Rom. xii. 20.

[2] Vide Deut. xxxii. 35. item 1 Reg. 25. 32, 33. item 26. 6. 7 8. 9. item 2 Reg. 19.
20. Ps. 7. 5. Eccl. xxviii. per totum. Isa. lviii. 6. Matt. vi. 14. et in Evangelio
passim. Vide item Tertul. in Apol. c. 31 et 37. Aug. in Joan tract. 81. lib. 50. hom.
Hom. 6. item ser. 61 et 169. de temp

[3] Vid. quæ citantur numero 18.   [4] Job i. 21.   [5] Gen. xlv. 5.

injuries inflicted on him by Semei.[1] To this also applies an
argument which St. Chrysostome has ably and learnedly
handled : it is that no man is injured but by himself.[2] Let the
man, who considers himself injured by another, consider the
matter calmly and dispassionately, and he will feel the justness
of the observation : he may, it is true, have experienced injury
from external causes ; but he is himself his greatest enemy, by
wickedly contaminating his soul with hatred, malevolence, and
envy.

    The second consideration to be explained by the pastor em-   II.
braces two advantages, which are the special rewards of those,
who, influenced by a holy desire to please God, freely forgive
injuries. In the first place, God has promised that he who
forgives shall himself obtain forgiveness ;[3] a promise which
proves how acceptable to God is this duty of piety. In the
next place, the forgiveness of injuries ennobles and perfects
our nature ; for by it man is, in some degree, assimilated to
God, " who maketh his sun to shine on the good and the bad,
and raineth upon the just and the unjust."[4]

    Finally, the disadvantages which arise from the indulgence   III.
of revenge are to be explained. The pastor will place before
the eyes of the unforgiving man a truth which has the sanction
of experience, that hatred is not only a grievous sin, but also
that a continued habit of indulgence renders it inveterate. The
man, in whose heart this passion has once taken deep root,
thirsts for the blood of his enemy : day and night he longs for
revenge : continually agitated by this perverse passion, his mind
seems never to repose from malignant projects, or even from
thoughts of blood ; and thus phrensied by hatred, never, or at
least not without extreme difficulty, can he be induced generously to pardon an offending brother, or even to mitigate his
hostility towards him. Justly, therefore, is revenge compared
to a festering wound, from which the weapon has never been
extracted.

    There are also many evil consequences, many sins which
follow in the train of this gloomy passion. Hence these words
of St. John : " He that hateth his brother is in darkness and
walketh in darkness, and knoweth not whither he goeth, because the darkness hath blinded his eyes."[5] He must therefore
frequently fall ; for how, possibly, can any one view in a
favourable light the words or actions of him whom he hates ?
Hence arise rash and unjust judgments, anger, envy, deprecia-
tion of character and other evils of the same sort, in which
are often involved those who are connected by ties of friendship
or blood ; and thus does it frequently happen that this one sin
is the prolific source of many.

    Hatred has been denominated " the sin of the devil," and Hatred de-
not without good reason : the devil was a murderer from the nominated
                                                    "the sin of
                                                    the devil."

[1] 2 Kings xvi. 10.
[2] Tom. 3. in hom. quod nemo læditur nisi a seipso.
[3] Matt. xviii. 33.   [4] Matt. v. 48.   [5] 1 John ii. 11.

beginning; and hence our Lord Jesus Christ, the Son of God, when the Pharisees sought his life, said, that " they were begotten of their father the devil."[1]

Remedies against hatred.
I.

But besides the reason already adduced, which afford good grounds for detesting this sin, other and most efficacious remedies are prescribed in the pages of inspiration; and of these remedies the first and greatest is the example of the Redeemer, which we should set before our eyes as a model for imitation. When scourged with rods, crowned with thorns, and finally nailed to a cross, he, in whom even suspicion of fault could not be found, " the sprinkling of whose blood speaketh better than that of Abel,"[2] poured out his last breath a prayer for his executioners: " Father," says he, " forgive them, for they know not what they do."[3]

II.

Another remedy prescribed by Ecclesiasticus is to call to mind death and judgment: " Remember thy last end, and thou shalt never sin;"[4] as if he had said: frequently and again and again reflect that you must soon die, and, as at the hour of death you will have occasion to invoke the infinite mercy of God, his pardon and peace, you should now, and at all times, place that awful hour before your eyes, in order to extinguish within you the consuming fire of revenge; for, than the forgiveness of injuries and the love of those who may have injured you or yours, in word or deed, you can discover no means better adapted, none more efficacious to obtain the mercy of God.

THE SIXTH COMMANDMENT.

" THOU SHALT NOT COMMIT ADULTERY."[5]

Order in which this commandment occurs, propriety of.

As the bond which subsists between man and wife is one of strictest union, nothing can be more gratifying to both than to know that they are objects of mutual and undivided affection; and as, on the other hand, nothing inflicts deeper anguish than the alienation of the legitimate love which they owe to each other, this commandment, which prohibits concubinage and adultery, follows with propriety, and in order, that which protects human life against the hand of the murderer. It prohibits to violate or sunder, by the crime of adultery, the holy and honourable union of marriage, a union which is generally the source of ardent affection and love.

John viii. 44.   [2] Luke xxiii. 34.   [3] Heb. xii. 24.
[4] Eccl. vii. 40.   [5] Exod. xx. 14.

In the exposition of this commandment, the pastor has oc- Extreme
cautiou
and pru-
dence ne-
cessary in
the exposi-
tion of this
command-
ment. casion for extreme caution and prudence, and should treat with great delicacy a subject which requires brevity rather than copiousness of exposition; for there is great reason to apprehend, that by detailing too diffusely the variety of ways in which men depart from the observance of this law, he may perhaps light upon those things, which, instead of extinguishing, serve rather to inflame corrupt passion. As however the precept contains many things which cannot be passed over in silence, the pastor will explain them in their proper order and place.

This commandment, then, resolves itself into two heads; the Resolves
itself into
two heads.
First head. one expressed, which prohibits adultery; the other implied, which inculcates purity of mind and body.[1] To begin with the prohibitory part of the commandment, adultery is the defilement of the lawful bed, whether it be one's own or another's: if a married man have criminal intercourse with an unmarried woman, he violates the integrity of his marriage bed; and if an unmarried man have intercourse with a married woman, he defiles the sanctity of the marriage bed of another.

But that every species of licentiousness and every violation Prohibits
every vio-
lation of
chastity. of chastity are included in this prohibition of adultery, is proved by the concurrent testimonies of St. Augustine and St. Ambrose,[2] and that such is the spirit of the commandment is an inference borne out by the authority of the Old as well as of the New Testament. In the writings of Moses, besides adultery, other sins against chastity are punished: the book of Genesis records the judgment of Judah against his daughter-in-law:[3] "that there should be no harlot amongst the daughters of Israel," is an excellent law of Moses, found in Deuteronomy:[4] "Take heed to keep thyself, my son, from all fornication,"[5] is the exhortation of Tobias to his son; and in Ecclesiasticus we read: "Be ashamed of looking upon a harlot."[6] In the Gospel, too, Christ the Lord says: "From the heart came forth adulteries and fornications, which defile a man;"[7] and the Apostle Paul expresses his detestation of this crime frequently, and in the strongest terms: "This," says he, "is the will of God, your sanctification; that you should abstain from fornication:"[8] "Fly fornication:"[9] "Keep not company with fornicators."[10] "Fornication, and all uncleanness and covetousness, let it not so much as be named among you, as becometh saints:"[11] "Neither fornicators, nor adulterers, nor the effeminate, nor liers

---

[1] Vide 32. q. 4. c. meretrices; item ibid. multa alia capita; item Amb. de Abraham. c. 4. Hier. contr. Jovin. lib. 1. et 2. item in cap. 5. epist. ad Gal. ad illa verba, manifest. autem; item in c. 5. ad Ephes. ad hæc verba, viri! diligite; Aug. de bono conjug. c. 16 et lib. 22. contra Faust. cap. 47, 48. item in quæst. Deut. q. 37. ad cap 23. iterum Amb. in seam. de St. Joan. qui sic incip. diximus superiore Dominica est, 65. item. Greg. in moral. lib. 12. c. 21. D. Thom. 1. 2. q. 100. a. 5. et 2. 2. q. 122. a. 6.

[2] Amb. lib. 1. officior. 1. c. 50. in fine. Aug. quæs. 71. super Exod.

[3] Gen. xxxviii. 14. [4] Deut. xxiii. 17. [5] Tob. iv. 13.

[6] Eccl. xli. 35. [7] Matt. xvi. 19. [8] 1 Thess. iv. 3.

[9] 1 Cor. vi. 18. [10] 1 Cor. v. 9. [11] Eph. v. 3.

Note.

with mankind shall possess the kingdom of God."[1] But adultery is thus strictly forbidden, because to the turpitude common alike to it and to other excesses it adds the sin of injustice, not only against our neighbour, but also against civil society. Certain it also is, that he, who abstains not from other sins against chastity, will easily fall into the crime of adultery. By the prohibition of adultery, therefore, we at once see that every sort of immodesty, impurity, and defilement is prohibited; nay that every inward thought against chastity is forbidden by this commandment is clear, as well from the very force of the law, which is evidently spiritual, as also from these words of Christ our Lord: "But I say to you, that whosoever shall see a woman to lust after her, hath already committed adultery with her in his heart."[2]

Admonition to the pastor.

This is the outline of those things which we have deemed proper matter for public instruction: to it, however, the pastor will add the decrees of the holy Synod of Trent against adulterers, and those who keep harlots and concubines;[3] omitting many other species of immodesty and lust, of which each individual is to be admonished privately, as circumstances of time and person may require.

Second head.

We now come to explain the positive part of the precept. The faithful are to be taught, and earnestly exhorted, to cultivate with zealous assiduity, continence and chastity, "to cleanse themselves from all defilements of the flesh and of the spirit, perfecting sanctification in the fear of God."[4] The virtue of chastity, it is true, shines with a brighter lustre in those who, with holy and religious fidelity, lead a life of perpetual continency: an ordinance in itself admirable, in its origin divine: yet it is a virtue which belongs also to those who lead a life of celibacy; or who, in the married state, preserve themselves pure and undefiled from unlawful desire. The Holy Fathers have delivered many important lessons of instruction, which teach to subdue the passions, and to restrain sinful pleasure: the pastor, therefore, will make it his study to explain them accurately to the faithful, and will use the utmost diligence in their exposition.[5]

Remedies against the violation of this commandment. I.

Of these instructions some relate to thoughts, some to actions. The remedy prescribed against sins of thought consists in our forming a just conception of the turpitude and evil of this crime; and this knowledge will lead more easily to the considerations which prompt to its detestation. The evil of this crime we may learn from this reflection alone; by its commission, the perpetrator is banished and excluded from the kingdom of God; an evil which exceeds all others in magnitude. This calamity is, it is true, common to every mortal sin; but to this sin it is peculiar, that fornicators are said to sin against their own bodies, according to the words of St.

II.

---

[1] 1 Cor. vi. 9. [2] Matt. v. 27, 28.
[3] Sess. 24. c. 24. de reform. [4] 2 Cor. vii. 1.
[5] Vid. D. Thom. 2. 2. q. 151. Trid. 24. de matrim. c. 3. et sess. 25. de regular.

Paul: "Fly fornication: every sin that a man doth is without the body; but he that committeth fornication, sinneth against his own body."[1] The reason is, that, by violating its sanctity, he does an injury to his own body; and hence the Apostle writing to the Thessalonians says: "This is the will of God, your sanctification; that you should abstain from fornication, that every one of you should know how to possess his vessel in sanctification and honour; not in the passion of lust, like the Gentiles that know not God."[2] Again, it is an aggravation of the sinner's guilt, that by the foul crime of fornication, the Christian makes the members of Christ the members of an harlot, according to these words of St. Paul: "Know you not that your bodies are the members of Christ? Shall I then take the members of Christ and make them the members of an harlot? God forbid; or know you not, that he who is joined to an harlot is made one body?"[3] Moreover, a Christian, as St. Paul testifies, is "the temple of the Holy Ghost;"[4] and to violate this temple, what is it but to expel the Holy Ghost?

III.

IV.

But the crime of adultery involves that of grievous injustice. If, as the Apostle says, they who are joined in wedlock are so subject to each other, that neither has power or right over his or her body, but both are bound, as it were, by a mutual bond of subjection, the husband to accommodate himself to the will of the wife, the wife to the will of the husband; most certainly if either dissociate his or her person, which is the right of the other, from him or her to whom it is bound, the offender is guilty of an act of flagrant injustice, and of a grievous crime.[5]

Adultery a grievous injustice.

As dread of infamy strongly stimulates to the performance of duty, and deters from the commission of crime, the pastor will also teach that adultery brands its guilty perpetrators with an indelible stigma: "He that is an adulterer," says Solomon, "for the folly of his heart shall destroy his own soul: he gathereth to himself shame and dishonour, and his reproach shall not be blotted out."[6]

Brands the adulterer with infamy.

The grievousness of the sin of adultery may be easily inferred from the severity of its punishment. According to the law promulgated by God in the Old Testament, the adulterer was condemned to be stoned to death;[7] and even for the criminal passion of one man, (the facts are recorded in the inspired Volume) not only the perpetrators of the crime, but also, as we read with regard to the Sichemites,[8] sometimes the inhabitants of an entire city have been destroyed. The Sacred Scriptures abound with examples of the divine vengeance invoked by such crimes; such as the destruction of Sodom and of the neighbouring cities,[9] the punishment of the Israelites who committed fornication in the wilderness with the daughters of Moab,[10] and

Its grievousness may be inferred from the severity of its punishment.
I.

---

1 1 Cor. vi. 18.   2 1 Thess. iv. 3—5.   3 1 Cor. vi. 15, 16.
4 1 Cor. vi. 19.   5 1 Cor. vii. 4.   6 Prov. vi. 32.
7 Levit. xx. 10. John viii. 5.   8 Gen. xxxiv. 25.   9 Gen. xix. 24.
10 Num. xxv. 4.

the slaughter of the Benjamites ;[1] examples which the pastor will adduce to deter from similar enormities.

II.   The punishment of death may not, it is true, always await such criminality ; but it does not therefore always escape the visitations of the divine wrath. The mind of the adulterer is frequently a prey to agonizing torture : blinded by his own infatuation, the heaviest chastisement with which sin can be visited, he is lost to all regard for God, for reputation, for hónour, for family, and even for life ; and thus, utterly abandoned and useless, he is undeserving of confidence in any matter of moment, and incompetent to the discharge of duty of any sort. Of this we find signal examples in the persons of David and of Solomon. David had no sooner fallen into the crime of adultery than he degenerated into a character the very reverse of what he had been before ; from the mildest of men becoming a monster of cruelty, and consigning to death Urias, a man who had deserved well of him ;[2] whilst Solomon, having abandoned himself to the lust of women, abandoned the true religion, to follow strange gods.[3] This sin, therefore, as Osee observes, plucks out the heart, and often blinds the understanding.[4]

Remedies against the concupiscence of the flesh.

I.   We now come to the remedies which are applicable to this moral disease.—The first is studiously to avoid idleness : for, according to Ezekiel, it was by yielding themselves up to its enervating influence, that the Sodomites plunged into all the turpitude of the most base and criminal lust.[5] In the next place,

II.   intemperance in eating and drinking is carefully to be avoided : "I fed them to the full," says the prophet, "and they committed adultery."[6] Repletion and satiety beget lust, as our Lord intimates in these words : "Take heed to yourselves, lest perhaps your hearts be overcharged with surfeiting and drunkenness ;"[7] "Be not drunk with wine," says St. Paul, "wherein

III.   is luxury."[8] But the eyes, in particular, are the inlets to criminal passion, and to this refer these words of our Lord ; "If thine eye scandalize thee, pluck it out, and cast it from thee."[9] The prophets, also, frequently speak to the same effect : "I made a covenant with mine eyes," says Job, "that I would not so much as think upon a virgin."[10] Finally, there are on record innumerable examples of the evils which have their origin in the concupiscence of the eyes : to it we trace the fall of David ;[11] the king of Sichem fell a victim to its seductive influence ;[12] and the elders, who became the false accusers of the chaste Susanna, afford a melancholy example of its baneful effects.[13]

IV   Too much ornamental elegance of dress, which solicits the eye, is but too frequently an occasion of sin ; and hence the

[1] Judges xx.   [2] 2 Kings xi. and xii.   [3] 3 Kings xi.
[4] Osee iv. 11.   [5] Ezek. xvi. 49.   [6] Jerem. v. 7.
[7] Luke xxi. 31.   [8] Ephes. v. 18.   [9] Matt. v. 29, 30.
[10] Job xxxi. 1.   [11] 2 Kings xi. 2.   [12] Gen. xxxiv. 2.
[13] Dan. xiii. 8.

admonition of Ecclesiasticus: "Turn away thy face from a woman dressed up."[1] A passion for dress often characterizes female weakness: it will not, therefore, be unseasonable in the pastor to give some attention to the subject; mingling reproofs with admonition, in the impressive words of the Apostle Peter: "Whose adorning," says he, "let it not be the outward plaiting of the hair, or the wearing of gold, or the putting on of apparel;"[2] and also in the language of St. Paul: "Not with plaited hair, or gold, or pearls, or costly attire."[3] Many females, adorned with gold and precious stones, have lost their only true ornament, the gem of female virtue.

Next to the excitement of desire, usually provoked by too studied an elegance of dress, follows another, which is indecent and obscene conversation. Obscene language is a torch which lights up the worst passions of the young mind; and an inspired Apostle has said, that "evil communications corrupt good manners."[4] Indelicate and lascivious songs and dances seldom fail to produce the same fatal effects, and are, therefore, cautiously to be avoided. In the same class are to be numbered soft and obscene books: possessing, as they do, a fatal influence in exciting to filthy allurements, and in kindling criminal desire in the mind of youth: they are to be shunned as pictures of licentiousness, and incentives to turpitude.[5]

V.

VI. & VII.

VIII.

But to avoid with the most scrupulous care the occasions of sin, which we have now enumerated, is to remove almost every excitement to lust; whilst frequent recourse to confession and to the Holy Eucharist operates most efficaciously in subduing its violence. Unceasing and devout prayer to God, accompanied by fasting and alms-deeds, has the same salutary effect. Chastity is a gift of God:[6] to those who ask it "aright" he denies it not; nor does he suffer us to be tempted beyond our strength.[7] But the body is to be mortified, and the sensual appetites to be repressed not only by fasting, and particularly, by the fasts instituted by the Church, but also by watching, pious pilgrimages, and other penitential austerities. By these and similar penitential observances is the virtue of temperance chiefly evinced; and in accordance with this doctrine, St. Paul, writing to the Corinthians, says: "Every one that striveth for the mastery, refraineth himself from all things; and they indeed that they may receive a corruptible crown, but we an incorruptible one;"[8] and a little after; "I chastise my body, and bring it into subjection, lest, perhaps, when I have preached to others, I myself should become reprobate;" and in another place; "Make not provision for the flesh in its concupiscence."[9]

IX. X.
XI. XII.
XIII.

---

[1] Eccl. ix. 8.   [2] 1 Pet. iii. 3.   [3] 1 Tim. ii. 9.   [4] 1 Cor. xv. 33.
[5] Parochus imprimis curet, ut quæ de sacris imaginibus a Sacrosancto Concilio Tridentino pie religioseque constituta sunt, ea sanctissime serventur. Vid. sess. 25. decret. de invocat, &c. vener. et. sacris imagin.   [6] 1 Cor. vii. 7.
[7] 1 Cor. x. 13. Vid. Tert. de Monog. in fine Nazianz. orat. 3. Basil. de virg. ultra. medium. Chrys. et Hieron. in c. 16. Matt. Aug. lib. 6. confess. c. 11.
[8] 1 Cor. ix. 25.   [9] Rom. xiii. 14.

THE SEVENTH COMMANDMENT.

"THOU SHALT NOT STEAL."[1]

The observance of this commandment strongly inculcated in the early ages of the church: the same practice to be followed in our days. THAT, in the early ages of the church, it was usual to impress on the minds of the faithful the nature and force of this commandment, we learn from the reproof uttered by the Apostle against some who were most earnest in deterring others from vices, in which they themselves were found freely to indulge : "Thou therefore," says he, "that teachest another, teachest not thyself : thou that preachest that men should not steal, stealest."[2] The salutary effect of such instructions was, not only to correct a vice which was then very prevalent, but, also, to repress turbulent altercations, and other causes of mischief, which generally grow out of theft. It is a melancholy truth, that in these our days men are unhappily addicted to the same vice : the peace of society is still frequently disturbed by the mischiefs and calamities consequent to theft; and the pastor, therefore, following the example of the Holy Fathers, and the masters of Christian discipline, will urge this point, and will explain with care and assiduity the force and meaning of this commandment.

This commandment, a proof of the love of God towards us, and a claim on our gratitude. In the first place, the care, diligence and industry of the pastor will be exercised in unfolding the infinite love of God to man : not satisfied with having fenced round our lives, our persons, our reputation, by means of these two commandments, " thou shalt not kill," " thou shalt not commit adultery;" he defends, and, as it were, places a guard over our property, by adding the prohibition, " Thou shalt not steal." Other meaning these words cannot have than that which has been already mentioned in expounding the other commandments : they declare that God forbids our worldly goods, which are placed under his sovereign protection, to be taken away or injured by any one.[3] Our gratitude to God, its author, should, then, be proportioned to the magnitude of the benefit conferred on us by this law ; and, as the truest test of gratitude, and the best means of returning thanks to God, consists not alone in lending a willing ear to his precepts, but, also, in putting forth in our lives practical evidence of our sincere approval of them, the faithful are to be animated and inflamed to a strict observance of this commandment.

Division of the commandment. Like the former precepts, this also divides itself into two parts : the one, which prohibits theft, is mentioned expressly ; of the other, which enforces kindliness and liberality, the spirit

---

[1] Exod. xx. 15.   [2] Rom. ii. 21.
[3] Vid. D. Thom. 1. 2. q. 100. art. 3 et 2. 2. q. 122. art. 6.

and force are implied in the former. We shall therefore begin with the first: " Thou shalt not steal." It is to be observed, that by the word " theft" is understood not only the taking away of any thing from its rightful owner, privately and without his consent; but also, the possession of that which belongs to another, contrary to the will, although not without the knowledge, of the true owner. That the detention of the property of another, under these circumstances, constitutes theft, is undeniable, unless we are prepared to say, that he who prohibits theft does not also prohibit rapine, which is accomplished by violence and injustice; whereas, according to St. Paul, " extortioners shall not possess the kingdom of God;"[1] and the same Apostle declares, that extórtion of every sort is to be avoided.[2] " Theft," definition of

Although rapine, which, besides the deprivation of his property, offers a violent outrage to the injured party, and subjects him to insult and contumely, is a more grievous sin than theft,[3] yet it cannot be matter of surprise, nor is it without good reason, that the divine prohibition is expressed under the lighter name of " theft," not under the heavier one of " rapine:" theft is more general and of wider extent than rapine; a crime of which they alone can be guilty, who are superior to their neighbour in brute force. It is obvious, however, that when lesser crimes are forbidden, greater enormities of the same sort are also prohibited.[4] "Rapine"a more grievous crime than theft: the latter why mentioned in the commandment.

The unjust possession and use of what belongs to another are expressed by different names. To take any thing private from a private individual is called " theft;" from the public, peculation: to enslave and appropriate the freeman or servant of another is called " man-stealing:" to steal any thing sacred is called " sacrilege;" a crime the most enormous and sinful of all, yet so common in our days, that what piety and wisdom had appropriated to the divine worship, to the support of the ministers of religion, and to the use of the poor, is employed in satisfying the cravings of individual avarice, and converted into a means of ministering to the worst passions. Different denomina- tions of theft.
I. & II.
III.
IV.

But, besides actual theft, the will and desire are also forbidden by the law of God: the law is spiritual: it regards the soul, the principle of our thoughts and designs: " From the heart," says our Lord, " come forth evil thoughts, murders, adulteries, fornications, thefts, false testimonies."[5] A desire of theft prohi- bited.

The grievousness of the sin of theft is sufficiently seen by the light of natural reason alone: it is a violation of justice which gives to every man his own. In order that every man, unless we dissolve all human society, may securely possess what he has justly acquired; it is necessary that stability be given to the distribution and allotment of property, fixed, as it has been, by the law of nations from the origin of society, and Grievous- ness of the sin of theft.
I.

---

[1] 1 Cor. vi. 10.   [2] Vid. Aug. q. 71. in Exod. et citatur. 32. q. 4. c. meretrices.
[3] 1 Cor. v. 10.   [4] Vid. D. Thom. c. 2. 66. art. 4 et 9. item 14, q. 4. c. pœnale.
[5] Matt. xv. 19.

25*

confirmed by human and divine laws. Hence these words of the Apostle, " Neither thieves, nor covetous, nor drunkards, nor railers, nor extortioners, shall possess the kingdom of II. God."[1] The long train of evils, however, which theft entails upon society, are an attestation at once of its mischievousness and enormity. It gives rise to hasty and rash judgments: it engenders hatred: originates enmities; and sometimes subjects the innocent to cruel condemnation.

Necessity and difficulty of restitution. What shall we say of the necessity imposed by God on all of satisfying for the injury done? " Without restitution," says St. Augustine, " the sin is not forgiven."[2] The difficulty of making such restitution, on the part of those who have been in the habit of enriching themselves with their neighbour's property, we may learn not only from experience and reflection, but also from the testimony of the prophet Habaccuc: " Wo to him that heapeth together what is not his own. How long also doth he load himself with thick clay?"[3] The possession of other men's property the prophet calls " thick clay," from which it is difficult to emerge and disengage one-self.

Different sorts of theft. Such is the variety of thefts, that it is difficult to enumerate I. them: to theft and rapine, however, as to their sources, all others may be traced; and the exposition of these two will therefore suffice. To inspire the faithful with a detestation of them, and to deter from such enormities, are objects which will engage all the care and assiduity of the pastor. But to proceed—They who buy stolen goods, or retain the property of others, whether found, seized on, or pilfered, are also guilty of theft: " If you have found, and not restored," says St. Augustine, " you have stolen."[4] If the true owner cannot, however, be discovered, whatever is found should go to the poor;[5] and if the finder refuse to yield it up for their use, he gives evident proof, that, were it in his power, he would make II. no scruple of stealing to any extent. Those who, in buying or selling, have recourse to fraud, and lying words, involve themselves in the same guilt: the Lord will avenge their frauds. But those who for good and sound merchandize sell bad and unsound, or who defraud by weight, measure, number, or rule, are guilty of a species of theft still more criminal and unjust: it is written, " Thou shalt not have divers weights in thy bag:"[6] " Do not any unjust thing," says Leviticus, " in judgment, in rule, in weight or in measure. Let the balance be just, and the weights equal, the bushel just, and the sextary equal:"[7] to which passages we may add these words of Solomon: " Divers weights are an abomination before the Lord: a deceitful balance is not good."[8]

III. It is, also, a downright theft, when labourers and artizans

---

[1] Cor. vi. 10.   [2] Epist. liv.   [3] Habac. ii. 6.
[4] Lib. 50. hom. Hom. 9. et de verbis Apost. serm. 19.
[5] It is unnecessary to remind the learned reader that human laws may affect this decision.—T.
[6] Deut. xxv. 13.   [7] Lev. xix. 35, 36.   [8] Prov. xx. 23.

exact full wages from those, to whom they have not given just and due labour; nor are unfaithful servants and stewards any other than thieves; nay they are more detestable than other thieves, against whom every thing may be locked; whilst against a pilfering servant nothing in a house can be secure by bolt or lock... They, also, who extort money under false pretences, or by deceitful words, may be said to steal, and their guilt is aggravated by adding falsehood to theft. Persons charged with offices of public or private trust, who altogether neglect or but indifferently perform the duties, whilst they enjoy the emoluments of such offices, are also to be reckoned in the number of thieves. To detail the various other modes of theft, invented by the ingenuity of avarice, which is versed in all the arts of gleaning together the fruits of injustice, were a tedious and complicated enumeration. The pastor, therefore, will next come to treat of the other general head, to which sins prohibited by this commandment are reducible; first, however, admonishing the faithful, to bear in mind the precept of the Apostle: "They that will become rich fall into temptation, and the snare of the devil;"[1] and also the words of the Redeemer: "All things whatsoever you will that men do to you, do you also to them;"[2] and finally the admonition of Tobias: "See thou never do to another what thou wouldst hate to have done to thee by another."[3]

Rapine is more comprehensive than theft: those who pay not the labourer his hire are guilty of rapine, and are exhorted to repentance by St. James in these words: "Go to now, ye rich men, weep and howl for your miseries which shall come upon you:" He subjoins the cause of their repentance; "Behold," says he, "the hire of the labourers, who have reaped down your fields, which by fraud has been kept back by you, crieth; and the cry of them hath entered into the ears of the Lord of Sabaoth."[4] This sort of rapine is condemned in terms of the strongest reprobation in Leviticus,[5] Deuteronomy,[6] Malachy,[7] and Tobias.[8] Amongst those who are guilty of rapine are also included persons who do not pay, who turn to other uses or appropriate to themselves, customs, taxes, tythes, and such revenues, which are the property of those who preside over the Church, and of the civil magistrate.

To this class also belong usurers, the most cruel and relentless of extortioners, who, by their usurious practices, plunder and destroy the poor. Whatever is received above the principal, be it money, or any thing else that may be purchased or estimated by money, is usury; for it is written in Ezekiel: "Thou hast taken usury and increase;"[9] and in Luke our Lord says: "Lend hoping for nothing thereby."[10] Even among the Gentiles usury was always considered a most grievous and odious crime; and hence the question, "What is usury?"

Marginal notes: V.   VI.   VII.   Note.   Different sorts of rapine.   I.   II.   III. Usury

---

1 1 Tim. vi. 9.   2 Matt. vii. 12.   3 Tob. iv. 26.   4 James v. 1, 4.
5 Lev. xix. 13.   6 Deut. xxiv. 14.   7 Mal. iii. 5.   8 Tob. iv. 15.
9 Ezek. xxii. 12. and xviii. 8.   10 Luke vi. 33.

which was answered by asking, "What is murder?" The reason why it was thus characterized is, that he who lends at usury sells the same thing twice, or sells that which has no real existence.[1]

IV. Corrupt judges, whose decisions are venal, and who, bought over by money or other bribes, decide against the poor and the necessitous, however good their cause, also commit rapine.

V. Those who defraud their creditors, who deny their just debts, and, also, those who purchase goods on their own, or on another's credit, with an engagement to pay for them at a certain time, and do not redeem their pledge, are guilty of the same crime of rapine; and it is an aggravation of their guilt, that, in consequence of their want of punctuality and their fraud, prices are raised, to the no small injury of the public. To such persons David alludes, when he says, "The sinner shall borrow and not pay again."[2]

VI. But, in what language of abhorrence shall we speak of those, who, themselves abounding in wealth, exact with rigour what they lend to the poor, who have not wherewithal to pay them; and who take as pledges even the necessary covering of their wretched applicants, in defiance of the divine prohibition; "If thou take of thy neighbour a garment in pledge, thou shalt give it him again before sunset, for that same is the only thing wherewith he is covered, the clothing of his body, neither hath he any other to sleep in: if he cry to me I will hear him, because I am compassionate."[3] Their rigorous exaction is justly termed "rapacity," and is therefore rapine.[4]

VII. Amongst those whom the Holy Fathers pronounced guilty of rapine are persons who, in times of scarcity, store up their corn, thus producing a dearth; and this also holds good with regard to all necessaries for food, and the purposes of life. These are they against whom Soloman hurls this execration, "He that hideth up corn, shall be cursed among the people."[5] Such persons the pastor will admonish of their guilt, and will reprove with more than ordinary freedom; and to them he will explain at large the punishments which await such delinquency.

Positive part of the precept: restitution; who are bound to. So far for the negative part of the precept—We now come to the positive part, in which the first thing to be considered is satisfaction or restitution; for without satisfaction or restitution the sin is not forgiven. But, as the law of restitution is binding not only on the person who commits theft, but also on the person who is a party to its commission, to determine who are indispensably bound to this satisfaction or restitution is a matter which demands explanation. These form a variety of classes.

I. The first ("imperantes") consists of those who order others to steal, and who are not only the authors and accomplices of theft,

[1] De usura vid. 14. q. 1. et q. 4. passim. vid. item titulum de usuris in Decretalibus et D. Thom. 2. 2. q. 78. item Amb. lib. de Tob. c. 14.
[2] Ps. xxxvi. 21.   [3] Exod. xxii. 26, 27.
[4] Titulum habes de pignor. in decretal. lib. 3. tit. 21. vid. Amb. lib. 5. de offic. c. 6.
[5] Prov. xi. 6.

but also the most criminal in its commission. Another class ("suasores") embraces those, who, like the former in will, but unlike them in power, are equally culpable; who, when they cannot command, persuade and encourage others to commit theft. A third class ("consentientes") is composed of those who are a consenting party to the theft committed by others. The fourth class ("participantes") is that of those who are accomplices in and derive gain from theft; if that can be called gain, which, unless they repent, consigns them to everlasting torments. Of· them David says : " If thou didst see a thief, thou didst run with him."[1] The fifth class of thieves ("non prohibentes") are those who, having it in their power to prohibit theft, so far from opposing or preventing it, fully and freely suffer and sanction its commission. The sixth class ("non indicantes") is constituted of those who are well aware that the theft was committed, and when it was committed; and yet so far from discovering it, are as silent on the subject as if it had never occurred. The seventh, and last ("custodes") comprises all who assist in the accomplishment of theft, who guard, patronise, receive or harbour thieves; all of whom are bound to make restitution to those from whom any thing has been stolen, and are to be earnestly exhorted to the discharge of so necessary a duty. Neither are those who approve ("approbantes") and commend thefts entirely innocent of this crime: children also and wives who steal from their parents and husbands are not guiltless of theft.

This commandment also implies an obligation to sympathize with the poor and the necessitous, and to relieve them under their difficulties and distresses from the means with which we have been blessed, and by rendering them the good offices which charity inculcates. On this subject, which cannot be urged too frequently or copiously, the pastor will find abundant matter to enrich his discourses in the works of those very holy men, St. Cyprian,[2] St. Chrysostome,[3] St. Gregory Nazianzen,[4] and other eminent writers on alms-deeds. It is theirs to inspire the faithful with an anxious desire and a cheerful willingness to succour the distresses of those, who depend for a precarious subsistence on the bounteous compassion of others.

The necessity of alms-deeds should also form the subject matter of the pastor's instructions: the faithful are to be strongly impressed with the obligation imposed on them of being really and practically liberal to the poor; and to this effect the pastor will urge the overwhelming argument that, on the day of final retribution, the Judge of the living and the dead will hurl against the uncharitable man the indignant sentence of irrevocable condemnation; and will invite in the language of eulogy, and intro-

Marginal notes: II.   III.   IV.   V.   VI.   VII.   VIII. & IX.

To relieve the necessitous, an obligation imposed by this commandment.

Alms-deeds.

[1] Ps. xlix. 18.   [2] Cypr. lib. de opera et eleemosyn.
[3] Chrysost. hom. 32. ad pop. Antioch. et hom. 33. et 34. in Math. vid. etiam nom. 16. 37. ad pop. Antioch.
[4] Nazianz. orat. de pauperum amore. August. serm. 50. et 227. de tempore: item hom. 18, 19, 28. 45.

2 P

duce into his heavenly country, those who have exercised mercy towards the poor. Their respective sentences have been already pronounced by the lips of the Son of God : " Come, ye blessed of my Father, possess the kingdom prepared for you ;"—" Depart from me, ye cursed, into everlasting fire."[1] The pastor will also cite those texts of Scripture which are calculated to persuade to the performance of this important duty : " Give and it shall be given to you."[2] He will cite the promise of God, than which imagination can picture no remuneration more abundant, none more magnificent : " There is no man who hath left house, or brethren, &c. that shall not receive an hundred times as much now in this time ; and in the world to come life everlasting ;"[3] and he will add these words of our Lord : " Make unto yourselves friends of the mammon of iniquity, that when you shall fail, they may receive you into everlasting dwellings."[4]

But the pastor will explain the different heads into which this duty naturally resolves itself; and will remind the faithful, that whoever is unable to give may, at least, lend to the poor wherewithal to sustain life, according to the command of Christ our Lord : " Lend hoping for nothing thereby."[5] The singular happiness, which is the reward of such an exercise of mercy, is attested by David in these words : " Acceptable is the man that sheweth mercy and lendeth."[6] But should it not be in our power otherwise to relieve distress, to seek, by labour and the work of our hands, to procure the means of doing so is an act of benevolence, by which we attain the double purpose of avoiding idleness and of discharging a duty of Christian piety. To this the Apostle exhorts all by his own example : " For yourselves," says he, writing to the Thessalonians, " know how you ought to imitate us ;"[7] and again, " Use your endeavour to be quiet, and that you do your own business, and work with your own hands, as we commanded you ;"[8] and to the Ephesians : " He that stole, let him steal no more ; but rather let him labour working with his hands the thing which is good, that he may have something to give to him that suffereth need."[9]

Frugality recommended. We should also practise frugality, and draw sparingly on the kindness of others, that we may not be a burden or a trouble to them. This exercise of temperance is conspicuous in all the Apostles, but pre-eminently so in St. Paul : writing to the Thessalonians he says : " You remember, brethren, our labour and toil ; working night and day lest we should be chargeable to any of you, we preached amongst you the Gospel of God ;"[10] and again : " In labour and in toil, we worked night and day, lest we should be chargable to any of you."[11]

Scriptural authority. To inspire the faithful with an abhorrence of all sins against this commandment, the pastor will recur to the prophets and the other inspired writers, to show the detestation in which God

---

[1] Matt. xxv. 34. 41.　　[2] Luke vi. 38.　　[3] Mark x. 29, 30.　　[4] Luke xvi. 9.
[5] Luke vi. 35.　　[6] Ps. cxi. 5.　　[7] 2 Thess. iii. 7.　　[8] 1 Thess. iv. 11.
[9] Eph. iv. 28.　　[10] 1 Thess. ii. 9.　　[11] 2 Thess. iii. 8.

holds the crimes of theft and rapine, and the awful threats which he denounces against their perpetrators: "Hear this," exclaims the prophet Amos, "you that crush the poor, and make the needy of the land to fail, saying, when will the month be over, and we shall sell our wares, and the Sabbath, and we shall open the corn; that we may lessen the measure, and increase the sickle, and may convey in deceitful balances?"[1] Many passages in Jeremiah,[2] Proverbs,[3] and Ecclesiasticus,[4] breathe the same spirit; and these, doubtless, are the seeds from which have sprung great part of the evils, which in our times overspread the face of society.

That Christians may accustom themselves to acts of gene- *Liberality* rosity and kindness towards the poor and the mendicant, an *to the poor.* exercise of benevolence inculcated by the second part of this commandment, the pastor will place before them those ample rewards which God promises, in this life and in the next, to the beneficent and the bountiful.

But, as there are not wanting those who would even excuse *Excuses of* their thefts, they are to be admonished that God will accept no *theft.* excuse for sin; and that their excuses, far from extenuating, *I.* serve only to aggravate their guilt. How insufferable the perversity of those men of exalted rank, who stand excused in their own eyes by alleging, that, if they strip others of what belongs to them, they are actuated not by cupidity or avarice, but by a desire to maintain the grandeur of their families, and the station of their ancestors, whose estimation and dignity must fall, if not upheld by the accession of another man's property. Of this mischievous error they are to be disabused; and are to be convinced, that to obey the will of God and observe his commandments is the only means to preserve and augment their wealth, and to enhance the glory of their ancestors. His will and commandments once contemned, the stability of property, no matter how securely settled, is overturned; kings are dethroned, and hurled from the highest pinnacle of earthly grandeur; whilst the humblest individuals in society, men towards whom they cherished the most implacable hatred, are sometimes called by God to occupy the thrones, which their rapacity had forfeited. The intensity of the divine wrath, kindled by such cruel injustice, God himself declares in these words, which are recorded in Isaias: "Thy princes are faithless, companions of thieves; they all love bribes; they run after rewards. Therefore, saith the Lord, the God of Hosts, the Mighty One of Israel: Ah! I will comfort myself over my adversaries; and I will be revenged of my enemies; and I will turn my hand to thee, and I will clean purge away thy dross."[5]

Some there are, who plead in justification of such conduct, n not the ambition of maintaining hereditary splendour and an-

---

[1] Amos viii. 4, 5.   [2] Jer. v. et xxi. et xxii.   [3] Prov. xxi.   [4] Eccl. x.
[5] Vid. Trid. sess. 22. decret. de reform. cap. 11. item Conc. Aurel. 3. c. 13. 22. Paris. 1. c. 1. Taron. 2. c. 25. Aurel. 5. c. 15. Mogunt. cap. 6. 11. Worm. c. 75. Aquisgr. c. 68. vid. et l. 2. q. 2. variis in capit.

cestral glory, but a desire of acquiring the means of living in greater ease, affluence and elegance. Such false excuses are also to be exposed and refuted: they are to be taught how impious is the conduct, how unacceptable to God the prayers, of those who prefer any earthly advantage to the will and the glory of God; and are to be made sensible of the magnitude of the offence, offered to him, by a neglect of his precepts.

Note. And yet what real advantage can there be in theft? Of how many very heavy curses is it not the source? " Confusion and repentance," says Ecclesiasticus, " is upon a thief."[1] But, suppose no temporal punishment to overtake the thief, does he not offer an insult to the divine name? does he not oppose the most holy will of God? does he not contemn his salutary precepts? is not this contempt of the divine precepts the source of all the error, and all the dishonesty, and all the impiety, which inundate the world?

III. But, do we not sometimes hear the thief contend that he is not guilty of sin, because, forsooth, he steals from the rich and the wealthy, who, in his mind, do not even perceive, not to

IV. say, suffer injury from the loss? Such an excuse is as wretched as its tendency is baneful. Others imagine that they should be acquitted of guilt, because they have contracted such a habit of stealing, as not to be able to gain an easy victory over the passion, or to desist from the practice. If such persons listen not to the admonition of the Apostle: " He that stole, let him now steal no more,"[2] let them recollect the awful punishment that awaits their obstinacy in crime, nothing less than an eter-

V. nity of torments.—Some excuse themselves by saying that it was impossible to resist the seasonable opportunity that presented itself: the proverb is trite; " those, who are not thieves, are made so by opportunity." Such persons are to be dissuaded and deterred from such wickedness, by reminding them that it is our duty to resist every evil propensity: were we to yield instant obedience to the impulse of inordinate desire, what measure, what limits to the most criminal and flagitious excesses? Such an excuse, therefore, is marked by more than ordinary turpitude, or rather is an avowal of unbridled licentiousness and unrestrained injustice. To say that you do not commit sin, because you have no opportunity of sinning, is almost to acknowledge, that you are always prepared to sin

VI. when opportunity offers.—There are some who say that they steal in order to gratify revenge, having themselves suffered the same injury from others. In answer to such offenders, the pastor will urge the unlawfulness of returning injury for injury; that no person can be a judge in his own cause; and that still less can it be lawful to punish one man for the crimes of another.

VII. Finally, some find a sufficient justification of theft in their own embarrassments, alleging that they are overwhelmed with

---

[1] Eccl. v. 17.   [2] Eph. iv. 28.

debt, which they cannot pay off otherwise than by theft. Such persons should be given to understand, that no debt presses more heavily than that from which, each day of our lives, we pray to be released in these words of the Lord's Prayer: " Forgive us our debts ;"[1] and to swell the debt which we owe to God, in order to liquidate that which is due to man, is the extreme of infatuation. It is much better to be consigned to an earthly prison than to be cast into the prison of hell : it is far a greater evil to be condemned by the judgment of God, than by that of man ; nor should it be forgotten, that, under such trying circumstances, it becomes our duty to have recourse to the assistance and mercy of God, that, in his goodness, he may relieve us from all our difficulties.

Other excuses are also preferred, which the judicious and zealous pastor will not find it difficult to meet; that thus he may one day be blessed with a people, " followers of good works."[2]

THE EIGHTH COMMANDMENT.

" THOU SHALT NOT BEAR FALSE WITNESS AGAINST THY NEIGH-
BOUR."[3]

THE great utility, nay the absolute necessity, of bestowing serious attention on the exposition of this commandment, and of impressing upon the minds of the faithful the obligation which it enforces, we learn from these words of St. James : " If any man offend not in word, the same is a perfect man ;" and again, " The tongue is indeed a little member, and boasteth great things. Behold how small a fire what a great wood it kindleth, &c."[4] From these words of St. James we learn two salutary truths : the one, that the vice of the tongue is of great extent, a truth which derives additional confirmation from these words of the prophet, " Every man is a liar ;"[5] whence this moral disease would seem to be almost the only one which extends to all mankind : the other, that the tongue is the source of innumerable evils. Through its wicked instrumentality are often lost the property, the character, the life, the salvation of the injured person, or of him who inflicts the injury ; of the injured person, whose feelings, impatient of control, impotently avenge the contumely flung upon them; of the person who inflicts the injury, because, deterred by a perverse shame and a false idea of what is called honour, he cannot be induced to

Importance of this precept; its salutary tendency a motive of gratitude to God.

[1] Matt. vi. 12. [2] Tit. ii. 14. [3] Exod. xx. 16.
[4] James iii. 2. 5. [5] Ps. cxv. 11.
26

satisfy the wounded feelings of him whom he has offended
Hence, the faithful are to be exhorted to pour out their souls
in thanksgiving to God, for a commandment of such salutary
tendency, a commandment which not only forbids us to injure
others, but also, on the same principle of obedience to its dictate, forbids others to injure us.

Note.

In its exposition we shall proceed as we have done with
regard to the others, pointing out in it two laws, the one prohibiting to bear false witness; the other commanding us, having
laid aside all dissimulation and deceit, to measure our words
and actions by the standard of truth; a duty of which the Apostle admonishes the Ephesians in these words: "Doing the
truth in charity, let us grow up in all things in him."[1]

*This pre-
cept man-
datory and
prohibi-
tory.*

With regard to the prohibitory part of this commandment,
although by false testimony is understood whatever is positively
but falsely affirmed of any one, be it for or against him, be it
in a public court or be it not; yet the commandment specially
prohibits that species of false testimony, which is given on oath
in a court of justice; because, the words of a person who thus
solemnly takes God to witness, pledging his holy name for his
veracity, have very great weight, and possess the strongest
claim to credit. Such testimony, therefore, because dangerous,
is specially prohibited. When no legal exceptions can be taken
against a sworn witness, and when he cannot be convicted of
palpable dishonesty and wickedness, even the judge himself
cannot reject his testimony, especially as it is commanded by
divine authority, that "in the mouth of two or three witnesses
every word shall stand."[2]

*What it
prohibits.*

In order that the faithful may have a clear comprehension
of this commandment, the pastor will explain who is our
"neighbour," against whom it is unlawful to bear false witness. According to the interpretation of Christ the Lord, our
neighbour is he who wants our assistance, whether bound to
us by ties of kindred or not, whether a fellow-citizen or a
stranger, a friend or an enemy.[3] To suppose it lawful to give
false evidence against an enemy, whom by the command of
God and of our Lord we are bound to love, were an error of
the worst description. Moreover, as in the order of charity
every man is bound to love himself, and is thus, in some sense,
his own neighbour, it is unlawful for any one to bear false witness against himself; he who does so is guilty of a suicidal
act, and, like the suicide, brands himself with infamy and disgrace, and inflicts a deep wound on himself and on the church
of which he is a member. This is the doctrine of St. Augustine: "To those," says he, "who understand the precept
properly, it cannot appear lawful to give false testimony against
one's-self, because the words 'against thy neighbour' are subjoined in the commandment: the standard of loving our neighbour is the love which we cherish towards ourselves; and,

*Who is our
"neigh-
bour:"
unlawful
to give
false testi-
mony
against our-
selves.*

[1] Eph. iv. 15.   [2] Deut. xix. 15. Matt. xviii. 16.   [3] Luke x. 36, et seq

therefore, as it is prohibited to bear false witness against our neighbour, it must also be prohibited to bear false witness against ourselves."[1]

But if we are forbidden to injure, let it not be inferred that we are therefore at liberty to serve our neighbour, by false testimony, however dear the relation in which he may stand towards us. We cannot compromise truth to consult for the feelings or the interests of any man. Hence, St. Augustine to Crescentius teaches from the words of the Apostle, that a lie, although uttered in unmerited commendation of any one, is to be numbered amongst false testimonies. Treating of that passage of the Apostle: " Yea, and we are found false witnesses of God, because we have given testimony against God, that he hath raised up Christ whom he hath not raised, if the dead rise not again,"[2] he says: " The Apostle calls it false testimony to utter a lie with regard to Christ, although it seems to redound to his praise."[3] It also not unfrequently happens, that by favouring one party we injure the other: false testimony is certainly the occasion of misleading the judge, who, yielding to such evidence, is sometimes obliged to decide against justice, to the injury of the innocent. The successful party, who has gained his suit by means of perjured witnesses, emboldened by impunity, and exulting in his iniquitous victory, is soon familiarized to the work of corruption and to the practice of subornation; and ultimately becomes so depraved, as to entertain a hope of attaining his ends, however iniquitous they may be, through the same wicked instrumentality. To the witness himself it must be a source of the most painful uneasiness, to be conscious that his falsehood and perjury are known to him by whom he has been purchased, and who has turned them to his own account; yet, encouraged by success, he becomes every day more practised; his mind is familiarized to its own audacious impiety; and his conscience is callous to all feelings of remorse. This precept, then, prohibits deceit and perjury on the part of witnesses; and the same prohibition extends also to plaintiffs, defendants and advocates, to relations and friends, to solicitors; in a word, to all who have any concern in suits at law.

Finally, God prohibits all testimony which may inflict injury or injustice, be it matter of legal evidence or not. In Leviticus, where the commandments are repeated, we read: " Thou shalt not steal; thou shalt not lie; neither shall any man deceive his neighbour."[4] To none, therefore, can it be matter of doubt, that this commandment condemns lies of every sort, as these words of David explicitly declare: " Thou wilt destroy all that speak a lie."[5]

This commandment forbids not only false testimony, but, also, the detestable propensity and practice of detraction; a moral

[Marginal notes:]
Forbidden to give false testimony in order to serve any one.
I.
II.
III.
All false testimonies, lies, &c. strictly prohibited.
It also prohibits detraction.

---

[1] Lib. 2. de civit. Dei. c. 20.   [2] 1 Cor. xv. 15.
[3] Ad Crescentium. cap. 12—14.   [4] Lev. xix. 11.   [5] Ps. v. 7.

pestilence, which is the poisoned source of innumerable and calamitous evils. This vicious habit of secretly reviling and calumniating character is reprobated in almost every page of the Sacred Scriptures: "With him," says David, "I would not eat;"[1] and St. James: "Detract not one another, my brethren."[2] The inspired Volume abounds not only with precepts on the

Illustration. subject, but, also, with examples which declare the enormity of the vice of detraction. Haman, by a crime of his own invention, had incensed Assuerus against the Jews ; and the consequence of the calumny was a royal mandate for the destruction of an unoffending people.[3] Innumerable examples, which illustrate the same wicked tendency of the sins of calumny and detraction, are to be found in the pages of sacred history ; and these the pastor will adduce, to deter his people from a crime of such magnitude.

Various sorts of detraction, and calumny.
I. & II.
But, to see in its full light the deformity of this sin, we must know, that reputation is injured not only by calumniating the character, but, also, by exaggerating the faults, of others. He who gives publicity to the secret sin of any man, at a time, in a place, or before persons, in which or before whom, the mischievous communication is unnecessary, incurs the just imputation of a detractor and a slanderer.

III.
IV.
But, of all sorts of calumnies the worst is that which is levelled against the Catholic doctrine and its teachers : persons who extol the propagators of error and of unsound doctrine are

V.
involved in similar criminality ; nor are those to be dissociated from their number, or their guilt, who, instead of reproving, lend a willing ear, and a cheerful assent, to the calumniator. As we read in St. Jerome,[4] and St. Bernard,[5] "Whether the detractor or the listener be the more criminal, it is not so easy to decide ; if there were no listeners, there would be no detractors."

VI.
To the same class of detractors belong those who continue to foment division, and excite dissension, and who feel a malignant pleasure in sowing discord ; dissevering, by fiction and falsehood, the closest friendships ; loosing the dearest social ties, and impelling to endless hatred and hostility the fondest friends. Of such pestilent characters the Lord expresses his detestation in these words : "Thou shalt not be a detractor nor a whisperer among the people."[6] Of this description were many of the advisers of Saul, who strove to alienate his affection from, and to exasperate his enmity against, David.[7]

VII.
Finally, amongst the transgressors of this commandment are to be numbered those wheedlers and sycophants, who insinuate their blandishments and hollow praises into the ears, and gain upon the hearts of those, after whose interest, money, and honours they hanker; as the prophet says, "calling good evil, and

[1] Ps. c. 5.   [2] James iv. 11.   [3] Esth. 13.
[4] St. Hieron. ep. ad Nepotianum circa finem.
[5] Bernard. lib. 2. de consider. ad Eugen. in fine.
[6] Lev. xix. 16.   [7] I Kings xxiv. and xxvi.

evil good."[1] Such characters David admonishes us to repel and banish from our society : " The just man," says he, " shall correct me in mercy, and shall reprove me ; but let not the oil of the sinner fatten my head."[2] This class of persons may not, it is true, speak ill of their neighbour; but they inflict on him the deepest wounds, causing him, by praising his vices, to continue enslaved to them to the end of his life. Of this species of flattery the most pernicious is that which proposes to itself for object the injury and the ruin of others. Saul, when, to procure the death of David, he sought to expose him to the ruthless sword of the Philistine, addressed him in these soothing words : " Behold my eldest daughter Merob, her will I give thee to wife : only be a valiant man, and fight the battles of the Lord ;"[3] and the Jews thus insidiously addressed our Lord : " Master, we know that thou art a true speaker, and teachest the way of God in truth."[4] *Note*

Still more pernicious is the language addressed sometimes by friends and relations to persons labouring under a mortal disease, and on the point of death ; flattering them that there is no danger of dying, telling them to be of good spirits, dissuading them from the confession of their sins, as though the very thought should fill them with melancholy, and, finally, withdrawing their attention from all concern about, and meditation upon, the dangers which beset them in their last perilous hour. In a word, lies of every sort are prohibited, but a lie uttered against or regarding religion, is one of extreme impiety. *Note.* *Note.*

God is also grievously offended by those opprobrious invectives which are termed lampoons and libels, and such contumelious slanders.[5] *VIII.*

To deceive by a jocose or officious lie, although neither useful nor injurious to any one, is, notwithstanding, altogether unworthy of a Christian ; and of this the Apostle admonishes us when he says, " Putting away lying, speak ye the truth."[6] This vile practice begets a strong tendency to frequent and serious lying, and from jocose, men contract a habit of uttering deliberate lies, lose all character for truth, and ultimately find it necessary, in order to gain belief, to recur to continual swearing. *Jocose and officious lies prohibited.* *Evil of such lies.*

Finally, the first part of this commandment prohibits dissimulation. It is sinful not only to speak but to act deceitfully. Actions as well as words are signs of our ideas and sentiments ; and hence our Lord, rebuking the Pharisees, frequently calls them " hypocrites."—So far with regard to the negative, which is the first part of this commandment.[7] *All dissimulation prohibited.*

We now come to explain the meaning of the second part— Its nature and the obligations which it imposes demand, that trials be conducted on principles of strict justice and according *Mandatory part of the precept: trials, on*

1 Isa. v. 20.   2 Ps. clx. 5.   3 1 Kings xviii. 17.   4 Matt. xxii. 16.
5 De libellis famosis vid. Bullam Pii V. 147. datam anno 1572. et Bullam Gregorii XIII. 4. datam eodem anno.
6 Eph. iv. 25.—Vid. D. Thom. 2. 2. q. 110. art. 3. et 4.
7 Vid. D. Thom. 2. 2. q. 311. per totam.

what prin-
ciples to be
conducted.

to law, and that men do not prejudge the cause, or usurp the
right of pronouncing on its merits; for, as the Apostle says,
" it were unjust to judge another man's servant."[1] Such an
assumption may lead men to decide without a sufficient knowledge of the case; and of this we have an example in the conduct of the priests and scribes, who passed judgment on St. Ste-
phen.[2] The magistrates of Philippi furnish another example
of the same criminal conduct: " They have beaten us publicly,"
says St. Paul, " uncondemned, men that are Romans, and have
cast us into prison; and now do they thrust us out privately."[3]

The obliga-
tion im-
posed on
judges.

This commandment also requires, that the innocent be not
condemned, nor the guilty acquitted; and that he who is invested with judicial authority suffer not his judgment to be
warped by interest, or biassed by hatred or partiality. This
is the admonition addressed by Moses to the elders, whom he
had constituted judges of the people : " judge that which is
just; whether he be one of your country or a stranger. There
shall be no difference of persons, you shall hear the little as well
as the great; neither shall you respect any man's person, because it is the judgment of God."[4]

On the
accused
when con-
scious of
their own
guilt.

With regard to an accused person, who is conscious of his
own guilt, when interrogated according to the forms of judicial
process, God commands him to confess the truth.[5] By that
confession he, in some sort, bears witness to, and proclaims the
praise and glory of God; and of this we have a proof in these
words of Joshua, when exhorting Achan to confess the truth :
" My son," says he, " give glory to the Lord the God of Israel."[6]

On wit-
nesses
bound to
tell the
whole
truth.

But, as this commandment chiefly regards witnesses, the pastor will also give to it, in this point of view, a due share of
attention. The spirit of the precept goes not only to prohibit
false, but also to enforce the obligation of giving true evidence.
In human affairs, to bear testimony to the truth is a matter of
the highest importance, because there are innumerable things
of which we must be ignorant, unless we arrive at a knowledge
of them on the faith of witnesses. In matters with which we
are not personally acquainted, and which, however, we have
occasion to know, what so important as true evidence ?—on this
subject we have the recorded sentiments of St. Augustine: " He
who conceals the truth, and he who utters falsehood, are both
guilty; the one, because he is unwilling to render a service; the
other, because he has the will to render a disservice."[7] We
are not, however, at all times, and under all circumstances,
obliged to disclose the truth; but when, in a court of justice, a
witness is legally interrogated, he is bound to tell " the whole

---

[1] Rom. xiv. 4.   [2] Acts vii. 59.
[3] Acts xvi. 37.—Vid. in 6 lib. c. tit. 7. de privilegiis c. 1. et ibidem lib. 2. tit. 2. de
foro competenti.   [4] Deut. i. 16.
[5] As these forms and their import differ in different countries, this decision is
conditional, and does not apply to the practice of our courts of justice.—T.
[6] Josh. vii. 19.—Vid. D. Thom. 2. 2. q. 96. per totas quatuor articulos.
[7] Hæc sententia citabatur olim a Gratiano ex Aug. sed apud Aug. non est in-
venta: similiter legitur apud Isid. lib. 3. c. 59.

truth." Here, however, witnesses should be most circumspect, Note. lest, trusting too much to memory, they affirm for certain what they have not fully ascertained.

Solicitors and counsel, plaintiffs and defendants, remain still On solicitors and counsel. to be treated of. The former will not refuse to contribute their services and legal assistance, when the necessities of others call for their interposition. In such circumstances, humanity will prompt them to plead the cause of suffering innocence, and a love of justice will prevent them from engaging in the defence of an unjust cause. They will not protract by cavils, or encourage through avarice, suits at law; and as to remuneration, in that they will be regulated by the principles of justice and of equity.[1] Plaintiffs and accusers are to be admonished, to avoid On plaintiffs and defendants. creating danger to any one by unjust charges, yielding to the influence of love, or hatred, or any other undue motive. Finally, to all conscientious persons is addressed the divine command, in all their intercourse with society, in every conversation, to speak the truth at all times from the sincerity of their hearts; to utter nothing injurious to the character of another, not even of those by whom they know they have been injured and persecuted; always recollecting, that so near is the relation that subsists between them, so close the social link that unites them, that they are all members of the same body.

In order that the faithful may be more disposed to avoid the Wretchedness and turpitude of lying. degrading vice of lying, the pastor will place before them the extreme wretchedness and turpitude of the liar. In the Sacred Scriptures the devil is called "the father of lies;" "Because he I. stood not in the truth, he is a liar and the father thereof;"[2] and, to II. banish from amongst the faithful so great an enormity, the pastor will subjoin the mischievous consequences of which this vice is the impure source. These consequences are without number; and the pastor, therefore, must be content with pointing out their principal heads. In the first place, he will inform them how III. grievously lies offend God, how deeply a liar is hated by God: "Six things there are," says Solomon, "which the Lord hateth, and the seventh his soul detesteth; haughty eyes, a lying tongue, hands that shed innocent blood, a heart that deviseth wicked plots, feet that are swift to run into mischief, a deceitful witness that uttereth lies, &c."[3] The man, therefore, who is IV. thus the object of God's sovereign wrath, who will shelter from the awful punishments which hang over his devoted head? Again, what more wicked, what more base than, as St. James V. says, "with the same tongue, by which we bless God and the Father, to curse men, who are made after the likeness of God, so that out of the same fountain flows sweet and bitter water."[4] The tongue, which was before employed in giving praise and VI. glory to God, by lying treats the Author of truth, as far as on it depends, with ignominy and dishonour; and hence, liars are

---

[1] Vid. 14. q. 5. c. non sane D. Thom. 2. 2. q. 71. art. 5.   [2] John viii. 44.
[3] Prov. vi. 16. &c.   [4] James iii. 9. 11.

excluded from a participation in the bliss of heaven. To David asking, " Lord ! who shall dwell in thy tabernacle ?" the Holy Spirit answers, " He that speaketh truth in his heart, who hath

VII.   not used deceit in his tongue."[1]   Lying is also attended with this very great evil; it is an almost incurable disease. The guilt of the calumniator cannot be pardoned, unless satisfaction be made to the calumniated person, a difficult duty to those who, as we have already observed, are deterred from its performance by false shame, and a foolish idea of dignity ; and hence, he who perseveres in this crime, perseveres in a course which must ulti-

Note.   mately lead to everlasting perdition.   Let no one indulge the delusive hope of obtaining the pardon of his calumnies or detractions, until he has repaired the injury which they have inflicted, be it offered in a court of justice, or in private and familiar conversation.

Evil conse-   But the evil consequences of lying are not confined to indi-
quences of.   viduals: they extend to society at large.   By duplicity and lying good faith and truth, which form the closest links of human society, are dissolved ; confusion ensues ; and men seem to differ in nothing from demons.

Loquacity   The pastor will also teach, that loquacity is to be avoided.
to be avoid-   By avoiding loquacity the other evils of the tongue will be ob-
ed.   viated, and a preventive opposed to lying, from which loqua-
cious persons can scarcely abstain.

Excuses   Finally, there are those who would seek to justify their
pleaded by   duplicity, and defend their violations of truth, on a principle
liars.
I.   of prudence, alleging that they lie in season.   To this erroneous
Note.   pretext the pastor will apply the divine truth; " The wisdom of the flesh is death ;"[2] he will exhort his people in all their difficulties and dangers to trust in God, not in the artifice of lying ; and will tell them that, in dangers and difficulties, to have recourse to subterfuge is to declare, that they trust more

II.   to their own prudence than to the providence of God.   Those who charge others with being the cause of their speaking false-hood, by having first deceived them, are to be taught the unlaw-fulness of avenging their own wrongs ; that evil is not to be rendered for evil, but rather that evil is to be overcome by good.[3] Were it even lawful, it would not be our interest, to make such a return : the man who seeks revenge by uttering falsehood

III.   inflicts very serious injury on himself.   Those who plead human frailty are to be taught, that it is a duty of religion to im-plore the Divine assistance, and not to yield to human infirmity.

IV.   Those who, in excuse of their guilt, allege habit, are to be admonished to endeavour to acquire the contrary habit of speaking the truth ; particularly as evil habit, far from extenu-ating, is an aggravation of guilt.   There are some who adduce in their own justification the example of others, who, they con-tend, constantly indulge in falsehood and perjury : such persons are to be reminded that bad men are not to be imitated, but

---

[1] Ps. xiv. 1. 3.　　　[2] Rom. viii. 6.　　　[3] Rom. xii. 17 21.

reproved and corrected ; and that, when we ourselves are addicted to the same vice, our admonitions have less influence in reprehending and correcting it in others. With regard to those who defend their conduct by saying, that to speak the truth is often attended with inconvenience ; these the pastor will meet by urging that, such an excuse is an accusation, not a defence ; whereas it is the duty of a Christian to suffer any inconvenience rather than utter a falsehood.

There are two other classes of persons who seek to justify a departure from truth ; the one who say that they tell lies for joke sake; the other who plead motives of interest, because, forsooth without having recourse to lies, they can neither buy nor sell to advantage. Both the pastor will endeavour to reform ; the first, by urging the inveteracy of the vicious habit which the practice of lying begets, and by strongly impressing a truth revealed by Jesus Christ, that " for every idle word that men shall speak, they shall render an account in the day of judgment :"[1] the second class, whose excuse involves their own accusation, he will reprove with greater severity, professing as they do, to yield no credit or authority to these words of our Lord : " Seek first the kingdom of God and his justice, and all these things shall be given you besides."[2]

THE NINTH AND TENTH COMMANDMENTS.

" THOU SHALT NOT COVET THY NEIGHBOUR'S HOUSE ; NEITHER SHALT THOU DESIRE HIS WIFE, NOR HIS SERVANT, NOR HIS HAND-MAID, NOR HIS OX, NOR HIS ASS, NOR ANY THING THAT IS HIS."[3]

IT is to be observed, in the first place, that these two precepts, which were delivered last in order, furnish a general principle for the observance of all the rest. What is commanded in these two amounts to this, that to observe the preceding precepts of the law, we must be particularly careful not to covet ; because he who covets not, content with what he has, will not desire what belongs to others, but will rejoice in their prosperity ; will give glory to the immortal God ; will render to him boundless thanks ; will observe the Sabbath, that is, will enjoy perpetual repose ; will respect his superiors ; and will in fine, injure no man in word or deed or otherwise ; for the root of all evil is concupiscence, which hurries its devoted victims into every species of enormity.[4] These considerations, if well weighed, must serve to

Meaning of these commandments; their efficacy in securing the observance of the others.

---

[1] Matt. xii. 36.   [2] Matt. vi. 33.   [3] Exod. xx. 17.
[4] Vid. Aug. lib. 1. Retract. c. 15. et epist. 200. et lib. 9. de civitate Dei, c. 4 et 5.

induce the pastor to explain what follows with increased diligence, and the people to hear his exposition with increased attention.

These two commandments why united; difference between them. But, although we have united these two commandments because, their object the same, the manner of treating them should be the same; yet the pastor, when exhorting and admonishing the faithful, will treat them conjointly or separately, as he may deem most convenient. If, however, he has undertaken the exposition of the Decalogue, he will point out in what these two commandments are dissimilar; how one concupiscence differs from another, a difference noticed by St. Augustine, in his book of questions on Exodus.[1] The one looks only to utility and interest, the other to unlawful desire and criminal pleasure; he, for instance, who covets a field or house, pursues profit rather than pleasure, whilst he, who covets another man's wife, yields to a desire of pleasure, not of profit.

Necessity of their promulgation.
I. Of these two commandments the promulgation was necessary for two reasons; the first is to explain the sixth and seventh, for, although reason alone is competent to inform us, that to prohibit adultery is also to prohibit the desire of another man's wife, because, were the desire lawful, its indulgence must be so too; yet blinded by sin, many of the Jews could not be induced to believe that such desires were prohibited by God. Nay, even after the promulgation, and with a knowledge of this law, many, who professed themselves its interpreters, continued in the same error, as we learn from these words of our Lord recorded in St. Matthew: "You have heard that it was said to them of old; 'thou shalt not commit adultery;' but I say to you, that whosoever shall see a woman to lust after her, hath already com-
II. mitted adultery with her in his heart."[2] The second reason for the promulgation of these two commandments is, that they distinctly, and in express terms, prohibit some things of which the six and seventh commandments contain but an implied prohibition. The seventh commandment, for instance, forbids an unjust desire or endeavour to take what belongs to another; but this prohibits even to covet it, on any account; although we may, without a violation of law or justice, obtain possession of that from which we know a loss must accrue to our neighbour.

Why added to the other commandments.
I. But, before we come to the exposition of the commandment, the faithful are first to be informed, that by this law we are taught not only to restrain our inordinate desires, but also to know the boundless love of God towards us. By the preceding commandments, God had, as it were, fenced us round with safeguards, securing us and ours against injury of every sort; but by the annexation of these commandments, he had for object principally, to provide against the injuries which we might inflict on ourselves by the indulgence of inordinate desires; and which should follow as a natural consequence, were we at liberty to covet all things indiscriminately. By this law, then, which forbids to covet, God has

[1] Quæst. 77. in Exod. Vid. item D. Thom. 2. 2. q. 122. a. 7. ad 3. et 4.
[2] Matt. v. 28.

opposed a resistance to the keenness of desire, which excites to every evil, but which, blunted in some degree by virtue of this law, is felt less acutely ; that thus freed from the annoying importunity of the passions, we may devote more time to the performance of the numerous and important duties of piety and religion which we owe to God.

Nor is this the only lesson of instruction which we derive from this commandment : it also teaches us that this divine law is to be observed not only by the external performance of the duties which it enforces, but also by the internal concurrence of the mind : so that between divine and human laws there is this difference, that human laws are fulfilled by an external compliance alone, whereas the laws of God (God sees the heart) require purity of heart, sincere and undefiled integrity of soul. The law of God, therefore, is a sort of mirror, in which we behold the corruption of our own nature ; and hence these words of the Apostle: " I had not known concupiscence, if the law did not say : ' thou shalt not covet.' "[1] Concupiscence, which is the fuel of sin, and which originated in sin, is always inherent in our fallen nature : from it we know that we are born in sin ; and, therefore, do we humbly fly for assistance to him, who alone can efface the stains of sin.

In common with the other commandments these also are partly mandatory, partly prohibitory. With regard to the prohibitory part, the pastor will make known to the faithful what sort of concupiscence is prohibited by this law, lest some may consider that which is not sinful to be sinful, such as the concupiscence mentioned by the Apostle, when he says : " The flesh lusteth against the spirit ;"[2] and that which was the object of David's most earnest desires : " My soul hath coveted to long for thy justifications at all times."[3] Concupiscence, then, is a certain commotion and impulse of the mind, urging to the desire of pleasures which it does not actually enjoy ; and as the other propensities of the soul are not always sinful, neither is the impulse of concupiscence. It is not, for instance, sinful to desire meat and drink, when cold to wish for warmth, when warm to wish to become cool. This species of concupiscence was originally implanted in the human breast by the Author of Nature ; but, in consequence of primeval prevarication, it passed the limits prescribed by Nature, and became so depraved, that it frequently excites to the desire of those things, which conflict with the spirit, and are repugnant to reason. However, if well regulated, and kept within proper bounds, it is still the source of many blessings to the world.

In the first place, it prompts us by fervent prayer to supplicate God, and humbly to beg of him those things, which are the objects of our most earnest desires. Prayer is the interpreter of our wishes ; and did not this well regulated concupiscence exist within us, Christians would not so often address the

Marginal notes:

II.

These commandments partly prohibitory, partly mandatory.

Concupiscence, twofold.

L

Advantages of the first sort of concupiscence.

I

---

[1] Rom. vii. 7.   [2] Gal. v. 17.   [3] Ps. cxviii. 20.

II. giver of all good gifts in prayer. It also imparts in our estimation a higher value to the gifts of God: the pleasure derived from the realization of our wishes, and the value which we set on the objects which they pursue, are proportioned to their intensity ;

III. and the gratification which we thus receive from the desired object serves also to increase our devotion and gratitude to God. If then, it is, at any time, lawful to covet, it will be readily conceded, that every species of concupiscence is not forbidden. St. Paul, it is true, says that "concupiscence is sin ;"[1] but his words are to be understood in the same sense as those of Moses, whom he cites ;[2] a sense conveyed by the Apostle himself, when, in his Epistle to the Galatians, he calls it " the concupiscence of the flesh :" " Walk in the spirit, and you shall not fulfil the lusts of the flesh."[3]· That natural, well regulated concupiscence, therefore, which passes not its proper limits, is not prohibited ; still less is that spiritual desire of the virtuous mind, which prompts to those things that war against the flesh, and to which the Sacred Scriptures exhort us : " Covet ye my

What sort of concupiscence is here prohibited. words :"[4] " Come over to me all ye that desire me."[5] It is not, then, the mere motion of concupiscence, directed equally, as it may be, to a good or a bad object, that is prohibited by these commandments : it is the indulgence of criminal desire ; which is called " the concupiscence of the flesh," and " the fuel of sin," and which, when it sways the assent of the mind, is always sinful. That which the Apostle calls " the concupiscence of the flesh" is alone prohibited ; that is to say, those motions of corrupt desire which are contrary to the dictates of reason, and outstep the limits prescribed by God.

Why prohibited.
I. This concupiscence is condemned, either because it desires what is evil, such as adultery, drunkenness, murder, and such heinous crimes, of which the Apostle says : " Let us not covet

II. evil things, as they also coveted ;"[6] or because, although the objects may not be bad in themselves, yet circumstances concur to render the desire of them criminal, when, for instance, they are prohibited by God or his Church. We are not warranted in desiring that which it is unlawful to possess; and hence, in the Old Law, it was criminal to desire the gold and silver from which idols were wrought, and which the Lord forbad "any

III. one to covet."[7] Another reason why this sort of concupiscence is condemned is, that it has for its object that which belongs to another, such as a house, servant, field, wife, ox, ass, and many other things; all of which, as they belong to another, the law

This concupiscence a sin ; when committed. of God forbids us to covet. The desire alone of such things, when consented to, is criminal, and is numbered among the most grievous sins. When the mind, yielding to the impulse of evil desires, is pleased with, or does not resist, evil, sin is necessarily committed, as St. James, pointing out the beginning and progress of sin, teaches, when he says : " Every man is

---

[1] Rom. vii. 20.   [2] Exodus xx. 17.   [3] Gal. v. 16.   [4] Wisdom vi. 12
[5] Eccl. xxiv, 26.   [6] 1 Cor. x. 6.   [7] Deut. vii. 25, 26.

tempted by his own concupiscence, being drawn away and allured: then, when concupiscence hath conceived, it bringeth forth sin; but sin, when it is completed, begetteth death."[1] When, therefore, the law says: "Thou shalt not covet," it means that we are to restrain our desires from those things which belong to others: a thirst for what belongs to others is intense and insatiable: it is written: "A covetous man shall not be satisfied with money;"[2] and of him Isaias says; "Wo to you that join house to house, and lay field to field."[3]

But a distinct explanation of each of the words, in which this commandment is expressed, will place the deformity and grievousness of this sin in a clearer light. The pastor, therefore, will teach that by the word "house" is to be understood not only the habitation in which we dwell, but, as we know from the usage of the inspired writers, the entire property of its owner. Thus to signify that God had enlarged their means and ameliorated their condition, he is said in Exodus to have built houses for the midwives.[4] From this interpretation, therefore, we perceive, that we are forbidden to indulge an eager desire of riches, or to envy others their wealth, or power, or rank, content with our own condition, be it humble or elevated. To desire the glory won by others is also prohibited, and is included in the word "house." Exposition of the words of the commandments: "house," what it signifies.

Next follow the words, "nor his ox nor his ass," from which we learn that it is unlawful to desire not only things of greater value, such as a house, rank, glory, because they belong to others; but, also, things of little value, whatever they may be, animate or inanimate. The words, "nor his servant," come next, and include slaves as well as other servants, whom it is not less unlawful to covet than the other property of our neighbour. With regard to freemen, who, induced by wages, affection or respect, serve voluntarily, it is unlawful, by words, or hopes, or promises, or rewards, to bribe or solicit them, under any pretext whatever, to leave those to whose service they have freely bound themselves; and if, before the period of their engagement has expired, they leave their masters or employers, they are to be admonished, on the authority of this commandment, to return by all means, until they shall have completed their full time of service. The word "neighbour" is mentioned in this commandment, to mark the wickedness of those, who covet neighbouring tenements, lands, houses and the like, which lie in their immediate vicinity; for neighbourhood, which consists in friendship, is transformed by covetousness from love into hatred. But this commandment is by no means transgressed by those, who desire to purchase or have actually purchased, at a fair price, from a neighbour, the merchandize which he has for sale: instead of doing him an injury, they, on "Nor his ox nor his ass." "Nor his servant." "Thy neighbour."

[1] James i. 14. Vid. D. Thom. 1. 2. q. 4. art. 78. 8. item August. lib. 12. de Trinit. c. 12. item de serm. Dom. in monte c. 23. Greg. hom. 19. in Evang. et lib. 4. Moral. c. 27. et in respons. 11. ad interrog. Aug. Hieron. in Amos. c. 1.   [2] Eccl. v. 9   [3] Isa. v. 8.   [4] Exod. i. 21.

the contrary, render him a considerable service, because to him the money is much more convenient and useful than the merchandize of which he disposes.

To covet our neighbour's wife, meaning of, grievousness of.

The commandment, which forbids us to covet the goods of our neighbour, is accompanied with another, which forbids to covet our neighbour's wife; and which prohibits not only that criminal concupiscence, which tempts the adulterer to desire the wife of another, but, also, the wish to be united to her in marriage. When, of old, a bill of divorce was permitted, it might easily happen, that she, who was repudiated by one husband, might be married to another; but this our Lord forbad, lest husbands might be induced to abandon their wives, or wives conduct themselves with such peevish moroseness towards their husbands, as to impose on them a sort of necessity of repudiating them. But, in the Gospel-dispensation, this sin acquires a deeper shade of guilt, because, the wife, although separated from her husband,

Note.

cannot marry another during his lifetime. To him, therefore, who wishes to be united in marriage to another man's wife, the transition from one criminal desire to another is easy; he will desire either the death of the husband or the commission of adultery.

The same principle applies to females who are betrothed, and to those who are consecrated to religion.

A particular case.

The same principle holds good with regard to females who have been betrothed to another: to covet them in marriage is also unlawful; and whoever strives to dissolve the contract, by which they are affianced, violates the most sacred engagements of plighted faith. And if to covet the wedded wife of another is highly criminal, it is no less so to desire in marriage the virgin who is consecrated to religion and to the service of God. But should any one desire in marriage a woman who is already married, supposing her to be unmarried, and not disposed, had he known that she was already married, to indulge such a desire, he does not violate this commandment. Pharaoh[1] and Abimelech,[2] as the Scripture informs us, were betrayed into this error; they wished to take Sarah to wife, supposing her to be unmarried, and the sister, not the wife of Abraham.

Remedies against covetousness.

In order to make known the remedies calculated to neutralize the evil consequences of the vice of covetousness, the pastor will explain the positive part of the commandment. God then commands, that " if riches abound, we set not our hearts upon them :"[3] that we be prepared to sacrifice them to a love of piety and religion: that we contribute cheerfully towards the relief of the poor; and that, if we ourselves are consigned to poverty, we bear it with patience and with a holy joy. And, indeed, liberality to the poor is a most effectual means of extinguishing in our own hearts the desire of what belongs to another. But, on the praises of poverty and the contempt of riches, the pastor will find little difficulty in collecting abundant matter, for the instruction of the faithful, from the Sacred Scriptures and the works of the Fathers.[4]

---

[1] Gen. xii.   [2] Gen. xx.   [3] Ps. lxi. 11.
[4] Vid. Hier. ep. 1. ad Heliod. et 8. ad Demetriadem, et 150. ad Hedebiam quæst 1. et 16. ad Pammach. item Basil. in regul. fusius disputatis, interrog. 9. Chrys. in

To desire, with all the ardour and all the earnestness of our Mandatory part of the commandment. souls, the consummation, not of our own wishes, but of the holy will of God, as it is expressed in the Lord's Prayer, is a further duty inculcated by this law. It is his will that we be made eminent in holiness; that we preserve our souls pure and undefiled; that we practise those spiritual duties which are opposed to sensuality; and that, having subdued our unruly appetites, and repressed the inordinacy of those senses which supply matter to the passions, we enter, under the guidance of reason and of the spirit, upon a virtuous course of life.

But, to extinguish the fire of passion, it will be found most Remedies against concupiscence. efficacious to place before our eyes the evils which are inseparable from its criminal indulgence. Amongst those evils the L first is our subjugation to the tyranny of sin: in him who is obedient to the impulse of passion, sin reigns uncontrolled; and hence the admonition of the Apostle: "Let not sin, therefore, reign in your mortal body, so as to obey the lusts thereof."[1] By resisting the ascendancy of the passions, we weaken the power and subvert the tyranny of sin; but by its indulgence we expel God from his throne, and introduce sin in his place. Again, concupiscence, as St. James teaches,[2] is the impure II. source from which flows every other sin: "All that is in the world," says St. John, "is the concupiscence of the flesh, the concupiscence of the eyes, and the pride of life."[3] A third III. evil of sensuality is, that it darkens the understanding: blinded by passion the sinner deems the objects of criminal desire, whatever they may be, lawful and even laudable. Moreover, IV. concupiscence stifles the seed of divine word, sown in our souls by God, the great husbandman: "Some," says St. Mark, "are sown among thorns; these are they who hear the word, and the cares of the world, and the deceitfulness of riches, and the lust after other things, entering in, choke the word, and it is made fruitless."[4]

But they who, more than others, are the slaves of concu Who are most enslaved to cupidity. piscence, and whom, therefore, the pastor will exhort with greater earnestness and assiduity, are those who are addicted to improper diversions, or who immoderately abuse such as L are in themselves lawful; and also, merchants, who wish for II. dearth, and, because they cannot sell at too high, and purchase at too low, a price, cannot bear that others, by engaging in business, contravene their oppressive monopoly. They, too, III. offend in this particular, who, with a view to gain by buying or selling, wish to see their neighbour reduced to want. Sol IV. diers, also, who thirst for war, in order to enrich themselves with plunder; physicians, who wish for the spread of disease; V. lawyers, who are anxious for a number of causes and litiga

---

ep. ad Rom. ad hæc verba. "salutate Priscam." Cassian. lib. de institut. Monach. c 13, et 33. et Collat. 24. c. 26. Greg. hom. 18. Ezech. Amb. in c. 6. Luc. Leon. mag. in serm. de omnibus Sanctis. Aug. lib. 17. de civ. Dei, et epist. 96. ad Hilar. et epist. 109.

[1] Rom. vi. 12.   [2] James iii. 14.   [3] 1 John ii. 16.   [4] Mark iv. 18, 19

VI.

VIII.

tions; and artizans who, greedy of gain, and with a view to increase their own profits, wish for a scarcity of the necessary articles for food and raiment, are all offenders against this commandment. They, too, who, envious of the praise and glory won by the achievements of others, strive to tarnish, in some degree, their fame, sin against this commandment; particularly if they themselves are worthless characters, persons of no estimation in society: fame and glory are the meed of virtue and industry, not of indolence and inexertion.

THE

CATECHISM

OF

THE COUNCIL OF TRENT.

PART IV.

ON PRAYER.

AMONGST the duties of the pastoral office, it is one of the highest importance to the spiritual interests of the faithful, to instruct them in Christian prayer; the nature and efficacy of which must be unknown to many, if not enforced by the pious and faithful exhortations of the pastor. To this, therefore, should the care of the pastor be directed in a special manner, that the faithful may understand how and for what they are to pray. Duty of the pastor.

Whatever is necessary to the performance of the duty of prayer is comprised in that divine form, which Christ our Lord vouchsafed to make known to his Apostles, and, through them and their successors, to all Christians. The sentiments which it expresses, and the words in which they are conceived, should, therefore, be so deeply impressed on the mind and memory, as to enable us to address it to God promptly and at all times. To assist the pastor, however, in teaching the faithful to pray, we have selected and set down from those writers, whose reputation for talents and learning on this head commands the highest respect, whatever appeared to us most instructive on the subject, leaving it to the pastor to draw upon the same source for further information, should he deem it necessary.[1] The Lord's prayer to be committed to memory.

In the first place, then, the pastor is to teach the necessity of prayer; a duty not only recommended by way of counsel, but also enforced by positive precept. Our Lord himself has said: " We should pray always ;"[2] and this necessity of prayer the Church deelares in the prelude, if we may so call it, prefixed to the Lord's prayer in her liturgy: " Admonished by salutary Necessity of prayer I.

n

---

[1] De oratione scripserunt Tertullian. Cyprian. Aug. ep. 111. ad. Probam. Chrysost. hom. 15. Cassian. lib. 9. Collat. D. Thom. in opusc. et 2. 2. q. 85. per 17. art. [2] Luke xviii. 1.

27* 317

III.

precepts, and taught by divine instruction, we presume to say, ' Our Father, &c.' "   Seeing, therefore, the necessity of prayer to the Christian, and at the solicitation of his disciples, " Lord teach us to pray,"[1] the Son of God gave them a prescribed form of prayer, and encouraged them to hope, that the objects of their petitions would be granted. He himself was to them a model of prayer : he not only prayed assiduously, but watched whole

IV.

nights in prayer.[2]   The Apostles, also, did not omit to deliver precepts on the subject : on this duty St. Peter,[3] and St. John[4] are incessant in their admonitions to the faithful; and St. Paul, not unmindful of its importance, frequently admonishes us

V.

of the salutary necessity of prayer.[5]   Besides, so various are our temporal and spiritual necessities, so numerous the blessings which we expect to receive, that we must have recourse to prayer as the best organ to communicate our wants, and the surest channel through which to receive whatever succour we need.   Of God nothing is due to us : it is ours, therefore, to

VI.

supplicate his goodness.   He has constituted prayer as a necessary means for the accomplishment of our desires ; and its necessity becomes still more obvious, when we reflect, that there are blessings which we cannot hope to obtain otherwise than through prayer.   Holy prayer, such is its efficacy, is a most powerful means of casting out demons : " this kind of demon is not cast out but by prayer and fasting."[6]

VII.

Those, therefore, who do not practise assiduous prayer, rob themselves of the means of obtaining from God gifts of singular value.   To succeed in obtaining the object of your desires, not enough that you ask that which is good ; your intreaties must also be assiduous : " Every one that asketh," says St. Jerome, " receiveth : if, therefore, it will not be given you, it is because you do not ask it : ' ask, therefore, and you shall receive.' "[7]

On the utility of prayer.

But prayer is not only a necessary, but also, a most pleasing and salutary exercise of devotion, from which we reap an abundant harvest of spiritual fruit.   On these fruits of prayer, the pastor will consult spiritual writers, and, when necessary for the instruction of the faithful, will draw copiously upon their labours.   We have, however, made a selection from their accumulated treasures, which appeared to us to suit the present purpose.

First fruit of prayer.

The first fruit which we receive from prayer is, that by prayer we honour God ; prayer is, in some sort, a proof of religion ; and is compared, in Scripture, to incense : " Let my prayer," says David, " be directed as incense in thy sight."[8] By prayer we confess our subjection to God, whom we acknowledge and proclaim to be the author of all good ; in whom alone we centre all our hopes ; who alone is our refuge, in all dangers ; and whose protecting care is the bulwark of our sal-

---

[1] Luke xi. 1.   [2] Luke vi. 12.   [3] 1 Pet. iii. 7. et iv. 19.   [4] 1 John iii. 21, 22
[5] Phil. iv. 6.   1 Thess. v. 17.   1 Tim. ii. 1.   [6] Matt. xvii. 20.
[7] Matt. vii. 8.   Luke xi. 10.   John xvi. 23, 24.   Hier. in cap. 7. Matt.
[8] Ps. cxl. 2.

vation. Of this fruit of prayer we are admonished, in these
words of the Psalmist; "Call upon me in the day of trouble;
I will deliver thee, and thou shalt glorify me."[1]

Another most pleasing and invaluable fruit of prayer, when
heard by God, is, that it opens to us heaven; "Prayer is the
key of heaven," says St. Augustine; "prayer ascends, and
mercy descends; high as are the heavens, and low as is the
earth, God hears the voice of man."[2] Such is the utility, such
the efficacy of prayer, that through it we obtain the plenitude
of heavenly gifts, the guidance and aid of the Holy Spirit, the
security and preservation of the faith, escape from punishment,
protection under temptation, victory over the Devil; in a word,
there is, in prayer, an accumulation of spiritual joy: "Ask,
and you shall receive, that your joy may be full."[3]

Nor can we, for a moment, doubt that God is, at all times,
ready to hear our petitions; a truth to which the sacred Scriptures bear ample testimony. As, however, the texts which go
to establish it are easy of access, we shall content ourselves
with citing a few from the Prophet Isaias. "Then," says he,
"shalt thou call, and the Lord will hear: thou shalt cry, and
he will say, ' here I am ;"[4] and again, "It shall come to pass,
that before they call, I will hear: as they are yet speaking, I
will hear."[5] With regard to instances of persons, who have
obtained from God the objects of their prayers, they are almost
innumerable, and too much within the reach of all to require
special mention.

But our prayers are sometimes unheard? True; and God
then consults, in a special manner, for our interests, bestowing
on us other gifts, of higher value, and in greater abundance;
or withholding what we ask, because, far from being necessary
or useful, its concession would prove not only superfluous, but
even injurious. "God," says St. Augustine, "denies some
things in his mercy, which he grants in his wrath."[6] Sometimes, also, such is the remissness and negligence with which
we pray, that we ourselves do not attend to what we say. If
prayer is an elevation of the soul to God,[7] and if, whilst we
pray, the mind, instead of being fixed upon God, is lost in
wandering distractions, and the tongue slurs over the words at
random, without attention, without devotion, with what propriety
can we give to such empty sounds the name of prayer? We
should not, therefore, be at all surprised, if God does not comply with our requests; we who, by our negligence, and by our
ignorance of the very object of our petitions, afford practical
proof that we are regardless of being heard by him; or who, if
we pray with attention, solicit those things, which, if granted,
must be prejudicial to our eternal interests. To those who
pray with devout attention, God grants more than they ask.

Marginal notes: Second fruit. God ever ready to hear our petitions. Why our prayers are sometimes unheard. To devout prayer God grants

---

[1] Ps. xlix. 15. [2] Sent. 226. de temp. [3] John xvi. 24. [4] Is. lviii. 9.
[5] Is. lxv. 24. [6] Aug. init. serm. 33, de verb. Domini; item in Joan. tract. 73.
[7] De orationis definitione vid. Damascen. libr. 3. de fid. orthod. c. 24. Aug. de
sermone Domini in monte, c. 7. et sermon. 230. de tempore.

more than is asked. This the Apostle declares, in his epistle to the Ephesians ;[1] and the same truth is unfolded in the parable of the prodigal son, who would have deemed it a kindness to be admitted into the number of his father's servants ; but who was received, by a forgiving parent, with more than a parent's fondness.[2] Nay, when we are properly disposed, God accumulates his favours on us. even when we ask them not; and this, not only with abundance, but also with a readiness, which anticipates our desires. Without waiting for their utterance, God prevents the inward and silent aspirations of the poor, according to these words of Scripture : " The Lord hath heard the desire of the poor."[3]

Third fruit of prayer.   Another fruit of prayer is, that it exercises and augments the Christian virtues, particularly the virtue of faith. As they, who have not faith in God, cannot pray as they ought; " How can they call on him, whom they have not believed ?"[4] so, the faithful, in proportion to the fervour of their prayers, possess a stronger and a more assured faith in the protecting providence of God, which requires, principally, that, in all things which we have occasion to supplicate from his bounty, we submit ourselves to his sovereign will. God, it is true, might bestow on us all things abundantly, although we asked them not, nor even thought of them, as he bestows on the irrational creation all things necessary for the support of life: but our most bountiful Father wishes to be invoked by his children; he wishes that, praying as we ought each day of our lives, we may pray with increased confidence ; by acceding to our petitions, he wishes, every day, to give fresh proofs and manifestations of his parental kindness towards us.

Fourth fruit.   Our charity is also augmented by prayer. Recognizing God as the author of every blessing, and the source of every good, we cling to him with the most devoted love. As those who cherish a sincere and mutual affection, become more ardently attached by frequent interviews and interchanges of sentiment, so the more frequent the aspirations which the pious soul breathes to God, and the closer the converse which she enjoys with him, by imploring his bounteous mercy, the more exquisite is the sense of delight which she experiences, and the more ardently is she inflamed to love and adore him. He will, therefore, have us to make use of the exercise of prayer, that, burning with the desire of asking what we are anxious to obtain, we may thus make such advances in spiritual life, as to be worthy to obtain those blessings, which the soul, before dry and contracted, was incapable of receiving.[5]

Fifth.

Sixth.   Moreover, God would have us to know, and always to keep in recollection, this revealed truth, that, unassisted by his heavenly grace, we can of ourselves do nothing, and should, therefore, apply ourselves to prayer, with all the powers of our

<hr>

[1] Ephes. iii. 20.   [2] Luke xxv.   [3] Ps. x. 17.
[4] Rom. x. 14.   [5] Vid. Aug. epist. 121. c. 8.

souls. The weapons which prayer supplies are most power- Seventh.
ful against our most implacable foes: " With the cries of our
prayers," says St. Hilary, " we must fight against the devil
and his armed hosts."[1]

From prayer, we also derive this important advantage, that, Eighth.
inclining as we do, to evil, by the innate corruption of our own
hearts, and to the indulgence of sensual appetite, God permits
us to bring him, in a special manner, present to our minds;
that, whilst we address him in prayer, and endeavour to merit
his gifts and graces, we may be inspired with a love of innocence, and, by effacing our sins, be purified from every stain
of guilt.

Finally, as St. Jerome observes, prayer disarms the anger Ninth.
of God. Hence, these words addressed to Moses, " Let me
alone,"[2] when Moses sought to interpose his prayer for the
protection of a guilty people. Nothing is so efficacious in
appeasing God, when his wrath is kindled; nothing so effectually averts his fury, when provoked; nothing so powerfully
arrests his arm, when already uplifted to strike the wicked, as
the prayers of the pious.

The necessity and advantages of Christian prayer being thus The parts
explained, the faithful should also know how many, and what and de-
are the parts of which it is composed. That this knowledge grees of
appertains to the perfect discharge of the duty of prayer we prayer.
learn from the Apostle, when, in his Epistle to Timothy, exhorting to pious and holy prayer, he carefully enumerates the
parts of which it consists: " I desire therefore first," says he,
" that obsecrations, prayers, postulations and thanksgivings be
made for all men."[3] Although the shades of distinction between these different parts of prayer are delicate and refined,
yet the pastor, should he deem the explanation useful to his
people, will consult, on the subject, the writings of St. Hilary and
St. Augustine.[4] But as there are two principal parts of prayer,
petition and thanksgiving, the sources, as it were, from which
all the other spring, they appeared to us of too much importance to be omitted. When we offer to God the tribute of our
worship, we do so either to obtain some favour, or to return
him thanks for those with which his bounty every day enriches
and adorns us; and each of these God himself declares to be
a necessary part of prayer: " Call upon me," says he, " in
the day of trouble: I will deliver thee, and thou shalt glorify
me."[5]

Who does not know how much we stand in need of the good- Goodness
ness and beneficence of God, if he but consider the extreme and benefi-
destitution and misery of man? Who that has eyes to see, and cence of
God, how
understanding to judge, and does not know how much the will necessary
of God inclines, and how liberal is his bounty towards us? to us.

---

[1] Hilar. in Psal. 63.   [2] Exod. xxxii. 10.   [3] 1 Tim. ii. 1.
[4] Hilar. in Psal. 140. ad illa verba, "dirigatur oratio." Aug. epist. 59. ad
Paulin. ante med. vid. item Cassian. Colla. 9. c. q. et seq. item D. Thom. 2. 2.
q. 83.   [5] Psal. xlix. 15. Vid. Basil. lib. Const. monast. c. 2.

Note.

Wherever we cast our eyes, wherever we turn our thoughts, the admirable light of the divine goodness and beneficence beams upon us. What have we that is not the gift of his bounty ? If, then, all things are the gifts and favours bestowed on us by his goodness, why should not every tongue, as much as possible, celebrate the praises of God, and every heart throb with the pulsation of gratitude, for his boundless beneficence ?

Subordinate degrees of the two principal parts of prayer.

I.

Of these duties of petition and thanksgiving each contains many subordinate degrees. In order, therefore, that the faithful may not only pray but also pray in the best manner, the pastor will propose to them the most perfect manner of praying, and will exhort them to it with the greatest earnestness. What, then, is the best manner and the most exalted degree of prayer ?—That which is made use of by the pious and the just, who, resting on the solid foundation of the true faith, rise successively from one degree of purity and of fervour in prayer to another, until, at length, they reach that height of perfection, whence they can contemplate the infinite power, beneficence, and wisdom of God ; where, too, they are cheered with a bright prospect, and animated with the assured hope, of obtaining not only those blessings which engage their desires in this life, but, also those unutterable rewards, which lie beyond the confines of this world, and which God has pledged himself to grant to him who piously and religiously implores his assistance.[1] Soaring as it were to heaven on these two wings, the soul approaches, in fervent desire, the throne of the Divinity ; adores with rapturous praise and thanksgiving, that Great Being from whom she has received such inestimable blessings ; and, like an only child, animated with singular piety and profound veneration, lays open to her most beloved Father all her wants. This sort of prayer the Sacred Scriptures express by the words " pouring out :" " In his sight," says the prophet, " I pour out my prayer, and before him I declare my trouble ;"[2] as if he had said ; "From him I suppress, from him I conceal nothing, but pour out my whole soul in prayer, flying with confidence into the bosom of God, my most loving father." To this holy exercise the Sacred Scriptures exhort us in these words : " Pour out thy heart before him,"[3] " and cast thy care upon the Lord."[4] This is that degree of prayer to which St. Augustine alludes when he says : " What faith believes, that hope and charity implore."[5]

II.

Another degree of prayer is that of those, who, pressed down by the weight of mortal guilt, strive, however, with what is called dead faith, to raise themselves from their prostrate condition, and to ascend to God ; but, in consequence of their languid state and the extreme weakness of their faith, cannot raise themselves from the earth. Impressed with a just sense of the enormity of their crimes, and stung with remorse of conscience,

---

[1] Vid. D. Bernard. serm. 4. de quadrag. et in serm. de quatuor modis orandi. et Basil. loco jam citato.
[2] Ps. cxli. 3.   [3] Ps. lxi. 9.   [4] Ps. liv. 23.   [5] Ench. cap vii

they bow themselves down with humility, and, far as they are removed from him, implore of God a penitential sorrow, the pardon of their sins, and the peace of reconciliation. The prayers of such persons are not rejected by God: they are graciously heard by him; nay, in his mercy, he generously invites such sinners to have recourse to him; "Come to me, all you that labour, and are heavily laden, and I will refresh you."[1] Of this class of sinners was the Publican, who, not daring to raise his eyes towards heaven, left the temple, as our Lord declares, more justified than the Pharisee.[2]

A third degree of prayer is that which is offered by those, who have not as yet been illumined with the light of faith; but who, whilst the divine goodness lights up in their souls the feeble glimmerings of the law of nature, are strongly excited to the desire and pursuit of truth, to arrive at a knowledge of which is the object of their most earnest prayers. If they persevere in such dispositions, God, in his mercy, will not neglect their earnest endeavours, as we see verified by the example of Cornelius the centurion;[3] against none who desire it sincerely are the doors of the divine mercy closed. III.

The last degree is that of those, who, not only impenitent but obdurate, adding crime to crime, and enormity to enormity, yet dare frequently to ask pardon of God for those sins, in which they are resolved to persevere. Under such circumstances, and with such dispositions, who would presume to ask pardon even of his fellow-man! To the prayer of such sinners God turns a deaf ear, as it is recorded in Scripture of Antiochus: "Then this wicked man prayed to the Lord, of whom he was not to obtain mercy."[4] Whoever lives in this deplorable condition should be exhorted to wean himself from all affection to sin, to turn to God in good earnest and from the heart. IV.

As, under the head of each petition, we shall point out in its proper place, what is, and what is not a proper object of prayer, it will here suffice to admonish the faithful, in general terms, to ask of God such things as are just and good; lest, suing for what is not conformable to his known will, they may be answered in these words: "You know not what you desire."[5] Whatever it is lawful to desire, it is lawful to pray for: the promise of our Lord is unlimited: "You shall ask whatever you will, and it shall be done unto you;"[6] words which ensure all things to pious prayer. Objects of prayer.

In the first place, then, to refer every thing to God, the Supreme Good, the great object of our love, the centre of all our desires, is the principle which should regulate all our wishes. I.

In the next place, those things which unite us most closely to God should be the objects of our most earnest desires; whilst those which would separate us from him, or occasion that separation, should have no share in them. From this principle we II.

[1] Matt. xi. 28.   [2] Luke xviii. 9. et seq.   [3] Acts x. 8.
[4] Mach. ix. 13.   [5] Matt. xx. 22.   [6] John xv. 7

III.   may learn how, after the supreme and perfect good, we are to
desire and ask from God our Father those other things which are
called goods. With regard to those which are called external
goods, and, as it said, belong to the body, such as health, strength,
beauty, riches, honours, glory, which often supply matter and
give occasion to sin, and which, therefore, it is not always either
pious or salutary to ask, they are not to be objects of our prayers
without this limitation, that we pray for them, because necessary, at the same time, referring to God the motive of our prayer.
It cannot be deemed unlawful to pray for those things for which
Jacob and Solomon prayed ; " If," says Jacob, " he shall give
me bread to eat and raiment to put on, the Lord shall be my
God ;"[1] " Give me," says Solomon, " only the necessaries of
life."[2] Whilst, however, we are supplied by the bounty of God
with food and raiment, we should not forget the admonition of
the Apostle : " Let them that buy, be as if they possessed not ;
and those that use this world, as if they used it not; for the
figure of this world passeth away ;"[3] and again, " If riches
abound, set not your hearts upon them."[4] To us, therefore,
belong only their use and advantage, with an obligation, however, as we learn from God himself, of sharing with the indigent. If we are blessed with health and strength, if we abound
in other external and corporal goods, we should recollect that
they are given to us in order to enable us to serve God with
greater fidelity, and as the means of lending assistance to the
wants and necessities of others.

But genius and the acquirements that adorn it, such as erudition and the arts, it is also lawful to pray for, provided our
prayers are accompanied with this condition, that the advantages
which they afford, serve to promote the glory of God, and our
own salvation. That, however, which is to be absolutely and
unconditionally the object of our wishes, our desires, our prayers, is, as we have already observed, the glory of God, and,
next to it, whatever can serve to unite us to that supreme good,
such as faith, the fear and love of God ; but of these we shall
treat at large, when we come to explain the petitions of the
Lord's Prayer.

Who are to
be prayed
for.   The objects of prayer known, the faithful are next to be taught
for whom they are pray. Prayer comprehends petition and
thanksgiving ; and we shall, therefore, first treat of petition.
We are, then, to pray for all mankind, without exception of
enemies, nation, or religion : every man, be he enemy, stranger,
or infidel, is our neighbour, whom God commands us to love,
and for whom, therefore, we should discharge a duty of love,
which is prayer. To the discharge of this duty the Apostle
exhorts when he says : "I desire that prayer be made for
all men."[5] In such prayers the spiritual interests of our
neighbour should hold the first, his temporal, the second place.

[1] Gen. xxviii. 20.   [2] Prov. xxx. 8.   [3] 1 Cor. vii. 30, 31.
[4] Ps. lxi. 11.   [5] 1 Tim. ii. 1.

This duty we owe to our pastors before all others, as we learn
from the example of the Apostle in his Epistle to the Colossians,
in which he solicits them to pray for him, "that God may open
unto him a door of speech;"[1] a solicitation which he also repeats in his Epistle to the Thessalonians.[2] In the acts of the
Apostles, we also read that "prayers were offered in the church
without intermission for Peter."[3] St. Basil, in his "Morals,"
urges to a faithful compliance with this salutary obligation:
"We must," says he, "pray for those who preside over the
word of truth."[4] That it is incumbent on us to offer up our
prayers for princes is obvious from the recorded sentiments of
the same Apostle. Who does not know what a singular blessing the Commonwealth enjoys in a religious and just prince?
We should, therefore, beseech God to make them such as they
ought to be, fit persons to rule over those who are subject to
their authority.[5]

To offer up our prayers also for the good and pious is a practice
sanctioned and supported by the authority of holy men. Even
the good and the pious have occasion for the prayers of others;
and this is a wise dispensation of Providence, that, aware of the
necessity they are under of being aided by the prayers of those
who are inferior to them in sanctity, they may not be inflated with
pride. Our Lord has also commanded us, "to pray for those that
persecute and calumniate us;"[6] and the practice of praying for
those who are not within the pale of the Church, is, as we know
on the authority of St. Augustine, of Apostolic origin.[7] We pray
that the faith may be made known to infidels; that idolators may
be rescued from the error of their impiety; that the Jews,
emerging from the darkness with which they are encompassed,
may arrive at the light of truth; that heretics, returning to soundness of mind, may be instructed in the true faith; and that schismatics, connected by the bond of true charity, may be united
to the communion of the Catholic Church, from which they
have separated. The great efficacy of such prayers, when poured
from the heart, is evinced by a variety of examples. Numerous
instances occur every day in which God rescues individuals of
every class which we have enumerated from the powers of darkness, and transfers them into the kingdom of his beloved Son,
from vessels of wrath making them vessels of mercy; and that,
in realizing so happy a consummation, the prayers of the pious
have considerable influence, no one can reasonably doubt.

Prayers for the dead that they may be liberated from the fire
of purgatory are of Apostolic origin; but this subject we have
already treated at large, when expounding the Holy Sacrifice
of the Mass.[8] Those who are dead in sin derive little advan-

I.

II.

III.

IV.

V.

VI.

VII.

---

[1] Col. iv. 3.   [2] 1 Thess. v. 25.   [3] Acts xii. 5.
[4] Basil. lib. Moral. Reg. 56. cap. 5. item. hom. in. Isaiam.
[5] Vid. Tertull. Apol. c. 30. et ad Scap. c. 2.   [6] Matt. v. 44.
[7] Vid. Aug. Epist. 10. ad Vital. Cypr. de Orat. Dom. Item Cœlestinum Papam
Epist. 1. c. 11.
[8] Dionys. cap. lib. de Eccles. Hierarch. c. 6, 7. Clem. Pap. ep. 1. et lib. Constit.
Apol. Tertul. de Ciron. milit. et in exhort. ad castit. et in lib. de monog. Cypr. ep. 66.

28

tage from prayers and supplications ; yet it is the part of Chris
tian charity to offer up our prayers and tears for them, in order

Note. if possible to obtain their reconciliation with God.   With regard to the execrations uttered by holy men against the wicked,
it is certain, from the concurrent exposition of the Fathers, that
they are either prophecies of the evils which are to befall them,
or denunciations against the crimes of which they are guilty,
that the sinner may be saved, but sin destroyed.[1]

Thanks-   In the second part of prayer, which is " thanksgiving," we
giving, of- render most grateful thanks to God for the divine and immortal
fered for   blessings which he has always bestowed, and still continues
whom.   to bestow on the human race.   This duty we discharge, principally, when we give singular praises to God for the victory
and triumph which, aided by his goodness, the saints have
The ange-   achieved over their domestic and external enemies.   To this
lical salu- sort of prayer belongs the first part of the Angelical Salutation.
tation.   When we say by way of prayer: " Hail Mary, full of grace,
the Lord is with thee, blessed art thou among women," we
render to God the highest praise and return him most grateful
thanks, because he accumulated all his heavenly gifts on the
most Holy Virgin ; and to the Virgin herself, for this her singular felicity, we present our respectful and fervent congratula-
Note.   tions.[2]   To this form of thanksgiving the church of God has wisely
added prayers to, and an invocation of, the most holy Mother
of God, by which we piously and humbly fly to her patronage,
in order that, by interposing her intercession, she may conciliate
the friendship of God to us miserable sinners, and may obtain
for us those blessings which we stand in need of in this life and
in the life to come.   Exiled children of Eve, who dwell in this
vale of tears, should we not earnestly beseech the Mother of
mercy, the advocate of the faithful, to pray for us ?   Should we
not earnestly implore her help and assistance ?   That she possesses exalted merits with God, and that she is most desirous
to assist us by her prayers, it were wicked and impious to
doubt.[3]

Prayers, to   That God is to be prayed to and his name invoked is the
whom ad-   language of the law of nature, inscribed upon the tablet of the
dressed.   human heart : it is also the doctrine of revelation, in which we
I.   hear God commanding: " Call upon me in the day of trouble ;"[4]
and, by the word " God," are to be understood the three per-
II.   sons of the adorable Trinity.   We must also have recourse to
the intercession of the saints who are in glory.   That the saints
are to be prayed to is a truth so firmly established in the church
of God, that the pious mind cannot experience a shadow of
doubt on the subject ; and as this point of Catholic faith
was explained in its proper place, under a separate head, to

---

[1] Vid. Aug. de serm. Dom. in monte lib. cap. 22. et serm. 109. de temp.
[2] Vid. Aug. Ench. c. 100. et 21. de civit. Dei, c. 24. et lib. 20. contr. Faust, c. 21.
[3] Aug. Serm. 18. de Sanctis. Ambr. in l. c. Lucæ. Bern. hom. 3. in " Missus est."
Item. lib. 5. c. 19. Athan. in Ev. de Sancta Deipara. Aug. Serm. 2. de annunt.
Nazianz. in orat. de St. Cyprian.   [4] Ps. xlix. 15.

that explanation we refer the pastor and others. To remove, however, the possibility of error on the part of the unlettered, it will be found useful to explain to the faithful the difference between the invocation of the saints, and the prayers which are offered to God.

We do not address God and the saints in the same manner ; God we implore to grant us the blessings of which we stand in need, and to deliver us from the dangers to which we are exposed ; but the saints, because they are the friends of God, we solicit to undertake the advocacy of our cause with him, to obtain for us, from him, all necessaries for soul and body. Hence, we make use of two different forms of prayer ; to God, we properly say, "Have mercy on us," "Hear us ;" but to the saints, "Pray for us." The words "Have mercy on us," we may also address to the saints, for they are most merciful ; but we do so on a different principle ; we beseech them to be touched with the misery of our condition, and to interpose in our behalf, their influence and intercession before the throne of God. In the performance of this duty, it is strictly incumbent on all not to transfer to creatures the right which belongs exclusively to God ; and when, kneeling before the image of a saint, we repeat the Lord's Prayer, we are also to recollect, that we beg of the saint to pray with us, and to obtain for us those favours which we ask of God, in the petitions of the Lord's Prayer ; in fine, that he become our interpreter and intercessor with God. That this is an office which the saints discharge, we read in the Apocalypse of John the Apostle.[1]

"Before prayer, prepare thy soul, and be not as a man that tempteth God,"[2] is an admonition which has all the weight and authority of revelation. He whose conduct is in direct opposition to his prayers, who, whilst he holds familiar converse with God, suffers his mind to wander, tempts God. As, therefore, the dispositions with which we pray are of such vital importance, the pastor will teach his pious hearers how to pray. The first disposition, then, which should accompany our prayers, is an unfeigned humility of soul, an acknowledgment of our unworthiness, and a conviction that, when we approach God in prayer, our sins render us undeserving, not only of receiving a propitious hearing from him, but even of appearing in his presence. This preparation is frequently mentioned in the inspired Volume : "He hath had regard to the prayer of the humble," says David, "and he hath not despised their petitions ;"[3] "The prayer of him that humbleth himself," says Ecclesiasticus, "shall pierce the clouds."[4] But on a condition of such obvious importance, we abstain from citing many texts of Scripture. Two examples, however, at which we have already glanced, and which are apposite to our purpose, we shall not pass over in silence. The publican, "who, standing

God and the saints addressed differently.

Note.

Preparation for prayer

I.

[1] Apoc. viii. 3.   [2] Eccl. xviii. 23.   [3] Ps. ci. 18.   [4] Eccl. xxxv. 21.

afar off, would not so much as lift up his eyes towards heaven,"[1] and the woman, a sinner, who, moved with sorrow, washed the feet of Christ our Lord, with her tears,[2] illustrate the great efficacy which Christian humility imparts to prayer.

II.

The next disposition is a feeling of poignant sorrow, arising from the recollection of our past sins, or, at least, some sense of regret, that we do not experience that poignancy of sorrow. If the sinner bring not with him to prayer both, or, at least one of these dispositions, he cannot hope to obtain the pardon of his sins.

III.

There are some crimes, such as violence and murder, which oppose the greatest obstacles to the efficacy of our prayers, and we must, therefore, preserve our hands unstained by outrage and cruelty: "When you stretch forth your hands," says the Lord, "I will turn away my eyes from you; and when you multiply prayer, I will not hear, for your hands are full of

IV.

blood."[3] Anger and strife we should also studiously avoid: they have great influence in preventing our prayers from being heard: "I will that men pray in every place," says St. Paul,

V.

"lifting up pure hands, without anger and contention."[4] Implacable hatred for injuries received is another obstacle to the efficacy of prayer, which we cannot be too cautious in avoiding: under the influence of such feelings, it is impossible that we should obtain from God the pardon of our sins. "When you shall stand to pray," says our Lord, "forgive, if you have aught against any man;"[5] "but if you will not forgive men, neither will your Father forgive you your offences."[6]

VI.

Insensibility and inhumanity to the poor we should also scrupulously avoid, if we hope that our prayers shall prove acceptable to God; "He that stoppeth his ear," says the book of Proverbs, "against the cry of the poor, shall also cry himself,

VII.

and shall not be heard."[7] What shall we say of pride? Its hatefulness in the sight of God, we learn from these words of St. James: "God resisteth the proud, and giveth grace to the

VIII.

humble."[8] What of the contempt of the divine oracles? "He that turneth away his ears," says Solomon, "from hearing the

Note.

law, his prayer shall be an abomination."[9] Here, however, we are not to understand that the humble acknowledgment of the injuries done to our neighbour, of murder, anger, insensibility to the wants of the poor, of pride, contempt of the divine oracles, in fine, of any other sin, is excluded from the objects of prayer, provided we implore pardon from God for these crimes.

IX.

Of this preparation of the soul, another essential quality is faith. Without faith, we can have no knowledge of the omnipotence or mercy of God, which are the sources of our confidence in prayer: "All things whatsoever you shall ask in prayer, believing," says the Redeemer, "you shall receive."[10]

[1] Luke xviii. 13.   [2] Luke vii. 37.   [3] Isa. i. 15.   [4] 1 Tim. ii. 8.
[5] Mark xi. 25.   [6] Matt. vi. 15.   [7] Prov. xxi. 13.
[8] James iv. 6. 1 Pet. v. 5.   [9] Prov. xxviii. 9.   [10] Matt. xxi. 22.

On these words of our Lord, St. Augustine, speaking of faith, says, " without faith, it is in vain to pray."[1] Prayer, then, as we have already said, to be efficacious, must be sustained by a firm and unwavering faith, as the Apostle shows by this strong antithesis: " How shall they call on him whom they have not believed?"[2] Believe, then, we must, in order to pray, and that we be not wanting in that faith which renders prayer available. Faith it is that prays, and unwavering prayer gives strength to faith. To this effect is the exhortation of the martyr Ignatius, to those who approach the throne of God in prayer: " Be not of doubtful mind in prayer; blessed is he who hath not doubted." To obtain from God the objects of our prayers, faith, and an assured confidence, are, therefore, of the first importance, according to the admonition of St. James; " Let him ask in faith, nothing wavering."[3]

There is much to inspire us with confidence in prayer. Amongst the motives to confidence, are to be numbered the beneficence and bounty of God, displayed towards us, when he commands us to call him " Father," thus giving us to understand that we are his children; the numberless instances on record of those whose prayers have been heard; and the mediation of our chief advocate, Christ the Lord, who is ever ready to assist us: We have an advocate with the Father, Jesus Christ, the just; and he is the propitiation for our sins;"[4] " Christ Jesus, that died, yea, that is risen also again, who is at the right hand of God, who also maketh intercession for us;"[5] "for there is one God, and one mediator of God and man, the man Christ Jesus."[6] " Wherefore, it behoved him in all things to be made like unto his brethren, that he might become a merciful and faithful high-priest before God."[7] Unworthy, then, as we are, of obtaining our requests, yet considering, and resting our claims upon, the dignity of our great Mediator and Intercessor, Jesus Christ, we should hope and trust most confidently, that, through his merits, God will grant us all that we ask in the proper spirit of prayer. Finally, the Holy Ghost is the author of our prayers; and under his guiding influence, we cannot fail to be heard. " We have received the spirit of adoption of sons, whereby we cry, Abba, (Father.)" This spirit succours our infirmity, and enlightens our ignorance, in the discharge of the duty of prayer; " and," continues the Apostle, " asketh for us with unspeakable groanings."[8] Should we, then, at any time waver, not being sufficiently strong in faith, let us say, with the Apostle, " Lord increase our faith;"[9] and, with the father of the blind man mentioned in the Gospel, " Help my unbelief."[10] But what most ensures the accomplishment of our desires, is the union of faith and hope with that correspondence on our part to the will of God, which makes us

Motives of confidence in prayer.
I.

II.
III.

IV.

Note.

Note.

---

[1] Epist. 10. ad Hier.   [2] Rom. x. 14.   [3] James i. 6.   [4] 1 John ii. 12.
[5] Rom. viii. 34.   [6] 1 Tim. ii. 5.   [7] Heb. ii. 17.   [8] Rom. viii. 15. 26
[9] Luke xvii. 5.   [10] Mark ix. 23.

regulate all our thoughts and actions, and prayers by the standard of his divine law, and the dictates of his sovereign pleasure: "If," says he, "you abide in me, and my words abide in you, you shall ask whatever you will, and it shall be done unto you."[1] In order, however, that all our prayers may be thus graciously heard, we must, as was previously observed, first bury in oblivion all injuries, and cherish sentiments of good will and beneficence towards all men.

The manner of praying:

The manner of praying is, also, matter of the highest moment. In itself prayer, it is true, is good and salutary ; yet, if not applied in a proper manner, it is unavailing : "You ask," says St. James, "and receive not ; because you ask amiss."[2] The pastor, therefore, will instruct the faithful in the best manner of private and public prayer, and in the rules which have been delivered on this subject, according to the discipline of Christ our Lord.

I.

We must, then, pray "in spirit and in truth ;"[3] and this we do when our prayers are the aspirations of an interior and intense ardour of soul.[4] This spiritual manner of praying does

Mental.

not exclude the use of vocal prayer ; but mental prayer, which is the outpouring of a soul inflamed with the vehemence of heavenly desires, deservedly holds the first place ; and, although not uttered with the lips, is heard by Him to whom the secrets of hearts are naked and open. He heard the prayer of Anna, the mother of Samuel, of whom we read, that she prayed, shedding many "tears and only moving her lips ?"[5] Such was, also, the prayer of David, for he says: "My heart hath said to thee, my face hath sought thee ;"[6] and in the perusal of the inspired Volume similar examples will frequently occur.

Vocal.

But vocal prayer has also its advantages, and is sometimes necessary : it quickens the attention of the mind, and kindles the fervent devotion of the heart. "We sometimes," says St. Augustine, "animate ourselves to more lively sentiments of devotion, by having recourse to words and other signs calculated to kindle the fervour of our desires ; filled with pious emotion we find it impossible to restrain the current of our feelings, and accordingly we pour them out in the fervid accents of prayer ; whilst the soul exults with joy, the tongue should also give utterance to that exultation."[7] Vocal prayer, as we know from numerous passages of the Acts of the Apostles, and of the Epistles of St. Paul, was used by the Apostles ; and, following their example, it become us also to offer to God the entire sacrifice

Private and public.

of soul and body. As, however, there are two sorts of vocal prayer, private and public, it is to be observed, that private prayer is employed in order to assist attention and devotion ; whereas, in public prayer, instituted, as it has been, to excite the piety of the faithful, the utterance of the words is, at certain fixed times, indispensably required.

---

[1] John xv. 7.   [2] James iv. 3.   [3] John iv. 23.
[4] De hac ratione orandi in spiritu et veritate vid. Cyrill. Alex. per. 17. libros integros ; item D. Thom. 2. 1. quæst. 83. art. 12.   [5] 1 Kings i. 10. 13.
[6] Ps. xxvi. 8.   [7] St. Aug. ad. Probam. cap. 8, 9, 10.

This practice of praying in spirit, a practice, too, peculiar to Christians, is unknown amongst infidels, of whom Christ our Lord has said, " When you pray, speak not much, as the heathens ; for they think that in their much speaking they may be heard. Be not you, therefore, like to them, for your Father knoweth what is needful for you before you ask him."[1] He therefore prohibits " much speaking ;" but long prayers, which proceed from the eagerness of devotion, and an ardour of soul, that burns with an enduring intensity, he not only does not reject, but on the contrary, recommends by his own example. Not only did he spend whole nights in prayer,[2] but also, " prayed the third time, saying the selfsame words,"[3] and the inference, therefore, to be drawn from the prohibition is, that prayers consisting of mere empty sounds are not to be addressed to God.[4]

To pray in spirit, peculiar to Christians.

" Much speaking" prohibited ; meaning of.

Neither do the prayers of the hypocrite proceed from the heart ; and from the imitation of their example, Christ our Lord deters us in these words : " When ye pray, ye shall not be as the hypocrites that love to stand and pray in the synagogues, and corners of the streets, that they may be seen by men : Amen I say, to you they have received their reward. But thou, when thou shalt pray, enter into thy chamber, and having shut the door, pray to thy Father in secret ; and thy Father who seeth in secret will repay thee."[5] Here the word " chamber" may be understood to mean the human heart, into which it is not enough to enter ; it should also be closed against every distraction ; and then will our Heavenly Father, who sees intuitively our most secret thoughts, hear our prayers, and grant our petitions.

The prayers of the hypocrite rejected by God.

Note.

Another necessary condition of prayer is importunity. The great efficacy of incessant solicitation, the Redeemer exemplifies by the conduct of the judge, who, whilst " he feared not God, nor regarded man," yet overcome by the importunity of the widow, yielded to her intreaties.[6] In our prayers to God we should, therefore, be importunate ; nor are we to imitate the example of those sluggish souls, who become tired of praying, if, after having prayed once or twice, they succeed not in obtaining the object of their prayers. We should never be weary of a duty, taught us by the authority of Christ our Lord and of his Apostles ; and should the mind at any time relax, we should beg of God by prayer the virtue of perseverance.

Importunity in prayer.

The Son of God will also have us present our prayers to the Father in his name : for, by his merits and the grace of his mediation, our prayers acquire such weight, that they are heard by our heavenly Father ; " Amen, Amen, I say unto you, if you ask the Father any thing in my name, he will give it you. Hitherto you have not asked any thing in my name : ask and you shall receive, that your joy may be full."[7] " If you shall ask me any thing in my name, that will I do."[8]

Our prayers to be addressed to God " through Christ."

---

[1] Matt. vi. 7, 8. [2] Luke vi. 12. [3] Matt. xxvi. 44.
[4] Vid. Aug. ep. 121. ad Probam. c. 9. [5] Matt. vi. 5, 6.
[6] Luke xviii. 2, 3. [7] John xvi. 23, 24. [8] John xiv. 14.

Fervour in
prayer.

Fasting.

Be it ours, therefore, to emulate the fervour of holy men in prayer; and to prayer let us unite thanksgiving, imitating the example of the Apostles, who, as may be seen in the Epistles of St. Paul, always observed this salutary practice. To prayer let us unite fasting and alms-deeds. Fasting is most intimately connected with prayer: When cloyed with meat and drink, the mind is so pressed down as not to be able to raise itself to the contemplation of God, or comprehend the utility of prayer.[1]

Alms-
deeds.

Alms-deeds have also an intimate connexion with prayer. What pretension has he to charity, who, blessed with the means of affording relief to those who depend for subsistence on the bounty of others, refuses to stretch forth the hand of mercy to a neighbour and a brother? With what countenance can he, whose heart is devoid of charity, demand assistance from the God of charity, unless he, at the same time, implore the pardon of his sins, and humbly beg of God to infuse into his soul the divine virtue of charity?

A triple re-
medy.

This triple remedy was, therefore, appointed by God to aid man in the attainment of salvation. When we offend God by sin, wrong our neighbour, or injure ourselves, we appease the wrath of God by prayer: by alms-deeds we redeem our offences against man; and by fasting we appease God, and efface from our own souls the stains of sin. Each of these remedies, it is true, is applicable to every sort of sin: they are, however, peculiarly adapted to those which we have specially mentioned.

THE LORD'S PRAYER.

"OUR FATHER WHO ART IN HEAVEN."

Prefatory
words to
the Lord's
Prayer.

As this form of Christian prayer, delivered by Jesus Christ, is of such importance as to have required the preceding prefatory words, which inspire those who approach God piously to approach him also more confidently, it becomes the duty of the pastor to premise a distinct and perspicuous exposition of them. The pious Christian will thus have recourse to prayer with increased alacrity, knowing that in prayer he communes with God, as with a father.[2] To consider the words alone,

---

[1] Vid. hac de re Aug. in Psal. 42. in fine et lib. de perfect. justitia resp. 17. item St. Leonis serm. 1. de jejunio septimi mentis. Petr. Chrys. serm. 43. Bern. in sent. sententia 11.

[2] Orationem Dominicam explicant Tertul. in lib. de ora. Cypr. in lib. de Orat. Domin. Cyril. Hierosp. Catech. 5. Mystag. Chrysost. hom. de orat. Dom. Hier. Theoph. Euthim. in cap. 6. Marc. Ambr. lib. 4. de sacram. c. 4. Aug. ep. 121. ad Probam. item de serm. Dom. in monte lib. 2. c. 5. 6, 7, 8. 16. et hom. 42. item de bono perseverantiæ c. 2. et seqq. et serm. 126. 135. et 182. de temp. item. Cassian collat. 7. c. 18, 19, 20, 21. D. Thom. in opuscul. et. 2. 2. q. 83. a. 9.

which compose this preface, they are, indeed, very few in number; but, looking to the matter, they are of the highest importance, and are replete with mysteries.

"FATHER"] The first word which, by the command and institution of our Lord, we utter in (the Greek and Latin forms of) this prayer is "Father." The Redeemer, it is true, might have commenced this prayer with a word more expressive of majesty, such as "Creator," or "Lord;" yet these he omitted, as they might be associated with ideas of terror, choosing rather an expression which inspires love and confidence. What name more tender than that of Father? a name at once expressive of indulgence and love.[1] God, why called "Father."

The propriety of the word "Father," as applied to God, the faithful may be taught from the works of Creation, Government and Redemption. God created man to his own image and likeness, an image and likeness which he impressed not on other creatures; and, on account of this peculiar privilege with which he adorned man, he is appropriately designated in Scripture the Father of all men, the Father not alone of the faithful but of all mankind. First proof of the propriety of the appellation.

His government of mankind supplies another argument for the propriety of the appellation. By the exercise of a special superintending providential care over us and our interests, he manifests the love of a Father towards us. But to comprehend more clearly the force of this argument, which is drawn from his paternal care over us, it may be necessary to say a few words on the guardianship of those celestial spirits whom he has appointed to watch over, and protect us. Second proof.

Angels are commissioned by Divine Providence to guard the human race, and be present with every man to protect him from injury. As parents, when their children have occasion to travel a dangerous way, infested by robbers, appoint persons to guard and assist them in case of attack; so has our Heavenly Father placed over each of us, in our journey towards our heavenly country, angels, guarded by whose vigilant care and assistance, we may escape the ambushes of our enemies, repel their fierce attacks, and proceed directly on our journey, secured by their guiding protection against the devious tracts into which our treacherous enemy would mislead us, and pursuing steadily the path that leads to heaven. Guardian angels, their ministry.

The important advantages which flow to the human race from this special superintending Providence, the functions and the administration of which are intrusted to angels, who hold a middle place between man and the Divinity, appear from numerous examples recorded in Scripture; which prove that angels, as the ministers of the divine goodness, have frequently wrought wonderful things in the sight of men; and from which we are to infer, that innumerable other important services are rendered to us by the invisible ministry of angels, the guar- Proofs.

[1] Vid. D. Leon. serm. 6. de nat. Dom. D. Thom. 1. p. quæst. 33. art. 1.

I.

dians of our safety and salvation. The angel Raphael, who was appointed by God the companion and guide of Tobias,[1] "conducted him and brought him safe again."[2] He assisted to save him from being devoured by a large fish, and pointed out to him the singular virtue of its gall and heart:[3] he expelled the evil demon, and, by fettering and binding up his power, protected Tobias from injury: he taught the young man the true and legitimate rights of marriage, and restored to the elder Tobias the use of his sight.[4]

II.

The angel who delivered the prince of the Apostles also affords abundant matter of instruction on the admirable advantages which flow from the care and guardianship of angels. To this event, therefore, the pastor will also call the attention of the faithful : he will point to the angel illuminating the darkness of the prison ; awakening Peter by touching his side ; loosing his chains ; bursting his bonds ; admonishing him to rise, and,

III.

taking his sandals and other apparel to follow him.[5] He will also direct their views to the same angel restoring Peter to liberty ; conducting him out of prison through the midst of the guards ; throwing open the door of his prison ; and ultimately placing him in safety without its precincts. The sacred Scriptures, as we have already observed, abound in examples which give us an idea of the magnitude of the benefits conferred on us by the ministry of angels, whose tutelary protection is not confined to particular occasions or persons, but extends to each individual of the human race, from the hour of his birth.

Utility of this exposition ; it evinces the goodness of God.

In the exposition of this point of doctrine, the diligence of the pastor will be rewarded with one important advantage : the minds of the faithful will be interested, and excited to acknowledge and revere the paternal care and providence of God.[6] In the first place, the pastor will here exalt and proclaim the riches of the goodness of God to man, of that God, who, notwithstanding that ever since the transgression of our first parents, who entailed upon us the evil consequences of sin, we have never ceased to offend him by innumerable crimes and enormities, even to the present hour, yet retains his love for us, and still continues his special care over us. To imagine that he is unmindful of his creatures were insanity, and nothing less than to hurl against the Deity the most blasphemous insult. God is angry with the people of Israel, because they suppose themselves deserted by his care: tempting the Lord, they said, "Is the Lord amongst us or not?"[7] And again, "The Lord seeth us not, the Lord hath forsaken the earth."[8] The faithful are, therefore, to be deterred by these authorities from the impiety of imagining that God can at any time be forgetful of man. The Israelites, as we read in Isaias, make the complaint against God ; and its unreasonableness God exposes by a similitude,

---

[1] Tob. v. 6.   [2] Tob. xii.   [3] Tob. vi.   [4] Tob. xii.   [5] Acts xii.
[6] Si de angelorum creatione et excellentia vis agere, redi ad primum symboli articulum supra. pag. 24.   [7] Exod. xvii. 7.   [8] Ezek. viii. 1.

which breathes nought but kindness: "Sion said, the Lord
hath forsaken me, and the Lord hath forgotten me:" to which
God answers, "Can a woman forget her infant, so as not to
have pity on the son of her womb? And if she should forget,
yet will not I forget thee. Behold, I have graven thee in my
hands."[1]

Indisputably as these passages establish this truth, yet, to Further
bring home to the minds of the faithful an absolute conviction, elucidation
that at no time does God forget man, or withdraw from him the of the same
offices of paternal love, the pastor will add to the evidence of truth.
this truth, by introducing the example of our first parents, by I.
which it is so strikingly illustrated. When you hear them
sharply reproved for having violated the command of God;
when you hear their condemnation pronounced in this awful
sentence, "Cursed is the earth in thy work: with labour and
toil shalt thou eat thereof all the days of thy life: thorns and
thistles shall it bring forth to thee; and thou shalt eat the herbs
of the earth;"[2] when you see them driven out of Paradise;
when, to extinguish all hope of return, you read that a fiery
cherub was stationed at the entrance, brandishing "a flaming
sword, turning every way;"[3] when you know, that to avenge
the injury done him, God consigned them to every affliction
of mind and body; when you see and know all this, would
you not be led to pronounce that man was lost irrecoverably?
That he was not only deprived of all assistance from God, but
also abandoned to every species of misery? But, although
the storm of the divine wrath burst over his guilty head, yet
the love of God shot a gleam of consolation across the darkness that enveloped him. The sacred Scriptures inform us,
that "the Lord God made for Adam and his wife garments of
skins, and clothed them,"[4] a convincing proof, that at no time
does God abandon his creature man.

That no injuries offered to God by man can exhaust the II.
divine love, is a truth contained in these words of David, "Will
God in his anger shut up his mercies?"[5] And Habaccuc, addressing himself to God, distinctly says, "When thou art
angry, thou wilt remember mercy."[6] "Who is a God like to
thee," says Micheas, "who takest away iniquity, and passest
by the sin of the remnant of thy inheritance? He will send
his fury in no more, because he delighteth in mercy."[7] When, Note.
therefore, we imagine that God has abandoned us, that we are
deprived of his protection, then, in an especial manner, does
he, of his infinite goodness, seek after and protect us; for in
his anger he stays the sword of his justice, and ceases not to
pour out the inexhaustible treasures of his mercy.

The creation and government of the world, therefore, display, Third
in an admirable manner, the singular love and protecting care proof.
of God; but amongst these, the great work of redemption

---

[1] Isa. xlix. 14—16.   [2] Gen. iii. 17, 18.   [3] Gen. iii. 23, 24.   [4] Gen. iii. 21.
[5] Ps. lxxvi. 10.   [6] Hab. iii. 2.   [7] Mich. vii. 18.

stands out so prominently, that this God of boundless benefi-cence, our Father, has by this third benefit, crowned, and shed a lustre on the other invaluable blessings bestowed on us by his bounty. The pastor, therefore, will announce to his spirit-ual children, and will sound continually in their ears, this over-whelming manifestation of the love of God towards us, in order that they may know that, by redemption, they are become, in an admirable manner, the children of God : " He gave them power," says St. John, " to be made the sons of God, who are born of God."[1] Therefore it is, that baptism, which we re-ceive as the first pledge and memorial of redemption, is called " the sacrament of regeneration ;" for thereby we are born children of God : " That which is born of the Spirit," says our Lord, " is spirit : we must be born again ;"[2] and the Apos-tle Peter says, " Being born again, not of corruptible seed, but incorruptible, by the word of the living God."[3] By virtue of our redemption, we have received the holy Spirit, and are dignified with the grace of God, by which we are adopted sons of God : " You have not received the spirit of bondage again in fear," says St. Paul, " but you have received the spirit of adoption of sons, whereby we cry, Abba, (Father.)"[4] Of this adoption, the force and efficacy are explained by St. John, in these words : " Behold what manner of charity the Father hath bestowed upon us, that we should be called, and should be the sons of God."[5]

Reciprocal affection due to God. These truths explained, the pastor will remind the faithful of the reciprocal affection which they owe to God, our most loving Father, because, by this means, they will comprehend what love and piety, what obedience and veneration, they should ren-der to their Creator, Governor, and Redeemer, and with what hope and confidence they should invoke his name.

God loves whilst he chastises. But to instruct the ignorance, and correct the perversity of such as may imagine that prosperity is the only proof of the love of God, and that adversity, with which he may please to visit us, indicates his hostility, and the utter alienation of his love ; the pastor will show, that when the hand of the Lord touches us,[6] it is not with hostile purpose, but to heal by strik-ing. If he chastises the sinner, it is to reclaim him by salutary severity, and to rescue him from everlasting perdition, by the infliction of present punishment. He visits our iniquities with a rod, and our sins with stripes ; but his mercy he taketh not away from us.[7] The faithful, therefore, are to be admonished to recognise, in such chastisements, a proof of his paternal love, to keep in their memory, and on their lips, these words of the patient Job : " He woundeth, and cureth : he striketh, and his hands shall heal ;"[8] and to adopt these sentiments, and repeat these words of the prophet Jeremiah, spoken in the name of the people of Israel : " Thou hast chastised me, and I was instruct-

---

[1] John i. 12, 13.   [2] John iii. 6, 7.   [3] 1 Pet. i. 23.   [4] Rom. viii. 15.
[5] 1 Ep. iii. 1.   [6] Job xix. 21.   [7] Ps. lxxxviii. 34.   [8] Job v. 18.

ed, as a young bullock unaccustomed to the yoke. Convert me, and I shall be converted, for thou art the Lord my God."[1] Let them also keep before their eyes the example of Tobias, who, when he felt the hand of God upon him, visiting him with blindness, exclaimed, "I bless thee, O Lord God of Israel, because thou hast chastised me."[2]

Here the faithful should guard with the utmost caution, against the error of believing, that any afflictions or calamities befall them, without the knowledge of God. He himself assures us, that a hair of our head shall not perish;[3] they should rather be cheered by these words, which we read in the Apocalypse: "Such as love, I rebuke and chastise;"[4] and all their apprehensions should be calmed by these exhortary words, addressed by St. Paul to the Hebrews, "My son, neglect not the discipline of the Lord, neither be thou wearied whilst thou art rebuked by him; for whom the Lord loveth, he chastiseth; and he scourgeth every son whom he receiveth."[5]

We are not to murmur against his will.

"Our"] When, under the name of Father, we all invoke God, calling him emphatically "our Father," we are taught that, as a necessary consequence of the gift and right of divine adoption, we are brethren, and should love one another as brethren: "You are all brethren," says the Redeemer, "for one is your Father, he that is in heaven;"[6] and hence, in their Epistles, the Apostles call all the faithful brethren. Another necessary conquence is, that, by the same divine adoption, not only are all the faithful united in one common brotherhood, but also called, and really are, brethren of the only begotten Son of God, who assumed our nature. Hence, the Apostle, in his Epistle to the Hebrews, speaking of the Son of God, says, "He is not ashamed to call them brethren, saying, 'I will declare thy name to my brethren.'"[7] This, David had, so many centuries before, prophesied of the Redeemer; and our Lord himself says to the woman mentioned in the Gospel, "Go, tell my brethren that they go into Galilee, there they shall see me."[8] This he said after his resurrection, when he had put on immortality, lest it should be supposed that this fraternal relation was dissolved by his resurrection, and ascension into heaven. So far is the resurrection of Christ from dissolving this bond of union and love, that, from the very throne on which he will sit on the last day, resplendent with majesty and glory, to judge a congregated world, even "the least" of the faithful shall be called by the name of brethren.[9]

We are all brethren of Christ.

I.

Note

But how, possibly, can we be other than brethren of Christ, called as we are, co-heirs with him? He is the first-begotten, appointed heir of all;[10] but we, begotten in the next place, are co-heirs with him, according to the measure of heavenly gifts, and according to the degree of love with which we approve our-

II.

[1] Jer. xxxi. 18.   [2] Tob. xi. 17.   [3] Luke xxi. 18.   [4] Apoc. iii. 19.
[5] Heb. xii. 5.   [6] Matt. xxiii. 8, 9.   [7] Heb. ii. 11, 12. Ps. xxi. 23.
[8] Matt. xxviii. 10.   [9] Matt. xxv. 40.   [10] Rom. viii. 17. Heb. i. 2.

selves servants and co-operators of the Holy Ghost. By the inspiration of the Holy Ghost we are animated to virtue, and to meritorious actions; supported by his grace, we are inflamed to engage with fortitude in the combat for salvation, the successful termination of which, and of our earthly career, will be rewarded by our Heavenly Father with that imperishable crown of justice, which is reserved for all who shall have run the same course; "for God," says the Apostle, "is not unjust, that he should forget our work and our love."[1]

The word "our" to be uttered with heartfelt piety.

But with what sentiments of heartfelt piety we should utter the word "our," these words of St. Chrysostome declare: "God," says he, "willingly hears the prayer of a Christian, not only when offered for himself, but for another. Necessity obliges us to pray for ourselves; charity exhorts us to pray for others. The prayer of fraternal charity," he adds, "is more acceptable to God than that of necessity."[2]

Our demeanour towards others should bespeak fraternal regard: our common brotherhood.

On the subject of prayer, a subject so important, so salutary, it becomes the duty of the pastor to admonish and exhort all his hearers, of every age, sex, and rank, to be mindful of this common brotherhood, and, instead of arrogating to themselves an insolent superiority over others, to exhibit in their conduct the bearing and the tone of fraternal regard. True, there are many gradations of office in the Church of God, yet that diversity of rank is far from severing the bond of this fraternal relationship; in the same manner as variety of use and diversity of office do not cause this or that member of the same body to forfeit the name or functions of a member. The monarch, seated on his throne, and bearing the sceptre of royal authority, as one of the faithful, is the brother of all who are within the communion of the Christian faith. There is not one God the Creator of the rich, another of the poor; one of kings, another of subjects; but there is one God, who is common Lord and Father of all. Considering their spiritual origin, the nobility of all is, therefore, the same, born, as we all are, of the same spirit, through the same sacrament of faith, children of God, and co-heirs to the same immortal inheritance. The wealthy and the great have not one Christ for their God, the poor and the lowly another; they are not initiated by different sacraments; they do not expect a different inheritance. No, we are all brethren; in the language of the Apostle, "We are members of Christ's body, of his flesh, and of his bones."[3] "You are all the children of God, by faith in Christ Jesus; for as many of you as have been baptized in Christ, have put on Christ. There is neither Jew nor Greek; there is neither bond nor free: there is neither male nor female; for you are all one in Christ Jesus."[4]

This doctrine to be forcibly inculcated by the pastor.

This is a subject which the pastor should handle with all possible care: on its consideration he cannot expend too much knowledge and ability: because it is not less calculated to fortify

[1] Heb. vi. 10.   [2] Chrys. hom. 14, operis imperfecti in Matt.
[3] Eph v. 30.   Gal. iii. 26, 27, 28.

and sustain the indigent and the lowly, than to restrain and repress the arrogance of the rich, and the pride of the powerful. It was to remedy this evil, that the Apostle so forcibly pressed on the attention of the faithful this principle of fraternal charity.

When, therefore, O Christian, you are about to address this prayer to God, remember that you, as a son, approach God your Father; and when you begin the prayer, and utter the words " our Father," reflect, for a moment, how exalted the dignity to which the infinite love of God has raised you. He commands you to approach him, not with the reluctance and timidity of a servant approaching his Lord, but with the eagerness and the security of a child flying to the bosom of his father. Consider, also, with what recollection and attention, with what care and devotion, you should approach him in prayer. You must approach him as becomes a child of God : your prayers and actions must be such, as not to be unworthy of that divine origin with which it has pleased your most gracious God to ennoble you ; a duty to which the Apostle exhorts, when he says, " Be ye, therefore, followers of God, as most dear children ;"[1] that of us may be truly said, what the Apostle wrote to the Thessalonians, " You are all the children of light, and the children of the day."[2] *In what spirit we should utter the words " our Father."*

" Who art in Heaven"] All who have a correct idea of the Divinity agree, that God is everywhere present. This, however, is not to be understood, as if he consisted of parts, filling and governing one place with one part, another place with another ; for God is a spirit, and is, therefore, indivisible. Who would presume to circumscribe within the limits of any place, or confine to any particular spot, Him, who says of himself, " Do I not fill the heavens and the earth ?"[3] Yes, by his power and virtue he fills heaven and earth, and all things contained therein. He is present with all things, creating them, or preserving them when already created ; whilst he himself is confined to no place, is circumscribed by no limits, is defined by nothing to prevent his being present everywhere by his immensity and omnipotence. " If," says the Psalmist, " I ascend into heaven, thou art there."[4] *God everywhere, in what sense*

God, although present in all places, and in all things, and, as we have already observed, circumscribed by no limits, is, however, frequently said in Scripture, to have his dwelling in the heavens, because the heavens which we see are the noblest part of the visible world, undecaying in splendour, excelling all other objects in power, magnitude, and beauty, and moving with uniform and harmonious revolution. To elevate the soul of man to the contemplation of his infinite power and majesty, which shine forth with such splendour in the expanse of heaven, God, therefore, declares that his dwelling is in the heavens. He also frequently declares that there is no part of creation *Why said to be specially in heaven.*
I.
II.

[1] Eph. v. 1.   [2] 1 Thess. v. 5.   [3] Jer. xxii. 24.
[4] Ps. cxxxviii. 8.   Aug. lib. 1. Conf. c. 3. D. Thom. 1. p. q. 8. art. 2.

III

that is not filled by his divinity and power, which are everywhere present. In the consideration of this subject, the faithful will, however, propose to themselves not only the image of the universal Father of mankind, but also that of God reigning in heaven, in order that, when approaching him in prayer, they may recollect that heart and soul are to be raised to heaven. The transcendant nature and divine majesty of our Father who is in heaven, should inspire us with as much Christian humility and piety, as the name of father should fill us with love and confidence.

IV.

These words also inform us what are to be the objects of our prayers. All our supplications offered for the useful and necessary things of this life, unless united to the bliss of heaven, and referred to that end, are to no purpose, and are unworthy

Note.

of a Christian. Of this manner of praying, the pastor, therefore, will admonish his pious hearers, and will strengthen the admonition with the authority of the Apostle: " If," says he, " you be risen with Christ, seek the things that are above, where Christ is sitting at the right hand of God. Mind the things that are above, not the things that are upon the earth."[1]

" HALLOWED BE THY NAME."

Objects and order of our prayers.

WHAT should be the objects and the order of our prayers, we learn from the Lord and Master of all; for as prayer is the envoy and interpreter of our wishes and desires, we then pray as we ought, when the order of our prayers corresponds with that of their objects. True charity admonishes us to consecrate stituting in himself alone the supreme good, he justly commands our particular and especial love; and this love we cannot cherish towards him, unless we prefer his honour and glory to all created things. Whatever good we or others enjoy, whatever, in a word, man can name, must yield to him, because emanating from him, who is the supreme good. In order, therefore, that our prayers may proceed in due order, our divine Redeemer has placed this petition, which regards our chief good, at the head of the others; thus teaching us that, before we pray for any thing for our neighbour or ourselves, we should pray for those things which appertain to the glory of God, and make known to him our wishes and desires for their accomplishment. Thus shall we remain in charity, which teaches us to love God more than ourselves, and to make those things which we desire for sake of God the first, and what we desire for ourselves the next object of our prayers.

[1] Coloss. iii. 1, 2.

But as desires and petitions regard things which we want, and as God, that is to say, his divine nature, can receive no accession, nor can the Divinity, adorned as he is, after an ineffable manner, with all perfections, admit not of increase, the faithful are to understand that what we pray for to God regarding himself, belongs not to his intrinsic perfections, but to his external glory. We desire and pray that his name may be better known to the nations ; that his kingdom may be extended; and that the number of his faithful servants may be every day increased; three things, his name, his kingdom, and the number of his faithful servants, which regard not his essence, but his extrinsic glory.

Object of this petition as it regards God.

When we pray that the name of God may be hallowed, we mean that the sanctity and glory of his name may be increased; and here the pastor will inform his pious hearers, that our Lord does not teach us to pray that it be hallowed on earth as it is in heaven, that is, in the same manner, and with the same perfection, for this is impossible; but that it be hallowed through love, and from the inmost affection of the soul. True, in itself, his name requires not to be hallowed ; " it is holy and terrible,"[1] even as he himself is holy ; nothing can be added to the holiness which is his from eternity ; yet, as on earth he is much less honoured than he should be, and is even sometimes dishonoured by impious oaths and blasphemous execrations ; we, therefore, desire and pray that his name may be celebrated with praise, honour, and glory, as it is praised, honoured, and glorified in heaven. We pray that his honour and glory may be so constantly in our hearts, in our souls, and on our lips, that we may glorify him with all veneration, both internal and external, and, like the citizens of heaven, celebrate, with all the energies of our being, the praises of the holy and glorious God. We pray that, as the blessed spirits in heaven praise and glorify God with one mind and one accord, mankind may do the same ; that all men may embrace the religion of Christ, and, dedicating themselves unreservedly to God, may believe that he is the fountain of all holiness, and that there is nothing pure or holy that does not emanate from the holiness of his divine name. According to the Apostle, the Church is cleansed " by the laver of water in the word of life;"[2] meaning by "the word of life," the name of the Father, of the Son, and of the Holy Ghost, in which we are baptized and sanctified. As, then, for those on whom his name is not invoked, there can exist no expiation, no purity, no integrity, we desire and pray that mankind, emerging from the darkness of infidelity, and illumined by the rays of the divine light, may confess the power of his name; that seeking in him true sanctity, and receiving by his grace the sacrament of baptism, in the name of the holy and undivided Trinity, they may arrive at perfect holiness.

What we solicit in this petition.
I.

II.

---

[1] Ps. xcviii. 3.   [2] Eph. v. 26.

III.   Our prayers and petitions also regard those who have forfeited the purity of baptism, and sullied the robe of innocence, thus introducing again into their unhappy souls the foul spirit that before possessed them. We desire, and beseech God, that in them also may his name be hallowed; that, entering into themselves, and returning to the paths of true wisdom, they may recover, through the sacrament of penance, their lost holiness, and become pure and holy temples, in which God may dwell.

IV.   We also pray that God would shed his light on the minds of all, to enable them to see that " every good and perfect gift, coming from the Father of light,"[1] proceeds from his bounty, and to refer to him temperance, justice, life, salvation. In a word, we pray that all external blessings of soul and body, which regard life and salvation, may be referred to him, whose hands, as the Church proclaims, shower down every blessing on the world. Does the sun, by his light, do the other heavenly bodies, by the harmony of their motions, minister to man? Is life maintained by the respiration of that pure air which surrounds us? Are all living creatures supported by that profusion of fruits, and of vegetable productions, with which the earth is enriched and diversified? Do we enjoy the blessings of peace and tranquillity, through the agency of the civil magistrate? All these, and innumerable other blessings, we receive from the infinite goodness of God. Nay, those causes, which philosophers term " secondary," we should consider as instruments wonderfully adapted to our use, by which the hand of God distributes to us his blessings, and showers them upon us with liberal profusion.

V.   But the principal object to which this petition refers is, that all recognise and revere the Spouse of Christ, our most holy mother the Church, in whom alone is that copious and perennial fountain, which cleanses and effaces the stains of sin; from whom we receive all the sacraments of salvation and sanctification, which are, as it were, so many celestial conduits, conveying to us the fertilizing dew which sanctifies the soul; to whom alone, and to those whom she embraces and fosters in her maternal bosom, belongs the invocation of that divine Name which alone, under heaven, is given to men, whereby they can be saved.[2]

Note.   The pastor will urge with peculiar emphasis, that it is the part of a dutiful child not only to pray for his father in word, but, in deed and in work, to endeavour to afford a bright example of the sanctification of his holy name. Would to God that there were none, who, whilst they pray daily for the sanctification of the name of God, violate and profane it, as far as on them depends, by their conduct; who are sometimes the guilty cause why God himself is blasphemed; and of whom

---

[1] James i. 17.
[2] Acts iv. 12. Vid. Aug. serm. 181. de tempore et Greg. lib. 35. Moral. c. 6.

the Apostle has said: "The name of God through you is blasphemed amongst the Gentiles,"[1] and Ezekiel: "They entered amongst the nations whither they went and profaned my holy name, where it was said of them, this is the people of the Lord, and they are come forth out of his land."[2] Their lives and morals are the standard by which the unlettered multitude judge of religion itself and of its founder: to live, therefore, according to its rules, and to regulate their words and actions according to its maxims, is to give others an edifying example, by which they will be powerfully stimulated to praise, honour, and glorify the name of our Father who is in heaven. To excite others to the praise and exaltation of the divine name is an obligation, which our Lord himself has imposed on us: "Let your light so shine before men, that they may see your good works, and glorify your Father who is in heaven;"[3] and the prince of the Apostles says: "Having your conversation good among the Gentiles, that, by the good works which they shall behold in you, they may glorify God in the day of visitation."[4]

"THY KINGDOM COME."

THE kingdom of heaven, which we pray for in this second petition, is the great end to which is referred, in which terminates, all the preaching of the Gospel: from it St. John the Baptist commenced his exhortation to penance, "Do penance, for the kingdom of heaven is at hand;"[5] and with it the Saviour of the world opens his preaching.[6] In that admirable discourse on the mount, in which he points out to his disciples the way to everlasting life, having proposed to himself, as it were, the subject-matter of his discourse, he commences with the kingdom of heaven: "Blessed are the poor in spirit, for theirs is the kingdom of heaven;"[7] and to those who would detain him with them, he assigned as the cause of his departure the necessity of preaching the kingdom of heaven: "To other cities, also, I must preach the kingdom of God; therefore am I sent."[8] This kingdom he afterwards commanded the Apostles to preach;[9] and to him who expressed a wish "to go and bury his father," he replied: "Go thou, and preach the kingdom of God;"[10] and after he had risen from the dead, "for forty days speaking to his Apostles, he spoke of the kingdom of God."[11] *The kingdom of heaven, the great end to which the Gospel is referred.*

This second petition, therefore, the pastor will treat with the greatest attention, in order to impress on the minds of the faithful its paramount importance and necessity. In the first place, *Duty of the pastor.*

1 Rom. ii. 24.   2 Ezek. xxxvi. 20.   3 Matt. v. 16.   4 1 Pet. ii. 12.
5 Matt. iii. 2.   6 Matt. iv. 17.   7 Matt. v. 3.   8 Luke iv. 43.
9 Matt. x. 7.   10 Luke ix. 60.   11 Acts i. 3

he will find its judicious and accurate exposition much facilitated by the reflection, that the Redeemer himself commanded this petition, although united to the others, to be also offered separately, in order that we may seek with the greatest earnestness the object of our prayer: "Seek first the kingdom of God and his justice, and all these things shall be given you besides."[1]

Comprehensiveness of this petition.

And, indeed, so great is the abundance of heavenly gifts contained in this petition, that it embodies all things necessary for the security of soul and body. The king, who pays no attention to those things on which depends the safety of his kingdom, we should deem unworthy of the name. What then must be the solicitude, what the providential care, with which the King of kings guards the life and safety of man! When, therefore, we say, "Thy kingdom come," we compress within the small compass of this petition all that we stand in need of in our present pilgrimage or rather exile, and all this God graciously promises to grant us: He immediately subjoins: "All these things shall be given you besides;" thus unequivocally declaring, that he is that king who, with bountiful hand, bestows upon man an abundance of all things; in the contemplation of whose infinite goodness David was enraptured when he poured out these words of inspired song: "The Lord ruleth me, and I shall want nothing."[2]

Means of obtaining what we ask in this petition.

Not enough, however, that we utter an earnest petition for the kingdom of God; we must also make use of all those means, by which it is sought and found. The five foolish virgins uttered the same earnest petition in these words: "Lord, Lord, open to us;"[3] but they used not the means necessary to secure its attainment, and were, therefore, excluded: "Not every one that says to me, Lord, Lord, shall enter into the kingdom of heaven."[4]

Motives to the adoption of these means.

I.

The priest, therefore, who is charged with the care of souls, will draw from the exhaustless fountain of inspiration those powerful motives, which are calculated to excite the faithful to the desire and pursuit of the kingdom of heaven; which portray in vivid colouring our deplorable condition; and which should make so sensible an impression upon them, that entering into themselves they may call to mind that supreme felicity and those unspeakable joys with which the eternal abode of God our Father abounds. In this nether world we are exiles, inhabitants of a land, in which, also, dwell those demons who wage against us an interminable warfare; who are the determined and implacable foes of mankind. What shall we say of those intestine conflicts and domestic battles in which the soul and the body, the flesh and the spirit, are continually engaged against each other?[5] in which we have always to apprehend defeat; nay, in which instant defeat becomes inevitable, unless we be defended by the protecting hand of God. Feeling this weight

II.

[1] Matt. vi. 33.   [2] Ps. xxii. 1.   [3] Matt. xxv. 11.   [4] Matt. vii. 21.
[5] Gal. v. 17.

of misery the Apostle exclaims: " Unhappy man that I am, who shall deliver me from the body of this death."[1]

The misery of our condition, it is true, strikes us at once of itself, but, if contrasted with that of other creatures, it strikes us still more forcibly. Although irrational and even inanimate, they are seldom seen to depart from the acts, the instincts, the movements imparted to them by nature, so as to fail of obtaining their proposed and determinate end. This is too obvious in the irrational portion of creation, in beasts, fishes, and birds, to require elucidation; but if we look to the heavens, do we not behold the verification of these words of David? " For ever, O Lord, thy word standeth firm in the heavens."[2] Constant in their motions, uninterrupted in their revolutions, they never depart in the least from the laws prescribed by the Creator. The earth, too, and universal nature, as we at once perceive, adhere strictly to, or, at least depart but very little from the laws of their being. But, unhappy man is often guilty of this deordination: he seldom realizes his good purposes, but generally abandons and despises what he has well commenced: his best resolutions, which pleased for a time, are often suddenly abandoned; and he plunges with blind precipitancy into designs as degrading as they are pernicious. What then is the cause of this misery and inconstancy? Manifestly a contempt of the divine inspirations. We close our ears to the admonitions of God, our eyes to the divine lights which shine before us, our hearts against those salutary precepts which are delivered by our heavenly Father.

To paint to the eyes of the faithful the misery of man's condition, to detail its various causes, and to point out the remedies prescribed for its removal, are, therefore, amongst the objects which should employ the most zealous exertions of the pastor; and, in the discharge of this duty, his labour will be not a little facilitated by pressing into his service what has been said on the subject by St. Chrysostome and St. Augustine, men eminent for sanctity; and still more by consulting our exposition of the Creed. Who so abandoned as, with a knowledge of these truths, and aided by the preventing grace of God, not to endeavour, like the prodigal son mentioned in the Gospel,[3] to rise from his abasement, and hasten into the presence of his heavenly Father and king?[4]

Having explained these matters, the pastor will proceed to point out the advantages to be derived by the faithful from this petition, and the objects for which it sues. This becomes the more necessary, as the words, " kingdom of God," have a variety of significations, the exposition of each of which will not be found without its advantages in elucidating other passages of Scripture, and is here indispensably necessary.

(marginal notes:) III.

Duty of the pastor.

Meaning of the words " kingdom of God."

---

[1] Rom. vii. 24.   [2] Ps. cxviii. 89.   [3] Luke xv.
[4] Vid. Chrys. in Ps. 118. et in c. 4. Isai. et hom. 62. ad pop. Antioch. item. et hom. 69. et in serm. de vanit. et brevit. vitæ. Aug. lib. 10. Confess. c. 28 et 31. et lib. 21. de civit. Dei, c. 14. et lib. 21. c. 22.

2 X

I.

The words " kingdom of God," ordinarily signify not only that power which he possesses over all men, and over universal creation, a sense in which they frequently occur in Scripture, but, also, his providence which rules and governs the world : " In his hands," says the Prophet, are all the ends of the earth.[1] The word " ends" includes those things, also, which lie buried in the depths of the earth, and are concealed in the most hidden recesses of creation ; and in this sense Mardochæus exclaims : " O Lord, Lord, Almighty King, for all things are in thy power, and there is none that can resist thy will : thou art Lord of all, and there is none that can resist thy majesty."[2]

II.

Note.

By " the kingdom of God" is also understood that special providence by which God protects, and watches over pious and holy men ; and of this David speaks, when he says : " The Lord rules me, I shall want nothing,"[3] and Isaias : " The Lord our king he will save us."[4] But, although, even in this life, the pious and holy are, as we have already observed, placed, in a special manner, under this kingly power of God ; yet our Lord himself informed Pilate, that his kingdom was not of this world,[5] that is to say, had not its origin in this world, which was created, and is doomed to perish. This is the temporary tenure on which empire is held by Kings, Emperors, Commonwealths, Rulers, and all whose titles to the government of States and Provinces is founded upon the desire or election of men, or who, in the absence of legitimate title, have intruded themselves, by violent and unjust usurpation, into sovereign power. Not so Christ our Lord, who, as the prophet declares, is appointed king by God,[6] and whose kingdom, as the Apostle says, is " justice :" " The kingdom of God is justice and peace, and joy in the Holy Ghost."[7] Christ our Lord reigns in us by the interior virtues of justice, faith, hope, and charity, which constitute us a portion, as it were, of his kingdom. Subject, in a peculiar manner, to God, we are consecrated to his worship ; and, as the Apostle said, " I live, yet not I, but Christ liveth in me ;"[8] so may we too say, " I reign, yet not I, but Christ reigneth in me."

This kingdom why called "justice."

This kingdom is called " justice," because it has for its basis the justice of Christ our Lord ; and of it our Lord says in St. Luke : " The kingdom of God is within you."[9] Jesus Christ, it is true, reigns by faith in all who are within the bosom of our Holy Mother, the church ; yet does he reign in a special manner over those, who animated by faith, enlivened by hope, and inflamed by charity, have yielded themselves pure and living members to God, and in whom the kingdom of God's grace is said to consist.

III.

By the words " kingdom of God" is also meant that kingdom of his glory, of which Christ our Lord says in St. Matthew :

---

[1] Ps. xciv. 4.   [2] Esth. xiii. 9.   [3] Ps. xxii. 1.   [4] Isa. xxxiii. 22.
[5] John xviii. 36.   [6] Ps. ii. 6.   [7] Rom. xiv. 15.   [8] Gal. ii. 29.
Luke xvii. 21.

" Come ye blessed of my Father, possess the kingdom which was prepared for you from the beginning of the world."[1] This kingdom the thief, acknowledging his crimes, begged of him in these words : " Lord, remember me, when thou comest into thy kingdom ;"[2] of this kingdom St. John speaks when he says ; " Unless a man be born again of water and the spirit, he cannot enter into the kingdom of God ;"[3] and of it the Apostle says in his epistle to the Ephesians : " No fornicator, or unclean, or covetous person (which is a serving of idols) hath inheritance in the kingdom of Christ and of God."[4] To it also refer some of the parables made use of by our Lord, when speaking of the kingdom of heaven.[5]

But the kingdom of grace must precede that of glory ; in him, in whom his grace does not reign, his glory cannot reign. Grace, according to the Redeemer, is " a fountain of living water springing up to eternal life ;"[6] nor can we designate glory otherwise than a certain perfect and absolute grace. Whilst we are clothed with this frail mortal flesh ; whilst, faint and wandering in this gloomy pilgrimage and dreary exile, we are separated from God, rejecting the aid of the kingdom of grace which supported us, we often stumble and fall ; but when the light of the kingdom of glory, which is perfect, shall have shone upon us, we shall stand for ever firm and immoveable. Then shall every imperfection be eradicated, and every inconvenience removed ; then shall every infirmity be strengthened and every weakness invigorated ; in a word, God himself will then reign in our souls and bodies. But on this subject we dwelt already at considerable length, in the exposition of the Creed.[7]

The kingdom of grace and of glory.

Having thus explained the ordinary acceptation of the words, " kingdom of God," we now come to point out the particular objects contemplated by this petition. In this petition we pray that the kingdom of Christ, that is, his Church, may be enlarged ; that Jews and infidels may embrace the faith of Christ, and the knowledge of the true God ; that schismatics and heretics may return to soundness of mind, and to the communion of the Church of God, which they have deserted ; and that thus may be fulfilled the words of the Lord, spoken by the mouth of Isaias : " Enlarge the place of thy tent, and stretch out the skins of thy tabernacles ; lengthen thy cords, and strengthen thy stakes, for thou shalt pass on to the right hand and to the left, for he that made thee shall rule over thee."[8] And again, " The Gentiles shall walk in thy light, and kings in the brightness of thy rising ; lift up thy eyes round about and see : all these are gathered together, they are come to thee : thy sons shall come from afar, and thy daughters shall rise up at thy side."[9]

Objects of this petition.
I.

But it is a melancholy truth, that, in the church of God,

II

---

[1] Matt. xxv. 34.   [2] Luke xxiii. 4.   [3] John iii. 5.   [4] Eph. v. 5.
[5] Matt. xiii.   [6] John iv. 14.
[7] See article, " Resurrection of the body."   [8] Is. liv. 2.   [9] Is. lx 3.

there are to be found those " who profess they know God, but in their works deny him ;"[1] whose conduct is a reproach to the faith which they glory to profess; who, by sinning, become the dwelling-place of the devil, where he exercises uncontrolled dominion. Therefore do we pray that the kingdom of God may also come to them, by which, the darkness of sin being dispelled from around them, and their minds being illumined by the rays of the divine light, they may be restored to their lost dignity of children of God ; that, heresy and schism being removed, and all offences and causes of sins being eradicated from his kingdom, our heavenly Father may cleanse the floor of his church ; and that, worshipping God in piety and holiness, she may enjoy undisturbed peace and tranquillity.

III.   Finally, we pray that God alone may live, alone may reign, within us ; that death may no longer exist, but may be absorbed in the victory achieved by Christ our Lord, who, having broken and scattered the power of his enemies, may, in his might, subject all things to his dominion.

Duty of the pastor.   The pastor will also be mindful to teach the faithful, and this the nature of the petition demands, the thoughts and reflections with which their minds should be impressed, in order to offer this prayer devoutly to God. He will exhort them, in the first place, to consider the force and import of that similitude of the Redeemer : " The kingdom of heaven is like a treasure hidden in a field : which a man having found, hid it, and for joy thereof, goeth and selleth all that he hath, and buyeth that field."[2] He who knows the riches of Christ the Lord will despise all things when compared to them : to him, wealth, riches, power, will appear as dross ; nothing can be compared to, or stand in competition with that inestimable treasure. Whoever, then, is blessed with this knowledge, will say with the Apostle, " I count all things to be but loss, and count them but as dung, that I may gain Christ."[3] This is that precious jewel of the Gospel, to purchase which, he who sells all his earthly goods shall enjoy an eternity of bliss.[4] Happy we, should Jesus Christ shed so much light on our minds, as to enable us to discover this jewel of divine grace, by which he reigns in the hearts of those that are his. Then would we be prepared to sell all that we have on earth, even ourselves, to purchase and secure its possession ; then might we say with confidence, " Who shall separate us from the love of Christ ?"[5] But would we know the incomparable excellence of the kingdom of God's glory, let us hear the concurring sentiments of the Prophet and of the Apostle : " Eye hath not seen, nor ear heard, neither hath it entered into the heart of man, what things God hath prepared for them that love him."[6]

To obtain the objects of our   To obtain the object of our prayers, it will be found most available to consider seriously who we are ; children of Adam,

[1] Tit. i. 16.   [2] Matt. xiii. 44.   [3] Phil. iii. 8.
[4] Matt. xxiii. 45.   [5] Rom. viii. 35.   [6] Is. lxiv. 2. 1 Cor. ii. 9.

exiled from Paradise by a just sentence of banishment, and deserving, by our unworthiness and perversity, to become the objects of God's hatred, and to be doomed to eternal punishment. This consideration should excite in us sentiments of unfeigned humility, sentiments, too, which our prayers should piously breathe. Diffiding entirely in ourselves, like the publican, we will fly to the mercy of God: attributing all to his bounty, we will render immortal thanks to him who has imparted to us his Holy Spirit; that Holy Spirit encouraged by whom we are emboldened to say, "Abba, Father."[1] We will also be careful to consider what is to be done, what avoided, in order to arrive at the kingdom of heaven. We are not called by God to lead lives of ease and indolence; he himself declares, that "the kingdom of God suffereth violence, and the violent bear it away;"[2] and if we will enter into life, we must keep the commandments.[3] Not enough, therefore, that we seek the kingdom of God: we must also use our best exertions for its attainment; and it is a duty incumbent on us to co-operate with the grace of God, in pursuing the path that leads to heaven. God never abandons us; he has promised to be with us at all times; and we have, therefore, only not to forsake God, or abandon ourselves.

In this kingdom of God, which is his Church, he has provided all those succours by which he defends the life of man, and accomplishes his eternal salvation; whether they are invisible to us, such as those which we receive from the ministry of the hosts of angelic spirits, or visible, such as we receive from the sacraments, those unfailing sources of celestial virtue. Defended by these safeguards, not only may we securely defy the assaults of our most determined enemies, but may even lay prostrate, and trample under foot the fell tyrant himself, with all his infernal legions.

In conclusion, let us, then, earnestly implore of God the effusion of his Divine Spirit, that he may command us to do all things in accordance with his holy will; that he may overthrow the empire of Satan, so as to have no power over us on the great accounting day; that Christ may be victorious and triumphant; that the divine influence of his law may be spread throughout the world; that his ordinances may be observed; that there be found no traitor to, no deserter from, his standard; and that all may so conduct themselves, as to come with joy into the presence of God their King, and may reach the possession of the celestial kingdom, prepared for them from all eternity, in the fruition of endless bliss with Christ Jesus.

Marginal notes: prayers, humility a necessary disposition: its fruits. Note. Succours to be found in this kingdom. IV.

[1] Rom. viii. 15. [2] Matt. xi. 12. [3] Matt. xix. 17.

30

"THY WILL BE DONE."

Propriety of placing this after the preceding petition.

THIS should be the prayer of all who desire to enter into the kingdom of heaven. Christ our Lord has said, "Not every one that says to me, Lord, Lord, shall enter into the kingdom of heaven; but he that doth the will of my Father who is in heaven, he shall enter into the kingdom of heaven;"[1] and therefore does this petition immediately succeed that which prays for the coming of his kingdom.

Its necessity; misery of man.
I.

But in order that the faithful may appreciate the necessity of the object of this petition, and may estimate the numerous and salutary gifts which we obtain through its concession, the pastor will direct their attention to the misery and wretchedness in which primeval guilt has involved mankind. From the beginning, God implanted in all creatures an inborn desire of pursuing their own happiness, that, by a sort of natural impulse, they may seek and desire their proper end, an end from which they never deviate, unless impeded by some external obstacle which opposes their progress. This propensity existed originally in man, and, endowed, as he is, with reason and judgment, was in him a noble and exalted principle, impelling him earnestly to desire God: but, whilst irrational creatures, which, coming from the hand of God, were good, preserved their instinctive impulse, and thus continued, and still continue, in their original state and condition, man, unhappy man, no longer guided by the innate principle of his being, ran into a devious course, and lost not only original justice, with which he had been supernaturally gifted and adorned, but also, weakened the predominant desire of the soul, infused into it by the Creator, the love of virtue. "All have gone aside: they are become unprofitable together; there is none that doth good, no, not one."[2] "Man is inclined to evil from his youth."[3] Hence, it is not difficult to perceive, that of himself no man is wise unto salvation; that all are prone to evil; and that man is a slave to innumerable corrupt propensities, which hurry him along with precipitancy to anger, hatred, pride, ambition, and almost to every species of evil.

II.

Although continually beset by these evils, yet, and this is the greatest evil of all, many of them appear to us not to be evils, a melancholy proof of the calamitous condition of fallen man, who, blinded by passion, sees not that what he deems salutary generally contains a deadly poison; whilst those things which are really good and virtuous, are shunned as the contrary. Of this false estimate and corrupt judgment of man, God thus expresses his detestation: "Wo to you that call evil good, and good evil; that put darkness for light, and light for darkness; that put bitter for sweet, and sweet for bitter."[4]

[1] Matt. vii. 21.   [2] Ps. lii. 4.   [3] Gen. viii. 21.   [4] Isa. v. 20.

In order, therefore, to delineate in vivid colouring the misery Scriptural illustration. I. of our condition, the sacred Scripture compares us to those who have lost the natural sense of taste, and who, in consequence, loathing wholesome food, relish only what is unwholesome. It also compares us to sick persons, for as they, whilst in a weak state, are unable to fill those offices, or discharge those duties, which require the vigour and activity of health ; so, neither can we, without the assistance of divine grace, perform those actions which are acceptable to God. Should we even, thus unassisted, be able to accomplish some good, it is but trivial, and of little or no advantage towards the attainment of salvation. To love and serve God as we ought is more than our natural strength can accomplish in our present feeble condition, unless assisted by the grace of God.

Another most appropriate comparison is that by which we II. are likened to children, who, with a fickleness characteristic of their age, are, if left to their own discretion, hastily caught by every thing that presents itself. We, indeed, are children, the moment we are destitute of the divine protection : like them we too are the dupes of our own imprudence ; and no less silly, we amuse ourselves with frivolous conversations, and fritter away our time in unprofitable pursuits. Wisdom, therefore, reproves us in the words : " O children, how long will you love childishness, and fools covet those things which are hurtful to themselves ;"[1] and the Apostle thus exhorts us : " Do not become children in sense."[2] We, however, are the dupes of Note. greater folly and grosser error than children : they may, as they advance in years, arrive at the wisdom of manhood ; but, unless guided and assisted from above, we can never aspire to the divine wisdom which is necessary to salvation. Unassisted by God, and having spurned those things which are really good, we rush on voluntary destruction.

Should, however, the soul emerge from the darkness in which Salutary effects of this knowledge. it is enveloped, and discover in the light of divine grace the miseries which encompass her ; should man, awakening from the lethargy which oppressed his faculties, feel the law of the members, and the desires of sense, opposed to the spirit ; should he despise the evil propensities of his nature which incline him to evil ; must he not seek an effectual remedy for the enormous mass of misery entailed on us by the corruption of nature ? Will he not sigh for the happiness which attends a conformity with the holy will of God, which is, and ought to be the rule of a Christian life. This it is that we implore, when we address these words to God : " Thy will be done." Having fallen into this state of misery by disobeying and despising the divine will, God vouchsafes to propose to us, as the sole corrective of all our evils, a conformity to his holy will, which by sinning we despised : he commands us to regulate all our thoughts and actions by this standard ; and for the accomplishment of

[1] Prov. i. 22   [2] James iv. 1.

this important end, we humbly address this prayer to God, "Thy will be done."

This petition necessary to the just.
I.

The same should also be the fervent prayer of those, in whose souls God already reigns; who have been already illumined with the divine light, which enables them to obey the will of God. Although thus gifted and thus disposed, they have still to struggle against the solicitations of passion, the offspring of innate degeneracy and corruption; and were we of their number, we should still be exposed to great danger from our own frailty, and should always apprehend, lest, drawn aside and allured by our concupiscences, "which war in our members," we should again stray from the path of salvation. Of this danger our Lord admonishes us in these words: "Watch ye and pray that ye enter not into temptation: the spirit indeed is prompt but the flesh weak."[1] It is not in the power of man, not even of him who is justified by the grace of God, to reduce the irregular desires of the flesh to such a state of utter subjection, as that they may never afterwards rebel. By justifying grace, God, no doubt, heals the wounds of the soul; but it is not true that he also removes the infirmity of the flesh, as we may infer from the words of the Apostle: "I know that there dwelleth not in me, that is to say, in my flesh, that which is good."[2]

II.

III.

The moment the first man forfeited original justice, which enabled him to bridle the passions, reason was no longer able to restrain them within the bounds of duty, or to repress those inordinate desires, which are repugnant even to reason. Hence the Apostle says, that sin, that is the incentive to sin, dwells in the flesh; giving us to understand that it does not, like a stranger, make a temporary stay with us, but, as an inhabitant of "our earthly house of this habitation,"[3] takes up its perpetual abode in our members. Continually beset, then, as we are, by domestic enemies, we see at once the necessity of taking refuge under the divine protection, and of praying that the will of God may be done in us.

Note

Meaning of the words "thy will."

In the next place, the pastor will explain to the faithful the force of this petition, and omitting many questions of scholastic disputation, which the erudition of some Doctors of the Church has discussed not less usefully than copiously, we shall content ourselves with saying, that, in the Lord's Prayer, the word "will" is that which is commonly called "the will of sign," ("voluntas signi,") and signifies what God commands or admonishes us to do or to avoid. Here, therefore, the word "will" comprehends all things which are proposed to us as the means of attaining heaven, whether they regard faith or morals; all things, in a word, which Christ our Lord has commanded or prohibited either in person or through his Church; and in the same sense are to be understood these words of the

---

[1] Matt. xxvi. 41.   Vid. Hieron. lib. 2. adversus Iovin. et Aug. de Hæresi, 6.
[2] Rom. vii. 18.   [3] 2 Cor. v. 1.

Apostle: "Become not unwise, but understanding what is the will of God."[1].

When, therefore we say, "Thy will be done," we first beseech our Heavenly Father to enable us to obey his divine commands, and to serve him all the days of our lives in holiness and justice; to do all things in accordance with his will and pleasure; to perform all those duties of which we are admonished in the pages of inspiration; guided and assisted by him, to conduct ourselves in every thing as becomes those "who are born, not of the will of flesh but of God;" following the example of our Lord Jesus Christ, who was made obedient unto death, even unto the death of the cross. Finally, we beseech him to enable us to be prepared to suffer all things rather than depart even in the least from his holy will. None desire or love more ardently the objects of this petition than they, to whom it is given to contemplate the surpassing dignity of him who obeys God. They, it is, who comprehend this truth, that to serve and obey God is to reign: "Whoever shall do the will of my Father who is in heaven; he is my brother and sister and mother;"[2] in other words: "To him am I most closely united by all the bonds of the tenderest love."

What we pray for in this petition.

I.
II.
III.
IV

V.

Note.

The saints, with scarcely a single exception, failed not to make the principal gift contemplated by this petition the object of their fervent prayers. All, indeed, have in substance made use of this admirable prayer; but not unfrequently in different words. David, whose inspired strains breathe such sweetness, pours out the same prayer in various aspirations: "O! that my ways may be directed to keep thy justifications:"[3] "Lead me into the path of thy commandments."[4] "Direct my steps according to thy word, and let no iniquity have dominion over me."[5] In the same spirit he says: "Give me understanding, and I will learn thy commandments:"[6] "Teach me thy judgments:"[7] "Give me understanding that I may know thy testimonies."[8] He often expresses the same sentiment in other words; and these passages the pastor will carefully notice, and explain to the faithful; that all may know and comprehend the plenitude and profusion of salutary gifts which are comprehended in the first part of this petition.

This petition very frequently used by the saints.

In the second place, when we say, "Thy will be done," we express our detestation of the works of the flesh, of which the Apostle says: "The works of the flesh are manifest, which are these, fornication, uncleanness, immodesty, &c."[9] "If you live according to the flesh you shall die."[10] In this prayer we also beg of God not to suffer us to yield to the suggestions of sensual appetite, of our lusts, or our infirmities, but to govern our will by the will of God. The sensualist, whose every thought is fixed on, whose every care is absorbed in, the tran

Of what we express our detestation in this petition.

Note.

---

[1] Eph. iv. 17. [2] Matt. xii. 50. Bernard. serm. 3. de S. Andrea.
[3] Ps. cxviii. 5. [4] Ps. cxviii. 35. [5] Ps. cxviii. 133.
[6] Ps. cxviii. 73. [7] Ps. cxviii. 108. [8] Ps. cxviii. 125.
[9] Gal. v. 13. [10] Rom. viii. 13.

sient enjoyments of this world, is far removed from the fulfilment of the will of God; borne along by the tide of passion, he indulges in the gratification of his licentious appetites: in this gratification he places all his happiness, and pronounces

VI. him blessed, who succeeds in its attainment. We, on the contrary, beseech God, in the language of the Apostle, that " we make not provision for the flesh in its concupiscence ;[1] but that his will be done."

Difficulty of offering this petition from the heart.
It is not without a struggle with corrupt nature, that we can bring ourselves to beg of God not to satisfy our inordinate appetites; this disposition of soul is difficult of attainment; and by offering such a prayer we seem in some sort to hate ourselves. To those who are slaves to the flesh such conduct appears folly ; but be it ours cheerfully to incur the imputation of folly for the sake of him, who has said : " If any man will come after me, let him hate himself."[2] Better to desire what is right and just, than to obtain what is opposed to reason and religion, and to the laws of God. Unquestionably the condition of the man, who attains the gratification of his rash and inordinate desires, is less enviable than that of him, who obtains not the object of his pious prayers.

VII Our prayers, however, have not solely for object, that God should deny us what accords with our inordinate desires, vitiated as they are in their source : but, also, that he would not grant us those things for which, under the persuasion and impulse of the devil, who transforms himself into an angel of

Scriptural illustrations.
light, we sometimes pray, believing them to be good. The desire of the prince of the Apostles, to dissuade our Lord from his determination to meet death, appeared not less reasonable than religious : yet our Lord severely rebuked him, because it originated, not in supernatural motives, but in natural feeling. What stronger proof of love towards the Redeemer than that evinced by the request of St. James and St. John, who, filled with indignation against the Samaritans for refusing to entertain their Divine Master, besought him to command fire to descend from heaven and consume those insensible and inhuman men ? Yet they were reproved by our Lord in these words, " You know not of what spirit you are; the Son of man came not to destroy but to save."[3]

VIII. We should beseech God that his will be done, not only when our desires are inordinate or appear to be inordinate, but, also, when they are not inordinate ; when, for instance, the will obeys the instinctive impulse which prompts it to desire what is necessary for our preservation, and to reject the contrary. When about to pray for such things, we should say from our hearts,

Scriptural illustration
" thy will be done ;" in imitation of the example of him, from whom we receive salvation and the discipline of salvation ; who, when agitated by a natural dread of torments, and of a cruel and ignominious death, bowed in that agonizing hour with meek

[1] Rom. xiii. 14.   [2] Matt. xvi. 24. Luke ix. 23.   [3] Luke ix. 54.

submission to the will of his Heavenly Father : " Not my will but thine be done."[1]

But, such is the degeneracy of our nature, that, even when we have contravened our inordinate desires, and subjected them to the will of God, we cannot avoid sin without his assistance, by which we are protected from evil, and directed in the pursuit of good. To this petition, therefore, we must have recourse, beseeching God to perfect in us those things which his grace has begun ; to repress the turbulent emotions of desire ; to subject our sensual appetites to the voice of reason ; in a word, to render us entirely conformable to his holy will. We pray that the whole world may receive the knowledge of his will ; that the mystery of God, hidden from all ages and generations, may be made known to all. We, also, pray for the form and model of this obedience, that our conformity to the will of God be regulated according to the rule observed by the blessed angels and the choirs of other celestial spirits ; that, as they spontaneously and with ecstatic pleasure, obey God, we too may yield a cheerful obedience to his will in the manner most acceptable to him.

Without grace we cannot avoid sin.

IX.

X.

XI.

XII.

XIII.

XIV.

God also requires, that in serving him we be actuated by the greatest love, and by the most exalted charity : that, whilst we devote ourselves entirely to him, with the hope of receiving heaven as the reward of our fidelity, we look forward to that reward, because it has pleased the Divine Majesty that we should cherish that hope. Let all our hopes, therefore, be based on the love of that God, who proposes as its reward the happiness of heaven. There are some who love to serve another, but who do so, however, solely with a view to some recompense, which is the end and aim of their love ; whilst others, influenced by love alone, and by generous devotedness, look to nothing else in the services which they render, than the goodness and worth of him whom they serve ; and in being able to render him these services deem themselves happy. This is the meaning of the terms appended to the petition, and of the apposition between the words, " On *earth* as it is in *Heaven.*"

God how to be served.

Imperfect love.

Perfect love.

Note.

It is, then, our duty to endeavour, as much as possible, to be obedient to God, as we have said the blessed spirits are, whose praises in the performance of this exercise of profound obedience are celebrated by David in the psalm in which occur the words, " Bless the Lord, all ye his hosts ; ye ministers of his that do his will." Should any one, however, adopting the interpretation of St. Cyprian, understand the words, " in heaven," to mean in the good and the pious, and the words " on earth," the wicked and the impious, we do not disapprove of the interpretation ; by the word " heaven" understanding " the spirit," and by the word " earth" " the flesh," that all creatures may in all things obey the will of God.[2]

What our obedience to God is.

<hr>

[1] Luke xxii. 42.   [2] Ps. cii. 21.

This petition contains thanksgiving. This petition also includes thanksgiving. We revere the most holy will of God, and in transports of joy celebrate all his works, with the highest praise and gratulation, knowing that he has done all things well. God is, confessedly, omnipotent; and the consequence necessarily forces itself on the mind, that all things were created at his command: he is the supreme good; we must, therefore, confess that all his works are good, for to all he imparted his own goodness. If, however, the human intellect cannot fathom all the mysterious depths of the divine economy, banishing every doubt from the mind, we unhesitatingly declare, in the words of the Apostle, that " his ways are unsearchable."[1]

Note.

A powerful motive to revere the will of God. We, also, find a powerful incentive to revere the holy will of God in the reflection, that by him we have been deemed worthy to be illumined by his heavenly light; who hath delivered us from the power of darkness, and hath translated us into the kingdom of the Son of his love."[2]

The disposition of mind in which this petition should be offered. But, to close our exposition of this petition, we must revert to a subject at which we glanced at its commencement: it is, that the faithful, in uttering this petition, should be humble and lowly in spirit; keeping in view the violence of inordinate and innate desire, which revolts against the will of God; recollecting that in this duty of obedience, man is excelled by all other creatures, of whom it is written, " All things serve thee;"[3] and reflecting, that he who, unsupported by the divine assistance, is unable to undertake, not to say, perform, any thing acceptable to God, must be, of all other beings, the weakest.

Obedience to the will of God, man's highest dignity. But, as there is nothing greater, nothing more exalted, as we have already said, than to serve God, and live in obedience to his law, what more desirable to a Christian, than to walk in the ways of the Lord; to think nothing, to undertake nothing, at variance with his will? In order that the faithful may adopt this rule of life practically, and adhere to it with greater fidelity, the pastor will recur to the pages of inspiration for examples of individuals, who, by not referring their views to the will of God, have failed in all their undertakings.

Important admonition. Finally, the faithful are to be admonished to acquiesce implicitly in the simple and absolute will of God. Let him, who thinks that he occupies a place in society inferior to his deserts, bear his lot with patient resignation: let him not abandon the sphere in which Providence has placed him; but abide in the vocation to which he has been called. Let him subject his own judgment to the will of God, who consults better for our interests than we can do, by adopting the suggestions of our own desires. If oppressed by poverty, harassed by distress, or goaded by persecution; if visited by troubles or afflictions of any sort: let us recollect, that none of these things happen without the permission of God, who is the Supreme Arbiter of all things. We should, therefore, not suffer our minds to be too

---

[1] Rom. xi. 33.   [2] Col. i. 13.   [3] Ps. cxviii. 91.

much disturbed by them, but bear up against them with fortitude ; having always on our lips the words of the Apostles,
"'The will of the Lord be done ;"[1] and, also, those of holy Job,
" As it hath pleased the Lord, so is it done : blessed be the
name of the Lord."[2]

"GIVE US THIS DAY OUR DAILY BREAD."

THE fourth and following petitions, in which we particularly Order of
and expressively pray for the necessary succours of soul and the peti-
body, have reference to those which preceded. According to tions.
the order of the Lord's Prayer, we ask for what regards the
body and its preservation, after that which regards God. As
man's creation and being terminate in God as his ultimate end,
so, in like manner, the goods of this life have reference to those
of the next ; and it is with a view to the former, that we should
desire and pray for the latter. This we should do, either because the divine order so requires, or because we have occasion
for these aids to obtain those divine blessings, and, assisted by
them, to attain our proposed end, the kingdom and glory of our
Heavenly Father, and the reverential observance of those commands which we know to emanate from his holy will. In this Note.
petition, therefore, we should propose to ourselves nothing but
God, and his glory.

In the discharge of his duty towards his people, the pastor, In asking
therefore, will endeavour to make them understand, that, in pray- for tempo-
ing for temporal blessings, our minds and our desires are to be ings, our
directed in conformity with the law of God, from which we are desires are
not to swerve in the least. By praying for the transient things to be con-
of this world, we but too often transgress ; for, as the Apostle the law of
says, " We know not what we should pray for as we ought."[3] God.
These things, therefore, " we should pray for as we ought," Note.
lest, praying for any thing as we ought not, we receive from
God for answer, " You know not what you desire."[4]

To ascertain what petition is good, and what the contrary, Means of
the purpose and intention of the petitioner is an infallible crite- ascertain-
rion. To pray for temporal blessings, under an impression that of intention
they constitute the sovereign good ; to rest in them, as the ulti- in offering
mate end of our desires, and to seek for nothing else ; this, this peti-
unquestionably, is not to pray as we ought ; for, as St. Augustine observes, " we ask not these temporal things as our good,
but as necessaries."[5] The Apostle, also, in his Epistle to the
Corinthians, teaches, that whatever regards the necessary pur-

---

[1] Acts xxi. 14.   [2] Job i. 21.   [3] Rom. viii. 26.
[4] Matt. xx. 22.   [5] Lib. 2. serm. Dom. in monte. c. 16. item. ep. 121. c. 6.

poses of life is to be referred to the glory of God: "Whether you eat or drink, or whatever else you do, do all to the glory of God."[1]

Importance of this petition.

In order that the faithful may see the importance of this petition, the pastor will advert to the necessity of external things, in order to support life; and this they will the more easily comprehend, by comparing the wants of our protoparent with those of his posterity. True it is, that, although in a state of spotless innocence, from which he himself, and, through his transgression, all his posterity fell, he had occasion to use food for the refection of the body; yet, between his wants, and those to which we are subject, there exists a wide diversity. He stood not in need of clothes to cover him, of a house to shelter him, of weapons to defend him, of medicine to restore health, nor of many other things which are necessary to us for the protection and preservation of our weak and frail bodies : to enjoy immortality, it had been sufficient for him to eat of the fruit which the.tree of life spontaneously yielded; whilst he and all his posterity should have been exempt from the labour of cultivating the earth in the sweat of their brow. Placed in that habitation of pleasure in order to be occupied, he was not, in the midst of these delights, to lead a life of listless indolence; but to him no employment could be troublesome, no duty unpleasant. Occupied in the cultivation of those beautiful gardens, his care would have been always blessed with a profusion of fruits the most delicious, his labours never disappointed, his hopes never blasted.

Difference between the state of innocence and of fallen nature.

Note.

His posterity, on the contrary, are not only deprived of the fruit of the tree of life, but also condemned to this dreadful sentence, " Cursed is the earth in thy work ; with labour and toil shalt thou eat thereof all the days of thy life; thorns and thistles shall it bring forth to thee, and thou shalt eat the herbs of the earth. In the sweat of thy face shalt thou eat bread, till thou return to the earth, out of which thou wast taken; for dust thou art, and into dust thou shalt return."[2] Our condition, therefore, is entirely different from what his and that of his posterity would have been, had he continued faithful to God. All things have been thrown into disorder, and have undergone a melancholy deterioration ; and of the evils consequent to primeval transgression, it is not the least, that the heaviest cost, and labour, and toil, are frequently expended in vain ; either because the crops are unproductive, or because the fruits of the earth are destroyed by noxious weeds, by heavy rains, by storms, hail, blight, or blast. Thus is the entire labour of the year quickly reduced to nothing, by the inclemency of the weather, or the sterility of the soil ; a calamity with which we are visited in punishment of our crimes, which provoke the wrath of God, and prevent him from blessing our labours ; whilst, at the same

Note.

[1] 1 Cor. x. 31.   [2] Gen. iii. 17.

time, the dreadful sentence first pronounced against guilty man is still recorded against us.[1]

In treating this subject, therefore, the pastor will exert him- *Duty of the* self to impress on the minds of the faithful, that if these mis- *pastor.* fortunes and miseries are incidental to man, the fault is entirely his own; that he must labour and toil to procure the necessaries of life, but that unless God bless his labours, all his hopes must prove illusory, all his exertions fruitless: "Neither he that planteth is any thing, nor he that watereth; but God that giveth the increase."[2] "Unless the Lord build the house, they labour in vain that build it."[3]

The pastor, therefore, will teach that those things which are *Necessity* necessary to human existence, or, at least, to its comforts, are *of this* almost innumerable; and this knowledge of our wants and *prayer.* weaknesses will stimulate the faithful to have recourse to their heavenly Father, humbly to solicit every blessing of soul and body, of heaven and of earth. They will imitate the example of the prodigal, who, when he began to experience want in a *Scriptural* strange land, unable to obtain even the husks of swine, on which *example.* to satisfy the cravings of hunger, at length, returning to himself, saw that, for the evils that oppressed him, he could expect no remedy from any one but from his father.[4] They will also *Motives to* have recourse to prayer with greater confidence, if they reflect *confidence* on the goodness of God, whose ears are always open to the cries of his children. Whilst he exhorts us to ask for bread, he promises to bestow it abundantly on us, if we ask it as we ought: by exhorting, he enjoins it as a duty: by enjoining it as a duty, he pledges himself to give it; and by pledging himself to give it, he inspires us with the confident expectation of obtaining it.

When the minds of the faithful are thus animated and en- *Objects of* couraged, the pastor will next evolve the objects of this petition; *this prayer.* and, first, what is the nature of the bread for which it prays. *I.* In the sacred Scriptures the word "bread" has a variety of meanings, but particularly the two following: first, whatever is necessary for the sustenance of the body, and for our other corporeal wants; secondly, whatever the divine bounty has bestowed on us for the life and salvation of the soul. In this petition, then, according to the interpretation and authority of the holy Fathers, we ask those succours of which we stand in need in this life; and those, therefore, who say that such prayers are unlawful, deserve no attention. Besides the unanimous concurrence of the fathers, many examples in the Old and New Testaments refute the error. Jacob, pledging a vow to heaven, prayed thus: "If God shall be with me, and shall keep me in the way by which I walk, and shall give me bread to eat, and raiment to put on, and I shall return prosperously to my father's house, the Lord shall be my God; and this stone, which I have set up for a title, shall be called the house of God; and of all

[1] Gen. iii. 17.   [2] 1 Cor. iii. 7.   [3] Ps. cxxvi. 1.   [4] Luke xv

things thou shalt give to me I will offer tithes to thee."[1]   Solomon prayed for a competency in these words: " Give me neither beggary nor riches; give me only the necessaries of life."[2] Nay, the Saviour himself commands us to pray for those things which, it will not be denied, are temporal blessings: " Pray that your flight be not in the winter, or on the Sabbath."[3]   St. James, also, says, " Is any one of you sad ? Let him pray. Is he cheerful in mind ?   Let him sing;"[4] and the Apostle thus addresses himself to the Romans ; " I beseech you, therefore, through our Lord Jesus Christ, and by the charity of the Holy Ghost, that you help me in your prayers for me to God, that I may be delivered from the unbelievers that are in Judea."[5] Since, then, God permits us to ask these temporal favours, and as this form of prayer was delivered by our Lord Jesus Christ, that it constitutes one of the seven petitions can no longer be matter of doubt.

I.

We, also, ask our daily bread, that is to say, necessary sustenance, and, under the name of bread, whatever is necessary for food and raiment. In this sense Elizeus makes use of the word, when admonishing the king to give bread to the Assyrian soldiers, who received a considerable quantity of flesh meat ;[6] and of Christ our Lord it is written, that " he entered into the house of a certain prince of the Pharisees on the Sabbath-day, to eat bread ;"[7] that is to say, to eat and drink.   To comprehend fully the meaning of the petition, it is also to be observed, that by the word bread, we are not to understand a profusion of exquisite meats, and of rich clothing, but what is in its quality simple, and in its object necessary, according to these words of the Apostle : " Having food and raiment, let us therewith be content ;"[8] and of Solomon, as already quoted ; " Give me only the necessaries of life."[9]   Of this frugality in diet and clothing, we are admonished in the next word of the prayer: when we say " our," we pray for the means of satisfying the necessary wants of nature, not of upholding extravagance, or pampering voluptuousness.

Note.

We do not, however, by using the word " our," imply that of ourselves, and independently of God, we can acquire these means : " All expect of thee," says David, " that thou give them food in season : what thou givest to them they shall gather up : when thou openest thy hand, they shall all be filled with good."[10] And again, " The eyes of all hope in thee, O Lord; and thou givest them meat in due season."[11]   Why, then, do we call that for which we pray " our bread ?"   The reason is, because it is necessary for our sustenance, and is given to us by God, the universal Father, whose providence feeds all living creatures ; and, also, because we are to obtain it, lawfully, not by fraud, or injustice, or theft.   Whatever we obtain by fraudulent means is not our property ; it is the property of another; and it very

Note.

---

[1] Gen. xxviii. 20 . [2] Prov. xxx. 8. [3] Matt. xxiv. 20. [4] James v. 13.
[5] Rom. xv. 30. [6] 4 Kings vi. 22. [7] Luke xiv. 1. [8] 1 Tim. vi. 8.
[9] Prov. xxx. 8. [10] Ps. ciii. 27. [11] Ps. cxliv. 15.

generally happens that the injustice is embittered·by the acquisition, the enjoyment, or, at least, by the loss of such ill-gotten property ; whilst, on the contrary, the fruits of honest industry are enjoyed in peace and happiness ;."Thou shalt eat the labours of thy hands," says the prophet ; "blessed art thou, and it shall be well with thee."[1]   To those, then, who strive, by honest industry, to procure the means of subsistence, God promises the fruit of his blessing in these words : "The Lord will send forth a blessing on thy storehouses, and on all the works of thy hands and will bless thee."[2]   The object of the   **III.** petition, however, is not solely to beg of God to grant us to make use of the fruits of our labour and industry, and of his bounty : these we truly call ours ; but we also pray that he may grant us enlightened judgment, to use with prudence and propriety what we have acquired by honesty and industry.

"DAILY"] This word also conveys an admonition to frugality, This word admonishes to frugality. of which we spoke in the preceding paragraph. We do not pray for delicacy, or variety of meats : we pray for that alone which satisfies the necessary demands of nature; and the Christian should blush, who, loathing with fastidious palate ordinary meat and drink, looks for the rarest viands and the richest wines.

The word "daily" conveys a no less severe censure on those, Condemns cupidity. against whom Isaiah holds out this awful menace : "Wo to you that join house to house, and lay field to field, even to the end of the place: shall you alone dwell in the midst of the earth ?"[3] The cupidity of such men is insatiable: "A covetous man," says Solomon, "shall not be satisfied with money."[4] "They that will become rich," says St. Paul, "fall into temptation, and the snare of the devil."[5]

We, also, call it "our daily bread," because we use it to regain Note. the waste of vital energy, which suffers a daily diminution from the natural heat of the human system.

Finally the word "daily" implies the necessity of unceasing Note. prayer, in order that we may not swerve from the practice of loving and serving God, and that we may be thoroughly convinced of this truth, that upon him we depend for life and salvation.

"GIVE US"] What ample matter for instruction is afforded These two words contain important matter of instruction. by these two words : what motives they supply to worship and reverence the infinite power of God, in whose hands are all things; what reasons to detest the execrable pride of Satan, who said, "To me all things are delivered, and to whom I will, I give them ;"[6] are reflections too obvious not to strike even the most superficial ; for by the sovereign pleasure of God are all things dispensed, and preserved, and increased.

But it may be asked, what necessity have the rich to pray In what sense applicable to the rich. for their daily bread, possessing, as they do, abundance of every

1 Ps. cxxvii. 2.   2 Deut. xxviii. 8.   3 Isa. v. 8.
4 Eccl. v. 9.   5 1 Tim. vi. 9.   6 Luke iv. 6.

thing. They are under the necessity of praying thus, not that those things in which they abound may be given them, but that they lose not what they possess. Let the rich, therefore, learn hence the lesson taught by the Apostle, " not to be high-minded, nor to trust in the uncertainty of riches, but in the living God; who giveth us abundantly all things to enjoy."[1] As a reason for the necessity of this petition, St, Chrysostome says, that in it we not only pray for the means of subsistence, but, also, that " our daily bread" may be supplied by the hand of God, which imparts to it a salubrious and salutary influence, rendering it nutritive, and preserving the body in subjection to the soul.[2]

Note.

Why "give us," not "give me."
I.

But why say " give us," in the plural number, not " give me," in the singular? Because it is a duty of Christian charity, that each individual be not only solicitous for himself, but, also, active in the cause of his neighbour; and that, whilst he attends to his own interests, he forget not the interests of others.

II.

Add to this, that the gifts which God bestows, he bestows, not with a view that he to whom they are given should possess them exclusively, or live luxuriously in their enjoyment; but that he may divide his superfluities with others. As St. Ambrose and St. Basil say, " It is the bread of the hungry that you withhold; it is the clothes of the naked that you lock up: it is the redemption, the freedom, the money of the wretched, that you hide under the earth."[3]

Force of.

" THIS DAY"] These words remind us of the common infirmity of mortals. Although distrustful of being able, by his own exertions, to procure permanent subsistence, who does not feel confident of being able to procure necessary food for one day at least? Yet even this confidence God will not permit us to cherish: he commands us to ask him even for our daily bread. As, then, we all stand in need of daily bread, it follows as a necessary consequence that we should make daily use of the Lord's prayer.

We here ask for spiritual food, and what.

We have thus far treated of that bread which we use to nourish and support the body, and which God, " who maketh his sun to rise on the good and the bad, and raineth upon the just and the unjust,"[4] bestows, in his admirable beneficence, indiscriminately on the good and the bad. It now remains to treat of that spiritual bread, which is, also, the object of this petition of the Lord's Prayer, and which comprehends every thing necessary for the safety and salvation of the soul. The soul, not less than the body, is nourished by a variety of food: the word of God, for instance, is the food of the soul; for Wisdom says, " Come, eat of my bread, and drink the wine which I have mingled for you."[5] When God deprives men of this his word, a privation frequently involved by our crimes, he is said to visit the human race with famine; " I will send forth," says he, " a

I

---

[1] 1 Tim. vi. 17.   [2] Hom. 14. oper. imperf. in Matt.
[3] S. S. Basil. hom. 6. variorum, Aug. et Ambr. serm. 81.
[4] Matt. v. 45.   [5] Prov. ix. 5.

famine into the land, not a famine of bread, or a thirst of water, but of hearing the word of the Lord."[1] And as an incapability of taking food, or, having taken it, of retaining it, is a sure sign of approaching dissolution ; so, it is a strong proof of the utter hopelessness of salvation, to reject the word of God, or, hearing it, to be unable to endure it, and to utter against God the blasphemous cry, "Depart from us, we desire not the knowledge of thy ways."[2]   Such is the infatuation, such the blindness of those who, disregarding the authority of the Catholic Church, of her legitimate pastors and prelates, and revolting against the spiritual power with which they are invested, have joined the standard of heretics, who corrupt the word of God.

An illustration.

Christ our Lord is, also, the bread of the soul: "I am," says he, "the living bread that came down from heaven."[3]   It is incredible with what exquisite pleasure and joy this bread fills devout souls, even when agitated by the rude shocks and afflictions of this life ; and of this we have a strong illustration in the holy choir of the Apostles, of whom it is recorded, that "they went out from the presence of the council rejoicing."[4]   The lives of the saints are replete with similar examples ; and it is of these interior delights, which replenish the souls of the just, that God speaks when he says, "To him that overcometh I will give the hidden manna."[5]

II.

But Christ our Lord, really and substantially present in the sacrament of the Eucharist, is pre-eminently this bread. Of this ineffable pledge of his love, which he bequeathed to us when about to return to his Father, he said, "He that eateth my flesh, and drinketh my blood, abideth in me, and I in him."[6] "Take ye and eat: THIS IS MY BODY."[7]   But, for those matters, which will serve to instruct the faithful on this subject, the pastor will revert to what we have already said, especially, on this sacrament.   The Holy Eucharist is called "our bread," because it is the spiritual food of the faithful only, that is, of those who, uniting charity to faith, cleanse their souls from sin in the sacrament of penance, and, mindful that they are children of God, receive and adore this divine mystery with all the holiness and veneration to which they can excite themselves.[8] It is called "daily" for obvious reasons : it is offered daily to God in the holy sacrifice of the altar, and is given to those who desire to receive it with piety and holiness ; and we should, also, receive it daily, or, at least, live in such a manner as to be worthy, as far as human infirmity will allow, to receive it daily.   Let him who, on the contrary, is of opinion, that the soul should not partake of this saving banquet but at distant intervals, hear the words of St. Ambrose : "If it is daily bread, why partake of it but once a year ?"[9]

III.

Note.

1 Amos viii. 11.   2 Job xxi. 14.   3 John vi. 41.   4 Acts v. 41·
5 Apoc. ii. 17.   6 John vi. 57.   7 Matt. xxvi. 26.   1 Cor. xi. 24.
8 Vid. Tertul. lib. de orat. Cypr. item de orat. Aug. et alios, locis citatis pag. 476.
9 Lib. 5. Sa. c. 4. vide etiam de consec. dist. 2.

The issue of this prayer to be confined to God.　　In the exposition of this petition the faithful are to be emphatically exhorted, when they have honestly used their best consideration and industry to procure the means of subsistence, to confide the issue to God, and to submit their own wishes to the will of him, " who shall not suffer the just to waver for ever."[1] God will either give what they ask, or he will not: if he does, their wishes are realized; if not, it is an unequivocal proof that what they desire would tend to promote neither their interests nor their salvation; whereas, it is denied to the pious, of whose salvation God is more careful than even they themselves.

Duty of the rich.　　Finally, in the exposition of this petition, the pastor will exhort the rich to recollect, that they are to look upon their wealth as the gift of God, bestowed on them in order that they may divide it with the necessitous; and with this truth the words of the Apostle, in his Epistle to Timothy, will be found to accord, and will supply the pastor with abundant matter to elucidate this subject in a manner conducive to the eternal interests of his people.[2]

" AND FORGIVE US OUR DEBTS, AS WE ALSO FORGIVE OUR DEBTORS."

The passion of Christ displays the love of God towards man.　　" FORGIVE US OUR DEBTS"] Many things display the infinite power of God, his wisdom and goodness. Cast our eyes, turn our thoughts, where we may, we are struck with unequivocal manifestations of his omnipotence and goodness; but if there be any one thing which, more than another, eloquently proclaims his boundless love for man, that most assuredly is the ineffable mystery of the passion of Jesus Christ, that perennial fountain which washes away the defilements of sin, and in which, under the guidance and goodness of God, we desire to be merged and purified, when we address him in these words: " Forgive us our debts."

Object of this petition.　　This petition comprises a summary, as it were, of those benefits which have been accumulated on the human race through the merits of Jesus Christ, as was foretold by Isaias: " The iniquity of the house of David shall be forgiven, and this is all the fruit, that the sin thereof should be taken away."[3] This is also the language of David, proclaiming those blessed who have the happiness to partake of that fruit: " Blessed are they whose iniquities are forgiven."[4] The pastor, therefore, will examine and explain, with minute attention, a petition so important to salvation.

Its exposition: the　　In it we enter on a new form of prayer: in the preceding peti-

[1] Ps. liv. 23.　　[2] 1 Tim. vi. 17.　　[3] Isa. xxvii. 9.　　[4] Ps. xxxi. 1.

tions, we ask from God not only spiritual and eternal, but also temporal and transient blessings; but in this we deprecate the evils of the body and of the soul, of this life, and of the life to come. As, however, to obtain the object of our prayers, we must pray as we ought, it appears expedient to explain the dispositions, with which this prayer should be offered to God. The pastor, then, will admonish the faithful, that he who comes to offer this petition must, first, acknowledge, and, in the next place, feel compunction for his sins. He must also firmly believe that God is willing to pardon the sinner when thus disposed, lest, possibly, the bitter remembrance and acknowledgment of his sins may lead the sinner to despair of mercy, as was the case with Cain,[1] and Judas,[2] who looked on God as an avenger of crime, and not, also, as a God of clemency and of mercy. In presenting this petition to the throne of God, we should, therefore, be so disposed as that, whilst we acknowledge our sins in the bitterness of our souls, we also fly to him as to a Father, not a Judge, imploring him to deal with us not in his justice but in his mercy.

We shall be easily induced to acknowledge our sins, if we but listen to God himself declaring by the mouth of David, "They are all gone aside; they are become unprofitable together; there is none that doth good, no not one."[3] Solomon speaks to the same effect; "There is no just man upon earth, that doth good and sinneth not;"[4] and to this subject are also applicable these words of Proverbs; "Who can say, my heart is clean, and I am pure from sin?"[5] St. John also makes use of the same sentiment as an argument against pride: "If we say that we have no sin, we deceive ourselves, and the truth is not in us;"[6] and the Prophet Jeremiah, "Thou hast said, I am without sin and am innocent; and therefore, let thy anger be turned away from me. Behold, I will contend with thee in judgment, because thou hast said, I have not sinned."[7] These sentiments Christ our Lord, who spoke by their lips, confirms in this petition, in which he command us to confess our sins; and the Council of Milevis forbids to interpret it otherwise: "Whoever says, that these words of the Lord's Prayer, 'forgive us our debts,' are to be said by holy men in humility, and not in truth, let him be anathema."[8] How wicked to pray, and at the same time to lie, not to men but to God; and yet this is the crime of him, who, with his lips, says that he asks to be forgiven, but, in his heart, that he has no debts to be forgiven.[9]

In the acknowledgment of our sins, it is not enough that we call them to mind lightly; we must recount them with bitter regret; the heart must be pierced with compunction; the soul must melt with sorrow. On this subject of compunction, therefore, the pastor will bestow his best attention, in order that his

---

[1] Gen. iv. 13. [2] Matt. xxvii. 4, 5. [3] Ps. xiii. 3. [4] Eccl. vii. 21.
[5] Prov. xx. 9. [6] John i. 8. [7] Jer. ii. 25. [8] Conc. Milev. c. 7—9.
[9] Vid. Trid. sess. 6. de justificatione c. 11. item Ang. in Ench. c. 17.

hearers may not only recall to their recollection their sins and iniquities, but may, also, recall them with tears of penitential sorrow ; that, penetrated with heartfelt contrition, they may betake themselves to God their Father, humbly imploring him to pluck from the soul the poisoned stings of sin.

Zeal of the pastor in this respect ; turpitude of sin.

The zeal of the pastor should not, however, content itself with sketching the turpitude of sin ; it should also depict the unworthiness and baseness of man, who, rottenness and corruption that he is, dares to outrage the majesty of God, which no created intelligence can comprehend, and his transcendant dignity, which no created tongue can describe. This picture of the baseness of man borrows a deeper shade from the consideration, that God has created us ; that he has redeemed us ; and that his goodness has heaped upon us countless blessings, the value of which is not to be appreciated. And why thus grossly outrage God? That, estranged from our Father, the supreme good, and lured by the base rewards of sin, we may devote ourselves to the devil, to become his wretched slaves. Language is inadequate to describe the cruel tyranny which he exercises over those, who, having shaken off the sweet yoke of Christ, and having broken the bond of love which binds the soul to God our Father, have gone over to their relentless enemy, the devil. Therefore, is he called in Scripture, " The prince and ruler of this world,"[1] " the prince of darkness,"[2] " and king over all the children of pride ;"[3] and to those who are thus the victims of his tyranny, apply with great truth these words of Isaias : " O Lord our God, other lords besides thee have had dominion over us."[4]

Calamities and miseries which sin entails.

Are we so insensible as to be unmoved by the base violation of the sacred covenant which bound us to God ? If so, let our insensibility yield, at least, to the calamities and miseries into which sin plunges its votaries. It violates the sanctity of the soul, which is wedded to Jesus Christ ; it profanes the temple of the living God ; and it thus involves the sinner in the awful denunciation conveyed by the Apostle in these words : " If any violate the temple of God, him shall God destroy."[5] Innumerable are the evils of which sin is the poisoned source ; their magnitude is thus expressed by David : " There is no health in my flesh, because of thy wrath ; there is no peace for my bones, because of my sins."[6] He marks the virulence of the disease, by declaring that it left no part of his frame uninfected ; the poison of sin entered even into his very bones ; in other words, it infected his understanding, and his will, the two great faculties of the soul. Describing this wide-spreading and destructive contagion, the sacred Scriptures designate sinners by " the lame," " the deaf," " the dumb," " the paralyzed."

The wicked are at war with God.

But, besides the anguish which he felt on account of the wickedness of his sins, David was afflicted yet more by the

---

[1] John xiv. 30. [2] Eph. vi. 12. [3] Job xli. 25.
[4] Is xxvi. 13. [5] 1 Cor. iii. 17. [6] Ps. xxxvii. 4.

consciousness of having provoked the wrath of God. The wicked are at war with God, whom their crimes so grievously offend. "Wrath and indignation," says the Apostle, "tribulation and anguish upon every soul of man that worketh evil."[1] The sinful act, it is true, is transient, but the guilt of sin remains; and that guilt the wrath of God pursues as the shadow follows the body. Pierced by these stings of the divine wrath, David was excited to sue for the pardon of his sins; and that the faithful, imitating the royal penitent, may learn to grieve, that is, to become truly contrite, and to cherish the hope of pardon, the pastor will place before their eyes and press upon their attention, the example of his penitential sorrow, and the lessons of instruction which it conveys.[2]

The importance of such instruction in teaching us to grieve for our sins, God himself declares by the mouth of his prophet: exhorting Israel to repentance, he admonishes her to awake to a sense of the evils which flow from sin: "Know thou, and see that it is an evil and a bitter thing for thee, to have left the Lord thy God, and that my fear is not with thee, saith the Lord the God of Hosts."[3] They who are strangers to these sentiments, who know not these feelings of heartfelt sorrow, are said by the Prophets Isaias, Ezekiel, and Zachary, to have "hard hearts,"[4] "stony hearts,"[5] "hearts of adamant;"[6] like stone they are insensible to all feeling of sorrow, and devoid of every principle of life, that is, of the salutary consciousness of their own infatuation and abandonment. *Utility of this instruction.*

But lest, terrified by the enormity of his crimes, the sinner despair of obtaining pardon, the pastor will animate him to hope by the following considerations; he will remind him that Christ our Lord gave power to his Church to remit sins, as is declared in one of the articles of the Creed; and that this petition makes known to us the extent of the divine goodness and bounty towards us, for if God were not disposed to pardon the penitent sinner, he would not have commanded him to ask for pardon: "Forgive us our debts." We should, therefore, be firmly convinced, that commanding us, as he does, to solicit, he will, also, extend to us his paternal compassion; the petition fully implies that God is so disposed towards us, that he is willing to pardon the truly penitent. True, he is that God against whom we sin by disobedience; the designs of whose wisdom we frustrate, as far as depends on us; whom we offend, whom we outrage in word and deed; but he is, also, a most beneficent Father, who has it in his power to pardon all our transgressions; and who not only declares his willingness to exercise this power, but also urges us to sue to him for pardon, and teaches us how to ask it. It cannot, therefore, be matter of doubt that, with his gracious assistance, we have it in our power to conciliate the divine favour. This attestation of the willing-
The sinner to be encouraged to hope for pardon.
I.
II.

III.

Note

---

[1] Rom. ii. 8, 9. [2] Ps. l. [3] Jer. ii. 19.
[4] Is. xlvi. 12. [5] Ezek. xxxvi. 26. [6] Zach. vii. 12

ness of God to pardon sin, increases faith, nurtures hope, and inflames charity; and it will, therefore, be found useful to enlarge upon this subject by citing Scriptural authorities to this effect, and by referring to examples of individuals whose repentance God rewarded with the pardon of the most grievous crimes. As, however, in our exposition of the prefatory words of the prayer, and of that part of the creed which speaks of the forgiveness of sins, we have been as diffuse on the subject as its matter required, the pastor will revert to those places for whatever he may deem necessary for further illustration; the rest he will draw from the fountains of inspired wisdom. He will also pursue the same plan of instruction which was followed in the other petitions, making known to the faithful the meaning of the word "debts;" without this knowledge they may ask for something different from the real objects which this petition contemplates.

What we do not pray for in this petition.

I.

II.

In the first place, then, we are to know that in it we pray not for exemption from the debt due to God on so many accounts, the payment of which is essential to salvation; that of loving him with our whole heart, our whole soul, and with all our strength. Neither do we ask to be exempted from the duties of obedience, worship, veneration, or any similar obligation included in the word "debt." We pray to be delivered from our sins: this is the interpretation of St. Luke, who, instead of "debt," makes use of the word "sins;"[1] for by their commission we become guilty before God, and incur a debt of punishment, which we must liquidate by satisfaction or by suffering. Such was the debt of which Christ spoke by the mouth of his prophet; "Then did I pay that which I took not away;"[2] from which we may infer that we are only debtors, but also unequal to the payment of the debts which we contract. Of himself the sinner is totally incapable of making satisfaction: we must, therefore, fly to the divine mercy; and as justice, of which God is most tenacious, is an equal and corresponding attribute to mercy, we must have recourse to prayer, and to the advocacy of the passion of Christ, without which, no one ever obtained the pardon of sin; from which, as from its source, flow all the force and efficacy of satisfaction. Such is the value of the price paid by Christ our Lord on the cross, and communicated to us through the sacraments received either actually or in desire, that it obtains and accomplishes for us the pardon of our sins, which is the object of our prayer in this petition. We ask pardon not only for our venial offences, for which pardon may be easily obtained, but also for grievous mortal sins, of which the petition cannot procure forgiveness, unless it derive that efficacy from the Sacrament of Penance received, as we have already said, either actually or in desire.

What we pray for.

Unable to satisfy for ourselves, we must have recourse to the merits of Christ.

Note.

Meaning of "our" in this dif-

The word "our," is here used in a sense entirely different from that in which we said, "our daily bread;" that bread is

[1] Luke xi. 4. [2] Ps. lxviii. 5.

"ours," because given us by the munificence of God ; the sins ferent from which we commit are "ours," because with us rests their guilt. that of "our" in They are our own free acts, otherwise they could not be imputed the pre- to us as sins ; sustaining, therefore, the weight, and confessing ceding the guilt of our sins, we implore the divine clemency, which is petition. necessary for their expiation. In this confession we seek not to palliate our guilt, nor to transfer the blame to others, as our first parents Adam and Eve did ;[1] no, we unbosom ourselves unreservedly, and as we really are, pouring out, if we are wise, the prayer of the prophet : "Incline not my heart to evil words, to make excuses in sins."[2]

We do not say, "forgive me," but "forgive us ;" because, Why each in virtue of the fraternal relation and mutual charity subsisting person between all men, we are each bound to be solicitous for the says, "for- give us," common salvation of all ; and, when we pray for ourselves, it not forgive is our duty to pray also for others. This manner of praying, "me." Note. delivered by our Lord, and subsequently received and always retained by the Church of God, was most strictly observed and enforced by the Apostles. In the Old and New Testaments we find this ardent zeal and intense earnestness in praying for the salvation of others, strikingly exemplified in the conduct of Moses and of Paul ; the former besought God in these words : "Either forgive them this trespass ; or, if thou dost not, strike me out of the book that thou hast written ;"[3] the latter : "I wished myself to be an anathema from Christ, for sake of my brethren."[4]

"AS WE ALSO FORGIVE OUR DEBTORS"] The word "as," The word may be understood in two senses : it has the force of a com- "as," may be under- parison when we beg of God to pardon us our sins, as we stood in pardon the wrongs and contumelies which we receive at the two senses, hands of those who injure us. It also marks a condition, and both meant here. in this sense we find it interpreted by Christ our Lord : "If you will forgive men their offences, your Heavenly Father will forgive you also your offences : but if you will not forgive men, neither will your Father forgive you your offences."[5] Either sense, however, equally implies the necessity of forgive- ness on our part, intimating, as it does, that, to obtain from God the pardon of our offences, we must also extend pardon to those from whom we may have received injury. Such is the rigour with which God exacts from us the pardon of inju- ries, and the tribute of mutual affection and love, that he rejects and despises the gifts and sacrifices of those who are not recon- ciled one to another. To conduct ourselves towards others, as we would have them to demean themselves towards us, is an obligation founded also upon the law of nature ; unparalleled, then, must be the effrontery of him, who, whilst feelings of hostility to a brother rankles in his breast, solicits from God the pardon of offences.

---

[1] Gen. iii. 12, 13.   [2] Ps. cxl. 4.   [3] Exodus xxxii. 32.
[4] Rom. ix. 3.   [5] Matt. vi. 14.

3 A

To be for-
given we
must for-
give.

Those, therefore, who have sustained injuries from others, should be prepared and prompt to pardon, urged to it as they are, by this form of prayer, and also by the command of God: " If thy brother sin against thee, reprove him; and if he sin against thee seven times in a day, and seven times a day be converted unto thee, saying, ' I repent,' forgive him."[1] The Apostle, too, and before him Solomon, said, " If thine enemy be hungry, give him to eat; if he thirst, give him to drink ;"[2] and we read in St. Mark: " When thou standest to pray, for-give, if thou hast ought against any man; that also your Father who is in heaven may forgive you your sins."[3]

Arguments
to enforce
forgive-
ness.

But as, owing to the corruption of our nature, there is no-thing to which man yields a more reluctant assent than to the pardon of injuries, the pastor will exert all the powers and all the resources of his mind to bend the obstinacy of the faithful to this exercise of mildness and mercy, so necessary to a Chris-tian.

I.

He will dwell on those passages of the divine oracles, in which we hear God himself commanding us to pardon our

II.

enemies; and will proclaim, and it is strictly true, that a dispo-sition to forgive injuries, and to love their enemies from the heart, is the strongest evidence of their being the children of God. By loving our enemies we image forth, in some sort, the loving forbearance of God, our Father, who, by the death of his Son, ransomed from everlasting perdition, and reconciled to himself the human race, who before were his avowed ene-

III.

mies. To close this instruction the pastor will urge the com-mand of Christ our Lord, to which the Christian cannot refuse obedience without degrading himself to the lowest degree, and bringing confusion on his guilty head: " Pray for them that persecute and calumniate you, that you may be the children of your Father who is in heaven."[4]

Caution to
the pastor;
forgiveness
of injuries
how to be
under-
stood.

This, however, is a subject which demands consummate prudence on the part of the pastor, lest, disheartened by the difficulty, and yet knowing the necessity, of observing this pre-cept, any of his hearers should yield to despondency. There are some, who, aware of the obligation of burying in voluntary oblivion the injuries which they may have sustained, and of loving those by whom they have been inflicted, desire to comply with these duties, and do comply with them as far as they are able, and yet find that they cannot entirely obliterate from their minds the recollection of the injuries which they have suffered. There still lurks in the mind some lingering grudge, which harrows up conscience, and fills the mind with alarming appre-hensions, lest, not having simply and sincerely forgiven, they may be guilty of disobedience to the command of God. The pastor, therefore, will here explain the opposite desires of the flesh and of the spirit; the one prone to revenge, the other pre-pared to pardon; from which contrariety arise continued strug

---

[1] Luke xvii. 3.   [2] Rom. xii. 20. Prov. xxv. 21, 22.
[3] Mark xi. 25.   [4] Matt. v. 44.

gles and conflicts. He will show that, if the appetites of corrupt nature are ever reclaiming against, and opposed to the dictates of reason, we are not, however, to yield to any misgivings regarding our salvation, provided the spirit perseveres in the duty and determination of forgiving injuries, and of loving every being stamped with the image of God.

Some, perhaps, there are, who, because they have not yet succeeded in bringing themselves to forgive injuries, and to love their enemies, are deterred by the condition contained in this petition, as already explained, from repeating the Lord's Prayer. To remove from their minds so pernicious an error, the pastor will adduce the two following considerations : first, that whoever belongs to the number of the faithful offers this prayer in the name of the entire Church, which must necessarily contain within its pale some pious persons, who have forgiven their debtors the debts mentioned in the petition ; and secondly, that when we offer this prayer to God, we also pray for whatever is necessary to enable us to comply with the petition. We pray for the pardon of our sins, and the gift of sincere repentance : we pray for a deep sense of sorrow : we pray for a hatred of sin ; and we pray for the grace of confessing our offences truly and piously to the minister of God. As, then, it is necessary that we pardon those who have done us injury or injustice, when we ask pardon of God, we also ask strength to be reconciled to those, against whom we harbour feelings of hatred. It, therefore, becomes the duty of the pastor to correct the gross and dangerous error of those, who fear that to utter this prayer would be to exasperate the anger of God ; an apprehension as groundless as it is mischievous. It is his to exhort them to the frequent use of this prayer, in which they beseech God our Father, to grant them grace to pardon those who have injured them, and to love those who have hated them.

But that our prayer be heard, we should first seriously reflect that we are suppliants at the throne of God, soliciting from him that pardon which he never refuses to the penitent ; that we should therefore, possess that charity, and that piety which become penitents ; and that it becomes us in a special manner to keep before our eyes our crimes and enormities, and to expiate them with our tears. To this consideration we should add the greatest circumspection in guarding for the future against the occasion of sin, and against whatever may possibly expose us to the danger of offending God our Father. Of these precautions David was not unmindful : "My sin," says he, "is always before me ;"[1] and again : "I will water my couch with my tears."[2] Let each one also propose to himself the glowing fervour which animated the prayers of those, who besought God to pardon their sins, and who obtained the object of their earnest entreaties ; such as the publican, who, through shame and grief, standing afar off, with eyes fixed on the ground, smote his breast,

Those who have not yet forgiven their enemies are to make use of this prayer; and why ?

I.

II.

Means of rendering our prayer efficacious.

I.

II.

III.

---

[1] Ps. l. 5. [2] Ps. vi. 7.

crying, " O God, be merciful to me a sinner;"[1] and also the woman, " a sinner," who, having washed the feet of our Lord, and wiped them with her hair, kissed them ;[2] and lastly, Peter the prince of the Apostles, who, "going forth wept bitterly."[3]

IV

They should next consider that the weaker men are, and the more liable to moral contagion, the greater the necessity they are under of having recourse to numerous and frequent remedies: the remedies of a soul labouring under spiritual disease are penance and the Holy Eucharist; and to these, therefore, they should have frequent recourse. The Sacred Scriptures inform us that alms-deeds are also an efficacious remedy for healing the wounds of the soul. Those, therefore, who desire to offer up this prayer with pious dispositions, should kindly assist the poor according to the means with which Providence has blessed them. That alms exert a powerful influence in effacing the stains of sin we learn from these words of Tobias: " Alms deliver from death, and the same is that which purgeth away sins, and maketh to find mercy and life everlasting."[4] To the same truth Daniel bears testimony, when, admonishing Nebuchodonoser, he says: "Redeem thou thy sins with alms, and thy iniquities with works of mercy to the poor."[5]

Note.

But the highest species of benevolence, and the most commendable exercise of mercy, is to forget injuries, and to cherish good-will towards those who injure us, or ours, in person, property, or character. Whoever, therefore, desires to experience in a special manner the mercy of God, let him present to God all his enmities, pardon every offence, and pray for his enemies from his heart, embracing every opportunity of deserving well of them. This, however, is a subject which we have already explained, when treating of murder, and to that exposition we, therefore, refer the pastor. He will, however, conclude what he has to say on this petition with the reflection, that nothing is or can be imagined more unjust than that he, who is so rigorous towards his fellow-man as to extend indulgence to no one, should demand of God to be gracious and merciful towards himself.

" AND LEAD US NOT INTO TEMPTATION."

Dangers of relapse.

When the children of God, having obtained the pardon of their sins, and being now inflamed with the desire of devoting themselves to the divine service, sigh for the coming of the kingdom of heaven; and when, engaged in the performance of all the duties of piety towards God, they depend entirely on his paternal will and providential care; then it is, no doubt, that the

[1] Luke xviii. 13.   [2] Luke vii. 38.   [3] Matt. xxvi. 75.
[4] Tob. xii. 9.   [5] Dan. iv. 24.

enemy of mankind employs all his artifices, and exerts all his powers against them, assailing them with such violence as to justify the apprehension, that, wavering in their good resolutions, they may relapse into sin, and their condition be thus rendered much worse than before their conversion to God. To them may be justly applied these words of the Apostle: "It had been better for them not to have known the way of justice, than, after knowing it, to turn back from that holy commandment which was delivered to them."[1] Therefore does our Lord command us to offer this petition, in order that we may commend ourselves daily to God, and implore his paternal care and assistance, well assured that when destitute of his protection, we must be caught in the ambushes of our crafty enemy. Nor is it in this petition alone that he commands us to beg of God not to suffer us to be led into temptation: addressing his Apostles on the eve of his death, and declaring them "clean,"[2] he says: "Watch ye and pray that ye enter not into temptation."[3] This admonition, reiterated by our Lord on so solemn and affecting an occasion, makes it particularly incumbent on the pastor to spare no pains in exciting the faithful to a frequent use of this prayer, that beset, as they all are, on every side and on each day of their lives, by the dangers in which their enemy the devil seeks to involve them, they may unceasingly cry out: "Lead us not into temptation;" thus supplicating the protection of God, whose arm is alone able to crush the efforts of the infernal enemy.

The necessity of the Divine assistance the faithful will understand, if they but reflect on their own weakness and ignorance; if they call to mind these words of Christ our Lord: "The spirit indeed is prompt, but the flesh weak;"[4] and if they consider the heavy calamities and misfortunes that must befall men through the instigation of the devil, if not upheld and assisted by the strong arm of the Omnipotent. Of this our frailty what more striking example than that which the holy choir of the Apostles affords? Evincing, as they had already done, such resolute courage, they however trembled at the first alarm; and abandoning the Saviour, fled from the scene of danger. A more instructive lesson still is presented to us in the conduct of the prince of the Apostles. Loud in professing more than ordinary fortitude, and singular love towards Christ our Lord, and confiding in his own strength, Peter said: "Though I should die with thee, I will not deny thee;"[5] yet in a few moments after, affrighted by the voice of a poor servant maid, he protested with an oath that he knew not the Lord. Doubtless, his strength was unequal to his ardour, when he professed such devotedness to his Lord: but if the confidence, which they reposed in the weakness of human nature, has betrayed men of eminent piety into the most grievous sins, what just cause

[Marginal notes:] Necessity of this petition. I. Illustrations. Note. Note.

---

[1] 2 Pet. ii. 21.　　[2] John xiii. 10.　　[3] Matt. xxvi. 41.
[4] Matt. xxvi. 41.　　[5] Matt. xxvi. 35.

32

of serious apprehensions to the mass of mankind, who are so far inferior to them in holiness.

II.   The pastor, therefore, will place before the eyes of the faithful the conflicts in which we have continually to engage, the dangers which we have to brave, assailed, as we are on all sides, by the world, the flesh, and the devil; and this as long as the soul shall dwell in the perishable tabernacle of the body. Who has not had melancholy experience of the evil effects of corrupt passion, of anger and concupiscence? Who is not harassed by their assaults? Who does not feel the poignancy of their stings? Who does not burn with these torches that smoulder within him? In truth, so numerous are these assaults, so varied these attacks, that it is extremely difficult to escape

III.   unhurt. Besides the enemies that dwell and live within us, there are also other most inveterate foes, of whom it is written: "Our wrestling is not against flesh and blood; but against principalities and powers, against the rulers of the world of this darkness, against the spirits of wickedness in the high places."[1] The efforts of our domestic enemies are seconded by the attacks of the devils from without, who assail us openly, and also insinuate themselves by secret stratagem into our souls; in so much, that it is not without extreme difficulty that we can elude

Note.   their malignity. These the Apostle calls "princes" on account of the excellence of their nature: (their nature is superior to that of man, and of every visible creature) he calls them "principalities and powers," because they excel not only by their nature but also by their power: he calls them "rulers of the world of this darkness," because they rule not the world of light and of glory, that is to say, the good and the pious; but the world of darkness and of gloom, that is, those who, blinded by the debasement and darkness of a wicked and flagitious life, are contented to be the slaves of the devil, the prince of darkness. He also calls the evil demons "the spirits of wickedness." There is a wickedness of the flesh and of the spirit: the former inflames to sensual lusts and criminal pleasures: the latter to wickedness of purpose and depravity of desire; and these belong to the superior part of the soul, and are more criminal than the former, in the same proportion that reason is superior to sensual impulse. This wickedness of Satan the Apostle denominates "in the high places," because his chief aim is to deprive us of the inheritance of heaven.

IV.   We may hence learn that the power of the infernal enemy is formidable, his courage undaunted, and his hatred cruel and implacable. He wages against us a perpetual war with such immitigable fury, that with him there is no peace, no cessation of hostilities. Of his audacity we may form an idea from the words of Satan recorded by the Prophet; "I will ascend into heaven;"[2] he attacked our first parents in Paradise; he assailed the Prophets; he beset the Apostles, and as our Lord declares,

[1] Eph. vi. 12.   [2] Isa. xiv. 13.

"he would sift them as wheat;"[1] in fine, his audacity was not deterred from aggression on the person of our Lord himself! His insatiable desire, his unwearied perseverance, are thus expressed by St. Peter; "your adversary the devil, as a roaring lion, goeth about, seeking whom he may devour."[2] Nor are we tempted by one demon only; sometimes a host of infernal spirits combine in the assault. This was avowed by the evil spirit, who, when asked his name by Christ our Lord, replied; "My name is legion,"[3] that is a host of demons, which tormented their unhappy victim; and of another it is written, that "he took with him seven other spirits more wicked than himself, and entering in they dwelt there."[4]

V.

There are many who, because they feel not the impetuous assaults of the devil, may imagine that this picture of his power is more fanciful than true. No wonder that such persons are not attacked by the devil, whereas they surrender to him at discretion. They possess neither piety, nor charity, nor any other Christian virtue; they are entirely subject to the dominion of the devil; and becoming, as they do, the willing abodes of the infernal tyrant, there needs no temptation to ensure their ruin. But those who have dedicated themselves to God, leading a heavenly life upon earth, are the chief objects of the assaults of Satan; against them he harbours the most malignant hatred; for them he is continually laying snares.

Its necessity to the wicked.

To the good.

The Sacred Scriptures abound in examples of holy men, who, although firm and resolute, fell victims to his open violence or his covert artifice. Adam, David, Solomon, and others, whom it were tedious to enumerate, have experienced the furious assaults and crafty cunning of the spirits of darkness, which human wisdom and human strength are unable to elude or combat. Who then can deem himself sufficiently secure, when abandoned to his own weakness? Hence the necessity of offering up pure and pious prayer to God, imploring him "not to suffer us to be tempted above our strength, but to make issue with temptation, that we may be able to bear it."[5]

Note.

But should any of the faithful, through weakness or ignorance, dread the power of the devil, they are to be exhorted to take refuge in the harbour of prayer, whenever they are overtaken by the storm of temptation. The power and pertinacity of Satan, however great, are not, in his unquenchable hatred of mankind, such as to enable him to tempt and torment as much, and as long, as he pleases; all his power is subject to the control and permission of God. Of this we have a conspicuous example in Job; the devil could have touched nothing belonging to him, if God had not said, "Behold, all that he hath is in thy hand;" whilst, on the other hand, he and his children, and all that he possessed, should have been entirely and at once destroyed by the devil, if God had not said, "Only put not

In temptation.

Note.

[1] Luke xxii. 31.　　[2] 1 Pet. v. 8.　　[3] Mark v. 9
[4] Matt. xii. 45.　　[5] 1 Cor. x. 13.

forth thy hand upon his person."[1] Nay, so restricted is the power of the devil, that he could not even enter into the swine mentioned in the Gospel, without the permission of God.[2]

"Tempta-
tion,"
meaning of.
I.

To understand the force of this petition, it is necessary to show the meaning of the word "temptation," as here employed, and also, what it is to be led into temptation. To tempt is to sound, to probe, him who is tempted, that, eliciting from him what we desire, we may extract the truth. In this meaning of the word, God does not tempt; for what is it that is unknown to God? "All things are naked and open to his

II.

eyes."[3] Another species of temptation consists in pushing our scrutiny far, having some further object in view, either for a good or a bad purpose; for a good purpose, as when worth is tried, in order that it may be rewarded and honoured, and its example proposed as a model for imitation, and as a motive to give glory to God. This is the only sort of temptation which consists with the divine attributes, and of it we have an illustration in these words of Deuteronomy: "The Lord your God tries you, that it may appear whether you love him or not."[4] In this sense, God is also said to tempt those who are his, when he visits them with want and infirmity and other calamities, with a view to try their patience, and in them to present to others an example of Christian virtue. Thus was Abraham tempted to offer his son in sacrifice,[5] and became a singular example of obedience and patience, worthy of being preserved in the records of all future ages; thus also Tobias, of whom it is written, "Because thou wast acceptable to God, it was necessary that temptation should prove thee."[6]

Man, how
tempted.

Man is tempted for a bad purpose, when impelled to sin or destruction. This is the peculiar province of the devil; he tempts mankind, to deceive and precipitate them into ruin; and is, therefore, called, in Scripture, "the tempter."[7] In these temptations, at one time stimulating us from within, he makes use of the agency of the passions; at another time, assailing us from without, he makes use of depraved men as his emissaries; and employs, with a fatal efficiency, the services particularly of heretics, who, "sitting in the chair of pestilence,"[8] which, instead of being the chair of truth, is converted into that of error, scatter, with profuse hand, the deadly seeds of false doctrine, unsettling and precipitating into the gulf of perdition their deluded adherents, who draw no line of distinction between vice and virtue, and who are of themselves but too much inclined to evil.

To be led
into temp-
tation,
meaning of.

We are said to be led into temptation, when we yield to its wicked suggestions. This takes place in a two-fold manner: first, when, abandoning our position, we rush into the evil to which we are allured by the agency of others. God tempts no man thus: he is the occasion of sin to none; "he hateth all

1 Job i. 12.   2 Matt. viii. 31. Mark liv. 12. Luke viii. 32.
3 Heb. iv. 13.   4 Deut. xiii. 3.   5 Gen. xxii. 1.
6 Tob. xii. 13.   7 Matt. iv. 3.   8 Ps. i. 1.

who work iniquity;"[1] and, accordingly, we read in St. James, "Let no man, when he is tempted, say that he is tempted by God; for God is not a tempter of evils."[2] The man, who, although he does not tempt us, nor co-operate in tempting us, has it in his power to prevent us from being tempted, or from yielding to temptation, and does not, is also said to lead us into temptation. God suffers the good and the pious to be thus tempted; but he does not leave them unsupported by his grace. Sometimes, however, we fall, being left to ourselves by the just and rigorous judgments of God, in punishment of our crimes.

II.

God is also said to lead us into temptation, when we abuse, to our own destruction, the blessings which he bestows on us as the means of promoting our eternal salvation, and, like the prodigal child, dissipate in voluptuousness our Father's substance, obedient to the impulse of our bad passions.[3] In such circumstances we may truly say what the Apostle says of the Law: "The commandment that was ordained to life, the same was found unto death to me."[4] Of this Jerusalem, as Ezekiel testifies, affords an apposite exemplification. Enriched and adorned by the Almighty with blessings of every sort, insomuch that God said, by the mouth of his Prophet, "Thou wast perfect through my beauty, which I had put upon thee;"[5] loaded with an accumulation of divine gifts, Jerusalem, far from evincing gratitude to God, from whom she had received, and was still receiving, so many favours; far from making use of those heavenly gifts for the end for which they were bestowed, the attainment of her own happiness, and laying aside all hope and every idea of deriving from them celestial fruit, ungrateful Jerusalem, sunk in luxury and abandonment, looked only to the enjoyment of her present superabundance. This is a subject on which Ezekiel dwells at considerable length, in the chapter to which we have already referred, and to which the pastor may recur. The inference, however, is obvious: it is, that those whom God permits to convert the abundant means, with which his Providence has blessed them, into instruments of vice, are equally guilty of ingratitude with the unhappy Jerusalem.

III.

Illustration.

Note.

The Sacred Scriptures sometimes express the permission of God in language, which, if understood literally, would imply a positive act on the part of God; and this scriptural usage also demands attention. In Exodus it is said, "I will harden the heart of Pharaoh;"[6] and in Isaias, "Blind the heart of this people;"[7] and the Apostle, writing to the Romans, says, "God delivered them up to shameful affections, and to a reprobate sense:"[8] but these, and similar passages, we are not to understand as implying any positive act on the part of God; they express his permission only.[9]

Scriptural phraseology explained.

[1] Ps. v. 5. [2] James i. 13. [3] Luke xv. 12. [4] Rom. vii. 10.
[5] Ezek. xvi. 14. [6] Ex. iv. et vii. [7] Isa. vi. 10. [8] Rom. i. 26.
[9] Vid. Iren. lib. 4. contra haeret. cap. 48. Tertull. lib. 2. contra Marc. 14. Aug. lib. de praedest. et gratia, c. 1. et de praed. sanct. cap. 9. et lib. de grat. et lib. arbit. cap. 21—23. D. Thom. 1. p. quaest. 87. art. 2 et 22. quaest. 15.

These observations premised, it will not be difficult to comprehend the object for which we pray in this petition. We do not ask to be totally exempt from temptation: human life is one continued temptation; and this state of probation is useful and advantageous to man. Temptation teaches us to know ourselves, that is, our own weakness, and to humble ourselves under the powerful hand of God; and by fighting manfully, we expect to receive a never-fading crown of glory; "for he that striveth for the mastery is not crowned, except he strive lawfully."[1] "Blessed is the man," says St. James, "that endureth temptation; for when he hath been proved, he shall receive the crown of life, which God hath promised to them that love him."[2] If we are sometimes hard pressed by the temptation of the enemy, it will also cheer us to reflect, "that we have a High-priest to help us, who can have compassion on our infirmities, tempted himself in all things."[3]

What, then, do we pray for in this petition? We pray that the divine assistance may not forsake us; that we yield not to temptation, deceived by the artifice of the wicked one; that we give not up the victory, worsted in the contest; and that the grace of God may be at hand to succour us when our strength fails, to refresh and invigorate us on the evil day. We should, therefore, implore the divine assistance, in general, under all temptations, and, in particular, when assailed by any particular temptation. This we find to have been the conduct of David, under almost every species of temptation: against lying, he prays in these words: "Take not thou the word of truth utterly out of my mouth:"[4] against covetousness, "Incline my heart unto thy testimonies, and not to covetousness:"[5] and against the vanities of this life, and the allurements of concupiscence, he prays thus; "Turn away my eyes, that they may not behold vanity."[6] We pray, therefore, that we yield not to evil desires, and be not wearied in enduring temptation; that we deviate not from the way of the Lord; that in adversity, as in prosperity, we preserve equanimity and fortitude; and that God may never deprive us of his protection. Finally, we pray that God may crush beneath our feet the head of the serpent.

Objects
of our
thoughts
and reflec-
tions in
presenting
this peti-
tion.
I. The pastor will next exhort the faithful to those things which, in offering this petition, should constitute the chief objects of their thoughts and reflections. It will, then, be found most efficacious, when offering this prayer, to distrust our own strength, aware of our extreme infirmity; and, placing all our hopes of safety in the divine goodness, and relying on the divine protection, to encounter the greatest dangers with greatness of soul; calling to mind particularly the many instances on record of persons animated with this hope, and thus arming themselves with resolution, who were delivered by Almighty God from the fangs of Satan. When Joseph was assailed

---

[1] 2 Tim. ii. 5.   [2] James i. 12.   [3] Heb. iv. 15.
[4] Ps. cxviii. 43.   [5] Ps. cxviii. 36.   [6] Ps. cxviii. 37

by the criminal solicitations of a maddening woman, did not Illustra-
tions.
God rescue him from the imminent danger, and exalt him to
the highest pitch of glory?[1] Did he not preserve Susannah,
when beset by the ministers of Satan, and on the point of
being made the victim of an iniquitous sentence? Nor should
the divine interposition in her behalf excite our surprise;
"her heart," says the Prophet, "trusted in God."[2] How
exalted the praise, how great the glory of Job, who triumphed over the world, the flesh, and the devil! There are
on record many similar examples, to which the pastor should
refer, in order to exhort with earnestness his pious hearers to
this hope and confidence.

The faithful should also reflect under whose standard they II.
fight against the temptations of the enemy: they should consider that their leader is no less a person than Christ the Lord,
who won the laurels of victory in the same combat. He overcame the devil: he is that "stronger man" mentioned in the
Gospel, who, "coming upon the strong armed man," overcame him, deprived him of his arms, and stripped him of his
spoils. Of his victory over the world, we read in St John:
"Have confidence: I have overcome the world:"[3] in the Apocalypse, he is called "the conquering lion;" and it is said that,
"conquering, he went forth to conquer:"[4] and by his victory he
has given power to others to conquer. The Epistle of St. Paul III.
to the Hebrews abounds with the victories of holy men, "who
by faith conquered kingdoms, stopped the mouths of lions."[5]
Whilst we read of such achievements, we should also take into IV.
account the victories which are every day won by men eminent
for faith, hope, and charity, in their domestic and exterior conflicts with the devil; victories so numerous and so signal, that,
were we spectators of them, we should deem no event of more
frequent occurrence, none of more glorious issue. Of the dis-
-comfiture of the wicked one, St. John says, "I write unto
you, young men, because you are strong, and the word of God
abideth in you, and you have overcome the wicked one."[6]
We must, however, recollect that Satan is overcome not by Note.
indolence, sleep, wine, revelling, or lust; but by prayer, labour,
watching, fasting, continence, and chastity: "Watch ye and
pray, that ye enter not into temptation,"[7] is, as we have already
said, the admonition of our Lord. They who make use of
these weapons in the conflict are sure to put the enemy to
flight: "From them who resist the devil," says St. James,
"he will fly."[8]

In these victories, however, which are achieved by holy men, Without
the divine
assistance
we can do
nothing.
let no one indulge feelings of self-complacency, nor flatter him-
self that, by his own single unassisted exertions, he is able to
withstand the hostile assaults of the devil. This is not within
the power of human nature, nor within the competency of

---

[1] Gen. xxix. 7.   [2] Dan. xiii. 61.   [3] John xvi. 33.   [4] Apoc. v. 5.
[5] Heb. xi. 33.   [6] 1 John ii. 13.   [7] Matt. xxvi. 41.   [8] James iv. 7

numan frailty. In order that we may ascribe to God alone the victory, and may thank him alone for its achievement, by whose guidance and assistance alone we can be victorious, the strength by which we lay prostrate the satellites of Satan, comes from God, "who maketh our arms as a bow of brass; by whose aid the bow of the mighty is overcome, and the weak are girt with strength; who giveth us the protection of salvation; whose right hand upholdeth us"[1] "who teacheth our hands to war, and our fingers to battle."[2] To this we are exhorted by the example of the Apostle: "Thanks to God," says he, "who hath given us the victory, through our Lord Jesus Christ."[3] The voice from heaven, mentioned in the Apocalypse, also proclaims God to be the author of our victories: "Now is come salvation, and strength, and the kingdom of our God, and the power of his Christ; because the accuser of our brethren is cast forth; and they overcame him by the blood of the Lamb."[4] That the victory obtained over the world and the flesh belongs to our Lord Jesus Christ, we learn from the same authority; "They shall fight with the Lamb, and the Lamb shall overcome them."[5] On the cause and the manner of conquering temptation, thus much will suffice.

The rewards which await our victories over temptation. These things explained, the pastor will propose to the faithful the crowns prepared by God, and the eternal and superabundant rewards reserved for those who conquer. To this effect he will cite divine authorities from the same inspired Epistle: "He that shall overcome shall not be hurt by the second death;" and in another place: "He that shall overcome, shall thus be clothed in white garments, and I will not blot out his name out of the book of life, and I will confess his name before my Father, and before his angels."[6] A little after, our divine Lord himself thus addresses John: "He that shall overcome, I will make him a pillar in the temple of my God; and he shall go out no more:"[7] and again: "To him that shall overcome, I will give to sit with me in my throne; as I also have overcome, and am set down with my Father in his throne."[8] Finally, having unveiled the glory of the saints, and the never-ending bliss which they shall enjoy in heaven, he adds, "He that shall overcome shall possess these things."[9]

[1] 1 Kings ii. 4. [2] Ps. xvii. 35. [3] 1 Cor. xv. 57.
[4] Apoc. xii. 10. [5] Apoc. xvii. 14. [6] Apoc. iii. 5.
[7] Apoc. iii. 12. [8] Apoc. iii. 21. [9] Apoc. xxi. 17.

" BUT DELIVER US FROM EVIL."

THIS petition, with which the Son of God concludes this prayer, embodies the substance of all the rest. To mark its force and weight, praying on the eve of his passion for the salvation of mankind, he thus concluded: "I pray thou keep them from evil."[1] The force and efficacy of the other petitions, he, as it were, epitomized in this form of prayer, which he delivered by way of precept, and confirmed by example. If we obtain what is comprehended in this prayer, the protection of God against evil, that protection which enables us to defeat, with security and safety, the machinations of the world and the devil, we are fortified by the authority of St. Cyprian in affirming, that nothing more remains to be asked.[2] *This petition an epitome of all the others.*

Such, then, being the nature of this petition, the diligence of the pastor in its exposition should be commensurate to its importance. The difference between it and the preceding petition consists in this, that in the one we beg to avoid sin, in the other, to escape punishment. It cannot, therefore, be necessary to remind the faithful of the numerous evils and calamities to which we are exposed, and how much we stand in need of the divine assistance. The picture of our misery has been drawn in lively colours by sacred and profane writers; but the dangers which beset himself and others have given each one a melancholy experience of the number and magnitude of the miseries incidental to human life. We are all convinced of the truth of these words of holy Job, which was exemplified in his own sufferings: "Man, born of woman, and living for a short time, is filled with many miseries. He cometh forth like a flower, and is destroyed, and fleeth as a shadow, and never continueth in the same state."[3] That no day passes without its own trouble or inconvenience is evinced by these words of our Lord: "Sufficient for the day is the evil thereof;"[4] and indeed, the condition of human life is pointed out by our Lord himself, when he admonishes us, that we are to take up our cross daily, and follow him.[5] *Diligence of the pastor in its exposition; difference between it and the preceding petition; to be often repeated.*

Feeling, therefore, as every one must, the labours and dangers inseparable from human life, it will not be difficult to convince them, that to implore of God deliverance from evil is an imperative duty: a duty to the performance of which they will be the more easily induced, as no motive exercises a more powerful influence on human action than a desire and hope of deliverance from those evils, which oppress, or impend over them. To fly to God for assistance in distress is a principle implanted in the human mind by the hand of nature; as it is written, "Fill their faces with shame, and they shall seek thy name, O Lord."[6] *Our dangers and difficulties serve to convince us of the necessity of prayer. Note.*

---

[1] John xvii. 15.   [2] Lib. de orat. citat.   [3] Job xiv. 1.
[4] Matt. vi. 34.   [5] Luke ix. 23.   [6] Ps. lxxxii. 17.

How to
pray; order
to be ob-
served in
our prayers.

• If, then, in calamities and dangers the unbidden impulse of nature prompts men to call on God, it surely becomes the duty of those, to whose fidelity and prudence their salvation is intrusted, to instruct them, in a special manner, in the proper performance of this duty. There are some who, contrary to the command of Jesus Christ, invert the order of prayer: he, who commands us to have recourse to him in the day of tribulation,[1] has also prescribed to us the order in which we should solicit the divine favours. It is his will that, before we pray to be delivered from evil, we pray that the name of God be sanctified; that his kingdom come, and so of the other petitions of the Lord's Prayer, which are so many gradations by which we ascend to this their summit. Yet there are those who, if their head, their side, or their foot, ache; if they sustain loss of property; if menaces or dangers from an enemy alarm them; if famine, war, or pestilence afflict them, omit all the other petitions of the Lord's Prayer, and ask only to be delivered from these evils. This preposterous practice is at variance with the express command of Christ: "Seek first the kingdom of God."[2] To pray, therefore, as we ought, when we beg to be delivered from calamities and evils, we should have in view the greater glory of God. Thus, when David offered this prayer: "Lord rebuke me not in thine anger," he subjoined the reason, "For there is no one in death, that is mindful of thee, and who shall confess to thee in hell;"[3] and, having implored God to have mercy on him, he added: "I will teach the unjust thy ways; and the wicked shall be converted to thee."[4]

Difference
between
the prayers
of the
infidel and
of the
Christian.

The faithful are to be excited to the adoption of this salutary manner of praying, and to an imitation of the example of the prophet; and at the same time, their attention should also be pointed to the marked difference that exists between the prayers of the infidel and those of the Christian. The infidel, too, begs of God to cure his diseases, and to heal his wounds, to deliver him from approaching or impending ills; but he places his principal hope of recovery, or deliverance in the remedies provided by nature, or prepared by art. He makes no scruple of using medicine no matter by whom prepared, no matter if accompanied by charms, spells, or other diabolical arts, provided he can promise himself some hope of recovery. Not so the Christian: when visited by sickness or other adversity, he flies to God as his sovereign refuge; in him does he centre all his hopes of returning health; him only does he acknowledge as the author of all good, adoring him as his deliverer, and ascribing to him whatever healing virtue resides in medicines, convinced that then only are they efficacious, when it is the divine will that they should be so. They are given by God to man to heal his corporal infirmities; and hence these words of Ecclesiasticus: "The Most High hath created medicines out of the earth, and a wise man will not abhor them."[5] He, therefore,

---

[1] Ps. xix. 15.   [2] Matt. vi. 33.   [3] Ps. vi. 6.   [4] Ps. l. 15.   [5] Eccl. xxxviii. 1.

who has pledged his fidelity to Jesus Christ, does not place his principal hope of recovery in such remedies: he places it in God the author of these medicines, and the Sacred Scriptures condemn the conduct of those who, confiding in the power of medicine, seek no assistance from God.[1] Nay more, those, who regulate their lives by the laws of God, abstain from the use of all medicines, which are not evidently intended by Almighty God to be medicinal; and, were there even a certain hope of recovery by using any other, they abstain from them as so many charms and diabolical artifices.

The faithful, then, are to be exhorted to place their confidence in God: our most bountiful Father has commanded us to beg of him our deliverance from evil; and commanded as we are, by him to implore his goodness, we must cherish a hope of obtaining the object of our prayers. Of this truth the Sacred Scriptures afford many illustrations, that they whom reasoning may not inspire with confidence, may be compelled to yield to a strong array of examples. Abraham, Jacob, Lot, Joseph, and David are unexceptionable attestations of the divine goodness; and the numerous instances recorded in the New Testament of persons rescued from the greatest dangers, by the efficacy of devout prayer, are so familiar as to supersede the necessity of crowding the page with citations. On this subject therefore, we shall content ourselves with one sentence from the prophet, which is sufficient to confirm even the weakest mind: "The just cried, and the Lord heard them; and delivered them out of all their troubles."[2] *In sickness our confidence should be placed in God.*

We now come to explain the force and nature of the petition, in order that the faithful may understand that in it we by no means solicit deliverance from every species of evil. There are some things which are commonly considered evils, and which, notwithstanding, are fraught with advantage to those who endure them: such was the sting of the flesh experienced by the Apostle, that, by the aid of divine grace, power might be perfected in infirmity.[3] When the pious Christian learns the salutary influence of such things, far from praying for their removal, he rejoices in them exceedingly. It is, therefore, against those evils only, which conduce not to our spiritual interests, that we pray; not against such as are auxiliary to our salvation. The full force of the petition, therefore, is, that freed from sin, we may also be freed from the danger of temptation, and from internal and external evils; that we may be protected from water, fire, and lightning; that the fruits of the earth may be preserved; that we be not visited by dearth, sedition, or the horrors of war; that God may banish disease, pestilence, desolation from us; that he may keep us from slavery, imprisonment, exile, treason, treachery; and from all those evils which fill mankind with terror and misery. Finally, we pray that God would remove all occasions of sin and iniquity. *Some things are commonly considered evils which are not real evils; meaning of the petition.*

---

[1] Paral. xvi. 12.   [2] Ps. xxxiii. 18.   [3] 2 Cor. xii. 17.

* We do not however pray to be delivered solely from those things, which all look upon as evils; with them we also deprecate those things which almost all consider to be good, such as riches, honours, health, strength, and even life itself, rather than that they should prove destructive or detrimental to our immortal souls. We also beg of God that we be not cut off by a a sudden death; that we provoke not his anger against us; that we be not condemned to suffer the punishments reserved for the wicked; that we be not sentenced to endure the fire of purgatory, from which we piously and devoutly implore the the liberation of others. This is the explanation of this petition given by the Church in the Mass and Litanies: in it we beseech God to avert from us all evil past, present, and to come.

God delivers us from evil in a variety of ways.

The goodness of God delivers us from evil in a variety of ways. He prevents impending evils, as we read with regard to the Patriarch Jacob: the slaughter of the Sichimites had exasperated the fury of his enemies; but God delivered him from their hands: "The terror of God fell upon all the cities round about, and they durst not pursue after them as they went away."[1] The blessed, who reign with Christ the Lord in heaven, have been delivered by the divine assistance from all evil; but, although the Almighty delivers us from some evils, it is not his will that, whilst journeying in this our mortal

Note.

pilgrimage, we should be entirely exempt from all. The consolations with which God sometimes refreshes those who labour under adversity are, however, equivalent to an exemption from all evil; and with these the prophet consoled himself when he said: "According to the multitude of my sorrows in my heart, thy consolations have rejoiced my soul."[2] God, moreover, delivers men from evil when he preserves them unhurt in the midst of extreme danger: thus did his protecting arm save the three children who were thrown into the fiery furnace,[3] and Daniel, who was cast into the lion's den, and who also escaped unhurt.[4]

The devil specially called "the evil one," and why. I.

According to the interpretation of St. Basil, St. Chrysostome, and Augustine, the devil is specially called "the evil one;" because he was the author of man's transgression, that is, of his sin and iniquity; and because God makes use of him as an instrument to chastise the impiety of sinners. The evils which mankind endure in punishment of sin are appointed by God; and this is the meaning of these words of the prophet Amos: "Shall there be evil in a city which the Lord hath not done?"[5] and also of Isaias: "I am the Lord and there is none else: I form the light and create darkness: I make peace and create

II.

evil."[6] The devil is also called evil, because, although we have never done any thing to provoke his hostility, he wages perpetual war against us, and pursues us with mortal hatred; but,

Note.

if we put on the armour of faith and the shield of innocence,

---

[1] Gen. xxxv. 5.   [2] Ps. lxiii. 19.   [3] Dan. vi. 22.
[4] Dan. iii. 50.   [5] Amos iii. 6.   [6] Isa. xlv. 7.

he can have no power to hurt us. He, however, unceasingly
tempts us by external evils and every other means of annoyance
within his reach; and therefore do we beseech God to deliver
us from evil.[1]

We say "from evil," not "from evils," because the evils We say
from evil,
not from
evils, and
why.
which we experience from others we ascribe to the arch enemy
as their author and instigator. This is also a reason why we
should be less disposed to cherish sentiments of resentment
towards our neighbour, turning our hatred and anger against
Satan himself, by whom men are impelled to inflict injuries. If,
therefore, your neighbour has injured you in any respect, when
you bend in prayer to God your Father, beg of him not only to
deliver you from evil, that is, from the injuries, which your
neighbour inflicts; but also to rescue your neighbour from the
power of the devil, whose wicked suggestions impel man to
deeds of injustice.[2]

Finally, we should know, that if by prayers and vows we Patience
under con-
tinued
affliction.
are not delivered from evil, we should endure our afflictions
with patience, convinced that it is the will of God that we
should so endure them. If, therefore, God hear not our prayers,
we are not to yield to feelings of peevishness or discontent: it
is ours to submit in all things, to the divine will and pleasure,
convinced that what happens in accordance with the will of
God, not that which, on the contrary, is agreeable to our own
wishes, is really useful and salutary to us. In fine, that during
our mortal career we should be prepared to meet every species
of affliction and calamity, not only with patience, but even with
joy, is a truth which the zealous Pastor should press upon the
attention of his pious hearers. "All that will live godly in Christ
Jesus," says St. Paul, "shall suffer persecution:"[3] "Through
many tribulations we must enter into the kingdom of heaven;"[4]
and again, our Lord himself says: "Ought not Christ to have
suffered these things, and so enter into his glory."[5] A ser- Examples.
vant, then, should not be greater than his master; and as St.
Bernard says, "Delicate members do not become a head
crowned with thorns."[6] The example of Uriah challenges our
admiration and imitation: when urged by David to remain at
home, he replied: "The ark of God, and Israel, and Judah,
dwell in tents; and shall I go into my house?"[7]

If to prayer we bring with us these reflections and these dis- Other
examples.
positions, although encompassed by evils on every side, like the
three children who passed unhurt amidst the flames, we shall
be preserved through the perilous ordeal; or at least, like the
Macchabees, we shall bear up against adverse fortune with firmness and fortitude. In the midst of contumelies and tortures we
shall imitate the blessed examples of the Apostles, who, after

---

[1] Isa. xlv. 7.
[2] Chrysost. hom. 20. in Matt. et hom. 5 in Job. Aug. in Ecclesiast. dogm. cap. 57.
Basil. in hom. quod Deus non sit auctor malorum, non procul a fine.
[3] 2 Tim. iii. 12.   [4] Acts xiv. 21.   [5] Luke xxiv. 26.
[6] Serm. 5. de omnibus Sanctis.   [7] 2 Kings xi. 1.

they had been scourged, "rejoiced exceedingly that they were accounted worthy to suffer reproach for the name of Jesus."[1] Like them, we too shall sing in transports of joy: "Princes have persecuted me without cause; and my heart hath been in awe of thy words; I will rejoice at thy words, as one that hath found great spoil."[2]

MEN.

The seal of the Lord's prayer; fruits of this concluding word; and of prayer in general.

THIS word "Amen," St. Jerome, in his commentary on St. Matthew, calls what it really is, "the seal of the Lord's prayer."[3] As then we have already admonished the faithful with regard to the preparation to be made before holy prayer, so we deem it necessary that they should know, why we close our prayers with this word, and also what it signifies: devotion in concluding does not yield in importance to attention in beginning, our prayers to God. The faithful, then, are to know that the fruits, which we gather from the conclusion of the Lord's prayer, are numerous and abundant; and of these, the richest is the attainment of the objects of our prayer, a matter on which we have already been sufficiently diffuse. By this concluding word, not only do we obtain a propitious hearing from God, but also receive other blessings of a higher order still, the excellence of which surpasses all powers of description. By prayer, as St. Cyprian observes, we commune with God; and thus the divine Majesty is, after an inexplicable manner, brought nearer to those who are engaged in prayer than to others, and enriches them with peculiar gifts. Those, therefore, who pray devoutly, may not be inaptly compared to persons who approach a glowing fire: if cold, they derive warmth; if warm, they derive heat, from its intensity. Thus, also, those who approach God in prayer depart with a warmth and ardour proportioned to their faith and fervour: the heart is inflamed with zeal for the glory of God: the mind is illumined after an admirable manner; and the soul is enriched

Example.

exceedingly with a plenteous effusion of divine grace, as it is written, "Thou hast prevented him with blessings of sweetness."[4] Of these astonishing effects of prayer, Moses affords an illustrious example; by intercourse and converse with God, Moses shone with the reflected splendours of the Divinity, so that the Israelites could not look upon his eyes or countenance.[5]

Note.

Those who pray with such fervour enjoy, in an admirable manner, the benignity and majesty of God: "In the morning," says the prophet, "I will stand before thee and will see; because thou art not a God that willest iniquity."[6] The more familiar

---

[1] Acts v. 4.   [2] Ps. cxviii. 161.   [3] In Matt. vi. 6.   [4] Ps. xx. 4.
[5] Exod. xxxiv. 35, 2 Cor. iii. 13.   [6] Ps. v. 5.

these truths are to the mind, the more piously do we venerate, and the more fervently do we worship God, and the more delightfully do we taste, "how sweet is the Lord, and how blessed is the man that hopeth in him."[1] Encircled by light from above, then do we also discover our own lowliness, and how exalted is the majesty of God: "Give me," says St. Augustine, "to know thee; give me to know myself." Distrusting our own strength, we thus throw ourselves unreservedly upon the goodness of God, not doubting that he, who cherishes us in the bosom of his paternal love, will afford us in abundance whatever is necessary to the support of life and the attainment of salvation. Thus do our hearts beat with warmest gratitude to God, and our lips, in accents of rapturous devotion, speak his praise; following the example of David, who commenced by praying; "Save me from all them that persecute me;" and concluded with these words: "I will give glory to the Lord according to his justice; and will sing to the name of the Lord the Most High."[2]

There are extant innumerable prayers of the saints, which breathe the same spirit, beginning with sentiments of reverential fear, and ending with consolatory and joyous hope. This spirit, however, is eminently conspicuous in the Psalms of David. Agitated by fear, he says: "Many are they who rise up against me: many say to my soul, there is no salvation for him in his God;" but at length, armed with fortitude, and filled with holy joy, he adds: "I will not fear thousands of the people surrounding me."[3] In another Psalm, after he had lamented his misery, reposing confidence in God, and rejoicing exceedingly in the hope of salvation, he says: "In peace in the selfsame, I will sleep, and I will rest."[4] Again, with what terror must he not have been agitated when he exclaimed: "O Lord, rebuke me not in thy indignation, nor chastise me in thy wrath;" yet, on the other hand, what confidence and joy must not have beamed upon him when he added: "Depart from me, all ye workers of iniquity; for the Lord hath heard the voice of my weeping."[5] When filled with dread of the divine wrath, with what lowliness and humility does he not implore the divine assistance: "Save me, O Lord, by thy name, and judge me in thy strength;"[6] and yet, in the same psalm he adds these words of joy and confidence; "Behold, God is my help; and the Lord is the helper of my soul." Let him, therefore, who has recourse to holy prayer approach God his Father, fortified by faith and animated by hope, not despairing to obtain, through the divine mercy, those blessings of which he stands in need.

The word "amen," with which the Lord's prayer concludes, contains, as it were, the germs of many of those reasons and reflections which we have already evolved. Indeed, so frequent was this Hebrew word in the mouth of the Saviour, that it

[margin:] The prayers of the saints breathe this spirit.

[margin:] Particular meaning of the word "amen" in this prayer, and in the Mass.

---

[1] Ps. xxxiii. 9.   [2] Ps. vii. 3—18.   [3] Ps. iii. 3. 7.
[4] Ps. iv. 9.   [5] Ps. vi. 2. 9.   [6] Ps. 53. 3.

pleased the Holy Ghost to have it still retained in the Church of God. Its meaning may be said to be: "know that thy prayers are heard;" it is in substance, as if God condescended to return an answer to the supplicant, and graciously dismissed him, after having heard his prayers with a propitious ear. This interpretation has been approved by the constant usage of the Church of God: in the sacrifice of the Mass, when the Lord's prayer is said, she does not assign the word "amen," to the assistant, who answers, "but deliver us from evil:" she reserves it as appropriate to the Priest himself, who, in quality of interpreter between God and man, answers "amen," thus intimating that God has heard the prayers of his people. This practice, however, is not common to all prayers, but is peculiar to the Lord's prayer. In every other instance the assistant answers "amen;" because, in every other, it only expresses the acquiescence of the people, and the community of their desires and prayers; in this it is an answer, intimating that God has heard the petition of his supplicant.

The word "amen," by many interpreted differently. By many, the word "amen" is differently interpreted: the Septuagint interprets it, "so be it:" others translate it, "verily," or "truly;" Aquila renders it, "faithfully." Which of these versions we adopt, is a matter of little importance, provided we understand it to have the force already mentioned, that of the Pastor confirming the concession of what has been prayed for; an interpretation to which the Apostle lends the weight of his authority in his Epistle to the Corinthians; where he says: "All the promises of God are in him it is;[1] therefore also by him, amen to God, unto our glory."

It fixes attention, and enlivens hope. To us also this word is very appropriate, containing, as it does, some confirmation of the petitions which we have already presented at the throne of God, and fixing our attention when engaged in holy prayer; for it not unfrequently happens that, in prayer, a variety of distracting thoughts divert the mind to other objects. Nay, more, by this word we most earnestly beg of God that all our preceding petitions may be granted, or rather, understanding that they have been all granted, and feeling the divine assistance powerfully present with us, we cry out in the inspired words of the prophet: "Behold God is my helper; and the Lord is the protection of my soul;"[2] nor can we for a moment doubt, that God is moved by the name of his Son, and by a word so often uttered by the divine lips of him, "who," as the Apostle says, "was always heard for his reverence."[3]

---

[1] 2 Cor. i. 20. ιν αυτω το ναι, in ipso, scilicet Christo, sunt est, that is to say, are ratified in Christ.—T.

[2] Ps. liii. 6.   [3] Heb. v. 7.

THE END.

PRAXIS CATECHISMI,

SEU

CATECHISMUS

IN

SINGULAS ANNI DOMINICAS DISTRIBUTUS, ET EVANGELIIS ACCOMMODATUS.

DOMINICA PRIMA ADVENTUS.

ERUNT SIGNA IN SOLE, ET LUNA, &c. Luc. xxi. 25, &c.]—Hoc Evangelium ad argumentum de judicio generali traducendum est. Quare hic recurrat Parochus ad articulum Symboli. " Inde venturus est judicare vivos et mortuos," p. 61, et seqq. prout. faciendum præcipitur, p. 18, vel secundum aliarum Ecclesiarum ritum.

ECCE REX TUUS VENIT TIBI, &c. MATT. xxi. 5, &c.]—Hic opportunè tractabit parochus ea, quæ de Incarnatione, et causis adventûs Christi Domini nostri habentur art. 2. et 3. Symboli Apostolici, p. 31, et 37.

INVENIETIS ASINAM ALLIGATAM, ET PULLAM CUM EA ; SOLVITE, &c.]—D. Athanasius in sermone de verbis hujus Evangelii ostendit ex hoc loco Apostolis et eorum successoribus factam esse potestatem solvendi eos qui, instar asinorum, peccatorum pondere pressi, ad eos confugerent. Quare hic populo exponet Parochus quæ habentur de confessione, p. 189, et seqq. et absolutione, p. 181, et de potestate remittendi peccata in Ecclesia, p. 82, et seqq.

DOMINICA SECUNDA.

CUM AUDISSET JOANNES IN VINCULIS, &c. TU ES QUI VENTURUS ES, &c. MATTH. xi. 2, &c.]—Ista Joannis interrogatio tam sedula, ostendit quanto cum studio curare debeamus, ut de rebus fidei, et nos, et ii, qui nobis subsunt, ritè, et à Catholicis doctoribus instruamur. Vide quæ huic argumento inserviunt initio Catechismi, usque ad primum Symboli articulum.

IN VINCULIS.]—Fides usque ad vincula, immò ad necem usque, cùm opus est, et a judice urgemur, profitenda est : nec est satis eam pectore inclusam habere, quantumvis rectam et sinceram, ut ostenditur, p. 22, et seqq. vel " Erunt signa in Sole et Luna," &c. ut Dominica præcedenti.

DOMINICA TERTIA.

CONFESSUS EST ET NON NEGAVIT, JOAN. i. 20, &c.]—Ex hoc loco simpliciter verum fateri docemur, nec intermiscere jusjurandum, ut nobis fides adhibeatur. Vide quanto, et sub quibus pœnis jurare prohibitum, in 2. præcepto, p. 254, et seqq.

QUID ERGO BAPTIZAS, SI TU NON ES CHRISTUS, &c.]—Agendum hic de ministris baptismi, de quo, p. 119, et seq. et quomodo sese habeant in dispensatione Sacramentorum Christus Dominus et minister, quantùm ad effectum Sacramenti, p. 108, et seqq.

CUJUS EGO NON SUM DIGNUS, &c.]—Hic monere parochus populum sibi creditum debet ut se pro festis natalitiis ad sacram synaxim præparet, et agere de condigna tanti hospitis (cujus corrigiam calceamenti solvere indignum se Joannes Baptista censet) susceptione, vide de præparatione ad Eucharistiam, p. 167, vel " Cum audisset Joannes in vinculis, ut in Dominica præcedenti."

DOMINICA QUARTA.

ANNO QUINTODECIMO IMPERII TIBERII CÆSARIS, &c. LUC. iii. 1.]—Cur hic

principum mundi fiat mentio, eadem
ratio afferri potest, quæ affertur in articulo 4. Symboli de eodem Pontio Pilato.

FACTUM EST VERBUM DOMINI SUPER
JOANNEM, &c.]—Quoniam Joannes non
nisi a Deo legitimè vocatus officium
verbi Dei prædicandi exercuit: ideo hîc
de legitimâ vocatione ministrorum Ecclesiæ parochus disseret, ut habetur de
sacram. Ordinis, p. 212, et seqq. legiti-
mosque, eos ministros non esse dicat,
qui missi non sunt, ut traditur in præ-
fatione.

IN DESERTO.]—Hîc de probitate et morum
integritate ministrorum verbi (qui sunt
sacerdotes) agatur ex eodem loco 212, et
seq. et de castitate, quæ eis, quando fiunt
subdiaconi, indicitur, ut hab. ibidem.

PRÆDICANS BAPTISMUM PŒNITENTIÆ.]—
Quomodo adulti, qui baptismum susci-
pere debent, affecti esse debeant, et præ-
teritæ eos vitæ pœnitere, traditur, p. 126,
et seqq.

PARATE VIAM DOMINI, RECTAS FACITE
SEMITAS DEI NOSTRI.]—Hîc de præparatione ad Eucharistiam, de qua in supe-
riori Dominica, et de necessaria mandatorum Dei observantia, de qua, p. 237,
et seqq. vel. "et confessus est, et non
negavit," ut in Dominica præcedenti.

IN DIE NATIVITATIS DOMINI.

PEPERIT PRIMOGENITUM FILIUM SUUM,
&c. LUC. ii. 7, &c.]—Explicetur articulus Symboli. NATUS EX MARIA
VIRGINE. Qui est hujus loci maximè
proprius, de quo, p. 38, et seqq. Eodem
die ad Missam majorem.

IN PRINCIPIO ERAT VERBUM, ET VERBUM
ERAT, &c. JOAN i. 1, &c.]—Quoniam hîc
locus dum agitur de æterna Christi Domini generatione adducitur, p. 35, hinc
parochus petet hujus loci expositionem.

ET VERBUM CARO FACTUM EST.]—Hîc exponatur mysterium Incarnationis prout
habetur, p. 36, et seqq.

GLORIAM QUASI UNIGENITI A PATRE.]—
Quomodo hîc unigenitus sit etiam patre
noster, vide p. 337.

DOMINICA INFRA OCTAVAM NATIVITATIS.

ET TUAM IPSIUS ANIMAM PERTRANSIBIT
GLADIUS, &c. LUC. ii. 35, &c.]—Ex hac
Simeonis prædictione ansam sumere
poterit parochus explicandi, cur Deus
fideles jam baptizatos, quos filios habet
carissimos, non eximat ab incommodis
vitæ hujus, qua de re agitur, p. 129, et

quò confugiendum tunc sit, de quo p
318, et seq.

NON RECEDEBAT A TEMPLO JEJUNIIS ET
ORATIONIBUS, &c.]—De privata et pub-
lica oratione habes, p. 330. Quomodo
ad orationem, et jejunium et eleemosyna
jungenda sint, p. 331, et quomodo ista
tria conducant ad satisfactionem peccatorum, p. 332, et seqq. et. 204.

IN CIRCUMCISIONE DOMINI.

ET POSTQUAM CONSUMMATI SUNT DIES
OCTO, UT CIRCUMCIDERETUR PUER, &c.
LUC. ii. 21, &c.]—Quoniam circumci-
sioni successit Baptismus, hîc in genere
dici poterit de vi, et efficientia Sacramentorum novæ legis supra antiquæ legis
Sacramenta, ut habetur, p. 111.

VOCATUM EST NOMEN EJUS JESUS, &c.]—
Quàm convenienter hoc nomen inditum
fuerit Christo Domino, et quare, vide p.
33.

Observandum hîc etiam est pueris nunc in
baptismo, et olim in circumcisione nomen
esse imponendum : cujus rei quænam sit
ratio, et quale nomen puero imponi debeat, habes, p. 136. Denique cum im-
positio nominis sit una ex cæremoniis in
baptismo usitatis, hîc de baptismi cæremoniis et ritibus apta concio haberi poterit,
p. 133, et seqq.

IN DIE EPIPHANIÆ.

VIDIMUS ENIM STELLAM EJUS IN ORIENTE,
&c. MATTH. ii. 2, &c.]—Quoniam non
ineptè per hanc stellam philosophica de
Deo scientia potest intelligi, sicut per re-
sponsum sacerdotum fidei lumen, non
malè hîc adaptari poterunt quæ de differentia sapientiæ Christianæ à Philosophica notitia habentur, p. 23.

ET PROCIDENTES ADORAVERUNT EUM, &c.
MATTH. ii. 11, &c.]—Hîc de adoratione
Dei, quæ LATRIA dicitur, et simul de veneratione Sanctorum, quæ DULIA nomi-
natur. Vide in expositione Decalogi p.
237, et 245, usque ad secundum præceptum. Hîc agi etiam potest de Eucharistiæ veneratione et adoratione. Nam si
eundem Christum, quem Magi adoraverunt præsentem in Eucharistia agnosci-
mus, et confitemur; ut disertis verbis
probatur, p. 159, et seqq. si pii esse vo-
lumus, cur non æque ac Magi eum ado-
rabimus ? Vide p. 146, et seqq.

DOMINICA INFRA OCTAVAM EPIPHANIÆ.

SECUNDUM CONSUETUDINEM NUPTIÆ FAC-
TÆ SUNT, LUC. ii. 42, &c.]—De observa-

tione dierum festorum, lego, p. 267, et seqq.

ET ERAT SUBDITUS ILLIS, &c.]—De officio liberorù erga parentes, vide p. 271, et seqq.

DOMINICA SECUNDA POST EPIPHANIAM.

NUPTIÆ FACTÆ SUNT IN CANA GALILÆÆ, &c. JOAN, ii. 1, &c.]—De Sacramento Matrimonii, vide p. 225, et seqq.

HOC FECIT JESUS INITIUM SIGNORUM SUORUM.]—Hæc conversio aquæ in vinum valet plurimùm ad confirmandos rudiores in fide Transsubstantiationis, quæ fit in augustissimo Altaris Sacramento: de qua vide p. 161, et seqq.

DOMINICA TERTIA.

ECCE LEPROSUS VENIENS ADORABAT EUM, MATTH. viii. 2, 3, &c.]—Per lepram hæresim significari dicunt Patres. Qui verò sunt censendi hæretici, et qui à castris Ecclesiæ, ut olim leprosi ejicendi, habetur, p. 70, et seqq.

VADE, OSTENDE TE SACERDOTI.]—De honore Sacerdotibus Domini, et Ecclesiæ præfectis exhibendo, vide p. 275.

VADE, OSTENDE TE SACERDOTI, &c.]— Longè excellentiorem virtutem nostris Sacerdotibus tributam docet Chrysostomus lib. 3, de Sacerd. quàm Mosaicis, quòd illi oblatos sibi leprosos non mundarent; sed mundatos tantùm esse declararent; nostri verò hominem peccati leprâ maculatum, dum absolutionis beneficium rite præparato inpendunt, verè emundant, et perfectè sanitati restituunt. Hîc de potestate clavium Sacerdotibus concessâ, ut habetur, p. 82, et sequentibus.

DOMINICA QUARTA.

ASCENDENTE JESU IN NAVICULAM, MATTH. viii. 23.]—Inter multa, quæ Ecclesiam repræsentant, est navicula illa seu arca Noe, de qua, p. 74. Hic ergo de Ecclesia Catholica, et notis, quibus internoscitur, parochus agere poterit: prout habetur, p. 73, seqq.

DOMINE SALVA NOS, PERIMUS.]—Quoniam nullum est tempus, in quo ita hominum vita, quam in propinquo animæ exitu, periclitetur; ideo parochus ex hoc loco hortari poterit suos subditos ut cùm mortis dies instabit, ad Deum maximè recurrant, et extremæ unctionis Sacramentum accipiant, de quo, p. 206, et sequentibus.

QUALIS EST HIC, QUIA VENTI ET MARE OBEDIUNT EI!]—Quomodo creaturæ omnes eum, quem à Deo ab initio acceperunt, cursum teneant homine dempto, vide p. 350.

DOMINICA QUINTA.

ET INIMICUS HOMO SUPERSEMINAVIT ZIZANIA, &c. MATTH. xiii. 25, &c.]—In Ecclesià duo sunt hominum genera, boni, qui tritici nomine designantur; improbi nomine zizaniorum, vide p. 72, et seqq. Vel per zizania intelliguntur odia, atque rixæ, quas pater dissentionis Diabolus seminare conatur in agro filiorum pacis, cujus morbi remedium habes, p. 281, 285, et 286.

INIMICUS HOMO HOC FECIT.]—De odio dæmonum in nos, et ad tentandum audacia et perversitate, vide p. 374; et ut omnis mali culpæ auctor, mali verò pænæ sit exactor, vide p. 378.

DOMINICA SEXTA.

SIMILE EST REGNUM CŒLORUM GRANO SINAPIS, MATTH. xiii. 31, &c.]—Quoniam juxta Doctores per granum sinapis fides intelligitur; hic tractanda sunt, quæ de ejus necessitate habentur, p. 24, et quomodo servanda sint ea quæ fide credenda proponuntur, p. 26, et 27, et ejus excellentia et quantum differat Christiana de Deo sapientia et philosophica divinarum rerum notitia, p. 23.

CUM AUTEM CREVERIT.]—Fidem augeri posse traditur, p. 329.

ITERUM SIMILE EST REGNUM CŒLORUM FERMENTO, QUOD ACCEPTUM MULIER.]— Hanc mulierem Ecclesiam interpretantur, quæ in doctrina fidei aut morum (per fermentum designata) errare non posse traditur, p. 77.

DONEC FERMENTATUM EST TOTUM.]—Hic de communione Sanctorum et meritorum participatione explicari possunt, quæ sunt, p. 79, et seq.

DOMINICA IN SEPTUAG

SIMILE EST REGNUM CŒLORUM HOMINI PATRIFAMILIAS, MATTH. xx. 1, &c.]—Hic paterfamilias est Deus, qui cur pater dicatur, habes, p. 25, et 26. 332, et 333.

RECEPERUNT IPSI SINGULOS DENARIOS.]— Denarii nomine cœlestis beatitudo designatur, quam hic paterfamilias alacriter et sinceré in vinea sua, id est, in cultura mandatorum divinorum laborantibus præstat. De hoc vitæ æternæ denario lege quæ diffusè traduntur, p. 92, et seq.

et 241, 343, et seqq. Hujus verò beatitudinis consequendæ certam viam, ac rationem habes, p. 346, et seqq. Item. exhortatio ad colendam hanc vineam mandatorum illustris habetur, p. 238, et seqq.

Singulos denarios, &c.]—In cœlo tamen varietas est mercedis, et gloriæ, pro ratione laboris et affectus, quo quis operatur, p. 88, et 99.

DOMINICA IN SEXAG.

Exiit qui seminat seminare semen suum, &c. Luc. viii. 5. &c.]—Semen hoc in terram sparsum est verbum Dei, exponente Domino, de quo, vide p. 362, et quomodo sit audiendum, vide præfet.

Venit Diabolus, &c.]—De dæmonis conatu, et impugnatione habes, p. 376, et seqq.

Et a sollicitudinibus et divitiis, &c.] —Quantùm divitiæ et effrænes rerum temporalium cupiditates impediant hujus divini seminis fructum habes, p. 350, et seq.

DOMINICA IN QUINQUAG.

Tradetur enim Gentibus, et illudetur, Luc. xviii. 32, &c.]—Ut Christi milites ejus crucem tamquam vexillum sui ducis contuentes, ad arma pœnitentiæ sumenda exstimulentur, ideo hoc Evangelium ineunte quadragesimâ legitur, quod passionis Dominicæ summam complectitur, quo loco non importunè parochus exponet, quæ de Passione Domini fusè traduntur, p. 43, et seqq. Vel si in aliud tempus commodius differre malit hoc argumentum ; hodie alteram Evangelii partem pertractabit, ut sequitur.

Cæcus quidam sedebat secus viam.]— Hic cœcus genus humanum denotabat, de cujus post peccatum statu misero, vide p. 350.

Jesu fili David miserere mei.]—Hic quomodo Deum aliter oremus ac Sanctos ex hac formula demonstrabis, ut habes, p. 327. Porrò si angustiis, aut tribulationibus premimur, aut re aliqua indigemus, ad Dominum cum hoc cæco nobis recurrendem est, precibusque sollicitandus Deus, ut nobis adsit. Vide de necessitate et utilitate orationis, p. 317.

Quid tibi vis faciam.]—Hic causas, ob quas clementissimus Deus vult à nobis rogari, etiam si sciat quibus rebus indigeamus, ex p. 318, et 319, proferes.

FERIA IV. CINERUM.

Cum autem jejunatis. &c. Matth. vi. 16, &c.]—Cùm quadragesimæ jejunium

eo nomine sit institutum, ut totius anni peccata hac quasi solemni mulctâ redimeremus, hodiè parochus excitare fidelem populum debebit ad pœnitentiam amplectendam, de cujus necessitate scribit, p. 81, et 180, docere quibus gradibus ad pœnitentiam licet ascendere, p. 179, et quibus operum generibus pro peccatis satisfacere possimus, p. 204, et seqq.

Nolite thesaurizare vobis thesauros in terra]—Vide adversus eos qui opes congerere undequaque studeant, p. 292, 294, et seq.

Thesaurizate vobis thesauros in cœlo.]—Quoniam parochi frequenter fidelem populù ad eleemosinas pauperibus erogandas excitare debent: hic hoc studiosè præstabunt ex his quæ habentur, p. 314, 315, et seq. et 372.

DOMINICA PRIMA QUADRAGESIMÆ.

Ut tentaretur a Diabolo, &c. Matth. iv. 11, &c.]—Cùm sit tentatio vita hominis super terram, ut dicit Job, vii. hic de tentatione agendum, de generibus tentationum, ad quid permittantur homines tentari, quibus armis tentationibus resistendum, et cætera hujusmodi, quæ habentur, p. 375, et seqq.

Non in solo pane vivit homo.]—De pane spirituali de quo hic agit Christus Dominus, vide p. 362, et seq.

Angelis suis Deus mandavit, &c.]—De Angelorum custodia erga homines, p. 333, et 334.

Dominum Deum tuum adorabis.]—De adoratione Dei quæ fide, spe et charitate, perficitur, vide p. 244.

DOMINICA SECUNDA QUADRAGESIMÆ.

Assumpsit Jesus Petrum, et Jacobum, et Joannem, et deduxit eos, &c. Matth. xvii. 1, &c.]—Hic afferri possunt ea, quæ de loco et tempore, quo homines ad divina contemplanda aptiores sunt, habentur, p. 243.

Bonum est nos hic esse.]—Hic tractari possunt, quæ de summa eorum dignitate, qui Deo obediunt, habentur, p. 358. Vel de intimis hominum sanctorum gaudiis, p. 363. Poterunt etiam Parochi de duodecimo articulo hic habere sermonem, de quo, p. 92, 93.

Hic est Filius meus dilectus, &c.]— Hic de æterna filii generatione latissimus sese offert dicendi campus, de qua, p. 35, et seq. vel secundum aliarum Ecclesiarum ritum.

MISERERE MEI FILI DAVID, MATTH. XV. 22, &c.]—Hic typum habes perfectæ orationis quantum spectat ad duas conditiones, quæ in oratione maximè desiderantur, fidem videlicet, et perseverantiam, de quibus, p. 329, et seqq.

FILIA MEA MALE TORQUETUR A DÆMONIO, &c.]—Hujus mulieris exemplo Parentes monentur diligentem liberorum curam gerere ; de quâ, p. 278.

DIMITTE EAM, QUIA CLAMAT POST NOS, &c.]—Si Apostoli in hac vita degentes, adhuc pro se soliciti pro Chananeâ interpellant, et exaudiuntur, et in cælo mutire non audebunt, inquit D. Hieron, contra Vigilantium. Hic de intercessione, Sanctorum, prout habetur p. 246, seqq.

DOMINICA TERTIA.

ET ERAT JESUS EJICIENS DÆMONIUM, ET ILLUD ERAT MUTUM, LUC. XI. 14., &c.] Dæmonis proprium est eum, quem possidet, reddere mutum, id est, á confessione peccati revocare. Sed tamen non est alia ratio ejiciendi Dæmonis, quam ut linguam solvas ad detegendum coram Sacerdote peccatum, vide quæ de Confessione habentur, p. 189, et seqq.

OMNE REGNUM IN SEIPSUM DIVISUM DESOLABITUR.]—Ecclesia est Christi regnum, ut habetur, p. 346. Id autem, ut in seipsum non sit divisum, unum esse necesse est, unde hic de unitate Ecclesiæ agendum est, ex p. 74, et seq.

REVERTAR IN DOMUM MEAM.]—De relabentium in peccati gravitatem, p. 47. Et quid post confessionem agendum, p. 204, et seq.

TUNC ASSUMIT ALIOS SEPTEM SPIRITUS NEQUIORES SE.]—Hic locus p. 374, inducitur ad probandum non unum tantum dæmonem, sed plures etiam interdum hominem tentare ; patet autem ex hoc loco dæmonem acrius eos tantare, qui ab eo defecerunt, ut est p. 375, et seqq.

BEATUS VENTER QUI TE PORTAVIT.]—Glorificatione B. Mariæ Virginis hoc Evangelium concluditur ; de quâ habes, p. 39, 40, 326.

DOMINICA QUARTA.

UNDE EMEMUS PANES, UT ET MANDUCENT HI ? &c. JOAN, VI. 5. &c.]—Hic aptè explicari poterit illa petitio Dominicæ orationis ; " Panem nostrum quotidianum da nobis," p. 357, et seqq.

Notandum prætereà quòd panis iste vim

etiam habebat sedandi sitim, ut tenent doctores. Ita et panis Eucharistiæ laicis pro calice est. Lege de Communione sub una specie, p. 171, 172.

HOC AUTEM DICEBAT TANTANS EUM.]— Quomodo Deus hominem tentet, vide p. 376, et seq.

DISTRIBUIT DISCUMBENTIBUS.]—Christus non distribuit, sed dedit Apostolis, et illi distribuerunt turbæ, Matth., xiv. 19. Sic á mundi initio per Patriarchas et Prophetas, et postea per Apostolos eorumque successores Deus verbum Dei et sacramenta subministrat, ut habetur p. 13, 14, et 108. Christus tamen est qui hæc omnia præcipuè efficit, p. 108.

HIC EST VERE PROPHETA.]—De gratiarum actione, p. 326.

DOMINICA IN PASSIO.

QUI EX VOBIS ARGUET ME DE PECCATO ? JOAN, viii. 46, &c.]—Innocentia Christi in hodierno Evangelio convenienter profertur in medium, ut In promtu sit nobis causa Dominicæ Passionis quam hodie repræsentare incipit Ecclesia, nimirum non propria illius delicta, sed nostra, De causis Passionis Christi habes, p. 47.

SI VERITATEM DICO VOBIS.]—Mendacio cavere docemur de quo multa p. 301, et seqq.

QUI EX DEO EST, VERBA DEI AUDIT, &c.] —De verbo Dei audiendo, p. 16, et 362.

NONNE BENE DICIMUS NOS QUIA SAMARITANUS, &c.]—Ex hoc loco Parochus ansam poterit arripere ad excitandos suos Fideles ad injurias condonandas, qua de re multa habentur, p. 364, et seqq.

SED HONORIFICO PATREM ET VOS INHONORASTIS ME.]—Christus sæpe, et á multis graviter inhonoratur, sed ab iis maximè qui ejus verbum vel malè interpretando, vel ad vana convertendo polluunt, de quo, p. 263.

TULERUNT ERGO LAPIDES, UT JACERENT IN EUM.]—Ex hoc loco perspici potest, et tempus et genus mortis á Christo delectum fuisse, qua de re, p. 43, et seqq.

DOMINICA IN RAMIS PALMARUM.

Evangelium ut in prima Dominica Advents, de quo ibid. Cœterum quoniam ad Eucharistiam percipiendam ex præcepto Ecclesiæ eo tempore omnes discretione præditi obligantur, ideo ex his Evangelii verbis " Ecce Rex tuus venit tibi mansuetus," ad ejus sumptionem Fideles hortari poterit parochus ex his quæ habentur, p. 147, 148, 163, et deinceps ;

3 D

et quoniam parentes utplurimum negligentissimi sunt ad liberos suos ad Eucharistiæ perceptionem præsentandos, ideo eis maximè Parochus inculcabit, quæ de cetate ad quam pueri ad eam percipiendam tenentur, et habentur, p. 171.

IN DIE SANCTO PARASCEVES.]—Hoc die quoniam solemnis de mysterio Passionis Domini nostri Jesu Christi concio haberi solet; ideo præterea, quæ in expositione art. 4. Symboli habentur, p. 43, et seqq. hæc insuper hoc die tractari posse videntur. De singulari amore, quo Deus genus humanum prosecutus est, cum illud morte unigeniti filii sui redimere voluerit, de quo, p. 336. De primi parentis lapsu et miseriis, quæ illum consecutæ sunt, de quibus, p. 32, 250, et seqq. quomodo ex passione Christi omnis remissio peccatorûm emanarit, de quo, p. 84, et 368, et proinde omnia Sacramenta ex hac Christi passione virtutem acceperunt, ut est, p. 110, et 111. De sacrificio Christi tam cruento quám incruento ex p. 175. De satisfactione et merito Christi, de quo, p. 202, et 203. Denique quomodo nulli unquam patuit, sed nec patere quidem potest aditus ad regnum cælorum sine hac de redemptionis humanæ per Christum fide, ut est, p. 31, idque esse summam et cardinem totius Christianæ religionis, scire Jesum Christum, et hunc crucifixum, ut habetur, p. 16.

DOMINICA PASCHÆ.

SURREXIT, NON EST HIC, &c., MARC. xvi. 6. &c.]—De resurrectione Domini exponetur artic. Symboli Apostolici, "Tertiâ die resurrexit à mortuis," p. 50.

FERIA SECUNDA POST PASCHA.

ET DUO EX DISCIPULIS JESU IBANT IPSA DIE IN CASTELLUM, xxiv. 13, &c.]—Quoniam fieri vix potuit ut Parochus omnia, quæ ad resurrectionem Christi pertinent pridiè explicuerit, ideo hoc die poterit ea quæ prætermisit, ex eo loco repetere.

OPORTUIT PATI CHRISTUM, ET ITA INTRARE IN GLORIAM SUAM.]—Hic locus est proprius causas exponendi ob quas necesse fuit Christum resurgere, quæ habentur, p. 55, et exemplo Christi fideles hortandi ut omni studio incumbant ut cælesti regno potiantur; quod habetur p. 343, et de commodis tribulationis, p. 378, et seq.

ET FACTUM EST DUM RECUMBERET CUM

IIS, ACCEPIT PANEM.]—Hic locus proprius est ad probandum utramque Eucharistiæ speciem laicis necessariò non exhibendam, de quo multa, p. 171, et seq.

FERIA TERTIA POST PASCHA.

STETIT JESUS IN MEDIO DISCIPULORUM SUORUM, LUC. xxiv. 36, &c.]—Hic de quatuor dotibus corporis gloriosi agi potest, ut habetur, p. 90, et seq.

PAX VOBIS.]—Quoniam regnum Dei, teste Apostolo, pax est et gaudium in Spiritu Sancto: Hic quale sit regnum Christi in pios tractari potest, ut habetur, p. 346.

PRÆDICARE IN NOMINE EJUS PŒNITENTIAM ET REMISSIONEM PECCATORUM.]—Quomodo pœnitentiæ prædicatio à Christo Apostolis injuncta sit ex hoc ipso loco probatur p. 81. Unde potes tam expositione articuli de remissione peccatorum, quam ex his quæ de Sacramento pœnitentiæ hic habentur, longissimam habere concionem.

DOMINICA PRIMA POST PASCHA.

CUM SERO ESSET DIE ILLA, UNA SABBATORUM, JOAN. xx. 19, &c.]—Christi resurrectio nostræ est resurrectionis exemplar, quam maxime stabilire necesse fuit, ut pariter nostra stabiliretur quibus autem tum Scripturis, tum rationibus nostra stabiliatur resurrectio, vide p. 55, 85, et seqq. "Una sabbatorum" autem quid sit vide, p. 265.

QUORUM REMISERITIS PECCATA, JOAN. xx. 23, &c.]—De potestate clavium sacerdotibus concessa, p. 82, et seq. et 350.

MITTE DIGITUM TUUM IN LOCO CLAVORUM, &c.]—Qualia futura sunt corpora post resurrectionem, et cur Christus et martyres cicatrices retinebunt, habes, p. 89, et seqq.

DOMINICA SECUNDA POST PASCHA.

EGO SUM PASTOR BONUS, x. 11, &c.]—Pastorum nomine comprehenduntur non solùm Episcopi et animarum rectores, sed etiam Reges, Magistratus, Parentes, et Magistri. Quid verò Pastores ejusmodí ovibus debeant, et quid vicissim oves Pastoribus, habes p. 273, et seq.

MERCENARIUS AUTEM, ET QUI NON EST PASTOR.]—Quis sit iste mercenarius et non pastor, vide p. 213, et seq.

ET FIET UNUM OVILE ET UNUS PASTOR.]—Hic de unitate Ecclesiæ, de qua p. 74,

et seqq. Unoque universali Ecclesiæ
Pastore D. Petro, et D. Petri successore
Rom. Pontifice, de quo p. 74, et seq. et
222, et 223.

DOMINICA TERTIA POST PASCHA.

MODICUM, ET NON VIDEBITIS ME, JOAN.
xvi. 16, &c.]—Efficax consolationis
genus, dum temporarius mæror pro
Christo susceptus, æternis gaudiis com-
pensatur. Vide quæ de vita æterna habentur, p. 92, et seqq.

Vos VERO CONTRISTABIMINI, MUNDUS
AUTEM GAUDEBIT.]—Quare perversi minus, pii verò acrius, á dæmonibus infes-
tentur, et proinde illi gaudeant, isti verò
tristentur, vide p. 375.

TRISTITIA VESTRA VERTETUR IN GAU-
DIUM, &c.]—Spe futurorum bonorum
quomodo alacri et constanti animo ad-
versa omnia toleraro debeamus, vide, p.
91, et seqq. et cur Deus sinat affligi
bonos, p. 378, et seq.

DOMINICA QUARTA.

SI ENIM NON ABIERO, PARACLITUS NON
VENIET, JOAN. xvi. 7. &c.]—De Spiritu
Sancto, deque admirandis ejus effectibus,
et donis habes, p. 66, 67, et seqq.

ARGUET MUNDUM DE PECCATO, &c.]—
Spiritûs Sancti proprium munus est,
corda et compunctionem movere, et pec-
cantem intrinsecus arguere. Quæ autem
contritio vera sit, quasquo res ea habere
debeat, p. 182, et seqq. Huic etiam re-
ferri possunt ea quæ, de peccatis quæ
remitti non possunt, habentur, p. 183.

DOMINICA QUINTA.

SI QUID PETIERITIS PATREM IN NOMINE
MEO, JOAN. xvi. 23, &c.]—De oratione,
et ejus adjunctis hic proprius est decendi
locus, de qua, p. 317, et seq.

USQUE MODO NON PETISTIS QUIDQUAM,
&c.]—Hic propriè de modo quo Deum
per Christum orare debemus, de quo, p.
329, et seqq. Hic etiam locus, p. 331,
adducitur ad probandum in nomine Christi
orandum esse.

IN FESTO ASCENSIONIS DOMINI.

ASSUMTUS EST IN CÆLUM, ET SEDET A
DEXTRIS DEI, MARC. xvi. 19, &c.]—
Hoc in loco artic. Symb. Apostolici qui
de Ascensione est, explicabitur, p. 57, et
seqq.

DOMINICA POST ASCENS.

CUM AUTEM VENERIT PARACLITUS, QUI
A PATRE PROCEDIT, JOAN. xv. 26, &c.]—
Hic de processione Spiritûs Sancti a Patre
et Filio, ex p. 68, et seqq.

UT OMNIS QUI VOS INTERFICIT, JOAN. xvi.
2, &c.]—Hic præceptum Decalogi " Non
occides," exponi poterit, de quo, p. 279,
et seqq.

ARBITRETUR SE OBSEQUIUM, &c.]—De
omnibus adversis et calamitatibus hujus
vitæ idem judicandum est quod he his,
quæ Christi causa patimur, nempe eas
esse magnum Dei in nos benevolentiæ
signum, ut habetur, p. 336.

IN FESTO PENTECOST.

SI QUIS DILIGIT ME SERMONEM MEUM SER-
VABIT, JOAN. xiv. 23, &c.]—Spiritus
Sanctus ideo credentibus datur, ut sermonem Dei qui Decalogo comprehendi-
tur, servare possint, ad quam rem, ut
promptiores sint, adferat parochus quæ
habentur initio explicationis Decalogi, p.
237, et seqq. vel quoniam, p. 240, hic
locus adducitur ad probandum Dei
mandata non esse impossibilia, ideo de
hac re aget ex, p. 239.

Vel hodié exponet quæ traduntur de Con-
firmationis Sacramento, p. 137, et seq.
Quandoquidem tali die Apostolos à
Spiritu Sancto confirmatos fuisse docent
Patres.

FERIA SECUNDA POST PENTA-COSTEN.

SIC ENIM DEUS DILEXIT MUNDUM, UT
FILIUM SUUM UNIGENTUM DARET,
JOAN, iii. 16.]—Hic locus proprius est
ad ea populo exponenda, quæ de eximia
charitate cælestis Patris in genus humanum, in creatione, et gubernatione de-
monstrata ; sed multo magis in Redemp-
tione habentur, p. 336, et seq.

UT OMNIS QUI CREDIT IN EUM, NON
PEREAT.)—Hic quomodo fides in Christum omnibus hominibus ab omni ævo
necessaria fuerit, docendum est ex, p. 31,
et seq.

QUI CREDIT IN EUM, NON JUDICATUR.]-
De verbo "credere" habes, p. 22, quæ hic
accommodare poteris : ex qua etiam dicendi forma Filium Dei vere Deum esse
demonstrabis, ex p. 67.

QUIA NON CREDIT IN NOMINE UNIGENITI
FILII.]—Quomodo Dei filius sit unigeni
tus poteris declarare ex his, quæ habentur,
p. 31, et contra qua ratione hic unigeni
tus fratres habeat, p. 337, et 338.

**FERIA TERTIA POST PENTE-
COSTEN.**

QUI NON INTRAT PER OSTIUM IN OVILE
OVIUM, JOAN. X. 1, &c.]—Hic locus proprius est ad ea explicanda, quæ de ligiti-
ma ordinatione ministrorum Ecclesiæ
habentur, p. 212, et seqq. de ligitimo
ministro Sacramenti ordinis, p. 223.

ET OVES VOCEM EJUS AUDIUNT.]—De
obedientia et honore, qui debetur Episcopis et sacerdotibus agitur, p. 275, et seq.

ALIENUM AUTEM NON SEQUUNTUR.]—
Hæreticorum ministros non esse sequen-
dos, vide p. 14, qui autem eos sequuntur,
non oves sed hædi sunt, p. 376.

IN FESTO SANCTISS. TRINITATIS.

DATA EST MIHI POTESTAS IN CŒLO ET
IN TERRA, MATTH. XXVIII. 18, &c.]—Hic
explicanda sunt quæ de regno Christi in
pios, et ratione quâ regnat in suis Fideli-
bus, habentur, p. 346, et seqq. de regno
ejam gloriæ ejusdem, p. 347, item de
potestate ipsius in Sacramentis tam in-
stituendis quam conferendis, p. 108, et
de potestate item clavium ejusdem, qua
remittuntur peccata, p. 82, et seqq.

BAPTIZANTES EOS.]—Hic locus adducitur
ad probandum, quo tempore baptismus
obligare cœperit, p. 118, et ideò necessitate ejusdem, et præsertim in infantibus
ea proferri possunt quæ habentur, p. 122,
et deinceps.

IN NOMINE PATRIS ET FILII ET SPIRITUS
SANCTI.]—Hic de materia et forma baptismi, quæ sunt, p. 114, 115, 116, et seq.
accurate agendum est. Hic etiam de
Sanctissimæ et gloriosissimæ Trinitatis
mysterio potorunt agere Parochi, de quo
p. 26, et seqq. Docebunt autem præsertim vulgus imperitum Sanctissimam
Trinitatem pingi et formari non posse,
atque adeo si quando pingatur, illam pic-
turam proprietates quasdam illius expri-
mere, ut habetur, p. 249, et seqq.

DOCENTES EOS SERVARE QUÆCUNQUE
MANDAVI.]—Hic de necessitate, et possi-
bilitate servandæ legis divinæ proferentur,
quæ habentur, p. 239, et seqq.

IN EADEM DOMINICA.

ESTOTE ERGO MISERICORDES SICUT ET
PATER VESTER CŒLESTIS, &c. LUC. vi.
36, &c.]—De hoc Evangelio in Dominica, 4. juxta aliarum Ecclesiarum
morem.

DATE ET DABITUR VOBIS.]—Hic de com-
municandis cum pioximis hujus vitæ

subsidiis produci possunt quæ habentur,
p. 361, et seq. vel de eleemosynis, p.
328, 332.

HYPOCRITA! EJICE PRIMUM TRABEM.]—
De hypocritis quorum orationes Dominus rejicit, habes, p. 331. Item secundum aliquos.

NISI QUIS VENATUS FUERIT, &c. JOAN. iii.
3, &c.]—Hic de necessitate baptismi,
qui in nomine Sanctissimæ Trinitatis con-
fertur, de ejus effectibus, et in universum
quicquid de eo habetur, p. 112, et seq.
explicabit.

IN FESTO CORPORIS CHRISTI.

CARO ENIM MEA VERE EST CIBUS, &c.
JOAN. vi. 56, &c.]—De Eucharistiæ Sacramento, p. 146, et seq.

DOMINICA SECUNDA POST PEN-
TECOSTEN,

Quæ est infra Octavam Corporis Christi.

HOMO QUIDAM FECIT CŒNAM MAGNAM,
&c. LUC. XVI. 1, &c.]—Cœnæ nomine,
quæ sub finem diei sumitur, cœlestis
gloria nobis significatur, quam hic paterfamilias in ipsa vitæ clausula beatis do-
nabit. In hoc argumentum, vide quæ
ponantur, p. 94, et seq. et 353. Vel
cœnæ nomine cum Paulo, 1 Cor. ii. intelligitur Sacrosanctum Christi corpus in
Sacramento altaris: de quo vide, ut
supra, p. 146, et seq.

ET CŒPERUNT OMNES SIMUL EXCUSARE.]
—Quoniam omnes hæ excusationes ex
mala concupiscentia proveniunt, ideo hic
adversus concupiscentias pravas agendum
erit, ex p. 309, et seq. Simulque miseria
nostra ob oculos ponenda, qui ea respui-
mus, quæ salutaria nobis sunt, rebus
autem perniciosis nos addicimus, ut hi
fecerunt, p. 350, et seq.

VILLAM EMI.]—Vide in superbos, et ambi-
tiosos, qui per hunc designantur, quæ
habentur, p. 299, et seq.

JUGA BOUM EMI QUINQUE.]—Vide in ava-
ros, p. 313, et seq.

UXOREM DUXI.]—Hic detestanda libido, et
commendanda continentia et castitas,
quæ aditum nobis ad cælorum regnum
facilem præbet, vide p. 288, et seq. Vel
secundùm alios.

HOMO QUIDAM ERAT DIVES QUI INDUEBA-
TUR, &c. LUC. XVI. 1, &c.]—De varie-
tate in vestibus fugienda, vide quæ habentur, p. 290, et 291. Et quomodo
necessariis tantum rebus ad victum et
vestitum pertinentibus contenti esse debeamus, p. 360.

Sepultus est in inferno.]—Ecce quæ pœna maneat improbos, qui morte præoccupati sceleribus pleni decedunt, de qua, p. 64, et 65.

Ut portaretur ab Angelis.]—Inter Angelorum officia hoc non postremum est, vide p. 333, et seq.

In sinum Abrahæ.]—De recaptaculis animarum post mortem habes, p. 51, et seq.

DOMINICA TERTIA POST PENTECOSTEN.

Gaudium erit in cœlo super uno peccatore pœnitentiam agente, &c. Luc. xv. 7, &c.]—Inter cætera, quæ ad pœnitentiam, agendam peccatorem exstimulare debent, est ista cœlitum lætitia, quâ perfruuntur ob peccatoris conversionem, Plura habes in hanc sententiam, p. 176, et 247, vel Homo quidam fecit ut in Dominica præcedenti.

DOMINICA QUARTA POST PENTECOSTEN.

Cum turba irruerent in Jesum ut aud. verbum, &c. Luc. v. 1, &c.]—Vide exhortationem ad audiendum diligenter verbum Dei, p. 14, et in præfat. Et quomodo pro captu cujusque tradenda sit doctrina Evangelii, ibidem infra ; idque præsertim diebus festis audiendum, p. 263.

Ascendens in unam navem, quæ erat. Simonis, &c.]—Petri navem non alterius ex Apostolis ingressus est Christus ut hoc suo facto insinuaret Petrum cum successoribus caput esse et principem pastorum Ecclesiæ : de hac tu, vide p. 74, et seq. et 222.

Exi a me Domine.]—Qui ad sacram synaxin accedunt, in Petri exemplo et centurionis, Matth. viii. agnoscant esse se tanti hospitis præsentiâ indignissimos: vide quæ de præparatione Eucharistiæ traduntur, p. 167, et seq. vel secundùm aliarum Ecclesiarum ritum.

Estote ergo misericordes sicut et pater, &c. Luc. vi. 36, &c.]—Ut Christus nobis condonet, prius condonare ipsi debemus iis à quibus læsi fuerimus. Vide explicationem illius petitionis : "Dimitte nobis debita nostra," &c. p. 364, et seq. Vide item de hoc Evang. in festo Trinit.

DOMINICA QUINTA POST PENTECOSTEN.

Audistis quia dictum est antiquis. Non occides, &c. Matth. v. 33, &c.]—Hujus loci erit hoc decalogi præceptum exponere, prout habetur, p. 279, et seq.

Ego autem dico vobis, omnis qui irascitur.]—Hæc verba exponuntur, p. 281, et seq.

Audistis quia dictum est antiquis. Non mœchaberis, &c.]—Hic similiter exponatur hoc præceptum, de quo habetur, p. 286, vel "cum turba irruerent in Jesum, ut supra."

DOMINICA SEXTA.

Misereor super turbam, quia ecce jam triduo sustinent me. Marc. viii. 2, &c.]—Præter ea, quæ notata sunt in Dominica quartâ Quadragesimæ poterit Parochus ea huc proferre, quæ de paterna Dei de hominibus cura habentur, p. 332, et seq.

Si dimisero eos jejunos deficient in via.]—Hic de imbecillitate hominum, qui nullum opus Deo gratum sine adjumento Dei possunt instituere, agendum est, ut habetur, p. 350, et seq. vel, "Audistis quia dictum est antiquis. Non occides, ut supra."

DOMINICA SEPTIMA POST PENTECOSTEN.

Attendite a falsis Prophetis, &c. Matth. vii. 15, &c.]—Hic cavendum præcipitur ab hereticis. Quis verò censendus sit hæreticus habes, p. 73. Quomodo autem hi, cùm in Ecclesia non sint, ab ea puniri possint, p. 73. Quibus autem artibus hi falsi prophetæ utantur ad impia sua dogmata infundenda, habes, p. 14.

In ignem mittetur, &c.]—De hoc igne infernali, p. 51.

Sed qui facit voluntatem Patris mei, &c.]—Hæc sententia est veluti methodus brevissima, docens qua ratione ad regnum cœlorum pervenire possimus : quare quicumque cupimus illud adipisci, hanc sententiam præ oculis habere debemus, vide p. 350, et deinceps, ubi hæc tertia petitio, "Fiat voluntas tua, sicut in cœlo et in terra," explicatur. Vel "Misereor super turbam," ut in præcedenti Dominica.

DOMINICA OCTAVA POST PENTECOSTEN.

Redde rationem villicationis tuæ, Luc. xvi. 2, &c.]—De ratione reddenda, cum unusquisque migrat è vita, vide p. 61.

Facite vobis amicos de mammona iniquitatis.]—Ideo divites à Deo bonis cumulantur, ut pauperibus ea erogent, p. 363. Hic ad eleemosynas suos poteris

exhortari Parochus, prout est, p. 298,
299, et 328. Hic etiam locus pro intercessione Sanctorum facit, de qua, p. 245,
et seq. 326, et 327 ; vel "Attendite à
falsis prophetis," ut in præcedenti Dominica, sicque deinceps omnia Evangelia
quæ consequenter in reliquis Dominicis
proponuntur, in quibusdam Ecclesiis, in
præcedenti Dominica legi consueverunt,
quod notare supersedimus.

DOMINICA NONA POST PENTE-
COSTEN.

FLEVIT SUPER ILLAM, LUC. xix. 41.]—Flevit
Christus, ut nos flere doceat. Quomodò
verò in pœnitudine erratorum sint adhi-
bendæ lacrymæ, et quam diligenter pro-
curandæ, habes, p. 186, ubi de contritione
agitur.

QUIA SI COGNOVISSES ET TU.]—Summa
est status nostri miseria nostram miseriam
non agnoscere, vide p. 350.

QUIA VENIENT DIES IN TE, ET CIRCUNDA-
BUNT TE, &c.]—Hierusalem in exemplum punitur hujus hominis, qui, multis
a Deo beneficiis ornatus, male eis in sui
perniciem abutitur, vide p. 377.

DOMINICA DECIMA.

HÆC APUD SE ORABAT, LUC. xviii. 11, &c.]
—Quibus virtutibus oratio debeat esse co-
mitata, ut Deo placeat, et ab eo exaudia-
tur, vide p. 327, et seq.

DEUS PROPITIUS ESTO MIHI PECCATORI.]—
Hoc veri pœnitentis exemplum inter alia
proponitur, p. 327. Quare cum istius
tum aliorum exemplo, qui habentur ibidem et p. 184, 185, ad veram pœnitentiam Parochi fideles excitabunt. Est
præterea exemplum eorum, qui, cùm pec-
catores sint, Deum orant et exaudiuntur,
p. 322. Denique quanta humilitate ad
Deum precaturi accedere debeamus hic
demonstratur, p. 328.

QUI SE EXALTAT, HUMILIABITUR.]—
Christi humilitatis exemplum maximum
pondus habet ad nostram superbiam de-
primendam, p. 43.

DOMINICA XI.

ET DEPRECABANTUR EUM, UT ILLI IMPO-
NAT MANUM, MARC. vii. 32, &c.]—Isto-
rum exemplo, qui Christum pro muto et
surdo ad eum adducto, ut sanaretur, interpellant, monemur pro aliis orare.
Quomodo vero id faciendum et pro quibus orandum habes, p. 324, et seq.

MISIT DIGITOS IN AURICULAS EJUS.]—
Christi exemplo pueris in baptismo,
aures, oculi, pectus, humeri signo crucis

recte insigniuntur. Vide de his et aliis
baptismi cæremoniis, et earum significa-
tione, p. 133, et seq.

SUSPICIENS IN CŒLUM INGEMUIT, &c.]—
Cùm Deus sit ubique, cur potius in cœlum quàm aliò oculos convertamus, et
cur in cœlis esse dicatur, p. 339. Præterea quoniam sacræ literæ nos surdos et
cæcos, et omnibus membris captos sæpe
appellant : ut habetur, p. 366, hic de
malis quæ peccatum invehit, ut ibidem
habetur, disserere Parochus commodè
poterit.

DOMINICA XII.

DILIGES DOMINUM DEUM TUUM EX TOTO
CORDE TUO, &c. LUC. x. 37, &c.]—In
hanc sententiam populo proponantur,
quæ habentur initio explicationis Decalogi, p. 237, usque ad secundum præceptum, vel quia hoc Evangelium concurrit
cum Dominica decima-septima, posterio-
rem hujus Evangelii partem priori præ-
termissæ exponet.

HOMO QUIDAM DESCENDERET AB HIERU-
SALEM IN HIERICO, &c.]—Hominis
hujus ita miserabiliter à latronibus vulne-
rati nomine, Doctores intelligunt hu-
manam naturam post Adæ lapsum, quæ,
quot, qualia, et quanta, vulnera acceperit,
habes, p. 31, 32, et 350, et seq. 358, et
seqq. et 382, et seq. sæpeque alibi.

SAMARITANUS AUTEM INFUNDENS OLEUM,
&c.]—Hic de Sacramentis agat Parochus, quæ à nostro Samaritano, id est à
Christo instituta sunt, tamquam remedia
contra vulnera humanæ naturæ, per Adæ
lapsum inflicta, ut habetur, p. 103, 104.

CURAM ILLIUS HABE.]—Nota genus humanum et Ecclesiam uni homini à
Christo commissam, qua de re vide, p.
74, et seq.

QUIS HORUM VIDETUR FUISSE PROXIMUS.]
Ex hoc loco quis sit proximus explicatur, p. 302.

DOMINICA XIII.

JESU PRÆCEPTOR, MISERERE NOSTRI, LUC.
xvii. 13, &c.]-De nomine Jesu, vide p. 33.

ITE, OSTENDITE VOS SACERDOTIBUS, &c.]
Vide quæ in hanc sententiam dicta sunt
Dominica secunda post Epiphaniam :
vide præterea, p. 191, ubi nominatim hic
locus adducitur. Quomodo item benefi-
cio contritionis peccata remittantur, ex
hoc loco probatur, p. 188, et 189. Quæ
tamen confessionem requirit, ut habetur,
p. 184, et 190.

NE SOLICITI SITIS ANIMÆ VESTRÆ, &c.
MATTH. vi. 25, &c.]—Quantum immo-
derata solicitudo congerendarum opum,

cæteræque cupiditates animæ saluti obsint, vide p. 312, et seq. et hujus morbi remedium habes, p. 314, et seq.

Scit pater vester quod omnibus his indigetis.]—Etiamsi Deus sciat desideria nostra et indigentiam, cur ei preces porrigamus, p. 320.

Primum quærite regnum Dei, &c.]— De iis quæ petenda sunt et quo ordine, habentur, p. 323, et seq. et 340, et seq. Porro hic commodé secunda petitio Dominicæ orationis tota explicabitur, ut habetur, p. 343, et seq.

Et huc omnia adjiientur vobis, &c.]— Quatenus temporalia petenda, p. 359, et 360.

DOMINICA XV.

Et resedit qui erat mortuus, Luc. vii. 15.]—Si hic mortuus et quidam alii sint revocati ad vitam, quomodo intelligendum quod Christus primus omnium resurrexerit, vide p. 53. Hic tractari poterit articulus Symboli Apostolici penult. de carnis resurrectione p. 85, et seq.

DOMINICA XVI.

Si licet Sabbato curare, Luc. xiv. 3, &c.]—De Sanctificatione dierum festorum, et á quibus tunc abstinendum, quidve agendum sit, habes, p. 268, et seq.

Cum invitatus feris ad nuptias, &c.] —Hic locus est cohortandi Christianos omnes, ne alii aliis se præferant, ut est, p. 338, neve ambitiosi sint honorumque cupidiores, ut est, p. 41.

DOMINICA XVII.

Diliges Dominum Deum tuum, Matth. xxii. 37, &c.]—Vide Evangelium Dominicæ xii. ut suprá.

Quid vobis videtur de Christo, &c.]— Christus quomodo sit David filius, vide p. 40. Quomodo item non sit filius David ratione Divinitatis, habes, p. 36.

DOMINICA XVIII.

Et videns autem Jesus fidem eorum, Matth. ix. 2, &c.]—Ecce quantum fide aliena moveatur Deus ad aliquod donum alteri non modo non petenti, sed ne cogitanti quidem impertiendum. Hinc fit ut in baptismo infantes regenerationis fiant participes, non quia mentis suæ assentione credant, sed quia susceptorum, vel parentum, (si fideles fuerint) sin minus, Ecclesiæ Catholicæ (ut sit Augustinus)

fide muniantur, p. 124, et de patrinis, p. 120, et seq.

Remittuntur tibi peccata tua, &c.]— Christum ut hominem primum omnium potestatem remittendorum peccatorum habuisse ex hoc loco probatur, p. 83. Porro dum Sacerdos, jurisdictionem habens vel órdinariam vel delegatam, rite pænitenti peccata remittit, non minus absolvitur, quàm paralyticus, quantum est ex parte Sacram. De forma absolutionis habes, p. 181, et 182.

Hic blasphemat, &c.]—De blasphemia habetur, p. 261, et de juramento, p. 251, et seq.

DOMINICA XIX.

Qui nuptias fecit filio suo, Matth. xxii. 2, &c.]—Quibus de causis vir et mulier conjungi debeant, vide p. 229, et quæ sponsæ magis sint quærendæ, p. 230, et de mutuis viri et mulieris officiis, p. 233, et seq. et quod Deum orandi causâ certis temporibus à matrimonii officio abstinere debeant, p. 236. Item de tribus matrimonii bonis ; p. 233.

Contumeliis affectos occiderunt, &c. —De contumelia, detractione, murmuratione, cæterisque vitiis quibus proximus læditur, vide p. 303, et seq.

Non habens vestem nuptialem, &c.]— Vestem hanc nuptialem vestis candida, vel sudariolum quod baptizatis datur, designat, de quo p. 135.

Mittite in tenebras exteriores, &c.] —De sententia et pæna damnatorum, p. 64.

DOMINICA XX.

Erat quidam Regulus, cujus filius infirmabatur, Joan. iv. 46, &c.]—Unde tot miseriæ et adversitates, et quæ quotque illæ sint, p. 358. Quò in malis et rebus adversis confugiendum, p. 375, et 380. Hic exponi poterit ultima petitio Dominicæ orationis : " Sed libera nos à malo," p. 381.

DOMINICA XXI.

Redde quod debes, Matth. xviii. 28, &c.] —Restitutio pænitenti est necessaria, antequam absolvatur, quia " non dimittitur peccatum, nisi restituatur ablatum," ut inquit Augustinus : vide de restitutione, p. 294, et 296. Item de furto, rapina, usuris et aliis illicitis rerum usurpationibus, p. 294, et seq.

Si non remiseritis, &c.]—Hic exponatur petitio illa orationis Dominicæ: "Dimitte nobis debita nostra, sicut et nos dimittimus," &c. p. 364, et seq.

DOMINICA XXII.

Magister! scimus quia verax es, Matth. xxii. 16, &c.]—Genus assentationis pessimum, quæ ad proximi calamitatem et perniciem adhibetur. De adulatione habes p. 304, et 305. "Quia verax es," &c. De mendacio vide, p. 303, et seq. ubi notatur hoc ipsum testimonium ex hoc Evangelio decerptum.

Reddite quæ sunt Cæsaris Cæsari, &c.]—Vide quæ debentur principibus et superioribus in potestate constitutis, p. 276.

DOMINICA XXIII. POST PENTECOSTEN.

Ecce princeps unus accessit et adorabat eum dicens, Matth. ix. 18, &c.]—Hic differentia, qua infideles et Christiani à morbis liberari cupiunt, de qua p. 382, et quomodo in morbis ad Deum, non ad præstigiatorum incantationes sit recurrendum, ibid p. 383.

Filia mea modo defuncta est.]—Hic de morte et novissimis, de quibus sæpe ad populum agendum esse præcipitur, p. 65, et 206.

Si tetigero tantum fimbriam vestimenti.]—Hic de reliquiis Sanctorum, et cultu, et veneratione earum aget Parochus ex, p. 320, et seq.

Et cum venisset Jesus in Domum principis, &c.]—Hic de ratione juvandi mortuos per sacrificium Missæ et orationes, de qua p. 175, et 326, vel in quibusbam Ecclesiis legitur Evangelium Dominicæ IV. Quadragesimæ, de quo ibidem. Si plures sint Dominicæ inter Pentecosten et Adventum, servetur quod de his in Breviarii rubricis habetur.

DOMINICA XXIV. POST PENTECOSTEN.

Cum ergo videritis abominationem desolationis stantem in loco sacro, Matth. xxiv. 15, &c.]—Hic de signis præcedentibus diem judicii agendum est, de quibus, p. 64.

Orate autem ne fiat fuga vestra, &c.]—Hic locus ad probandum temporalia à Deo peti posse inducitur, p. 360, unde de hoc argumento Parochi etiam agere poterunt, de quo tum ibidem, tum p. 323, et 324, agitur.

Sed propter electos breviabuntur dies illi.]—Hic de dæmonum potestate poterit agi qui quantum possunt, et quamdiu volunt, homines tentare non possunt. ut habetur, p. 375, et seq.

GENERAL INDEX.